LAW AND MEDICINE

CURRENT LEGAL ISSUES 2000

Volume 3

LAW AND MEDICINE

CURRENT LEGAL ISSUES 2000
Volume 3

Edited by

MICHAEL FREEMAN
Professor of English Law
University College London

and

ANDREW D. E. LEWIS
Senior Lecturer in Laws
University College London

OXFORD
UNIVERSITY PRESS

OXFORD
UNIVERSITY PRESS

Great Clarendon Street, Oxford OX2 6DP

Oxford University Press is a department of the University of Oxford.
It furthers the University's objective of excellence in research, scholarship,
and education by publishing worldwide in

Oxford New York

Athens Auckland Bangkok Bogotá Buenos Aires Calcutta
Cape Town Chennai Dar es Salaam Delhi Florence Hong Kong Istanbul
Karachi Kuala Lumpur Madrid Melbourne Mexico City Mumbai
Nairobi Paris São Paulo Shanghai Singapore Taipei Tokyo Toronto Warsaw
with associated companies in Berlin Ibadan

Oxford is a registered trade mark of Oxford University Press
in the UK and in certain other countries

Published in the United States
by Oxford University Press Inc., New York

British Library Cataloguing in Publication Data

Data available

Library of Congress Cataloging in Publication Data

Law and medicine / edited by Michael Freeman, Andrew D.E. Lewis.
p. cm.—(Current legal issues; .3)
Includes bibliographical references.
1. Medical laws and legislation. 2. Medical ethics. I. Freeman, Michael D.A.
II. Lewis, Andrew D.E. III. Series.
K3601.L39 2000
344′.041—dc21   00–037463

ISBN 0–19–829918–4

1 3 5 7 9 10 8 6 4 2

Typeset in Sabon by
Cambrian Typesetters, Frimley, Surrey

Printed in Great Britain
on acid-free paper by
Biddles Ltd., Guildford and King's Lynn

CONTENTS

EDITORS' PREFACE

UCL's third annual international interdisciplinary colloquium hosted by the Law Faculty brought together the disciplines of law and medicine and their various satellites, health care, medical ethics, the sociology and history of medicine, mental health, and psychiatry. The interdiscipline is better established than law and science and law and literature, the subject of the first two colloquia. It attracted over 100 participants from some twelve countries and there were nearly forty papers presented. This volume collects together thirty-one of these on a broad range of contemporary issues and controversies. The colloquium coincided with the implementation of the Health Act 1999 and the Bristol Infirmary Inquiry was in full swing. Debates about the ethics of cloning, forced caesareans, Viagra, medical malpractice, and reform of mental health legislation hogged the headlines and are well-reflected in the papers presented here.

The colloquium was convened by Michael Freeman and Andrew Lewis with the assistance, gratefully acknowledged, of administrative staff, in particular Lisa Penfold and Jacqui Bennett.

The next colloquia are on Law and Religion in July 2000, Law and Geography in July 2001 and Law and History in July 2002. Law and Art is the likely subject for 2003. Anyone interested in any of these colloquia should contact, initially, Andrew Lewis (e-mail a.d.e.lewis@ucl.ac.uk)

April 2000

Michael Freeman
Andrew Lewis

NOTES ON CONTRIBUTORS

Rebecca Bailey-Harris is Professor of Law at the University of Bristol. She is an editor of the *Family Law Reports*.

Peter Bartlett is a Lecturer in Law at the University of Nottingham and author of *The Poor Law of Lunacy* and (with D. Wright) the editor of *Outside The Walls of the Asylum: The History of Care In The Community 1750-2000*.

Belinda Bennett is Senior Lecturer in the Faculty of Law at the University of Sydney. She is the author of *Law and Medicine*, and is currently working on the impact of the new genetics on women.

Erwin Bernat is Professor of Law at the University of Graz in Austria.

Hazel Biggs is Lecturer in Law at the University of Kent.

Meredith Blake is Lecturer in Law at the City University, London.

Elizabeth Boetzkes is Professor of Philosophy at McMaster University, Hamilton, Ontario.

Cynthia Daniels is Associate Professor of Political Science and Women's Studies, Rutgers University, and a Research Associate at Princeton University. She is the author of *At Women's Expense: State Power and the Politics of Fetal Rights*, and is currently working on a book entitled *Exposing Men: The Science and Politics of Male Reproduction*.

Robert Dingwall is Professor of Sociology and Director of the Genetics and Society Unit at the University of Nottingham. He is one of the authors of *Medical Negligence: Compensation and Accountability*.

Rebecca Dresser is Professor of Law and Ethics in Medicine at Washington University – St Louis. She is writing a book about the public's role in determining and implementing biomedical research policies.

Howard Ducharme is Professor of Philosophy at Akron University, Ohio, U.S.A.

Abul Faal Mohsin Ebrahim is Professor in Islamic Studies at the University of Durban - Westville. He is the author of *Abortion, Birth Control and Surrogate Parenting – An Islamic Perspective.*

Michael Farrell is an Instructor at the Yale University School of Medicine. He was formerly Robert Wood Johnson Clinical Scholar at the University of Michigan.

Anne Flamm is Fellow in the Department of Clinical Ethics at the M.D. Anderson Cancer Center in Houston.

Heidi Forster is Fellow in the Department of Clinical Bioethics at the National Institute of Health, Bethesda, Maryland. She was formerly a Visiting Assistant Professor at Case Western Reserve University.

Michael Freeman is Professor of English Law at University College London. He is Editor of *Current Legal Problems*, General Editor of the *International Library of Medicine, Ethics and Law*. He is writing a book on cultural pluralism and the rights of the child.

Janet Golden is Associate Professor and Director of the Graduate Program in History at Rutgers - Camden. She is currently working on a cultural history of foetal alcohol syndrome.

Vivienne Harpwood is a Reader in Law at Cardiff Law School and Director of the LL.M degree (Legal Aspects of Medical Practice). She was a member of the NHS Complaints Review Committee and currently serves on the Silicone Gel Breast Implant Review Group.

John Harris is Sir David Alliance Professor of Bioethics at the University of Manchester and Research Director at the Centre for Social Ethics and Policy, University of Manchester. He is the author of *Wonderwoman and Superman*. He is directing a project for the European Commission on Communicable Diseases and Lifestyle Choices.

Jonathan Herring is a Fellow of Exeter College, Oxford.

Diana Kloss is Senior Lecturer in Law at the University of Manchester.

Athena Liu is Associate Professor of Law at the University of Hong Kong. She is the author of *Artificial Reproduction and Reproductive Rights* and of *Family Law for the Hong Kong SAR*.

Robin MacKenzie is Lecturer in Law at the University of Kent.

Sheila McLean is the International Bar Association Professor of Law and

Ethics in Medicine at the University of Glasgow and is the Director of the Institute of Law and Ethics in Medicine. She has acted as a consultant to the World Health Organization and the Council of Europe.

B Mahendra is a Consultant Psychiatrist and a Barrister. He is the author of *Depression: The Disorder and its Associations* and *Dementia: A Survey of the Syndrome*, and a regular contributor to the *New Law Journal*.

Frances Miller is Professor of Law at Boston University School of Law; Professor of Public Health, Boston University School of Public Health; Professor of Health Care Management, Boston University School of Management. She is the Editor of the *American Journal of Law and Medicine*.

Debbie Mortimer is a member of the Victorian Bar, practising in public law. She was formerly a lecturer in the Monash University Law School.

Linda Mulcahy is Reader in Law at Birkbeck College London. She is the author of *Mediating Medical Negligence Claims*, and (with Judith Allsop) of *Regulating Medical Work* and (with Marilynn Rosenthal and Sally Lloyd-Bostock) of *Medical Mishaps*.

Christopher Newdick is Reader in Health Law at the University of Reading. He is the author of *Who Shall We Treat?*

Kenneth Norrie is Professor of Law at the University of Strathclyde.

Nicola Peart is Senior Lecturer in Law at the University of Otago, and formerly Chairperson of the Otago Ethics Committee.

Carl Schneider is Chauncey Stillman Professor of Law and Professor of Internal Medicine at the University of Michigan. He is the author of *The Practice of Autonomy*.

Françoise Shenfield is Clinical Lecturer – Infertility in the Reproductive Medicine Unit at University College London.

Bonnie Steinbock is Professor of Philosophy at the State University of New York, Albany. She is a Fellow of the Hastings Center, and a Past President. She is the author of *Life Before Birth: The Moral and Legal Status of Embryos and Fetuses*.

Harvey Teff is Professor of Law, University of Durham. He is the author of *Reasonable Care: Legal Perspectives on the Doctor/Patient Relationship*.

Anton Vedder is a senior Research Fellow and Research Co-ordinator at the Faculty of Law at Tilburg University. His research and publications are in moral epistemology, law and globalization, ethics and information and communication technologies, and bioethics.

Louis Waller, A.O. is Sir Louis Cussen Professor of Law at Monash University. He chaired the Committee to Consider the Social, Ethical and Legal Issues Arising from In Vitro Fertilization, which reported in 1984.

TABLE OF CASES

TABLE OF STATUTES, CONVENTIONS, ETC

INTRODUCTION

MEDICINE, HEALTH AND THE LAW AT THE MILLENNIUM'S END

As the millennium closed, medical and health issues dominated the headlines in the press in Britain. The trial and conviction of a GP of the murder of fifteen of his elderly female patients and subsequent speculation that he may have murdered many more, coupled with the revelation that the General Medical Council had allowed him to continue to practise despite a drug theft conviction and evidence that he had falsified prescriptions, sent shivers through the whole population.[1]

The trial of Harold Shipman was played out against a background of an inquiry into the deaths of twenty-nine babies at the hands of heart surgeons at Bristol Royal Infirmary[2]—the most public and most sensitive inquiry ever into alleged medical malpractice—and the revelation that bodies of children who died at Alder Hey hospital in Liverpool were subjected to routine stripping of their organs on a scale unequalled elsewhere.[3]

And it occurred at a time when the health service appeared to be in crisis: overstretched, underfunded, laid low by a flu epidemic. That Britain spent less of its GDP than its immediate neighbours on health was widely discussed—that the news seemed to shock suggests how badly informed the public is.[4]

It appeared the public wanted more to be spent on the National Health Service: even, perhaps, that it was willing to forgo a tax cut to subsidize health spending.[5] The question of waiting lists—what they meant and what was to be done to reduce them—and of health spending priorities (with debates over new drugs such as Viagra and Relenza)[6] exercised both

---

[1] See *The Times*, 1 February 2000; see also Lois Rogers *The Sunday Times*, 6 February 2000, 1.21. He was struck off the register after his murder conviction: *The Guardian*, 12 February 2000. See also Bill O'Neill, 'Doctor As Murderer' (2000) 320 *British Medical Journal* 329.

[2] The inquiry is being conducted by Professor Ian Kennedy.

[3] *The Independent*, 22 December 1999. On the inquiries into this see Richard Woodman, 'Storage of Human Organs Prompts Three Inquiries', (2000) 320 *British Medical Journal* 77.

[4] Annabell Ferriman, 'Blair Will Have Difficulty in Matching European Spending' (2000) 320 *British Medical Journal* 267.

[5] Elias Mossialos, Anna Dixon and Martin McKee, 'Paying for the NHS', (2000) 320 *British Medical Journal* 197.

[6] And see R. v. *Secretary of State for Health* [1999] Lloyd's Rep Med. 289.

government and its critics. Hard choices about the future of health care provision (in particular about the NHS) are unavoidable.

There will continue to be debates over needs and choices. Biggs and Mackenzie address these in the context of Viagra.

Both medical science and health care provision are in a state of flux. The position of GPs has changed. From being the primary provider of health care on a needs-related basis only, they found themselves subject, in the 1990s, to market incentives and their position will change again as the Health Act 1999 and institutions it has spawned, like the National Institute for Clinical Excellence (NICE), make themselves felt.7 The impact of private finance initiatives has yet to be calculated and the law will be forced to respond too. Are either private law remedies or those within public law well-adapted to tackle the problems that will arise? Neither, Newdick argues, is fit for the task and he looks to other solutions, particularly in regulation.

There will be calls for greater accountability and increased transparency of decision-making. The greater use of technology—on-line information, for example—may, as Miller argues—heighten accountability. Will it lead also to English transplanting the 'transatlantic' doctrine of informed consent?[8] Medical guidelines have (in 1999) encouraged doctors of adopt a reasonably prudent patient test,[9] but the law, it seems, lags behind, still committed to an ideology of 'doctor knows best'.[10] The publication of 'league tables', leaving patients in little doubt as to the risk they are taking and that the risks are surgeon-related, may accelerate the adoption of 'informed consent'.[11] Different experiences and interpretations of this are recounted by Miller, but, as Schneider and Farrell show, patients do not appraise evidence or assimilate or assess information. Instead, they rely uncritically on culturally powerful but inapt axioms. They would not abandon informed consent but their research shows it is clear that it has real limits.[12]

Doctors themselves have greater access to research findings. We are into an evidence-based, guidelines culture. It is clear, as Teff notes, that courts place importance on this. But what is the status of guidelines? Clearly, they do not constitute legal standards. The Woolf report,[13] as Teff notes, proposed a single court-appointed expert. But this has not happened. Can it be long in the future?

---

7 See also Michael L. Millenson, *Demanding Medical Excellence* (Chicago, 1997).

8 *Canterbury* v. *Spence* 464 F 2d 772 (1972) DC Cir.

9 General Medical Council, *Seeking Patients' Consent: The Ethical Considerations* (London, 1999).

10 *Sidaway* v. *Bethlem Royal Hospital* [1985] A C 871.

11 *The Independent*, 17 June, 1999.

12 See further Carl Schneider, *The Practice of Autonomy* (Cambridge, Mass, 1998).

13 Lord Woolf, *Access To Justice* (London, 1996).

14 The NHS is reported as having at least 15,000 cases of clinical negligence on its books. The report on the 1997–8 NHS expenditure for England recorded that £79m had been paid out that year on negligence cases.

Meanwhile, there has been a growth in negligence claims.[14] As Mulcahy points out, the gap with the United States is closing. But the costs remain enormous, and the success rates are low. English law clings to its sociological *Bolam* test.[15] The judges see their role as sustaining respect for clinical autonomy. *Bolitho*[16] has come and gone. In effect has probably been little more than marginal. Whether NICE can offer a normative framework, as Harpword suggests, remains to be seen. How the courts would then react is a question of major significance.

A key value in medical law and in bioethics is patient autonomy.[17] Englehardt[18] would not be alone in assigning it priority over the principle of beneficence.[19] Its implications, its limitations are explored in a number of the essays in this collection. The *St George's* case[20]—which tests its limits graphically—is discussed by Bailey-Harris, by Herring and by Blake. None of the three sees only unqualified good in its upholding of a woman's right to refuse a caesarean section.[21] One problem of focusing on autonomy is that it necessitates the employment of tests of competence. The *Gillick* case[22]—and the retreat therefrom[23]—demonstrates both the problems of establishing this and the implications of so finding. Bailey-Harris looks at *St George's* in relation to adolescent autonomy. Herring, although he concedes that the mother's voice must prevail, looks to construct other models, including one which emphasizes relationship, which might better enable us to understand the dynamics of the decision-making involved. And Blake, for whom the unrestrained emphasis on autonomy is as dangerous as an emphasis on the unborn child would be, looks to whether (and how) such cases might be decided differently when the Human Rights Act 1998 comes into operation. The reasoning might be different (discussions for example of proportionality) but not, she concludes, the end results.[24]

US courts have come to similar conclusions and Flamm and Forster in their paper distinguish such cases from those such as *Saikewicz*[25] where autonomy has been trumped by countervailing state interests. They show

---

[15] *Bolam v. Friern Hospital Management Committee* [1957] 2 All ER 118.

[16] *Bolitho v. City and Hackney HA* [1997] 3 WLR 1151. However, see *Penney, Palmer and Cannon v. East Kent HA* [1999] Lloyds Rep Med 123.

[17] *Schloendorff v. Society of New York Hospital* (1914) 211 NY 125.

[18] *Foundations of Bioethics* (New York, 1995).

[19] See, for example, Tom Beauchamp and James Childress, *Principles of Biomedical Ethics* (New York, 1994) and Robert Veatch, *A Theory of Medical Ethics* (New York, 1981).

[20] *St George's Health Care NHS Trust v. S* [1998] 2 FLR 728.

[21] See also Margaret Brazier, 'Liberty, Responsibility, Maternity' (1999) 52 *Current Legal Problems* 359.

[22] *Gillick v. West Norfolk and Wisbech Area Health Authority* [1986] AC 112.

[23] *Re R* [1992] Fam 11; *Re W* [1993] Fam 64.

[24] For another example see Michael Freeman, 'Death, Dying and the Human Rights Act 1998' (1999) 52 *Current Legal Problems* 218.

[25] *Superintendent of Belchertown State School v. Saikewicz* 370 N.E. 2d 417 (1977).

that the courts protect a concept of autonomy grounded in bodily integrity, but not a broader right of non-interference in all personal and intimate decisions: hence the refusal of the Supreme Court to challenge legislation banning physician assisted suicide.[26]

Those who lack competence cannot exercise autonomy. Such persons have, of course, a right to bodily integrity, hence the dilemma faced when there is a request to harvest gametes from a dying, unconscious or comatose person or to keep a pregnant woman alive so that her baby can come to term.[27] The former dilemma was famously posed in the *Blood*[28] case and arose also in Victoria, Australia. Shenfield discusses the *Blood* case—drawing on a distinction between intent and consent—and Waller and Mortimer the Australian decision. Neither decision employs human rights jurisprudence, in particular the right to bodily integrity. In *Blood* this is hardly surprising: English judges have been more convinced by utilitarian considerations than appeals to human rights.[29] The Australian court's omission is more surprising, given Brennan J's ringing espousal of the right to bodily integrity in *Marion's* case.[30]

Of all medical science developments in recent years the one to have provoked the most interest, and concern, has been cloning.[31] Like IVF, twenty years earlier, the debate about the propriety of human cloning is shrouded in fear. But, as Bennett asks, is the deliberate creation of sameness wrong? There may be, as she acknowledges, a perceived threat to individuality, but identity cannot be reduced to genetics. As Dingwall also argues, neither science nor law can exist in a social vacuum. It is important to ask, she believes, what the impact of new technologies will be, in particular, since they carry the reproductive burden, what the impact will be on women. It is equally important for the law to ensure that the processes of law reform are informed by 'social and scientific versions of vision'.

McLean, writing of gene therapy, offers a similar message. The future of medicine may well lie in gene therapy and she believes in germ-line therapy, though this has generally been frowned upon.[32] But we must control rather than fear genetic information. The crucial questions are who controls it and for what purposes. This essentially optimistic message is,

[26] Margaret P. Battin, Rosamond Rhodes and Anita Silvers, *Physician Assisted Suicide— Expanding The Debate* (New York, 1998).

[27] See the German case reported in (1982) 2 *Bioethics* 135.

[28] R. v. *Human Fertilisation and Embryology Authority ex p. Blood* [1997] 2 WLR 806 and see Timothy Murphy, 'Sperm Harvesting and Postmortem Fatherhood' (1995) 9 *Bioethics* 380.

[29] For example, contrast Laws J and the Court of Appeal in R. v. *Cambridge D H A, ex p. B* [1995] 1 FLR 1056.

[30] *Department of Health and Community Services* v. *JWB and SMB* (1992) 66 A L J R (High Court of Australia).

[31] And see Glenn McGee, *The Human Cloning Debate* (Berkeley, Calif., 1998).

[32] In England in the *Report of the Committee on the Ethics of Gene Therapy* Cm., 1788 (the Clothier report) (London, 1992).

however, subjected to an important reservation, the often overlooked fact that germ-line therapy means that tomorrow's child's genetic make-up may be determined by today's treatment.

Bennett's concerns about the impact of technology on women are matched by the socio-historical investigation by Daniels and Golden into the politics of pregnancy. Pointing out, as Troy Duster did,[33] that the temperance crusade was a cultural enterprise, they draw attention to the ways women are targeted by images of foetal risk. Although men's sperm can also show defects as a result of drug use (and pollutants to which war and industry has exposed them), men are pitied and women are blamed. Warnings are not directed to men as to women. They conclude that 'it is the population targeted, not the nature of the risk, that determines the public and scientific responses to evidence of foetal risk'. But is this scientific ignorance rather than gender bias? Of course, if it is, the reasons for this ignorance may also need to be explained. Boetzkes too examines the impact of medical technology on women, in particular the symbolic harms women as a group suffer.

A number of the articles in this volume address research and experimentation. Peart looks at health research with children. She addresses three principal questions. She has no doubt children should be involved in health research, pointing to the need to uncover the causes of health problems principally or only suffered by children (for example, Sudden Infant Death Syndrome). She has no doubt also that parents should be able to consent in order that their children might participate, or that children themselves when competent—she approves *Gillick* criteria—have the right to consent.[34] Harris, addressing the AIDS epidemic in sub-Saharan Africa, argues that progress in research has been hampered by images and events of the past, for example Tuskegee,[35] and urges a more expansive interpretation of the Helsinki Declaration to include one that acceptance of the provision of inducements to research subjects is neither coercive nor otherwise unethical or inappropriate as long as the research is well-founded and in the public interest. Dresser's concern is what is researched. Clearly there are priorities but it is not clear, nor can any consensus be expected, as to what these are. The case for going beyond distributive justice criteria to embrace fair procedures is advocated.[36] And this includes an expansion of those able to participate in the choice process. To take just one example, HIV activists might well be incorporated into the decision making process, an instance perhaps of affirmative action in a new context.

---

[33] *The Legislation of Morality* (New York, 1970).

[34] Cf. Lainie Friedman Ross, *Children, Families and Health Care Decision Making* (Oxford, 1998), ch. 6.

[35] See also Allen M. Hornblum, *Acres of Skin* (New York, 1998) on experiments at Holmesburg Prison.

[36] See Norman Daniels, *Just Health Care* (Cambridge, 1985).

Children—or at least prospective children—feature in a number of articles other than Peart's. Steinbock examines the moral status of the embryo and takes an intermediate position. Rejecting both the right of life view and that espoused both famously by Peter Singer which offers a vision of a 'factory in a dish',[37] she argues for our according respect for embryos. On this view they can be used but only in important ways. It is easy to cite examples of unimportant uses, indeed, abhorrent ones: their use as jewellery is fairly uncontentious.[38] Deciding what is important and who is to decide what is important is not so easy (and see Dresser). Islamic jurisprudence has a very clear answer, as Ibrahim shows. But would it want to profit from the results of research carried out in its view immorally? As has been asked in relation to the Human Genome Project, to whom do the findings of research projects belong?[39] Norrie examines various ways of protecting the unborn child outside the context of abortion. He stresses the importance of the United Nations Convention on the Rights of The Child[40]—a document curiously neglected by medical lawyers and medical ethicists. Some of the issues he addresses are also addressed, from a different angle, by Daniels and Golden. We have become so used to repeating the legal conclusion (of English law, for example) that a foetus lacks legal status[41] that it is salutary to be reminded by Norrie that this lack of legal personality is an artificial legal construct, and not a matter of natural fact. That the unborn child lacks legal rights does not mean that we do not have responsibilities (and these may be legal as well as moral) towards her. Freeman examines decisions at the edge of life where the subjects are very sick children and concludes that these life or death decisions are too important to be left to parents. The recent liver transplant dilemma[42] is used as a case study to invigorate the debate.

Life or death decisions feature also in contributions to this volume from Bernat, Ducharme and Liu. Bernat critiques an Austrian Supreme Court decision to authorise an abortion where the pregnant woman was in a persistent vegetative state and was thus unable to consent. Bernat's main concern is as to the lawfulness of the operation. The ethical issues are equally troubling. It was very probably in the family's best interest and they wanted the pregnancy to be terminated. But is this a justification? We have been rightly critical when sterilisations of learning disabled women have been authorised to convenience others.[43] Ducharme's wide-ranging

---

[37] See *The Guardian*, 21 August 1999.

[38] As in *R. v. Gibson* [1990] 3 WLR 595.

[39] Darryl Macer, 'Whose Genome Project?' (1991) 5 *Bioethics* 183.

[40] This dates from 1989. It has been ratified by all states except Somalia and the United States.

[41] See *Re F* [1988] 2 All E R 193.

[42] *Re T* [1997] 1 FLR 502. And see Nicholas A. Pace and Sheila A. M. McLean, *Ethics and the Law in Intensive Care* (Oxford, 1996).

[43] Though it has been constantly denied that this is the reason: for example in *Re B* [1988] 1 A C 199.

essay explores, what he calls, 'thrift euthanasia' in all its forms. His insights into Kevorkian's 'medicide' and into the pre-mortum activities of doctor and state in China and Japan[44] are as troubling as they are revealing. The juxtaposition of Kevorkian's van and Joseph Fletcher's 'situation ethics'[45] will undoubtedly provoke debate—perhaps also examination questions! Liu writes of organ acquisitions in Hong Kong. As elsewhere there are concerns about the mismatch of demand and supply and discussions about the legitimacy of introducing market principles.[46] Given Hong Kong's new status, concerns about the role of the state and of consent, which both Ducharme and Liu examine, will increase.

A number of presentations at the Colloquium, but only two contributions to this volume, addressed mental health issues. Bartlett offers both socio-historical context (where we have come from) and a critique of current policies and reform agenda including its political context (where we are going to). He stresses the importance of non-discrimination. His concerns are with over-definition (who is brought within categories) and with over-prediction (of dangerousness). Mahendra's essay explores the philosophical foundations of the mind/body dualism and its implications in current legal analysis looking at such issues as Viagra (also discussed by Biggs and Mackenzie), senile dementia, ME and conversion hysteria.

Many of the issues discussed in this volume are relatively new. Those which relate to the relationship between doctor and patient are not. They can be traced back to Hippocrates.[47] They do, however, arise in new forms today, Newdick's account of the impact of the private finance initiative has already been alluded to in this introduction. Two other contributions which examine this perennial issue in a contemporary context are the essays by Kloss and by Vedder. Kloss addresses important legal questions which arise in the employment context from pre-employment health screening. Vedder discusses the implications of data mining and shows how our current conceptions of privacy are deficient. There are, Miller notes, over 25,000 websites devoted to health. An increase in knowledge can lead to greater patient care. It can also increase power.

No one theme pervades this collection but the power of medicine—as also its limits—and the control of health care professionals are recurrent and nagging concerns.

---

[44] See Carl Becker, 'Money Talks, Money Kills—The Economics of Transplantation in Japan and China' (1999) 13 *Bioethics* 236.

[45] As in Joseph Fletcher, *The Ethics of Genetic Control* (Buffalo, New York, 1988).

[46] See Pranlal Manga, 'A Commercial Market for Organs? Why Not' (1987) 1 Bioethics 321.

[47] See Roy Porter, *The Greatest Benefit to Mankind* (London, 1997).

The Provision of
Health Care

THE NHS IN PRIVATE HANDS?
REGULATING PRIVATE
PROVIDERS OF NHS SERVICES *

Christopher Newdick

The boundary that has traditionally separated public and private law is being eroded. At least in part, this is because governments all over the western world have sought the assistance of private, commercial interests in the provision of public services. One reason for this trend is explained by the OECD: '[c]apital resources and key groups of highly skilled labour have become very mobile. Multinational businesses have flourished. The freedom of national governments to act individually is significantly restrained. Internationalism has also put pressure on the public sector to improve its own performance.'[1] 'Internationalism', or globalization, requires governments to create an attractive environment for investors by balancing low levels of taxation with high standards of public services, particularly education and health care. Within these constraints, nation states are no longer free to decide entirely for themselves appropriate levels of taxation or public spending policies. The risk of failure is that inward investment will decline with inevitable economic and social consequences to national prosperity.[2] In this new economic environment, large capital-intensive projects,

* With the usual caveats, I thank Professors Tony Prosser and Mike Taggart, and my colleagues Professor Paul Jackson and Dr Chris Hilson for their helpful comments during the preparation of this paper.

[1] *Governance in Transition* (Paris, 1995), 26. See also D. Andrews, 'Capital Mobility and State Autonomy' (1994) 38 *International Studies Quarterly* 193 and A. Marr, *Ruling Britannia—The Failure and Future of British Democracy* (Harmondsworth, 1996), ch. 4. The emphasis of these explanations is economic. For a more political perspective see D. Oliver and G. Drewry, *Public Service Reforms—Issues of Accountability and Public Law* (London, 1996).

[2] See the discussion in *Governance in Transition*, n. 1 above, 10. Note however that to a more limited extent governments have always depended on private finance for the provision of public services. 'It has at no time been possible for the civil government or the foreign and

such as new hospitals, pose significant challenges to the Treasury. Clearly, this development is important in the National Health Service.

One solution has been to encourage private investors to bear the costs of such projects, taking an entirely commercial view of their prospects. [3] In doing so, government may not be in a position simply to impose its own particular requirements. Given the level of investment and commercial risk involved, investors will require a significant margin for profit.[4] Naturally, the Treasury puts a rather more optimistic emphasis on the matter: '[p]rivate firms become the long term providers of services rather than simply upfront asset builders, combining the responsibilities of designing, building, financing and operating the assets in order to deliver the service demanded by the public sector'.[5] In truth, however, if sufficient numbers of hospitals are not built, it will be the government, not private interests, which will be criticized for failing to safeguard the NHS. In this way, economic and political factors may impose significant pressures to enter agreements of this nature.

When commercial organizations collaborate to provide public services, how should their activities be supervised and regulated? Previously these services have been provided by public bodies and subject to judicial review. So far as the beneficiaries of the service (the public) are concerned, nothing has changed, other than the powers and identity of the provider. Should we seek to import similar public, or constitutional values into the activities of private providers of public services?[6] For example, in the future, large numbers, perhaps the majority, of new hospitals may be financed privately because, in an environment of low taxation, public funds will not be capable of undertaking such projects alone. In the light of these developments, the following examines (1) collaboration and the regulation of public services, (2) what is happening in the NHS, (3) public and private law responses to the problem, and (4) governance and accountability in the 'mixed economy' of public welfare.

---

domestic wars of the United Kingdom to be conducted without recourse to private individuals and firms for the supply of goods and services.' See C. Turpin, *Government Procurement and Contracts* (London, 1989), 257.

[3] See the discussion of the first such hospital project by the National Audit Office in *The PFI Contract for the Dartford and Gravesham Hospital* (HC 423, Session 1998–9) which expresses uncertainty whether PFI achieved better value than public funding (para. 2.49). Given the lessons of the past, future schemes may be able to achieve improved economies.

[4] For a pessimistic view of the advantages offered by the PFI, see D. Gaffney and A. Pollock, *Can the NHS Afford the Private Finance Initiative?* (London, 1997) and J. Shaoul, 'Charging for Capital in the NHS Trusts: To Improve Efficiency?' (1998) 9 *Management Accounting Research* 95.

[5] *Partnerships for Prosperity: The Private Finance Initiative* (London, 1998), para. 3.01.

[6] See M. Freedland, 'Government by Contract and Public Law' [1994] *PL* 86 and 'Public Law and Private Finance—Placing the Private Finance Initiative in a Public Law Frame' [1998] *PL* 228.

(1) Collaboration and the Regulation of Public Services

These developments pose the most profound problem of regulation. Both GPs in primary care, and hospitals in secondary care, will exercise control over resources as private parties to contracts (or, perhaps, quasi-contracts in the case of GPs[7]). On the one hand, if their agreements are of an essentially private nature and governed by contractual terms, private law is the relevant mechanism under the law of contract. On the other, if the purpose of the contract is to promote public interest in co-operation with a public authority, public law is an attractive means of regulating conduct, together with the flexibility of judicial review. The traditional 'Diceyan' approach would be clear cut:

Whether a particular decision or activity was subject to the High Court's supervisory jurisdiction depended entirely on the source of the power being exercised. If it was statutory, judicial review was available; but if its source lay in private law, such as contract, administrative law remedies were excluded by the availability of private law remedies.[8]

On this analysis, the essence of the duty imposed on a GP, or private financier, is a private contract. Of course, the contract is to provide services to the public, but the duty to do so is not imposed by public law. It is a private agreement, and any failure in the provision of public services which arises as a result should be the sole responsibility of the public authority. It, in turn, may have its own remedies in contract against the private party for any failure with respect to contractual performance. On the other hand, as the state has withdrawn from many aspects of public service in which it was the natural provider—as public utilities have been nationalized, and services increasingly contracted out to private providers—it has become clear that we live in a 'mixed economy' of public services:

The legal relationships that arise out of these new forms of service provision are neither wholly 'public' nor 'private'. They involve a complex mixture of regulatory activity on the traditional 'command and control' model, intertwined with regulation based on contractual-type arrangements between the direct provider of services and the ultimate purchaser, consumer or customer.[9]

Many would agree that the 'Diceyan' dichotomy is too crude to distinguish the appropriate remedy. Most significantly, of course, as against a private party performing a public service, many beneficiaries of the service,

---

[7] See *Roy v. Kensington, Chelsea and Westminster FPC* [1992] 1 All ER 705.

[8] M. Hunt, 'Constitutionalism and the Contractualisation of Government in the United Kingdom' in M. Taggart (ed.), *The Province of Administrative Law* (Oxford, 1997), 27.

[9] S. de Smith, Lord Woolf and J. Jowell, *Judicial Review of Administrative Action* (5th edn., London, 1995), para. 3–019. See also I. Harden, *The Contracting State* (Buckingham, 1992) and C. Harlow and R. Rawlings, *Law and Administration* (London, 1997), 328–52.

be they patients, schoolchildren, or residents of homes for elderly people, will have no contractual relationship on which to sue. And for those who do have such a relationship, for example 'customers' of private utility companies, proof of damage may be difficult, or impossible, to show, particularly if the complaint is that goods or services have been diluted or withdrawn altogether. In these circumstances, De Smith, Lord Woolf, and Jowell suggest that judicial review ought to be available when the body in question is providing 'a public function', i.e. 'when it seeks to achieve some collective benefit for the public or a section of the public and is accepted by the public or that section of the public as having authority to do so'.[10] Is this a suitable yardstick for determining which bodies should be subject to judicial review? What is the 'collective benefit' and accepted 'authority' concerned? Would a manufacturer of important medicines, a private nursing home, or a GP's practice qualify? The following examines the matter generally, but with particular reference to the private providers in the NHS, namely GPs and privately financed hospitals.

(2) What is Happening in the NHS?

What role should private interests play within the National Health Service and how ought they to be regulated? Aneurin Bevan, the architect of the NHS, considered that: '[t]he field in which claims of individual commercialism come into most conflict with reputable notions of social values is that of health'.[11] He continued: '[s]ociety becomes more wholesome, more sensitive and spiritually healthier, if it knows that its citizens have at the back of their consciousness the knowledge that not only themselves, but all their fellows, have access, when ill, to the best that medical skill can provide'.[12] This notion of social solidarity is not unique to the United Kingdom. Many of the countries of Europe express similar commitments in the field of health care.[13] This common ideal, however, of providing appropriate care simply on the basis of clinical need is continually under pressure from scarce resources. Until 1990, the usual response within the United Kingdom was to insert further links in the chain of command and control, and to seek to improve efficiency, or output, by improved systems of management.[14] But this never delivered the desired improvements and the demands imposed on the NHS continued to exceed supply.

---

[10] De Smith, Woolf, and Jowell, n. 9 above, para. 3–024. See also S. Fredman and G. Morris, 'The Costs of Exclusivity—Public and Private Re-examined' [1994] *Public Law* 69.

[11] *In Place of Fear* (London, 1955) 73.   [12] *Ibid.* 75.

[13] See, e.g., *Choices in Health Care* (Government Ctte on Choices in Health Care, The Netherlands, 1992), *Priorities in Health Care* (Final Report of the Swedish Parliamentary Priorities Commission, 1995) and generally R. B. Saltman and J. Figueras, *European Health Care Reform—Analysis of Current Strategies* (1997).

[14] See R. Klein, *The New Politics of the NHS* (3rd edn, 1995).

A significant break with this 'managerial' response was adopted in the 1990s with the introduction of market incentives to improve output. The central idea was to devolve decision-making authority downwards, so that, for example, GPs themselves, or NHS trust hospitals, became responsible for managing their own funds.[15] The extent to which these changes expanded the influence of the private sector in the NHS, however, was very limited for two reasons. First, NHS hospitals continued to play the predominant role in the provision of secondary care so that private hospitals could never exert significant pressure on NHS resources. Secondly, although, in principle, GP fund-holders had the capacity to influence the allocation of NHS resources,[16] their power to do so was limited both by the numbers of those who chose fund-holding status and the limitations imposed on the financial resources placed at their disposal. To a large extent, therefore, the 'internal market' was truly 'internal'. It continued to depend on institutions within the NHS and did not dramatically expand the contribution of private providers.[17]

Since the election of the Labour government in 1997, however, there have been two significant developments which dramatically enlarge the impact of private finance within the NHS.

(A) PRIMARY CARE

The first is in the field of primary care. Under the Health Act 1999, all GPs have become members of primary care groups (PCGs) and, from the year 2000, may apply to become members of primary care trusts (PCTs). The policy which supports this development is to abolish the divisive element of fund-holding, which encouraged hospitals to prefer to admit the patients of some doctors over others simply on the basis of the status of the referring doctor. At the same time, however, the policy seeks to preserve the incentive to doctors to manage with prudence the funds allocated to them. Thus, PCGs and PCTs will be entitled to retain a proportion of the savings allocated to them in order to improve their premises and the services available to patients. This is an incentive to a private provider within the NHS. GPs are, as a rule, not employees of health authorities. They are independent contractors in business on their own account. Their legal relationship with health authorities is contractual, or 'quasi'-contractual and, like any other business, they have to generate sufficient revenue in order to remain afloat.

---

[15] National Health Service and Community Care Act 1990, s. 5 and Sched. 2. See K. Walsh, N. Deakin *et al.*, *Contracting for Change—Contracts in Health, Social Care and other Local Government Agencies* (Oxford, 1997).

[16] National Health Service and Community Care Act 1990, ss. 14 and 15.

[17] J. Le Grand, N. Mays, and J. Mulligan, *Learning from the NHS Internal Market—A Review of the Evidence* (London, 1998).

Thus, the position of GPs has changed. Now all are encouraged to become managers of funds, and the more effectively they do so, the more they will generate for themselves. Of course, I do not suggest that GPs will participate in the exercise cynically or selfishly. The point is that the environment in which they work will change. This is the more so if GPs supply services under a 'pilot scheme' approved under the National Health Service (Primary Care) Act 1997. Since 1948, responsibility for providing NHS services has vested with local health authorities. Effect has been given to the duty by means of statutory regulations known as the Terms of Service, upon which health authorities engage GPs.[18] The purpose of the 1997 Act, however, is to explore the benefits of a range of other mechanisms for providing primary care to patients. Included amongst the range of possibilities is a private company limited by shares.[19] Clearly, the possibility of creating such a private company could affect doctors' attitudes to their practices, particularly if their decisions concern the value of the shares in the company. Presumably, entire primary care groups, or trusts, could become companies in this way with all the incentives and disincentives such an environment would create. In this case, primary care groups and trusts in the UK would resemble health maintenance organizations in the USA, in which financial considerations are more prominent.[20] Like Aneurin Bevan, we might be concerned about the extent to which commercial interests could undermine the relationship between doctor and patient in the NHS.

(B) SECONDARY CARE

Similar forces are emerging in secondary care as a result of the private finance initiative (PFI). This has profound implications for any capital intensive public welfare programme. Clearly, a new hospital, for example, costing (say) £300 million presents a level of expenditure that governments may be reluctant to underwrite. The proposed solution is the PFI. In this way, private interests contract to finance, design, build, manage, and own the hospital.[21] In return, the NHS trust hospital agrees to occupy and use the hospital for the payment of rent. PFI contracts will last for a period of between twenty and sixty years.

[18] See the National Health Service (General Medical Services) Regs. 1992, SI 1992 No. 635.

[19] See s. 2(1) of the National Health Service (Primary Care) Act 1997. Such shares must be legally and beneficially owned by those engaged in the NHS.

[20] See, e.g., G. Annas, 'Patients' Rights in Managed Care—Exit, Voice and Loyalty' (1997) 337 *New England Journal of Medicine* 219; M. Rodwin, 'Consumer Protection and Managed Care: Issues, Reform, Proposals and the Trade-offs' (1996) 32 *Houston Law Review* 1319; D. Orentlicher, 'Paying Physicians More to do Less: Financial Incentives to Limit Care' (1996) 30 *University of Richmond Law Review* 155.

[21] See the National Health Service (Private Finance) Act 1997 under which, subject to the agreement of the Secretary of State, NHS trusts may enter 'externally financed development agreements': see s. 1.

Originally, the Labour government (unlike its Conservative predecessor) proposed to exclude PFI employees from clinical functions by confining the contracts to managerial and non-clinical functions. However, this separation of 'clinical' responsibilities is difficult to sustain. The distinction is by no means clear-cut. How does it affect the non-touching departments such as radiology, pathology, and pharmacy services? Also, since NHS patients can already be referred to private hospitals for all and any of their care,[22] it is not obvious why similar care cannot be offered by doctors and nurses employed privately in a PFI hospital. Current plans, therefore, do not distinguish the services which may, and may not, be provided privately within a PFI hospital. One would expect a Labour administration to give most sympathetic response to applications which prefer using NHS employees in principle, whilst allowing private provision of clinical services if a sufficiently persuasive case can be made to justify it. A Conservative minister, on the other hand, might be more inclined to approach the matter pragmatically, as one of best value for money, rather than as an issue of principle.

The present focus of PFI is secondary care and the construction of hospitals. So far, some thirty-two major hospitals have been approved, providing capital investment of over £2.5 billion, and the first PFI hospital is expected to become operational by the end of 2000.[23] But there is no reason why it should not operate in primary care. As the Department of Health says: '[t]he next challenge is to replicate the success of big hospital PFI in non-acute settings, and to explore the scope for PFI-type solutions in primary care, especially in those areas where it has proved difficult to improve the standard of existing premises'.[24] There is significant potential for private finance in primary care. The controversy surrounding treatment for erectile dysfunction demonstrates that, although the NHS may be relatively under-funded, there are considerable numbers of patients and potential patients who are prepared to pay for medical treatment themselves. It is precisely the policies which impose resource constraints on public services which have the effect of increasing levels of disposable income for private individuals. Further, there is no reason in principle why PFI should not be extended to *purchasing* responsibilities within the NHS.[25] Demand for care is likely to increase, and some may see advantage in permitting non-governmental bodies to take responsibility for allocating health resources. Hard choices about the future of the NHS, and publicly funded welfare systems in general, are unavoidable.[26] Certain categories of illness

---

[22] National Health Service Act 1977, s. 23.

[23] *The Government's Expenditure Plans 1999–2000, Department of Health Report* Cm. 4203 (London, 1999) para. 4.40.   [24] *Ibid.* para. 4.36.

[25] Indeed, one could contemplate a 'virtual' NHS, financed from general taxation, in which neither purchasers, nor providers were public bodies. See C. Ham, *Public, Private, or Community?* (London, 1996).   [26] See *Making a Difference* (Paris, 1999).

could be excluded from the NHS altogether, or levels of taxation will steadily increase. Alternatively, and, perhaps, least unattractive in political terms, systems of co-payments might be introduced, in which patients share the costs of some categories of treatment.

If this is correct, and particularly with respect to the last of these alternatives, there is very considerable scope for the private sector to increase its contribution to the NHS. In these circumstances, how should we regulate private providers of NHS services?

(3) Public and Private Law Responses

In one sense, equally effective remedies are available to claimants irrespective of whether they pursue remedies in public or private law. If they seek simply an order of the court that the body take, or reverse, a particular decision which affects them, such a solution is available both in private and public law. Private law provides the equitable remedies of specific performance, injunctions, and declarations. And in public law the prerogative writs of certiorari, mandamus, and declarations may achieve the same purpose. But this similarity of result should not mask the *grounds* on which each of the remedies will be granted. Considerable difference exists between the rights conferred by public and private law and, therefore, the responses available to them. In public law government departments should adhere to the highest standards. They are subject to the doctrine of legitimate expectation, they must act impartially and consistently between citizens,[27] and occasionally have to be open, or transparent, in the process by which they do so.[28] Further, in order to prevent public authorities being unduly hampered by litigation, applications must observe strict time limits and obtain the leave of the court under Order 53 before proceeding.[29] By contrast, private law permits contracting parties latitude in deciding with whom they wish to contract. Subject to unlawful discrimination, they are entitled to exclude parties from contracts for good reason or bad, to enforce contractual terms in ways that appear unfair and unreasonable, and (subject to the law of misrepresentation and estoppel) to go back on their non-contractual promises. Further, in cases of breach of contract, specific performance is generally not available to enforce contractual performance,[30] no matter how reprehensible the conduct of the defendant.

---

[27] R. v. IRC, ex p. National Federation of Self-Employed [1981] 2 All ER 93 and R. v. Secretary of State, ex p. Mowla [1992] 1 WLR 70. See generally A. Harding, Public Duties and Public Law (Oxford, 1989), ch. 2.

[28] e.g. R. v. Civil Service Appeal Board, ex p. Cunningham [1991] 4 All ER 310 and Doody v. Secretary of State for the Home Department [1993] 3 All ER 92.

[29] See generally H. W. R. Wade and C. F. Forsyth, Administrative Law (Oxford, 1994), ch. 18.

[30] See Attica Sea Carriers Corp. v. Ferrostaal Poseiden [1976] 1 Lloyd's Rep. 250 and Clea Shipping Corp. v. Bulk Oil International [1984] 1 All ER 129.

The claimant's remedy is confined to damages, even if they are nominal only.[31] To this extent, private law takes a largely amoral view of the conduct of the parties. Thus, it is important to know where the claim arises.

In the following, I will not attempt to describe or define the line that separates public from private law.[32] Instead, I will describe the somewhat random and inconsistent way in which disputes concerning private providers of public services have been categorized by the courts and discuss whether a more coherent and effective mechanism of regulation might be developed.

(A) PUBLIC LAW SOLUTION—*EX PARTE DATAFIN* AND ITS LIMITATIONS

Private bodies may be subject to public law review when they perform a public function. They may be treated as if they are public bodies and have public law standards applied to their conduct. The starting point for analysis is the case of *Ex parte Datafin* and its recognition that judicial review is available to supervise the activities of some private bodies in the context of their regulatory activities. The precise circumstances in which the remedy is appropriate are impossible to define. The need for judgment in this matter is explained by Lloyd LJ as follows:

if the source of power is a statute, or subordinate legislation under statute, then clearly the body in question will be subject to judicial review. If, at the other end of the scale, the source of power is contractual, as in the case of private arbitration, then clearly the arbitrator is not subject to judicial review. . . . But in between these extremes there is an area in which it is helpful to look not just at the source of the power but at the nature of the power. If the body in question is exercising public law functions, or if the exercise of its functions have public law consequences, then that may . . . be sufficient to bring the body within the reach of judicial review. It may be said that to refer to 'public law' in this context is to beg the question. But I do not think it does. The essential distinction, which runs through all the cases . . . is between the domestic or private tribunal on the one hand and a body of persons who are under some public duty on the other.[33]

What is the nature of this 'public duty'?[34] This question has caused difficulty principally in relation to the supervisory functions of private regulators. Rose J has suggested that 'the ratio of the decision [in *Ex parte Datafin*] is that a body may be subject to judicial review if it regulates an important aspect of national life and also with the support of the state in

[31] See *Surrey CC* v. *Bredero Homes Ltd* [1992] 3 All ER 302.

[32] See C. Harlow, 'Public and Private Law: Definition Without a Distinction' (1980) 43 *MLR* 241.

[33] *R.* v. *Panel on Take-overs and Mergers, ex p. Datafin plc* [1987] 1 All ER 564, 583.

[34] See the helpful discussion by P. Craig, 'Public Law and Control over Private Power' in Taggart, n. 8 above.

that, but for its existence, the state would create a public body to perform its functions . . .'.[35] And Hoffmann LJ has observed: '[w]hat one has is the privatisation of the business of government itself'.[36] On the other hand 'the mere fact of power, even over a substantial area of economic activity, is not enough. In a mixed economy, power may be private as well as public. Private power may affect the public interest and the livelihoods of many individuals. But that does not subject it to the rules of public law.'[37] Clearly, the line that divides the two is not clear and will be influenced by judicial instinct.[38]

A great deal more could be said about the ambit of public law in the context of private regulatory activities. I do not propose to do so, however, because its concern is essentially procedural—with the processes that ought to be in place before adjudications are made or complaints resolved by private bodies. Of course, matters of procedure will often be crucial to those in receipt of public services. On the other hand, the existence of perfect *procedures* for screening claims may not satisfy those for whom care has been delayed, or denied. In the NHS, for example, it may be more important to review the decisions of clinicians and managers in the alloca-tion of resources. The more common complaint, therefore, may be that a primary care group has restricted patients' access to care, or that a hospital has underfunded some of its units, so that waiting lists are unacceptably long. When such a decision is made by a private body under contract with a health authority or NHS trust, to what extent can the interventionist approach apply? In *Ex parte Collier*,[39] for example, a 4-year-old boy was denied the surgery to his heart that he 'desperately needed' because suffi-cient nurses could not be made available. He was not treated or referred elsewhere in sufficient time to save his life. The issue in the case was substantive, not procedural—was the boy entitled to care? Similarly, *Ex parte Fisher*[40] concerned a right of access to expensive medicine. The claim was not to the benefit of a procedure, but the substantive right to the drug itself—should the medicine have been stocked in the hospital pharmacy? How would these matters have been dealt with had they arisen in the context of a *privately* owned hospital providing NHS services? Indeed, the

[35] R. v. Fooball Association, ex p. Football League [1993] 2 All ER 833, 845, per Rose J.
[36] R. v. Jockey Club, ex p. Aga Khan [1993] 2 All ER 853, 874.
[37] Ibid. 875.
[38] In R. v. Disciplinary Committee of the Jockey Club, ex p. Massingberd-Mundy [1993] 2 All ER 207, 221, Roch LJ identified the following as relevant to the question, although 'no one test is decisive': (1) the source of the power, (2) the nature of the source of the power, (3) the role fulfilled: does the body hold a position of major national importance. Does it exercise monopolistic or near monopolistic powers in an area in which the public generally or a large section thereof have an interest? (4) Is there an alternative remedy if judicial review is refused? See also Scott v. National Trust for Places of Historic Interest or National Beauty [1998] 2 All ER 705.
[39] R. v. Central Birmingham HA, ex p. Collier (Court of Appeal, unreported, 1988).
[40] R. v. North Derbyshire HA, ex p. Fisher (1997) 8 Med. LR 327.

matter may arise in respect of those who are not patients at all in respect of (say) the visiting hours permitted to visitors. Similar questions arise in relation to GPs allocating resources within their practices, or primary care groups, or striking patients from their lists. How would *Ex parte Datafin* respond, not to applications in respect of regulatory authorities dealing with procedural complaints, but to substantial claims to tangible benefits?

Judicial Review of Substantive Decisions

There has been a suggestion that the principle in *Ex parte Datafin* should be extended to the activities of non-regulatory private bodies. Thus in two education cases Dyson J reviewed the decisions of private schools to admit or exclude their local-authority-assisted students. His Lordship accepted that in principle 'such decisions, if made by private schools, are not subject to judicial review. This is because the source of power of such schools is not statute but consensual, and the decisions are not made in the exercise of public law duties or functions.'[41] However, as the interest of the state in the enterprise increases, together with the degree of statutory supervision which it imposes upon the private provider, judicial review becomes more likely. Thus, in a case concerning the power of a private school to dismiss a pupil who had been admitted under the assisted places scheme (in which local authorities were empowered to pay for students to attend fee-paying schools)[42] His Lordship said:

In relation to the 15 assisted pupils, the school was performing functions very similar to those of a publicly maintained school. I accept the analogy is not exact. One point of difference is that within the parameters of the criteria for eligibility stipulated by the regulations the school was free to select or not select a child for an assisted place. But it seems to me that in relation to pupils who have been selected, the analogy is close. The state has an interest in the education of the assisted pupils at public expense. Parliament has reflected that interest by imposing significant controls over the way in which assisted pupils are educated by an independent school. Those controls take two forms. First, the controls imposed directly by the regulations by which the schools are bound. Secondly, by giving the Secretary of State considerable powers of control. . . . All these factors lead me to conclude that the respondent exercises public functions in relation to its assisted pupils.[43]

His Lordship concluded that the court did have jurisdiction to reinstate the pupil on a non-paying basis. One of his concerns was the absence of any alternative remedy. In *Ex parte Tyrell*, he said: '[i]f CTCs [City Technology Colleges] are not susceptible to judicial review, pupils . . . will be left without a remedy if they are victims of a wrong . . . unless they have private law rights. . . . There is no contractual relationship between

---

[41] See *R. v. The Governors of Haberdashers Aske's Hatcham College Trust, ex p. Tyrell*, *The Times*, 19 Oct. 1994.

[42] Under the Education (Schools) Act 1997. The powers have since been repealed.

[43] *R. v. Cobham Hall School, ex p. S*, *The Times*, 13 Dec. 1997.

parents and CTCs. That is not, of course, determinative of the issue that I have to decide. It does, however, reinforce the conclusion that I have reached.'[44]

Taken alone, these considerations have the potential of embracing commercial institutions which would not traditionally have been considered to fall within the arena of public law supervision. For example, the state has a significant interest in the pharmaceutical industry. In the UK, the NHS is its only significant purchaser. This interest is reflected both in the systems by which drug prices are regulated and the powers vested in the Secretary of State in the licensing process. Under the Medicines Act 1968, he must determine which drugs should be granted a product licence and which should be withdrawn from circulation if they are no longer safe. Such a network of regulation, however, would not render drug companies subject to the public law supervision of Order 53. It seems most improbable, for example, that a company which withdrew, for commercial reasons, a medicine which offered significant public benefit would be subject to an order of mandamus ordering it to make it available. Indeed, such an order seems improbable even in relation to a body established by statute in respect of its commercial responsibilities.[45] Thus, the National Coal Board (established under the Coal Industry Nationalization Act 1946) was for some purposes to be regarded as a public body subject to judicial review. But a decision to close a colliery was of a different character. It was:

An executive, or business, or management decision in exactly the same category as a decision in similar circumstances made by a public company. Of course it has public interest. Of course it deals with the public . . . But it is not . . . a decision in the field of public law when made by a nationalised industry created by statute any more than it would be if it had been made by a commercial company in public ownership.[46]

Which response most appropriately governs GPs? NHS patients have no private rights in contract with their doctors. GPs are engaged by health authorities under regulations made pursuant to the National Health

---

[44] R. v. *The Governors of Haberdashers' Aske's Hatcham College Trust, ex p. Tyrell, The Times,* 19 Oct. 1994. By contrast, in R. v. *Jockey Club, ex p. Aga Khan* [1993] 2 All ER 853, 873, Farquharson LJ said: '[i]n the present appeal there is no hardship to the applicant in his being denied judicial review. If his complaint that the disciplinary committee acted unfairly is well founded there is no reason why he should not proceed by writ seeking a declaration and an injunction.' See also R. v. *Fernhill Manor School, ex p. Brown* (1992) 5 ELR 159, Brooke J.

[45] Precisely such an application occurred in France when, in the face of hostility from pressure groups, Roussell-Uclaf Laboratories refused to make available the morning-after pill RU 486 (mifegyne). The Minister of State for health purported to instruct the company to do so but the Conseil d'Etat declared the order void. See *Confédération Nationale des Associations Familiales Catholiques et autres* (25 Jan. 1991, no. 103.143).

[46] R. v. *National Coal Board, ex p. National Union of Mineworkers* [1986] ICR 791, 795.

Service Acts.[47] Regulations govern, amongst other things, the circumstances of their admission onto, and removal from, the health authority's medical list; the nature of the services to be made available to patients; rights to accept, reject, or strike off patients from the doctor's list; the compulsory assignment of patients to doctors; the scale of fees by which they are remunerated; and the procedures to be adopted in matters of complaints and discipline.[48] Perhaps the nature and extent of their regulation indicate that, as a general rule, they fall within the jurisdiction of public law. Equally, different considerations may apply to those who practise as limited companies under the National Health Service (Primary Care) Act 1997. Clearly, there is no precise test by which the matter may be resolved. However, allowance must be made for a further difficulty in determining the nature of the supervision suitable for public authorities. The decision that a body is subject to judicial review may leave unresolved the question of the nature and intensity of the review itself.

The Intensity of Review

The question of the appropriate level of intensity of review in these cases is illustrated in respect of the refusal of a private water company to act on the recommendations of its local health authority to fluoridate its water supply. Section 87 of the Water Industry Act 1991 permits water authorities wide discretion whether to fluoridate water supplies. In *R. v. Northumbrian Water Ltd, ex parte Newcastle and North Tyneside HA*,[49] there was no dispute about the scientific and medical evidence that fluoridation was of substantial public benefit, particularly in the prevention of childhood tooth decay. Following a request by the local health authority that it do so, was the company under a duty to fluoridate the supply in the public interest? Collins J dealt with the case as follows. His Lordship accepted that 'the decision of the respondent water company is amenable to judicial review. That, of course, is because it carries out functions which can be described as public. . . . It may be that 50 years ago the Respondent would not so readily have been considered to be within the scope of the judicial review and it might have been considered that it was analogous to, for example, a nationalised industry which the courts in those days did not regard in the same way. But we have moved on since then and the scope of a judicial review is very much wider. . .'.

His Lordship then addressed the issue of the nature of the obligations imposed by public law in the circumstances of this case. Within the frame-

---

[47] See principally the National Health Service (General Medical Services) Regs. 1992, SI 1992 No. 635 and the National Health Service (Service Committees and Tribunal) Regs. 1992, SI 1992 No. 664, both have been substantially amended.

[48] See my discussion in I. Kennedy and A. Grubb (eds.), *Principles of Medical Law* (Oxford, 1998) ch. 1.

[49] LEXIS, ENGGEN file, 1998.

work of its statutory duties, he was careful to balance the private interests
of the company and its shareholders. His reasoning deserves careful attention. He said:

It is perfectly clear that as a commercial organisation the respondent company
cannot be said to possess powers solely in order to use them for the public good.
It has its commercial obligations to its shareholders. It must exercise its powers in
accordance with those obligations. Equally it must comply with any statutory
duties imposed upon it by Parliament. It must also exercise any discretion that it
may be given within the scope of the statute which confirms it. Thus if it is clear
that the discretion given by the statute is to be confined because of the particular
wording of the statute, then it would be wrong to exercise it outside those
confines. . . .[50]

Thus a water authority is entitled to say no [to fluoridation], even though it has
no reason to doubt that it would be in the interests of the health of its customers,
that its customers want it, that the health authority wants it and that it is in accordance with the policy of the government. It is entitled to say to itself 'it would
involve us in expense. It will involve us in a potential liability if things go wrong,
and it is quite impossible to be sure that there will not be a mistake made by an
employee which creates a liability in those circumstances. We are very sorry but we
do not think that we wish to take the risk.'
. . . that would be a perfectly proper approach for a water company to take and
that is because it does not have the same duty that a public body, which is not a
commercial undertaking, has. It is entitled to look to the interests of its shareholders and that is something which is inevitable, as it seems to me, when privatised
bodies, are given control of matters such as the provision of water, and something
which no doubt Parliament has recognised. If Parliament wishes to ensure that a
discretion is exercised on particular principles, then it must set out those principles
in the statutory provisions.

Strikingly, therefore, although the company was exercising a public function, its obligations were owed only to its shareholders and not to the
public. Although it was subject to the procedural supervision of judicial
review, the substantive principles regulating it were entirely private in
origin. Minimalist reasoning of this nature would clearly have the most
profound implications for those who agree to provide private services
within the NHS. The logic of construing the nature and extent of the
obligation in accordance with the empowering statute is impeccable,
although one might question the very limited construction put on the
intention of Parliament. This approach is also consistent with the rule of

---

[50] To the same effect see *Mercury Energy Ltd* v. *Electricity Corporation of New Zealand
Ltd* [1994] 1 WLR 521, 528, *per* Lord Templeman: '[t]he express statutory duty of the defendant is to pursue its principal objective of operating as a successful business, by becoming profitable and efficient, by being a good employer and by exhibiting a sense of social
responsibility. It was for the defendant to determine whether its principal objective would
best be served by allowing the contractual arrangement to continue or by terminating the
contractual arrangements'.

statutory interpretation that private law rights remain intact unless they are expressly and unambiguously taken away by statute.[51]

This range of responses clearly leaves in doubt the question of the nature and extent of the public law supervision appropriate to private providers of public services. In view of this uncertainty could private law provide a better vehicle for redress?

(B) PRIVATE LAW REGULATION ACCORDING TO 'PUBLIC' VALUES?

A number of arguments support the proposition that private providers of public services are, as a general rule, more appropriately regulated by private law. The first is that the exercise of the discretion to contract out to private bodies does not necessarily engage the public authority in an activity regulated by public law.[52] Thus, in *Ex parte Hibbit and Saunders*, Waller J said that if a governmental body carrying out its governmental functions enters into a contract with a third party, including another public body, 'the obligations that it owes will be under the contract, *unless there also exists some other element that gives rise in addition to a public law obligation*'.[53] The exact nature of the additional element referred to is not entirely clear.[54] The mere fact of statutory underpinning is neither a necessary nor a sufficient criterion for imposing public law standards upon a statutory body. It is not a necessary precondition because the principle of legitimate expectations may arise independently of statute.[55] Nor is it a sufficient condition for at least two reasons. First, the statutory body may be acting in an area which is properly the subject of private law, such as matters concerning contracts of employment.[56] Secondly, statutory duties may be imposed in ways which permit varying degrees of discretion. There comes a stage when the ambit of the authority's discretion is, or has become, so narrow or technical that the applicant's right to a benefit is no longer subject to discretion.[57] Thus, the exercise of a health authority's discretion in relation to disciplinary matters is a matter of public law,[58] but the issue of proper rates of remuneration is not.[59] Here, the matter is properly resolved by a trial of fact within private law. The additional element required has been said to be 'one of overall impression and degree.

[51] See *Pierson* v. *Secretary of State for the Home Department* [1997] 3 All ER 577, 592, *per* Lord Browne-Wilkinson. See also *Raymond* v. *Honey* [1982] 1 All ER 756.

[52] See the discussion in S. Arrowsmith, 'Judicial Review of the Contractual Powers of Public Authorities' (1990) 106 *LQR* 277.

[53] *R.* v. *The Lord Chancellor, ex p. Hibbit and Saunders, The Times*, 12 Mar. 1993 emphasis added.

[54] See A. Harding, *Public Duties and Public Law* (Oxford, 1989), 12–14.

[55] See *Council for Civil Service Unions* v. *Minister for the Civil Service* [1985] AC 374.

[56] e.g. *R.* v. *East Berkshire HA, ex p. Walsh* [1984] 3 All ER 425.

[57] *Trustees of the Dennis Rye Pension Fund* v. *Sheffield CC* [1997] 4 All ER 747.

[58] *R.* v. *Secretary of State for Health, ex p. Hickey* (1993) 10 BMLR 12.

[59] N. 7, above.

There can be no universal test',[60] although 'the instinctive reaction that there should be a remedy does not lead to the conclusion that there must be a public law remedy'.[61]

Thus,[62] it cannot be assumed that the public authority's discretion to engage a private provider will itself be amenable to judicial review. It would be odd, therefore, if the private provider were presumed to be regulated by public law principles when the discretion of the public authority to delegate its power in this way was subject to no such presumption.

Secondly, PFI agreements appear by their nature to be private commercial agreements. Detailed Treasury guidance on the supervision of the terms of private finance agreements has the flavour of a private contract. PFI contracts should contain disincentives against under-performance which have the appearance of liquidated damage clauses;[63] there should be provision for break clauses to enable the parties to withdraw from the contact;[64] rights to step in temporarily or terminate the contract following a breach of contract;[65] and procedures for varying the agreement as circumstances require.[66] Notable for their absence are any of the public law requirements that might be expected of public authorities. The 'Nolan' Committee, for example, identified seven 'principles of public life', namely, selflessness, integrity, objectivity, accountability, openness, honesty, and leadership. It recommended that these principles should permeate the appointment and conduct of public boards and quangos which, in addition, should be governed by specific codes of conduct.[67] Matters of this nature are not included in private finance agreements with private providers. These considerations, therefore, appear to convey a private contractual intention to enter a commercial agreement for mutual benefit.[68] They do not suggest overwhelmingly that the relationship should be governed by principles of public law.

Regulating 'Discretion' in Private Law

Private law, then, may be the more appropriate mechanism for regulating the PFI contracts. Does it possess sufficient flexibility to adapt itself to the difficulties presented in these circumstances? If the control of discretion is a persistent problem in public law, the question is also central to private finance agreements. Many contracts between public and private bodies to

---

[60] R. v. *Legal Aid Board, ex p. Donn & Co* [1996] 3 All ER 1, 11, *per* Ognall J.

[61] R. v. *The Lord Chancellor, ex p. Hibbit and Saunders*, n. 53 above, *per* Waller J.

[62] For criticism of the uncertainty created by this distinction, which arose in the wake of the decision of the House of Lords in *O'Reilly* v. *Mackman* [1983] 2 AC 237, see Wade and Forsyth, n. 29 above, 684–95.

[63] See *Practical Guidance to the Private Finance Initiative—Further Contractual Issues* (London, 1997), ch. 3.

[64] *Ibid.* ch. 6.   [65] *Ibid.* chs. 7–9.   [66] *Ibid.* ch. 10.

[67] *Standards in Public Life* Cm. 2850-I (London, 1995), ch. 4.

[68] See generally Turpin, n. 2 above.

design, build, and operate large projects will be for long periods of time.[69] Obviously, such contracts will have to accommodate the possibility of large alterations and adjustments. They will need to be expressed in the most flexible terms to allow the parties discretion in their performance of their obligations. How should discretion of this nature be regulated? From a purely private perspective, the exercise of the power to choose presents the problem of regulating the freedom which is inherent in the law of contract. 'In a contractual context, discretion is often taken to mean that a matter is remitted to the unrestricted choice of a person.'[70] As Lord Reid said:

> It might be, but it never has been the law, that a person is only entitled to enforce his contractual rights in a reasonable way and that the court will not support an attempt to enforce them is an unreasonable way . . . that is not the law, no doubt because it would cause too much uncertainty.[71]

Nevertheless, mechanisms for regulating the exercise of discretion between parties to contracts have been developed, as Lord Hoffmann has said, in the law of contract, the doctrine of restraint of trade, the EEC Treaty, 'and all the other instruments available in law for curbing the excesses of private power'.[72] For example, the *regulatory and supervisory* responsibilities of private authorities should be conducted to standards similar to those imposed upon public authorities. It was said, for example, with respect to the adjudicatory functions of the London Metal Exchange that there was 'no reason why rules developed in public law as being applicable to administrative or regulatory bodies acting in the public domain should not, in principle, be applied to administrative or regulatory bodies acting in circumstances to which only the private law applies'.[73] Thus, in the same way that administrative action is subject to control by judicial review, so the exercise of private adjudicatory power must be:

> fair in the circumstances, in accordance with the rules of natural justice; . . . legal; and . . . not . . . unreasonable in the sense of what is called *Wednesbury* unreasonable.[74]

---

[69] On the problems presented by long-term contracts see E. McKendrick, 'The Regulation of Long-Term Contracts in English Law' in J. Beatson and D. Friedmann (eds), *Good Faith and Fault in Contract Law* (Oxford, 1995).

[70] See J. Beatson, 'Public Law Influences in Common Law' in *ibid.* 267 for a helpful account of the regulation of private discretion.

[71] *White and Carter (Councils) Ltd* v. *McGregor* [1962] AC 413, 430. See also *Walford* v. *Miles* [1992] 2 AC 128 (HL); a pre-contractual duty to negotiate in good faith was unenforceable for being inherently repugnant to the adversarial position of the parties. Note, however, the right to exercise discretion may be restricted by an implied term that the choice will be made reasonably, as a reflection of the presumed intention of the parties. See *Paula Lee Ltd.* v. *Robert Zeehill* [1983] 2 All ER 390.

[72] N. 36, above.

[73] *Shearson Lehman Hutton Inc* v. *Maclaine Watson & Co. Ltd* [1989] 2 Lloyd's Rep. 570, 625, col. 2. [74] *Ibid.* 627, cols. 1–2.

This use of public law language and concepts as a means of regulating private parties is striking. Indeed, the difference between this private law approach and the public law response in *Ex parte Datafin* may amount to nothing. To what extent, however, may it be applied *beyond* the regulatory context?

Professor Oliver has argued that 'the common law is ready to develop its supervisory jurisdictions by imposing duties of fairness and rationality in private law on those exercising private power that will be similar in many respects to the duties imposed in judicial review'.[75] She identifies in particular 'five key values' of autonomy, dignity, respect, status, and security as notions which permeate both sides of the public–private divide. Thus, for example, the law concerning the duties imposed upon common callings,[76] businesses affected with a public interest, and the prime necessity doctrine are cited as means by which, quite independently of the law of contract, common law has restricted the freedom of private parties to act as they please. In addition, within the law of 'defective' contracts, the law of restraint of trade will declare void in the public interest restrictions imposed on individuals which are unreasonable, it refuses to recognise the validity of agreements entered into after a misrepresentation has been made, or following the duress or undue influence of one party over another,[77] and it protects employees from some forms of unfair treatment by their employers.[78] In equity, it modifies the inflexibility of the law of consideration by means of promissory estoppel, it superimposes public interest considerations over duties of confidentiality to protect public safety,[79] or to encourage the exposure of wrongdoing.[80] It demands *Wednesbury*-type duties of trustees of pension funds,[81] and may impose other fiduciary duties when circumstances require it to do so.[82]

To what extent, however, do these cases really provide a mechanism for

[75] D. Oliver, 'Common Values in Public and Private Law and the Public/Private Divide' [1997] *PL* 630, 630. See also D. Oliver, 'The Underlying Values of Public and Private Law' in Taggart, n. 8 above, and W. Friedmann, 'Public and Private Law Thinking: The Need for Synthesis' (1959) 5 *Wayne Law Review* 291 for previous recognition of the arguments in this area.

[76] e.g. *Constantine* v. *Imperial Hotels Ltd* [1944] 1 KB 693.

[77] See P. Finn, 'Controlling the Exercise of Power' (1996) 7 *Public Law Review* 86.

[78] See generally R. Rideout, 'Implied Terms in the Employment Contract' in R. Halson (ed.), *Exploring the Boundaries of Contract* (Aldershot, 1996). In *Provident Financial* v. *Hayward* [1989] IRLR 84, it extended to preventing an employer from putting the employee on 'garden leave' during the currency of the contract of employment.

[79] e.g. *W* v. *Egdell [1990] 1 All ER 835.*

[80] e.g. *Initial Services* v. *Putterhill* [1968] 1 QB 396.

[81] e.g. *Cowan* v. *Scargill* [1984] 2 All ER 750.

[82] On the other hand, the existence of a fiduciary relationship between doctor and patient is far from certain. Contrast the views of I. Kennedy, 'The Fiduciary Relationship and its Application to Doctors and Patients' in P. Birks (ed.), *Wrongs and Remedies in the Twenty First Century* (Oxford, 1996), with A. Grubb, 'The Doctor as Fiduciary' [1994] 47 *Current Legal Problems* 311.

introducing into private law principles analogous to those governing public bodies? Overwhelmingly, the focus of their concern is to demand minimum standards of conduct between individuals, particularly in connection with contracts. Admittedly, there is reference to public interest considerations in some of the cases, for example on common callings, businesses affected with a public interest, and prime necessities, but, perhaps owing to the existence of the welfare state and the growth of public services generally in the United Kingdom, these have largely fallen into disuse. As a result, they provide a rather narrow and fragile basis for a new law of accountability in private law. The same observation may be made of the law of restraint of trade. There may once have been a time when the courts were genuinely concerned with the security of employment of large sectors of the community, and in an age when trade barriers were more common, could be persuaded to uphold such restraints of trade 'in the public interest'.[83] More recently, however, it has become difficult to discover cases in which the public interests have prevailed over a reasonable agreement between the parties. Thus, even when a doctor, who had left his partnership subject to a restraint of trade clause, presented the court with a large petition signed by his patients that he should be permitted to remain and practise within the area forbidden by the restraint 'in the public interest', the court upheld the clause against him.[84] His private agreement prevailed over the public interest of permitting his patients to be treated by the doctor of their choice.

Even if this private law jurisdiction were to revive and expand, how would it apply to bodies responsible for public services? Take the example of a general practice which has established itself as a private company, or a primary care group, or trust. It is wrestling with the demands made upon its limited financial allocation. It might attempt to balance a number of competing considerations in deciding how to allocate its funds, for example the different demands made upon it from central and local authorities; the conflicting priorities identified by clinical, managerial, or lay interests; and the different merits of promoting fewer individual or larger collective interests.[85] Given that each of these strategies may provoke complaint, how could private law respond? What procedural mechanism would be available to the complainant and what substantive principles of review would be applied? Even if a public law response is directly transplanted into the private law to resolve the matter, Collins J has given some indication of the sort of response that might be anticipated in the *Northumbrian Water Ltd* case. Companies enter business with a variety of objectives; any

---

[83] e.g. *McEllistrim v. Ballymacelligott Co-operative and Dairy Society Ltd* [1919] AC 548.

[84] *Kerr v. Morris* [1986] 3 All ER 217.

[85] See C. Lupton, S. Peckham, and P. Taylor, *Managing Public Involvement in Healthcare Purchasing* (Buckingham, 1998) 31, and R. Klein, P. Day, and S. Redmayne, *Managing Scarcity—Priority Setting and Rationing in the National Health Service* (Buckingham, 1996).

application of judicial review must take this into consideration. Precisely this observation applies to manufacturers of valuable pharmaceutical products and the owners of private nursing homes. Both make a substantial contribution to the NHS,[86] but their supervision in law is most appropriately conducted within the sphere of private law. To involve the judges in balancing the need of a company to make a profit against the social needs of the community without further guidance would be a truly radical, indeed revolutionary, step.[87] Though private law appears to be the most appropriate forum for resolving disputes in this area, by comparison to public law, it offers no coherent system for supervising private providers of public services.

(4) Governance and Accountability in the Mixed Economy of Public Welfare

Neither public law nor private law is well adapted to the new problems created by the 'mixed economy' of public welfare, in which commercial interests undertake responsibility for providing public services. A more systematic response is required to impose a specific statutory scheme for all arrangements in which statutory services are provided by private providers. Equally, within the current framework of law, effective solutions to the problem are not readily available.

(A) CAN WE AVOID THE 'PUBLIC/PRIVATE' LAW DISPUTE?

We have become accustomed to dealing with the problem of determining when public bodies are acting within their 'private' or 'public' domains of discretion. Ideally, we should seek to avoid similar difficulties in relation to private providers of public services. As Lord Woolf MR has observed, this preliminary question causes a disproportionate drain on time and resources in disputes involving public authorities.[88] It would be preferable to presume that private providers are subject to private law unless the circumstances demand otherwise. Also, the reasons for giving public bodies the procedural safeguards of Order 53 are less obvious in relation to private companies acting within the terms of a contract. In practice, however, the distinction is so deeply engrained that a policy which sought to reduce its application to 'private' bodies would be bound to fail. Indeed,

---

[86] See Laing's *Healthcare Market Review* (London, 1998), ch. 1. The NHS purchases over £1 billion from the independent sector, over half of which is on residential care and day care for those with learning disabilities. See *The Regulation of Private Medicine and other Independent Healthcare* (HC 281–I, Session 1998–9), para. 2.12.

[87] See M. Taggart, 'State-Owned Enterprises and Social Responsibility: A Contradiction in Terms' [1993] *NZ Recent Law Review* 343, discussing *Auckland Electric Power Board* v. *Electricity Corp. of NZ Ltd* [1993] 3 NZLR 53.

[88] See *Trustees of the Dennis Rye Pension Fund* v. *Sheffield CC* [1997] 4 All ER 747.

the concept of public law supervision of private bodies performing public functions is now developing both in European law[89] and the European Court of Human Rights.[90] Far from contracting, the scope of the concept is likely to expand.

(B) CAN WE CLARIFY THE POSITION OF THE PUBLIC AUTHORITY?

Parliament should address more precisely the nature and extent of the public authority's residual responsibilities. One technique available for doing so is adopted by the Deregulation and Contracting-out Act 1994. This fixes the public authority from which the service has been contracted out with liability for any failure of the private provider ('the authorised person'). Thus:

> Anything done or omitted to be done by . . . the authorised person . . . in connection with the exercise or purported exercise of the function shall be treated for all purposes as done or omitted to be done . . . by or in relation to the Minister or office-holder in his capacity as such. [91]

By this principle, when statutory services are provided privately, the source of the responsibility for any failure is not in doubt. Consequently, action against the public authority remains intact and the public authority, in turn, may recover its own losses from the private provider under the terms of its contract.[92] The major limitation of the 1994 Act, however, is that it is limited to specific cases in which the relevant minister has issued an order contracting out the relevant service.[93] No such order is required within the NHS, however, because both health authorities and NHS trust hospitals have powers of their own to contract out to private providers entirely independent of the 1994 Act.[94] Could the common law adopt an analogous approach to statutory duties contracted out to private providers? A public authority may be permitted to contract out the performance of those services to private providers. What it cannot do is enter a contract which varies or restricts the extent or nature of the statutory duty

[89] The approach has developed in European law as a means of enforcing Community dir. directly against private bodies performing public functions as 'an emanation of the state'. See *Foster* v. *British Gas* [1990] 3 All ER 897, 917–18 and V. Kvjatkovski, 'What is an "Emanation of the State"? An Educated Guess' (1997) 3 *European Public Law* 329.

[90] The European Court of Human Rights has indicated its willingness to extend the scope of the European Convention to some private bodies exercising public functions. See *Costello-Roberts* v. *United Kingdom* [1994] EHRR 112 for a discussion of corporal punishment within a private school and A. Clapham, 'The Privatisation of Human Rights' (1995) 1 *European Human Rights Law Review* 20 and P. R. Ghandi and J. A. James, 'Parental Rights to Reasonable Chastisement and the ECHR' (1999) 3 *Int. J H R* 97.

[91] S. 72(2) of the 1994 Act.   [92] S. 72(3) of the 1994 Act.

[93] S. 69(2) of the 1994 Act.

[94] See s. 23(1) National Health Service Act 1977 (with respect to health authorities) and s. 72(3) National Health Service and Community Care Act 1990 (with respect to NHS trust hospitals).

imposed upon it. Statutory bodies have no common law powers of their own. As Lord Denning MR has said with respect to a local authority, '[t]he local council here are a public authority established by statute to exercise statutory powers and to perform statutory duties. They have no power to do anything except such power as Parliament has given them.'[95] Thus, although the duties imposed by the National Health Service 1977 are notoriously vague and are sometimes referred to as 'targets', rather than duties,[96] in principle actions for judicial review and breach of statutory duty are available against the public authority regardless of the arrangements it has made with a private provider.

Of course, this assumes that there is some residual *public* authority which is responsible for the service in question. If, as in the case of public utilities, the authorities responsible have been privatized, or (as in the *Northumbrian Water* case) the private company is ostensibly subject to public law supervision, but the intensity of the review is extremely slight, alternative mechanisms of regulation must be developed. (In addition, even when there is a residual public authority against whom action may be taken, many may feel that the responsible private body should also be subject to direct action by those they purport to serve.)

(C) REGULATE THE PRIVATE PROVIDER

Clearly, public and private remedies seek to react to complaints after something is alleged to have gone wrong. An alternative, indeed an unavoidable, solution is to introduce further layers of regulation as a means of defining the standards of service to be achieved and, thereby, avoiding disputes.[97] The difficulty presented by 'regulation', however, is the immense variety of systems and objectives it may embrace.

Regulation involves three different tasks. The first is that of regulating monopoly, mimicking the effect of market forces through implementing controls on prices and on quality of services. The second is regulating for competition, creating the

---

[95] R. v. *Basildon DC, ex p. Brown* (1981) 79 LGR 655, 661. See similarly R. v. *Somerset CC, ex p. Fewings* [1995] 1 All ER 513, 524, *per* Laws J: '[f]or private persons, the rule is that you may do anything you choose which the law does not prohibit. It means that the freedoms of the private citizen are not conditional upon some distinct and affirmative justification for which he must burrow in the law books. Such a notion would be anathema to our English legal traditions. But for public bodies to rule is opposite, and of another character altogether. It is that any action to be taken a must be justified by positive law. A public body has no heritage of legal rights which it enjoys for its own sake. . . . The rule is necessary in order to protect the people from arbitrary interference by those set in power over them.'

[96] e.g. *Danns* v. *Department of Health* (1995) 25 BMLR 121.

[97] See C. Hood and C. Scott, 'Bureaucratic Regulation and New Public Management in the United Kingdom: Mirror-image Developments' (1996) 23 *Journal of Law and Society* 312. As Tony Prosser has said, 'it can be suggested that on some crucial matters the industries were more autonomous under nationalisation than under regulation after privatisation'. See his *Law and the Regulators* (Oxford, 1997), 42.

conditions for competition to exist, and policing it to ensure that it continues to exist. . . . Thirdly, there is social regulation, where the rationale is not primarily economic but is linked to notions of public service. [98]

Naturally, these objectives may be pursued singly or in combination. In addition, varying degrees of formality may be employed to promote them. At one end of the spectrum is the degree of control surrounding GPs. It is statutory in origin, highly detailed, and prescriptive, and it provides a range of sanctions against poor performance.[99] Should a regulator be provided with powers to step in when circumstances require to suggest, or impose, solutions of his own? Recall the case of *Ex parte Collier*, in which a 4-year-old boy was effectively abandoned by his health authority. We ought to be sensitive to the need to regulate such a case in respect of private providers in the NHS. Procedures could be provided within the PFI contract indicating how such a case should be resolved; indeed, an independent tribunal might be considered as a mean of resolving disputes.[100] The *Northumbrian Water Ltd* case amply illustrates the need for more care in this regard. Given the absence of privity of contract with the patient, consideration ought to be given to the question of how patients themselves could rely on such an undertaking.[101]

Less intensive regulation of the medical profession is illustrated by the Medical Act 1983, under which the General Medical Council is given broad discretion on matters of professional discipline concerning doctors.[102] Still more distant control is illustrated by the Registered Homes Act 1984 which requires private nursing homes and hospitals to register their activities with a statutory authority and to be subject to periodic inspections.[103] Equally, statutes may adopt a more generic approach

---

[98] *Ibid.* 6. See also T. Prosser, 'Theorising Utility Regulation' (1999) 62 *MLR* 196 and P. Jackson and C. Price, *Privatisation and Regulation* (Oxford, 1994).

[99] Providers of private prisons are similarly obliged to operate their prisons 'subject to and in accordance with . . . the 1952 [Prison] Act . . . and prison rules'. See s. 84 of the Criminal Justice Act 1991.

[100] For such a suggestion in the United States, see G. Annas, 'Patient's Rights in Managed Care—Exit, Voice and Loyalty' (1997) 337 *New England Journal of Medicine* 210 and the discussion in C. Newdick, 'Public Health Ethics and Clinical Freedom' (1998) 14 *Journal of Contemporary Health Law and Policy* 335.

[101] e.g. the jurisdiction of the Health Service Ombudsman extends to private providers of NHS services. Persons are subject to his investigation if '(a) they are persons (whether individuals or bodies) providing services in England under arrangements with health service bodies or family health service authorities, and (b) they are not themselves health service bodies or family health service providers'. See s. 2, of the Health Service Commissioners Act 1993, inserted by s. 2A of the Health Service Commissioners (Amendment) Act 1996. Thus, lawful though it may be, the Health Service Ombudsman proposes to 'name and shame' GPs who strike patients from their lists without good reason, see *Annual Report of the Health Service Ombudsman*, HC 54 (Session 1998–9), xx. [102] See s. 36.

[103] For discussion of the inadequacy of the regulation provided by the Registered Homes Act 1984, see *The Regulation of Private Medicine and other Independent Healthcare*, HC 281–I (Session 1998–9). This system is to be reformed, see *Regulating Private Healthcare* (London, 1999).

by imposing standards on a variety of different bodies and activities. Thus, the Human Rights Act 1998 applies to 'public authorities', namely 'any person certain of whose functions are functions of a public nature'. The Act provides that 'it is unlawful for a public authority to act in a way which is incompatible with a Convention right'.[104] Clearly, providing services on behalf of the NHS would, *prima facie*, be a public function within the 1998 Act. Equally effective forms of regulation may also be available from entirely informal systems.[105] Increasing interest is expressed in systems of governance which seek to regulate institutions by principles which reflect the legitimate expectations of those they serve.[106] Thus, for example, grievance procedures, performance monitoring, citizen's and patient's charters, and chartermark recognition may operate on an informal basis, and achieve their objectives more quickly and effectively than formal legal mechanisms. Obviously, responsible organizations will often use procedures of this nature as a means of promoting customer confidence and satisfaction and, indeed, enhancing the quality of its service.

In devising such systems of regulation, however, we should be sensitive to two further matters. Regulatory power, be it public or private, remains subject to judicial review if the regulator acts illegally, irrationally, or with procedural impropriety.[107] To this extent, so long as regulators remain subject to residual judicial supervision, the problem of the proper framework remains. 'Regulation', therefore, may serve only to postpone, rather than resolve, the problem. Secondly, provisions of this nature may create obstacles to claimants. They require us to consider whether the existence of a public procedure against a body should negate further alternative remedies. In Australia, for example, telecommunications services have been privatized and contracts awarded to private contractors supervised by a statutory regulator. In response to an application for review of a decision not to extend particular services to certain parts of the country, the Federal Court of Australia declined to intervene, reasoning that 'seeing that is the remedy given by the statute, I do not think there is any other remedy'.[108] In seeking to provide additional protection to individuals, we should be careful not to undermine the statutory duties owed to intended beneficiaries.[109]

---

[104] S. 6.

[105] See J. Allsop and L. Mulcahy, *Regulating Medical Work—Formal and Informal Controls* (Buckingham, 1996).

[106] See P. Vincent-Jones, 'The Regulation of Contractualisation in Quasi-markets for Public Services' [1999] *PL* 304 and P. Vincent-Jones, 'Responsive Law and Governance in Public Services Provision: A Future for the Local Contracting State' (1998) 61 *MLR* 362.

[107] For such an example of a successful challenge in the context of statutory authority, see *R. v. Parliamentary Commissioner for Administration, ex p. Maurice and Audrey Balchin* [1997] JPL 917. For judicial review of private regulatory power, see *Ex p. Datafin*, n. 33, above.

[108] *Yarmirr v. Australian Telecommunications Corporation* (1990) 96 ALR 739, 750, quoting Lord Denning MR in *Southwark LBC v. Williams* [1971] Ch. 734, 743.

[109] The preferable explanation may be that statutory duties do not necessarily create duties

Conclusion

We have no systematic response, either in common law or statute, to the problems presented by the expansion of the private provision of public services. At present, the reaction to the erosion of the public/private divide in law, brought about by the mixed economy of public welfare has been random. Central to the discussion are the issues of democracy, openness, and civic responsibility, rather than merely private systems of accountability and governance.[110] We have no readily available response capable of providing a satisfactory solution. As public and private 'partnerships' become more common, we must be sensitive to the problems they create and the range of solutions available to resolve them. The problem is one of supervision, created by the need to permit commercial contractors discretion in the performance of their contracts, both as an inducement to enter partnerships of this nature and because of the long periods of time during which the contracts are designed to run. More extensive layers of regulation offer a partial solution, but this too presents uncertainty and may not exclude the need for litigation and further judicial exploration of the issue in any case.

Ideally, we might prefer all our public services to be funded from general taxation and provided by public bodies subject to public law supervision. Alternatively, we might accept the need for private contractors of public services, provided they are held to comparable standards of supervision by specific statutory or contractual undertakings. In reality, however, neither may be available. The degree to which we can insist on standards of this nature is not simply a matter of dictating which constitutional and public service values we consider important. Ultimately, this reconfiguration of public services reflects a political response to economic pressure. The greater the dependency of government on 'partnerships' of this nature, the less it will be in a position to impose unilateral requirements of its own. The distribution of rights and duties between commercial providers of public services and those they serve has to accommodate this fact.

---

in private law: see in relation to actions in negligence, Lord Browne-Wilkinson's discussion in *X* v. *Bedfordshire CC* [1995] 3 All ER 353 and *Stovin* v. *Wise* [1996] 3 All ER 801.

[110] T. Prosser, 'Bringing Constitutional Values Back In' in R. Bellamy, V. Bufacchi, and D. Castiglione (eds.), *Democracy and Constitutional Culture in the Union of Europe* (Edinburgh, 1995).

HEALTH CARE INFORMATION TECHNOLOGY AND PROVIDER ACCOUNTABILITY: A SYMBIOTIC RELATIONSHIP

Frances H. Miller*

Introduction

As the century turns, health care accountability issues have penetrated public consciousness on both sides of the Atlantic,[1] and have surfaced to a lesser extent in Australia as well.[2] In the UK, the Bristol Royal Infirmary Trust proceedings have trained the spotlight on management deficiencies associated with hospital clinical care.[3] In the USA, public dissatisfaction with managed care is driving the current state and federal legislative push for greater health insurer accountability to subscribers.[4] Such high-profile 'political' controversies are the tip of a trans-oceanic iceberg of health sector accountability pressures.[5] These address every imaginable medical-legal

---

* Professor of Law, Boston University School of Law; Professor of Public Health, Boston University School of Public Health; and Professor of Health Care Management, Boston University School of Management. Heather Burkhardt, Boston University School of Law Class of 2000, provided invaluable research assistance and editorial commentary for this article, for which she has my deepest thanks.

[1] 'Study Reveals Nations Face Public Discontent with Health Care', *U.S. Newswire*, 1998 WL 13606662, 22 Oct. 1998; Michael L. Millenson, *Demanding Medical Excellence: Doctors and Accountability in the Information Age* (Chicago, 1997).

[2] For background see, Gwen Gray, 'Access to Medical Care under Strain: New Pressures in Canada and Australia' (1998) 23 *Journal of Health Politics, Policy & Law* 905, 935–41; Tanya Ahmed, 'The Move Towards Evidence-based Medicine: Doctors, Educators, Administrators and Patients must Commit to Health Care Decisions based on Valid Scientific Research' (1995) 163 *The Medical Journal of Australia* 60.

[3] *Roylance* v. *General Medical Council Council (No. 2)* Privy Council, Judgment of 24 March 1999.

[4] William M. Sage, 'Regulating Through Information: Disclosure Laws and American Health Care' (1999) 99 *Columbia Law Review*; James Sabin, 'The Ethics of Accountability in Managed Care Reform' (1998) 17 *Health Affairs* No. 5, 50; Marc Rodwin, 'Managed Care and the Elusive Quest for Accountable Health Care' (1996) 1–SPG *Widener Law Symposium Journal* 65.

[5] Leona Markson and David Nash, *Accountability and Quality in Health Care: The New Responsibility* (Joint Commission on the Accreditation of Healthcare Organizations, Terrace IL, 1995); Donald Irvine, 'The Performance of Doctors: The New Professionalism' (1999) 353 *The Lancet* 1174; Marnix Elsenaar, 'Law, Accountability and the Private Finance Initiative in the National Health Service' [1999] *Public Law* 35; David Nash, 'Renegotiating

question, from ensuring that doctors disclose the risks of proposed therapy to patients realistically (which may entail doing so in statistical terms),[6] to maintaining the privacy of e-mail communications between providers and patients,[7] to monitoring the ethical conduct of clinical research.[8]

This paper will first briefly describe the increasing connection between information technology and accountability in the health sector. It will then review recent legal proceedings in Britain, the USA, and Australia, wherein health care provider accountability was a core issue, and the legal analysis was significantly affected by evidence that information technology can produce. The paper will then describe selected examples of health service databases about providers, easily accessible to almost anyone over the internet. It takes the position that information technology functions as a powerful stimulus to health care quality improvement. The data this technology is capable of generating have already greatly enhanced the accountability of health service providers, but sometimes in ways that were not entirely expected. Rather than functioning primarily as an aid to third parties in monitoring, improving and policing the quality of care, US experience demonstrates that information technology turns out to be an equally powerful stimulus to provider self-improvement and quality innovation.[9] Finally the paper concludes that making the fruits of information technology more widely accessible to all can substantially improve overall patient health.[10]

The Symbiosis Between Information Technology and Accountability

Information technology advances have been a primary catalyst for the burgeoning 'accountability movement' in medicine, for they are adept at detecting health service problems.[11] They are also tailor-made for identifying

Medicine's Contract with Patients' (1998) 316 *British Medical Journal* 1622; 'Study reveals nations face public Discontent with Health Care', *U.S. Newswire*, 22 Oct. 1998.

[6] *Chappel v. Hart*, (1998) 156 ALR 517, High Court of Australia (HCA) 55; *Johnson v. Kokemoor*, 545 NW 2d 495 (Wis. 1996); *Arato v. Avedon*, 858 P 2d 598 (Cal. 1993).

[7] Alissa R. Spielberg, 'Online Without a Net: Physician–Patient Communication by Electronic Mail' (1991) 25 *American Journal of Law & Medicine* 267.

[8] Evan M. Melhado, 'Innovation and Accountability in Clinical Research' (1999) 77 *The Milbank Memorial Quarterly* 111, predicting that public accountability will require clinical research to incorporate outcomes research and clinical science and decision-making—subjects that were traditionally thought to compromise basic research.

[9] Thomas M. Burton, 'HMO Rates Hospitals: Many Don't Like It, But They Get Better', *Wall Street Journal*, 22 Apr. 1999, 1; Linda O. Prager, 'Spotlight Spurs Improvement', *American Medical News,* July 1999, 11 (managed care plans); E.L. Hannan *et al.*, 'The Decline in Coronary Artery Bypass Surgery Mortality in N.Y. State' (1995) 273 *Journal of American Medical Association* 209; Cf. 'The Outcome of Outcomes Releases: A Report Card on Report Cards', *Medical Utilization Management*, 16 Apr. 1998, (pg unavailable online @ 1998 WL 10321875).

[10] A recent National Committee for Quality Assurance report confirms this point. See Linda O. Prager, 'Spotlight Spurs improvement', *American Medical News*, July 1999, 11.

[11] See generally, Susan M. Wolf, 'Quality Assessment of Ethics in Health Care: The Accountability Revolution' (1994) 20 *Am. JL & Med.* 105.

non-productive therapeutic practices, and for uncovering promising avenues to better patient care.[12] High-speed networked computers, in concert with increasingly sophisticated software applications for health care, have already spawned quantum advances in knowledge about basic science, as the Human Genome Project has already graphically demonstrated.[13] These advances have also shed new light upon the appropriateness and effectiveness—as well as the baseline costs—of health service delivery.[14] These systems are capable of breaking out complex cost and quality information on a per-provider basis, regardless of whether that provider is an institution or an individual. Moreover, modern information technology has vastly enhanced the ease and speed with which an astonishing wealth of health care information can be acquired and disseminated by almost any savvy person with access to a computer terminal.[15]

This plethora of knowledge about what health services seem effective, not to mention cost-effective (and which seem not to be), coupled with data indicating which institutions and/or clinicians seem particularly good (or bad) at providing those services, inexorably points toward intensified accountability for health sector providers and managers. Computer-facilitated aggregation of clinical data tends to raise quality and cost of care questions which cannot reasonably—or morally—be ignored by any thinking person. It makes little sense to persist in medical practices which have been demonstrated not to benefit patient health—or worse, to harm it—particularly since the funds spent on ineffective therapy could be far better spent elsewhere. Similarly, when evidence produced with the aid of information technology reveals that better modes of treatment are presumptively feasible, only the myopic would disregard it without a strong rationale for doing so. Accountability and health care information technology thus fit hand in glove to further the interests of better overall patient health services. At its best, the law functions as handmaiden to their symbiotic relationship.

---

[12] Elizabeth A. McGlynn *et al.*, *Health Information Systems: Design Issues and Analytic Application* (Rand Health, Santa Monica CA, 1998).

[13] Eric S. Lander, 'Scientific Commentary: The Scientific Foundations and Medical and Social Prospects of the Human Genome Project' (1998) 26 *Journal of Law, Medicine and Ethics* 184; Daniel L. McKay, 'Patent Law and Human Genome Research at the Crossroads: The Need for Congressional Action' (1994) 10 *Santa Clara Computer and High Technology Law Journal* 465.

[14] Derek F. Meek, 'Telemedicine: How an Apple (or Another Computer) May Bring Your Doctor Closer' (1998–9) 29 *Cumberland Law Review* 173.

[15] See, e.g., http://www.guideline.gov (current clinical practice guidelines clearing-house, with standardized abstracts, appropriateness analyses, scientific basis of the guideline graded, etc.); see generally, Symposium 'Electronic Medical Information: Privacy, Liability & Quality Issues' (1999) 25 *Am. JL & Med.* Nos. 1 & 2.

Legal Proceedings Where Information Technology Plays a Central Role

Information technology has unequivocally enlarged the sphere of human knowledge about all aspects of health care. And knowledge matters greatly when it comes to legal analysis. The law has always recognized that what an individual knows—or ought to know—is a critical component of liability for common law negligence.[16] In medical malpractice litigation doctors are thus held to the standard of professional knowledge (including knowledge generated by information technology) that is possessed by 'a similar doctor in similar circumstances'.[17] Quasi-criminal sanctions can also be imposed on professionals who are aware, thanks to information technology, about problems within their spheres of responsibility, if they shirk professional obligations to ameliorate them. For example, a physician-manager knowing (or who ought to know) of a situation statistically shown to be detrimental to patient health and having responsibility for ensuring that the entity delivers good quality care, can lose a professional licence to practise medicine for failure to correct the problem.[18] Finally, an individual with a statutory duty to act who knows (or ought to know) of statistically validated health and safety hazards can be considered criminally liable if appropriate corrective action is not forthcoming.[19] The recent highly-publicized prosecution of French government officials controlling that country's HIV-tainted blood supply is a case in point.[20]

UK LEGAL PROCEEDINGS

The General Medical Council (GMC), which licenses British physicians, recently found[21] (and the Privy Council has confirmed[22]) that the Bristol Royal Infirmary Trust's physician-administrator, faced with mortality statistics indicating grave problems within the paediatric cardiac surgery unit, had a clear duty to inquire aggressively into the reasons for the unit's poor performance. These statistics showed, among other things, that

---

[16] *Restatement (Second) of Torts* (St Paul Minn., 1965) §290; W. Page Keeton *et al.*, *Prosser and Keeton on the Law of Torts* (5th edn. West Publishing Co St. Paul, Minn. 1984) §32, at 182.

[17] *Bolam* v. *Friern Hospital Management Committee* [1957] 1 WLR 582; *Klisch* v. *Meritcare Medical Group, Inc.*, 134 F.3d 1356 (8th Cir. 1998).

[18] See note 3, above.

[19] See American Law Institute Model Penal Code Official Draft, 1962, Art. 2 (3): '[l]iability for the commission of an offense may not be based on an *omission* unaccompanied by action unless: (a) the omission is expressly made sufficient by the law defining the offense; or (2) a duty to perform the omitted act is otherwise imposed by law'.

[20] Douglas Starr, 'The World AIDS the Misguided Idealism Behind France's Tainted-Blood Affair', *Los Angeles Times*, 21 Mar. 1998, M2.

[21] General Medical Council, *Announcement on Findings of Fact (in the Case of Wisheart, Dhasmana, Roylance)* 29 May 1998.

[22] *Roylance* v. *General Medical Council Council (No. 2)* Privy Council, Judgment of 24 Mar. 1999.

between 1990 and 1994 the nationwide mortality rate for hole-in-the-heart repairs was 14 per cent, while the mortality rate for repairs done by Bristol's chief of medicine (who headed the unit) was 60 per cent.[23] With respect to arterial switch operations, the nationwide mortality rate at the time was 10 per cent, while the rate for the surgeon performing the same procedure at Bristol was 66 per cent.[24]

Furthermore, the GMC found that had the hospital's administrator undertaken the rigorous investigation the situation called for, he would have faced a clear obligation to prevent unnecessary infant deaths in the future. His failure to investigate and to take remedial action, in light of ominous statistics indicating life-threatening clinical shortcomings in the paediatric cardiac surgery unit, warranted negating the administrator's licence to practise medicine.[25] The chief of medicine, who happened to be one of the operating surgeons, lost his licence as well, in part for his administrative failure to rectify the situation.[26] The other paediatric cardiac surgeon involved was severely sanctioned,[27] which effectively ended his medical career.[28]

In post-Bristol England greater public accountability for the health sector has become a political imperative, since the medical profession demonstrated itself woefully inadequate to the task of policing its own members before the GMC stepped in.[29] The highly visible Bristol Royal Infirmary Inquiry chaired by Professor Ian Kennedy[30] was the Labour government's response to the clamor for better public oversight over the quality of British clinical care once the GMC findings were released. The government also established the National Institute for Clinical Effectiveness[31] and its companion Commission for Health Improvement,[32]

---

[23] General Medical Council, *Announcement on Findings of Fact (in the Bristol proceedings)* para. 2, Sched. A, 29 May 1998.

[24] *Ibid.* at Case No. 1B, para. 2, Sched. C.

[25] Frances H. Miller, 'Doctors in the Executive Suite: Should the US and UK be Putting MD Licensure at Risk for Shortfalls in Institutional Quality of Care?' [1998] *Journal of Health Law* 217.

[26] General Medical Council, *Announcement of Findings of Fact (in the Bristol proceedings)*, Case No. 1–A, 29 May 1998.

[27] The surgeon's continued licensure was conditioned on his refraining from performing pædiatric cardiac surgery for three years. General Medical Council Professional Conduct Committee, *Case of Wisheart, Dhasmana, Roylance*, Day 74, at 74–7.

[28] The surgeon was subsequently sacked by the Bristol Trust. 'Bristol Heart Doctor Sacked', *The Guardian*, 10 Sept. 1998, *The Guardian* 9.

[29] R. Smith, 'All Changed, Changed Utterly: British Medicine will be Transformed by the Bristol Case' (1998) 316 *British Medical Journal* 1917.

[30] The inquiry's web site is accessible at http://www.bristol-inquiry.org.uk.

[31] NHS Executive, *A First Class Service: Quality in the New NHS* (London, 1998). See also Richard Thomson, 'Quality to the Fore in Health Policy—at Last: But the NHS Musn't Encourage Quality Improvement with Punitive Approaches' (1998) 317 *BMJ* 95; Rudolf Klein, 'Competence, Professional Self-regulation, and the Public Interest' (1998) 316 *The Lancet* 1740.

[32] NHS Executive, *A First Class Service: Quality in the New NHS* (London, 1998).

in reaction to widespread dissatisfaction about the British medical profession's relatively slow take-up of the advances that evidence-based medicine have to offer. Moreover, both the Royal College of Physicians and the GMC have recently proposed that physician competence be evaluated annually, a radical departure from the relatively *laissez-faire* attitudes toward self-governance of the past. [33]

Britain is not the only country to have experienced recent medical-legal proceedings wherein the fruits of health care information technology have played a pivotal role. For example, computers have long been critical to the economic analysis central to understanding whether a practice challenged as anticompetitive has in fact restrained trade. Thus in antitrust litigation complex computerized market-share analysis has always been essential to calculating whether a proposed hospital merger would (or would tend to) give the new entity monopoly power in the USA's health sector.[34] But in the past few years both the USA and Australia have also decided tort cases in which computer-generated morbidity and mortality statistics were central to the reasoning of the court.

LEGAL PROCEEDINGS IN THE USA

The two most well-known US cases to discuss medical statistics in the context of tort litigation, *Johnson* v. *Kokemoor*[35] and *Arato* v. *Avedon*,[36] both broke new ground in discussing the kinds of statistical information which patients might consider material to a fully-informed consent before undergoing recommended therapy. *Kokemoor* went even further to suggest that at some point comparative morbidity and mortality data might give rise to a physician's duty to refer patients elsewhere, to those providers with better success rates at performing the recommended procedure than the referring doctor.

In *Arato* v. *Avedon*, the deceased suffered from pancreatic cancer, which is almost invariably fatal within a matter of months after diagnosis. Mr Arato had filled out a form on his first visit to the defendant oncologists, affirming that he 'wish[ed] to be told the truth about [his] condition' rather than having his doctors 'bear the burden' for him. However, none of his doctors informed him or his family about the extremely high statistical mortality rate for his disease following a short period of illness, although they did tell him that most pancreatic cancer patients eventually died of their disease, regardless of therapy. The plaintiff contended that had Mr Arato been aware of the grim survival statistics, he would have

---

[33] 'Consultant Physicians should be Appraised Annually' (1999) 318 *BMJ* 419.

[34] *Federal Trade Commission* v. *Freeman Hospital*, 69 F.3d 260 (8th Cir. 1995); *United States* v. *Mercy Health Services*, 902 F.Supp. 968 (ND Iowa, 1995).

[35] *Johnson* v. *Kokemoor*, 545 NW2d 495 (Wis. 1996).

[36] *Arato* v. *Avedon*, 858 P2d 598 (Cal. 1993).

foregone the fruitless therapy he endured that diminished his quality of life. Moreover, he would have paid more attention to settling his financial and professional affairs so that his estate would not have suffered avoidable tax and business losses.

The jury found for the defendant physicians on a claim for failure to secure Mr Arato's informed consent, but the California Court of Appeal reversed. Its opinion held that the doctors had a duty to disclose Mr Arato's statistical life expectancy *as a matter of law* in order to secure his informed consent to radiation and chemotherapy.[37] The California Supreme Court reversed the Court of Appeal's decision. It held that, notwithstanding that a Californian patient is entitled to all information *material* to a decision about whether to undergo therapy before giving informed consent, the 'propriety' of a doctor's disclosing life expectancy statistics to a cancer patient must be judged by the professional standard of disclosure. In other words, the standard depends on what other doctors tell their other patients about their life expectancies.

The California Supreme Court opted for a relatively abstract formulation of the informed consent doctrine, focused on the materiality (to the patient's decision) of the information that a doctor must disclose. The opinion rejected the idea that a particular *type* of information—in this case mortality statistics—be disclosed as a matter of law. Citing the language in its landmark *Cobbs* v. *Grant* opinion, the Supreme Court reiterated that juries are best situated to determine whether the doctor has disclosed 'adequate information to enable [the patient to make] an intelligent choice'.[38] However, it noted that *Cobbs*' patient-centered materiality standard of disclosure applied only to the *risks* of proposed therapy. Holding that statistical life expectancy data fall outside the scope of risk *per se*, the court considered that disclosing such data should be governed by the professional standard instead. Thus, what other doctors tell their pancreatic cancer patients about life expectancy is the standard against which the defendant doctor's disclosure to Mr Arato should have been measured.

One could certainly take issue with Mr Arato's doctors' position that most patients contemplating submitting to experimental procedures would not consider life expectancy data (both with and without recommended therapy) to be material information, particularly when the contemplated therapy would seriously impair their quality of life. This author has in fact challenged such reasoning in another article.[39] However, the California Supreme Court's decision that doctors should not be compelled to provide such statistics *as a matter of law* seems intuitively correct. Some patients

[37] *Arato* v. *Avedon*, 11 Cal. Rptr. 2d 169, 177–8 (Cal. App. 1992).
[38] 502 P 2d 1 (1972).
[39] Frances H. Miller, 'Health Care Information Technology and Informed Consent: Computers and the Doctor–Patient Relationship', 31 *Indiana Law Review* 1019, 1033 (1998).

prefer having their doctors make medical decisions for them, and the law supports their right to remain uninformed if they so choose.[40] In addition, the therapeutic privilege still retains some importance for the small subset of emotionally fragile other patients whose physical health would be significantly compromised by knowledge of rapidly impending death.[41]

The Wisconsin Supreme Court's opinion in *Johnson* v. *Kokemoor* probed much more deeply into the materiality, for informed consent purposes, of comparative morbidity and mortality statistics related to performing surgical repairs of basilar bifurcation aneurisms. The plaintiff in *Kokemoor* was operated on in a community hospital by the defendant doctor, who had performed approximately forty aneurism repairs previously. Most of these procedures had been undertaken during medical training, when he was under direct supervision, and none of them had been repairs of the highly complex type of lesion with which the plaintiff presented. Although the operation was a technical success, the plaintiff emerged an incomplete paraplegic with seriously compromised bodily functions, speech, sight, and mobility. A jury found in her favour, based on the defendant's failure to secure her informed consent before proceeding with such technically demanding surgery.

Evidence the plaintiff produced at trial showed that Dr Kokemoor not only exaggerated her need for surgery, but exaggerated his experience in performing it as well. He told her that the procedure carried a 2 per cent risk of morbidity and mortality. Her expert witnesses testified, however, that even surgeons having extensive experience with the particularly complicated aneurism with which she was afflicted encountered 10.7 per cent morbidity and mortality risks. Moreover, her experts showed that a surgeon having the defendant's limited range of experience would be more likely to have rates 'closer to the 30 per cent range'.

Like California, Wisconsin has adopted a 'materiality' standard of disclosure for informed consent, holding that a doctor must disclose all information which would be material to a reasonable patient's decision whether to undergo recommended therapy.[42] The Wisconsin statute embodying the materiality requirement explicitly states that a physician must inform patients of 'the availability of all alternate, viable medical modes of treatment and about the benefits and risks of these treatments'.[43] The defendant argued that the trial court erred in admitting evidence about the doctor's own projected risk statistics, claiming that the statutory language required that the risks *generally* involved with the procedure be

---

[40] See David E. Ost, 'The Right Not to Know' (1984) 9 *Journal of Medicine & Philosophy* 301, 306–7.

[41] See Alaska Statutes, sec. 09.55.556(b)(4)(1983).

[42] *Scaria* v. *St Paul Fire & Marine Ins. Co.*, 227 NW2d 627 (Wis. 1975), codified at Wis. Stat. at §448.30.

[43] Wis. Stat at §448.30.

communicated, but not those that might be associated with any particular physician.

The Wisconsin Supreme Court rejected the defendant's 'bright line' formulation of the statutory mandate, citing its own previous holding that the statute 'should not be construed so as to unduly limit the physician's duty to provide information that is reasonably necessary under the circumstances'.[44] The plaintiff had introduced sufficient evidence to show that had a reasonable person in her position known of Dr Kokemoor's relative inexperience in performing the surgery, she would not have permitted him to operate. The Supreme Court held that the trial court therefore did not err in concluding that 'when different physicians have substantially different success rates with the same procedure' those statistical facts are material and therefore admissible. In the context of this case, Dr Kokemoor's inexperience constituted an independent risk factor which a reasonable patient could well deem material on the basis of comparative surgical success rates.[45]

Finally the defendant physician asserted that the trial judge should not have admitted expert testimony that he should have referred the plaintiff to a nearby tertiary care facility for surgery because she needed such a complicated procedure, asserting that any failure to refer had no relevance to an informed consent claim. The court disagreed, holding that when a surgeon's experience significantly affects the morbidity/mortality calculus, the doctor's failure to *refer* may 'be material to the ability of a reasonable person in plaintiff's position to render an informed consent'.[46] This statement is a potential bombshell for informed consent cases, for all physicians during the course of their medical training and practice must at some point perform procedures for the 'first' time. Few procedures carry the serious risks of death and disability that aneurism repairs do, but presumably few patients in such situations who were aware of the experience issue would be willing to assume guinea pig status if they could possibly avoid it.

Previously US courts had generally steered clear of requiring physicians to tell patients about their own comparative risk factors, on the theory that medicine is hardly an exact science.[47] Judges also shied away from requiring doctors to disclose any personal 'failings' that might be thought to increase patient risk, such as their alcoholism[48] and drug dependency.[49] They justified this on the theory that alcoholism and drug dependency are addictions, and impaired physicians should be encouraged to undergo

---

[44] *Martin v. Richards*, 192 Wis.2d 156, at 175, n. 30 (1995).

[45] The court gave short shrift to the defendant's claim that admitting evidence pertaining to his limited experience with the procedure was unfairly prejudicial. 199 Wis.2d 615, 642–7 (1996).   [46] *Ibid.* at 648, emphasis added.

[47] *Kennedy v. St Charles General Hospital*, 630 So. 2d 888, 892 (La. App. 1993).

[48] *Ornelas v. Fry*, 727 P 2d 819 (Ariz. Ct. App.. 1986).

[49] C. Morrow, 'Doctors Helping Doctors' (1984) 14 *Hastings Center Report* 32.

rehabilitation.[50] Requiring doctors to disclose their addictions to patients would theoretically deter them from seeking help. The *Kokemoor* logic, however, implies that physicians should indeed reveal this information to patients, regardless of its impact on patient willingness to be treated by them. If one takes seriously the idea that a patient must be fully informed of all facts material to a decision about whether to proceed with recommended therapy in order for consent to be valid, *Kokemoor* signals that these decisions are ripe for overruling. With regard to a doctor's HIV-positive status, US courts have been more willing to require doctors to disclose that fact to their patients,[51] notwithstanding scholarly opinion to the contrary.[52]

For the purposes of this paper, the *Kokemoor* and *Arato* decisions are important because they directly address the issue of informing patients about what information technology reveals concerning the promise and perils of modern health care. Without doubt, future US case law will carry this discussion of the relevance and materiality of complex medical data in medical malpractice litigation a great deal further.

Legal Proceedings in Australia

Informed patient consent and full disclosure by physicians have also been at the heart of recent medical negligence litigation in Australia.[53] The extent to which patients in Australia should be informed of statistical risks presented by their own physicians has yet to be determined. Judging from Australia's High Court 1998 decision in *Chappel* v. *Hart*,[54] however, disclosure of medical data in general, and perhaps even data relating specifically to the skills of a particular physician recommending a procedure, may become the required standard for securing informed consent. The High Court's three to two decision, upholding a $172,000 damages award for a patient the jury deemed to be uninformed,[55] underlines the responsibility of medical personnel to inform patients fully about the risks of therapy. The increasing adoption of information technology by the Australian health care sector will presumably reinforce the thrust of the disclosure requirement.

In *Chappel* v. *Hart*, the patient suffered from a serious throat ailment and underwent elective surgery on her aesophagus, without being warned by her physician of the possible consequences should perforation and

---

[50] W. E. McAuliffe *et al.*, 'Psychoactive Drug Use among Practicing Physicians and Medical Students' (1986) 315 *New England Journal of Medicine* 805.

[51] *Behringer* v. *The Medical Center at Princeton*, 592 A 2d 1251 (NJ 1991).

[52] Leonard H. Glantz *et al.*, 'Risky Business: Setting Public Health Policy for HIV-infected Individuals' (1995) 70 *The Milbank Quarterly* 43.

[53] Paul Gerber, 'Has Informed Consent become a Legal Nightmare?' (1995) 163 *The Medical Journal of Australia* (*Med. J Aust.*) 262.

[54] N. 6, above.   [55] *Ibid.*

subsequent infection occur. These did in fact ensue, paralyzing the patient's right vocal cord and causing her to lose her voice. Although surgery was apparently inevitable at some point, the plaintiff argued that had she been aware of the serious risks involved, she would have postponed the procedure as long as possible. She also asserted that she would have had it eventually performed only by the most experienced surgeon in the field. The defendant physician argued that any failure to inform the plaintiff adequately of the risks involved was not causally related to her medical problem. The High Court made '[t]he onus on doctors to fully inform their patients of any risks associated with their treatment . . . significantly heavier',[56] by following the modern trend of requiring full information disclosure to ensure provider accountability to patients exercising their autonomy.

This is not the first time that Australian courts have faced the issue of informing patients about the statistical risks associated with treatment. In the 1983 case of *F* v. *R*,[57] the Full Court of South Australia held that doctors had a duty to warn patients of the 1 per cent failure rate associated with tubal ligation. The court held that 'people had a right to make their own life decisions and a doctor should not lightly make the judgment that a patient does not wish to be fully informed'.[58] It rejected, for informed consent purposes, the physician-centred standard of care established in the landmark British *Bolam* case.[59] This rejection of the *Bolam* principle for informed consent cases was later adopted by the Australian High Court in *Rogers* v. *Whitaker*.[60] That judgment held that doctors have a duty to warn patients of material risks in order to secure their informed consent, regardless of whether their peers actually do so.[61]

The patient-centred standard of disclosure set forth in *Rogers* v. *Whitaker* was found to have been breached by the defendant in *Chappel* v. *Hart*. Kirby J stated in his majority opinion '[t]his is the duty which all health care professionals . . . must observe: the duty of informing patients about risks, answering their questions candidly and respecting their rights, *including (where they so choose) to postpone medical procedures and to go elsewhere for treatment*'.[62] As noted by Kirby J, one of the difficulties in this case was the lack of statistical evidence to support the plaintiff's contention that the more experienced the surgeon the less the risk of resultant complications. 'Although no statistical or other evidence was called to

---

[56] Roderick Campbell, 'Heavier Onus on Doctors to Tell Patients of Risks', *Canberra Times*, 3 Sept. 1998, 6.
[57] *F* v. *R* (1983) 33 SASR 189.   [58] Gerber, n. 54 above, 262.
[59] *Bolam* v. *Friern Hospital Management Committee* [1957] 1 WLR 582 (a doctor is not negligent if complying with standards set forth by a responsible body of medical opinion).
[60] *Rogers* v. *Whitaker* (1992) 175 CLR 479.
[61] Gerber, n. 54 above, 262; see also Philip W. Bates, 'Social and Legal Changes in Medical Malpractice Litigation' (1995) 163 *Med. J Aust.* 264.
[62] *Chappel* v. *Hart*, n. 6 above, emphasis added.

demonstrate that recourse to a more experienced surgeon would necessarily have reduced the risk of the kind of injury that occurred ... intuition and commonsense suggest that the higher the skill of the surgeon, the less is the risk. ...'[63] Although no statistical data were presented to quantify the particular risk involved in the case, one can infer from Kirby J's judgment that had such information been available, it would have been used to illustrate a physician's duty to inform patients of all potential risks involved in the proposed therapy.

Australian case law has increasingly recognized the patient's right to know of all surrounding risks involved in medical treatment. One of those risks may relate to the physician's lack of skills or experience in handling the patient's problem. That being so, the expanding use of information technology can be expected to further the Australian physician's responsibility to divulge information, and ultimately perhaps to disclose statistical evidence about provider-specific risks of proposed therapy.[64]

Basic Principles of Legal Accountability

When an individual or an institution is held legally accountable for a situation causing harm to persons or property, we mean that the actor involved must have possessed some control over the relevant circumstances, and had an obligation to exercise that control. That duty can be imposed by statute,[65] arise from a fiduciary relationship between the parties,[66] or emanate from a common law source of obligation inhering in the nature of their relationship.[67] Individuals must possess a degree of responsibility for proper performance of activity causally related to perceived problems before they will be held liable for any detrimental results.[68] The accountability principle applies to an expanding group of potentially responsible health sector players, beyond the conventional physician and hospital targets. Prominent among these are now certain corporate managers of health services, on both sides of the Atlantic.[69] Government is increasingly being brought into the accountability fray as well, with some limited success.[70] And as previously noted, the concept of accountability applies to a constantly expanding range of health care issues, as well as to the growing number of parties.

---

[63] *Chappel* v. *Hart*, n. 46 above, 55, emphasis added.

[64] Martin B. Van Der Weyden, 'The Bristol Case, the Medical Profession and Trust: An Open Professional Culture Promoting the Quality of our Work and the Safety of our Patients is Paramount' (1998) 169 *Med. J Aust.* 352.   [65] See n. 20 above.

[66] *Moore* v. *Regents of University of California*, 793 P 2d 470 (1990).

[67] *Cortes* v. *Baltimore Insular Line*, 287 US 367 (1932).   [68] See n. 4 above.

[69] See, n. 4 above, and *Murphy* v. *Board of Medical Examiners of the State of Arizona*, 949 P 2d 536 (Ariz. App. 1997).

[70] R. v. *North Derbyshire Health Authority, ex parte Fisher* (1997) 38 BMLR 76.

The accountability principle is fundamentally bottomed on disclosure, for without information about the quality and/or cost of health services, performance evaluation, and appropriate remedial action are impossible. In the UK, the relatively recent pressure for health information disclosure is heavily weighted toward a newly-heightened determination to hold medical professionals and institutions more responsible for their actions in the wake of *Bristol*.[71] In the USA, the push for information disclosure encompasses both traditional provider accountability issues and the special conditions required in order for competitive health care markets to function efficiently.[72]

Serious market-based choice among health services is impossible without reliable information about the quality and costs of care. The pressure for public disclosure of medical data—because it aids purchaser choice of health care—has accordingly been much stronger and of longer duration in the market-oriented US health sector than it has in the government-provided UK system.[73] In both countries, however, modern information technology facilitates the trend toward greater accountability for all those involved with health service delivery.

Computerized Health Services Information

Edith Mumford once quipped that knowledge is power—provided one has it about the right person.[74] Computers potentially shift the power that knowledge confers toward the end-users of information technology, for computers give anyone with a terminal access to mind-boggling stores of intelligence about health services. How good that information is,[75] and how well it is understood and used,[76] are separate questions entirely. However, computerization plainly creates the potential for a global expansion of awareness about the merits of specific health services.[77] It also promotes evaluating the merits of the individual professionals and institutions providing those services.[78]

SELECTED HEALTH CARE PROVIDER DATABASE EXAMPLES

As at 1997, an estimated 25,000-plus web sites were devoted to the subject

---

[71] Bruce E. Keogh *et al.*, 'Public Confidence and Cardiac Surgical Outcomes: Cardiac Surgery: The Fall Guy in Medical Quality Assurance' (1998) 316 *BMJ* 7147.

[72] Leslie W. Hann, 'Keeping Score', *Best's Review—Life-Health Insurance Edition*, 1 Nov. 1998.

[73] Webster's *New World Dictionary of Quotable Definitions* (2nd edn., 1988) 307.

[74] Seth M. Powsner *et al.*, 'Opportunities for and Challenges of Computerization' (1998) 352 *The Lancet* 1617. [75] Miller, n. 40 above, 1019.

[76] *Ibid.* [77] *Ibid.*

[78] Judy Foreman, 'It's a Tangled Medical Web They Weave on the Internet', *The Boston Globe*, 13 Oct. 1997, C1.

of health care,[79] and a significant portion of these sites constituted gateways to databanks of health service data and information. Search engine rankings of health data web sides are easy to perform through such popular programs as Yahoo, Webcrawler, Lycos and Infoseek using the keywords 'health data'. They quickly reveal the most heavily used data sources. The sophisticated health data researcher will mentally sort the sites by domain, and will evaluate the reliability and potential bias nuances of databank information accessible via, for example, .com (commercial), .org (not-for-profit), .edu (educational), and .gov (governmental) domains accordingly. Many guides to the intelligent use of computerized health data can guide the neophyte toward efficient use of the abundant resources available.[80] Educational systems in developed countries now teach children of all ages to be ever more relaxed and skilled in using computers, and many of today's eager students will mature into the increasingly computer-literate patients, providers, and health service managers of the twenty-first century. Their future proficiency in moving quickly and easily among various goldmines of health information ensconced in computerized systems seems inevitable.

At the turn of the century the USA has far more health service information available on-line than does the UK. The USA's historical legacy of fee-for-service medicine, financed in large part through the medium of private health insurance, explains much of that phenomenon. A system originally based on payment by unit of medical service generates compelling needs for computerization because of the high transaction costs involved in piecemeal billing. Although capitated payment systems have made astonishingly deep inroads on the US fee-for-service model in the past decade or so,[81] American physicians are by now thoroughly accustomed to justifying their fees by documenting specific services they render. They generally do not consider having to provide basic information about the patient care they deliver an unacceptable intrusion on clinical autonomy, although they often rail against the administrative burden.[82]

America's history of billing for health services generated a serendipitous by-product in the form of computerized information about the (reported) clinical inputs to patient care. This has facilitated profiling providers' patterns of practice, which served as the initial base for health insurers and others to start 'managing' patient care more than two

---

[79] See, e.g. *http://www.healthfinder.gov/* (US government health portal, linking to quality on-line health information resources, and *http://www.lawlib.slu.edu/centers/healthlaw/hlthlnk.htm* (Selected Internet Resources in Health Law and Policy).

[80] Frances H. Miller, 'Capitation & Physician Autonomy: Master of the Universe or Just Another Prisoner's Dilemma?' (1996) 6 *Health Matrix* 89.

[81] Roz D. Lasker *et al.*, 'The Intensity of Physicians' Work in Patient Visits: Implications for the Coding of Patient Evaluation and Management Services' (1999) 341 *The New England Journal of Medicine* 337.

[82] Peter R. Kongstvedt, *The Essentials of Managed Care* (Aspen Publishers, Gaithersburg MD, 1997) 182.

decades ago.[83] Provider profiling has revealed wide variations in physician practice patterns unexplainable on any ground other than that doctors tend to continue practising medicine the way they were originally taught.[84] The implication that physicians have seemed to pay relatively little—or belated—attention to medical advances in turn served as an important stimulus for the US practice guidelines movement.[85] Widespread physician awareness of these findings has also conditioned the medical profession to the need for improving its knowledge and skills on a continuous basis. Professional resistance to the benefits of evidence-based medicine is less vociferous in the US than in the UK. The UK has trailed behind America in computerizing information about health services and providers, but British physician resistance will predictably diminish over time, as it did in the USA, when the quality-enhancing benefits of holding input and outcome data up to the light become uncontrovertible.

Physicians

Physician profiling of one sort or another has in fact been taking place for many years in both the UK and the USA. For example, almost a decade ago in the early days of the Conservative government's internal market in the National Health Service (NHS), the NHS was utilizing general practitioners' drug prescription profiles in calculating financial incentive structures for GP fundholders.[86] In another widely-known practice, New York has since 1991 ranked all cardiac surgeons practising in the state on the basis of their patients' risk-adjusted mortality data following coronary artery bypass grafting.[87]

Although some sceptics predicted, *inter alia*, that heart surgeons would flee the state or refuse to perform cardiac surgery rather than submit to the 'statistical vagaries' of New York's profiling, the most significant result of publicizing mortality data turned out to be a dramatic increase in the quality of cardiac care.[88] Doctors, no surprise to learn, in fact respond quite quickly to data, particularly about themselves. More pointedly, when the New York heart surgeons were presented with data revealing some of them to be mortality outliers in comparison with colleagues having more

---

[83] John E. Wennberg *et al.*, 'Hospital Use and Mortality Among Medicare Beneficiaries in Boston and New Haven' (1990) 323 *The New England Journal of Medicine* 1202; John E. Wennberg *et al.*, 'Are Hospital Services Rationed in New Haven or Over-Utilized in Boston?' (1987) 330 *The Lancet* 1185.

[84] John E. Wennberg, 'Dealing with Medical Practice Variations: A Proposal for Action' (1984) 3 *Health Affairs* 6.

[85] Christopher Newdick, 'Public Health Ethics and Clinical Freedom' (1998) 14 *Journal of Contemporary Health Law and Policy* 335.

[86] See *http://www.health.state.ny.us/nysdoh/consumer/heart/homehear.htm* (New York State cardiac surgery reporting system).

[87] E. L. Hannan *et al.*, 'The Decline in Coronary Artery Bypass Surgery Mortality in N.Y. State' (1995) 273 *Journal of American Medical Association* 209.

[88] *Ibid.*

favourable clinical results, those at the bottom of the list appear to have sought ways to reduce risk and bring their outcome statistics back in line with those of their peer group.[89] Instead of avoiding elderly high-risk patients or declining to do risky cardiac procedures to avoid jeopardizing their profiles, as some had predicted, these doctors strove successfully to improve the quality of all their patients' care once they saw where they stood in comparison with their peers.[90] The result was a classic win/win scenario for doctors and patients alike.[91]

A more recent example of relatively comprehensive physician data available to the public can be found on the Massachusetts State Board of Registration in Medicine's website.[92] The website maintains profiles on all doctors licensed in the state, setting forth the basic building blocks of physician competence such as education, years of training, and where it took place, specialty certification, institutions at which the doctor enjoys staff privileges, honours, and awards, publications, and the like. However, Massachusetts was the first US state also to profile any 'negative' information that might exist in licensing board files concerning the doctor's malpractice payouts (not malpractice *claims*, however), criminal convictions (but not *charges*), and hospital and licensing board disciplinary sanctions.[93]

The Massachusetts Medical Society supported legislation mandating MD profiling, because it recognized a rapidly changing public climate with regard to physician accountability, particularly in the US's competitive health sector theoretically based on market 'choice'. Moreover, by co-operating in the legislation's passage, the Society was able to forestall enactment of a statute that might have mandated, for example, that all malpractice *claims* against a physician also be publicly disclosed. It argued successfully on fairness grounds against including any negative information in physician profiles unless the report constituted a final decision after an adversarial proceeding, at which the doctor had been provided with a full opportunity to present any relevant defences. Organized medicine also persuaded Massachusetts legislators that any information in the negative category more than ten years old was no longer relevant to a physician's current competence, and thus should no longer appear on the profile.

---

[89] Elizabeth R. DeLong, *et al.*, 'Publicizing Bypass Surgery Outcomes has not Prompted Doctors to deny Surgery to Elderly High-risk Patients' (1988) 32 *Journal of the American College of Cardiology No 4*, 993.

[90] Similar managed care health insurance plan improvements have been observed following publication of quality measures. Linda O. Prager, 'Spotlight Spurs Improvement', *American Medical News*, July 1999, 11.

[91] http://www.docboard.org/MA/df/masearch.htm

[92] See generally, Jeffrey P. Donohue, 'Developing Issues Under the Massachusetts "Physician Profile" Act' (1997) 23 *Am. JL & Med.* 115; Frances H. Miller, 'Illuminating Patient Choice: Releasing Physician-Specific Data to the Public' [1995–6] *Loyola Consumer Law Reporter* 125.

[93] Donohue, n. 82 above, 115.

Once again sceptics predicted that giving potentially negative information to the public would deter malpractice settlements, drive doctors from the state, and serve only to confuse patients.[94] However, Massachusetts-licensed MD profiling went on line in May of 1997, and the phase-in has been remarkably smooth. In fact, only 8 per cent of Massachusetts doctors show anything untoward in their profiles at all,[95] and patients have seemed quite capable of evaluating this information sensibly. The website is widely used, and few problems have been reported associated with its use.[96] Other states have begun following the Massachusetts profiling example, sometimes to a lesser but not yet greater degree, and the trend is decidedly toward increased disclosure nationwide.[97]

No such comprehensive physician profiling information appears to be publicly available in the UK at the time of writing, but many indications of serious momentum toward increased accountability for UK doctors exist.[98]

Hospitals

The federal government shook the hospital establishment badly when it first published relatively raw hospital mortality statistics relating to Medicare patients in the mid-1980s.[99] The hospital information genie was by then out of the bottle, however, because New York state began collecting data on morbidity and mortality surrounding cardiac surgery in the mid-1980s, and was making it public by 1991.[100] Since 1997, New York has also publicly released data categorizing, by each of the thirty-one hospitals in the state performing angioplasty as at that date, rates of complications and heart attacks following the procedure.[101] (Few patients

[94] Bruce Mohl, 'Now Consumers Can Give Their Doctors a Checkup', *The Boston Globe*, 9 Nov. 1996, A1.

[95] The Massachusetts MD profiling web site was averaging 700 'hits' a day, as at early 1998: statistics furnished by the Massachusetts Board of Registration in Medicine, copy on file with the author.

[96] http:\\www.docboard.org is the health professional licensing database maintained by the Association of State Medical Board Executive Directors.

[97] Donald Irvine, 'The Performance of Doctors: The New Professionalism', *The Lancet*, 2 Apr. 1999, 1174; Huw Talfryn Davies *et al.*, 'Public Disclosure of Performance Data: Does the Public Get what the Public Wants?' (1999) 353 *The Lancet* 1639; J. N. Johnson, 'Making Self Regulation Credible: Through Benchmarking, Peer Review, Appraisal and Management' (1998) 316 *BMJ* 7148.

[98] *Medicare Hospital Mortality Information* (1987), Health Care Financing Administration, Publication 01.002; *cf.* Mark Chassin, *et al.*, 'The Accuracy of Medicare's Hospital Claims Data: Progress has been Made, but Problems Remain' (1992) 82 *American Journal of Public Health* 243.

[99] Edward L. Hannan *et al.*, ' Adult Open Heart Surgery in New York State: An Analysis of Risk Factors and Hospital Mortality Rates', (1990) 264 *Journal of the American Medical Association* 2768.

[100] 'The Outcome of Outcomes Releases: A Report Card on Report Cards', *Medical Utilization Management*, 16 Apr. 1998.

[101] Edward L. Hannan *et al.*, ' Adult Open Heart Surgery in New York State: An Analysis

die as a result of undergoing angioplasty, so morbidity data per hospital were not deemed a statistically significant measure of analysis.)

All 250 New York hospitals deliver at least some trauma care during the course of a year, however, and state officials plan soon to release risk-adjusted data on hospital performance in handling trauma as well.[102] The state of Pennsylvania has been making public hospital-specific information on mortality, lengths of stay, complications and average charges for coronary artery bypass grafts, heart attacks, and C-sections for the past decade,[103] and populous states such as Michigan[104] and California have released hospital-specific comparative information about specified procedures to the public as well.

Although the poorer-performing hospitals usually resist scorecard rankings, and occasionally succeed in suppressing them,[105] the public appetite for comparative data about hospital quality is likely to increase.[106] As the costs of health care continue to climb, those who finance it will more and more insist on value for the prodigious sums of money it takes. Moreover, knowledgeable patients will demand information about the quality of the institutions (and professionals) to whom they entrust their lives. Value can be assessed only on the basis of good information, and computer-based comparative statistics about hospital quality fit the bill better—and more efficiently—than many other quality assessment measures. Strategic hospital behaviour would thus entail putting the products of information technology to work for improvement purposes, as many hospitals have already done, especially when the statistical news is unpleasant.[107]

Conclusion

The trend toward according significant weight to health care information technology products in litigation (and regulation) can only be expected to accelerate as we move on into the twenty-first century.[108] Making such

of Risk Factors and Hospital Mortality Rates', (1990) 264 *Journal of the American Medical Association* 2768.

[102] See, n. 101 above.

[103] James Jollis and Patrick Romano, ' Pennsylvania's *Focus on Heart Attack*—Grading the Scorecard' (1998) 338 *New England Journal of Medicine* 983.

[104] See, e.g., http://mha.org/performance.2.

[105] Patrick S. Romano *et al.*, 'Grading the Graders: How Hospitals in California and New York Perceive and Interpret Their Report Cards', (26 May, 1999) *Journal of the American Medical Association*.

[106] E. J. Topol and R. M. Califf, 'Scorecard Cardiovascular Medicine: Its Impact and Future Directions' (1994) 120 *Annals of Internal Medicine* 65.

[107] See, Thomas M. Burton, 'HMO Rates Hospitals: Many Don't Like It, But They Get Better', *Wall Street Journal*, 22 Apr. 1991, 1.

[108] See generally Aaron D. Twerski *et al.*, 'Comparing Medical Providers: A First Look at the New Era of Medical Statistics' (1992) 58 *Brooklyn Law Review* 5; Jesse Green, 'Problems in the Use of Outcome Statistics to Compare Health Care Providers' (1992) 58 *Brooklyn LRev.* 55.

data available to providers and managers has already been demonstrated to serve as a strikingly strong incentive for physician, hospital and managed care organization self-improvement in the USA.[109] The prospect—or threat—of public access to this same information functions as an even more powerful stimulus for health service quality improvement. Notwithstanding somewhat questionable analyses of data and reputation, *US News & World Report's* annual publication of the '100 best' hospitals and managed care plans in the country has had a profound impact on the practices of those institutions.[110] No provider or managed care health insurer wishes to appear a quality outlier when it comes to protecting vulnerable patient health. Indeed, in a competitive health sector, it cannot afford to do so if it wishes to survive. Therefore, if public and private incentives to disclose reliable data are structured carefully to promote better medical practice, the need for law to intervene for purposes of policing health care quality should be significantly diminished.[111]

[109] See, Thomas M. Burton, 'HMO Rates Hospitals: Many Don't Like It, But They Get Better', *Wall Street Journal*, 22 Apr. 1999, 1; Linda O. Prager, 'Spotlight Spurs Improvement', *American Medical News*, July 1999, 11 (managed care plans); E. L. Hannan *et al.*, 'The Decline in Coronary Artery Bypass Surgery Mortality in N.Y. State' (1995) 273 *Journal of American Medical Association (JAMA)* 20.

[110] See, 'America's Best Hospitals', *U.S. News And World Report*, 19 July 1999, 58–102; 'America's Top HMOs', *U.S. News And World Report*, 5 Oct. 1998, 64–91.

[111] Frances H. Miller, 'Medical Discipline in the Twenty-First Century: Are Purchasers the Answer?' (1997) 60 *Law and Contemporary Problems* 31.

THE MANIPULATION OF
MEDICAL PRACTICE

Vivienne Harpwood

Introduction

The Ancient Greek model of clinical autonomy was that of the doctor as a beneficent paternalist, in sole possession of specialist skills and knowledge. The only constraints on the individual doctor's freedom of action were those imposed by the medical profession itself, in line with its perception of the best interests of the patient.[1] With this autonomy, there resided an assumption that external regulation was unacceptable, and that self-regulation would be carried out competently. Indeed, self-regulation has long been regarded as one of the main distinguishing features of the professions. Although this model was largely unchallenged for millennia, developments during the second half of the twentieth century have introduced greater concern for the autonomy of the patient, and the most recent trends threaten to circumscribe the doctor's traditional and jealously-guarded freedom to practise with the minimum of external intervention.

This paper presents a broad overview of the way in which medical practice is being manipulated by extraneous forces, with a view to controlling the level of clinical negligence litigation. It explores recent encroachments on traditional professional freedoms of individual doctors in the UK, pointing to a range of convergent and cumulative pressures for greater accountability and monitoring of medical practice and clinical judgement.

Some of these pressures are the product of technological advances in terms of data collection and evaluation; others are the result of the open acknowledgement of financial limitations in the provision of healthcare, a growing climate of empowerment of consumers generally, and powerful media. These elements will be examined in the course of the discussion, and likely future developments will be considered in the light of the changed political and legal climate which promotes intervention in what had for centuries been regarded as a private professional domain.

Factors Eroding Clinical Autonomy

There are three main factors which have created the impetus for change

---

[1] E. D. Pellagrino and D. C. Thomasma, *For the Patients' Good* (New York and Oxford 1990), 3.

during the 1990s. First, the manifest failure of the medical profession to regulate itself successfully,[2] which has been a grave cause for concern and is likely to result in interventionist measures[3] and greater external regulation of the profession as a whole;[4] secondly, the problems involved in delivering increasingly expensive healthcare to an ageing population within a finite budget, have produced a regime of healthcare 'rationing' which involves limits on prescribing and treatment; thirdly, the need to provide high quality healthcare on a uniform basis and the proliferation of clinical negligence claims have led to the introduction into the NHS of 'clinical governance' and official guidelines on clinical practice. In each of these areas, it will be observed the powerful influence of the media has led to high-profile action by the government. Even the courts, which have traditionally defended medical decision-making, are succumbing, allowing for 'cultural lag', to the pressures for change.

This paper focuses on exploring the clinical negligence problems in depth. However, it should be noted that there have been claims that '[t]he Bristol case will probably prove much more important to the future of healthcare than the reforms suggested in the White Papers'[5] which have now been enacted in the Health Act 1999.

The Proliferation of Clinical Negligence Claims

It is evident from figures released by the Department of Health and by the doctors' defence organizations that clinical negligence claims are increasing rapidly.[6] There has been much speculation about the reasons for the proliferation of claims. Public services, including healthcare services, have become consumer-driven. A new patient-centred culture has developed in the NHS following changes introduced by the NHS and Community Care

---

[2] The Medical (Professional Performance) Act 1995 amends earlier legislation and gives the GMC power to screen doctors whose poor performance is 'so serious as to call into question a doctor's registration'. In 1998, the GMC Professional Conduct Committee found three doctors guilty of serious professional misconduct, following events surrounding an unacceptably high level of deaths and injuries in children undergoing heart surgery at Bristol Royal Infirmary. Following this, the government took the view that a review of the internal professional regulatory system was necessary.

[3] To meet this concern, the GMC has announced continuing education and stricter monitoring of the performance of doctors in the document *Maintaining Good Medical Practice* (1998).

[4] A public enquiry is currently being held into the Bristol case (above). This enquiry was established under s. 84 of the National Health Service Act 1977, and is chaired by Prof. Ian Kennedy. It is anticipated that the result of this Enquiry will be greater external regulation of the medical profession. Provision is made in the Health Act 1999 for changing the regulatory system of the health-care professions without the need for further primary legislation.

[5] R. Smith, 'All Changed, Changed Utterly' (1998) 316 *BMJ* 1917–1918.

[6] In Apr. 1998 the government indicated that £235 million had been spent on clinical negligence litigation in 1996–7, an increase of 17% on the previous year. That figure was expected to double by the year 2002.

Act 1990, and expectations of patients about the quality of NHS care have been raised. This factor together with cultural changes, has led many to become less deferential to doctors. The NHS complaints system invites users of NHS services to express their dissatisfaction by complaining.[7] This leads some people to litigation. Media coverage of higher awards of damages, since the basis for compensating claimants for the cost of future care was changed in favour of claimants in 1998, is encouraging more people to bring claims.[8] Perhaps the best recent evidence is that published by the Centre for Policy Studies in April 1999.[9] This suggests that the steady increase in the number of solicitors from 32,700 in 1986 to 75,000 in 1999 has created an expanding market for legal services from among accident victims of all kinds, including victims of medical accidents. By means of aggressive marketing and advertising, this has generated greater awareness among consumers of the possibility of claiming large sums of compensation.

There follows an overview of some of the measures intended to provide a solution to the clinical negligence problem. Not all of these measures are explicitly intended to address the issue of clinical negligence. The official rationale for some of the reforms is stated to be a general attempt to ensure high quality NHS care, but one need not look far beneath the surface to find a hidden agenda which attempts to reduce claims against NHS staff. This paper attempts to assess the effect of these measures on the clinical autonomy of individual doctors, as opposed to the profession as a whole.

In April 1998, Frank Dobson, Health Secretary, made the now famous statement that 'the best place for a lawyer is on the operating table', because, he claimed, lawyers are milking the NHS millions of pounds— 'money which would otherwise be spent on caring for patients'.[10] He invited suggestions from members of the public and professions as to how this problem could be solved, but in reality, behind the public facade of blaming lawyers, the government was already attempting to solve the problems within the NHS itself, by introducing institutional changes which will target and control the way in which medicine is practised in order to stem the rising tide of litigation against the NHS.

At the time that Frank Dobson made this statement, the White Paper entitled *The New NHS: Modern Dependable*[11] had been in existence for more than six months. Proposals for formalizing central government control over medical practice made in that document have now been published as the centrepiece of the Health Act 1999 which received the

---

[7] NHS Complaints Procedures operational since Apr. 1996.
[8] *Wells* v. *Wells* [1998] 3 WLR 329.
[9] As reported in the *Sunday Times*, 18 Apr. 1999.
[10] Department of Health Press Release, 29 Apr. 1998.
[11] Cm 3807 (London, 1999).

Royal Assent on 30 June 1999. External pressures introduced by the Act will result in close monitoring of the performance of individual doctors, and will impose guidelines which will be virtually impossible for them to ignore. It is inevitable that this proposed new framework for the delivery and monitoring of healthcare will have an effect on clinical negligence litigation.

At about the same time, the government was in the process of implementing many of Lord Woolf's proposals for the reform of civil procedure, which in April 1999 were brought into operation in the Civil Procedure Rules.

The Health Act 1999: Enforcing Clinical Governance, Controlling Litigation

The Health Act 1999 sets out to implement the policies set out in that White Paper, and in two further White Papers entitled *Designed to Care*,[12] and *Putting Patients First*.[13] More detailed proposals were made in a consultation document, *A First Class Service*,[14] in July 1998, and in a discussion document published in September 1998 entitled *Partnership in Action*. In Wales, proposals concerning quality and partnership were set out in two further consultation documents, *Quality Care and Clinical Excellence* (July 1998) and *Partnership for Improvement* (October 1998). While it had been possible to implement many of the proposals for change through statutory instruments, some of the changes can be introduced only by primary legislation—hence the Act, which was introduced as a Bill into the House of Lords on 28 January 1999.

The monitoring of standards and the quality of medical practice are dealt with in sections 18 to 25. A statutory duty of quality is placed on all NHS Trusts and Primary Care Trusts, as they will be called, and this duty will operate alongside the duty of care already owed to patients at common law in the law of negligence. NHS Trusts and Primary Care Trusts must establish plans for monitoring and improving the quality of the care which they provide to patients, and central to this will be the requirement that 'clinical governance' arrangements be implemented. 'Clinical governance'[15] is defined as:

A framework through which NHS organisations are accountable for continuously improving the quality of their services and safeguarding high standards of care by creating an environment in which excellence in clinical care will flourish.[16]

---

[12] Cm 3811 (London, 1999). [13] Cm 3841 (London, 1998).
[14] HSC 1998/113.
[15] Many of the policies with clinical governance are drawn from the US system of managed care which was an attempt to respond to, and to manage, costs and variations in quality of health-care—see J. Iglehart, *Physicians and the Growth of Managed Care* (London, 1994) 1167–71.
[16] The White Paper, *A First Class Service: Quality In The New NHS* (London, 1998).

In the context of healthcare, clinical governance, which is essentially a risk-management system, uses ideas drawn from business and corporate governance and applies them to the management and regulation of clinical teams and the management of healthcare services. The word 'governance' is defined in the same context as 'the control and direction of behaviour, with authority'.[17] This is the antithesis of the clinical autonomy and discretion traditionally enjoyed by doctors. Although the focus in this paper is on the role of the doctor, clinical governance applies to entire healthcare teams, involving clinicians, nurses, laboratory workers, other professionals, and their interactions with agencies outside the NHS. Clinical governance is both pervasive and structured, imposing rigid monitoring regimes and a framework of accountability, which it is impossible for doctors to evade without incurring penalties for themselves or their organizations. Despite the government's enthusiastic espousal of clinical governance, there must be some reservations about imposing a risk-management system originally intended to regulate commercial organizations on the healthcare system. The main requirements of clinical governance are:

(1) The establishing of clear lines of responsibility and accountability for the entire system of care. The Chief executives of every NHS Trust are to have ultimate responsibility for ensuring quality of services in their organizations, and a senior clinician will be responsible for establishing systems of clinical governance and ensuring that they are continuously monitored;

(2) The implementation of a comprehensive programme to improve quality systems, including clinical audit, the use of evidence-based medicine, and the implementation of evidence-based clinical guidelines. Among other factors, participation by all hospital doctors in audit, and in the National Confidential Enquiries will be required, together with the routine application of clinical standards and guidelines which are evidence-based and effectively monitored;

(3) The setting up of policies of risk management and the practical means of identifying and remedying poor performance of healthcare staff. This has been facilitated by the GMC in its latest advice to doctors, and by the Public Interest Disclosure Act 1998.[18]

The Department of Health maintains the official view that clinical governance is necessary to overcome the fact that there are regional variations in the quality of healthcare throughout the UK, as is the case in all healthcare systems throughout the civilized world, and to prevent healthcare which is 'inappropriate', but the additional hidden agenda is the need to reduce the number of clinical negligence claims. Although the

---

[17] See *Clinical Governance: Clinician, Heal Thyself*, IHSM Policy Document (London, Oct. 1988).   [18] See n. 4, above.

monitoring of healthcare has become common practice since the introduction of medical and clinical audits in the 1990s, under what was then a new framework for the delivery of healthcare, the government was not satisfied with the level of accountability achieved by that process,[19] and sees the introduction of a statutory duty of quality as a means of overcoming the problems presented by that earlier system of audit.

THE NATIONAL INSTITUTE FOR CLINICAL EXCELLENCE

The National Institute for Clinical Excellence (NICE), which has been established by Statutory Instrument,[20] will have a central role in the process of raising standards. It is this body which will appraise and issue guidelines on the clinical effectiveness and cost-effectiveness of drugs, technologies, and treatments. Its three main functions will be the appraisal of new and existing health technologies, the development of clinical guidelines, and the promotion of clinical audit and confidential enquiries. The government has announced proposals to strengthen the four standing National Confidential Enquiries, which monitor deaths after surgery, maternal deaths, stillbirths and infant deaths, and suicides. Speaking in the House of Lords, in answer to a question about the GMC enquiry into the Bristol case, Baroness Jay said:

There are four national Confidential Enquiries, but participation is voluntary. The disturbing result is that in some NHS regions, for example, over a third of surgeons and anaesthetists do not take part in the National Confidential Enquiry into Perioperative Deaths. Even in the best performing regions, one in five did not participate in the NCEPOD report published last year.

In future the government will take action to require all relevant clinicians to participate in these professionally-led external audits, and will further take action to bring the enquiries under the aegis of the new National Institute for Clinical Excellence, so that their findings can be properly incorporated in the national standards and guidance which NICE will promulgate.[21]

---

[19] Comptroller and Auditor General, *Clinical Audit in England*, HC 27 Session 1995–6 (London, 1995).

[20] The National Institute For Clinical Excellence (Establishment and Constitution) Order 1999 was laid before Parliament on 3 Feb. 1999, and came into force on 26 Feb. 1999: SI 1999 No. 220. This Order makes provision for the setting up and constitution of the National Institute for Clinical Excellence which is to have the role of promoting excellence throughout the NHS. A list of the members who are to be appointed is stated in the Order. The functions of the Institute are '[s]ubject to and in accordance with such directions as the Secretary of State may give, the Institute shall perform such functions in connection with the promotion of clinical excellence in the health service as the Secretary of State may direct'.

[21] The National Confidential Enquiry into Perioperative Deaths (NCEPOD), since 1988, has been concerned with maintaining high standards of clinical practice in anaesthesia and surgery, auditing hospital deaths occurring within 30 days of surgery. The Confidential

NICE is a Special Health Authority with its own legal identity, with direct responsibility to the Health Secretary Alan Milburn and the Secretary of State for Wales.[22] In effect, NICE will be the mechanism by which standards are set, using 'National Service Frameworks' (NSFs), with panels of experts drafting guidelines on specified areas of healthcare.

The first four NSFs have been announced, covering mental health, coronary heart disease, care of the elderly, and diabetes. The frameworks, which will be developed over a period of about two years, will set national quality standards which will be required to be met across the NHS. The Commission for Health Improvement, established under the Health Act 1999, will have powers to visit every hospital to ensure that these standards are being met.

NICE will advise on the clinical and cost effectiveness of both new and existing health technologies, including medicines, diagnostic tests, and surgical procedures. Modern information technology will allow details of innovation to be disseminated quickly and effectively, helping to ensure that all health professionals have guidelines available. NICE is expected to influence prescribing decisions and the rationing debate, as the allocation of resources is a matter which NICE must address when formulating clinical guidelines. Although the general understanding has been that NICE would recommend the most effective treatments, irrespective of the cost, Sir Michael Rawlins, chairman of NICE, has stated frankly, '[i]t is no good us recommending a therapy if there is not the money available.... Although some will find this distasteful, it is what doctors have done since time immemorial'. This admission has been greeted with indignation by the medical profession, and the indications are that doctors are unhappy about accepting guidelines which will suit the Treasury rather than the best interests of patients. The Chief Executive of the NHS Confederation pointed out that 'these are political value-judgements, not the technical ones which are the proper responsibility of NICE'. After NICE failed to approve the flu drug Relenza in October 1999, the government accepted its recommendation, and the drug is not available on the NHS.

THE COMMISSION FOR HEALTH IMPROVEMENT

Section 19 and Schedule 2 of the Act deal with the setting up of the

---

Enquiry into Stillbirths and Deaths in Infancy (CESDI) seeks to identify ways of preventing stillbirths and deaths in infancy, and indicating areas where more research is needed. The Confidential Enquiry into Maternal Deaths (CEMD), since 1951, has assessed the causes of maternal deaths, identifies inadequate care, recommends improvements and directions for future research. The Confidential Inquiry into Suicide and Homicide by People with Mental Illness (CISH), established in 1991, carries out a national audit of suicide and homicide by people who have had a history of contact with mental health services, making recommendations to Ministers on measures to reduce such deaths.

[22] The NICE website is www.nice.org.uk.

Commission for Health Improvement, (CHI), a new body which will have oversight of the entire quality system in the NHS, and ensure that local systems for monitoring and up-grading the quality of healthcare are working satisfactorily. The Commission will be accountable to the government through Parliament, will be required to produce an annual report, and will be treated as an executive non-departmental government body. It will fall within the jurisdiction of the Parliamentary Commissioner for Administration. Schedule 2 contains details about the staff and membership of the Commission For Health Improvement. The main functions of CHI are :

(1) to provide national leadership and to develop the principles of clinical governance;
(2) to provide advice and information about monitoring arrangements and improvements in healthcare;
(3) to review the implementation of NSFs and guidance issued by NICE;
(4) to investigate, advise, and report on specific matters concerning the management of healthcare and its delivery, and on clinical problems;
(5) to conduct national reviews of particular kinds of healthcare provided by the NHS.

The Secretary of State will have the power to draw the attention of health service bodies to the advice given by CHI. If necessary, he may require them to act on that advice using his powers under the National Health Service Act 1977. The Secretary of State will also be able to direct CHI to deal with specific issues which are of particular concern.

CHI will have important statutory powers to monitor the performance of all NHS Trusts and report on how local services are implementing NICE guidelines and National Service Frameworks. It will be given the task of providing independent assurance about local activity to improve and assure quality. It will also be able to offer expert help to services with serious or persistent clinical problems. Where serious problems are not being properly addressed, the Secretary of State will be able to instruct it to investigate and make recommendations. In extreme cases, the Secretary of State will have the power to dismiss Trust boards.

Officers of CHI will be able to gain entry to NHS premises in the exercise of their functions, and will have access to documents and information by the healthcare bodies whose work it reviews. Details of these powers will be set out in regulations, but it will not normally have the power to obtain documents or information where access to such matters is prohibited by another Act (section 23).

The Secretary of State will have the power to draw the attention of health service bodies to the advice given by CHI. If necessary, he may require them to act on that advice using his powers under the 1977 Act. The Secretary of State will also be able to direct the Commission to deal with specific issues which are of particular concern.

The controls imposed by the Health Act will be far-reaching, and will affect areas of care outside the traditional scope of the NHS. The duty of partnership between local authorities and health bodies found in the National Health Service Act 1977 is extended by the Act. An explicit duty of co-operation between Health Authorities, NHS Trusts, and Primary Care Trusts is introduced by section 26. By section 27 the concept of partnership is extended to a duty to secure and advance the health and welfare of the population. Co-operation is required in the commissioning of healthcare, in its delivery, and in strategic planning. This includes areas such as housing, education, environment, and social services. There is a statutory requirement for all Health Authorities to plan for improving health and healthcare provision for people living in their areas, and a duty for Primary Care Trusts, NHS Trusts, and local authorities to take part in this planning exercise.

Although each area is expected to develop specialized local plans for health improvement, involving local communities, voluntary bodies, employers, educational establishments, etc., the Secretary of State is to have power to issue directions which will ensure that effective programmes can be set in place. Provision is also made for Health Authorities and Primary Care Trusts to transfer monies for health-related purposes to local authorities, for social services, education, and housing functions as part of the concept of partnership. Section 31 contains detailed provisions for the removal of barriers between the various agencies allowing them to pool resources and staff to develop flexible packages of care for particular individuals in need of special kinds of care. Regulations may be made to establish the criteria which must be met for these purposes. Already reforms are being introduced to monitor the quality of social work care in line with the introduction of clinical governance in healthcare. Plans are in place, in the Care Standards Bill introduced in November 1999, for establishing measures to improve the quality of social services, in the light of new partnerships between social and health care to be introduced when the Health Act becomes law. A quality strategy for social services will be published for consultation towards the end of the year. As in the health care setting, measures will be established to assess performance and monitor progress much more actively.

Controls Beyond the Health Act 1999

Measures outside the ambit of the Health Act will support the new climate of control, and will further erode the clinical autonomy of the individual physician, creating greater openness in healthcare. It is likely that these will have an indirect impact on the clinical negligence cases. The measures, which are outlined briefly below, include the publication of new league tables for clinical outcomes and cost efficiency, the introduction of a computerized prescribing system, called PRODIGY, and proposals to introduce tighter regulation of private healthcare.

LEAGUE TABLES FOR CLINICAL PERFORMANCE

A Performance Assessment Framework[23] is being established, backed up by forty-one indicators, looking at the work of the NHS across six areas: health improvement, fair access, effective delivery of appropriate healthcare, patient and carer experience, health outcomes of NHS care, and efficiency. This framework is intended to be a powerful tool to enable Health Authorities, Primary Care Groups, and NHS Trusts to monitor and compare their performance. The information will, it is hoped, encourage services to be improved systematically across the NHS, and will operate in conjunction with the new duty for all parts of the NHS to implement clinical governance. As one of these six elements involves measuring the health outcomes of treatment and care, sophisticated assessment methods will need to be developed on a specialty-by-specialty and hospital-by-hospital basis. Clinical performance indicators will be collected, published, and monitored in every NHS hospital for each major medical condition, which will enable experts to identify potential problems at an early stage and to take appropriate measures if necessary. A ten-year rolling programme to improve clinical performance information is planned.

Amid a storm of criticism and controversy, the first league tables of clinical performance covering named hospitals in England have now been published. The publication covers a range of aspects of clinical care including hospital death and complication rates after an operation, death rates after heart attacks, and death rates after fractured neck or femur. The main criticism stems from the fact that the figures do not necessarily represent a fair and accurate reflection of clinical quality. It is essential to ensure accurate comparability so that, for example, doctors who are attempting to treat seriously ill elderly patients are not compared with those who are dealing with younger, fitter patients. All the figures will need to be 'risk adjusted' to standardize for factors such as age, severity, and concurrent illnesses.

Individual hospital doctors will be able to compare their own clinical performance with national averages which will be risk-adjusted, and all hospital doctors will be required to participate in a national audit programme appropriate to their specialty or subspecialty externally endorsed by the Commission for Health Improvement. Audits will typically

[23] Following a Consultation Paper issued in Jan. 1998.

be run by the relevant Royal College, university, faculty, or special interest group. In many specialties these national audits are already under way. Doctors whose results are unsatisfactory will be required to take urgent action to improve their results. Where the outcome is an unacceptable mortality rate, it may be necessary for the clinician to stop work in that procedure. Fellow professionals will then provide extra training, supervision, and support. In appropriate circumstances the GMC will be involved.

To ensure that results of audit are translated into action to raise standards, individual doctors will be required to share their results confidentially with the medical director of their Trust and the Trust's lead clinician responsible for clinical governance. In turn, doctors on the Commission for Health Improvement will have access to these data when they visit the Trust to review local standards. It is intended that GPs and the new Primary Care Groups will be able to offer better advice to patients on treatment options. Patients will be able to ask their hospital doctor for increasingly comprehensive information on the success rates of their unit's procedures compared with national figures. These proposals are consistent with the developing notion of 'openness' in the NHS, and should mean that in future patients will be able to consent to treatment in the light of much more comprehensive information.

COST-EFFICIENCY RANKING

An additional control mechanism lies in the fact that each NHS Trust will publish the costs of treatments and services it delivers. The new National Schedule of Reference Costs and National Reference Cost Index will deal with significant variations in cost for the same service or treatment across the NHS. The National Schedule of Reference Costs will show the range of costs in each treatment category, ranking all NHS Trusts from those with the lowest to the highest costs. This will allow for the ranking of all NHS Trusts on a scale of efficiency, allowing comparison between all Trusts, even if they provide different treatments and services. National benchmarks for each type of treatment will be set and will form the basis of targets for NHS Trusts. This move is seen as part of the government's drive for an open, accountable, and more efficient health service, and is part of the fast-moving process of establishing greater central control over the NHS.

THE PRODIGY SYSTEM

There are further measures being introduced which are likely to make inroads into clinical autonomy and to impact on the standard of care in clinical negligence disputes. 'PRODIGY',[24] a computer software system, gives

---

[24] Which stands for **P**rescribing **R**ationally with **D**ecision Support **I**n **G**eneral Practice Study.

the latest prescribing advice to doctors while they see their patients. The system has been developed by a partnership between the NHS Executive, GP clinical systems suppliers, and a team at the University of Newcastle, and will be the first national prescribing system in the world.

During consultations, GPs will be able to type the patient's diagnosis into the system, which will then suggest an appropriate treatment. All recommended treatments have been validated by a national panel, and chosen on the basis of clinical effectiveness and safety. The cost of the products recommended is considered where more than one drug with similar clinical effect exists, or where the benefits of one drug over another are marginal. Patient information leaflets for many conditions can be printed out on the spot for the patient to take home. PRODIGY combines the government's aims for developing uniform efficient and acceptable standards in the NHS with its aim of using modern technology as a means of implementing its policies. Although the government emphazises that GPs will still have complete freedom of choice in prescribing, and that PRODIGY will merely help to ensure consistent, high-quality standards in prescribing for patients, there must be some dismay at what might appear to be interference with clinical discretion. However, there will be a strong incentive to use the system because it will be supplied free to GPs.

The PRODIGY project was commissioned in 1995 by the NHS Executive, and an independent evaluation of the system has been undertaken. There have been two phases in the trials in nearly 200 GP practices across England. A continuous updating programme of the clinical recommendations will be carried out, as well as a programme of education for the users of the new system. The legal implications of the implementation of this new system are significant, and will be discussed later in this paper, yet its introduction appears to be passing virtually without comment. The fact that an eminent panel with representatives from the Royal College of General Practitioners (RCGP), the General Practitioners' Committee, the Royal College of Physicians, and the Royal Pharmaceutical Society of Great Britain validates PRODIGY guidance will give the system a high status. This will place its guidelines in a similar category to NICE guidelines, with similar implications for clinical negligence litigation.

PRIVATE SECTOR REGULATION

It might be thought that doctors practising in the private sector would be immune from threats to their professional freedom. However, so great is the concern that the quality of care in the NHS will not be matched by private healthcare providers that a consultation document has been launched which proposes new regulations which will help protect patients against substandard private health-care. Under current arrangements regulation of private clinics and hospitals is through the Registered Homes Act

1984, under which Health Authorities register and inspect private health-care premises, such as specialist private clinics and nursing homes. The consultation proposes that a single, independent body be established to regulate the private health sector. The body will oversee the registration and inspection of private health-care providers. The proposal suggests that private patients should have access to clinical and non-clinical information on areas such as staffing, facilities available, and the range of services provided, and that private health-care providers should, as a condition of registration, have a clearly laid-out complaints procedure. Details should be published annually of all complaints received, and made available to prospective patients, and measures be introduced to help prevent private hospitals and clinics from continuing to work with poor quality doctors who have been suspended from the NHS. The proposals would need to be implemented by primary legislation, now introduced as the Care Standards Bill 1999.[25]

Sustaining the Attack on Clinical Autonomy: The Role of the Judges

The traditional role of the law has been to sustain the respect for clinical autonomy which doctors had grown to expect over the centuries. It is still possible to find recent examples of this in cases involving complex ethical issues, where the courts tend to leave decision-making to the medical profession,[26] despite the much-publicized change of approach in favour of patient autonomy in cases concerning refusal of medical treatment.[27] However, in the context of clinical negligence, there is a real possibility that judges are in the process of changing their attitudes towards the clinical autonomy of doctors.

From 1957, the *Bolam* test[28] for determining the standard of care in clinical negligence cases ensured that doctors would be judged according to the standards laid down by the profession, and that judges would almost never be free to choose which of two or more opposing bodies of medical opinion was correct. Despite a flood of criticism, his test was seldom challenged judicially,[29] and was repeatedly reaffirmed by courts at all levels, including the House of Lords.[30] The main criticisms centered on the fact that the test was too heavily weighted in favour of doctors, and it approved practices which were on the fringe of what was acceptable to the

---

[25] *Regulating Private and Voluntary Healthcare: A Consultation Document* (London 1999).

[26] *Re F (Mental Patient: Sterilization)* [1990] 2 AC 2.

[27] *Re C (A Minor)* (1997) 40 BMLR 31.

[28] *Bolam* v. *Friern Hospital Management Committee* (1957) 1 WLR 582.

[29] But see *Newell* v. *Goldburg* (1995) 6 Med LR 371; *Hucks* v. *Cole* (1993) 4 Med LR 393.

[30] *Whitehouse* v. *Jordan* [1981] 1 All ER 267; *Maynard* v. *West Midlands Regional Health Authority* [1985] 1 WLR 634.

majority of the profession, as long as medical experts could confirm that they were approved by a 'responsible' body of medical opinion. The elusive word 'responsible' was never satisfactorily defined, and it was unclear from the many conflicting cases exactly how many doctors would have to approve a practice for it to be regarded as responsible.[31]

At long last, in November 1997, in *Bolitho* v. *City and Hackney Health Authority*[32] the House of Lords modified the test to allow a judge to choose in circumstances when a particular body of medical opinion was not 'logically defensible'. Lord Browne-Wilkinson, in the course of a speech paying due deference to the medical profession, acknowledged the importance of risk management when he stated the modified approach:

In particular, in cases involving as they often do, the weighing of risks and benefits, the judge, before accepting a body of opinion as responsible, reasonable or respectable, has to be satisfied that, in forming their view, the experts have directed their minds to the question of comparative risks and benefits, and have reached a defensible conclusion on the matter. . . . It is only where a judge can be satisfied that the body of expert opinion cannot be logically supported at all, that such opinion will not provide the benchmark by reference to which the defendant's conduct falls to be assessed.

Although this new approach is to be welcomed, this modification is unlikely to have more than a marginal effect on clinical negligence claims. Cases in which the treatment of a patient falls within the narrow range of what experts would regard as 'logically indefensible' are almost always settled out of court, and although the *Bolitho* case may lead to an increase in the number of settlements, it is unlikely to make a significant difference. Nevertheless, the decision does signify a departure from the previous virtually impregnable position of doctors in clinical negligence cases, and a more recent development indicates that there may be a movement towards greater respect for patient autonomy, and consequently further inroads into clinical autonomy, in the law of consent.

In *Bolitho*, Lord Browne-Wilkinson expressly excluded from the discussion any modification of the use of the *Bolam* peer-group test for deciding how much information should be provided in the course of obtaining a patient's consent to treatment. However, more recently, the Court of Appeal, in *Pearce* v. *United Bristol Healthcare Trust*,[33] again considered this matter. The decision was based upon analysis of the speeches in the House of Lords in the difficult and complex case of *Sidaway* v. *Governors of Bethlem Royal Hospital*,[34] and the *Bolitho* case. The Court of Appeal took the view that it will normally be the legal duty of the doctor to advise the patient about any 'significant risks' which may affect the judgement of

---

[31] See V. Harpwood, *A Chink in the Armour of Bolam* (London, 1996).
[32] [1998] AC 232, (1997) 39 BMLR 1.
[33] [1999] PIQR 53.   [34] [1985] 1 A.C. 871 (HL).

a reasonable patient in making a decision about treatment. It appears that the *Bolitho* test *is* likely to be of relevance in consent cases. More significantly, Lord Woolf indicated in *Pearce* that it is for the court and not for doctors to decide on the appropriate standard as to what should be disclosed to a patient about a particular treatment. He stated:

If there is a significant risk which would affect the judgment of a reasonable patient, then in the normal course it is the responsibility of a doctor to inform the patient of that risk if the information is needed so that the patient can determine for him or herself as to what course he or she should adopt.

This is an indication that there may be a move by the UK courts towards adopting an approach similar to that taken in the Australian case of *Rogers* v. *Whittaker*,[35] in which the Australian High Court ruled in favour of doctors disclosing all material risks which the reasonable patient might regard as significant, taking into account the particular patient. In future UK cases, the crucial issues are likely to centre around what risks are to be regarded as 'significant' or relevant in the view of a reasonable patient to the decision whether to agree to the proposed treatment. We now await more cases concerning information disclosure to be brought before the courts so that the judges will have the opportunity to consider, clarify, and develop the new approach which was adumbrated in *Pearce*.

THE IMPACT OF THE NHS CHANGES: THE EFFECT OF GUIDELINES ON CLINICAL NEGLIGENCE LITIGATION AND CLINICAL AUTONOMY

The medical profession has been developing guidelines on clinical practice for fifty years, and it is possible to find guidance on treatment spanning many centuries. However, since the changes in the delivery of healthcare introduced by the National Health Service and Community Care Act 1990, there has been an enormous proliferation of guidelines and protocols issued to doctors from a variety of sources, such as managers within the NHS, professional bodies, and the Department of Health. Although the medical profession has been cautious about accepting such guidelines, not least because they threaten clinical autonomy and flexibility, it is facing growing government pressure to adopt 'evidence-based' medical practice.[36] With the advent of clinical audit and the growing awareness of the importance of basing clinical practice on evidence derived from systematic reviews of clinical trials, this pressure has increased, and guidelines have, for some time, been identified as providing a possible solution to the problem of defining the standard of care in clinical negligence. The Medical Defence Union spokesman stated as long ago as 1993:

[35] (1992) 175 CLR 479.
[36] See A. Cochrane, *Effectiveness and Efficiency: Random Reflections on Healthcare Services* (London, 1972).

If guidelines have been produced from a respected body and they have been accepted by a large part of the profession, a doctor will have to have a strong reason for not following the guidance.

In 1994 the Scottish Office issued the following statement:

With the increasing use of guidelines in clinical practice, they will be used to an increasing extent to resolve questions of liability. Those who draft, use and monitor guidelines should be aware of these legal implications.

However, in addition to suspicions based on the inflexibility of guidelines, a particular problem has been determining which guidelines have the greatest authority, especially where guidelines conflict.

A potential solution to this problem lies in the Health Act 1999. The guidelines, to be issued under the auspices of NICE, will be drafted by approved panels from the Royal Colleges and will have an official status and imprimatur. They will be disseminated throughout the entire NHS, and will be expected to be implemented by all doctors and other health-care professionals working within the specialist areas to which they apply. There will be regular monitoring by CHI to ensure that guidelines are implemented and observed, and this is likely to have a significant impact on patterns of treatment and clinical outcomes. The evidence produced as a result of audit and systematic review of clinical trials suggests that certain treatments are so beneficial to some classes of patients that it is essential that doctors make them available to all who fall within those groups.[37]

It is many years since Montrose[38] identified one of the main criticisms of the *Bolam* test as lying in the fact that it is a 'sociological' test, measuring a doctor's performance and the standard of care according to what *is* done by other doctors, rather than a 'normative' test, which considers what ought to have been done in the circumstances. In other areas of negligence a normative test is applied, and to single out the professions for privileged treatment is unjust and unduly deferential.

The opportunity now arises, within the new legislative framework established in the Health Act 1999, for a normative test to be applied to the medical profession by using guidelines to measure the standard of care for the purposes of clinical negligence litigation. The idea that guidelines drafted as a result of clinical audit could determine the standard of care in clinical negligence cases was suggested by the author in 1994.[39] However, NICE will establish a normative framework which is more impressive than that arrived at through audit, and it is a strong possibility that NICE guidelines will determine the standard of care to which doctors must conform. Indeed, Sir Michael Rawlins, newly appointed as the first

[37] e.g. the use of prophylactic antibiotics after caesarean section.
[38] J. Montrose, 'Is Negligence an Ethical or Sociological Concept' (1958) 21 *MLR* 259.
[39] V. Harpwood, 'NHS Reform, Audit, Protocols and Standard of Care', (1994) 1 *Medical Law International* 241–59.

Chairman of NICE, recently informed a conference[40] that: 'NICE guidelines are likely to constitute a reasonable body of opinion for the purposes of litigation', and that 'doctors are advised to record their reasons for deviating from guidelines'. He advised that in a clinical negligence case, a doctor who does not, without good reason, follow NICE guidelines, may be found to have fallen below the standard of care. Similar advice was given by Frank Dobson, then Health Secretary, in March 1999.

It follows that any deviation from NICE guidelines may not be regarded by a court as 'logically defensible'; the crucial question is what view the courts will take of this matter in the future. Even before NICE was conceived, there was a case in which a doctor who ignored Department of Health guidelines was found negligent. In 1996, in *Thomson* v. *James*,[41] a GP was held to be have been negligent because he had ignored DOH guidelines on vaccinating children (though the decision was reversed on appeal on another point—causation). In another more specialized case, *Re C (A Minor) (Medical Treatment)*,[42] the President of the Family Division accepted without question the guidelines of the Royal College of Pædiatrics and Child Health on withdrawing medical treatment from terminally ill children. However, this case, although much publicized, is very unusual. In the general run of clinical negligence litigation, there will be scope for the courts to endorse high-level decision-making by the Royal Colleges as part of the new framework of standards, and to give these priority over decisions of individual doctors who choose to cling to their clinical autonomy by ignoring NICE guidelines.

It should be emphasized that what is at stake is not the autonomy of the medical profession as a whole, since leaders of the profession will be involved in drafting the guidelines to be disseminated by NICE. This involvement will enable clinicians to control the content of, though not the agenda for, NICE guidelines. It is the individual doctor who wishes to ignore the guidelines or who chooses not to follow them whose clinical autonomy is threatened.

Practising lawyers are now forced to take clinical guidelines seriously. In clinical negligence cases where the plaintiff is legally aided,[43] solicitors are expected to make a preliminary assessment of the viability of the medical evidence in cases. Clinical guidelines are available to them and can assist in this process. The Civil Procedure Rules, discussed below, which were introduced in April 1999, demand fast response times in the early stages of claims and a reduction in the number of expert witnesses used in the course of litigation. These and other factors connected with the introduction of the new

---

[40] Reported in *Pulse*, 29 May 1999, 4.   [41] (1996) 31 BMLR 1.

[42] [1998] 1 Lloyd's Rep. Med 1.

[43] Legal aid will still be available for the time being for clinical negligence cases, despite being withdrawn from other personal injury claims.

rules will encourage lawyers, doctors, complaints managers, and, eventually, judges to rely heavily on NICE guidelines in the process of resolving disputes.

CO-ORDINATED STRATEGIES FOR DEALING WITH CLINICAL NEGLIGENCE

It has been pointed out that the development of the new framework for regulating healthcare, although officially an attempt to drive up standards and to improve the quality of healthcare, may hold the key to a solution, at least in part, to reducing the number of clinical negligence claims. But there is also evidence of co-ordinated strategies between different branches of government for dealing with the clinical negligence explosion, which draw upon the new NHS structure. The Pre-Action Protocol for the Resolution of Clinical Negligence Disputes relies heavily on references to clinical governance in its advice to lawyers and health-care professionals on the early conduct of claims.

This Protocol accompanies the Civil Procedure Rules, introduced on 26 April 1999 as part of a package of reforms to improve the conduct of civil litigation. The reforms are the result of recommendations made by Lord Woolf, who had identified numerous problems in the old system which led to high costs, delays, inequalities in access to justice, uncertainties, poor organization, and many injustices. The Civil Procedure Rules introduce a strict regime for the conduct of civil claims which is intended to overcome many of the difficulties inherent in the previous civil procedure.

The Protocol (whose title refers to 'clinical negligence' in preference to 'medical negligence') was drafted by the Clinical Disputes Forum, a multi-disciplinary body established in 1997. This document encourages openness when it is apparent that there has been a mishap of some kind in the treatment of a patient, and provides general guidance on how this new culture of co-operation may be achieved, recommending a timed sequence of measures for all those involved in a clinical negligence case to follow. Its aim is to resolve disputes in ways which are appropriate to both parties, to reduce delays and costs, and to reduce the need for litigation.

What is of particular interest is that the Protocol makes specific reference to 'clinical governance' within health-care, and that it is as much concerned with risk and claims management issues as with the early steps in the conduct of claims. In fact much of the document is addressed to claims handlers and risk managers and is at least as important to them as it is to lawyers.

For example, the protocol sets out 'Good Practice Commitments' for health-care providers, which include advice about training of staff in health-care law and dealing with complaints; adverse outcome reporting; a sound approach to clinical governance; good systems for storing and retrieving records; and a proper response to complaints, including the offer of compensation where appropriate. It recommends that alternative forms of dispute-settlement be used where appropriate, including the NHS complaints system. It is remarkable that advice to lawyers on the conduct of claims should also contain advice to health-care providers. The document states that health-care providers should:

- ensure that key staff, including claims and litigation managers, are appropriately trained and have some knowledge of health-care law,[44] of complaints procedures, and civil litigation practice and procedure;
- develop an approach to clinical governance which ensures that clinical practice is delivered to commonly accepted standards and that this is routinely monitored through a system of clinical audit and clinical risk management;
- set up adverse outcome reporting systems in all specialties;
- use the results of adverse incidents and complaints positively as a guide to improve services;
- ensure that patients receive clear and comprehensible information in an accessible form about how to raise their concerns or complaints;
- establish efficient and effective systems of recording and storing patient records;
- advise patients of a serious adverse outcome and provide on request an explanation of what happened, including, where appropriate, an offer of future treatment to rectify the problem, and apology and changes in procedure, and/or compensation.

A Practice Direction has been issued by the Lord Chancellor dealing with the question of non-compliance with protocols. This indicates that the court will expect all parties to have complied in substance with the terms of an approved protocol. If, in the opinion of the court, non-compliance leads to the commencement of proceedings which might not have needed to be commenced, or leads to costs having been incurred which would not have been incurred otherwise, the court may make a number of orders which impose heavy penalties on the party at fault.

Conclusion

This review has focused on clinical negligence as one context within which the clinical autonomy of the individual doctor is being eroded. However, there are so many convergent pressures on clinical autonomy that it would be difficult to isolate the relative contributions made by each individual factor. Matters such as the growing presure for strict external regulation of the medical profession and the open acknowledgement by the government of rationing within the NHS also need to be considered.

---

[44] Health-care law is already a compulsory subject in the core curriculum for undergraduate medical education, and for hospital Registrars.

It seems that the erosion of clinical autonomy is over-determined. Sustained efforts on several fronts to control and contain the explosion of litigation will inevitably mean that there will be further inroads into professional freedom, but it is also necessary to consider the wider context, and the continued dismantling of the doctor's clinical discretion which will become inevitable as the drive towards patient autonomy gathers momentum in the context of the Human Rights Act 1998. Patient empowerment is limited by financial and market constraints, and patients will never have a realistic prospect of demanding whatever they want from the NHS. However, despite cultural factors within the medical profession, which prevent some doctors from embracing fully the new normative framework, the continuing empowerment of patients will almost inevitably mean that clinical autonomy is circumscribed as medical practice and is further manipulated by external processes.

CLINICAL GUIDELINES, NEGLIGENCE, AND MEDICAL PRACTICE

Harvey Teff

The Perceived Authority of Guidelines

One of the more prominent features of modern governance is its increasing reliance on guidelines. Sometimes they acquire such an aura of authority that they are assumed to be part of the general law. This misperception is not uncommon among health-care personnel; it is likely to become more widespread as a result of new arrangements for 'clinical governance' in the NHS,[1] as further extended and reinforced by the Health Act 1999. In particular, the National Institute for Clinical Excellence (NICE),[2] by developing clinical guidelines with an expectation of routine adherence, could have a significant impact on the nature of medical practice and also influence outcomes in medical negligence litigation. Yet there is legitimate concern about the extent to which guidelines reflect considerations other than the improvement of patient care; about their applicability in clinical settings, and their potential for inhibiting clinical discretion and innovation. More generally, a pervasive 'guidelines mentality' could serve to undermine the valuable, and officially endorsed, goal of encouraging more collaborative doctor–patient relationships.

Health professionals may follow clinical guidelines[3] and protocols[4] too slavishly, either in the mistaken belief that they *are* the law, or taking the prudential view that non-compliance might have serious consequences for their jobs. The perception of guidelines *as* law is partly attributable to the prescriptive tone typical of the genre and the tendency for general guidance

---

[1] Clinical governance has been defined as 'a framework through which NHS organisations are accountable for continuously improving the quality of their services and safeguarding high standards of care by creating an environment in which excellence in clinical care will flourish': Department of Health, *A First Class Service: Quality in the New NHS* (London, 1998).

[2] See M. Rawlins, 'National Health Service: In Pursuit of Quality: The National Institute for Clinical Excellence' (1999) 353 *Lancet* 1079.

[3] Typically defined as 'systematically developed statements to assist practitioners and patients about appropriate health care for specific circumstances': M. Field and K. Lohr (eds.), *Clinical Practice Guidelines: Directions for a new Program* (Washington, DC, 1990) 8. Cf NHS Executive, *Clinical Guidelines* (Leeds, 1996) 4.

[4] Relatively detailed plans for the conduct of a clinical trial or course of treatment.

from prestigious professional bodies to elide distinctions between political, moral, and legal rights.[5] The misconception is reinforced by the cavalier use of the word 'rights' in the Patient's Charter,[6] and by some recent pronouncements emanating from the new institutional machinery within the NHS. When the aim is to ensure that clinicians improve quality and maintain standards of care within a framework of 'clinical governance', exhortation can easily shade into prescription.

It is true that most such guidance contains caveats. Thus, the National Health Service Executive (NHSE), not wishing to incur the wrath of the profession, has said that even clinical guidelines endorsed by leading professional bodies or by the NHSE itself:

can still only assist the practitioner; they cannot be used to mandate, authorise or outlaw treatment options. Regardless of the strength of the evidence, it will remain the responsibility of the practising clinicians to interpret their application. . . . It would be wholly inappropriate for clinical guidelines to be used as a means of coercion of the individual clinician, by managers and senior professionals.[7]

Similarly, the chairman of NICE has indicated that the Institute's guidance 'will not be mandatory'. However:

Its guidelines will cover most clinical circumstances for which they have been developed; and, although it is widely acknowledged that strict adherence to clinical guidelines is not in the best interests of some patients, health professionals would be wise to record their reasons for non-compliance in patients' medical records.[8]

Moreover, as Hurwitz points out, '[o]fficially, there may be no managerial or legal expectation that doctors should automatically follow guidelines, but purchasers may adopt a different view'.[9]

In fact, it appears that in England guidelines have not so far been much used as part of the contracting process.[10] However, their increased use in

---

[5] e.g. doctors '*must* give patients the information they ask for or need about their condition, its treatment and prognosis; give information to patients in a way they can understand; [and] respect the rights of patients to be fully involved in decisions about care': General Medical Council, *Good Medical Practice* (London, 1995), para 11, emphasis added. Cf '[t]he surgeon's clinical duties of care are based on an understanding of the rights of patients'. And again, 'surgeons should: Inform competent adult patients . . . of the nature of their condition, along with the type, purpose, prognosis, common side effects and significant risks of any proposed surgical treatments. Where appropriate, alternative treatment options (including non-surgical) should also be explained, together with the consequences of no treatment. This information should be provided in the detail required by a reasonable person in the circumstances of the patient to make a relevant and informed judgement': Senate of Surgery of Great Britain and Ireland, *The Surgeon's Duty of Care* (London, 1997) 4 and 6, respectively.

[6] H. Teff, *Reasonable Care: Legal Perspectives on the Doctor/Patient Relationship* (Oxford, 1994) 106–8.   [7] NHSE, n. 3, above, 10.

[8] Rawlins, n. 2, above, 1079.

[9] B. Hurwitz, 'Clinical Guidelines: Legal and Political Considerations of Clinical Practice Guidelines' (1999) 318 *BMJ* 661, 664.

[10] P. Day, R. Klein, and F. Miller, *Hurdles and Levers: A Comparative US–UK Study of Guidelines* (London, 1998) 28.

health-care delivery seem irresistible. Alongside the pivotal role of NICE within clinical governance, there is now an intense focus on evidence-based medicine (EBM), facilitated by the growth in randomized controlled trials and advanced methods of analysing and systematising data. All of this is happening in the context of a purchasing/commissioning process, funded and run by the state,[11] in which the pursuit of cost-effective treatment is a major aim, as specified in NICE's own remit. This is not to say that these developments are simply reducible to a government agenda imposed on the profession to control profligate practitioners. As Day, Klein, and Miller point out, to the extent that guideline production and implementation have been introduced by the Royal Colleges and remain medically led, 'the guidelines movement can be seen as a successful strategy by the medical profession which, in its own self-interest, has sought to control the outliers within its own ranks in order to fend off managerial pressure'.[12] At all events, the more authoritative clinical guidelines are perceived to be by the profession, the more likely is it that adherence or non-adherence to them will be invoked as a measure of medical negligence.[13] Before this cultural shift becomes too entrenched, it is desirable to consider how it is viewed by those called upon to subscribe to it, and what might be the implications for legal decision-making and medical practice.

The Limits to Implementation of Guidelines

Although evidence on the use and impact of guidelines in clinical practice is limited, experience in England and elsewhere suggests that, when they are not incorporated into the general law or contractual arrangements, the level of actual compliance, especially by *doctors*, is noticeably low.[14] Thus a recent Ontario study revealed that (voluntary) 'Clinical Guidelines have had no ostensible effect on practice patterns or medical service costs'.[15] In

---

[11] D. Light, 'Managed Care in a New Key: Britain's Strategies for the 1990s' (1998) 28 *International Journal of Health Services* 427, 433.

[12] See n. 10, above, 13.

[13] See, e.g., 'there is no doubt that clinical guidelines will be used as evidence in legal cases and are likely to be referred to more and more by the courts': K. Bloor and A. Maynard, *Clinical Governance: Clinician, heal thyself?* (London, 1998) 10. Cf. I. Kennedy, 'Medicine in Society, Now and in the Future' in S. Lock (ed.), *Eighty-five Not Out: Essays to Honour Sir George Godber* (London, 1993), 74. See also C. Havighurst, 'Practice Guidelines as Legal Standards Governing Physician Liability (1991) 54 *Law and Contemporary Problems* 87.

[14] Some managed care organizations in the United States achieve high levels of compliance. Due to a surplus of physicians they can recruit selectively, and the use of comparative performance profiling maximizes conformity of practice, with deselection as the ultimate sanction: Day, Klein and Miller, *Hurdles and Levers*, n. 10 above, 57–63. Cf. '[c]linicians in managed care organisations have much less discretion about the use of guidelines than other US (and UK) clinicians. However, many . . . are based on "expert opinion" and are lacking hard evidence of effectiveness and cost effectiveness': Bloor and Maynard, n. 13, above, 20.

[15] S. Rappolt, 'Clinical Guidelines and the Fate of Medical Autonomy in Ontario' (1997) 44 *Social Science and Medicine* 977, 983. Cf. R. Lawton and D. Parker, 'Procedures and the

part, our concern is with why this is so, and why, in some respects, circumspection about the 'clinical guidelines movement' can be defended as a rational response.

Some of the reasons for non-compliance are fairly predictable. There is inevitably a degree of knee-jerk antipathy and apathy among established individual clinicians, which may be reinforced by negative peer group attitudes. Equally predictable is the conspicuous lack of funding and of effective mechanisms to boost levels of compliance.[16] There is evidence that passive dissemination—by means of journals, postal communication, and conferences—rarely leads to changes in the behaviour of health professionals.[17] But it would be an over-simplification to explain non-compliance purely in the above terms. Managers keen to further 'clinical governance and the drive for quality improvement'[18] can appear at once too convinced of the rightness of the cause and unduly cynical about the motivation of those who resist or question it. Nor is the cause itself advanced by the vacuous 'managementspeak' in which the message is all too often couched.[19]

As viewed by many health-care professionals, the introduction of guidelines and protocols is driven more by risk-management considerations—in the sense of the organization's desire to fend off complaints and the threat of litigation—than by a desire to improve patient care.[20] Hospital staff resent being blamed when guidelines incorporate expectations that are locally unattainable, especially where managers are perceived as remote from day-to-day pressures. At the same time, it is easy to understate the strong propensity to accommodate change within current and preferred working practices rather than alter them. As Caper put it, writing in 1988 of the American experience: 'as fast as regulations and review protocols are written physicians learn to circumvent them, resenting the intrusion into their clinical autonomy'.[21] The problem is exacerbated by the

Professional: The Case of the British NHS' (1999) 48 *Social Science and Medicine* 353, 354, noting that 'little has been written about the percentage of practitioners who actually comply with the guidelines', and citing various studies, in none of which did compliance exceed 54%. In several, it was well below that.

[16] R. Grol, 'Beliefs and Evidence in Changing Clinical Practice', (1997) 315 *BMJ* 418, 420.

[17] See N. Freemantle *et al.*, 'The Effectiveness of Printed Educational Materials in Changing the Behaviour of Health Care Professionals' in Cochrane Collaboration. *Cochrane Library*. Issue 3. (Oxford, 1996).

[18] See G. Scally and L. Donaldson, 'Clinical Governance and the Drive for Quality Improvement in the New NHS in England' (1998) 317 *BMJ* 61.

[19] See N. Goodman, 'Clinical Governance' (1998) 317 *BMJ* 1725, deprecating Scally and Donaldson's vision for 'clinical governance' as 'rigorous in its application, organisation-wide in its emphasis, developmental in its thrust, and positive in its connotations': n. 18, above, 61.

[20] Lawton and Parker, n. 15 above, 355. Cp. '[c]linical guidelines are produced for one reason, and one reason only: to improve the quality of care': NHSE, n. 3, above, 7.

[21] P. Caper, 'Solving the Medical Dilemma' (1988) 318 *New England Journal of Medicine* 1535, cited in Lawton and Parker, n. 15 above, 360. Cf. much of the empirical evidence on implementation of the Police and Criminal Evidence Act 1984 and its codes. See, e.g.,

constant need to monitor and update guidelines. Naturally, creatures of habit, wedded to manifestly inferior, outdated methods of treatment, are open to criticism. Equally, for certain screening procedures and clinical conditions, as well as for a number of nursing routines, there is a compelling case for developing standardized guidelines. Yet, often, other tried and tested approaches can be perfectly appropriate, while many situations will call for the use of intelligence and initiative—the exercise of clinical autonomy—in ways not anticipated by the guidelines.

The experience of medical audit is instructive in this context, not least because guidelines could, in principle, act as a benchmark for the good performance standards to which it aspires. Medical audit has thus been one of the catalysts for the production of guidelines. Developed by the Royal Colleges in the 1980s, it was incorporated into consultants' contracts and GPs' terms of service following the 1990 health-care reforms,[22] although individual clinicians were not compelled to participate. Black and Thompson have observed that '[i]n general, audit will be shaped by the prevailing, established environment rather than the converse',[23] and they point to the risk of doctors *appearing* to change their clinical practice to produce better audit results, and even some instances of junior doctors modifying their case-note entries in order to influence the audit results. The point of interest—irrespective of the merits or demerits of the preferred procedure—is how the *appearance* of compliance can so easily take the place of *actual* compliance. This phenomenon is explored at length in Powers' *The Audit Society*,[24] where he portrays the malign consequences of a world in which the audit must be shown to have been a success; where trust is disparaged, and where, crucially, no one audits the auditors. The fact that doctors are much more likely than nurses to pay lip-service to guidelines raises the further problem of tensions within the health-care team.[25]

Even when guidelines are followed in good faith, we may still see adverse consequences, again prefigured in Black and Thompson's study on audit:

D. Dixon, A. Bottomley, C. Coleman, M. Gill, and D. Wall, 'Reality and Rules in the Construction and Regulation of Police Suspicion' (1989) 17 *International Journal of the Sociology of Law* 185.

[22] National Health Service and Community Care Act 1990. Medical audit was defined in the White Paper, *Working for Patients*, as 'the systematic, critical analysis of the quality of medical care, including the procedures used for diagnosis and treatment, the use of resources, and the resulting outcome and quality of life for the patient': Secretary of State for Health, *Working for Patients* (London, 1989) Cmnd 555, 39.

[23] N. Black and E. Thompson, 'Obstacles to Medical Audit: British Doctors Speak' (1993) 36 *Social Science and Medicine* 849, 855. See also J. Lowas *et al.*, 'Do Practice Guidelines Guide Practice? The Effect of a Consensus Statement on the Practice of Physicians' (1989) 321 *New England Journal of Medicine* 1306, 1310.

[24] M. Powers, *The Audit Society* (Oxford, 1997).

[25] Lawton and Parker, n. 15, above, 357.

there was a common, recurring perception that audit sought to turn medical practice from an individualised, subtle art into an unthinking, routine activity based
largely on guidelines and rules. Many doctors believed that such dependency upon
guidelines would have adverse effects for doctors, destroying the initiative of
juniors who would no longer think through the logistics of treatment but pick up a
form and tick the appropriate box. Some doctors also believed that the presence of
guidelines meant that they were obliged to comply with them, even when they felt
that it was not appropriate in a particular case.[26]

If hard-pressed clinicians become too wedded to the checklist, too driven
by the 'average' outcomes predicted by randomized controlled trials, in
which the participants' conditions and circumstances might have borne
little resemblance to that of their particular patients, they may well find
themselves providing inappropriate treatment. With the advent of NICE,
this risk is compounded by the suspicion that, where there is a conflict
between fiscal restraint and optimal therapeutic provision, guidelines
developed by a governmental agency accountable to the Department of
Health may be less credible than those developed by bodies of experts
within the relevant specialty.

It may be objected that such reactions reflect a misunderstanding of the
proper role of clinical guidelines (and of EBM) in medical practice; that far
from *displacing* individual clinical expertise, they should, wherever possible, incorporate or allow for clinical judgement, so that, ideally, the two
perspectives can function as an integrated whole.[27] It is just such a blend
that is advocated by the Senate of Surgery in its recent Guidance.[28] Plainly,
clinical guidelines do have a valuable part to play over a wide range of
medical activities. They can, within limits, assist rational and responsible
prescribing,[29] help reduce the incidence of inappropriate care, and serve as
a valuable aid in routine procedures, especially for new and inexperienced
staff. At least in theory, they could also help improve the performance of
longer-serving, deficient practitioners. Certainly, in the wake of such
events as the deaths from paediatric heart surgery at Bristol and the cancer
screening failures in Kent, the demand for stricter monitoring and for a
more systematic approach to raising standards and encouraging better
practice has never been stronger.[30] However, there remains the concern

---

[26] See n. 23 above, 851.

[27] See T. Greenhalgh, 'Narrative Based Medicine in an Evidence Based World' (1999) 318
BMJ 323.   [28] See n. 5 above, 3.

[29] The mandatory 'selected list' restrictions on prescribing for certain conditions are
broadly accepted within the profession, despite the inroad on clinical freedom. See National
Health Service (General Medical and Pharmaceutical Services) Amendment Regs. 1985 SI
1985/290 (as amended).

[30] See, respectively, *The Inquiry into the Management of Care of Children Receiving
Complex Heart Surgery at the Bristol Royal Infirmary* (I. Kennedy, Chairman): Hansard,
HC, 18 June 1998, cols. 529–530; *Penney, Palmer and Cannon v. East Kent HA*, BENF
1999/0294/AZ (16 Nov. 1999). And see Department of Health, *Supporting Doctors,*

that seeking to impose, or even inculcate, a guidelines *culture* would in some respects reduce the quality of health-care provision, not least by undermining doctor–patient relationships.[31] At the same time, one might question the wisdom of allowing guidelines a dominant role in legal decision-making.

The Legal Status of Guidelines

If, in some areas of medical practice, use of clinical guidelines becomes a standard expectation, what will be the impact on liability in negligence? Could the guidelines acquire the status of a *legal* standard, displacing the lowest common denominator of acceptable care which the '*Bolam* test' still appears to permit?[32] The current status of guidelines as regards the tortious liability of health-care professionals is clear.[33] Like any codified standards of professional conduct, they are not, as such, conclusive, although they may be significant, even very strong, evidence of what constitutes reasonable care. Let us suppose that a patient suffering from a condition for which apparently relevant guidelines exist has been injured in the course of treatment. The most basic issues which can arise, regarding the guidelines, are whether the relevant health professional is negligent for not having complied with them, or immune from liability as a result of having done so. Since guidelines alone are not dispositive, the short answer to both questions must be 'no'—*Bolam*, as explicated in *Bolitho* v. *City and Hackney Health Authority*,[34] remains the test.

Guidelines, then, can be only *one* element in the equation, to be weighed alongside expert evidence, textbooks, other relevant literature, and primary medical evidence, such as test results and symptoms. Traditionally, courts have valued the oral evidence of expert witnesses on 'reasonable practice' above guidance in prestigious works of reference, and formal guidelines could be perceived as comparable reference material presented in a different form. In *Vernon* v. *Bloomsbury Health Authority*,[35] the plaintiff's prescribed drug dosage was higher than that recommended by the Product Data Sheet, the British National Formulary (BNF), the Monthly Index of Medical Specialities (MIMS), and

Protecting Patients. A Consultation Paper on Preventing, Recognising, and Dealing with Poor Clinical Performance of Doctors in England (London, 1999).

[31] See 'The Impact on Medical Practice and the Doctor–Patient Relationship', below.

[32] *Bolam* v. *Friern Hospital Management Committee* [1957] 1 WLR 582.

[33] It is not proposed to explore here any contract of employment issues which may arise: see V. Harpwood, 'Guidelines in Medical Practice: The Legal Issues' [1998] *Cephalalgia*, Suppl 21, 56. As regards the scope for action against purchasers of health care, and the remote possibility of guideline producers being held liable in negligence, see K. Stern, 'Clinical Guidelines and Negligence Liability' in M. Deighan and S. Hitch (eds.), *Clinical Effectiveness: From Guidelines to Cost-effective Practice* (Brentwood, 1995) 127.

[34] [1997] 3 WLR 1151 (HL) See n. 38, below.   [35] (1995) 6 Med. LR 297.

Martindale's Extra Pharmacopoeia, and it was prescribed for longer than recommended by MIMS and Martindale. In finding that 'the dosage was a proper one', the judge said, 'I agree with the defendants' experts that the guidelines laid down by the manufacturers and, for example, MIMS, are too conservative and that they err on the side of caution'.[36]

In a nutshell, for some thirty years after *Bolam*, the courts largely deferred to expert testimony supporting or condoning the practice of medical defendants. Although, in the last ten years or so, they have been more willing to probe and challenge the *credibility* of such evidence, they will very rarely override clinical judgement.[37] *Bolitho* seems to encourage, or at least invite, judges to reach their own conclusions on the *reasonableness* of clinical conduct, and to find negligence in the 'rare case' where the expert's professional opinion is not *'logically* defensible'. It remains unclear, however, whether this formulation envisages no more than judicial determination as to the internal consistency of expert testimony, as distinct from substantive judicial evaluation of reasonableness, in risk-benefit terms.[38]

HAS *BOLITHO* MADE A DIFFERENCE?

Can we now expect more independent and rigorous judicial evaluation of expert medical evidence adduced on behalf of the defence? Granted the clear indication in *Bolitho* that rejection of such evidence would be very uncommon, there is now, in the Court of Appeal as well as at first instance, increasing use of phrases such as 'logically supported' and 'stands up to logical analysis', as well as acknowledgement of 'the principle that, in some circumstances, a judge is entitled to form her own view upon the logic of medical evidence'.[39] Moreover, in the medical sphere it is proving difficult to fulfil Lord Woolf's objective of neutrally provided expert evidence, which would not be readily susceptible to judicial criticism.[40] Judges are becoming increasingly intolerant of partisan testimony in medical litigation, a problem that has attracted considerable adverse comment.[41] However, the new Civil Procedure Rules[42] have, at least

---

[36] Cf The reference to a surgical rule as 'a useful guideline, but not one which had to be followed in every case': *Ratty* v. *Haringey HA* (1994) 5 Med LR 413, 416. And see *Early* v. *Newham HA* (1994) 5 Med. LR 214, 216.

[37] See J. Montgomery, *Health Care Law* (Oxford, 1997), 169–76.

[38] See H. Teff, 'The Standard of Care in Medical Negligence—Moving on from *Bolam?'* (1998) 18 *Oxford Journal of Legal Studies* 473, 479–81.

[39] e.g., respectively, *Wisniewski* v. *Central Manchester HA* [1998] Lloyd's Rep. Med. 223, 237 (CA); *Penney, Palmer and Cannon* v. *East Kent HA* [1999] Lloyd's Rep. Med. 123, 130, and *Ian Leslie Marriott* v. *West Midlands HA* [1999] Lloyd's Rep. Med. 23, 30 (CA).

[40] Lord Woolf, *Access to Justice* (Final Report) (London, 1996) ch. 13.

[41] e.g. *Hepworth* v. *Kerr* (1995) 6 Med. LR 139, 165, and see commentary by M. Puxon Q.C., *ibid., 171*. Cf. Lord Woolf, *Access to Justice*, n. 40 above, 144.

[42] Civil Procedure Rules 1998, SI 1998 3132, Part 35.

temporarily, stopped short of Lord Woolf's original proposal for a single court-appointed expert; meanwhile, resort to a single joint expert, appointed by the parties, is likely to be relatively rare in complex medical negligence cases.

Bolitho's emphasis on quality of evidence, rationality, and coherence does argue a shift in *legal* decision-making which mirrors the quest in medicine itself for more defensible *clinical* decisions—more evidence-based and systematic, and less dependent on proclaimed medical experience. It veers between making rigorous professional standards the effective legal determinant—an advance on the early interpretation of *Bolam*—and allowing leeway for enhanced external control, based on the court's view of what is 'logically' defensible, albeit blurring the line between reason and reasonableness. As forensic medical evidence becomes more accessible to the non-specialist, through increasingly sophisticated computerized techniques, judges may prove less reluctant to make independent judgements on clinicians' conduct. At the same time, the very growth of 'authoritative' clinical guidelines may make them more disposed to question the failure to follow them. Certainly, post-*Bolitho*, experts and legal practitioners specializing in the field are increasingly conscious of the need for rigorously researched reports which include a risk analysis and address the significance of any relevant guidelines.

THE JUDICIAL RESPONSE

The courts' traditional preference for the oral evidence of experts over medical works of reference or guidance could change, following the recent reform of civil procedure[43] and if clinical guidelines attain greater prestige. Already there is evidence of them playing an influential role—especially in 'life or death' and other highly charged contexts, where resort to 'authoritative' guidance is an understandable source of relief for judges confronted with hard choices. For example, in 1997, a non-resuscitation order was granted in respect of a 16-month-old baby suffering from spinal muscular atrophy. The judge indicated that he had been greatly assisted by the '*amicus curiae*' who had the advantage of having been a party to the preparation of relevant *guidelines* produced a few weeks earlier, adding; 'it is clear that what is being proposed by the doctors has the support of the Royal College of Paediatrics and Child Health'.[44]

Comparable judicial respect for, and endorsement of, clinical guidelines can now be found across a wide range of medical contexts, including the limits of confidentiality,[45] withdrawal of treatment from patients in a

---

[43] See Civil Procedure Rules 1998, SI 1998 3132, pursuant to Civil Procedure Act 1997 (the 'Woolf Reforms').

[44] *Re C (a minor) (medical treatment)* [1998] 1 FCR 1, 10.

[45] *W v. Egdell* [1990] 2 WLR 471.

persistent vegetative state,[46] and authorization of caesarean sections when consent has been withheld.[47] There may be an acknowledgement that they are not the law, as in *St George's Healthcare* v. *S*: '[t]he guidelines should be approached for what they are, that is, guidelines'. And again, 'formulaic compliance' can be inappropriate.[48] Yet, sometimes the very insistence on their non-conclusive nature seems to reflect an awareness that others may have thought differently. For example, in a recent appeal on quantum in a negligent diagnosis case, Staughton LJ specifically addressed the relevance of the Judicial Studies Board Guidelines on quantum.[49] He referred to an earlier case,[50] in which he had said: '[t]hey are not in themselves law', adding that though this had 'provoked some magisterial comment', 'I remain of that opinion; and it is worth saying, as the very title "Guidelines" might be thought to suggest that they have some special authority of their own'.[51]

Although English law has not adopted the dispositive stance, there are recent pointers in this direction in a number of jurisdictions. One example can be found in the Canadian case of *Pierre* v. *Marshall*.[52] The defendant was found negligent in not having followed guidelines of the Alberta Medical Association and of the Society of Obstetricians and Gynaecologists of Canada, recommending universal screening of pregnant women for gestational diabetes. He was found negligent, despite controversy about the cost-effectiveness of the guidelines. In the United States, there are a number of legislative schemes whereby compliance with an officially adopted guideline can act as an affirmative defence to a medical malpractice claim,[53] quite apart from the extensive imposition of guidelines by the managed care organizations which finance and organize the bulk of private American health-care delivery.[54] In France, between 1994 and 1996, some 150 mandatory practice guidelines were introduced for non-hospital medicine and surgery, diagnosis and treatment, with fines of up to £2,000, for non-compliance.[55]

---

[46] *Airedale National Health Service Trust* v. *Bland* [1993] 2 WLR 316.
[47] *St George's Healthcare Trust* v. *S* [1998] 3 WLR 936.   [48] *Ibid.* 970.
[49] *Reed* v. *Sunderland HA* (1998) (LEXIS, 12 Oct. 1998).
[50] *Arafa* v. *Potter* [1994] PIQR 73, 79.   [51] *Reed* v. *Sunderland HA*, n. 49, above, 9.
[52] (1994) 8 WWR 478 (Alta QB).
[53] Most notably, Maine: Me. Rev. Stat. Ann. tit. 24, paras. 2971–2979 (West Supp. 1995). See also B. Bennett 'Setting the Standard? Clinical Practice Guidelines and Medical Negligence Litigation' (1997) 20 *University of New South Wales Law Journal* 707; A. Hyams *et al.*, 'Practice Guidelines and Malpractice Litigation: A Two-way Street' (1995) 122 *Annals of Internal Medicine* 450.
[54] Cf. '[p]urchasers in US health care, unlike in the UK, are driven to rigorous purchasing by the profit motive. These arrangements curtail the freedoms of clinicians and hospitals by establishing and implementing strict protocols and guidelines (not always evidence based) . . . which restrict the choice of patients and providers': Bloor and Maynard, n. 13, above, 20.
[55] I. Durand-Zaleski, C. Colin, and C. Blum-Boisgard, 'An Attempt to Save Money by Using Mandatory Practice Guidelines in France' (1997) 315 *BMJ* 943.

At present, the National Health Service Executive acknowledges that, in the medical context, *Bolam* 'continues to be a valid and important evidentiary rule ... whether or not national clinical guidelines have been published'. Even where they are seen as authoritative, cases may be argued to be outside the 'defined selection criteria for applicability';[56] or 'preferences of the individual patient' could justify alternative options, as might widespread, but supported, variations. And again, '[a]dvances in care come through the efforts of people who are prepared to take risks, and clinical guidelines must not be constraining, and must not stop change'.[57] Yet as they do become more 'authoritative', the perceived epitome of 'best practice', they could, even without displacing *Bolam*, create pressure to reverse the onus of proof, requiring the doctor to establish that failure to adhere to guidelines was not negligent.[58] Granting such a high level of putative authority to guidelines would, it is submitted, be undesirable. They are not designed *as* legal rules. Depending on their provenance, they may offer a counsel of perfection that is locally unattainable, or be too undemanding, perhaps unduly influenced by considerations of cost-containment. Equally, there are often reasonable grounds for arguing that seemingly controlling guidelines, derived from population studies, are either not meant to, or did not in fact, cover the particular clinical circumstances.

In view of such inevitable limitations, it would be inappropriate for guidelines to become the sole basis of liability, and imprudent to make them a key, or even, *prima facie*, determinant, especially if this would encourage more people to initiate misconceived claims when guidelines had not been followed. The NHSE's caveats about not letting guidelines become a straightjacket might not survive intact in a 'guidelines culture'. This concern is underscored by the new statutory duty of quality introduced in the Health Act 1999.[59] It was originally contemplated that Chief Executives should be statutorily accountable for their Trusts' failure to attain the relevant standards. The Act is less stringent, requiring 'each Health Authority, Primary Care Trust and NHS trust to put and keep in place arrangements for the purpose of monitoring and improving the quality of health care which it provides to individuals'.[60] However, subsequent guidance and the advent of National Service Frameworks could extend the scope of liability.[61] In any event, clinical discretion is increasingly likely to be constrained, whether by purchaser- or Trust-driven demands, or through doctors' fears that, in the era of clinical governance, non-conformity will invite legal sanction. As 'learned intermediaries', clinicians (or

---

[56] NHSE, n. 3, above, 10. [57] *Ibid.*, 11.
[58] See V. Harpwood, 'NHS Reform, Audit, Protocols and Standards of Care' (1994) 1 *Medical Law International* 241, 252.
[59] Health Act 1999, s. 18. [60] *Ibid.*, s. 18(1).
[61] See further V. Harpwood, 'The Manipulation of Medical Practice', this vol.

institutions vicariously liable for them) are much more vulnerable to a finding of negligence than health-care purchasers or the even more causally remote guideline developers, who are highly unlikely to be seen as owing a duty to a particular patient.

The Impact on Medical Practice and the Doctor–Patient Relationship

There are serious implications for health-care provision if clinical discretion is unduly constrained by the developments outlined above. The clinical guidelines and EBM movements are disarming. If one begins with the inarticulate premise that guidelines are intrinsically desirable, it is all too easy to assume that they will be appropriately developed, widely applicable, and properly applied. Thus beguiled, we are tempted to understate the hold of established working practices, and to minimize the possible chilling effect of a guidelines mentality on medical expertise and innovation. Reluctance to innovate for fear of litigation may become more pronounced because, by definition, it is normally hard to demonstrate that *new* health technologies are evidence-based. We are also tempted to play down the inescapable role of value judgement in their production, which is not necessarily, or exclusively, cost-related. Whether through 'occupational imperialism by particular specialties'[62] or subconscious preferences, guideline developers may unduly favour particular approaches to treating medical conditions. Their conclusions may gloss over legitimate differences of view, not only on the relative merits of rival modes of treatment, including the cases for and against interventionist measures, but also about appropriate types and levels of medication. More broadly, guidelines are liable to divert the attention of the clinician from what constitutes 'health' for the particular patient.

Such factors account for the reservations of many experienced practitioners who are not, in principle, averse to guideline development.[63] Hence the 'call for the research community to value observational methods and to see applicability as an issue that is as important to trial design as statistical power'.[64] In similar vein, there is the criticism that EBM, coming as it does from population studies, reflects decisions 'distant from the patient and the consultation' and interpretation which is 'almost always doctor centred'. It 'diminishes the importance of human relationships and the role of the other partner in the consultation—the patient'.[65] Many patients suffer

[62] Day, Klein, and Miller, n. 10, above, 38.

[63] See, e.g., A. Hopkins, 'Some Reservations about Clinical Guidelines' (1995) 72 *Archives of Disease in Childhood* 70. Cf. Sir D. Black, 'The Limitations of Evidence' (1998) 32 *Journal of the Royal College of Physicians of London* 23.

[64] D. Mant, 'Evidence and Primary Care: Can Randomised Trials Inform Clinical Decisions about Individual Patients?' (1999) 353 *Lancet* 743, 745.

[65] K. G. Sweeney, D. MacAuley, and D. P. Gray, 'Personal Significance: The Third Dimension' (1998) 351 *Lancet* 134.

from a complex mix of *chronic* medical and social problems, not readily accommodated in the form of guidelines or ameliorated by applying them. Thus, to the statistical and clinical significance of research findings there needs to be added a 'third dimension'—*personal significance*.[66] But how realistic is it to expect such a blend to emerge in the doctor–patient encounter? The guidelines mind-set is apt to produce a style and method of communication which makes it more difficult to achieve a shared medical message at the critical point of delivery.

In *Clinical Guidelines and the Law*, Hurwitz draws attention to one of Plato's *Dialogues*, which presciently addresses the respective merits of skills grounded in practical expertise and those based merely upon instruction or obeying rules.[67] Plato warns against the perils of de-skilling in medicine, which he sees as the inevitable outcome of health-care provision dominated by prescribed techniques. Alongside the 'clinical guidelines movement' and the 'EBM movement', there exists a 'medical humanities' movement, pointing to the benefits of arts and humanities courses for doctors, and consequently for their patients. Their potential value in helping to instil the human skills of medicine is another of the messages coming from leaders of the profession[68] and prestigious medical institutions. In *Tomorrow's Doctors*,[69] the General Medical Council recommended adding special study modules drawn from non-medical disciplines to the formal curriculum. In 1998, a number of medical students at Glasgow University opted for a module on Plato's *Republic*. They reported that learning how to formulate an argument and how to identify and criticize the arguments of others was a revelation to them, as they had been used to accepting much of what they were told.[70]

If EBM becomes the 'new deity in clinical medicine',[71] it could herald the dominance of a new kind of medical paternalism—'*the guideline knows best*'—at the very time that the new generation of medical students is being encouraged to adopt a more questioning approach, and when the medical profession is encouraging us to see the doctor–patient relationship as collaborative and to become more actively involved in our own health care. In the pressurised world of modern medical practice, a 'guideline mentality' could exacerbate concerns about medicine becoming increasingly 'dehumanised', which are unlikely to diminish in the new era of 'walk in' health centres and clinics, NHS Direct, and telemedicine. This is

---

[66] *Ibid.*

[67] Plato in J. Annas and R. Waterfield (eds.), *Statesman* (Cambridge, 1995), 59–77. Cited in B. Hurwitz, *Clinical Guidelines and the Law* (Abingdon, 1998), 74–7.

[68] See Sir K. Calman, 'Why Arts Courses for Medical Curricula?' (1996) 347 *Lancet* 1499.

[69] General Medical Council, *Tomorrow's Doctors. Recommendations for Undergraduate Medical Education* (London, 1993).

[70] R. Downie and J. Macnaughton, 'Should Medical Students Read Plato?' (1999) 170 *Medical Journal of Australia* 125.

[71] Sweeney *et al.*, n. 65, above, 134.

not, of course, to deny that such developments have positive features. Yet they do threaten to undermine doctor–patient relationships. The risks are perhaps most apparent in general practice, and in the context of chronic illness: '[t]he fact that the doctor sometimes chooses to place more weight on the patient's agenda than on clinical evidence seems to be a rational strategy aimed at maintaining an important relationship', which, in terms of the overall 'healing' process, may make more sense than 'staying within the bounds of a statistically defined consensus on clinical effectiveness'.[72] Crudely stated, 'bullet point' care is inimical to therapeutic alliance. It minimizes the very patient involvement which the profession's leaders also rightly exhort clinicians to foster, not least for its *therapeutic* benefits. If medicine sends out mixed messages to its exponents and to the public about its preferred model of health care provision, it should not surprise us if individual patients are confused by the messages they receive in the clinical encounter.

[72] Z. Tomlin, C. Humphrey, and S. Rogers, 'General Practitioners' Perceptions of Effective Health Care' (1999) 318 *BMJ* 1532, 1534.

THREATENING BEHAVIOUR? THE CHALLENGE POSED BY MEDICAL NEGLIGENCE CLAIMS

Linda Mulcahy

Introduction

This chapter considers the threat to the medical profession posed by medical negligence claims. It develops an important argument made by Dingwall that the threat of litigation is best understood in terms of the symbolic challenge that this form of consumer activism poses to medical autonomy. The chapter draws on new data about the characteristics of law-suits against doctors collected as part of a three-year evaluation of the use of mediation in the resolution of medical negligence claims, and reported elsewhere.[1] The study was commissioned by the Department of Health and directed by the author. To date few reliable data have been collected by the Department about the incidence and characteristics of medical negligence claims. Despite this, the medical profession, media and other commentators have commonly claimed that the UK is facing an American-style litigation crisis, and that the financial and social costs of medical negligence have become unbearable.[2] Most recently the Secretary of State has indicated that something must be done about the problem of compensation-hungry patients and their lawyers. His approach and that of those constructing the issue as a crisis is summed up in his contention that the best place for lawyers in the NHS is on the operating table. The notion of a crisis and vexatious litigants sits in the popular imagination alongside the equally extreme treatment of the tragic cases of those injured as a result of iatrogenic injury. Media representations of the medical profession have veered from portraying doctors as the saint-like saviours of lives or restorers of good health to criticizing doctors for medical negligence, avarice, and sexual harassment. This chapter questions assumptions made in the context of such debate and considers the ways in which conceptual-

---

[1] L. Mulcahy, with M. Selwood, L. Summerfield, and A. Netten, *Mediating Medical Negligence Claims—an option for the future?* (Norwich, 1999).

[2] C. Ham, R. Dingwall, P. Fenn and D. Harris, *Medical Negligence: Compensation and Accountability*, briefing paper 6 (Oxford and London, 1988); E. Willis, 'The Medical Profession in Australia' in F. Hefferty and J. McKinley (eds.), *The Changing Medical Profession: An International Perspective* (New York and Oxford, 1993); D. Lupton, 'Doctors on the Medical Profession' (1997) 19 *Sociology of Health and Illness* 480–97.

izing the incidence of medical negligence claims as a crisis can serve to enhance the interests of the medical profession.

Negligence claims clearly do have the potential to threaten the medical profession in a number of ways. They can expose doctors to external scrutiny by colleagues, solicitors, barristers, the judiciary and increasingly to managers within the health service with responsibility for overseeing claims and risk management. In turn they may fear that this exposure could affect their career prospects. Claims can involve doctors in activities such as case conferences and meetings with claimants which take them away from their clinical activities and private practice. Whether or not a claim has actually been received by a doctor the fear of litigation may encourage him or her to adopt risk-averse strategies such as defensive medicine or the avoidance of high risk specialties. Additionally, the high costs of some claims and the fact that such costs are now met from local budgets may expose doctors to pressure from managers to manage the claims in a way which is not acceptable to them. Where they see the allegations as justified doctors may have to come to terms with their own incompetence. At the very least they will have to come to terms with a breakdown in the relationship with a patient. Finally, allegations about clinical competence are a form of calling to account in which the expert is asked to explain and justify his or her activity to the laity. This poses a threat to the individual doctor but can also be viewed as a symbolic threat to the principle of clinical autonomy and a challenge to the doctor's professional, social and economic power.

This chapter is in three main parts. The first section will review what is known about medical negligence claims. The second section will then draw on data collected for the evaluation study which shed some new light on the threat posed by claims. The third section will consider the symbolic threat of medical negligence and argue that it is this factor more than any other which explains the reaction of doctors to medical negligence.

What do We Know about Medical Negligence?

Since the emergence of a distinct profession of doctors in the last century actions against health-care professionals have been relatively rare. However, the number of claims has risen considerably since the inception of the National Health Service, although the incidence of claims appears to vary considerably between regions.[3] In the United Kingdom, Ham et al. found, in their review of claims rates for two English regions between 1977 and 1987, that the number of claims per 100,000 population had

---

[3] P. Hoyte, 'Unsound Practice: The Epidemiology of Medical Negligence' [1995] 3 Medical Law Review 53–73; R. Dingwall and P. Fenn, 'Risk Management: Financial Implications' in C. Vincent (ed.), Clinical Risk Management (London, 1995).

risen from four in 1977–8 to twenty-one in 1986–7 in one region. The Medical Protection Society has suggested that 2.5 per cent of its membership has a claim or complaint against it in any one year.[4] Moreover, in their review of 142 district health authorities Fenn *et al.* estimated that the approximate rate of new claims per 100 hospital doctors was 10.5.[5] They suggest that, although litigation rates clearly remain much higher in the United States than in Britain, the gap is narrowing. In their important review of available data, Dingwall and Fenn surmise that the frequency of claims increased by about 500 per cent during the 1980s.[6] Allowing for inflation, the cost of settling claims increased by about 250 per cent over the same period.

Research suggests that the cost of medical negligence claims to the state is rising. In 1987, one case alone, handled by the Medical Defence Union (MDU), was settled for £1,032,000, a sum 97 per cent greater than the MDU spent on all damages and settlements in 1975.[7] Recent announcements from the Department of Health suggest that payments to victims of medical negligence have soared by 56 per cent in two years and are currently costing the NHS £125 million a year. However, other estimates of the cost of medical negligence have been more conservative, and doubt has been cast on the accuracy of the Department of Health calculations which are based on sparse data. Dingwall and Fenn estimate that the direct cost of claims to the NHS is around £52million,[8] about 0.4 per cent of its total budget,[9] and this approximate figure was confirmed during a parliamentary question to Dr Brian Mawhinney based on financial returns. In light of these discrepancies and the high cost of claims, the collection of more accurate data has become imperative.

Part of the medical negligence 'crisis' in the 1980s appeared to revolve around the issue of who should pay for the escalating costs. In the past, as crown bodies, health authorities did not take out insurance against damages and legal expenses but met such costs from their own budgets. All hospital doctors were contractually bound to subscribe to a defence organization approved by the government in order to cover possible liability for damages. These organizations defended members accused of negligence and provided compensation to victims who had proved negligence. Health authorities and the societies co-ordinated their defences of cases and shared damages in proportion to the contribution of each party to the negligent acts. As the costs of membership fees, for which doctors were traditionally held personally responsible, rose dramatically, health authorities were forced to subsidize them. Dingwall and Fenn report that there

---

[4] M. Ennis and C. Vincent, 'The Effects of Medical Accidents and Litigation on Doctors and Patients' (1994) 16 *Law and Policy* 97–122.

[5] Fenn *et al.*, n. 2, above.　　　　　　　　[6] Dingwall and Fenn, n. 3, above.

[7] Hoyte, n. 3, above.　　　　　　[8] This includes a 20% administrative loading.

[9] Dingwall and Fenn, n. 3, above.

was a staggering 2,700 per cent increase in subscriptions between 1978 and 1988.[10] Further disruption was caused in 1989 when medical defence organizations (MDOs) announced their intention to charge differential subscription rates, with high risk specialties having to pay the most. This led to calls from the profession for differential salaries to be set to reflect this.

Since the conduct of most litigation was in the hands of the defence organizations, health authorities increasingly realized that they were being held financially responsible without being able to control fully the litigation and its financial consequences.[11] Since January 1990, at the instigation of the government, health authorities and trusts have taken over financial liability for claims.[12] The introduction of crown indemnity reflects the move towards the notion of an internal market in the NHS. In the words of Dingwall and Fenn:

In effect, the economic analysis of tort as a mechanism designed to provide appropriate incentives for loss prevention has been directly incorporated into the logic of the system. Units with high litigation costs will be obliged to charge higher prices, losing business to competitors who are more successful at managing their risks or delivering better quality services.[13]

The majority now subscribe to the Clinical Negligence Scheme for Trusts, a voluntary mutual assurance scheme which sets premiums by reference to a trust's scale of operations, its case mix and its risk-management procedures. The rationale behind the reforms was that the costs of negligence would be charged to the relevant clinical area and built into its prices rather than those of individual units. Thus, a breakdown of claims by severity assumes a new importance, and specialty groups are encouraged to implement effective risk-management programmes.[14]

The move towards crown indemnity was an important one, shifting as it did the locus of control over claims from the medical to the managerial sphere. The shift has been seen as a highly significant threat by the medical profession.[15] It has moved the responsibility for the management of claims to the trust level and provided financial incentives for managers and clinicians to handle medical negligence claims in the most cost-efficient way.

[10] Dingwall and Fenn, n. 3, above.

[11] I. Kennedy and A. Grubb, *Medical Law* (London, 1994).

[12] In addition to their budgets, local units have been able to make a call on funds from the NHS Litigation Authority for claims which arose before the introduction of the scheme.

[13] Dingwall and Fenn, n. 3, above, at 77.

[14] With the introduction of this scheme it will become increasingly important for accurate data to be collected so that contributions to the scheme can be set by reference to actual claims rather than just the scale of a Trust's operations. Over time, the scheme will develop a comprehensive database of claims and settlements and should greatly ease the case flow problems of smaller units.

[15] I. Harvey and R. Chadwick, 'Compensation for Harm: The Implications for Medical Research' [1992] 34 *Social Science and Medicine* 1399–1404.

The financial incentive *may* mean that early settlement of a case is deemed to be the most efficient solution, whether or not the doctor involved believes there has been a fault and wants to defend the case. This has been seen as an infringement of clinical freedom by many doctors. Mason and McCall Smith note:

Health Authorities may, as a consequence, felt obliged to settle cases on the grounds that this is the cheapest, if not the fairest, option; moreover, there is a strong suspicion that compensation for the injured party may be bought at the expense of limitations in treatment facilities for the remainder—but this is, perhaps to take too pessimistic a view.[16]

A Personal Crisis?

The making of a claim can also prompt a personal crisis for the doctor being accused of substandard care. Claims clearly have the potential to prompt strong reactions amongst doctors because they challenge the core assumption that healthcare professionals heal or alleviate pain. Basic tenets of the relationships between patients and doctors, and managers and doctors are called into question, and this can lead to a breach of trust, suspicion, and anger.[17] Commentators have suggested that doctors are often emotionally devastated by causing serious medical mishaps and suffer a mixture of fear, guilt, anger, embarrassment, and humiliation.[18] Particular emphasis has been put on anger. In the context of medical negligence, Lavery has argued:

The response is anger . . . By bringing legal action, the patient also assaults the physician's credibility, insinuating faulty judgement or treatment. Self-esteem and status as a successful practitioner in the community or member of the academic environment are suddenly jeopardized. A malpractice suit challenges professional reliability and authority.[19]

In their important review of the literature on doctors' responses to medical negligence, Ennis and Vincent have also suggested that feelings of anger and betrayal are not unusual in doctors reporting on the personal effects of litigation.[20] They place particular emphasis on the feelings of isolation caused by claims and the ways in which litigation and the threat

---

[16] J. Mason and R. McCall Smith, *Law and Medical Ethics* (4th edn., London, 1994) 206.

[17] L. Mulcahy and M. Rosenthal, 'Beyond Blaming and Perfection—A Multi-dimensional Approach to Medical Mishaps' in M. Rosenthal, L. Mulcahy and S. Lloyd-Bostock (eds.), *Medical Mishap—Pieces of the Puzzle* (Buckingham, 1999).

[18] R. Smith, 'Foreword' in A. Wu, S. Folkman, J. McPhee, and B. Lo, 'Do House Officers Learn from Their Mistakes?' [1991] 265 *Journal of the American Medical Association*: 2089–94.

[19] P. Lavery, 'The Physician's Reaction to a Malpractice Suit' (1988) 70 *Obstetrics and Gynaecology* 138–41 at 139.

[20] Ennis and Vincent, n. 4, above.

of litigation subtly change doctors' relationships with all patients, and not just those who actually initiate claims against them. Other research has demonstrated that doctors are likely to experience a host of symptoms characteristic of stress-induced illness in response to legal claims.[21] Lavery has drawn an analogy between these reactions and grief reactions flowing from the death of a close family member.[22] Many doctors take litigation as a personal affront and argue that this can cause a loss of confidence in their own ability or their enjoyment of their professional work.[23] Doctors have reported insomnia, appetite change, irritability, headaches, and many other symptoms of stress as responses to having made mistakes.[24]

Research also suggests that doctors are not well supported in their plight by medical colleagues or by the normative frameworks of the profession into which they are socialised at medical school. Many suffer severe reactions to having a claim made against them and in coming to terms with medical mishap. Authors of recent large-scale studies of error in medicine suggest that the incidence of mishap is high and that intense reactions to these events have to be understood within the context of the 'perfectibility model' to which doctors are taught to aspire in the course of their education.[25] Doctors are trained to function at high levels of proficiency. They are social-ized in medical schools to strive for error-free practice. As Leape explains:

There is a powerful emphasis on perfection, both in diagnosis and treatment. In everyday hospital practice, the message is equally clear: mistakes are unacceptable. Physicians are expected to function without error, an expectation that physicians translate into the need to be infallible. One result is that physicians . . . come to view error as a failure of character—you weren't careful enough, you didn't try hard enough.[26]

It seems that strong emotional reactions to claims do not just reflect concerns about the personal risks to promotion prospects or standing, but also induce self-criticism and introspection.

[21] S. C. Charles, 'A Different View of Malpractice' (1984) 87 *Chicago Medicine* 338–42.
[22] Lavery, n. 19, above.
[23] S. C. Charles, and E. Kennedy, *Defendant: A Psychiatrist on Trial for Medical Malpractice* (New York, 1988); Charles, n. 21, above.
[24] M. Ennis and J. Grudzinskas 'The Effect of Accidents and Litigation on Doctors', in C. Vincent, M. Ennis, and R. Audley (eds.), *Medical Accidents* (Oxford, 1993) 142—65.
[25] V. Nathanson, 'Medical Mistakes: A View from the British Medical Association' in M. Rosenthal, L. Mulcahy, and S. Lloyd-Bostock (eds.), *Medical Mishaps—Pieces of the Puzzle* (Buckingham, 1999); R. McL. Wilson, R. Gibberd, J. Hamilton, and B. Harrison, 'Safety of Healthcare in Australian Adverse Events to Hospitalised Patients' in M. Rosenthal, L. Mulcahy and S. Lloyd-Bostock (eds.), *Medical Mishaps—Pieces of the Puzzle* (Buckingham, 1999). T. Brennan, L. Leape, N. Laird, L. Herbert, A. Localio, A. Hawthers, 'Incidence of Adverse Events and Negligence in Hospitalised Patients: The Results of the Harvard Medical Practice Study' (1991) 324 *New England Journal of Medicine* 370–6; L. Leape, T. Brennan, N. Laird, *et al.* 'Incidence of Adverse Events in Hospitalised Patients: Results of the Harvard Medical Malpractice Study II' (1991) 324 *New England Journal of Medicine* 377–84.
[26] Leape, n. 25, above, 22.

When individuals are criticized, it is a common reaction to look to others for support. Disputants often utilize networks of kin, affinity, and close patronage.[27] Other commentators have identified how support networks can provide emotional backup and act as 'sounding boards', as well as taking on the roles of go-betweens or champions in disputes.[28] Patterns of help-seeking are a form of protection in which individuals may talk to others who share the same framework of meaning and knowledge-base. But, in a medical context, writers have emphasized the barriers and difficulties to doctors in approaching others for help. Despite the intensity of reactions, doctors have demonstrated a reluctance to get help from psychiatrists or counsellors, most commonly because it could be viewed as a sign of weakness.[29] Leape claims that doctors are typically isolated by their emotional responses to medical mishap because there are rarely support networks which can serve to facilitate 'emotional healing for the fallible physician'.[30] Sociological studies, based on empirical work in the USA and undertaken in the 1950s and 1960s, showed how doctors are socialized into the norms of biomedical culture. This serves to create distance between themselves and others.[31] In their empirical study of house doctors' responses to complaints, Wu *et al.* found that only 50 per cent of house officers discussed their most significant mistakes with attending physicians.[32]

Developing a Profile of Claims—the Methods

Research conducted as part of the evaluation of the mediation pilot involved the collection of a unique dataset with details of over 4,000 claims. It is hoped that this will contribute to the rather blurred picture of the threat posed by claims which emerges from much of the existing literature. The data reported here are mainly quantitative and there is much work to be done in exploring doctors' emotional reactions to claims in more depth. However, the data presented in this chapter suggest that, although claims clearly pose a challenge, once placed in context the material threat of claim is less daunting than is often suggested.

[27] P. Caplan (ed.), *Understanding Disputes: The Politics of Argument* (Oxford, 1995).
[28] D. Black and M. Baumgartner, 'Towards a Theory of the Third Party' in K. Boyum and L. Mather (eds.), *Empirical Theories about Courts* (New York, 1983).
[29] Ennis and Grudzinskas, n. 24, above.
[30] L. Leape, 'Error in Medicine' in M. Rosenthal, L. Mulcahy, and S. Lloyd-Bostock (eds.), *Medical Mishaps—Pieces of the Puzzle* (Buckingham, 1999) 20, 23.
[31] J. Stelling and R. Bucher, 'Vocabularies of Realism in Professional Socialisation' (1973) 7 *Social Science and Medicine* 661–75; H. Becker, B. Geer, E. Hughes, and A. Strauss, *Boys in White: Student Cultural in Medical School* (Chicago, Ill., 1961); R. Bucher and A. Strauss, 'Professions in Process' (1961) 66 *American Journal of Sociology* 325–54; R. Fox, 'Training for Uncertainty' in R. Merton, G. Reader, and P. Kendall (eds.), *The Student Physician* (Cambridge, Mass., 1957).
[32] Wu *et al.*, n. 18, above.

The Department of Health has never collected detailed information on the incidence of claims, their characteristics, or the level of damages paid out, and at the time of the study had recently discontinued the central monitoring of claims. These problems have been compounded by structural changes in the NHS introduced in 1990 which acted as an incentive against the pooling of data. In time the centralization of claims management through the Clinical Negligence Scheme for Trusts should mean that a comprehensive database of claims and settlements will eventually be developed, although this appears to be taking longer than was originally anticipated and the data produced still leave gaps in a historic overview of trends.

It was a basic tenet of the evaluation of the Department of Health's mediation pilot scheme that it was necessary to develop a profile of traditional claims-handling which could be compared with mediated claims. However, there were many difficulties in developing a profile of medical negligence claims and the gathering and 'cleaning' of data took over a year before analysis could begin. Across the country information on claims is collected in different formats, using different databases. For these reasons a profile of existing claims was undertaken using three databases held from three areas in the two Regions which participated in the pilot scheme. In these Regions reliable data were stored electronically only from 1990–1 onwards. The database held by Area B has proved to be much more extensive than those held in the other Areas and goes back over twenty years. The design of the other two databases was such that the evaluators were obliged to input raw data supplied into their own customized database using the Statistical Package for Social Scientists (SPSS). This allowed for a more detailed analysis of the data. Table 6.1 shows the breakdown of claims by database.

Table 6.1: To show total number of closed claims in participating regions 1990–1995

Region	Number of claims recorded on each database	Number of claims per outpost
Database A	2906*	2906
Database B	742	
		947
Database C	205	
Total	*3853*	*3853*

* To date we have been granted access to only 2,406 cases. All subsequent calculations take this figure as their base point.

An exact match between the data held by participating authorities has been difficult to achieve. However, it has been possible to create a core of data which is comparable across Regions. Access to the data held by the regions was successfully negotiated with trusts and health authorities in the vast majority of cases. The research team gained permission to check data on 2,406 cases which amounted to 83 per cent of the data held on the databases. Unfortunately certain types of information which would have been of great interest were not available. In particular, data on legal aid were either not collected or unreliable in all the participating regions and none of the regions collected information on the internal costs of claims-handling on their claims database.[33]

In addition to the data provided by the participating Regions, the Research and Policy Planning Unit of the Law Society kindly gave the research team access to data collected during a survey of medical negligence practitioners conducted in March 1995. The data were collected with a view to assessing whether the insurance contracts used in conditional fee-funded personal injury cases could be extended to cover medical negligence cases. The Law Society sampled the firms which would be eligible to provide the cover—that is, those on the Action for Victims of Medical Accidents panel of solicitors considered by the organization to be competent in the field.[34] Each of the firms on the panel was asked to provide data on a maximum of twenty cases completed in 1994. Twenty-four firms provided details of 395 cases with which they had been involved. The data were not, and were not meant to be, representative of medical negligence cases generally but they do provide a profile of a significant group of specialist firms. The data have assumed a new importance since policy-makers are increasingly encouraging the use of only specialists in this complex field of litigation. Where possible I have used the information gleaned from these extra data to complement those collected from the two Regions.

The Nature of the Threat Posed

As has been indicated by the discussion above, fears of a litigation crisis are often couched in terms of the number of claims made and the costs of high awards. Such discussion fails to reveal how representative the high value awards are of all claims and the stage of the litigation process to

[33] However, in the Northern and Yorkshire Region some information on the time spent by fee earners in handling claims is held by the accounts department which is responsible for billing Trust clients. We are currently exploring access to these data.

[34] The firms which took part in the survey varied in size from one to 35 equity partners and one to 18 salaried partners, the average being 11 and five respectively. A total of 37 (14%) equity partners and 24 (19%) salaried partners from all the firms were regularly conducting medical negligence litigation. There were 49 members of the Law Society's Personal Injury Panel in the participating firms.

which most claims progress. Socio-legal scholars have drawn attention to the fact that very few litigants pursue their cases as far as the court, and that most personal injury actions are settled rather than won or lost.[35] New reforms introduced in the wake of the Woolf Report now further encourage the earlier and speedy settlement of claims.

Because settlements occur informally there are hardly any statistics relating to them, and it can be very difficult to distinguish between those cases which are settled and those which are abandoned. Important work on the characteristics of claims undertaken by Genn for the Woolf Report has provided a profile of what happens to cases once proceedings are issued, but it has been impossible to determine from previous studies and official statistics what happens to cases where a claim is made but proceedings have not been issued. Figure 6.1 presents a unique dataset which serves to fill many of these gaps in information about medical negligence claims.

It can be seen from this figure that settlement or abandonment of a claim can occur at any stage and the vast majority of claims are abandoned. Interviews with claims managers conducted for the evaluation study revealed that the majority of abandoned cases are considered closed after one letter from the claimant and one response from a defence solicitor or claims manager. Abandonment may also occur after the release of medical records. It appears that the provision of additional information allows most claimants to reassess their claims and make the decision not to pursue them. In many of these cases the doctor involved may not even have been informed that a claim had been made. At most he or she will have been asked to prepare a statement.

Data provided by the three databases demonstrate that service of a writ is a relatively unusual event. In Database A, for instance, writs were served in just 71 (11 per cent) out of 674 cases in which data are available. Similarly, in database C writs were served in just 17 (8 per cent) cases. Again, the vast majority of claims were abandoned before the issue of proceedings. It can also be seen from Figure 6.1 that a very small minority of cases proceed to trial.

Of those cases which are pursued, out-of-court settlement is the most likely outcome. Out-of-court settlement of claims is likely to advantage doctors in a number of ways. First, although their activity may well be scrutinized by solicitors, barristers, and managers they are able to avoid the resolution of the dispute in a public forum and media attention. Experienced litigators such as health authorities and trusts are likely to be advantaged in the negotiating process. Many commentators assume that out-of-court settlements anticipate the outcome of full trial but this represents an overly simplistic and optimistic view of bargaining dynamics. All

---

[35] See, in particular, H. Genn, *Hard Bargaining* (Oxford, 1987).

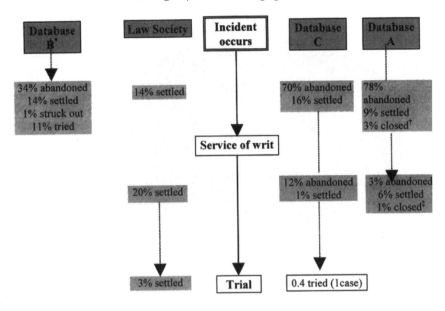

* No stage defined
† Classified on database as closed, completed, won
‡ As previous footnote.

Figure 6.1: Summary of Stages Reached by Claims on the Four Databases

the parties suffer from problems of uncertainty in legal rules and medical prognosis, and the pressures of costs and delay. Particular attention has been paid to the problems faced by claimants[36] and their lawyers who tend to be 'one shotters' against 'repeat player' health authorities. Claimants have difficulties accessing expert lawyers, suffer the consequences of delay in a greater proportion than defendants, and may often be ill.[37] In particular 'rational' decisions about risk can be made only when the parties are furnished with credible information which it is difficult for lay persons to obtain.

It is interesting to note that the specialist firms represented by the Law Society data set were more likely to pursue cases and settle later. It contradicts many of the assumptions of the Woolf Report that rational litigation actors will settle early as long as they are in receipt of sufficient information

[36] M. McMahon, G. Roberts, J. Daly, M. Evans, C. Lowy, and G. Coventry, 'The Quest for Recompense: Claimants' Experience of Medical Negligence Compensation in Victoria, Australia' (1994) 16 *Law and Policy* 209–34; Genn, note 36, above; O. M. Fiss, 'Against Settlement' (1984) 93 *Yale Law Journal* 1073–90.
[37] Galanter, 'Why The Haves Come Out Ahead: Speculation on the Limits of Legal Change' (1974) 9 *Law and Society Review* 95–160. Genn, n. 36, above.

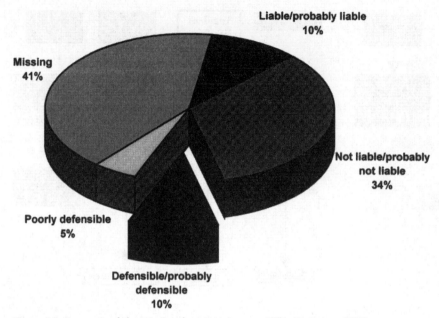

Figure 6.2: Prognosis of claim in Database B (1 January 1991–31 August 1995)

to be able to assess the value of their claims. One explanation supported by earlier research is that expert solicitors are less likely to accept the first offer made. When compared with the other datasets it suggests that the majority of claimants' solicitors are less experienced and less likely to pursue a bullish negotiatory stance.

A proportion (618) of cases in the three databases had been assessed according to the risk they posed to the hospital defending the claim. Four hundred and thirteen (56 per cent) of the Database A claims were classified according to whether there was a good or bad chance of the claim succeeding. Seven major categories were used: not liable; probably not liable; defensible; probably defensible; poorly defensible; liable; and probably not liable. These have been collapsed into four major categories and are shown in Figure 6.2. Database B also recorded a case prognosis. This was done according to four categories—low, medium, and high risk, and none. Figure 6.3 shows how the 205 cases were classified. It can be seen that the classifications of risk follow similar patterns in both Regions. It is significant that the largest portion of cases is considered low risk or defensible by the defence.

Who is at Risk?

Further analysis of these data shows that the risk of medical negligence claims is not evenly spread in terms of NHS units or specialties. A relatively

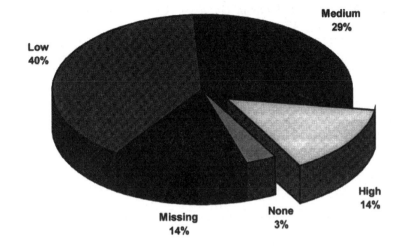

Figure 6.3: Estimate of risk in Database C (1 January 1991–31 August 1995)

small number of hospitals in each region account for the majority of claims, and these tend to be acute units. In Database A out of a total of 34 major units identified, seven acute units accounted for 89 per cent of the claims and three hospitals accounted for 58 per cent of all the claims from 1990–5.

The risk is also unevenly spread when it comes to specialty. Dingwall and Fenn reported that five specialties—obstetrics and gynæcology, orthopædics, accident and emergency, general surgery and anæsthetics—accounted for two-thirds of the claims between 1974 and 1988.[38] In the present study the top five[39] 'at risk' specialties were obstetrics and gynæ-cology, accident and emergency, general surgery, trauma and orthopædics and radiology . Together these accounted for 60 per cent of all claims, and in Region A obsterics and gynæcology and surgery together accounted for 62 per cent of all claims. Table 6.2 shows that in Area A 80 per cent of claims from two specialties proceeded to the issue of proceedings. Further, by comparing the data on claims for all specialties with those on the specialties of cases that get to writ, it is evident that surgical are more likely and radiological cases are less likely to reach this stage than other specialty groupings.

As Ham and colleagues[40] suggest in order to provide an appropriate context data on the incidence of negligence actions, such statistics need to

---

[38] N. 3, above.

[39] Obstetrics and gynaecology are technically separate specialties, but they can be conveniently grouped together for the purposes of analysis.

[40] Ham *et al.*, n. 2, above.

Table 6.2: To show all claims in Database A by specialty and progress to writ by specialty (n=742)

Specialty grouping	% of all claims	% cases to writ
Medical	14	14
Obstetrics and gynaecology	24	28
Pathology	2	1
Psychiatry	6	2
Radiology	13	0
Surgical	40	52
Other clinical	2	0
Other	0	1
Total	101	99

be compared with data on the amount of activity within specialties. This allows for an assessment of the risk of a claim being made per patient contact. Determining the level of doctors' contact with patients was not an easy task. First, very little information is available on doctors' activity for those below the rank of consultants. Secondly information on patient contact is recorded in a variety of ways for a variety of different purposes and provides only a broad indication of activity.[41] However, these data, though crude, do at least provide us with a way of contextualizing the data on claims. Table 6.3 shows data gleaned from the mediation evaluation study on the number of negligence claims per consultant–patient contact in one of the regions involved in the pilot scheme.

Table 6.2 suggested that specialists in surgery and obstetrics and gynæcology were most at risk from claims. However, it is clear from Table 6.3 that taking into account the level of consultant activity, obstetrics and

---

[41] When patients first enter hospital they are given a READ code which provides a narrative description of their condition from which a certain level of hospital activity might be predicted. Thereafter, they are categorized by an ICD code, a detailed diagnosis code which reflects the type of procedures undertaken. The only dataset which records the specific activity of consultants appears to be DoH data dealing with Finished Consultants Episodes (FCEs), Referral Attendances to consultants and Consultant Initiated Attendances.There are difficulties in using these figures as a yardstick against which to judge activity. Only one episode of any kind is recorded per patient treatment, so that in procedures where more than one consultant is concerned with the care, only one of them will have the FCE recorded. Thus, consultants whose service diagnosis and treatment, such as laboratory-based specialties and haematology, are hardly represented at all. A particular concern is that a very large specialty like anaesthetics appears extremely under-represented. Some of these difficulties can be overcome. By using generic categories of specialties, it is more probable that teams of consultant activity will be reflected. For instance, by using the category surgical, the work of anæsthetists is captured in the figures. Finally, particular emphasis can be placed on comparing levels of activities with complaints in those specialties where these data are more reliable indicators of patient contacts.

Table 6.3: To show consultant activity in 1993–4 by specialty in Oxford Region[42] and number of patient contacts per claim in 1990–95

Specialty	Activity	% activity (n=2,108,059)	Total claims	% all claims (n=742)	Patient contacts per claim
All specialties	2108059	100%	742	100%	2841
Obs. and gynae.	281,089	13%	177	24%	1,589
General medicine	207,501	10%	25	3%	8,300
General surgery	206,231	10%	53	7%	3,891
Paediatrics	106,217	5%	23	3%	4,618
Dermatology	79,528	4%	5	1%	15,906
Mental illness	61,025	3%	26	4%	2,347
Haematology	56,928	3%	5	1%	11,386
Geriatrics	29,530	1%	3	0%	9,843
Orthopaedics	23,140	1%	61	8%	379
Psychiatry	19,509	1%	12	2%	1,626

gynaecology, mental illness, orthopædics and psychiatry receive more claims per patient contact than other specialties and general medicine, general surgery, paediatrics, dermatology, hæmatology and geriatrics receive less. Most notably, although only accounting for 1 per cent of activity in hospitals, orthopaedics receives 8 per cent of all claims and treatment by orthopaedic specialists is much more likely to prompt a claim than that given by colleagues in other specialties.

A Financial Threat?

Dingwall and Fenn have argued that the cost of medical negligence is relatively low when seen as a percentage of the NHS budget. They claim that average losses of around £234,000 per district per year is a minor irritant to most hospitals:

It is important to emphasise the modest scale of medical negligence litigation as a financial problem for the NHS. There has been a good deal of alarmist talk, which mainly reflects the confusion and uncertainty within the service arising from the limitations of its own financial information systems in this area.[43]

The current study confirmed their findings. Of the 742 claims in Database A from 1991–5 some financial data were available on 669 (90

---

[42] Source: Department of Health. Figures are an amalgamation of Finished Consultant Episode, Outpatient Referrals and Consultant Initiated Attendances for Oxford Region, 1993–4.

[43] Dingwall and Fenn, n. 3, above, 79.

per cent) of them. Damages were paid to claimants in 142 or just over a fifth (21 per cent) of these cases. For the minority of cases which settled the average payout was in the range of just under £10,000 to £13,000 from 1991–4 but increased in 1995 to an average of £17,368. A figure which is less likely to be reported in the medical press that record damages of over £1 million. Data on costs from Database C were not as complete or reliable as those of Database A but the data available reflect the same general trend. Payout to the plaintiff was made in just 25 (12 per cent) cases, the average payout being £11,138. Database B data show that, of the 2,406 cases, no compensation was paid out in 2,040 (85 per cent) of cases. The range of damages awarded was from £28–£1,156,348, the average payout being much less than that for the other Regions at £4,374.

The research team was also interested to explore the percentage of the Region's overall expenditure which was taken up by negligence claims. Table 6.4 below shows the cost of these medical negligence claims as a percentage of total expenditure.

The range reported is not far from that reported by Dingwall and Fenn. One research participant remarked that the sums spent on compensating the victim of medical negligence fell far short of the government's annual subsidy to the Royal Opera House.

Table 6.4: Cost of medical negligence claims as a percentage of total expenditure

Region	Total spent on claims in one year*	Approx. total expenditure 1993–4	Claims as % of total expenditure
Database B**	£894,106	£882,141,000	0.1%
Database A	£2,103,897	£2,790,983,000	0.7%
Database C	Not reliable	£773,543,000	–

  * For Database A the figure reflects 12 consecutive months in 1993–4 as this most closely tallies with the financial data provided by the Department of Health. For Database B the figure represents an average yearly pay out for 1991–5 as closure dates for files were not available.
  **Database B figures do not include solicitors' costs, overheads or administration costs.

Different Ways of Looking at the 'Crisis'

So far in this chapter data collected for the mediation evaluation project have drawn attention to the characteristics of claims and considered the ways in which they might be considered a threat. The data show that most specialties do not have a high incidence of claims and that the risk of claims is located in surgical specialties and obstetrics and gynaecology. The data show that the majority of claims are abandoned at a very early stage of proceedings, most commonly before the issue of proceedings, and that in many of these cases the doctors involved might not even be troubled by notification of the claim. The vast majority of those claimants who pursue their suit beyond the issue of proceedings settle their claims, thus ensuring a private resolution which cannot be held up to public scrutiny. Only a minute proportion end up in court. Over four-fifths of claims involve no payment whatsoever, and for those where there is payment the average settlement is £11,095. The costs of claims amounts to much less than 1 per cent in the two areas.

These data provide a useful setting for a more in-depth discussion of the threat posed by claims. Why has the claims rate been constructed as a crisis and prompted so much activity from the profession? In the sections which follow I will draw on my data and other studies to suggest alternative images of the problems posed by medical negligence claims.

A Crisis of Conflicting Narratives?

Part of the solution to the question why claims pose such a symbolic threat to the profession is explained by reference to clinicians' views of what prompts disputes. Elsewhere I have argued that doctors commonly discuss the root cause of grievances as a manifestation of the illness being experienced. They argue that disputes are more likely to arise in some specialties than others because of the nature of the illness or disease being treated, the characteristics and invasive nature of treatment plans, the likely length of the relationship between doctor and patient, and the intimacy of relationship. It has been suggested that certain specialists, especially those involved in diagnosis, are more likely to receive a complaint because they impart bad news which is more likely to invoke intense emotional reactions and criticism of care. This is viewed as a way of coming to terms with the news. Such accounts have a tendency to deflect blame away from the medical profession.[44]

However others have argued that the propensity to complain may be more complex. A recent study in Florida sought to find out why more than 85 per cent of 963 lawsuits concerning obstetric care in the State were filed against 3–6 per cent of doctors. The researchers rejected the contention that these doctors were caring for the more seriously ill patients. They found that severity of illness was virtually the same amongst those sued and those who were not. They also rejected the argument that those doctors sued were less competent. Instead, they found that poor communication and insensitivity accounted for much of the difference in patterns.

---

[44] L. Mulcahy, 'From Fear to Fraternity; Doctors' Construction of Accounts of Complaints' (1996) 18 *Journal of Social Welfare and Family Law* 397–412.

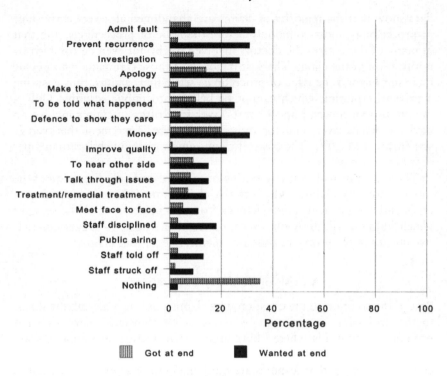

Figure 6.4: What did claimants get versus what they wanted?

Thus, a doctor may not have done anything technically wrong but could have generated enough ill-feeling to provoke a claim.

Similarly, in their study of 227 patients and relatives, Vincent, Young, and Phillips found that the decision to take legal action was determined not only by the original injury, but also by insensitive handling and poor communication after the original event.[45] Claimants were motivated not only by a desire for an explanation, a wish for retribution, and the need for compensation, but also concerns about standards of care. Both patients and relatives wanted to prevent similar accidents happening in the future and believed that staff or the organization should have to account for their actions. In a survey of 128 claimants conducted for the evaluation research project claimants were asked what they had wanted to achieve as a result of making a claim and what they had actually achieved.[46] The results are presented in Figure 6.2.

It is not surprising that all claimants do not receive financial

---

[45] C. Vincent, M. Young, and A. Phillips, 'Why do People Sue their Doctors? A Study of Patients and Relatives taking Legal Action?', (1994) 343 *Lancet* 1609–13.
[46] This represented a 23% response rate.

compensation, since not all of their claims will have been substantiated. What is surprising is the number of remedies which relate to communication such as an explanation, a desire to meet face to face, to be told what happened, for the defence to show they cared, that patients in the study did not receive, whether or not their case is substantiated. The figures reveal that undue emphasis may be being placed on risk-avoidance strategies at the cost of effective claims management.

A more sociologically orientated explanation of these data might suggest that the high incidence of disputes relating to or triggered by poor communication does not necessarily result from inattentiveness or insensitivity, but from a more fundamental disagreement about the nature of illness. Williams and Popay argue that the differences between the ways in which medicine and everyday thinking represent matters of health and illness have been well documented in recent years and that this body of work has clearly demonstrated that the ways of seeing illness and talking about it that sociologists call lay beliefs are often quite distinctive in form and content.[47] It has been argued that, rather than representing a shared reality between doctor and patient, illness represents two distinct realities. Tombs has argued that there is a systematic distortion of meaning in the doctor–patient relationship resulting largely from the fact that illness is experienced in significantly different ways by each party.[48] This makes it particularly difficult for the parties to construct a world of shared meaning. In her words:

The physician is trained to perceive illness essentially as a collection of physical signs and symptoms which define a particular disease state. He or she thematizes the illness as being a particular case of multiple sclerosis, diabetes, peptic ulcer, and so forth. The patient, however, focuses on a different reality. One does not see one's own illness primarily as a disease process. Rather one experiences it essentially in terms of its effects upon everyday life.

However, Williams and Popay suggest that this lay challenge to medical knowledge is not a complaint about the aesthetics of discourse but is more accurately seen as a political challenge to the status of scientific knowledge and the power of those whom we are encouraged to trust with such knowledge.[49]

A Legitimation Crisis?

The challenge posed by claims can also be seen as part of a series of threats to the medical profession in the latter part of the last century.

---

[47] G. Williams and J. Popay, 'Lay Knowledge and the Privilege of Experience' in J. Gave, D. Kelleher, and G. Williams (eds.), *Challenging Medicine* (London, 1994).

[48] S. Tombs, *The Meaning of Illness—A Phenomenological Account of Physician and Patient* (Norwell, Mass., 1992), 11.

[49] Williams and Popay, n. 48 above.

Since the beginning of the twentieth century doctors have increased their social, cultural, and economic power in society. Kelleher *et al.* argue that this has been facilitated by rising concern about public health, the decline of organized religion, the development of pharmacological products to which the profession has acted as gatekeeper, the growth of research laboratories, and the increase in notions of the scientific foundations of medical practice.[50] But as well as enjoying the achievement of a successful professional project the medical profession has also suffered certain crises of credibility, although the sociological exploration of change has not been extensively explored.[51]

Recent research on the incidence of medical mishap has demonstrated that medical error and mistakes are common[52] and this has provided an incentive for the introduction of more stringent risk management and clinical audit protocols.[53] More recently the profession has faced the challenge of an influx of new politically led external regulatory structures such as clinical governance; the setting up of the Commission for Health Improvement; the National Institute for Clinical Excellence; and the reform of the GMC's poor performance procedures. Moreover, inquiries into systemic mismanagement of risk and poor practice, such as the Bristol Royal Infirmary Inquiry, continue to provide windows of opportunity in which the government can press for more radical mechanisms for accountability than might normally be possible in their negotiations with the profession.[54] It is clear that public support and outrage remain important bargaining tools in the negotiation process.

A series of structural changes such as privatization and contracting out took place in the 1980s and have caused a radical transformation of public administration.[55] New notions of accountability and public service have come about as a result of the Next Steps Programme,[56] the creation of internal markets, the Citizen's Charter; the publication of information about NHS Trusts. These have all aimed to increase efficiency and to provide greater accountability to 'consumers' at the level of service delivery. The 1990 reforms of the service have provided a significant new set of incentives for doctors and managers to work together in the workplace and have encouraged a new wave of managerialism. These challenges clearly pose a new threat to clinical autonomy and the profession has been

[50] D. Kelleher, J. Gabe, and G. Williams (1994) 'Understanding Medical Dominance in the Modern World' in Gabe, Kelleher and Williams, n. 48, above.
[51] *Ibid.*   [52] Brennan, n. 28, above.
[53] Mulcahy and Rosenthal, n. 17, above.
[54] Rosenthal, Mulcahy and Lloyd-Bostock (eds.), n. 17, above.
[55] R. Austin, 'Administrative Law's Reaction to the Changing Concepts of Public Service' in P. Leyland and T. Woods (eds.), *Administrative Law: Facing the Future—Old Constraints and New Horizons*, Blackstone (London, 1997).
[56] Cabinet Office, *Improving Management in Government: The Next Steps* (London, 1988).

critical of the reforms. Paradoxically, managers and doctors are now compelled to join in the common corporate pursuit of the winning of contracts for their services. But evidence about the willingness of doctors to participate in hospital-wide risk management and audit structures suggests that, despite these moves, a culture of tribalism continues to exist.[57]

Other professional groups have also provided challenges. Kelleher *et al.* argue that the nursing elite have been embarking on a process of occupational development which has forced a redefinition of the relationship between medicine and nursing.[58] In a similar vein Saks has charted the growth of complementary medicine as a direct attack on the bio-medical model of care.[59] Such developments have led to claims that medicine is being de-professionalized as part of a more general trend of rationalization and codification of expert knowledge.[60] Others have argued that professionalism is being proletarianized in line with the requirements of advance capitalism.[61] According to this view people no longer believe in doctors' special status.

But it is challenges to medical power from lay persons which have probably been most prominent. The emergence of a consumer movement, especially the women's movement, and better education amongst lay persons has provided an impetus for alterations in the ideal form of the doctor–patient relationship. These challenges have expressed themselves in a number of ways, through complaints, non-compliance with treatment plans, and more obviously through political action. The medical negligence action is another form of consumer activism in which individual members of the profession are called to account. The very act of making a claim assumes that patients have a right to medical decisions, a notion which is out of line with the dominant bio-medical model of medicine in which clinical autonomy is paramount.

Those arguing from a consumerist perspective have suggested that claimants getting compensated for injuries wrongly sustained should never be labelled a crisis. In this vein Rosenthal argues:

Medical injuries and medical malpractice have now become perennial public concerns in the United States. Public discussion—often in the mass media—usually focuses on the high court awards in selected malpractice cases, exposés of 'bad' doctors and recently, the soaring cost of malpractice premiums that physicians pay.

---

[57] J. Allsop and L. Mulcahy, *Regulating Medical Work—Formal and Informal Controls* (Buckingham, 1996).

[58] Kelleher *et al.*, n. 48, above.

[59] M. Saks, 'The Alternatives to Medicine' in Gabe, Kelleher, and Williams (eds.), n. 48, above.

[60] M. Haug and B. Lavin, *Consumerism in Medicine: Challenging Physician Authority* (Beverley Hills, Cal., 1983).

[61] J. McKinley and J. Arches, 'Towards the Proletarianisation of Physicians' (1985) 15 *International Journal of Health Services* 161–95.

How concerns are expressed is very much a function of who is complaining: the public, the medical profession, the legal profession, the insurance carriers.[62]

She goes on to suggest that whilst the crisis for doctors may be 'one of capricious lawsuits, an avaricious legal profession, ungrateful patients, and soaring malpractice premiums' the crisis for consumers may be one of confidence in the medical profession and of having adequate resources to pursue an action through the courts.[63] Recent research suggests that the majority of those injured in the course of receiving medical care do not sue. Viewed in this way it could be argued that the problem with medical negligence is that not enough people sue. It is known from the Harvard Study of 31,000 medical records that there were more adverse events than were ever reported in complaints or claims. By matching individual clinical records with individual claims records, researchers found that the number of patients (5,400) who had serious disability injuries as a result of negligent care, and who did not file claims, exceeded the number of patients (3,570) making malpractice claims. About half of those making claims were expected to receive compensation. For a variety of reasons—such as gratitude, low expectations, lack of information, poor advice, fear of retribution, and deference to health professionals, most dissatisfaction remains unvoiced.[64] The problems of claimants' lack of knowledge are compounded by difficulties in gaining expert advice, and defendants tend to be represented by a dispersed, heterogeneous group of lawyers whose infrequent involvement in medical negligence cases diminishes their effectiveness.[65]

The resources needed by claimants in terms of time and money in their pursuit of a case are large.[66] In addition to the direct costs of funding their case, claimants in the British tort system have been exposed to a double risk of having to pay their opponent's costs under the guise of the so-called 'costs rule' should they lose their case. Moreover, the 'payment-in rule' further penalizes claimants who reject reasonable offers of compensation before a trial. Additionally, proof that an injury was caused by the negligence of a doctor has been identified as one of the most difficult hurdles for the claimant to negotiate.[67] There may be a number of causes of injury; the patient may not know what has happened; the medical records may not contain all the details of the case;

---

[62] M. Rosenthal, *Dealing with Medical Malpractice: The British and Swedish Experience* (London, 1987) 2.   [63] *Ibid.*

[64] L. Mulcahy and J. Tritter, 'Pathways, Pyramids and Icebergs? Mapping the Links between Dissatisfaction and Complaints', (1998) 20 *Sociology of Health and Illness*; W. Felstiner, R. Abel, and A. Sarat, 'The Emergence and Transformation of Disputes: Naming, Blaming, Claiming . . .', (1986) 43 *Law and Society Review* 1161.

[65] Ham *et al.*, n. 2, above.   [66] *Ibid.*

[67] M. Mildred, 'The View of the Plaintiff's Lawyer' in R. Mann and J. Harvard (eds.), *No-Fault Compensation in Medicine* (London, 1989).

and there are considerable difficulties in getting a medical expert to review another doctor's work. The problems of fault are such that in some countries the burden of proof is reversed, and it rests on the defendant to prove that there was no negligence where a *prima facie* case has been made. Available evidence suggests that the claimant in a medical negligence action is less likely to succeed at trial than other litigants using the civil litigation system. Other writers have commented on policy-based judicial reluctance to award damages against doctors.[68]

Little research has focused on how doctors view challenges by consumers but in a small-scale empirical study of Australian doctors and patients Lupton found that the discourse of consumerism is commonly employed by doctors to describe the changes they have noticed in patient attitudes and that this has served to make them more accountable. Most of the doctors interviewed agreed that their status had diminished in recent years, although some made a distinction between feelings about the medical profession as a whole and personal doctors.

The development of a consumer movement has been symbiotic with the growth in media coverage of doctors and a tendency for the media to be more critical of doctors than in the past. In particular the media have given more extensive coverage to the failings of medicine and the mistakes made by them.[69]

Strong has argued that the media's role in the transformation of views about the medical profession rarely gets the attention or credit it deserves.[70] Not only has press coverage of health matters increased, but so too have the use of lay, as opposed to medical, perspectives.[71] All these factors are seen to contribute to an erosion of the traditional power of doctors, an increase in their economic vulnerability and alienation in the workforce.[72] This development has, in turn, empowered readers, listeners, and viewers to challenge medical decision-making.

The increasing challenge to self-regulation of consumerism is said to be most apparent in the increasing number of claims being made about doctors. In the UK consumers of health care are being encouraged to become more active in voicing their views and concerns, and health care providers are increasingly expected to canvass user views and respond appropriately. This policy initiative has been underpinned by legislative reforms which have expanded the role of management and encouraged the generation of information about quality and risk in order to facilitate the better regulation of medical work and improvements in service. These have

---

[68] J. K. Mason and R. McCall-Smith, *Law and Medical Ethics* (4th edn., London, 1994).
[69] Kelleher *et al.*, n. 48 above.
[70] P. Strong, 'The Rivals' in R. Dingwall and P. Lewis (eds.), *The Sociology of the Professions*, (London, 1983).
[71] Kelleher *et al.*, n. 48, above.
[72] P. D. Lupton, n. 2, above.

led policy-makers to encourage a proactive approach to complaints, welcoming the voicing of dissatisfaction as a useful management tool.

Conclusion

Medical negligence claims are one aspect of broader consumer challenges to medicine which have brought changes to the context in which medicine is practised. There is evidence across a number of countries that medical negligence claims are increasing, and this is commonly viewed in terms of a crisis. The reasons for the increase in claims are diverse. Expectations of medical care, sometimes fuelled by the medical profession itself, continue to rise. Other factors include the greater availability of information and extensive media coverage of medical developments and mishaps, as well as the growth of consumer groups. In many countries, governments have encouraged consumerism. For example, in Britain the Patient's Charter has provided an outline of expectations, performance targets, and the means for redress which aim to facilitate user involvement.

Medical negligence claims also serve to change the usual rules of the doctor–patient relationship. Typically, doctors control interactions since they determine the flow of knowledge and the resources of time and space in the encounter. By voicing their dissatisfaction, people attempt to hold a doctor to account. I suggest this has a transformative effect on the doctor–patient relationship. A response is required from the doctor who may have to justify, or at least explain, his or her decision-making and in so doing may well be called upon to articulate what is involved in their work and answer questions different from those posed by fellow professionals. This may be in the privacy of the consulting room or may be through a written response or a meeting with the complainant and managers. It may even require an appearance in the public arena of a tribunal or, if a claim is pursued, in a court. Thus, the doctor loses the power to define core issues and initiate further contact on his or her terms.

The notion of a crisis is not a given, and much depends on the perspective from which the 'problem' of rising claims is viewed. It has been argued here that consumers could equally well argue that the crisis is that not enough claims are being made, given the level of iatrogenic injury which occurs. Equally, it might be argued that the crisis is that the same mistakes occur repeatedly or that doctors are held hostage to a perfectability model of care. But whatever the perspective adopted, the study of doctors' responses also allows an examination of the *process* of how professional work is accomplished in everyday practice and how the boundaries are maintained or reconstituted in response to a challenge by user-led initiatives. Each medical negligence case will have a radiating effect within the medical profession and responses from the profession may also have a symbolic importance. The profession's success at labelling the increasing incidence of claims a crisis could be viewed as a reflection of the level of power it wields. Moreover, the construction of a shared threat to the profession may well serve to increase professional solidarity and demonstrates how a defence of expertise is accomplished on a broader basis.

Questions of Autonomy

INFORMATION, DECISIONS, AND THE LIMITS OF INFORMED CONSENT

Carl E. Schneider and Michael H. Farrell

> The human understanding is not a dry light, but is infused by desire and emotion, which give rise to 'wishful science'. For man prefers to believe what he wants to be true. He therefore rejects difficulties, being impatient of inquiry; sober things, because they restrict his hope; deeper parts of Nature, because of his superstition; the light of experience, because of his arrogance and pride, lest his mind should seem to concern itself with things mean and transitory; things that are strange and contrary to all expectation, because of common opinion.
>
> Francis Bacon
> *Novum Organum*

The Problem

For many years, the heart's wish of bioethics has been to confide medical decisions to patients and not to doctors. The favoured key to doing so has been the doctrine of informed consent. The theory of and hopes for that doctrine are well captured in the influential case of *Canterbury* v. *Spence*: '[t]rue consent to what happens to one's self is the informed exercise of a choice, and that entails an opportunity to evaluate knowledgeably the options available and the risks attendant upon each'.[1]

Anxious as bioethicists and courts have been to promulgate this doctrine, they have been less anxious to discover how well it works; the bioethical tradition has been more interested in articulating principle than testing practice. But, as Don Herzog drolly warns, 'theory had better not

---

[1] 464 F 2d 772, 780 (DC Cir. 1972).

be what you get when you leave out the facts'.[2] So in this paper we will briefly review some of the empirical literature on informed consent and present findings of a study on the way men decide whether to use PSA screening to detect prostate cancer. This will lead us to reflect on the limits of informed consent.

The success of informed consent depends on two things. First, patients must be able to understand and remember the information doctors give them. Secondly, patients must be able to analyse that information and use it to make a decision. The first of these requirements has been studied extensively. Despite prolonged struggles to improve informed consent, the kind of success hoped for remains elusive. As Cassileth *et al.* wrote some years ago, '[i]t is well known that many patients, despite all efforts to the contrary, remember or understand little of what they agree to during the consent process'.[3] And as Cassileth *et a* different *al.* said, studies of informed consent 'have shown that patients remain inadequately informed, even when extraordinary efforts are made to provide complete information and to ensure their understanding. This appears to be true regardless of the amount of information delivered, the manner in which it is presented, or the type of medical procedure involved'.[4] Furthermore, the sicker patients become, the less they understand and retain.

The second requirement for the success of informed consent—that patients be able to analyse the information they are given—has, in contrast, been virtually unstudied.[5] Scholars have been interested in what patients hear, but not in how they consider what they hear. Yet what evidence we have is unsettling. As Irving Janis says, '[t]he stresses of making major decisions and the various ways people deal with those stresses . . . frequently result in defective forms of problem solving that fail to meet the standards of rational decision making'.[6]

Yet this should not be surprising. In a recent book, *The Practice of Autonomy: Patients, Doctors, and Medical Decisions*,[7] Schneider suggests a number of reasons to expect that patients' decisions will not easily meet 'the standards of rational decision making'. To begin with, many people regard making decisions of all kinds as forbidding work, and medical decisions are exceptionally challenging. Doctors themselves must often

---

[2] 'I Hear a Rhapsody: A Reading of *The Republic of Choice*' (1992) 17 *Law & Social Inquiry* 147, 148.

[3] Barrie R. Cassileth *et al.*, 'Attitudes Toward Clinical Trials Among Patients and the Public' (1982) 248 *Journal of the American Medical Association* 968, 970.

[4] Barrie R. Cassileth *et al.*, 'Informed Consent—Why Are Its Goals Imperfectly Realized?' (1980) 302 *New England Journal of Medicine* 896, 896.

[5] See Carl E. Schneider, *The Practice of Autonomy: Patients, Doctors, and Medical Decisions* (New York, 1998), 92–9.

[6] Irving L. Janis, 'The Patient as Decision Maker', in W. Doyle Gentry (ed.), *Handbook of Behavioral Medicine* (New York, 1984), 333.

[7] Schneider, n. 5, above, chap. 3.

struggle to draw sound conclusions from unreliable data and problematic theories. Thus the information patients receive is often frustratingly uncertain. Worse, doctors most comfortably speak the language of medicine, a tongue that dismays even the brightest and best-educated patients. What is more, information can never be put in completely objective terms, yet often neither doctor nor patient recognizes the assumptions and preferences reports and recommendations silently incorporate.

The Practice of Autonomy further suggests that medical decisions are made yet harder because of their social and moral context. The practice of medicine is becoming bureaucratized. This means that an astonishing number of people may have information and opinions to contribute to medical decisions, that the players change rapidly, and that responsibility is diffused. In addition, while some medical decisions present a single issue at a single moment, more often patients face a series of decisions over days or even months whose individual importance is often not apparent at the time. Even the non-technical aspects of medical decisions may baffle patients. For instance, people's 'values' are often more obscure than the theory of informed consent assumes, and (reasonably enough) they change over time and with experience. Nor will it always be clear what conclusions are to be drawn even from well-established and stable preferences.[8]

Furthermore, most medical decisions are made by sick people, and sickness impairs thought. When you are ill you are weary. When you are ill you are distracted by a regiment of unfamiliar problems, not least reconciling yourself to your disease, reconstructing your future, and coping with the quotidian. You may want to avoid facing the dismal facts of your illness. You may even want to 'deny' your condition (often a wise deception). You may not find your medical condition absorbingly interesting. (We even have a pejorative term—valetudinarian—for people too fascinated by their illness.) And you may be so frightened that you cannot think lucidly and dispassionately.

All this may help us understand why Janis speaks so discouragingly about how patients address decisions. It also helps explain the emerging evidence about how patients go about making decisions. One of the plainest elements of that evidence suggests that patients often make decisions with a rapidity that forecloses the systematic deliberation many students of decisions prescribe and the doctrine of informed consent presupposes. This has been most extensively studied among people asked to donate a kidney. They tend to decide instantly whether to donate or to decline. As one study put it, '[n]ot one of the donors weighed alternatives and rationally decided. Fourteen of the donors and nine of the ten donors waiting for surgery stated that they had made their decision immediately

[8] *Ibid.*

when the subject of the kidney transplant was first mentioned over the telephone, "in a split-second", "instantaneously", and "right away" '.[9] In short, 'all the donors and potential donors interviewed . . . reported a decision-making process that was immediate and "irrational" and could not meet the requirements adopted by the American Medical Association to be accepted as an "informed consent" '.[10]

The most detailed, circumstantial, and vivid descriptions of how patients make medical choices appear in the memoirs so many of them have written about the experience of illness. Many of these memoirs, like the studies of kidney donors, report truncated decisions. For one lymphoma patient, for example, '[n]ot even a split second was needed to opt for chemotherapy despite all I had heard about it'.[11]

Such instantaneous decisions are possible partly because many patients seem to fix on one factor, make it the basis of decision, and then close their minds to new data. (This psychological conservatism is often called the 'anchoring heuristic'.) Penny Pierce, one of the closest students of how patients make medical decisions, reports such thinking among many of the breast cancer patients she studied.[12] Schneider frequently observed it among people asked to choose a dialysis modality. Such patients:

often seem to listen until they hear some arresting fact and then make it the basis of their decision. For instance, as soon as some patients hear that hemodialysis requires someone to insert two large needles into their arm three times a week, they opt for whatever the alternative is. When some other patients hear peritoneal dialysis means having a tube protruding from their abdomen, they choose 'the other kind of dialysis'.[13]

Not only do many patients decide quickly and consult only a few criteria—or even a single criterion—but even patients well educated and reflective enough to write memoirs regularly describe no decisional process at all. Instead, they invoke intuition, instinct, and impulse. An AIDS patient, for example, wrote, 'I've learned to listen to my inner voice for guidance when choosing treatments. If I get what Louise refers to as a "ding" (a strong instinct) about a vitamin, herb, drug, or other treatment, I try it'.[14] A multiple sclerosis patient 'got a flash', found that a 'little light flashed inside my head', came to 'trust my own intuition', and asked why

---

[9] Carl H. Fellner and John R. Marshall, 'Kidney Donors—The Myth of Informed Consent' (1970) 126 *American Journal of Psychiatry* 1245, 1247.

[10] *Ibid.*, at 1250.

[11] Mary Alice Geier, *Cancer: What's It Doing in My Life?* (Pasadena, Calif., 1985) 18.

[12] Penny F. Pierce, 'Deciding on Breast Cancer Treatment: A Description of Decision Behavior' (1993) 42 *Nursing Research* 20, 23.

[13] Schneider, n. 5, above, 94–5.

[14] Louie Nassaney with Glenn Kolb, *I Am Not a Victim: One Man's Triumph Over Fear & AIDS* (Santa Monica, Cal., 1990) 86.

she should not 'play my hunches'.[15] Even patients particularly committed to making their own decisions on rational bases often cannot, even in retrospect, explain their choices. For instance, a Rice sociologist with prostate cancer who tried as hard as anyone could to make decisions systematically wrote, '[w]ithout knowing precisely why or being able to provide a clear rationale, I decided I would ask Peter Scardino to perform my surgery'.[16]

A Case Study: Screening for Prostate Specific Antigen

Our survey of the evidence about the two requirements for successful informed consent suggests two things. First, we have a great deal of evidence about how much patients understand and retain of what they are told by their doctors about their medical choices: In brief, troublingly little. Secondly, we have only scant evidence about how patients analyse what they hear and remember. But that evidence gives us good reason to doubt that their analyses meet the expectations of the bioethicists who advocate informed consent or the judges who demand it.

To gain further insight into the way patients think about their medical choices, let us examine a case study. The most common cancer among men attacks the prostate. Traditionally, physicians tried to detect prostate cancer before its symptoms became acute by 'digital rectal examination', that is by trying to feel the cancer in the prostate. However, this method is roughly as effective as it is pleasant, at least where the cancer is in its early stages. This has made it seem desirable to find another way of identifying men with this common and potentially fatal disease. The best current way to do so arises from the fact that distressed prostates emit abnormally high levels of a protein called prostate-specific antigen. A number of physicians thus favour screening men by testing their blood for elevated PSA levels and then, where the PSA is elevated, performing an ultrasound examination and, usually, a biopsy.

Other physicians, however, disagree. These PSA sceptics make several points. First, they observe that many things besides prostate cancer can distress a prostate and that therefore the PSA test provokes numerous biopsies that reveal no cancer. Indeed, at least 70 per cent of the men with elevated PSA levels do not have cancer. The 30 per cent who do are generally distinguished from the 70 per cent who do not through a biopsy. While the PSA test is relatively inexpensive and only trivially burdensome (it is a blood test often performed on men who are already having blood drawn for other purposes), few men find the biopsy agreeable. Furthermore, it is both expensive and fallible.

---

[15] Rachelle Breslow, *Who Said So?: How Our Thoughts and Beliefs Affect Our Physiology* (Berkeley, Cal., 1991).

[16] William Martin, *My Prostate and Me: Dealing with Prostate Cancer* (New York, 1994) 114.

Secondly, opponents of PSA screening say that prostate cancer often grows so slowly that most men who have the disease do not die from it. Autopsies of men who were not known to have prostate cancer found evidence of the disease in up to a quarter of the 65-year-olds and 40 per cent of the 85-year-olds. One estimate is that 10 per cent of all men contract prostate cancer but only 2 to 3 per cent of these actually die or suffer seriously from it. This suggests that, for most men, the best reaction to a diagnosis of prostate cancer may be not to treat it but to monitor it to try to discover whether it is developing rapidly enough to threaten the patient's well-being seriously.

Thirdly, opponents of PSA screening note that the treatments for prostate cancer—surgery and radiation—can be painful and that they are likely to cause quite trying complications. In some studies, up to 60 per cent of the men treated became temporarily impotent or incontinent, and 30 per cent of those treated suffered from one of these conditions permanently. Others had persistent infections, and some had permanent rectal problems. Some even died. Since the treatment will be unnecessary for many men, this means that these complications would—for those men—have been pointless. For a number of other men, treatment cannot vanquish the cancer. For these men, too, the unpleasantness and complications of treatment may well outweigh its benefits.

The studies necessary to determine whether PSA screening is on balance worthwhile are under way but are years from completion. Meanwhile, opponents of screening say, there are hints that screening—on the average—increases life expectancy by only a few days and that screening may even *reduce* one's 'quality adjusted' life expectancy by a few days. In short, the PSA sceptics fear that, on average, screening does not improve health and longevity and thus is not worth the cost. The PSA proponents, on the other hand, are more hopeful that studies will eventually show that the cost-benefit analysis favours screening, and they tend to believe that it is better to try and fail to treat all the victims of the disease than to let those who could be saved die.

Several attempts have been made to resolve this controversy among physicians by bringing them together to write guidelines. These attempts, however, have failed. Instead, these groups have recommended that each patient be given the evidence and decide for himself.[17] In short, the medical dispute among doctors has been deferred to their patients under the aegis of informed consent.

How well will this work? How will men confronted with these conflicting arguments analyse them? To find out, we interviewed forty men who were 40 to 65 years old. They varied widely in income and occupation. However, they were on average better educated than the American population. Only

[17] See, e.g., 'Screening for Prostate Cancer' (1997) 126 *Annals of Internal Medicine* 480.

nine of them had no college experience (three of whom did not finish high school).[18]

The interviews were generally held in the interviewee's home or office and lasted from one to two hours. A central feature of the interview was an attempt to give the men the kind of information about whether to be screened for PSA that an exceptionally conscientious physician striving to be as neutral as possible would offer. In other parts of the interview, the men were asked about their health, their experience with prostate problems and tests, their relationships with physicians, their views about participating in medical decisions, and their skill in handling simple arithmetic.

In general, these were not men who shrank from the burden of decision. A number of them not only aspired to make sound decisions, but felt obliged to do so. They disparaged friends or even spouses who had avoided the responsibility of making medical choices. They often spoke contemptuously of such people and their dangerous course.

[When] they don't decide ... they abdicate their responsibility. They would do *anything* anybody told them, any crackpot idea that a brand-new, greenhorn doc might dream up.

My wife goes to the doctor, and if her doctor told her to eat a bushel of horse manure a week, she'd do it, and she wouldn't question it.

The thinking of forty men over a prolonged discussion is not easily summarized. When humans speak, their ideas are fluid, incomplete, and even contradictory. These men were no different. Nevertheless, two central and significant generalizations are inescapable: first, only two of the forty seemed to change their minds about PSA screening despite all the information they were given. This may be partly because three-quarters of them had already had a PSA test and because prostate cancer and screening for it have by now entered into public discourse.[19]

Secondly, even though the interviews offered patients an exceptionally favourable basis for making well informed and well reasoned decisions, the men seemed to have considerable difficulty in doing so. More specifically, participants frequently seemed swayed by unexamined assumptions which led them to ignore or misunderstand the information they were

---

[18] More complete information about this study and its results will be published in subsequent papers.

[19] This is in interesting distinction to an earlier study which found that, 'compared with controls, patients who received the information intervention were much more likely to indicate no interest in pursuing PSA screening ... and were much less likely to indicate high interest in screening ...': Andrew M. D. Wolf *et al.*, 'The Impact of Informed Consent on Patient Interest in Prostate-Specific Antigen Screening' (1996) 156 *Archives of Internal Medicine* 1333, 1333. At least two factors may account for the difference between our results and Wolf's. First, Wolf's respondents began the study less well informed about PSA. Secondly, public discussion of prostate cancer and PSA screening has proliferated in the years between the two studies.

given. More specifically still, the interviewees relied crucially on what might be called principles of folk wisdom which often seemed to repel, rather than induce, thought. An examination of some of these principles will reveal much about the way these men thought about the problem they confronted.

Prevention is good. Public-health and cancer education have done their job almost too well. Our interviewees had fully imbibed the principles that 'prevention' is better than treatment, that nothing is more crucial to combating cancer than catching it early, and that screening is vital to early detection. Thus one respondent said:

My mother is a retired registered nurse. I've got a lot of health professionals in my family. I've been aware of health and health care all my life. . . . I've been blessed with good health, for the most part, and I just did not want to run the risk. I didn't want to do something stupid. . . . [I]f there's a test, or an exam, or something, I'm going to take it. . . . I just want to be preventive, instead of [regretting] after the fact.

And another:

[My body's] like a machine. . . . [I]f there's a flat tire, I'll go ahead and change it. If the oil's low, I'll go ahead and change it. . . . It's by taking preventive measures like this [test] I've been able to maintain a reasonable amount of good health. . . .

And in like vein:

Respondent: I honestly believe the knowing, and having the option of prevention, outweighs all the other risks [of PSA screening]. . . . [I]f you do the proper things, it's just like starting a car. You can have the key, and if you don't unlock the door and stick it in the ignition, you're not going anywhere. But if you do the proper things—stick the key in the door, unlock the door, stick it in the ignition, put the seat belt on for safety— . . . you're going to go somewhere. . . .This is good sense, this is good medicine.

Interviewer: So you've said that 'prevention' really overrides this uncertainty about PSA?

Respondent: The availability of prevention has to be part of the system, part of the schedule of benefits [for an HMO]. . . . I mean, I think of prevention. I'm not always that way, but prevention—you're always in control of prevention.

Of course, the interviewees were commonly doing more than applying the general lesson of prevention and screening. The advocates of PSA screening have had much the better of the controversy in the media, and the blessings of such screening seem to have been well preached by celebrities like Bob Dole, Norman Schwarzkopf, and Arnold Palmer. As one of the participants remarked, prostate cancer 'is all over the TV now'. This has had its effects.

PSA screening may well be wise because it may make it possible to detect disease early and thus to treat it more effectively. Screening is controversial precisely because many estimable authorities accept that view. But such a position is reasonable only after one has grappled with the proposition that, in the particular case of PSA screening, the general argument in favour of screening does not work. Many of the interviewees seemed so powerfully driven by an idealized version of 'prevention' that they had difficulty hearing, understanding, and analysing any reason PSA screening might be undesirable.

To put the point a bit differently: screening often works just as it is supposed to. It works for easily apprehended reasons. The virtues of screening have been drummed into the public over many years of virtuous advertising. As the passages quoted a moment ago suggest, screening is easily analogized to familiar and desirable practices, like routine maintenance of one's car. All one's educated intuitions, in short, make PSA screening seem like common sense and the arguments against screening seem foolish. Taking those arguments seriously requires an uncomfortable and burdensome re-examination of what feel like settled questions. Personal experience suggests to most people that such re-examinations are rarely worth the effort, and they are thus resisted.

Many of these men were also diverted from thinking clearly about their choices by their tendency to call PSA screening 'prevention'. But PSA screening does not prevent disease, it reveals it. Effective prevention relieves people of the consequences of disease and treatment, and prevention is often virtually free of risk. Thus prevention can be much more effective than screening, and conflating the two ordinarily makes screening unduly attractive.

Control is good. Some years ago, 'control freak' was a term of disparagement. Today, Americans feel with increasing conviction that people should seize and keep control over their circumstances.[20] Control even takes on a moral dimension, for 'taking responsibility' often means taking control. PSA testing appealed to a number of men because it seemed to be a way of taking control of and responsibility for their health: '[t]here are a limited number of things that you can control in your life. . . . I like to keep as many of those as possible'. PSA screening looked attractive because it was seen as a form of 'prevention', and prevention was seen as a way of having control: '[p]revention—you're always in control of prevention'. More than half the participants used negative stories about other people who had failed to assume responsibility for their health by using PSA screening.

Now, if they don't get a PSA, and then they get [cancer], I have no sympathy for 'em. That's just stupid on their part. They could have prevented it, but didn't. They could all die for all I care. . . . [W]hy should we pay for *their* unnecessary medical

---

[20] See generally, Schneider, n. 5, above.

care? No doubt it's their doctor's fault too. A doctor is supposed to prevent things, not ignore them.

The association of PSA screening with 'control' suggests another reason men may be reluctant to grapple with the argument against screening. That argument disturbingly suggests that, in the present state of knowledge, medicine fights prostate cancer ineptly. Taking that argument seriously means confronting medicine's limits with disquieting directness. In addition, that confrontation challenges another idea of psychological importance—that if you live right, you will live long, that you can avoid all harm if you are just careful enough. As one interviewee said, '[i]f you avoid all these things that are bad they got these days, you'll be rewarded with life. You have to take care of yourself, get the proper checkups and test'. In short, the desire for control provides another reason to accept PSA screening with little thought and to resist examining the argument against it.

Information is good. The survey literature now insistently suggests that most patients believe they want a good deal of information about their illnesses.[21] The participants in this study shared a nearly axiomatic belief that information is always good to have. Some of them had quite comprehensible reasons. For example, some of them saw PSA testing not as a way of detecting cancer but as a way of hearing comforting news: '[i]f you have a negative test, then you say, hey, you're really reassured that nothing is going to happen'.

Another common reason for wanting information is a belief that forewarned is forearmed:

Everything affects your life, but that [prostate cancer] affects the end of your life, so you need to know. . . . Nobody anticipates when they're gonna die. . . . If it happens, it happens, but if you *know* it's going to happen, you put yourself into an advantage situation of being able to accomplish things that you've put off, things that you've wanted to do, or . . . maybe experimental medication. . . .

Or, as another man put it:

I would rather know what information's available, and which way to go, so I've got all the information to make some kind of a sensible decision of what I'm gonna do with myself. . . .

Other men seemed committed to 'more information' even if its usefulness might be obscure. These men might acknowledge the possible disadvantages of PSA testing but then suggest that even a misleading PSA is better than no test. One man said that a PSA test is:

not a gamble. I'm mean, do it. It's silly not to. . . . [L]ogic would dictate the tests are there, they're available, and they're reasonably accurate, even if they're not a hundred percent.

[21] See generally, Schneider, n. 5, above.

As another interviewee said:

You're attempting to try and find out what's going on [with the prostate]. . . . [T]he PSA may not be exact, but at least it is some measure, and as time goes on it will become more precise, but nonetheless, it's something.

These men are recruiting a standard aphorism from common sense—that half a loaf is better than none, that some information is better than none. Yet the aphorism is inappropriate, since the uncertainty lies not just in the accuracy of the test, but also in what to do if cancer is diagnosed. The argument against screening is that men may be best off doing nothing when diagnosed with cancer. The interviewees seemed to have difficulty examining this argument, however, since little seemed more counter-intuitive to them than the suggestion that information might not be useful.

Even participants who seemed to acknowledge some of the arguments against PSA screening emphasized how important 'knowing' is:

I didn't understand [PSA statistics before], to be honest with you. I didn't realize about all these numbers, and it may sound silly, but I still like the idea of doing the blood test, only because I'm always curious about these things. I just like to see.

The same man said:

But if I get a positive result, I'm not sure I'll do anything. The potential [adverse effects of treatment] here, which would make life very unpleasant, outweigh the small possibility of dying.

He saw PSA screening, then, as a way of putting off a decision about how to respond to prostate cancer until the evil moment of knowledge actually arrived.

But if I start to get a positive result, then that's something I should find additional information about, look into, you know, really make a decision about.

The independent worth of knowing is further suggested by the fact that, although three-quarters of the participants wanted to be screened, almost none thought he would want to be treated for cancer should it be discovered. This states a plausible position—I *really* want to know if I have cancer—but it also raises intriguing questions with which the interviewees may not fully have engaged. Was this actually what these men believed? If they were not going to be treated, would they really be happier burdened by the knowledge of their disease? Was their desire for information *simpliciter* strong enough to lead them to endure the risks and disadvantages of trying to discover whether they had prostate cancer? Would they stick with their decision not to be treated were cancer discovered?

Other participants put their preference for information in yet starker terms. As one frankly said, 'I can't explain why [I want screening]. I just like to see tests'. And another participant felt so intensely that information is good and ignorance bad that he angrily saw the argument against PSA screening as part of a conspiracy to keep him in ignorance:

You can't put the genie back in the bottle. The awareness is there. People like myself are spreading the word, of advantages of PSA. I don't care if [the cancer] is latent or active. . . . [W]ho do you think shows up at those meetings [on cancer screening nights]? Opinion leaders, people that want the information. Now, you [showed] your statistical work [to me], but it's the opinion leaders that tell ten others. You unleashed the dragon. [The speaker at the screening night] said, pure and simple, just like that— . . . he knows how many other groups are talking about [PSA].

There is, of course, much to be said for knowing about one's health. However, here, as with the other two axioms we have explored, the danger is that the simple principle 'information is good' operates so powerfully and is accepted so uncritically that men do not hear and consider the arguments that the information provided by PSA tests may be bought at a high price (because the PSA test itself produces so many false positives) and is unexpectedly uninformative (because there is—PSA sceptics argue—no satisfactory evidence about what men with prostate cancer should do and thus reason to think they should do nothing).

Technology is good. Another common axiom of American folk wisdom is the steady progress of technology and medical science. Some of the interviewees saw PSA screening as the 'state of the art' and believed they should take advantage of the best medical science had to offer:

We already know about heart disease. We already know about certain forms of cancer that are caused by smoking. We know about emphysema—that's usually a by-product of smoking. Right now, prostate cancer is a treatable problem. You know, [PSA] is a tool. Right now there isn't anything else.

Some saw being screened as a necessary best step toward the next technology:

If I were presented with a positive PSA test, I guess the most logical thing is to get a second confirming PSA test. But there will be another test that the medical community will come up with in the future, and that will work better than the PSA. . . . If I don't get the PSA, then I won't know to get that [other] test, I won't be able to benefit from the advance. . . . There was a time when the PSA didn't exist, after all, and men were subject to cancer without warning. Now, the PSA is here, and something else will be discovered soon.

The folk wisdom is right—medicine surely has made gratifying progress. Here again, however, the problem is to apply that wisdom discriminatingly. Sometimes the best medicine can do is not worth doing. Sometimes progress comes slowly. It now appears, for example, that studies which will determine the usefulness of PSA screening will take many years to complete.

Statistics are lies. Several of the participants scorned the arguments against PSA screening because they shared folk wisdom's scepticism of, and even contempt for, statistics. That scepticism is epitomized by one man's use of the cliché 'you can prove anything you want with statistics'. Another man said scornfully, '[t]hey can take the statistics and bend them any way you want to'. Similar doubts led other men to such conclusions as a belief that all statistical uncertainty was automatically a 'fifty-fifty chance', so that either choice was appropriate, or a 'toss-up'.

Respondent: The numbers [don't matter]. . . . I don't want to take chances with all that stuff. I might die, I might not. I might get those [side effects of impotence and incontinence], I might not. Either way, I got a fifty-fifty chance, you know, I might as well guess!

Interviewer: Hmm. Remember those numbers here aren't exactly fifty-fifty, your chances could be worse, maybe of getting a side effect, or maybe a lot better, like living for years without problems [from the cancer].

Respondent: Yeah, I hear you. But I figure it's a gamble, an even chance either way, you know, fifty-fifty. Since you don't know, you know you're saying thirty percent here, you might as well guess either way. You got an even chance of good or bad.

This scepticism of statistics could shade into an acid distrust of those who use them:

Now the person [who is] saying the PSA tests aren't that valid. . . . What would happen if their mother went in and got a pap smear, and it was positive, or their father went in and got a PSA that was a 5 [somewhat elevated]? By God, right then and there they'd want to do everything possible to see what was going on. Yet it's very easy for them to say, 'Joe Blow down there, he may not have it 'cause he's got a PSA of five'. When you start throwing statistics around, I think it's a copout, in a way, for these people. I always say, '[I]f [I] was your mother or father, or your son or your daughter, what would you do?' And if they're telling the truth, they're gonna say, '[W]ell I'd do everything possible'. . . . You place it in a personal context—bullshit! Hey, you know, statistics.

'I knew someone once who . . .'. One of the best-studied defects in human reasoning is the tendency to prefer a few vivid examples to systematic but dry statistics. Our interviewees were as prone to this failing as the rest of us. Almost every participant cited stories of friends, relatives, and celebrities who had been saved by testing:

I think my impression initially was that [my physician] didn't want to do the test, and I insisted that we do it. . . . I think about Bo Schembechler [once the University of Michigan football coach and a sainted name in Ann Arbor]. He had a prostate operation, and [a friend of mine], and somebody else, too, a pretty renowned citizen—oh! Schwarzkopf, General Schwarzkopf.

Often these stories did not even involve PSA screening, but rather involved quite different kinds of cases, from other blood tests (e.g. for cholesterol) to decisions about children with congenital heart disease.

You know, a one in 1000 chance may not sound like much, but I had an aunt that was told she had a one in 1000 chance of having a blood clot go to her brain through a procedure she was going to have, and it happened. . . . [I]t's all risky, but I still think it provides a framework for decision making even if it's not totally accurate, because you can't have complete accuracy.

'If it weren't for bad luck, I'd have no luck at all.'[22] Finally, some men implicitly relied on folk beliefs about a purposive fortune. A quarter of the participants complained quite seriously about their bad luck. From this they concluded that PSA testing might be bad for the general population but necessary for themselves:

Respondent: Oh, I understand you all right, and I don't think *most* people should have a PSA. . . . I still want it because bad things happen to me. I'm the guy with bad luck, the 1%.

Interviewer: You told me you don't have a family history of cancer, right?

Respondent: Yeah, but I'm just like [the men with a family history], [or] just like the black people. . . . I'll get cancer because I get everything else.

The Lessons of the PSA Study

It is never wise to make too much of a single study, especially a small one in an underdeveloped field—here, how patients make decisions. We certainly do not believe that in this short paper we have fully described the way even these few men thought. Nevertheless, the results we have reported are reassuringly plausible, and they are consonant with and help explain what we know about how patients think about medical choices. We are thus emboldened to address the irresistible question—did these men evaluate the information they were given well?

The answer, of course, depends crucially on what 'well' means. One approach is to ask whether they evaluated the information well by what we might call 'public' standards, by the criteria of medical rationality. Did they, in other words, appraise the evidence in the way we would expect from, say, a panel of experts asked to establish guidelines for screening? The answer to the question thus defined seems to be no.

The problem lies not in the men's substantive decisions, for experts themselves have failed to find a basis for agreement about screening. The problem, rather, lies in what we might call procedure, in the *way* many of the men handled the information they were given. For they often did not

---

[22] Perhaps we should say that we borrow this quotation not from an interviewee but from the classic TV show *Hee-Haw*.

seem to assimilate and assess it. Instead, they seemed to short-circuit their evaluation of the data by falling back on axioms current in American culture. These axioms were not necessarily problematic in themselves, although some of them were (like the facile dismissal of all statistics). Axioms usually gain currency because they capture important truths. However, the axioms our interviewees relied on could seem so right (and could in the proper circumstances be so unexceptionable) that they made it seductively easy for the participants confronted with an unappealing and counter-intuitive proposition (PSA screening is not a good bet) to dismiss the information without reflecting on it and instead to leap to a conclusion.

Our hypothesis, then, is that even patients whose informed consent is solicited in virtually ideal circumstances may be misled in analysing the data by their tendency to rely too uncritically on culturally powerful but inapt axioms. This hypothesis gains credence from the evidence we reviewed earlier that patients often make medical decisions unreflectively. In particular, our study suggests one quite plausible explanation of the evidence that patients reach conclusions with a rapidity that virtually excludes reflection, namely, that patients can decide quickly because they rely on cultural axioms to make scrutiny of complexity unnecessary.

If our description of the interviewees' reasoning is correct, they did not, *pro tanto*, analyse their choices in the way American public policy has generally tried to encourage. First, their reasoning does not seem consonant with the animating assumptions of informed consent as they have ordinarily been understood. That doctrine assumes that patients will grapple as directly as possible with the advantages and disadvantages of their medical choices. Why proffer thorough recitals of complex information about troubling choices if consideration of them is thus to be short-circuited? (And if you do not provide such recitals, how are patients to make wise choices?) Similarly, we have devoted untold dollars and effort on public health education intended to persuade people to make decisions about their health (about safe sex, about smoking, about cancer, and so on) in an unashamedly conventional and rational way.

We have been suggesting that, judged by 'public' standards, the interviewees' methods of evaluating the evidence they were given seem unsatisfactory, that if panels writing guidelines for screening used such methods, indignation would be the reaction. Obviously, however, these men are private citizens who may make private decisions in whatever way seems best to them. In other words, one interpretation of the PSA study is that informed consent was a success, that the men took the information they were given, applied their own 'values' to it, and reached the results those values dictated. This is true at least in the narrow (but not trivial) sense that people formulate and evince their values by making decisions.

But there are important senses in which this interpretation of the study seems false. It is quite unlikely that many of the men wanted to make decisions in the way they seem to have done. For one thing, most people believe at least in principle in the usefulness of conventional rationality in analysing scientific problems. And indeed, the interviewee's occasional comments at least hinted that they generally espoused just such views of how to approach medical problems. One man, for example, said that 'people should not just make irrational, emotional decisions'. Another man—a mathematician—was avowedly afraid of making a bad decision because of his fear of the disease: 'I could never look at the numbers and decide like I do at work'. Yet another man found satisfaction in being 'more with-it now, . . . more rational'.

Furthermore, the problem with the men's methods was not just that they fell short of widely shared standards of rationality. It was that the axioms seemed often to preclude the men from confronting the contending arguments directly. Few people believe this is a good way to approach difficult and dangerous decisions. Most people believe that making good decisions requires listening to the arguments on both sides carefully enough to understand them. (Another cultural axiom is that there are two sides to every question.) Certainly the participants insisted vigorously on being given 'the proper information of what I need' and felt that 'the only way for him [the patient] to make a decision is to be well informed' with the kinds of information usually thought necessary for making conventionally rational decisions.

This raises the question why men could make decisions in ways they themselves regarded as undesirable. There are at least two cogent possibilities. First, people regularly fail to meet their own standards in many areas, particularly where, as here, performance is difficult. Secondly, these men probably did not realize just how they were making decisions, since the psychological mechanism at work is one which ordinarily does not reveal itself to its user.

In short, it is unlikely that the interviewees would have chosen to rest their decisions on these cultural commonplaces in so significant a way. When bioethicists and lawyers discuss informed consent, they speak of patients making decisions by applying their 'values' to the data they are given. But whatever 'values' denotes, it connotes someone's deepest beliefs. And it is that connotation that gives the principle of informed consent so much of its force. The axioms that often figure prominently in the interviewees' thinking, however, will rarely reflect their more basic and considered beliefs. Rather they tend to be convenient generalizations which people find useful in ordinary affairs but which they are not much committed to. Analogously, for example, Nisbett and Ross report that, while people regularly depend on unreliable 'heuristics' in reasoning about unfamiliar subjects, they abandon them when dealing with familiar ones.[23] Indeed, it

[23] Richard Nisbett and Lee Ross, *Human Inference: Strategies and Shortcomings of Social Judgment* (Upper Saddle River, NJ, 1980).

is all too likely that the 'values' represented by these axioms may conflict with other beliefs which represent more truly what the interviewees ultimately think.

The Cure for the Ills of Informed Consent

The problems patients have in understanding and retaining what they are told are well known. And evidence is beginning to accumulate about the difficulty patients have in analysing the information they are given and making decisions about it. The hypothesis we investigated in the preceding section helps substantiate the suggestion that patients often seem to resolve medical questions with a speed that would inhibit thoughtful consideration of the information they are given. Added to the other doubts we have already reviewed about how patients receive and process information, the hypothesis raises questions about what can be hoped for from informed consent.

The conventional response to concerns of this kind has most typically been: '[t]he only cure for the ills of informed consent is more informed consent'. Many of these suggestions have to do with ways to convey information more effectively, as by improving the way forms are worded, or by having people other than doctors explain choices to patients, or by making educational videos part of informed consent. As it has become clear that such changes do less than had been hoped, doctors have been urged to expand the range of information they impart, and the range of situations in which they offer informed consent. (The movement away from guidelines and toward patient choice in PSA screening exemplifies the latter tendency.) A sense of the ambition—one might almost say desperation—of these proposals is to be found by examining a recent article by Geller *et al.* in the *Hastings Center Report*.[24] Among its recommendations are:

(1) There should be an 'in-depth exploration by providers of patients' affective and cognitive processes', since '[p]roviders who rely on a discrete or short-term approach to informed consent are unlikely to succeed at understanding fundamental patient beliefs and preferences and thereby have little hope of obtaining truly informed consent'.
(2) Providers should 'explore uncertainties and limitations both in the provider's own knowledge and in the state of the science'.
(3) '[I]f they are to facilitate truly informed decisionmaking on the part of their patients, providers must understand and disclose their own motivations, beliefs, and values to patients'.

---

[24] Gail Geller *et al.*, ' "Decoding" Informed Consent: Insights from Women regarding Breast Cancer Susceptibility Testing' (1997) 27 *Hastings Center Report* 28.

(4) '[P]roviders ought to explore what kind of role expectations [about how decisions should be made] the patient has for herself and her provider'.

(5) Finally, 'informed consent ought to be individualized . . . and take place in the context of an ongoing relationship with a trusted health care provider'.

People are driven to such effulgent visions of informed consent in part by the strength of the autonomist ideal in American life, law, and medicine. More particularly, they are not insubstantially motivated by the rise of the view among some bioethicists and even some doctors and patients that, as a matter of good medical practice and even as a matter of moral duty, patients ought to make their own medical decisions even if they would rather delegate them to someone else.[25] Those who espouse this 'mandatory autonomism' must hope to perfect informed consent for want of a better way of achieving their goals. But is such perfected informed consent practicable?

Confronting the Limits of Informed Consent

Before we answer the question we have just posed, we should pause for a stipulation and reassurance: the doubts the paper has expressed about informed consent do not require anything like abandoning it. There are many reasons for this but space for only a few. First, sometimes informed consent works in something like the way bioethicists and courts envisage. Some people are well-situated to make medical decisions. Some 'medical' decisions can be well made by many patients. (The choice of dialysis modality—which often raises more questions about the patient's social and professional life than about medicine—is one example.) Secondly, most people want at least some of the information the doctrine of informed consent intends for them to have, even if they do not want to make decisions themselves. Thirdly, some of the information given in informed consent helps patients care for their illness better even if it does not help them make medical decisions. Fourthly, some people may want to make their own decisions even if they do so clumsily. Fifthly, informed consent may have value even if it is only a ritual, for it reminds doctors of their duties of concern and deference to their patients, duties it is easy for them to forget and neglect in the press of the other duties that surround them.

The question, then, is not whether to discard informed consent, but what to expect of it. The material we have surveyed raises the possibility that there are real limits to our ability to solve the two problems of informed consent, and thus real limits to what we may reasonably hope

---

[25] See Schneider, n. 5, above.

for from it. The PSA study illustrates a number of those limits. Not the least of these is time. In the artificial setting of this study, time could be lavished on a single medical question in a way that would be flatly impossible in most ordinary medicine (and that would have been impossible even in that imagined Eden before health management organizations). Yet interviewees still came away from this educational extravagance without having fully understood and confronted the arguments presented to them.

But why is this surprising? Teaching and learning are both humblingly difficult, as any student and any teacher knows. Yet teachers teach and students learn in virtually ideal settings compared to those in which doctor and patient must labour. In the earlier pages of this paper we sketched a few of the intellectual and social factors that make medical decisions forbiddingly and even repellently difficult for patients. And when the subject of the teaching and learning is as fraught with disturbing ideas and with unrecognized and unreliable assumptions as medical decisions, it is inevitable that people should almost struggle to avoid the labour of learning and the chore of choosing.

Indeed, a substantial number of patients expressly say, when asked, that they do not want to make their own medical decisions.[26] And the sicker patients are, the less likely they are to want to make their own medical decisions. The task of education is always daunting. How much more daunting must it be when the learners do not wish to use what is being taught?

The PSA study suggests another practical limit to the scope of informed consent. The participants in that study seemed often to rely on powerful cultural axioms that allowed them to dismiss much of what they were being told. Yet they probably did not fully realize what they were doing, and it seems likely that physicians trying to inform them would likewise not realize all that they were thinking. Furthermore, patients must often be influenced by misapprehensions of whose existence or strength their physicians are unaware. For example, patients who have agreed to become research subjects considerably over-estimate their chances of benefiting from the experimental treatment even when they have been told what those chances actually are.[27] These research subjects 'systematically misinterpret the risk/benefit ratio of participation in research because they fail to understand the underlying scientific methodology'.[28] Like our interviewees, they are

---

[26] The evidence for this proposition is displayed and dissected at length in Schneider, n. 5 above.

[27] See, e.g., Christopher Daugherty et al., 'Perceptions of Cancer Patients and Their Physicians Involved in Phase I Trials' (1995) 13 *Journal of Clinical Oncology* 1062; Nancy E. Kass et al., 'Trust: The Fragile Foundation of Contemporary Biomedical Research' (1996) 26 *Hastings Center Report* 25; Sjoerd Rodenhuis et al., 'Patient Motivation and Informed Consent in a Phase I Study of an Anticancer Agent' (1984) 20 *European Journal of Cancer & Clinical Oncology* 457.

[28] Paul S. Appelbaum et al., 'False Hopes and Best Data: Consent to Research and the Therapeutic Misconception' (1987) 17 *Hastings Center Report* 20, 21.

saved from difficult choices by misplaced reliance on a cultural truth: '[m]ost people have been socialized to believe that physicians (at least ethical ones) always provide personal care. It may therefore be very difficult, perhaps nearly impossible, to persuade subjects that *this* encounter is different . . .'.[29]

What is more, it appears that even willing physicians have had trouble in overcoming this kind of misapprehension:

The investigator in one of the projects we studied offered his subjects detailed and extensive information in a process that often extended over several days and included one session in which the entire project was reviewed. Despite this, half the subjects failed to grasp that treatment would be assigned on a random basis, four of twenty misunderstood how placebos would be used, five of twenty were not aware of the use of a double-blind and eight of twenty believed that medications would be adjusted according to their individual needs.[30]

Doctors should surely do their best to give patients the information they want. But it is time to consider the possibility that doctors will never be able to communicate to patients all the information they need in a way that they can use effectively. It is the rare physician who has the skill and the time to probe deeply enough into the patient's mind to discover the misapprehensions of fact and the inapt reliance on truths that distort what patients hear and think about the problems they face. It may therefore be time to chart the limits of informed consent and to consider what other approaches might help patients secure what they want and need from medicine.[31]

[29] Paul S. Appelbaum *et al.*, 'False Hopes and Best Data: Consent to Research and the Therapeutic Misconception' (1987) 17 *Hastings Center Report* at 23.

[30] *Ibid.*

[31] For thoughts on how to proceed, see chap. 6 of Schneider, n. 5, above.

PATIENT AUTONOMY—A TURN IN THE TIDE?

Rebecca Bailey-Harris

Introduction

The genesis of this paper was the decision of the Court of Appeal in *St George's Healthcare NHS Trust* v. *S; R.* v. *Collins and Others, ex parte S* (hereafter *St George's*).[1] That decision highlighted a number of classic debates in medical ethics: autonomy versus paternalism, consequentialism versus deontological absolutism, and the nature of personhood. The particular factual context was that of refusal of medical and surgical treatment by a woman in a late state of pregnancy, but the decision is of a wider significance. The decision is concerned primarily with the power of the patient against the medical profession, rather than any conflict between mother and unborn child.[2] This interpretation[3] is based on three particular aspects of the judgment: (i) the absolute nature of the autonomy right as framed by the Court of Appeal and its contextualization as a necessary freedom within a democratic society which will brook no erosion; (ii) the reasoning technique which denies the foetus the status of personhood, and thus deliberately eschews a conflict of rights analysis; and (iii) the issuing by the court of guidelines[4] which are intended, at least procedurally, to tip the balance back in favour of the competent patient in future situations. Hence the title of this paper: the decision represents a landmark for patient autonomy generally.

The facts are crucial to an interpretation of the general significance of the decision, for they dramatically illustrate an abuse of power by health professionals against the patient concerned, which the decision was intended to rectify. S, a woman aged 28, had a deep-seated aversion to medical intervention. She consulted a general practitioner for the first time when she was thirty-six weeks pregnant and was diagnosed as suffering from severe pre-eclampsia. She was told by the doctor that this condition posed a risk of death or disability both to herself and the unborn child, but nevertheless she consistently refused treatment, believing that nature

---

[1] [1998] 2 FLR 728.

[2] Judge LJ expressly stated that '[i]n the present case there was no conflict between the interests of the mother and the foetus': at 742.

[3] Other interpretations stress the maternal/foetal conflict: see Herring's ch. later in this vol.

[4] The guidelines are included in full in an appendix to this ch., 137.

should take its course. On application by a social worker under section 2 of the Mental Health Act 1983, S was against her will admitted to and detained in one hospital and subsequently transferred to another. The general practitioner's diagnosis that she was depressed was confirmed by hospital doctors. The evidence did not suggest that there was a question about her competence. After consulting solicitors she repeated both orally and in writing her refusal of treatment. Unknown to her or to her solicitors, the hospital authority applied *ex parte* to the High Court for a declaration that treatment, including caesarean section by general anaesthetic, was lawful, notwithstanding S's refusal. The judge, who had been incorrectly given the impression that S had been in labour for twenty-four hours, granted the declaration. A caesarean section was successfully performed and S was delivered of a daughter. Within a few days her section 2 detention was terminated and S discharged herself. S subsequently sought to challenge her admission, detention, and treatment and to appeal the declaration. In *Re S (Application for Judicial Review)*[5] the Court of Appeal granted leave to apply for judicial review notwithstanding delay. The court on that occasion made it clear that this was an exceptional case where the issues involved were of genuine public importance and merited ventilation in the public law context. It recommended that the appeal against the declaration and the application for judicial review be heard together, which subsequently occurred.

In an earlier line of cases, the High Court had been prepared to declare lawful a caesarean section (and where necessary the use of reasonable force) performed on a woman despite her refusal of consent, on the grounds that it was in her best interests: *Re S (Adult: Surgical Treatment)*;[6] *Norfolk and Norwich Healthcare (NHS) Trust v. W;*[7] *Tameside and Glossop Acute Services Trust v. CH (A Patient);*[8] *Re L (Patient: Non-Consensual Treatment.*[9] Earlier in *Re T (Adult: Refusal of Medical Treatment)*[10] Lord Donaldson had suggested obiter that the absolute nature of the competent adult's right to refuse treatment might be qualified where the life of a viable foetus was in issue. In the subsequent cases cited above, saving the life of the unborn child (as well as that of the mother) was certainly a consideration which weighed with the court. The lack of jurisprudential justification for the decisions where a caesarean section was carried out against the woman's wishes was the subject of much academic debate, although the paternalistic approach was not without its defenders.[11] The judicial technique adopted in order to reach the stage of

---

[5] [1998] 1 FLR 790; comment in [1997] *Fam Law* 790.
[6] [1993] 1 FLR 26.   [7] [1996] 2 FLR 613.   [8] [1996] 1 FLR 762.
[9] [1997] 2 FLR 837.   [10] [1992] 4 All ER 649 at 652–3.
[11] See, e.g., J. K. Mason and R. McCall Smith, *Law and Medical Ethics* (5th edn., London, 1999), 265–6; A. Grubb, 'Commentary' (1996) 4 *Med Law Rev.* 193; K. Stern 'Court-Ordered Caesarean Sections: In Whose Interests?' (1993) 56 *MLR* 238–43; Thorpe LJ, 'The Caesarean Section Debate' [1997] 27 *Fam Law* 663.

the 'best interests' enquiry was to hold the woman temporarily incompetent and therefore incapable of exercising her autonomy right. However, a marked change of approach, at least jurisprudentially, was signalled by the judgment of the Court of Appeal in *Re MB (Medical Treatment)*,[12] although in the end the result was the same as in the earlier cases. Here a woman who was forty weeks pregnant with her unborn child in the breech position initially consented to a caesarean section but later on two occasions refused to consent to anaesthesia; she had a phobia of needles. Hollis J declared that it was lawful for the caesarean, anaesthesia by needle, and reasonable force to be administered. The woman appealed immediately. The Court of Appeal[13] in obiter dicta robustly reasserted the general principle of patient autonomy and the absolute right of a competent patient to refuse to consent to medical treatment for any reason, rational or irrational, or for no reason at all, even where that decision may lead to death. Significantly, the Court stated that where a competent woman refuses medical intervention, it has no jurisdiction to consider the interests of the unborn child; a foetus up to the moment of birth does not in this situation have separate interests capable of being taken into account. Nevertheless, on the facts, the woman was held, applying the test in *Re C (Refusal of Medical Treatment)*,[14] to be temporarily incompetent and therefore unable to exercise her autonomy right. Her fear of needles rendered her incapable of making a decision about medical treatment and at that moment she was faced with an impairment of her mental function which disabled her. The proposed treatment was in her best interests. Thus it was necessary to await a subsequent opportunity for correlation between the rhetoric of autonomy and the reality of judicial protection of that right.

St George's provided just that opportunity.[15] The Court of Appeal, allowing the appeal against the order of Hogg J, held that caesarean section and accompanying medical procedures performed on S amounted to a trespass and that in the extraordinary circumstances of the case the declaration provided no defence to the claim for ordinary damages in that action against the hospital. A declaration obtained *ex parte* was ineffective to determine the patient's rights and should be set aside. In holding that the admission, detention, and treatment of S under the Mental Health Act 1983 had been unlawful, the Court of Appeal adopted a strict construction of the relevant provisions consistent with the minimum erosion of patient autonomy necessary. Mental disorder must be of such a nature and degree as to warrant detention in hospital for assessment, and treatment to be

---

[12] [1997] 2 FLR 426.
[13] See the comment by R. Bailey-Harris in [1997] 27 *Fam Law* 542–4.
[14] [1994] 1 FLR 31.
[15] See R. Bailey-Harris, 'Pregnancy, Autonomy and Refusal of Medical Treatment' (1998) 114 *LQR* 550.

lawful under the Act must be integral to the mental disorder.[16] S had effectively been detained in order to treat her pregnancy. Any treatment outside the scope of the Act must be subject to the normal requirements of competence and consent. The Court of Appeal subsequently issued detailed guidelines[17] (elaborating on those given earlier in *Re MB (Medical Treatment*[18])) for hospital authorities for the prevention of problems in future cases involving questions of capacity where *any* surgical or other invasive treatment may be in a patient's best interests. The Court of Appeal emphasized that these guidelines are of *general* application and *not* confined to the particular factual context in *St George's* itself.

Autonomy

The reason the Court of Appeal stated the autonomy right of S in absolute terms was to resolve the conflict between the competent patient and medical paternalism. The protection afforded to the competent patient is reinforced by setting the right of individual autonomy in the context of freedom in a democratic society:

Even when his or her own life depends on receiving medical treatment, an adult of sound mind is entitled to refuse it. This reflects the autonomy of each individual and the right of self-determination. Lest reiteration may diminish the impact of this principle, it is valuable to recognise the force of the language used when the right of self-determination was most recently considered in the House of Lords in *Airedale NHS Trust* v. *Bland* [1993] AC 789, [1993] 1 FLR 1026.[19]

It is significant that Judge LJ chose to cite Lord Reid in *S* v. *McC; W* v. *W*,[20] thereby invoking the language of political freedom beyond the particular context of S's own circumstances:

There is no doubt that a person of full age and capacity cannot be ordered to undergo a blood test against his will. . . . The real reason is that English law goes to great lengths to protect a person of full age and capacity from interference with his personal liberty. We have too often seen freedom disappear in other countries not only by coups d'état but by gradual erosion: and often it is the first step that counts. So it would be unwise to make even minor concessions.

According to Judge LJ, the importance of this salutary warning remains undiminished.[21] If a right is characterized as absolute, no other right can conflict with or prevail against it; there is simply no scope for a balancing exercise between competing or conflicting rights. In *St George's,* as in

---

[16] Thus reversing the trend of earlier authority: see, e.g., *Tameside and Glossop Acute Services Trust* v. *CH (A Patient)* [1996] 1 FLR 762; 'Caesarean Section: A Treatment for Mental Disorder?' (1997) 314 *BMJ* 1183.

[17] [1998] 2 FLR 728 at 758–60. They are set out in full as an appendix to this ch., at 137.

[18] [1997] 2 FLR 426.

[19] [1998] 2 FLR 728 at 739.

[20] [1972] AC 25.

[21] [1998] 2 FLR 728 at 740.

other cases in different contexts,[22] the sanctity of life of the adult patient himself or herself is not regarded as an absolute. It was necessary for the Court of Appeal to cast the right of self-determination of a competent patient in absolute terms in order to empower the patient against the medical profession. The conflict thereby resolved (by eliminating any 'right' of medical paternalism from the equation) is that between patient autonomy and medical paternalism—*not* that between conflicting rights of mother and unborn child.

The Non-personhood of the Unborn Child

The second aspect of the Court of Appeal's reasoning which supports an interpretation in terms of patient autonomy upheld against medical paternalism is the construction of the status of the unborn child. Only persons have rights; hence there can be no conflict of rights if two persons are not involved. The court (consistent with earlier authority[23]) held that a child acquires legal personality only at birth. On the other hand, '[w]hatever else it may be a 36-week old foetus is not nothing: if viable it is not lifeless and it is certainly human'.[24]

The Court of Appeal *deliberately* refrained from pronouncing on the precise status of the unborn child between the parameters of full legal personality and nothingness. It should not be criticized for so doing, precisely because the conflict in issue was *not* perceived by the court as one between the mother and the unborn child. Further, the subordination of the unborn child's interests (as opposed to rights) is an inevitable consequence of the absolute nature of the mother's autonomy right and the political necessity of safeguarding it from any erosion:

In our judgment while pregnancy increases the personal responsibilities of a woman it does not diminish her entitlement to decide whether or not to undergo medical treatment. Although human, and protected by the law in a number of different ways set out in the judgment in *Re MB*, an unborn child is not a separate person from its mother. Its need for medical assistance does not prevail over her rights. She is entitled not to be forced to submit to an invasion of her body against her will, whether her own life or that of her unborn child depends on it. Her right is not reduced or diminished merely because her decision to exercise it may appear morally repugnant. The declaration in this case involved the removal of the baby from within the body of her mother under physical compulsion. Unless lawfully justified this constituted an infringement of the mother's autonomy. Of themselves the perceived needs of the foetus did not provide the necessary justification.[25]

---

[22] See, e.g., *Airedale NHS Trust* v. *Bland* [1993] AC 789; *Re C (Medical Treatment)* [1998] 1 FLR 384; *Re JT (Adult: Refusal of Medical Treatment)* [1998] 1 FLR 48.

[23] *Paton* v. *British Pregnancy Advisory Service Trustees* [1979] QB 276; *Re F (In Utero)* [1988] Fam. 122; *Attorney-General's Reference (No 3 of 1994)* [1997] 3 WLR 421; *Re MB (Medical Treatment)* [1997] 2 FLR 426.

[24] [1998] 2 FLR 728 at 741.　　　　　　　　　　[25] *Ibid., per* Judge LJ at 746.

Equality of Autonomy Between Women and Men

It is implicit—if not explicit—in the judgment in *St George's* and in the guidelines issued by the Court of Appeal that the autonomy right must be enjoyed equally between women and men patients. Gender, or physical conditions which are gender-specific,[26] does not justify differential treatment. After all, one could observe (although the Court of Appeal did not, because the point was not raised) that the father of an unborn child has the absolute right to refuse treatment which is essential to preserve his life (and therefore his parental responsibility obligations). The right to equal access to substantive human rights will in future be reinforced domestically by the implementation of the Human Rights Act 1998, in October 2000. Patient autonomy should be reinforced by Article 5 of the European Convention ('[e]veryone has the right to liberty and security of person') and Article 8 ('[e]veryone has the right to respect for his private . . . life').[27] It is important to appreciate that Article 14 is essentially an *access* provision and does not in itself create a substantive equality right: '[t]he enjoyment of the rights and freedoms set forth in this Convention shall be secured without discrimination on any ground such as sex . . .'. Equality between men and women patients in the application of the test of competence is discussed below.

The Duty to Warn and the Doctrine of Informed Consent

The judgment and the guidelines issued in *St George's* may mark a step forward for patient autonomy in the context of the doctrine of informed consent and the duty to warn in the tort of negligence. Traditionally, the non-observance of patient autonomy in relation to the medical profession's duty to warn of risks inherent in medical and surgical interventions has been notorious in English law. In applying the *Bolam* test[28] to the duty to warn[29] of risks as well as to diagnosis and to the entire range of treatment,[30] English law has to date eschewed the 'prudent patient' approach[31] in favour of the test of accepted medical practice, albeit that some change of approach may be evident in the judgment of the Court of Appeal in *Pearce* v. *United Bristol Healthcare Trust.*[32] In *Bolitho* v. *City and Hackney HA*[33] the House of Lords expressed no view on whether, in

---

[26] Note that in *Brown* v. *Rentokil* [1998] 2 FLR 649 it was held that dismissal on the basis of pregnancy-related illness was discrimination based on sex under the Equal Treatment Dir.

[27] For a discussion of maternal/foetal conflict from a human rights perspective, see Blake's ch. in this volume.   [28] [1957] 2 All ER 118.

[29] *Sidaway* v. *Board of Governors of Bethehem Royal Hospital and the Maudsley Hospital* [1985] AC 871.

[30] *Gold* v. *Haringey H.A.* [1988] QB 481; *Blyth* v. *Bloomsbury HA* (1993) 4 MLR 151.

[31] *Rogers* v. *Whitaker* (1992) 109 ALR 625.   [32] [1999] PIQR 53.

[33] [1997] 3 WLR 1151.

the context of the duty to warn, the court was permitted to examine the logical basis of an accepted medical practice.[34] However, *St George's* may be interpreted as suggesting that a patient should be told more than is to be inferred from the *Sidaway* line of authority. Here the guidelines[35] handed down by the Court of Appeal are of particular relevance. According to Professor Douglas it may be implicit from the guidelines:

that the patient must be given the same information as will be given to the judge— i.e. all the accurate and relevant information in the case. If so, then together with the court's emphasis upon the need to provide a patient with information about the consequences of consent or refusal, such a requirement appears to go beyond what has previously been required by English medical law.[36]

Defending the Autonomy Approach: The Uncertainty and Unpredictability of Paternalism

The Court of Appeal's characterization in *St George's* of the autonomy right as absolute may be defended *inter alia* on the basis of the certainty which it produces. This may be illustrated by exploring the hypothetical consequences of adopting a paternalistic 'best interests' approach to the facts of the case. Looking at best interests purely (and narrowly) in terms of physical health, there was no conflict between the interests of the mother and the unborn child;[37] the life and health of both were at risk if a caesarean was not performed. The unborn child's non-person status would not necessarily preclude the consideration of his or her interests under a paternalistic approach. What if there were a conflict between the two interests? Even on the facts of *St George's* itself, such a conflict would arise if a broader construction of 'best interests' were adopted, to include consideration of the mother's wishes and her possible future rejection of a child born other than by natural means. Even the unborn child's best interests could have been construed as including the broader social setting and potential rejection. There is ample authority for the wide interpretation of best interests.[38] The paternalistic approach would therefore involve a balancing exercise by the court and the inevitable exercise of a value judgement where conflict between competing interests is irreconcilable. The autonomy approach, by virtue of its very absolutism, has the advantage of certainty, and moreover the moral judgement has already been made in the abstract before the individual case arises for determination.

---

[34] 'I am not here considering questions of disclosure of risk': *per* Lord Browne-Wilkinson at 1160. [35] See the Appendix to this ch., at 137.

[36] [1998] Fam Law 663–4.

[37] As Judge LJ himself observed: [1998] 2 FLR 728 at 742.

[38] See, e.g., recently *Re Y (Mental Incapacity: Bone Marrow Transplant)* [1996] 2 FLR 787; *Re T (Wardship: Medical Treatment)* [1997] 1 FLR 502; *Re C (Medical Treatment)* [1998] 1 FLR 384.

Critique: The Limitations of the Decision

It is time to ask whether the decision in *St George's* really represents so significant a turn in the tide back in favour of patient autonomy. What are the limitations inherent in the judgment and in the guidelines? It is axiomatic that the autonomy right can be owned and exercised only by a *capable* patient: the precondition for autonomy is capacity. It is debatable whether the judgment or the guidelines *in practice*—rather than in theory—really reduce the power of the medical profession. Mason and McCall Smith have observed the guidelines are procedural and not clinical in nature, and take a somewhat pessimistic view of their real potential in curbing the power of health professionals:

[the Court of Appeal] emphasised that the guidelines were, at the end of the day, guidelines only and advised that rigid compliance with them was inappropriate if to do so would put the patient's health at risk. The ball thus remains firmly in the health carers' court—subject, of course, to it being played according to the rules.[39]

Where there is serious doubt about the capacity of a patient, the primary determination is to be made by a psychiatrist (see Guideline 5). Only if doubt remains thereafter will the court become involved, with the consequential protection of the patient through appointment of a guardian *ad litem*, notification of his or her solicitors and, where necessary, of the Official Solicitor.

Capacity—the prerequisite for the exercise of autonomy—remains to be determined by the test formulated by Thorpe J (as he then was) in *Re C (Refusal of Medical Treatment)*[40] and applied in subsequent cases.[41] The test is drawn from clinical psychiatry. The decision is *St George's* itself on the issue of capacity is to be welcomed by feminists, since it put paid to any notion that a woman's mental condition in advanced pregnancy is synonymous with incapacity. The judgment was also significant in holding that:

The [Mental Health] Act cannot be deployed to achieve the detention of an individual against her will merely because her thinking process is unusual, even apparently bizarre and irrational, and contrary to the overwhelming majority of the community at large.[42]

However, on the facts of *St George's* the question of S's capacity was remarkably clear. In other cases there is more doubt, the factual decision as to capacity can be a fine one and the result of applying the *Re C* test can be unpredictable. In *Re MB (Medical Treatment)*[43] the Court of Appeal,

---

[39] *Law and Medical Ethics*, n. 11, above, 269. [40] [1994] 1 FLR 31.
[41] *Re MB (Medical Treatment)* [1997] 2 FLR 426; *Re JT (Adult: Refusal of Medical Treatment)* [1998] 1 FLR 48.
[42] [1998] 2 FLR 728 at 746. [43] [1997] 2 FLR 426.

despite its resonant obiter rhetoric on the absolute autonomy of a competent woman in the late stages of pregnancy to refuse treatment, nevertheless on the facts found the woman to be incompetent. The same occurred in *Rochdale Healthcare NHS Trust* v. *C*.[44] Thus, despite the emphatic statements in both *Re MB* and *St George's* that irrationality is not *per se* sufficient evidence of incapacity, the test of capacity in *Re C* may lead to seemingly capricious results.

Adults and Adolescents: Time to Reconsider?

The strength of the *adult* autonomy principle asserted in *St George's* invites a reconsideration of the autonomy rights of *near*-adults. The decision of the Court of Appeal may provide the necessary impetus to re-evaluate the stark contrast under the present law between the absolute autonomy accorded to adults to refuse treatment and that denied to adolescents. The former indicates an extreme rights approach, the latter extreme paternalism. Is the difference in approach justified?

A well known and controversial line of authority has denied the teenager the right to refuse life-saving treatment. Whilst the decision in *Gillick* v. *West Norfolk and Wisbech Area HA*[45] represented a significant advance in the recognition of the autonomy of the competent minor, subsequent cases have narrowed its scope by drawing the distinction between *consent* to treatment and *refusal* of treatment by a minor. How do the courts arrive at the conclusion in these cases that the treatment is lawful despite the teenager's refusal? The usual device is to hold that the teenager lacks *Gillick* competence in the context of the particular treatment refused. However, such is the strength of the paternalism operating that many of the judgments deny that capacity is the decisive issue, and proceed to weigh a range of considerations in the best interests equation.

Thus in *Re R (a minor)*[46] a young woman of 15 who suffered hallucinations was given anti-psychotic treatment. The Court of Appeal held that a parent's consent can override child's refusal—in other words, that *Gillick* competence is not decisive of the issue—but it distinguished *Gillick* on the facts: the girl here was not competent because of fluctuations in her mental state. In *Re W (a Minor: Medical Treatment)*[47] it was held to be lawful to treat a 16-year-old anorexic against her wishes on the basis that (a) anorexia destroys capacity and the treatment was in her best interests, and (b) section 8(1) of the Family Law Reform Act 1969 does not confer absolute right to refuse medical treatment. In *Re E (A Minor: Wardship) (Medical Treatment)*[48] a Jehovah's Witness aged $15^3/_4$ would not consent to a blood transfusion and knew that he would die as a consequence;

[44] [1997] 1 FCR 274.   [45] [1986] AC 112.   [46] [1992] Fam. 11.
[47] [1992] 4 All ER 627.   [48] [1993] 1 FLR 386.

however, the doctors and the court withheld information from him on precise details of the probable mode of death. Ward J (as he then was) held the young man had no capacity to withhold his consent because he did not fully understand consequences of refusal, but that capacity was in any event not decisive; it was one factor—as was the young man's wish—to be weighed in the 'best interests' exercise. *Re L (Medical Treatment: Gillick Competence)*[49] concerned a Jehovah's Witness of 14 who was mature for her age and a sincere adherent to the faith. She had suffered serious burns which would have led to gangrene and slow death without surgery involving a blood transfusion. The doctor did not explain to her in detail the consequences of refusal, on the ground that they were too shocking. The girl had signed written refusals to blood transfusion and was supported in that by her parents. Sir Stephen Brown P held that the young woman lacked capacity and held that surgery involving blood transfusions was lawful as being in her best interests. She lacked capacity because she did not have all the details necessary to make an informed decision about refusal of treatment. Most recently in *Re M (Medical Treatment Consent)*[50], Johnson J held that it was lawful to transplant a heart into a 15-year-old who had refused her consent on the basis that she did not want to have someone else's heart.

Is this denial of autonomy to adolescents justifiable, when the autonomy right of a person aged 18 is now stated in absolute terms? Mason and McCall Smith have attempted to explain the distinction between consent and refusal:

It is reasonable to suppose, paternalistic though it may sound, that a qualified doctor knows more about the treatment of disease than does a child. Thus, while consent involves acceptance of an experienced view, refusal rejects that experience—and does so from a position of limited understanding. Furthermore, a refusal of medical treatment may close down the options. . . .'[51]

But is this really convincing? One worrying aspect of certain of the decisions mentioned above is that the adolescent is effectively denied capacity by having information withheld. This occurred in both *Re E*, and *Re L*, above, and makes the attainment of *Gillick* competence—which requires a proper appreciation of the treatment consented to or refused—an impossibility.

More fundamentally, the whole issue of refusal of treatment by teenagers invites reconsideration in the light of Professor Freeman's arguments for recognising the autonomy rights of children in 'Taking Children's Rights More Seriously'.[52] Freeman there argues for the equal treatment of children with adults and for their recognition as autonomous beings:

[49] [1998] 2 FLR 810; see McCafferty [1999] *Fam Law* 335.
[50] [1999] 2 FLR 1097.   [51] *Law and Medical Ethics*, n. 11 above, at 260.
[52] In P. Alston, S. Parker, and J. Seymour (eds.), *Children, Rights and the Law* (Oxford, 1992) 52–71.

To believe in autonomy is to believe that anyone's autonomy is as morally significant as anyone else's. Nor does autonomy depend on the stage of life that a person has reached. . . . To respect a child's autonomy is to treat that child as a person and as a rights-holder.[53]

He recognises the need to recognise the welfare rights of children and to 'treat them as persons entitled to have both their present autonomy recognised and their capacity for future autonomy safeguarded',[54] and acknowledges the need particularly for younger children to be protected. In the cases of attempted refusal of treatment by adolescents, however, we are not talking of younger children. It can be argued that the courts should reconsider the extent of the paternalism being exercised in such cases, for all paternalism must be justified. How then to delineate an acceptable boundary for paternalism? Freeman himself suggests[55] the benchmark of principles that would enable children to mature into independent adulthood. Applied literally to the cases mentioned above, such an approach could deny to a teenager the right to refuse life-saving treatment—precisely what the courts do at present. But such a literal application is over-simplistic. Arguably the correct approach is to regard these teenagers with deeply held convictions as already mature and therefore entitled to their full autonomy rights. It remains to be seen whether the decision in *St George's* has repercussions in this sensitive area.

Appendix

GUIDELINES

St George's highlighted some major problems which could arise for hospital authorities when a pregnant woman presented at hospital, the possible need for Caesarean surgery was diagnosed, and there was serious doubt about the patient's capacity to accept or decline treatment. To avoid any recurrence of the unsatisfactory events recorded in this judgment, and after consultation with the President of the Family Division and the Official Solicitor, and in the light of written submissions from Mr Havers and Mr Gordon, we shall attempt to repeat and expand the advice given in *Re MB (Medical Treatment)*.[56] This advice also applies to any cases involving capacity when surgical or invasive treatment may be needed by a patient, whether female or male. References to 'she' and 'he' should be read accordingly. It also extends, where relevant, to medical practitioners and health practitioners generally, as well as to hospital authorities.

The guidelines depend upon basic legal principles which we can summarize:

---

[53] *Ibid.*, at 64–5.   [54] *Ibid.*, at 66.   [55] *Ibid.*, at 67.
[56] [1997] 2 FLR 426.

(i)   They have no application where the patient is competent to accept or refuse treatment. In principle a patient may remain competent notwithstanding detention under the Mental Health Act.

(ii)   If the patient is competent and refuses consent to the treatment an application to the High Court for a declaration would be pointless. In this situation the advice given to the patient should be recorded. For their own protection hospital authorities should seek unequivocal assurances from the patient (to be recorded in writing) that the refusal represents an informed decision: that is, that she understands the nature of and reasons for the proposed treatment, and the risks and likely prognosis involved in the decision to refuse or accept it. If the patient is unwilling to sign a written indication of this refusal, this too should be noted in writing. Such a written indication is merely a record for evidential purposes. It should not be confused with or regarded as a disclaimer.

(iii) If the patient is incapable of giving or refusing consent, either in the long term or temporarily (e.g. due to unconsciousness), the patient must be cared for according to the authority's judgement of the patient's best interests. Where the patient has given an advance directive, before becoming incapable, treatment and care should normally be subject to the advance directive. However, if there is reason to doubt the reliability of the advance directive (for example it may be sensibly be thought not to apply to the circumstances which have arisen), then an application for a declaration may be made.

CONCERN OVER CAPACITY

(iv)   The authority should identify as soon as possible whether there is concern about a patient's competence to consent to or refuse treatment.

(v)   If the capacity of the patient is seriously in doubt it should be assessed as a matter of priority. In many such cases the patient's general practitioner or other responsible doctor may be sufficiently qualified to make the necessary assessment, but in serious or complex cases involving difficult issues about the future health and well-being, or even life, of the patient, the issue of capacity should be examined by an independent psychiatrist, ideally one approved under section 12(2) of the Mental Health Act 1983. If following this assessment there remains a serious doubt about the patient's competence, and the seriousness or complexity of the issues in the particular case may require the involvement of the court, the psychiatrist should further consider whether the patient is incapable by reason of mental disorder of managing her property or affairs. If so the patient may be unable to instruct a solicitor and will require a guardian *ad litem* in any court proceedings. The authority should seek legal advice as quickly as possible. If a declaration is to be sought the patient's solicitors should be informed immediately, and if practicable they should have a proper opportunity to take instructions and apply for legal aid where necessary. Potential witnesses for the authority should be made aware of the criteria laid down in *Re MB* and this case, together with any guidance issued by the Department of Health and the British Medical Association.

(vi) If the patient is unwilling to instruct solicitors, or is believed to be incapable of doing so, the authority or its legal advisors must notify the Official Solicitor and invite him to act as guardian *ad litem*. If the Official Solicitor agrees he will no doubt wish, if possible, to arrange for the patient to be interviewed to ascertain her wishes and to explore the reasons for any refusal or treatment. The Official Solicitor can be contacted through the Urgent Court Business Officer out of office hours on 0207 936 6000.

THE HEARING

(vii) The hearing before the judge should be *inter partes*. As the order made in her absence will not be binding on the patient unless she is represented either by a guardian *ad litem* (if incapable of giving instructions) or (if capable) by counsel or solicitor, a declaration granted *ex parte* is of no assistance to the authority. Although the Official Solicitor will not act for a patient if she is capable of instructing a solicitor, the court may in any event call on the Official Solicitor (who has considerable expertise in these matters) to assist as an *amicus curiae*.

(viii) It is axiomatic that the judge must be provided with accurate and all the relevant information. This should include the reasons for the proposed treatment, the risks involved in the proposed treatment, and in the proceedings with it, whether any alternative treatment exists, and the reason, if ascertainable, why the patient is refusing the proposed treatment. The judge will need sufficient information to reach informed conclusion about the patient's capacity, and, where it arises, the issue of best interest.

(ix) The precise terms of any order should be recorded and approved by the judge before its terms are transmitted to the authority. The patient should be accurately informed of the precise terms.

(x)   Applicants for emergency orders from the High Court made without first issuing and serving the relevant applications and evidence in support have a duty to comply with the procedural requirements (and pay the court fees) as soon as possible after the emergency hearing.

CONCLUSION

There may be occasions when, assuming a serious question arises about the competence of the patient, the situation facing the authority may be so urgent and the consequences so desperate that it is impractical to attempt to comply with these guidelines. The guidelines should be approached for what they are, that is, guidelines. Where delay may itself cause serious damage to the patient's health or put her life at risk then formulaic compliance with these guidelines would be inappropriate.

LEGAL LIMITS: WHEN DOES AUTONOMY IN HEALTH CARE PREVAIL?

Anne Flamme and Heidi Forster

Introduction

Both law and bioethics are concerned with articulating and justifying the permissible scope of individual autonomy in health-care decision-making. While bioethical analysis recognizes values and factors, including autonomy, that influence health-care decision-making, United States case law and statutory doctrines address the extent to which the state may intervene in or regulate individuals' autonomous choices with regard to profound moral decisions about their health and bodies. We first discuss the tension arising between interests that the state asserts in protecting its citizens and the interests of individuals in making their own choices about what happens to their bodies. In an attempt to locate the boundary between individual autonomy and the state's power to intervene in health-care decision-making, we describe: (1) how particular courts understand or depict autonomy in the context of health-care decision-making; (2) the state interests courts recognize that conflict with autonomy; and (3) the analyses courts use to reconcile these interests. We review United States statutory and common law doctrines governing four different health-care decisions: organ donation, refusal of life-sustaining treatment, abortion, and physician-assisted suicide.

Our review of the judicial balancing of individual autonomy against state interests illuminates two concepts of autonomy in health-care decision-making. The first is a physical one, grounded in the notion of bodily integrity and freedom from invasion of one's physical being. The second is a more abstract concept of self-determination, encompassing the liberty to define meaning for oneself and control one's destiny and finding legal protection in the doctrine of substantive due process. We conclude that courts are consistently willing to protect the concept of autonomy grounded in bodily integrity, but are not willing to protect a broader right of non-interference in all personal and intimate decisions. While courts generally will not interfere in individuals' thoughts, values, and beliefs about the quality of their life or their reasons for making their personal choices, courts will place limits on the actualization of those beliefs.

The Tension: Autonomy v. State Interests

INDIVIDUAL AUTONOMY IN HEALTH CARE

In the past twenty-five years, promoting and protecting individual autonomy within health-care has become the paramount concern in bioethics.[1] The principle of autonomy declares that each person has the right to self-determination. In the context of health-care, autonomy is exercised by directing what happens to one's body. Also in the past twenty-five years, patients have been given greater control over their own medical care. Many patients feel they have the right to make their own choices about whether to refuse or accept treatment, whether to have an abortion, and even whether to receive assistance in suicide. Proponents of such autonomy believe that these types of profound, moral decisions are so intimate and personal that interference by the state is both unwelcome and unjust.

As articulated by courts, personal autonomy in health-care decision-making derives from two legal doctrines: a traditional right of bodily integrity, and the constitutional doctrine of substantive due process. The notion of bodily integrity is rooted in the historic, common law right to be free from non-consensual bodily touching or invasion. The legal doctrine of informed consent developed from this physical notion of autonomy: a patient's right to self-determination could only be effectively exercised if the patient possessed the appropriate information to make choices about his medical care.[2] Only when a patient consents may a physician invade the personal being of that individual by providing medical treatment. The right to refuse treatment, another expression of the physical notion of autonomy, is a corollary to the law of informed consent.[3] Treatment without proper consent should not be administered because the 'touching' is an invasion of personal, physical, bodily integrity.

In addition to a clear foundation in the right of bodily integrity, the judiciary's concept of self-determination in health-care decision-making may also be grounded in the constitutional doctrine of substantive due process.[4] While early substantive due process analysis depended upon judicial interpretation of a constitutional right to privacy,[5] the modern

---

[1] See generally T. Beauchamp and J. Childress, *Principles of Bioethics* (4th edn., New York, 1994), 120–41.

[2] *Ibid.* at 142–6. See also W. Curran, M. Hall, M. A. Bobinski, and D. Orientlicher, *Health Care Law and Ethics* (5th edn., New York, 1998), 213–84.

[3] *Cruzan* v. *Dir. Missouri Dep't of Health*, 497 US 261, 270 (1990).

[4] For a discussion of modern substantive due process and related case law, see D. Lively, P. Haddon, D. Roberts, and R. Weaver, *Constitutional Law: Cases, History, and Dialogues* (Cincinnati, Ohio, 1996), 98–185.

[5] *Eisenstadt* v. *Baird*, 405 US 438 (1972); *Stanley* v. *Georgia*, 394 US 557 (1969); *Griswold* v. *Connecticut*, 381 US 479 (1965) (finding the unwritten constitutional right of privacy to exist in the prenumbra of specific guarantees of the Bill of Rights).

doctrine is based upon the Due Process Clause of the Fourteenth Amendment to the United States Constitution,[6] which prohibits the state from depriving citizens of life, liberty, or property without due process of law. Modern substantive due process analysis reflects a court's interpretation of what rights are encompassed within the term 'liberty': whether a particular activity is so crucial to individual liberty, dignity, and autonomy that, even though the right to that activity is not explicitly granted in the Constitution, the court may limit the extent to which a state may regulate it. Those personal rights that are 'implicit in the concept of ordered liberty'[7] attain the status of fundamental rights, and a court will examine any state action that interferes with such rights under its strictest scrutiny. Under the 'strict scrutiny' test, a state must prove that any limitation upon the fundamental right is both justified by a compelling state interest and narrowly drawn to serve that interest. If the court concludes the right at stake is anything less than fundamental, it reviews state action with lesser scrutiny, and in most cases will apply the 'rational relation' test requiring only that a regulation be rationally related to a legitimate state interest.[8]

COUNTERVAILING STATE INTERESTS

Even when state intervention is subjected to strict scrutiny, an individual's legal ability to make personal, intimate, and profound medical decisions is not absolute. States may assert countervailing interests that may be sufficiently compelling to overcome individuals' autonomous choices. As articulated in 1977 in *Superintendent of Belchertown State School* v. *Saikewicz*,[9] countervailing state interests often implicated in cases involving health-care decision-making include the preservation of life, the prevention of suicide, the protection of third parties, and the maintenance of the ethical integrity of the medical profession. As case law has developed and new bioethical issues enter the courtroom, states have asserted these and other related interests.

The asserted state interests stem from the state's power to protect the health, safety, and welfare of its citizens.[10] This power constitutes legal justification for limitations on individual liberty, including restrictions on individuals' rights to make choices about their own bodies. The state may

---

[6] US Const. amend. XIV.

[7] *Palko* v. *Connecticut*, 302 US 319, 325 (1937).

[8] *Meyer* v. *Nebraska*, 262 US. 390, 400 (1923); *Doe* v. *Bolton*, 410 US 179, 194–5, 199 (1973).

[9] *Superintendent of Belchertown State Sch.* v. *Saikewicz*, 373 Mass. 728, 370 NE 2d 417 (1977).

[10] See *Jacobson* v. *Commonwealth of Massachusetts*, 197 US11 (1905) which established the constitutional basis for constraining individual liberties to protect the public health. In both *Casey* and *Cruzan*, the Supreme Court cites *Jacobson* as the authoritative statement of the scope of the state's police power.

also assert that it is attempting to preserve the moral worth of society (e.g. to promote respect for life), or the state may claim it acts to protect citizens who are vulnerable and could easily be victimized by societal influences upon health-care decision-making. Court decisions and statutes establish the permissible scope and terms of individual liberty both by protecting certain personal health-care decisions and by prohibiting others. Courts and legislatures, in their role as developers of the law, balance the rights of the parties involved in health-care decisions.[11] And while courts attempt to protect individual autonomy, they also apply limitations when the exercise of a person's autonomy threatens the liberty of another or conflicts with other legitimate state interests.

The Preservation of Human Life

The preservation of human life frequently constitutes the basis for state intervention in individual health-care decisions. As stated by the *Saikewicz* court, the preservation of human life is the most significant of the asserted state interests.[12] However, courts disagree about its scope and strength. The different analyses generally revolve around whether the state's interest in the preservation of human life is independent and unqualified, or whether certain characteristics of or considerations related to the particular life at issue impact or limit the significance or strength of the state's interest.

The *Saikewicz* court asserted that the state's interest in preserving life was dependent upon the hardship that prolonging the life would impose upon the individual: '[t]he interest of the State in prolonging a life must be reconciled with the interest of an individual to reject the traumatic cost of that prolongation'.[13] The court also reasoned that '[t]here is a substantial distinction in the State's insistence that human life be saved where the affliction is curable, as opposed to the State interest where . . . the issue is . . . when, for how long, and at what cost to the individual that life may be briefly extended'.[14] According to the *Saikewicz* court, the state's interest in preserving human life was strongest when a person was relatively healthy or his or her affliction was curable, but when the person was dying, the state's interest waned.[15] The court mandated that the state's interest in preserving life be balanced against a comparably sacred right of autonomy. The right to act autonomously, characterized by the court as the constitu-

---

[11] For a discussion of court approaches to balancing patient autonomy and countervailing state interests, see A. Meisel, *The Right to Die* (2nd edn., New York, 1995), §§ 8.14–8.19.

[12] *Saikewicz*, n. 9, above, at 741.

[13] *Ibid.*, at 742.   [14] *Ibid.*

[15] Similar to the *Quinlan* court, in the recent *Gilgunn* case in Massachusetts, the judge explained to the jury that the state's interest in life wanes as a patient's condition is terminal and becomes incurable and that the state's interest is strongest when a patient is relatively young, healthy, and curable: *Gilgunn* v. *Massachusetts General Hospital*, No. 92–4820 (Mass. Super. Ct. Suffolk Cty., 22 Apr. 1995).

tional right to privacy, was described as 'an expression of the sanctity of individual free choice and self-determination'.[16]

In its earlier case of *In the Matter of Karen Quinlan*,[17] the New Jersey Supreme Court had also rendered the state's interest in preserving human life dependent upon the patient's condition, opining that the right to refuse life-sustaining treatment should grow as the degree of bodily invasion required to prolong life increased and the patient's prognosis dimmed. The New Jersey Supreme Court, in *In re Conroy*,[18] further limited the significance of the state's interest in preserving life by finding that the state's interest arose only when a patient wanted his life preserved. The state's purpose was only to protect patients from having their lives taken involuntarily; the state did not have an interest in preserving an individual's life apart from the individual's own autonomous desire to continue living.[19]

As suggested in *Conroy*, if the state's interest in preserving a person's life exists only in so far as the patient wishes to continue living, then the court has no need to balance the state's interest against the individual's interest because the patient's own interest in continuing life will be the determining factor.[20] If the state's interest in preserving life has some content that is independent of the individual's interest, as the *Saikewicz* and *Quinlan* courts suggest, then the challenging task of how to balance the competing interests arises.[21] For example, if a patient's right to refuse life-sustaining treatment is balanced against countervailing state interests, how should the right be limited? Should courts limit patients' rights based upon, for example, the type of treatment at issue (ventilator *v.* antibiotics) or the patient's medical condition (end stage *v.* acute event)?

The perception that the state's interest in preserving human life depended on the patient's condition and desire to live was rejected by the United States Supreme Court in its landmark case, *Cruzan v. Director, Missouri Dep't of Health*.[22] The Court stated in dicta that 'a state may properly decline to make judgments about the "quality" of life that a particular individual may enjoy, and simply assert an unqualified interest in the preservation of human life to be weighed against the constitutionally protected interests of the individual'.[23] Unlike the lower courts, the Supreme Court deemed that the state did possess an unqualified interest in preserving human life that was independent of the wishes of the individual.[24]

---

[16] *Saikewicz*, n. 9, above, at 742.
[17] *In the Matter of Karen Quinlan*, 355 A 2d 647 (NJ 1976).
[18] *In re Conroy*, 486 A 2d 1209 (NJ 1985).   [19] *Ibid.*
[20] Curran *et al.*, n. 2, above, 584.   [21] *Ibid.*
[22] *Cruzan*, 497 US 261 (1990).
[23] *Ibid.*, at 282. Compare with Stevens J's dissent. Stevens objected to the Missouri policy of 'equating [Cruzan's] life with the biological persistence of her bodily functions'; *ibid.* at 345 (Stevens J dissenting).
[24] In the dissent in *Cruzan*, however, Brennan J was offended by the notion that a general-

Cruzan decided, however, that the state's interest in preserving life carried little weight when balanced against a competent person's right to refuse treatment.[25] Almost without exception,[26] in the context of life-sustaining treatment refusals, 'the right to self-determination ordinarily outweighs any countervailing state interests, and competent persons are generally permitted to refuse medical treatment, even at the risk of death. ... A competent person's common-law and constitutional rights do not depend on the quality or value of his life.'[27] Related to the idea that courts allow patients' autonomous choice to prevail over a state interest in preserving life, courts also consistently refuse to impose quality of life judgements on patients. For example, in *Bouvia* v. *Superior Court*,[28] the court stated that it was Ms Bouvia's choice to decide alone whether her life had meaning; it was not a choice for the state, doctors, or lawyers to make. 'A person of adult years and in sound mind has the right, in the exercise of control over his own body, to determine whether or not to submit to lawful medical treatment. ... It follows that such a patient has the right to refuse *any* medical treatment, even that which may save or prolong her life.'[29]

Despite this consensus that the individual's interest in refusing treatment prevails over the state's interest in preserving life, courts continue to recognize the weight of the state's interest in preserving life in the contexts of abortion, in which the state asserts an interest in preserving the foetus's potential life, and of physician-assisted suicide. As will be discussed below, courts consider the preservation of life to be a legitimate state interest which, if sufficiently compelling, may prevail over individual autonomy.

The Prevention of Suicide

The second state interest developed in *Saikewicz* is the prevention of suicide. In refusal of treatment cases, this interest is now often considered anachronistic.[30] Attempting suicide is not a crime in any state, although all

---

ized state interest in life could overcome a person's liberty interest to forego life-sustaining treatment. One's rights, he argued, may not be sacrificed to make society feel good. He said 'the state has no legitimate general interest in someone's life, completely abstracted from the interest of the person living that life, that could outweigh the person's choice to avoid medical treatment': see *Cruzan*, at 313–14.

[25] See below, 150.

[26] On rare occasions a patient's right to refuse treatment is subordinated to the state's interest in preserving life. See, e.g., *In re Caulk* 480 A 2d 93 (NH 1984) (state ordered prisoner to be forcibly fed).

[27] *Ibid.*, at 1225–6. Similarly, a New Jersey court in *In re Peter* stated that '[m]edical choices ... are not to be decided by societal standards of reasonableness or normalcy. Rather, it is the patient's preferences—formed by his or her unique personal experiences—that should control': *In re Peter*, 529 A 2d 419 (NJ 1987).

[28] *Bouvia* v. *Superior Ct.* 179 Cal. App. 3d 1127 (1986).

[29] *Ibid.*, at 300 (emphasis in original).

[30] B. Furrow, T. Greaney, S. Johnson, T. Jost, and R. Schwartz, *Bioethics: Health Care Law and Ethics* (3rd edn., St. Paul, Minn., 1997), 239.

states do have policies discouraging suicide. Courts almost summarily dismiss the prevention of suicide as an objection to the autonomous choice of a competent individual to withdraw life-sustaining treatment. In *Saikewicz*, the court stated that '[t]he interest in protecting against suicide seems to require little if any discussion. . . . There is no connection between the conduct here in issue and any state concern to prevent suicide.'[31] Courts also claim that refusing medical treatment does not necessarily constitute suicide. In *Saikewicz* and *Conroy* cases, the courts focused on causation. The patient's underlying disease constituted the cause of the death, not the physical act of removing mechanical ventilation. The courts in those cases also focused on the intent of the patient. The patient had no specific intent to die or commit suicide, but rather to remove the burdens of the medical treatment or to relieve suffering. In addition, *Saikewicz* claimed that the state interest in this area lies in the prevention of 'irrational self destruction',[32] which would not include the rational choice of a competent person to remove life sustaining treatment when death is inevitable and the treatment burdensome.[33]

The state's interest in the prevention of suicide is not compelling in refusal of treatment cases mainly because the cause of death and the patient's intent are distinguishable from the general understanding of suicide. In the context of physician-assisted suicide, however, the state's interest in preventing suicide carries greater weight. Although the patients requesting their physicians' assistance are terminally ill, the cause of death is the lethal medication ingested by the patients. In addition, the patient takes an active role in bringing about his or her death by intentionally ingesting the drugs. As opposed to the context of patient refusal of treatment, there is no burdensome, invasive medical treatment which is being refused—the patient simply intends to end his or her life. Therefore, the state's interest in preventing suicide and in preventing physicians from assisting in suicide has more force, as discussed below.

The Protection of Innocent Third Parties

The third interest of the state involves protecting the interests of innocent third parties. The *Saikewicz* court stated that when 'the State's interest in preserving an individual's life [is] not sufficient, by itself, to outweigh the individual's interest in the exercise of free choice, the possible impact on minor children would be a factor which might have a critical effect on the outcome of the balancing process'.[34] States generally assert this interest when an adult patient chooses to refuse life-sustaining treatment, and, the

---

[31] *Saikewicz*, 373 Mass. at 743, n. 11.   [32] *Ibid.*

[33] Compare with *Cruzan*, 497 US at 294–8. Scalia J in his *Cruzan* concurrence claimed that there is no distinction between refusing life sustaining treatment and committing suicide.

[34] *Saikewicz*, 373 Mass. at 742–3 (quoting *Holmes* v. *Silver Cross Hosp. of Joliet, Ill.*, 340 F Supp. 125 (D Ill. 1972)).

state anticipates, the patient's minor child would suffer 'from the emotional and financial damage which may occur as a result of the decision of a competent adult to refuse life-saving or life-prolonging treatment'.[35] In some cases involving the refusal of a blood transfusion by a Jehovah's Witness patient, courts have ordered the transfusion to avoid a child's loss of a parent.[36] This state interest in preventing the abandonment of children held more force in the past. In more recent cases, courts have generally recognized a patient's right to refuse life-sustaining treatment despite her minor dependents.[37]

The Ethical Integrity of the Medical Profession

The last state interest developed in *Saikewicz* was the maintenance of the ethical integrity of the medical profession. Courts have recognized this interest as asserted by states in two different manners. First, states might assert this interest when they perceive an individual's autonomous health-care decision to conflict with a medical professional's societal role and purpose. In *Saikewicz*, the state argued that permitting a patient to refuse life-sustaining treatment contrasted with the physician's goal of healing and preserving life. As noted by the court, 'the force and impact of this interest [has been] lessened by the prevailing medical ethical standards'.[38] Because current ethical standards permitted discontinuation and refusal of medical treatment by competent patients, the court found the interest to be unsubstantiated.[39] This interest has been upheld, however, in the contexts of abortion and physician-assisted suicide, in which states have argued that physicians' participation in patients' decisions to terminate pregnancy or take action to end life desecrates the physician's role as healer and protector of life.[40]

The state's interest in the ethical integrity of the medical profession has also arisen in cases in which patients make autonomous choices about their care to which their physicians have personal, moral objections. In *Brophy* v. *New England Sinai Hospital*,[41] the court stated that 'there is nothing in *Saikewicz* and its progeny which would justify compelling

---

[35] *Ibid.*, at 742.

[36] See *Application of the President and Directors of Georgetown College, Inc.* 331 F 2d 1000, 9 ALR 3d 1367 (DC. Cir., 1964) (stating that '[t]he state, as *parens patriae*, will not allow a parent to abandon a child, and so it should not allow this most ultimate of voluntary abandonments. The patient had a responsibility to the community to care for her infant. Thus the people had an interest in preserving the life of this mother').

[37] See *In re Debreuil* 629 So.2d 819 (1993); *Fosmire* v. *Nicoleau* 551 NE 2d 77 (NY 1990); *Stamford Hospital* v. *Vega* 674 A 2d 821 (Conn. 1996). Also see *Pub. Health Trust of Dade County* v. *Wons* 541 So.2d 96 (Fla. 1989). In this case although the trial judge ordered a transfusion and reasoned that 'minor children have a right to be reared by two loving parents, a right which overrides the mother's rights of free religious exercise and privacy', the case was overturned. The appellate court ruled that while it is important for children to have two parents, the state's interest in protecting children 'is not sufficient to override fundamental constitutional rights': *ibid.*

[38] *Saikewicz*, 373 Mass. at 743.   [39] *Ibid.*   [40] See below, 153.

[41] *Brophy* v. *New England Sinai Hosp.*, 497 NE 2d 626 (Mass. 1986).

medical professionals ... to take active measures which are contrary to their view of their ethical duty toward their patients'.[42] When a patient's autonomous choices conflict with a physician's or hospital's ethical views, courts have advocated the patient's transfer to another physician or hospital.[43]

Judicial Resolution in Four Types of Health Care Decisions

Cases in which states exercise their police power to limit or intervene in individual health-care decision-making reflect the clash between the individual's right of self-determination in health care and the state's countervailing interests. In this section, we explore how courts resolve this tension between individual autonomy and state interests in four types of health-care decisions: organ donation, refusals of life-sustaining treatment, abortion, and physician-assisted suicide. Reviewing cases in each of these arenas, we analyse the scope of autonomy recognized by the courts, their consideration of the countervailing state interests, and the analyses they employ to determine whose interests prevail.

ORGAN DONATION

The context of organ donation offers a clear example of the pre-eminence of the physical, bodily concept of individual autonomy over countervailing state interests. In *McFall* v. *Shimp*,[44] a Pennsylvania court refused to order one individual to donate bone marrow necessary to save the life of his cousin. While the court characterized the refusal to donate as 'morally indefensible', it upheld the individual's autonomous interest in doing so. Compelling submission to a bodily intrusion for the sake of another would 'defeat the sanctity of the individual' which constituted 'the very essence of our free society'.[45] According to the court, protecting the bodily integrity of the potential donor outweighed the state's interest in preserving the life of the would-be recipient. Even when the donation was needed to preserve a life, the court ruled, an individual was not required to sacrifice control over his physical body for the sake of another.

---

[42] *Ibid.*, at 639.
[43] See also *Gray* v. *Romeo* 697 F Supp. 580 (DRI 1988) (court allowed hospital to transfer patient but held that the hospital must respect patient's wish to refuse artificial nutrition and hydration if the patient could not be promptly transferred). In other cases, such as *In re Jobes*, 529 A 2d 434 (NJ 1987), the court forced the hospital to respect the patient's wishes, although a transfer may have been possible, because the hospital's policies on refusal of artificial feeding were not disclosed to patient before entering the hospital.
[44] *McFall* v. *Shimp* 10 Pa. D & C 3d 90 (1978).
[45] *Ibid.*, at 91.

REFUSAL OF LIFE-SUSTAINING TREATMENT

In some of the most critiqued and heralded cases in the past thirty years, courts have struggled to establish and articulate a right on behalf of patients to choose to refuse life-sustaining medical treatment. Individuals' exercise of this right to refuse medical treatment has been challenged by claims of state interests in protecting human life.[46] The right to refuse treatment is usually based on the premise that a person rationally may decide that death is preferable to the pain, expense, and inconvenience of life.[47] This process of weighing the value of life and death is generally based on the person's personal history, religious, and moral factors, and individual sensitivity to a number of different factors.[48] The right to make personal choices finds its philosophical basis in the principle of autonomy and has been given legal substantiation in several court cases.

As detailed above, lower court cases addressing individual treatment refusals such as *Quinlan* and *Saikewicz* described the state's interest in preserving life as qualified and dependent upon certain characteristics of the individual whose life was at issue, such as the gravity of the patient's condition and his desire to continue living. In *Cruzan*, the United States Supreme Court rejected the idea that the state's interest was necessarily so qualified. While the Court's conclusion on this point suggested a broader range for the assertion of the state's interest in life and a narrower scope of individual autonomy, the manner in which the Court depicted autonomy, in its physical, bodily sense, resulted in its ruling to affirm an individual's right to refuse life-sustaining treatment.

The majority opinion in *Cruzan* explored whether the right to refuse treatment derived either solely from the common law right to bodily integrity and informed consent, or from both the common law right and the constitutional privacy right.[49] The Court explicitly declined to hold that a generalized, constitutional fundamental right of privacy encompassed a right to refuse treatment. Instead, the Court analysed the issue in terms of a Fourteenth Amendment liberty interest, implicitly finding that the right of bodily integrity and informed consent was not itself sufficient to substantiate the right of a competent individual to refuse life-saving medical treatment.

The Court avoided a direct answer to the question whether a constitutional right to die existed, but it permitted an inference to be drawn from prior cases that competent adults have a constitutionally protected liberty interest in refusing all unwanted medical treatment.[50] The historical common law prohibition against the unwanted touching of one person by

---

[46] See above, 144.   [47] Furrow *et al.*, n. 29, above, 241.
[48] *Ibid.*
[49] *Cruzan* 497 US 271–2 (describing *Saikewicz, Storar*, and *Conroy*).
[50] *Ibid.*, at 278.

another became the basis for the Court's characterization of a decision to refuse life-saving medical treatment as an individual liberty interest protected by the Fourteenth Amendment. Thus the Court collapsed an individual's right to be free of unwanted bodily invasion with the liberty right to make important personal decisions. While expressing that the state's interest in preserving life might exist independently of the patient's interest in that life, the Court ruled that the individual's autonomous decision to avoid a violation of bodily integrity must prevail so long as that preference could be established according to procedural safeguards. As stated by the Court, 'no right is held more sacred, or is more carefully guarded . . . than the right of every individual to the possession and control of his own person'.[51]

<h2 style="text-align:center">ABORTION</h2>

Whether a woman's autonomy encompasses the right to terminate her pregnancy by abortion has been one of the most controversial issues courts in this country have been asked to decide. How the United States Supreme Court perceived the scope of autonomy in *Roe* v. *Wade*[52] and *Planned Parenthood* v. *Casey*[53] drew out the more subtle debate about whether autonomy in health care encompasses simply the right to control one's physical body and to protect oneself from bodily invasion, or whether autonomy includes the broader ability to control one's destiny and act on one's beliefs regarding the meaning of one's existence. The Court's conclusions in these cases support that *autonomy* understood in its limited, physical sense obtains greater protection against state intervention than the latter, broader right to self-determination.

In *Roe*, the Court compared a woman's abortion decision to other personal choices that have obtained historical protection from state interference, including marriage, procreation, and family relationships. The Court recognized numerous harms to the individual that might arise from state prohibition of abortion, noting the distress, psychological harms, and stigma that might arise from forcing women into a life and future of

---

[51] *Ibid.*, at 269 (quoting *Union Pac. R.R. Co.* v. *Botsford* 141 US 250, 251 (1891)). Despite *Cruzan*'s failure explicitly to affirm a fundamental right to refuse life-sustaining treatment, subsequent courts and commentators commonly rely upon *Cruzan* when asserting that such a constitutional right does exist. Some commentators have criticized *Cruzan* for this failure, and for the Court's resulting conclusion that the state could properly impose a higher evidentiary standard for the incompetent patient's wishes before discontinuing treatment. The Court, however, perceived the state's clear and convincing requirement as a procedural safeguard that enhanced individual autonomy by ensuring accurate understanding of an individual's wishes. 'The choice between life and death is a deeply personal decision of obvious and overwhelming finality. We believe Missouri may legitimately seek to safeguard the personal element of this choice through the imposition of heightened evidentiary requirements': *ibid.* at 281.

[52] 410 US 113 (1973).   [53] 505 US 833 (1992).

unwed motherhood in addition to specific and direct threats to the
woman's physical health.[54] Unwilling to deny women the choice of avoiding such harms, the Court concluded that the abortion decision fell within
a fundamental right of privacy that emanated from the Fourteenth
Amendment's guarantee of personal liberty.[55]

The right was not absolute, however. Because of the foetus's physical
dependence upon the pregnant woman for its potential life, the pregnant
woman 'cannot be isolated in her privacy'.[56] The Court recognized the
important state interests in the woman's decision: safeguarding her own
health and life, maintaining the ethical integrity of the medical profession
(as argued by the state, an interest not served if medical professionals
participate in the destruction of potential human life), and protecting the
life of the unborn foetus.[57] Weighing the state interests against the
woman's autonomy, the Court enacted the trimester framework and
concluded that the state's respective interests became sufficiently
compelling to sustain regulation of factors governing a woman's abortion
decision at the point of foetal viability.[58]

In *Casey*, the Supreme Court found that the nature of autonomy implicated in a woman's abortion decision was even broader than that articulated in *Roe*. Yet, simultaneously, the Court endorsed heightened
regulation of that decision. *Casey* described the liberty interests at issue in
the abortion context in extremely expansive language that supported a
fuller, richer conception of individual autonomy than that derived from
the right of bodily integrity alone. Recognizing the interests protected in
earlier decisions related to marriage, procreation, contraception, and
family, the Court stated:

These matters, involving the most intimate and personal choices a person may
make in a lifetime, choices central to personal dignity and autonomy, are central to
the liberty protected by the Fourteenth Amendment. At the heart of liberty is the
right to define one's own concept of existence, of meaning, of the universe, and of
the mystery of human life. Beliefs about these matters could not define the attributes of personhood were they formed under compulsion of the State.[59]

Thus while the Court upheld greater restrictions on the decision to
terminate a pregnancy, *Casey* suggested that the liberty protected by the
Due Process Clause encompasses an individual's definition of meaningful-
ness for her own existence. As the Court stated, liberty required that a
woman's own understanding of her role shape her destiny. 'Her suffering
is too intimate and personal for the State to insist, without more, upon its
own vision of the woman's role. . . . The destiny of the woman must be
shaped to a large extent on her own conception of her spiritual imperatives

---

54 410 US at 153.   55 *Ibid.*, at 152–3.   56 *Ibid.*, at 158.
57 *Ibid.*, at 154.   58 *Ibid.*, at 162–4.   59 505 US at 851.

and her place in society.'[60] In *Casey*, the autonomy protected by substantive due process was broader than an individual's physical boundaries: the woman's claim 'to retain the ultimate control *over her destiny* and her body' was 'implicit in the meaning of liberty'.[61]

Even as its expression of the scope of autonomy expanded, the Court permitted heightened regulation of its exercise based on important and legitimate state interests. Abandoning the trimester framework of *Roe*, the Court developed the 'undue burden' standard to define the boundary between the permissible exercise of autonomy and the state's countervailing interests.[62] The woman's right to autonomy existed alongside the state's interest in protecting the unborn child throughout the entire pregnancy. Thus the state's interest could be expressed in the form of regulations at any time, prior to viability or after, though the regulations could never unduly burden the woman's right. Any state law that acted as a substantial obstacle to, or placed an undue burden on, a woman's access to an abortion and her exercise of autonomy was deemed unconstitutional.

PHYSICIAN-ASSISTED SUICIDE

In *Washington v. Glucksberg*,[63] one of two companion cases upholding state bans against physician-assisted suicide decided in 1997,[64] the Supreme Court continued its exploration of the scope of individual autonomy and its relationship to state interests in health-care decision-making. Depending heavily on history and tradition to substantiate its conclusions both about the nature of autonomy and the legitimacy of the state's asserted interests, the Court denied constitutional protection to a concept of autonomy that was not firmly bounded by the limits of bodily integrity, and explicitly rejected the idea that substantive due process encompassed a sweeping liberty right to make personal, intimate health-care decisions.

The portion of the Court's analysis that is most interesting for exploring the scope of individual autonomy is its response to the plaintiffs' contention that the asserted interest in assistance in suicide was consistent with the Court's substantive due process precedents. The plaintiffs argued that the right to die and the choice regarding the manner and time of one's death were analogous to two personal rights of self-determination previously

---

[60] *Ibid.*, at 852.   [61] *Ibid.*, at 869 (emphasis added).   [62] *Ibid.*, at 875–6.
[63] 117 S Ct. 2258 (1997).

[64] In both *Glucksberg* and *Vacco v. Quill*, 117 S Ct. 2293 (1997), the Supreme Court upheld state statutes banning physician-assisted suicide. Both cases involved similar statutes that defined assisted suicide as either knowingly or intentionally causing or aiding another to attempt or commit suicide, and subjected those convicted under the statutes to monetary penalties and/or imprisonment. Also in both cases, the plaintiffs were dying patients and the physicians who cared for them. The cases differed, however, in the constitutional arguments set forth. The plaintiffs in *Quill* argued that the ban unconstitutionally violated the Equal Protection Clause of the Fourteenth Amendment, which we will not address here.

upheld by the Court: (1) the right inferred in *Cruzan* to refuse unwanted medical treatment, and (2) a woman's right to reproductive choice protected in *Casey*.

The plaintiffs argued that these cases described a general tradition of 'self-sovereignty', and directed that the choice to die, and assistance in realizing that choice, were among the 'basic and intimate exercises of personal autonomy'[65] that obtained the status of fundamental rights protected by the Due Process Clause. According to the plaintiffs, because the constitutional principle behind recognizing the patient's liberty to direct the withdrawal of artificial life support applied at least as strongly to the choice to hasten impending death by consuming lethal medication, *Cruzan* directed constitutional protection of assisted suicide. Moreover, citing *Casey*, ' "[l]ike the decision of whether or not to have an abortion, the decision how and when to die is one of 'the most intimate and personal choices a person may make in a lifetime,' a choice 'central to personal dignity and autonomy' " '.[66]

In response, the Court explicitly and flatly denied that *Cruzan* and *Casey* had protected individual decisions in those cases because they were important, intimate, and personal.[67] As stated by the Court, the right assumed in *Cruzan* was not simply deduced from abstract concepts of personal autonomy. Again, it derived from historical and traditional protection of bodily integrity and informed consent.

And in *Casey*, the Court explained, it may have employed language that was descriptive of intimate and personal choices but it did so to reflect the depth of the roots of protected decisions and activities in our history and traditions. While *Casey* recognized that liberty necessarily included freedom of conscience and belief about ultimate considerations, the Court said, the opinion had concluded that the abortion decision was more than a philosophic exercise; it was an act 'fraught with consequences for others', which might include consequences for the life or potential life that was aborted.[68] According to the Court, '[t]hat many of the rights and liberties protected by the Due Process Clause sound in personal autonomy does not warrant the sweeping conclusion that any and all important, intimate and personal decisions are so protected ... and *Casey* did not suggest otherwise'.[69] Requiring entrenchment in historical tradition such as the right of bodily integrity, the *Glucksberg* Court protected a notion of individual autonomy that was limited by the body's physical properties.

Though the decision to commit suicide might well be personal and profound, the Court asserted, the act obtained no historical legal protection.

[65] 117 S Ct. at *36.
[66] *Ibid.*, at *41 (citing *Compassion in Dying* v. *Washington* 79 F 3d 790, 813–14 (1996)).
[67] *Ibid.*, at *42.
[68] *Ibid.* (citing *Casey*, 505 US at 852).
[69] *Ibid.* (citing *San Antonio Indep. Sch. Dist.* v. *Rodriquez* 411 US 1, 33–5 (1973)).

The Due Process Clause protected only those fundamental rights and liberties that were objectively, deeply rooted in the nation's history and tradition.[70] Moreover, the Court stated, substantive due process analysis required a careful description of the asserted fundamental liberty interest. Rejecting the numerous descriptions provided by the respondents in the case, which included 'a right to "determine the time and manner of one's death," the "right to die," a "liberty to choose how to die," and right to "control of one's final days," "the right to choose a humane, dignified death," and "the liberty to shape death" ',[71] the Court characterized the interest at stake as the right to assistance in suicide.[72] Because neither suicide nor assistance in suicide obtained the status of a fundamental liberty interest, the state needed to establish only that its ban was rationally related to legitimate state interests.[73]

The Court recognized several state interests as relevant in the assisted suicide context. The state of Washington had posited that the ban furthered the state's interest in preserving life, maintaining the integrity of medical professionals as healers in society, and protecting vulnerable groups against abuse and neglect. Warding against a slippery slope from assisted suicide to euthanasia, the Court agreed that these were legitimate state interests.[74]

The Court's analysis to determine which interest prevailed echoed the majority in *Cruzan*. The Court concluded that the state's interest in preserving life was unqualified, and that the lives of the terminally ill, disabled, and elderly must be no less valued than lives of young and healthy individuals. As the choice to receive assistance in dying did not obtain protection as a fundamental right, the interests of the state prevailed.[75]

Despite the Court's rejection of constitutional protection to individuals' right to make personal, intimate health-care decisions, *Glucksberg* reveals that a majority of the Supreme Court Justices do espouse a broader description of personal autonomy in health-related decisions. Stevens J described *Cruzan* as 'embrace[ing] a far broader and more basic concept of freedom that is even older than the common law . . . her interest in dignity, and in determining the character of the memories that will survive long after her death'.[76] Whatever the outer limits of the concept of protected liberty may be, Stevens stated, 'it definitely includes protection for matters "central to personal dignity and autonomy" '.[77] In O'Connor J's concurrence, joined by Stevens, Souter, Ginsburg and Breyer, she aligned with the majority opinion because she agreed there is no right to commit suicide, and therefore the right to assistance in suicide cannot exist. However,

[70] *Ibid.*, at *36, *39–40.   [71] 117 S Ct. 2258, syllabus, paragraph (b).
[72] *Ibid.*, at *35.   [73] *Ibid.*, at *43.   [74] *Ibid.*, at *54.
[75] *Ibid.*, at *50–6.   [76] *Ibid.*, at *68–9.
[77] *Ibid.*, at 71 (citing *Casey* 505 US at 851).

O'Connor's concurrence suggested that liberty might include a terminally ill, competent individual's effort to seek to end his suffering, so long as the 'laboratory' of state democratic processes established appropriate procedures for negotiating individual liberty rights with the state's interest in protecting vulnerable citizens.[78]

Finally, Souter J emphasized that the liberty protected by the Due Process Clause 'compris[es] a continuum of rights to be free from "arbitrary impositions and purposeless restraints" ',[79] and demands justification from states in proportion to the importance of the interest being asserted by the individual.[80] Moreover, specifically addressing individual decisions in health care, Souter cites *Roe*'s acknowledgment that 'the good physician is not just a mechanic of the human body whose services have no bearing on a person's moral choices, but one who does more than treat symptoms, one who ministers to the patient'.[81] According to Souter J, the idea of the physician serving the whole person, a 'source of the high value traditionally placed on the medical relationship',[82] grounded the individual decisions involved in abortion and assisted suicide in the historical traditions of the USA that were requisites of the substantive due process analysis.[83]

Conclusion

Throughout fluctuations in courts' views on the scope of personal autonomy in health-care decision-making, the right of self-determination that has consistently been protected by the courts has remained bounded by an individual's right to control his physical body. Individual liberty may encompass the right to believe whatever one does about one's destiny, and the meaning of one's existence. But when actualizing one's concept of autonomy or implementing the beliefs requires the contribution or participation of another individual, courts have not been willing to afford the shield of constitutional protection to that component of autonomy.

The case of organ donation demonstrates most clearly that autonomy in the sense of protecting one's bodily integrity is pre-eminent; even where the state might preserve a life it may not compel an individual to donate an organ. And courts consistently affirm individuals' rights to protect their bodies from unwanted physical intrusions by refusing even life-sustaining medical treatment. But in the abortion context, where the choice to terminate a pregnancy extends beyond the limits of the woman's body, requiring, in the state's view, the sacrifice of the foetus's potential life, individual

---

[78] 117 S Ct. 2258, syllabus, paragraph (b) at *58.
[79] *Ibid.*, at *107 (citing *Griswold* v. *Connecticut*, 381 US at 500, and *Poe* v. *Ullman*, 367 US at 543 (Harlan J dissenting)).
[80] *Ibid.*, at *102.   [81] *Ibid.*, at *129.
[82] *Ibid.*, at *129 (citing *Roe* 410 US at 153; *Griswold* 381 US at 482).
[83] *Ibid.*, at *129–30.

decision-making can be regulated or even restricted entirely. Regardless of whether the foetus obtains the rights and protections of personhood, courts and legislatures accord the foetus protection of its own bodily integrity. And where an individual must make a positive claim soliciting the assistance of another in actualizing his belief that the intrusions of medical treatment upon his body and the extent of his suffering are intolerable, such as in the context of physician-assisted suicide, the claim is excluded from the United States Supreme Court's conception of the protected sphere of autonomy. Autonomy as a broad right to determine one's own destiny fails to reach fundamental status, and states may impose limitations in furtherance of asserted, countervailing interests.

In some ways, this rule makes sense. It mirrors First Amendment doctrine that affords unlimited protection to belief but justifies limitations on realizing those beliefs through conduct by invoking the principle of doing no harm to others and others' negative liberty rights not to participate in objectionable activity. The rule is also consistent with the concept of ordered liberty in a constitutional democracy, in which one's freedom is bounded when it interferes with the freedom of another or violates societal mandates.

However, as ongoing debate over assisted suicide suggests, the modern analysis is not entirely satisfying. The Supreme Court has continued to insist that the law look backward to history and tradition for guidance on whether a right is fundamental. In the Court's view, this backward-looking approach limits the subjectivity that is necessarily present in due-process judicial review. Moreover, the Court has expressed, by establishing a threshold requirement before requiring more than a reasonable relation to a legitimate state interest to justify state action, the approach also avoids the need for complex balancing of competing interests in every case.

However, the requirement that a right must have a foundation in history and tradition before it may be deemed fundamental in some ways seems mismatched to current questions of autonomy in health care. Courts and analysts may wish to consider whether the capacities created by modern medical technology—to sustain existence in ways that some see as being suspended between life and death, to derive benefits from the use of human tissue and organs in ways once thought impossible, even to create human existence where previously it could not be done—may require inquiry into values and rights that cannot be found in history and tradition.

Genetics and Cloning

LAW, SOCIETY, AND THE NEW GENETICS

*Robert Dingwall**

It has been suggested that, if the nineteenth century was the century of chemistry and the twentieth the century of physics, the twenty-first will be the century of biology. The technologies unlocked by the specification of the structure of DNA and subsequent fundamental advances in molecular biology promise—or threaten—to reshape human relations with the natural world as much as have the contributions of organic chemistry and nuclear physics. Alongside this science of small entities, we have also seen an upsurge in the corresponding science of large entities or systems which has at different times variously been termed social biology, sociobiology, or population biology. In the space between these levels, we find a science of the interaction or, more particularly, of the implications of the micro for the macro. Much confusion can arise, and has arisen, from the assimilation of these levels to one perceived social or scientific movement, the so-called 'New Genetics'. This paper attempts to demonstrate a sociological perspective on the social implications of this new technology and to contrast this with the currently dominant voices of bioethical commentary originating from philosophy, theology, and critical theory. The first section defines and distinguishes the levels of the scientific movement. The following sections examine each level in turn through a socio-legal lens to identify the issues that they seem to raise for law, policy, and social analysis. The final section considers the extent to which these issues can be resolved by reference to some disinterested body of ethical analysis or whether the claims of bioethics should be seen as part of the problem as much as part of the answer.

The 'New Genetics'

The scientific movement known loosely as the 'New Genetics' can be seen as three different enterprises with different agendas and inspirations. One

* I am grateful to Peter Bartlett, Kath Melia, Paul Martin, and Alison Pilnick for their comments and suggestions on previous versions of this paper.

is the research in molecular biology inspired by Watson and Crick's specification of the structure of DNA in 1953 and the subsequent development
of techniques to study the arrangement of genes within genomes, the isolation of particular genes, the comparison of genomes from different species
or kingdoms, the asexual reproduction of genes or genomes (cloning), and
the cutting and pasting of genes from one genome to another in order to
transfer desired properties. Ultimately, the science promises an ability to
correct 'faulty' genes and to assemble genomes which contain constella-
tions of desired properties rather than an individual one—tomatoes, for
example, which not only rot more slowly but also have a particular size,
shape, and skin colour, process fertilizers more efficiently, and tolerate
lower night-time temperatures. The second is the research for which I shall
use the older term 'social biology', a study of the distribution of traits
believed to have a genetic foundation at a population level. The third over-
laps with both of the others but is more conveniently distinguished. It may
be termed socio-molecular biology and summed up in the notion that
certain behaviours have a foundation in specific genes. Socio-molecular
biology seeks to explain specific dimensions of human behaviour in terms
of specific genes or combinations of genes. It might be caricatured as the
'gene for . . .' science as in 'the gene for alcoholism', 'the gene for criminality', 'the gene for homosexuality', etc. To the extent that such associations
can be identified, various kinds of intervention may be proposed.

Molecular Biology

The bioethics agenda for molecular biology has been concerned primarily
with the normative questions that are thought to arise from the manipulation of the 'essence of life' and from the implications of selective reproduction. There is, for example, a critique of the extension of patenting to the
specification of genes which argues that it should not be possible to establish private property rights in what may be perceived either as Divine
Creation or as the common heritage of humankind.[1] Another instance may
be the questioning of cloning on the basis that it undermines the natural
lottery of mating and the benefits that this brings in terms of the promotion of social relations and interdependency, to say nothing of the possible
abuse of the technology to reproduce autocrats or other undesired egoists.

Neither of these instances is actually quite as straightforward as is
sometimes supposed. The notion of property rights in genetic material is
well-established, as any breeder of dogs or horses will appreciate. The
owner of the animal also owns the right to its gametes and to their use in
reproduction. More recently, this principle has been extended to confer on

---

[1] A. L. Caplan, 'What's So Special About the Human Genome?' (1998) 7 *Cambridge
Quarterly of Health Care Ethics* 422.

plant breeders similar rights. Reproductive cloning is also a less than novel challenge. Plant breeders have been doing it for generations, for example, by reproducing from cuttings, a process now assisted by hormonal agents, and, more recently, by F1 hybridization to produce genetically identical seed. The extension of the technology to humans is a matter of concern only for those who do not understand the extent to which the expression of genotypes is influenced by environments. Cloning's capacity to produce even physically identical beings is limited by the conditions of growth and development. In the human case, for example, we know that the uterine environment exerts an effect on the foetus which, in certain respects, may be the consequence of experiences during the mother's own growth and development. Once born, a child is no less subject to modification by its material, biological, and psychological environment. Although monozygotic twins may be more alike than dizygotic twins, they are rarely identical in every respect. The same influences will ensure that a clone from an adult is no more similar than a monozygotic twin and, indeed, is likely to be less similar because of the difficulty in reproducing the exact conditions under which the adult's genotype was expressed. Therapeutic cloning, for the production of replacement tissues and, possibly, organs, raises different questions, particularly if it comes to involve the creation, manipulation, and destruction of embryos. However, the arguments here are also familiar, even if it is a paradox that there may be more reason to be morally troubled by cloning to produce parts of a human being than to produce a whole.

For a sociologist, however, discussion of the ethics of molecular biology must be founded on practical understanding of what this technology is actually doing and how people are dealing with the problems that it throws up on an everyday basis. Two particular issues suggest themselves as focal points for law and society studies.

The first is the idea of the molecule as intellectual property. The sociological analysis of capitalism and the place of law within it has always owed much to the work of Max Weber.[2] However, there is a curious gap in his examination of the constitutive powers of law in relation to the nature of property. It is, though, prior to any discussion of contract or bookkeeping. Before you can transfer goods or services by contract or count the movements of items from credit to debit, you need a definition of property itself. Although intellectual property has become an exciting area of legal development, this is reflected only to a limited extent in the ethical debates over patenting. A recent exchange in the *Cambridge Quarterly of Healthcare Ethics* is a case in point. McGee outlines the case for patenting in anticipated rebuttal of a position which is taken by two

---

[2] D. M. Trubek, 'Max Weber on Law and the Rise of Capitalism' [1972] *Wisconsin Law Review* 720.

critical responses, by Caplan and by Merz and Cho, and addressed from slightly different directions by a representative of the pharmaceutical industry, Tribble, and a clinician, Magnus.[3]

Caplan notes that arguments over the morality of patenting may be motivated either by the self-interest of the laggards in the scientific race or by antipathy to technology as such. He identifies three main objections: an argument that no-one should be allowed to own the 'blueprint for humanity'; an argument that patenting is comparable to slavery and prostitution in commercializing something which should be outside the realm of commerce; and an argument that the human genome is already owned in the sense of being the common property of humankind. Such objections cannot be met by arguments about economic efficiency. Merz and Cho restate the traditional legal argument that a patent should properly relate only to an innovation rather than a discovery. From a social constructionist perspective, however, McGee argues that the difference between a discovery and an invention is not so clear-cut. Genes are no more a 'simple, self-evident library of data' than the State of Nebraska is pre-given in the landform of the midwestern United States. They are as much the invention of the scientists who discover them as Nebraska was the invention of the nineteenth-century surveyors who delineated its boundaries for the US government. Moreover, if genes are merely a convention for organizing the sense data of science, they cannot simultaneously be a sacred mystery of nature. Tribble and Magnus's contributions focus on the practical objectives of the pharmaceutical industry rather than philosophical or legal theory. The industry wants to get a reasonable return on its R&D investment. If a patent, a temporary licence to extract an economic rent from an invention, is a way to achieve that, fine: if not, then any functional equivalent will do. Clinicians fear getting into legal tangles because the way in which patenting splits up a complex interacting biological system makes infringements almost impossible to avoid.

The move to a more practical level is significant because it allows some issues to be seen as interesting but of limited relevance. As Caplan notes, people with theological objections or a straightforward anti-technology position are unlikely to be satisfied with anything that creates property rights in the human genome. However, as McGee points out, patenting is not the only way to control intellectual property rights in genetic material and, indeed, there are analogies which may work better, like water rights or air rights. An alternative approach might start from recognizing three basic interests which may conflict: the desire of investors—whether public

---

[3] G. McGee, 'Gene Patents Can Be Ethical' (1998) 7 *CQHCE* 417; Caplan, n. 1, above; J. F. Merz and M. K. Cho, 'Disease Genes Are Not Patentable: A Rebuttal of McGee' (1998) 7 *CQHCE* 425. J. L. Tribble, 'Gene Patents—A Pharmaceutical Perspective' (1998) 7 *CQHCE* 429; D. Magnus, 'The Clinician's Dilemma' (1998) 7 *CQHCE* 433.

or private—to recover their investment together with a rate of return that reflects the risks and opportunity costs of this use of their money; to encourage research; and to apply research advances in clinical practice. Law may be able to provide a framework for recognizing and reconciling these interests which is sufficiently authoritative to minimize conflicts and which can resolve those which do arise with a minimum of fuss and cost.

The sociology of law can make a contribution to designing appropriate legal and policy responses. In this case, for example, there are the questions about who invests, how and why, and about what they expect in return. Is there a real difference between government money, venture capital money, and corporate money from large pharmaceutical companies? How do the stereotypes of the cleanliness of government or foundation money versus the dirtiness of industrial or mercantile money stand up to empirical investigation? Is there a kind of Gresham's Law where bad money drives out good? What are the effects of property regimes on scientific research? Does a concern for commercial exploitation stimulate research or draw it in directions which are profitable rather than innovative? What is the impact on communication or peer review? How does research filter into clinical practice? Do legal regimes really affect uptake more than many physicians' *a priori* indifference or scepticism about any innovation—or others' uncritical adoption of any novelty?

The application of patent law to genetic material may be simply a holding operation until the constellation of rights and interests around this developing area of science and technology are better understood and a more specific legal regime can be created—much as happened with the railways in the nineteenth century and their stimulus to legal innovation.[4]

The second area of sociological interest relates to the regulation of the technology. In the UK, regulation studies have become narrowly identified with economic analysis rather than the broad interdisciplinary project found in the USA. Regulation is not purely about costs and efficiency incentives but also about social accountability. It is sensible to ask about both the opportunity and the transaction costs of regulation: what are we giving up as a result and are the costs of enforcement proportionate to the benefits delivered? These can be expressed in financial terms, although it may not always be appropriate to do so. The opportunity cost of rejecting genetically modified food, for example, may be expressed in the extra expenditure by farmers to produce comparable yields per acre from less efficient plants, leading to higher prices and consumers either reducing consumption of food or reducing consumption of other goods or services in order to sustain their existing diet, with consequential losses elsewhere in the economy. At the same time, we may also see a metaphorical cost in terms of the displacement of existing plant varieties, a disruption of the

---

[4] R. W. Kostal, *Law and English Railway Capitalism 1825–1875* (Oxford, 1997).

'natural' food chain if more efficient crop predator control starves out higher species or an increased dependence of farmers on multinational corporate suppliers.[5] There are standard economic techniques for expressing these costs in money terms but their correspondence with the values involved often seems arbitrary. Similarly, the transaction costs of regulation are not just those of enforcement and compliance but of their whole impact on the quality of the organization being regulated.

From a bioethics perspective, Baroness Warnock has some sense of these issues. Discussing regulation in the context of cloning, for example, she argues against over-hasty legislation in terms of the value of protecting the freedom of scientific inquiry.[6] The opportunity cost of regulating science is the loss of a liberty which she regards as fundamentally important in and of itself. This deontological position can be contrasted with the utilitarian argument that the regulation of scientific inquiry slows innovation and leads to loss of competitiveness. In principle, this argument is empirically testable, although there are non-trivial difficulties in measuring the 'rate of innovation' and 'competitiveness'. There may still be room to debate the weighting of the outcomes but it is surely important to have some sense whether regulation leads *both* to reduction in freedom of inquiry *and* to a less affluent society.

Historians, sociologists, and political scientists have produced a wealth of studies about the different strategies that may be used to regulate industries and about their implications. Some regulatory bodies rely heavily on producing detailed rulebooks and an enforcement strategy focused on penalizing each infraction. Others produce less detailed rules but seek to negotiate compliance with the spirit of their regulatory mission in ways which suit the circumstances of each particular enterprise? The tension between equality and equity in dealing with cases that are formally alike under these regimes will be familiar to lawyers. How much discretion should be available to enforcement agents, particularly when dealing with potentially catastrophic technologies? Is it better to police enterprises, and chance the development of strategies for creating the appearance of compliance that make little impact on everyday practice?[7] Is it better to seek the co-operation of enterprises and make their personnel partners in a joint effort to promote standards, at the cost of fuelling criticism that an agency which is not issuing lots of fines and prosecutions has been captured by the industry. Baroness Warnock seems to be hinting at this

---

[5] There has, of course, been no such thing as a 'natural' food chain since the Stone Age when settled farmers began to select plants for their germ line properties and to collect them in convenient locations where they could be fertilized to encourage growth and protected from predators.
[6] M. Warnock, 'The Regulation of Technology' (1998) 7 *CQHCE* 173.
[7] J. M. Johnson, 'The Practical Uses of Rules' in R. A. Scott and J. D. Douglas (eds.), *Theoretical Perspectives on Deviance* (New York, 1972), 215.

when she discusses the 1970s moratorium on research into the genetic manipulation of plants until problems of risk to the investigators and containment of experimental organisms had been adequately resolved. Scientists themselves perceived the danger and internalized a safety regime that acknowledged it. With hindsight, of course, this may not look the best example to choose, given the 1999 moral panic about genetically-modified food.[8] Nevertheless, the observation remains true—the most effective form of discipline is self-discipline, since all other techniques are reactive and can only intervene after a rule has been breached or a standard broken.

Although there is a considerable accumulation of regulatory studies, crucial empirical gaps remain. There is, for example, relatively little work at the intersection of the sociology of science and the sociology of law. Most work on regulation has concentrated on hazardous industries and technologies rather than on the process of science itself. Although the sociology of science has been increasingly interested in laboratory work, this has mainly been linked to questions about the social construction of knowledge.[9] How do scientists come to agree what counts as legitimate practice and valid knowledge? As is common with social constructionist approaches, the material and extra-situational constraints on practice have received less attention. Laboratory science is, however, subject as much as industry to health and safety and environmental regulation. In the health field, there are the additional regulatory constraints of Institutional Review Board or ethical committee review. What it is possible to propose as scientific knowledge is fundamentally conditioned by the regulatory environment within which research is undertaken.

The scientific laboratory is a crucial new domain for studies of regulation, exploring its impact on scientific practice and considering the questions of efficiency and effectiveness. It may be, for example, that this is an area where an adversarial relationship between regulators and regulated is desirable: does an internalization of regulatory constraint lead to the production of less innovative science? Could it be that a degree of friction between regulators and scientists is actually in the latter's interest by compelling them to be more inventive or creative in their attempts to find ways round regulations?

Social Biology

The second area of interaction between law, society, and genetics is that of the implications of understanding more about the distribution of traits

---

[8] The theoretical literature on moral panics is summarized in E. Goode and N. Ben-Yahuda, *Moral Panics: The Social Construction of Deviance* (Oxford, 1994).

[9] e.g. B. Latour and S. Woolgar, *Laboratory Life: The Social Construction of Scientific Facts* (Beverly Hills, Cal., 1979).

believed to have a genetic foundation at population level. The issues here also have a long history: the idea of managing the national gene pool by regulating the reproduction of individuals goes back to the earliest years of genetic science as the principles of Mendelian inheritance and Darwinian evolution were taken up by nineteenth-century racial science. Even before the basis of inheritance was understood, physical anthropologists were trying to distinguish racial types by means of body measurements and to classify them into an evolutionary hierarchy, usually with North Europeans at the top. Criminologists like Lombroso extended these techniques into the study of deviant groups, seeking correlations between body measurements and criminal behaviours. The case for active management of reproduction by encouraging the fittest to breed with each other and discouraging or preventing the unfit from breeding at all was widely accepted in both progressive and conservative circles by the early part of the twentieth century. In many parts of Europe and North America, it became the basis of legislation, particularly to encourage the sterilization of people with mental or physical impairments. The excesses of the National Socialist regime in Germany were one end of a continuum with countries like the USA, Canada, Finland, and Sweden positioned rather closer than many people now care to recall: the Swedes, for example, were still compulsorily sterilizing people with learning disabilities until the 1960s.

The United Kingdom was something of an exception. As Kevles notes, the legislative proposals to promote the sterilization of the 'unfit' that were brought forward from the early 1900s until the 1930s were consistently rejected, despite the strength of social biology in Britain and the activity of the Eugenics Society.[10] It must be acknowledged that the actual treatment of people in institutional care did not always match the legal standards and that the terms of the legislation offered only limited protection against the enthusiasm of individual medical superintendents. However, the reasons for parliamentary scepticism bear some examination, both because they reflect the scepticism of contemporary British social biologists and because much of their critique remains valid. Kevles summarizes the objections to the active management of reproduction under three general statements:

1. definitions of reproductive fitness were based on expressions of class, race, and gender prejudice concealed in scientific rhetoric: the apparent rise in the number of the unfit had to do with the demands of industrial society, the spread of testing, and the intensification of class and other conflicts, rather than being a deterioration of the gene pool;

---

[10] D. J. Kevles, *In the Name of Eugenics: Genetics and the Uses of Human Heredity* (Berkeley, Cal., 1985).

2. the expression of genotypes was subject to environmental influence at all stages from conception, or possibly even pre-conception, onwards: eugenic reformers claimed far too much for heredity in ignorance of the scope and intensity of environmental effects;
3. breeding between adults defined as phenotypically superior did not necessarily reproduce those characteristics in their offspring: it could be shown mathematically that regression to the population mean was more likely.[11]

To the extent that these objections could be modified today, they would reflect a broader range of concerns about the incorporation of prejudice into definitions of reproductive fitness and the rather small number of autosomally dominant single-gene disorders that have been identified—of which the best known is Huntington's Chorea—where reproductive management might have some prospect of reducing the frequency of affected births. However, it has also become clear that most of the influences on human phenotypes are polygenic, involving a number of genes in complex interactive processes, and that the simple Mendelian notions of dominance and recession are less straightforward than originally thought. The expression of a single gene is also subject to its penetrance—the extent to which its potential for action is actually realized in the presence of other genes or environmental influences.

The best-documented debates about the implications of the difference between analysis at population level and at individual level are those around IQ. However, given the controversies over the heritability of intelligence and the complexity of interactions with the environment in which a person grows up, it is not the best case for a brief discussion. Physical disabilities are better because we can be clearer both about their genetic basis and about the extent to which disability is disability-in-a-particular-environment.[12] The development of genetic science has considerably increased the ability to examine individual genotypes prenatally. Although many current tests have limited sensitivity and specificity and many disabilities are still undetectable prenatally, it is argued that they are

---

[11] On the implications of this for societies see particularly M. Young, *Rise of the Meritocracy* (Harmondsworth, 1961).

[12] The same point about disability-in-an-environment can also be made for learning disabilities or low-range measured IQ. These may be problems only in a society that tests people, especially children, regularly and classifies some of them as below a 'normal range' of functioning: see L. H. Dexter, 'On the Politics and Sociology of Stupidity in Our Society' in H. S. Becker (ed.), *The Other Side* (New York, 1967) 37. In practice, once they escape from the testing environment, many of these people prove to be entirely capable of managing their everyday lives and developing highly inventive strategies for passing—covering their limited literacy or numeracy by cover stories which enlist the help of others without disclosing their spoiled identity: see R. B. Edgerton, *The Cloak of Competence: Stigma in the Lives of the Mentally Retarded* (Berkeley, Cal., 1967).

changing societal views of people with disabilities.[13] The birth of a child with a disability is no longer the result of a natural lottery but potentially the result of a parental choice.

As bioethicists have noted, prenatal genetic screening may reverse the recent movement towards seeing people with disabilities as people rather than as disabilities. A wide range of human potential has been revealed that was previously neglected or ignored. It may reinforce the drive in modern obstetrics for the 'perfect baby', who may now be defined not just in terms of avoidance of disability but also by parental preferences for sex, eye, skin, and hair colour, and overall physique. The true 'designer baby' may be far in the future but current decisions about the selective termination of genetically screened pregnancies are its moral precursor. Is the result a society which is as intolerant of disability, as a result of the aggregated private decisions of parents, as some of those societies which incorporated eugenic objectives into law as a result of collective legislative decisions?

This questions the common assumption in bioethics that private decisions are necessarily preferable to collective ones. As recent critics have noted, bioethical thought is strongly influenced by American liberal individualism. They have challenged its applicability outside the cultural context of the USA and its indifference to the social and distributional consequences of emphasizing autonomy above community.[14] Such a bias may, of course, be understandable in terms of the history of prioritizing the collective interest over the individual in the experiments of Nazi scientists or, indeed, in studies like the Tuskegee project on the natural history of untreated syphilis by the US Public Health Service.[15] However, the bioethics paradigm has yet to find an adequate response to the communitarian and civic republican versions of liberalism which have emerged in recent years, partly from the perception that the strong emphasis on autonomy and individual rights in US liberal thought was profoundly destructive of the environment within such rights could have value and be exercized. Responsible citizens assert their rights in ways which are sensitive to their impact on others and on the community as a whole. This may involve a personal choice not to bear a child with a disability out of consideration for the costs it would impose on others. Even if we would consider it improper for the community to *require* that choice to be made, it may not be illegitimate for the community to *remind* the choice-maker of their responsibility towards fellow-citizens. At the same time, it may also be appropriate for both bioethicists and human biologists to remind the community of the advantages of diversity: a society that allows the repro-

---

[13] K. O. Steel, 'The Road That I See: Implications of New Reproductive Technologies', (1995) 4 *CQHCE* 351; A. Asch, 'Distracted by Disability' (1998) 7 *CQHCE* 77.

[14] S. R. Benatar, 'Just Health Care Beyond Individualism: Challenges for North American Bioethics' (1997) 6 *CQHCE* 397.

[15] A. R. Jonsen, 'The Birth of Bioethics' (1993) 23 *Hastings Center Report* S1.

ductive choices of its members to impose greater homogeneity on its gene pool may suffer not only cultural or economic disadvantages but also physical ones. If we are concerned about the loss of biodiversity in the plant or animal kingdoms, why should we exempt our own species? How do we know what genetic material will be of value to us in the future as the co-evolution of the species around us changes our biological environment?

Bioethics have provided an important forum for identifying and clarifying some of these issues. As a sociologist of law, however, I might be more concerned to explore the ways in which they have made a difference to the environment of practice. In some contexts, medical decision-making clearly operates within a framework of anti-discrimination law, a context which is likely to expand considerably in the UK with the domestic incorporation of the European Convention on Human Rights.[16] Asch's discussion of the use of the Americans with Disabilities Act by a 34-year-old woman with Down's syndrome to secure access to a heart-lung transplant may foreshadow a range of litigation here: although the UK courts have historically been reluctant to intervene in medical discretion, it seems arguable that some existing practice in relation to the treatment of people with disabilities will be unacceptable in the future.[17] Although some concern for the equitable distribution of available health-care resources within a community is unavoidable, this clearly cannot be based solely on crude assumptions about quality of life, even when they are expressed in apparently technical measures. One of the important contributions from sociology and psychology is to demonstrate just how difficult it is to determine quality of life in any valid or reliable sense.[18] All the methodological difficulties of intelligence tests apply to the various attempts to construct measurement scales. Nevertheless, equity requires some consideration of both need and ability to benefit and it is likely that some combination of statute and judge-made law will be ultimately be required if we aspire to a measure of uniformity in approach across our national community.[19]

---

[16] It has to be said that much of this framework is also flawed by a one-sided emphasis on individual rights and that it may be necessary to revisit it in a generation which is less haunted by the spectre of totalitarianism in search of a better compromise between the individual and the community.

[17] Asch, n. 14, above; D. Silverman, 'The Child as a Social Object: Down's Syndrome Children in a Paediatric Cardiology Clinic' (1981) 3 *Sociology of Health and Illness* 254.

[18] On the difficulty of determining the quality of life for families with disabled children by qualitative methods, see M. Voysey, *A Constant Burden: The Reconstitution of Family Life* (London, 1975). On quantitative methods for quality of life measurement see C. Jenkinson, 'Death by Questionnaire: Quality of Life Measurement Could Seriously Damage your Health' (1999) 4 *Journal of Health Services Research and Policy* 129.

[19] We may, of course, define 'community' at different levels. The UK National Health Service has traditionally left a considerable degree of discretion in clinical decision-making to relatively local levels, if not to individual doctors. Although the autonomy of individual clinicians is diminishing, even in general practice, current structures leave room for significant

The front line of reproductive management is genetic counselling. Although it is possible legally to regulate the actions of doctors, as shown by the Abortion Act 1967 and subsequent amendments, reproductive choices around genetics are shaded in a slightly different way. We have not created a 'right to choose' termination of pregnancy in general: in those parts of the UK where the Act applies it remains a medical decision whether to accede to a patient's request and compliance with this protocol is carefully regulated. However, it does seem in practice that such a right has been created *de facto*, where the termination can be justified on genetic grounds. It is in the activity of genetic counselling that the moral issues outlined above and discussed at length by bioethicists must achieve a practical resolution. At the end of a counselling process, prospective parents cannot avoid a momentous decision—to avoid reproduction, to terminate a pregnancy, or to risk a genetically-impaired child. Within this essentially invisible process, the counsellor has to reconcile the interests of parents, kin, existing and possible offspring, and the community at large in a morally defensible fashion. The formal ethical training of counsellors is very limited and dogged by a simple-minded faith in the virtues and possibility of non-directiveness.[20] As McGee and Arruda point out, there may well be circumstances where it is entirely appropriate for a counsellor to persuade a client towards a course of action, particularly where treatments are available, as in mutations related to haemachromotosis or in neonatal phenylketonuria (PKU) screening.[21] Moreover, they acknowledge, even at a common-sense level, that the presentation of data by counsellors is not a neutral act especially in reproductive contexts. Unless genetic counsellors can find a way to deal rigorously with these issues, they suggest, it may be hard to argue that this process is any more effective than a well-designed information leaflet, while being a good deal more expensive. Pilnick and colleagues have recently completed a literature review on genetic counselling research which bears out many of these criticisms.[22] A huge variety

variation between the local group structures—Trusts, specialty directorates, or Primary Care Groups—through which care is allocated and delivered. While there are good organizational reasons for this in terms of the impossibility of national governments having sufficiently detailed knowledge of the circumstances of every locality, let alone every patient, this does not sit comfortably alongside a legal structure with a growing emphasis on the uniform treatment of similarly placed individuals, not simply within the nations of the United Kingdom but between the nations of Europe.

[20] A. L. Caplan, 'Neutrality is Not Morality' in D. M. Bartels, B. S. LeRoy, and A. L. Caplan (eds.), *Prescribing Our Future: Ethical Challenged in Genetic Counseling* (New York, 1993).

[21] G. McGee and M. Arruda, 'A Crossroads in Genetic Counseling and Ethics' (1998) 7 *CQHCE* 97. This study reports a survey of the 22 genetic counselling programmes accredited in the USA. An inspection of the literature relating to the programmes established in the UK to date does not suggest that the picture would be very different.

[22] A. M. Pilnick, R. Dingwall, E. Spencer, and R. Finn, *Genetic Counselling: A Review of the Literature* (Sheffield: 1999).

of activities seem to go on under the general rubric of 'counselling' and practically nothing is understood about the processes that are involved in any of them, let alone sufficient to develop a coherent specification of counselling models and an assessment of their strengths and weaknesses. As work in cognate areas like mediation has already shown, however, neutrality and non-directiveness are intensely problematic concepts to operationalize in a situation where the professional is better informed than the clients and the clients may be actively looking for guidance—whatever the professional intends may be read for its directionality and have that effect.[23] McGee and Arruda challenge bioethics to produce more rigorous training for counsellors but the research effort necessary to translate this ethical awareness into interactional behaviour capable of realizing the more considered goals of the counsellors they envisage will be a massive challenge to the sociological community.

Socio-molecular Biology

The third dimension of the 'New Genetics' to which I have given a label of my own invention relates to the explicit or implicit project of behavioural control embedded in some contributions. It is proposed that human behaviour is genetically determined to the extent that it will be possible for prenatal testing to identify those individuals likely subsequently to behave in certain ways and either to terminate a pregnancy or to subject their lives to specific legal interventions intended to control this risk or, at some future date, to modify their genotype to eliminate this 'faulty' gene. Clearly, many of the problems which arise from this argument have already been touched on. It is somewhat implausible to see behaviour as controlled by single genes when almost all other genetically-determined human characteristics seem to be polygenic. The notion of a 'faulty' gene is just as culturally determined as the notion of 'reproductive fitness' when used in social biology. To the extent that single-gene causes could be determined, this tells us nothing directly about the moral implications that we should draw from this.

We may take as an example the suggestion, since withdrawn, in some early 1990s studies that homosexuality in both men and women may have a genetic basis.[24] Some gays and lesbians welcomed this work as a means of demonstrating that their sexual orientation was not a matter of choice, while others saw it as a possible basis for genocide, much as some people with disabilities have seen prenatal testing and selective termination of

---

[23] D. Greatbatch and R. Dingwall, 'Selective Facilitation: Some Preliminary Observations on a Strategy Used by Divorce Mediators' (1989) 23 *Law and Society Review* 613.
[24] This paragraph is based on T. F. Murphy, 'Abortion and the Ethics of Sexual Orientation Research' (1995) 4 *CQHCE* 340 where full citations to the original papers can be found.

pregnancy. Discussing these responses, Murphy has pointed out that a genetic test might equally be used to select for or to select against homosexual offspring—gay or lesbian couples might wish to bear or adopt children who shared their orientation. On the other hand, he is reluctant to condemn selective abortion. There is, he suggests, no moral theory which requires the presence of a particular proportion of gays or lesbians in the population and there are good arguments for not imposing on parents the care and upbringing of children they would not choose to bear and raise. If a reduction in the number of homosexuals is the result of a morally defensible process of personal choice, so be it. Murphy's argument lies within the mainstream of bioethical liberal individualism and its prioritization of personal choice. It might equally be challenged by the argument about the value of diversity and of ensuring that private decisions do not add up to a homogenization of society.

He touches a more fundamental issue, however, when he refers to the problem of determining what homosexuality is, which is logically prior to determining that we have found a gene, or genes, for it. Of course, just as it is a disciplinary deformation of biology to assume that all behaviour can be reduced to genetic foundations, so too is it the deformation of sociology and anthropology to assume that only culture and social structure matter. In both cases, the result has been to perpetuate a variety of fallacies, misconceptions, and downright stupidities. Some *rapprochement* between these fields in the hope of producing a better synthesis is undoubtedly overdue.[25] However, the current conceit that this will be achieved by genetic determinism, or its close relative, evolutionary determinism, seems misplaced. There are three fundamental truths of sociology and anthropology which this argument has to confront.

First, there is the meaningful nature of human social behaviour. Homosexuality, criminality, alcoholism, and whatever are not copies of Platonic ideals. They are locally determined judgements about the meaning of observed or reported behaviour in the light of whatever theories about conduct and its disorders are considered reasonable, sensible, and legitimate in that context. Consensual sodomy may be a definable behaviour. However, its significance to the participants and those around them may be very different in, say, an eighteenth-century naval vessel or a twentieth-century prison, where it is an alternative to heterosexual expression or a means of acquiring specific benefits, and participation has no identity significance, among a traditional society, where it may be part of the ritual attainment of a social status, or in a San Francisco bathhouse of the 1980s, where it was a self-conscious declaration of self. In the same way, what constitutes criminality has long been recognized as depending upon what constitutes legality in a particular social environment—what theft is

[25] W. G. Runciman, *The Social Animal* (London, 1998).

depends upon what property is. Alcoholism or other addiction depends on the recognition of an association between whatever psychoactive substances are in use in a particular society and the experience of deprivation or withdrawal.

Secondly, there is the contextual quality of the meaning of human behaviour. This is particularly relevant to the attempt to generalize evolutionary explanations to human societies by postulating 'memes', cultural units, which are fixed and combined in patterned ways, on the model of the lexemes or phonemes identified by linguists in the analysis of language. There is an important distinction to be made between the use of the phoneme in linguistics and the meme in evolutionary analysis. Linguists do not reify phonemes or their related concepts. Memes, however, are objectified—indeed that is the whole point. They are a reincarnation of the cultural trait approach which expired in anthropology about forty years ago as the problems of the Human Relations Area Files (HRAF) project became apparent. The HRAF was a scheme for classifying ethnographic reports according to standard codes with a view to developing testable propositions about the relationships between these elements. Unfortunately, it rapidly became clear that this unitization destroyed the intelligibility of the units in the context of the cultures in which they were found. To the extent that correlations could be found, their predictive value was limited and their social, as opposed to their statistical, significance was negligible. This is not to suggest that evolutionary thinking may not be useful within sociology but that a much more sophisticated approach may be needed. As the English sociologist, Herbert Spencer, showed at the end of the nineteenth century, Darwinian thinking can be very helpful in understanding the dynamics of the relationships between groups within societies, between societies themselves, and, indeed, between societies and their material environment.[26] There are important differences though: social evolution can be Lamarckian as well as Darwinian, for example, in that individuals, groups, and societies can study what makes others effective and systematically set about copying and reproducing it.

The third is set out most systematically in G. H. Mead's critique of Watsonian behaviourism.[27] J. B. Watson's influence dominated psychology, particularly in the USA and, to a slightly lesser extent, the UK for the best part of half a century from the early 1920s onwards. Watson sought to strip out what he saw as the metaphysical elements which psychology had inherited from the introspective studies of the late nineteenth and early twentieth centuries and their preoccupation with quasi-philosophical questions about

[26] H. Spencer, *Principles of Sociology* (London, 1876, 1882, 1896) 3 vols. A good modern exposition of Spencer's work can be found in J. Turner, *Herbert Spencer: A Renewed Appreciation* (Newbury Park, Cal., 1985).

[27] G. H. Mead, *Mind, Self and Society from the Standpoint of a Social Behaviorist* (Chicago, Ill., 1934).

the nature of the mind. He proposed an alternative model based on the proposition that actions could be understood as an unmediated chain of stimuli and responses, where an environmental input, a stimulus, triggered a series of brain reactions which automatically produced a response. Later writers merged this with Pavlov's work on operant conditioning to propose a biological basis for these chains in terms of the particular patterns of sanction and reward, negative and positive reinforcement, experienced by an individual. Mead's criticism began from a discussion of the difference between human action and that of chickens pecking at corn or dogs squaring up for a fight. Human action, he showed, was necessarily symbolic in character, which required the modelling of a mind and a self as processes for the production and interpretation of symbols, particularly language. Mead was primarily a philosopher but his model had a strong influence on sociological work, particularly in its stimulus to studies of the use of language and its structuring of experience.

The problems of free will and determinism are familiar ones to lawyers and philosophers. They are, however, also central to sociology. Since the demolition of naïve functionalism and notwithstanding the attempts to resuscitate this in cybernetic and rational choice theory, the mindedness of action has been a prominent concern in sociological theorizing. The attempts to dismiss mind as a species conceit about its escape from the grinding mills of evolution show little awareness of the attention that has been paid to this topic by sociologists in their theoretical work from the earliest years of the discipline.

Bioethics as a Social Movement

A final consideration might be the contribution of sociology to a reflexive analysis of the claims and arguments of bioethics. This paper has already hinted at the cultural biases and professional interests which may make bioethics a less disinterested activity that some of its practitioners might acknowledge. Many of those stakeholdings bring bioethics and sociology into competition, of course, so that even this discussion cannot be seen to be entirely dispassionate. However, in an open society, it is the interaction between interests that checks the territorial ambitions of each.

David Rothman has portrayed the rise of bioethics as a defensive response by the US medical profession in the face of continuing challenges from politicians and the courts over its social accountability.[28] The alliance between medicine, philosophy, and theology served the interests of each. Medicine developed a supplier of ideological legitimacy while philosophy and theology saw ethics rescued from its role as an arid and technical

---

[28] D. J. Rothman, *Strangers At the Bedside: A History of How Law and Bioethics Transformed Medical Decision Making* (New York, 1991).

field and the creation of career roles as public intellectuals.[29] The relationship may not have begun as an easy one under some of the influences of the counter-cultural currents of the late 1960s and 1970s but the degree of incorporation of bioethics has both struck and troubled a number of its most prominent figures. In contributing to a special 1993 supplement of the *Hastings Center Report* to mark the thirtieth anniversary of the 'God Committee' at the University of Washington, Seattle, Daniel Callahan, one of the founders of the Hastings Center, noted the contrast between the partnership of bioethics and medicine and the oppositional relationships which marked the environmental field.[30] Bioethics meshed neatly with the market liberalism of educated Americans as it worked out in the medical setting. Almost inevitably, the result has been the professionalization of the field, both academically and clinically.[31] Yoder, and Casarett, Daskal and Lantos, in a more recent *Hastings Center Report*, discuss the current status of clinical ethics as a specialty and the foundation of its expertise.[32] Although clinical ethicists may not be moral legislators, it is argued that they may have a particular expertise in the process of conflict resolution. The value of conflict resolution is, however, itself the result of a particular moral theory stressing the virtues of participation and harmony—in this case, Habermas's discourse ethics. Others are less sure about this. Pellegrino, one of the pioneers of the field as an academic discipline, has noted the lack of a methodology for dealing with 'the increasing polarization that authentic convictions bring to the debates . . . our deepest philosophical and religious convictions about right and wrong are frequently in conflict and sometimes even incommensurable'.[33] However, medicine's prolonged romance with positivism and the evident desire of at least some bioethicists to prescribe a matching Utopia represent a dangerous combination. The coalescence of 'evidence-based' rules of medical practice and the authority of clinical ethics, however philosophically untenable either might be, threatens to produce an institution which is even more insensitive to the needs and circumstances of individual citizens than the one

[29] S. Toulmin, 'How Medicine Saved the Life of Ethics' (1982) 25 *Perspectives in Biology and Medicine* 736.

[30] D. L. Callahan, 'Why America Accepted Bioethics', (1993) 23 *HCR* S8. The 'God Committee' was a body created in 1961 at the University of Washington in Seattle to decide which patients should receive dialysis treatment. Chronic dialysis had just become possible through the invention of the arteriovenous shunt and cannula but demand rapidly exceeded supply. The committee, mostly non-physicians, reviewed the medical and social histories of potential patients in order to determine priority for treatment in the knowledge that those given a low priority were likely to die.

[31] See G. R. Scofield, 'Ethics Consultation: The Least Dangerous Profession?' (1993) 2 *CQHCE* 417 and the responses following in the same issue.

[32] S. D. Yoder, 'The Nature of Ethical Expertise' (1998) 28 *HCR* 6; D. J. Casarett, F. Daskal, and J. Lantos, 'The Authority of the Clinical Ethicist' (1998) 28 *HCR* 11.

[33] D. C. Thomasma, 'Edmund Pellegrino on the Future of Bioethics' (1997) 6 *CQHCE* 373.

challenged by the bioethics pioneers of the 1960s and 1970s.[34] At the same time, the problems of the untrammelled and optimistic market liberalism of those pioneers are becoming apparent in the face of challenges from communitarian versions of liberal theory, many of which, of course, have their roots in the works of sociologists like Etzioni or Selznick.[35]

The professionalization of any field makes it an obvious terrain for study by the sociologist of work and occupations and, since professions are legal formations, by the sociologist of law. Yoder's citations point to the movement towards standard-setting, if not actual accreditation. At what point, if any, will we see the emergence of a self-appointed monopoly and what interests and values will it institutionalize? Rothman's study of the rise of bioethics brings the skills of a social historian but leaves many of the critical theoretical questions unarticulated. How would we understand the export of bioethics to the United Kingdom and elsewhere? Is this yet another piece of cultural imperialism, the McDonaldization of morality? How comfortably does the liberalism of US medical ethics sit within the social democratic traditions of a National Health Service, let alone the more collectivity-oriented traditions of some parts of mainland Europe? Suppose we were to accept the normative claims of at least some parts of the bioethics movement. What kind of society are they modelling? Are we in danger of installing a caste of philosopher-kings and queens in the name of democratic participation?

Conclusion

No one academic discipline holds all the answers to everything. Whatever the claims to dominance and technical or moral superiority that each advances in the market-place for ideas, it is inherently improbable that any will have absolute right on its side. Many of the observations in this paper are neither original nor uniquely sociological. Nevertheless, I hope that the sum total will persuade you that, even if we sociologists are latecomers to the party, it might still be worth buying us a round of drinks or listening to our chat-up lines!

---

[34] The 'evidence-based medicine' programme is based on the assumption that research evidence, preferably from randomized controlled trials, can be used to develop rule-based algorithms for medical practice, unequivocally specifying the best available treatment in any particular case. Lawyers will be more familiar than doctors with the philosophical unsoundness of the idea that one can write unequivocal rules about anything.

[35] A. Etzioni, The Spirit of Community: Rights, Responsibilities and the Communitarian Agenda (London, 1995); A. Etzioni, The New Golden Rule: Community and Morality in a Democratic Society (New York, 1996); P. Selznick, The Moral Commonwealth: Social Theory and the Promise of Community (Berkeley, Cal., 1992).

THE ETHICS OF HUMAN CLONING

Bonnie Steinbock *

'Human cloning' is an ambiguous expression. It might refer to the creation of new human beings through the technology Ian Wilmut used to create Dolly the sheep: somatic cell nuclear transfer (SCNT) cloning. The technique involved transplanting the nucleus, which contains the genetic material, of one sheep, from an adult differentiated cell (in this case, a cell from a mammary gland), into the egg of another sheep, from which the nucleus had been removed or enucleated. The resulting egg cell was 'tricked' into acting like an embryo, that is, dividing and becoming all the differentiated cells of a new individual. The creation of 'Dolly clones' (in Alta Charo's evocative expression) is what is meant by this sense of 'human cloning': the cloning of human beings. It is the possibility of cloning humans that has received intense media attention, and spurred legislation all over the world to prevent its occurrence.[1]

There is another meaning of 'human cloning', namely, the creation via cloning technology of human tissue of varying kinds (skin, bone marrow, organs) for purposes of transplantation. In its 1997 report, *Cloning Human Beings*, the National Bioethics Advisory Commission (NBAC)[2] emphasized the importance of distinguishing between human cloning and cloning humans, so that, as legislators introduced Bills to ban the cloning of human beings, they would not inadvertently ban human cloning.[3] The

* I wish to thank Erik Parens for long telephone conversations in which he attempted to help me understand the science of embryonic stem cell research, and for helpful written comments on earlier drafts of this paper.

[1] On 12 Jan. 1998, 19 European nations (Denmark, Estonia, Finland, France, Greece, Iceland, Italy, Latvia, Luxembourg, Macedonia, Moldova, Norway, Portugal, Romania, San Marino, Slovenia, Spain, Sweden, and Turkey) signed an agreement to prohibit reproductive cloning. Britain and Germany did not sign the cloning protocol. Britain rejected the measure as too strict and liable to ban therapeutic cloning, not just reproductive cloning, which is prohibited in the UK. Germany rejected the protocol as too weak. German law already forbids all research on human embryos.
   Unlike Britain, Spain, Germany, and Denmark, among other countries, the US has no national law that bans the cloning of humans, although there is a ban on federal funding for human cloning experiments.

[2] *Cloning Human Beings: Report and Recommendations of the National Bioethics Advisory Commission* (Washington, DC, 1997) (hereinafter NBAC Report).

[3] A Republican measure to ban human cloning was rushed to the Senate floor on 11 Feb. 1998 after Dr Richard Seed said that he wanted to open a human cloning clinic. The Senate,

usual objections to cloning humans, such as damage to human uniqueness or individuality, violations of the child's right to an open future, the threat to free will and so forth, do not apply to the use of cloning technology to create human tissue for transplant. Nevertheless, careless wording could prohibit both kinds of cloning, both the 'good' therapeutic kind and the 'bad' reproductive kind.[4] It was this kind of confusion that NBAC was anxious to avoid.

In an earlier paper on the ethics of cloning,[5] I assumed that the distinction between cloning humans and human cloning was all-important.That is, while both kinds of cloning raise the usual concerns about health and safety, it seemed that only cloning human beings was ethically problematic (although, I argued, less so than many people assume). By contrast, using cloning technology to create tissue for transplant would be, I thought, an easily-solved moral problem.

I was wrong. As recent events in Britain and the United States have shown, human cloning, as well as cloning humans, raises important ethical questions. Human cloning requires us to think about the nature of a human embryo, the moral status of the human embryo, what is required by respect for human embryos, and whether the distinction between 'spare' embryos (that is, those left over from *in vitro* fertilization or IVF) and embryos deliberately created for research purposes has moral significance.

Embryonic Stem Cell Research

One of the most exciting potential uses of SCNT cloning technology is to produce embryos, which can serve as sources of human embryonic stem (ES) cells. ES cells have great medical potential because they are pluripotent, that is, they have the property of being able to become any kind of cell in the body. If ES cells could be grown in the laboratory, scientists

by a 54 to 42 vote, refused even to bring the bill to the floor for debate. A majority of the senators, including some Republicans, said they were unwilling to enact sweeping restrictions on cloning experimentation, which could ban therapeutic as well as reproductive cloning, because of the potential value in medicine of therapeutic research: L. Alvarez, 'Senate, 54–42, Rejects Republican Bill to Ban Human Cloning', *New York Times*, 12 Feb. 1998, A20.

[4] This assumes that cloning for reproductive purposes would be morally wrong, a very widely held view. Baroness Onora O'Neill, chair of the HGAC, reported that the commission found that 'there are no circumstances in which the reproductive cloning of human beings would be acceptable'. Although its recommendation to permit cloning for therapeutic purposes was rejected by the British government, Baroness O'Neill was reportedly 'pleased' that the government shares its rejection of reproductive cloning. Many individuals and states have called for a permanent and universal ban on the cloning of human beings for reproductive purposes. I have my doubts about the arguments made in favour of such a ban, but addressing that issue goes beyond the scope of this paper.

[5] Bonnie Steinbock, 'Cloning Human Beings: Sorting Through the Ethical Issues' in B. MacKinnon (ed.), *Human Cloning: Science, Ethics, and Public Policy* (Champaign, Ill., 1999).

might be able to grow replacement human tissue at will. According to one science writer,' [t]he ES cell could, scientists hope, be a factory-in-a-dish that turns out cardiac muscles to patch heart attack victims, neurons to mend paralysis or pancreatic cells to battle diabetes'.[6]

Until recently, ES cells were derived either from discarded human embryos left over from IVF or from the germinal ridge of aborted foetuses. Not surprisingly, considering their source, ES cell research has been vigorously opposed by right-to-life groups. However, such opposition does not translate into law or government policy. Not only is abortion legal in the United States,[7] but one of President Clinton's first acts in office was to lift the moratorium on federal funding of foetal tissue research. However, in 1995 Congress passed a ban on federal financing of research on embryos. This raises the following legal question: is research on embryonic stem cells 'embryo research'? If it is, then it comes under the congressional ban and laboratories getting federal money cannot do the research, though such research can be done if privately funded.

Harold Varmus, director of the National Institutes of Health (NIH), responded by saying that it would be a shame if the law prohibited ES cell research, which has extremely promising health benefits. Federal lawyers opined that NIH support of stem-cell research would not violate the ban on support for embryo research, so long as researchers use stem cells that have already been isolated. The ban on embryo research is not violated because embryonic stem cells are not embryos and do not have the potential to develop into embryos.

Critics have called this interpretation of the law sophistical. The ban on embryo research, they argue, applies to the initial collection of cells from the embryo, even if the stem cells themselves are not and could not become embryos.[8] As Douglas Johnson, legislative director for the National Right to Life Committee, told the *Los Angeles Times*, the NIH 'may think it can protect itself by requiring that the embryos actually be killed by someone not receiving federal funds, or by requiring the federally funded researcher to clock out when he kills the embryos, but these would be subterfuges and do violence to the clear intent of the law'.[9]

The right-to-life objection to ES cell research derives from the source of stem cells, that is, killed embryos and foetuses. But what if you could

---

[6] Antonio Regalado, 'The Troubled Hunt for the Ultimate Cell,' *Technology Review* (July/August 1998), 35.

[7] *Roe* v. *Wade*, 410 US 113 (1973) legalized abortion until foetal viability, after which time states may, if they choose, restrict or even prohibit abortion, except when necessary to preserve the life or health of the pregnant woman. Despite some post-*Roe* restrictions, the basic idea of abortion as a constitutional right or protected liberty interest has been retained.

[8] This criticism is not limited to anti-abortion advocates. See, e.g., L. Andrews, 'Legal, Ethical, and Social Concerns in the Debate Over Stem-Cell Research', *The Chronicle of Higher Education*, 29 Jan. 1999, B4–B5.

[9] Quoted in Andrews, n. 7 above, B4.

derive human embryonic stem cells without relying on discarded embryos or aborted foetuses? What if you could use SCNT cloning to derive ES cells directly from an adult somatic cell, without going through an embryonic stage? If this were possible, it would have two advantages. First, because the ES cells would be derived from cells from the patient's own body, they would not be rejected, a problem that occurs with stem cells derived from foreign embryos or foetuses. Secondly, if ES cells could be created without the need to derive them from discarded human embryos or aborted foetuses, the objections from right-to-life groups to ES cell research could be sidestepped.

In June 1999, a biotechnology firm, American Cell Technology (ACT), announced that it had taken a human somatic cell (from a man's leg) and a cow's egg cell from which the nucleus was removed, and created an embryo via somatic cell nuclear transfer. It is not clear from news reports why ACT used a cell from a cow's egg to create the embryo. Possibly, it was to allay fears that it was creating (and destroying) a (fully) human embryo. But some people are more bothered by the idea of creating hybrid embryos than they are by the idea of creating and destroying a very early human embryo, so it is not obvious that this would avoid controversy, if that was indeed the intent. In any event, the embryo was destroyed after being allowed to develop for twelve days. According to a BBC report:

> Dr. Robert Lanza, ACT's director of tissue engineering, told the *Daily Mail* newspaper that the embryo cannot be seen as a person before 14 days. . . . ACT say they have no intention of attempting to use a cloned embryo to start a pregnancy—their aim is 'therapeutic cloning', not 'reproductive cloning'.[10]

Another company interested in ES cell research is the Geron Corporation. In May 1999 Geron formed a $20 million research alliance with the Roslin Institute of Scotland, called Roslin Bio-Med. Whereas ACT claims to be interested only in therapeutic cloning, not reproductive cloning, Geron denies that it has any interest at all—at least at this time—in cloning embryos as a source of ES cells.

Rather, its recently announced collaboration with the Roslin Institute of Scotland, the cloner of Dolly the sheep, was an effort to understand how eggs 'reprogramme' the nucleus of an adult cell, said Dr. Thomas Okarma, Geron's vice president for research.

If the reprogramming process was understood, biologists might be able to take an ordinary cell from a patient and convert it into a stem cell, using the reprogramming factor found in an egg. A group of the stem cells might then be used to repair the patient's tissues.[11]

---

[10] BBC Report of 17 June 1999, http://news.bbc.co.uk/hi/english/sci/tech/newsid 371000/371378.stm.

[11] N. Wade, 'No Research on Cloning of Embryos, Geron Says', *The New York Times*, 15 June 1999, A21.

However, to study the reprogramming process in somatic cell nuclear transfer, it is necessary to create embryos, or so it would appear. Geron denies that it is creating embryos because it uses only non-viable human eggs, eggs which contain a defect in their cytoplasm which would prevent them from developing into embryos. Therefore, Geron maintains, the entities they are creating are not true embryos.

How plausible is Geron's claim that it is not creating human embryos as part of its research? That depends on one's view about what is produced by taking the nucleus of a somatic cell and putting it into a non-viable enucleated egg cell. Is the resulting entity something other than an embryo? Some say that it is an embryo, albeit a non-viable embryo. So is a non-viable embryo a kind of embryo or is it ontologically something altogether different? And does this matter? That is, is there a moral difference between an embryo and a non-viable embryo?

Some observers are sceptical of Geron's claim that it has no interest in cloning human embryos to derive ES cells. Why, they ask, would Geron pour resources into research that might possibly someday enable somatic cells to be converted directly into ES cells when a much more promising use of SCNT is to create human embryos from which ES cells can be derived? They suspect that Geron is putting a spin on its research to avoid the charge that it is doing something wrong, that is, creating human embryos for research. But is it ethically wrong to create human embryos as a source of ES cells?

Most supporters of ES cell research are impressed by the promise of remarkable medical advances. For example, if this technology works, a doctor may one day cure heart disease by taking the nucleus of a somatic cell from a patient and injecting that nucleus into an enucleated egg cell. The cytoplasm of an egg cell, it is theorized, could reprogramme the genes in the inserted nucleus, and create new, disease-free heart cells. The new heart cells would be treated with the human enzyme, telomerase, which enables cells to grow and divide an unlimited number of times, and then injected into the person's ailing heart, which would then *repair itself.* 'Genomic medicine' might make invasive heart surgery a thing of the past. The technology has the potential for treating Parkinson's, juvenile diabetes, stroke, and many other diseases.

The Human Fertilisation and Embryology Authority (HFEA) and the Human Genetics Advisory Commission (HGAC) recommended to the British government that the law in Britain be changed to allow the creation of embryos for medical research, including research into whether human tissue could be grown for transplants. Both agree that the creation of human embryos as a source of stem cells is morally permissible, so long as they are not allowed to develop beyond fourteen days, the point at which the primitive streak is formed which is the basis of the nervous system.

The British government rejected the recommendation to allow cloning embryos for therapeutic purposes, saying that more evidence is needed of the potential benefits to human health before the use of cloning techniques for therapeutic purposes is allowed in research. What explains the government's position? It might be based on practical considerations. Why put resources into research unless there is strong evidence of health benefits? However, it seems clear that such pragmatic concerns were not behind the rejection of the recommendation. Rather, the government's cautious position reflected a certain conception of the moral status of the embryo.

The Moral Status of the Embryo

How one views creating embryos for therapeutic purposes depends on one's view of the moral status of embryos. Typically, three possibilities are presented:

THE RIGHT-TO-LIFE POSITION

This position maintains that embryos have the same moral status as born humans, regardless of their age or stage of development. So anti-abortion groups in Britain, such as *Life*, oppose cloning embryos, even though they would not be allowed to develop beyond fourteen days, much less transferred to uteruses or brought to birth. Nor does *Life* care how much benefit to sick and dying people might result from stem-cell research. On their view, cloning a human embryo to harvest stem cells would be equivalent to creating a baby to harvest its organs. Both would be immoral, regardless of how many lives might be saved. In fact, *Life* takes the view that this is precisely what will happen if scientists are permitted to clone embryos. According to a BBC report, Peter Garrett, research director of *Life*, said, 'If they had gone ahead today, they would have said yes to sick patients deliberately constructing tiny twin and triplet replicas of themselves, then those twin and triplet replicas would have been killed to provide tissue for transplantation'.[12]

THE PERSON VIEW

The person view[13] is that moral status is not a matter of species membership, but rather of psychological features, such as the ability to think or feel or experience. Human embryos, on this view, are not persons, or even close to persons. Yes, they are alive, yes, they're human. But that is not enough, so this argument goes, to endow embryos with the special moral status we think belongs to people. Early embryos cannot feel or experience

---

[12] BBC Report of 24 June 1999, http://news.bbc.co.uk/hi/english/sci/tech/newsid 377000/377425.stem.

[13] This view is explained in detail in my book, *Life Before Birth: The Moral and Legal Status of Embryos and Fetuses* (New York, 1992), 51–8.

anything, much less think or want anything. Nothing you do to an embryo, including killing it, can harm it or set back its interests because embryos do not have any interests.[14] In this respect, embryos are more like gametes than developed foetuses or born babies, and they may be used in research as long as their progenitors give informed consent.

RESPECT FOR EMBRYOS

Moderating between the right-to-life view and the person view is the view that while human embryos do not have moral status, or full moral status, or human moral status, they are a form of human life and, as such, deserving of respect. This is the view that virtually every commission that has considered the issue has taken, including the Human Embryo Research Panel of the National Institutes of Health (NIH)[15] and the Warnock Committee in Great Britain.[16] (It is also consistent with my own view, a variation on the person view, which I call the interest view.[17])

But what does 'respect for embryos' mean? Does the notion have any definitive content? Daniel Callahan argues that 'respect for embryos' is often an empty phrase, solemnly invoked to make us feel better about killing embryos. Callahan takes the NIH Human Embryo Research Panel to task for failing to demonstrate (as opposed to merely asserting) that progress in scientific research depends on using human embryos.[18] Callahan's point is not that respect for embryos entails that they *never* be destroyed or used in research. Rather, it is that the interests or goals to be accomplished by using human embryos in research must be shown to be *compelling*, and *unreachable by other means*. For if less than compelling purposes can justify the destruction of embryos, or if compelling goals could be reached without destroying embryos, the idea that embryos are due 'profound respect' rings hollow.

Callahan's objections are reflected in the rationale given by the British government for rejecting the recommendation that therapeutic cloning research be allowed to proceed. According to the Minister for Public Health, Tessa Jowell, the pros and cons of such a move need to be carefully weighed. 'We believe that more evidence is required of the need for such research, its potential benefits and risks and that account should be

---

[14] For a fuller presentation of the connection between moral status and interests, see Steinbock, *Life Before Birth*, n. 10, above, ch. 1.

[15] Ethics Advisory Board, Department of Health, Education and Welfare, *Report and Conclusions: HEW Support of Research Involving Human In Vitro Fertilization and Embryo Transfer* (Washington, DC, 1979), 35–6.

[16] Mary Warnock, *A Question of Life: The Warnock Report on Human Fertilisation and Embryology* (Oxford, 1985), 63–4.

[17] See Steinbock, *Life Before Birth*, n. 10, above, 208–9.

[18] Daniel Callahan, 'The Puzzle of Profound Respect' (1995) 25(1) *Hastings Center Report*: 39–40, at 39.

taken of alternative approaches that might achieve the same ends', she said.[19]

The government's decision was attacked by scientists and the British Medical Association. Professor Lord Winston, a leading fertility expert and Labour peer, told the BBC the delay would impinge on research for incurable diseases like Parkinson's disease, cancer, and burns. 'I think that there is a risk that by delaying this research people in this country will die unnecessarily. So in my view this is an immoral decision', he said.[20]

It may be that Professor Winston views embryos as having no moral standing at all (the second position). But he might endorse the third view, which requires respect for embryos, so long as such respect does not entail prohibiting or even delaying potentially life-saving research. By contrast, Callahan (and by implication the British government) suggests that any meaningful concept of respect for embryos *requires* some delay in order to ensure that cloning embryos is necessary to benefit human health; otherwise the phrase 'respect for embryos' is empty rhetoric. On the one conception of respect for embryos, delay is not necessary, and indeed would be immoral; on the other, delay is necessary if we are serious about the idea of respect for embryos. Can this conflict be resolved? Or should we just drop the idea of 'respect for embryos' as being either vapid or immoral? In that case, we could take either option 1 (and oppose embryo research) or option 2 (and support it). In my view, seeing these as the only options reflects a failure to understand what respect for embryos as a form of human life entails.[21]

Respect for embryos is not like respect for persons. Respect for *persons* means, as Kant instructs us, never treating persons as mere means to our ends, but always treating them as ends in themselves. This obscure phrase means that we must take seriously the ends—the projects, the goals—that other people have (at least if they're morally permissible ends). Now we cannot do this with embryos since they do not have ends of their own. Without the ability to feel or think, there can be nothing that they want. Without wants, they have no goals or ends. They simply develop, as do other living, non-sentient beings, like plants. When trees send out roots deep into the ground, we can say that they are 'searching' for water. When sunflowers turn to face the sun, we can say that they 'want' light. But if these are ends or goals at all, they are not the kinds of ends that people have. They are not chosen ends, or even ends of which these entities are in any sense aware. Lacking the kinds of ends that persons have, embryos cannot be given the respect that is due to persons. At the same time,

---

[19] 24 June 1999, http://news.bbc.co.uk/hi/english/sci/tech/newsid 3777/377–31.stm.

[20] *Ibid.*

[21] This idea is developed in my article, 'Respect for Human Embryos' in Paul Lauritzen (ed.), *Cloning and the Future of Human Embryo Research* (Oxford, forthcoming).

embryos are not just things, but potential human beings. This potential gives them a significance and importance that does not belong to other cells of the body, and imposes restrictions on what it is permissible to do to embryos. The significance and importance of embryos is, in my view, symbolic. They are owed respect because they are 'potent symbols of human life'.[22] In this respect, embryos are like dead bodies, which also do not have interests.

So, how do we display respect for embryos and corpses? We show respect for dead bodies by burying them in accordance with certain social or religious traditions, instead, say, of putting them out with the trash. However, context and purpose are morally significant. Thus, respect for the dead is consistent with letting medical students dismember them.[23] It is not consistent with letting people use dead bodies as targets in a shooting gallery. Similarly, we show respect for human embryos by not using them in unimportant or frivolous ways, say, to teach high school biology or to make cosmetics or jewelry. However, respect for embryos does not require refraining from research likely to have significant benefits, such as treating disease and prolonging life. Moreover, when symbolic values conflict with important interests of people, in my view, those interests should prevail.

Is respect for embryos simply respect for *other people's* views of embryos?[24] That is, given that some people regard embryos at all stages of development as moral human beings or persons, we might refrain from doing certain things to embryos as a way of respecting *their* view of the moral status of embryos. I do think that it is important to respect others' views, even when we disagree with them. We show respect for people's views by listening to them, by not dismissing them, by giving reasons for our disagreement with them. This is part of respecting other people, which is certainly a moral requirement, as well as being essential in a democracy, where all parties are entitled to be heard. However, I do not think that respect for the embryo is nothing but respect for the views of others. Respect for embryos entails that it is wrong to use embryos in frivolous or non-essential ways. This reflects our own attitude toward human embryos, as distinguished from other entities. Condemning certain uses of embryos as frivolous expresses our *own* symbolic valuing of embryos as potential human life. Respecting symbols is not, in my view, as important as, say, saving lives, but that is not to say that it is unimportant or simply a matter of consideration for the views of *other* people.

---

[22] John A. Robertson, 'Symbolic Issues in Embryo Research' (1995) 25(1) *Hastings Center Report*: 37–8, at 37.
[23] Erik Parens, 'What Has the President Asked of NBAC? On the Ethics and Politics of Embryonic Stem Cell Research,' to be published in the volume of background papers for the forthcoming NBAC ES cell report.
[24] This was suggested by Dena Davis at the Law and Medicine Colloquium at which this paper was presented, 5 July 1999.

Morally Permissible Sources of Stem Cells

Another issue raised by stem cell research is whether there is a moral difference between deriving stem cells from cloned embryos (assuming this could be done) and deriving stem cells from embryos left over from *in vitro* fertilization (IVF) or from the germinal ridge of aborted foetuses.[25] Again, we get three possible views:

(1) The right-to-life position is that both sources of stem cells are morally bad, although bad in different ways. Right-to-life advocates who view embryos as human persons consider cloning embryos and then destroying them—for whatever purpose—to be murder. By contrast, using already killed embryos or foetuses is not murder (since murder requires the killing of a living human being). Nevertheless, the wrongness of killing embryos and foetuses has implications for the use of discarded embryos and aborted foetuses. Research that utilizes the results of these wrongful practices is 'tainted' by the original wrong, and therefore is morally unacceptable.

Some commentators have argued that it is possible to think abortion is morally wrong and yet not oppose deriving tissue or stem cells from aborted foetuses.[26] The idea is that so long as abortion is legal, it would be wasteful not to put foetal tissue to some good use. Using aborted foetuses for transplant or research 'salvages some good from evil' and is therefore acceptable. It seems to me that this is not a plausible argument for those who implacably oppose abortion and think it should be outlawed. Someone who regards abortion as murder can no more condone the use of aborted foetuses in research than vegetarians who regard killing animals as murder can condone wearing clothing made from the hides of animals killed for food. [27]

---

[25] There is actually another issue which I will not discuss in depth, as it concerns specifically US law: whether US law regards deriving stem cells from discarded embryos differently from deriving them from aborted foetuses. While deriving stem cells from aborted foetuses is generally regarded as a federally fundable form of foetal tissue research, some think that deriving stem cells from discarded embryos falls under the ban on embryo research. NBAC's report on stem cell research, due in July 1999, but which is not out at the time of writing, is expected to argue that the ban should be lifted so that it will be possible to derive ES cells from discarded embryos. President Clinton has said that, contrary to NBAC's preliminary suggestions, he will not make any effort to lift the ban on embryo research. Instead, he will suggest that insofar as the ban applies to embryos, as opposed to ES cells, researchers may use ES cells derived from discarded embryos, so long as they do not themselves derive the ES cells from the embryos (personal communication from Erik Parens). This is the approach Harold Varmus has taken and which, as I discussed above, has been severely criticized both by right-to-life groups and other commentators who find it facetious.

[26] This was the position taken by a majority of the Human Fetal Tissue Transplantation Panel in the United States. *Report of the Human Fetal Tissue Transplantation Panel* (Washington DC, December 1988), i, 2.

[27] For a fuller presentation of this argument, see Steinbock, *Life Before Birth*, n. 10, above, 180–3.

(2) Another view distinguishes between deriving stem cells from already killed embryos and aborted foetuses and cloning embryos to get stem cells, holding that the first is morally permissible, but the second impermissible.

The rationale for the distinction is that using discarded embryos in therapeutic research is morally comparable to using foetal tissue in research which, as I noted above, has been legal in the United States since the first days of the Clinton administration.

Foetal tissue research is not morally acceptable to those in the right-to-life movement because of their implacable opposition to abortion. However, most Americans think that abortion should remain legal and view it as morally permissible in many cases. For these people, the 'salvage good from evil' argument is plausible. It is consistent both to support reducing the number of abortions and using foetuses that are aborted as a source of tissue or as a source of stem cells. Indeed, it is morally better to use aborted foetuses for beneficial purposes than to throw them away.

This provides the justification for using aborted foetuses (or discarded embryos) as a source for stem cells. But this is only half of the second position. It says not only that it is permissible to use discarded embryos or aborted foetuses to derive stem cells, but that it would be impermissible to clone embryos for the express purpose of deriving stem cells. Why is *that* wrong? Presumably the argument is that while it is wasteful and pointless to throw away embryos that have already been killed when they could be used in beneficial research, the same cannot be said of deliberately creating embryos to derive stem cells. The deliberate creation of human embryos for research purposes goes beyond 'salvaging good from evil', or making the best of an unfortunate situation.

This view distinguishes between creating embryos for reproductive purposes and then using the ones that are not needed for reproduction in research, and creating embryos specifically for research purpose. But why should there be a moral difference between using 'spare' embryos in research, as opposed to creating embryos for research? This brings me to the third position, and the one that I endorse.

(3) Whether you create an embryo for reproductive purposes, but end up using it in research or therapy, or whether you create an embryo for the explicit purpose of research or therapy, *makes no moral difference*. Both reproductive and therapeutic uses for embryos can be justified.

That is, creating embryos for reproductive purposes serves a morally good end: to enable couples to have children.[28] But equally, research to improve

---

[28] For simplicity's sake, I simply assume that enabling infertile couples to have children via IVF is a good thing. There are of course many arguments against infertility treatment which I

fertility treatment or to cure disease also serves a morally good end. The goodness of the ends does not justify regarding differently the creation of embryos for reproductive purposes from the creation of embryos for research or therapeutic purposes. And if, as I argue, respect for embryos is demonstrated by restricting their use to important ends, likely to benefit people, then respect for embryos is displayed whether they are used for reproduction or for research.

The acceptability of the third position depends, of course, on one's view on the moral status of the embryo. If embryos are *people*, then there is a moral difference between creating embryos for reproductive purposes and creating them for research or therapeutic purposes. Creating embryos for birth *benefits* the embryo, while creating them for research purposes *harms* (kills) the embryos to benefit others. But if you reject the idea that pre-implantation embryos are the kinds of beings who can be benefited or harmed (much less that they are people), then creating embryos for research or therapeutic purposes is just as acceptable as creating them for reproductive purposes. Both are valid; neither is frivolous. Therefore, neither contravenes the principle of respect for embryos as a form of human life.

Conceivably, there are non-symbolic, interest-based considerations against cloning embryos. Peter Garratt, the research director of *Life*, thinks that legalizing 'so-called "therapeutic" cloning will provide the ideal bridge across which scientists and pharmaceutical companies will march toward full pregnancy cloning, which will yield massive profits. Individual cloned children will sell for thousands of pounds'.[29] Most people would agree that this would be a terrible outcome. However, no evidence is given to think that allowing the cloning of embryos for research purposes will result in the cloning and selling of children. Moreover, there are already laws preventing the sale of children. If it is the cloning, as opposed to the sale, of children that ought to be banned, we should direct our efforts toward preventing that, not preventing the cloning of very early embryos for valuable research or therapeutic purposes.

here ignore. For a thoughtful treatment of many of these arguments, see P. Lauritzen, *Pursuing Parenthood: Ethical Issues in Assisted Reproduction* (Indianapolis, Indiana, 1993).

[29] BBC Report, n. 9, above.

WRITTEN IN CODE: DIVERSITY
AND THE NEW GENETICS

Belinda Bennett *

In July 1996 in Scotland, Dolly the sheep was born. The announcement of Dolly's birth in early 1997 attracted international scientific and media attention—not the usual way of marking the birth of one more sheep in the world. However, Dolly was different. Born at the Roslin Institute in Scotland, Dolly was a clone. With the birth of one sheep, cloning moved from the realm of futuristic science fiction into the realm of the present and possible. The furore that followed was, in many ways predictable, for Dolly's birth appeared to open a Pandora's box of ethical dilemmas about the cloning of human beings. International concern over the potential for human cloning-motivated governments and other bodies to consider its implications. Overwhelmingly, cloning of whole individuals has been condemned.

While the significance of Dolly's birth must not be understated, it is also important to see debates over cloning within the broader context of debates over developments in genetic science generally. It was in 1953 that James Watson and Francis Crick unlocked the key to modern genetics when they discovered the structure of DNA. Since then genetic research has brought discoveries which have helped us to understand the genetic basis of some diseases and conditions. Through the Human Genome Project, an international scientific effort to map the entire human genome by 2005, there is the promise of further developments.[1]

Modern genetic research holds out the promise of a bold new future in which humanity has identified and conquered the genetic roots of many diseases. It also holds out the promise of a successful 'archaeological dig' of human genetics that will reveal humanity's ancestral history through a genetic tracing of the development of the human species. Genetic science

* An earlier version of this paper was presented at the Feminist Legal Academics Workshop (F-LAW) in Sydney, Feb. 1999, as a seminar at the Faculty of Law, University of Sydney, Mar. 1999, and at the Law and Medicine Colloquium at University College London, July 1999. I am grateful to the participants at these seminars for their comments on this paper. I also wish to thank the Ian Roller Foundation and the University of Sydney for travel grants that supported my attendance at the Law and Medicine Colloquium.

[1] For an analysis of the history of genetics see W. Bodmer and R. McKie, *The Book of Man* (London, 1994). On the history of cloning and its implications see G. Kolata, *Clone: The Road to Dolly and the Path Ahead* (London, 1997).

also promises to shed light on who we are, what it is that makes us tick, what it is that makes us the way we are—in short, what it is that makes us human.

Yet while genetics are a potential saviour (saving us from disease), it also appears as a threat that at the extremes appears to be the stuff of our worst nightmares,[2] such as the prospect, probably more imagined than real, of rows of cloned individuals. The new genetics hold out the promise that through genetics we will be able to determine what we are, a promise that is simultaneously appealing and terrifying.[3] Between the extremes of saviour and horror there are many other concerns along the spectrum about issues such as privacy and genetic testing, discrimination, and the potential eugenic uses of genetics.[4]

Cloning of People and Parts

Works of fiction have long warned of the dangers of attempting to play God by tinkering with human nature. Both Mary Shelley's *Frankenstein* and Aldous Huxley's *Brave New World* warn, in very different ways, of the horrors that can be unleashed when we seek to control the processes of creating human life. More recently, films such as *The Boys From Brazil* and *Jurassic Park* have shown us what can happen if we play with genetics.

The birth of dolly the sheep seemed to have the potential to blur the distinction between science fiction and science fact. Suddenly, cloning of mammals was real. Taking the step from cloning sheep to cloning humans seemed frighteningly possible, with concerns fuelled by media reports that one US scientist was '90% ready' to clone a human.[5] The process that led to Dolly's birth truly was an enormous development in medical science. Dolly's birth resulted from the transfer of the nucleus of a somatic[6] cell from an adult sheep, into another sheep's egg from which the nucleus had

---

[2] For analysis of this point see George Annas, 'Mapping the Human Genome and the Meaning of Monster Mythology' (1990) 39 *Emory Law Journal* 629.

[3] As one commentator put it: 'Our children may be able (I hope, I fear) to choose their kids' traits: to select their gender and eye color; perhaps to tinker with their IQs, personalities and athletic abilities. They could clone themselves, or one of their kids, or a celebrity they admire, or maybe even us after we've died,'; Walter Isaacson, 'The Biotech Century', *Time*, 11 Jan. 1999, 24.

[4] These issues have received widespread analysis. See, e.g., Privacy Commissioner, *The Privacy Implications of Genetic Testing* (Canberra, 1996); Sheila A. M. McLean, 'Interventions in the Human Genome' (1998) 61 *Modern Law Review* 681; Deryck Beyleveld and Roger Brownsword, 'Human Dignity, Human Rights, and Human Genetics' (1998) 61 *Modern Law Review* 661; Donald Chalmers, 'The Challenges of Human Genetics' in I. Freckelton and K. Petersen (eds.), *Controversies in Health Law* (Sydney, 1999), 202.

[5] Rick Weiss and Julie Delvecchio, 'Scientist "90% Ready" to Clone First Human', *Sydney Morning Herald*, 8 Jan. 1998. See also Marshall Froker, 'Seed of Doubt on Clones', *Sydney Morning Herald*, 14 Jan. 1998.

[6] A somatic cell is a non-reproductive cell.

been removed. The significance of this achievement is that it showed that genetic material could be removed from a differentiated somatic cell (a cell containing two sets of chromosomes), and that that genetic material could be 'reprogrammed' or 'reactivated well into the chronological life of the cell'.[7]

Yet within the cloning controversy it is necessary to distinguish between cloning of people (reproductive cloning) and cloning of parts (therapeutic cloning). While much of the debate over cloning has focused on cloning of whole individuals, there is also potential for cloning of human cells for therapeutic purposes. It has been suggested, for example, that cell nucleus transfer techniques could be used for cell or tissue therapy. As the United Kingdom's Human Genetics Advisory Commission noted:

People who have tissues or organs damaged by injury or disease (e.g. skin, heart muscle, nervous tissue) could provide their own somatic nuclei and, by using these to replace nuclei in their own or donated eggs, individual stem cells (not embryos) could be produced in culture. These cells could then be induced (by exposure to appropriate growth factors) to form whichever type of cell or tissue was required for therapeutic purposes with no risk of tissue rejection and no need for treatment of the patient with immunosuppressive drugs.[8]

While there are clearly enormous benefits to medical advances of these kinds, potential research into these areas is limited by legal regulation of research using human reproductive material. The cloned child could be the ultimate solution to infertility, and cloning may hold the promise of therapeutic uses such as organs or tissue that will not be rejected by the body when transplanted (and indeed this form of therapeutic cloning has encountered less opposition than reproductive cloning), yet it is the prospect of a cloned individual that strikes fear into the hearts and minds of many. Concern has been expressed over the potential for cloning to undermine the individuality of the cloned child through the deliberate creation of a delayed genetic 'twin'. Concerns have also been expressed over the potential for the life expectations and autonomy of cloned individuals to be diminished by the expectations others will have of their behaviour or personality,[9] for the change in social values that will occur in a world where cloning is permitted,[10] or for the potential for individuals to become objectified, particularly if the cloned child is brought into existence for the benefit of another person, such as where a bone marrow donor is needed.[11] Finally, the spectre of eugenics raises its head in a world

---

[7] National Bioethics Advisory Commission, *Cloning Human Beings* (Rockville, Mld., June 1997), i.

[8] Human Genetics Advisory Commission and Human Fertilization and Embryology Authority, *Cloning Issues in Reproduction, Science and Medicine* (Issued Dec. 1998) available at <http://www.dti.gov.uk/hgac/papers/papers_d.htm>, 5.3.

[9] Discussed in National Bioethics Advisory Commission, n. 7 above, 68.

[10] *Ibid.*, 69.   [11] *Ibid.*, 73.

where cloning is possible, with parents choosing the characteristics of their offspring.[12]

The pace of the genetic revolution is driving a push for considered legal responses to the dilemmas presented by applications of genetic technology in areas ranging from insurance coverage and genetic testing through to the cloning of whole individuals. Before we embark on the processes of legal reform it is vital that we give critical consideration to the social meanings of these new technologies and both the limits and possibilities that they may present for legal reform.

The Law's Response to Cloning

It is the potential for undesirable or even scary developments that has led to such caution over cloning. In Australia, cloning was prohibited in three states even before the birth of Dolly. Given the techniques involved in cloning, legal regulation of cloning practices arises in the context of regulation of reproductive technologies. Under Australia's federal system, legislation regulating reproductive technology is a state matter.[13] Three Australian states, Victoria, South Australia, and Western Australia, have reproductive technology legislation. In New South Wales the introduction of legislation is under consideration,[14] and the government has announced that it intends to ban cloning.[15]

In each of the states with reproductive technology legislation, cloning is specifically prohibited and research on human embryos is tightly regulated. Under the Victorian Infertility Treatment Act 1995 human embryo research must not be carried out without prior approval,[16] and approved research may be conducted only in a place licensed for that purpose.[17] The Act bans destructive research on human embryos[18] and the Infertility Treatment Authority must not approve destructive research on embryos.[19] In addition, the legislation prohibits the alteration of the

[12] Discussed in National Bioethics Advisory Commission, n. 7 above, 74.

[13] For an excellent overview of Australian laws on reproductive technology see H. Szoke, 'Regulation of Assisted Reproductive Technology: The State of Play in Australia' in Freckelton and Petersen, n. 4, above, 240.

[14] NSW Health, *Review of the Human Tissue Act: Discussion Paper: Assisted Reproductive Technologies* (Sydney, Oct. 1997).   [15] *Ibid,.* 3.

[16] Infertility Treatment Act 1995 (Vic) s. 22.   [17] *Ibid.,* s. 23.

[18] *Ibid.,* s. 24 which provides:

A person must not carry out research, outside the body of a woman, involving the use of an embryo—
    (a) if the embryo is unfit for transfer to a woman; or
    (b) in the case of an embryo which is fit for transfer to a woman, if the research would—
        (i)   harm the embryo; or
        (ii) make the embryo unfit for transfer to a woman; or
        (iii) reduce the likelihood of a pregnancy resulting from the transfer of the embryo.

[19] *Ibid.,* s. 25.

genetic constitution of a gamete that will be used in a treatment procedure or to form a zygote or embryo, and prohibits altering the genetic, pronuclear, or nuclear constitution of a zygote or embryo except where somatic cells are altered for therapeutic purposes.[20] The legislation also specifically bans cloning or attempted cloning.[21]

In South Australia, research using human reproductive material can be carried out only in pursuance of a licence.[22] The licence is subject to a condition that prohibits 'research that may be detrimental to an embryo',[23] as well as a condition requiring the licensee to ensure adherence to the code of ethical practice formulated by the Reproductive Technology Council.[24] The Code of Ethical Research Practice prohibits the alteration of the 'genetic structure of a cell while the cells forms part of an embryo or ovum in the process of fertilisation'.[25] The Code also specifically prohibits cloning.[26]

In Western Australia, the Human Reproductive Technology Act 1991 creates a number of offences relating to reproductive technology. These offences include:

- causing or permitting the conduct of research on human embryos (or an egg in the process of fertilization) without prior approval of the Western Australian Human Reproductive Technology Council or all the approvals required by the Act;[27]
- causing or permitting 'any procedure to be carried out directed at human cloning';[28]
- causing or permitting the replacement of the nucleus of a cell of an egg in the process of fertilization or an embryo;[29]
- and causing or permitting the alteration of the genetic structure of any cell while the cell forms part of an egg in the process of fertilization or any embryo.[30]

At a national level the National Health and Medical Research Council (NHMRC) has issued *Ethical Guidelines on Assisted Reproductive Technology*. The Guidelines list a number of practices which are 'ethically unacceptable and should be prohibited' including:

Experimentation with the intent to produce two or more genetically identical individuals, including development of human embryonal stem cell lines with the aim of producing a clone of individuals.[31]

---

[20] *Ibid.*, s. 39.   [21] *Ibid.*, s. 47.
[22] Reproductive Technology Act 1988 (SA), s. 14.
[23] *Ibid.*, s. 14(2)(b).   [24] *Ibid.*, s. 14(2)(c).
[25] Reproductive Technology (Code of Ethical Research Practice) Regs. 1995 (SA), cl 8.
[26] *Ibid.*, cl 6.
[27] Human Reproductive Technology Act 1991 (WA), s. 7(1)(a).
[28] *Ibid.*, s. 7(1)(d)(i).   [29] *Ibid.*, s. 7(1)(e).   [30] *Ibid.*, s. 7(1)(f).
[31] National Health and Medical Research Council, *Ethical Guidelines on Assisted Reproductive Technology* (Canberra, 1996), 11.3.

The NHMRC Guidelines also impose limitations on embryo research. The Guidelines provide that embryo research 'should normally be limited to therapeutic procedures which leave the embryo, or embryos, with an expectation of implantation and development'.[32] Non-destructive, non-therapeutic research may be approved by an institutional ethics committee (IEC).[33] Research which is non-therapeutic and which is destructive of the embryo 'or which may otherwise not leave it in an implantable condition, should only be approved by an IEC in exceptional circumstances'.[34]

In December 1998 the Australian Health Ethics Committee of the NHMRC published a report on cloning,[35] the recommendations of which, *inter alia*, noted that Victoria, South Australia, and Western Australia have legislation regulating embryo research and prohibiting human cloning, and recommending that the Federal Minister urge the other states and territories to introduce legislation on embryo research according to the principles in the NHMRC *Guidelines on Assisted Reproductive Technology*.[36] In August 1999 the House of Representatives Standing Committee on Legal and Constitutional Affairs was given a reference by the Federal Minister for Health to inquire into the scientific, ethical, and regulatory aspects of human cloning.[37]

Caution over cloning has also been expressed internationally.[38] The United States National Bioethics Advisory Commission concluded in its June 1997 report on human cloning that 'at this time it is morally unacceptable for anyone in the public or private sector, whether in a research or clinical setting, to attempt to create a child using somatic cell nuclear transfer cloning'.[39] The Commission was of the view that at this time cloning was not safe for human use and, furthermore, that the ethical concerns over cloning required 'much more widespread and careful public deliberation' before cloning is used.[40] The Commission also recommended the enactment of federal legislation, with a sunset clause, to prohibit attempts at creating a child through somatic cell nuclear transfer cloning, either in a research or a clinical setting.[41]

In 1998 the Council of Europe passed an Additional Protocol to the

---

[32] National Health and Medical Research Council, *Ethical Guidelines on Assisted Reproductive Technology* (Canberra, 1996), 6.2.

[33] *Ibid.* 6.3.   [34] *Ibid.* 6.4.

[35] National Health and Medical Research Council, Australian Health Ethics Committee *Scientific, Ethical and Regulatory Considerations Relevant to Cloning of Human Beings* (1998) nhmrc/ethics/clone.pdf>.

[36] *Ibid.*, Recommendation 2, at 43.

[37] Details available at <http://www.aph.gov.au/house/committee/laca/humancloning.inqinf.htm>.

[38] For an excellent analysis of international responses to cloning see Dean Bell, 'Human Cloning and International Human Rights Law' (1999) 21 *Sydney Law Review* 202. See also Beyleveld and Brownsword, n. 4, above.

[39] National Bioethics Advisory Commission, n. 7 above, 108.

[40] *Ibid.*   [41] *Ibid.*, 109.

Convention for the Protection of Human Rights and Dignity of the Human Being with Regard to the Application of Biology and Medicine, on the Prohibition of Cloning Human Beings.[42] Part of the Preamble to the Protocol notes that 'the instrumentalisation of human beings through the deliberate creation of genetically identical human beings is contrary to human dignity and thus constitutes a misuse of biology and medicine'. Article 1 of the protocol prohibits '[a]ny intervention seeking to create a human being genetically identical to another human being, whether living or dead'.

The United Nations Economic, Scientific and Cultural Organisation (UNESCO) has approved a Universal Declaration on the Human Genome and Human Rights.[43] Article 1 of the Declaration highlights the value of diversity:

The human genome underlies the fundamental unity of all members of the human family, as well as the recognition of their inherent dignity and diversity. In a symbolic sense, it is the heritage of humanity.

The Declaration also opposes cloning, stating 'practices which are contrary to human dignity, such as reproductive cloning of human beings, shall not be permitted'.[44]

In the United Kingdom, the Human Genetics Advisory Commission and the Human Fertilisation and Embryology Authority published *Cloning Issues in Reproduction, Science and Medicine*.[45] This report suggested that the government consider legislation explicitly banning reproductive cloning.[46] In addition, the Report recommended that the Secretary of State for Health consider regulations covering two purposes for which the Human Fertilisation and Embryology Authority could issue licences: (i) 'developing methods of therapy for mitochondrial diseases' and (ii) 'developing methods of therapy for diseased or damaged tissues or organs'.[47] In June 1999 the British government announced that an independent, expert advisory group would be established to assess therapeutic cloning.[48]

Genetics and Diversity

What is so fascinating about the debate over cloning is that opposition to cloning is often articulated by an appeal to diversity. There is concern that the deliberate creation of a delayed twin through cloning represents an affront to the rights of the cloned individual by robbing them of their

---

[42] Available at <http://www.coe.fr/eng/legaltxt/168e.htm>.

[43] Available at <http://www.biol.tsukuba.ac.jp/-macer/unseco.html>.

[44] UNESCO, *Universal Declaration on the Human Genome and Human Rights*, Art 11.

[45] Human Genetics Advisory Commission and Human Fertilization and Embryology Authority, n. 8 above.

[46] *Ibid.* 9.2.   [47] *Ibid.* 9.3.

[48] Roger Highfield, 'Government Rejects Advice and Blocks Human Cloning', *Daily Telegraph*, 25 June 1999, 1.

potential (or right?) to genetic uniqueness. So the appeal to diversity rests on a view that there is something ethically suspect about the deliberate creation of an individual who is the genetic twin of another person—that the deliberate creation of sameness is wrong.

The difficulty with this approach is that it relies on a form of 'genetic essentialism'. As Dreyfuss and Nelkin argue, '[g]enetic essentialism posits that personal traits are predictable and permanent, determined at conception, "hard-wired" into the human constitution'.[49] At its extreme forms, genetic essentialism would see people purely as the products of their genes. Even if the relevance of culture and environment in forming an individual is acknowledged, the appeal of the apparent certainty and neutrality of science is very strong. As Evelyn Fox Keller has pointed out, forty years ago biology and culture were clearly divided. Today however, 'the very notion of "culture" as distinct from "biology" seems to have vanished'.[50]

What is evident in the debate over cloning is the conflation of identity with genetics. Just as in the broader debates over genetics we are all the products of our genes (at least to some degree), the cloned individual is also genetically determined, but even more so since his or her genes are already 'owned' by someone else. While we are all now seen as the products of our genes, the clone in particular seems to be characterized as an asocial creation. As Valerie Hartouni says:

The individual of the cloning controversy emerges rather as a self-evident fact of nature or a fixed, stable, noncontingent value. It is an utterly nonrelational entity, indeed, an entity whose definitive features—whose individuality, authenticity, unique difference, or thoroughly contained and autonomous self—are regarded as genetically inscribed, guaranteed, and given properties, the potential theft or (unauthorized) appropriation of which may now require policing.[51]

Yet to the extent that concerns over cloning are founded on the perceived threat to individuality by the owning of DNA that is identical to another's, those concerns succumb to a view of humanity in which one's life story is written in DNA code, inscribed in our makeup in the same way that computer software comes pre-installed and defines the scope of the tasks that may be performed on that particular machine. The appeal of genetics is, as I have already pointed out, very strong. Yet in a world of genetic determinism where is the space for the influence of culture and environment in forming an individual? Where is the space for individual agency, for our ability to write our own lives, or to install new 'software'?

[49] Rochelle Cooper Dreyfuss and Dorothy Nelkin, 'The Jurisprudence of Genetics' (1992) 45 *Vanderbilt Law Review* 313, 320–1.
[50] Evelyn Fox Keller, 'Nature, Nurture and the Human Genome Project' in D. J. Kevles and L. Hood (eds.), *The Code of Codes: Scientific and Social Issues in the Human Genome Project* (Cambridge, Mass., 1992) 281, 297.
[51] V. Hartouni, *Cultural Conceptions: On Reproductive Technologies and the Remaking of Life* (Minneapolis, Minn., 1997) 125.

The limits of the notion that someone's identity is genetically deter-mined and that cloning means that an individual's identity is already predefined quickly become apparent if we consider the case of identical twins. Identical twins have the same DNA, they are the product of the splitting of one fertilized egg. Yet while we often accept that there is a special bond between twins, we do not necessarily expect them to have identical personalities or identical lives. Yet in the cloning debate there often appears to be the assumption that the clone will be the same as its earlier twin. Little account seems to be made for the impact of social and environmental factors in the development of personality. It is also true that we do not regard the lives of identical twins as somehow diminished because they have a twin with the same DNA—if anything, we regard them as having something extra in the special bond that often exists between twins. In its 1998 report on human cloning, the British Human Genetics Advisory Commission referred to the case of identical twins and said that [p]ersonhood derives from a humanity that is expressed through relationships with others'.[52] As the Commission noted, in the case of iden-tical twins, the existence of a natural clone is not regarded as threatening the identity of the individual. The Commission concluded that 'the claim that each person is entitled to a unique genetic make-up is a correspond-ingly questionable assertion. Of itself, it could not prove an adequate eth-ical objection to human reproductive cloning.'[53] The Commission did note however, that with cloning it is possible to create a delayed twin that could present 'novel problems'.[54]

I am not suggesting that everyone assumes a clone will have a personal-ity that is identical to his or her earlier twin. In most discussions of cloning and identity there is an acknowledgment of the relevance of cultural and environmental factors in shaping an individual. Yet even where there is this recognition, the magnetic pull of science is very strong, and the tendency to slide towards biological determinism remains.

To return to my earlier point, since a large part of the unease over cloning rests on the deliberate creation of genetic sameness, opposition to cloning makes an appeal to diversity.[55] The fascinating thing about this appeal is that it is so strikingly at odds with the general cultural push away from the particular and towards the universal. The appeal to diversity in the cloning debate stands in stark contrast to the way that diversity has been problema-tized in other areas. Contemporary debates over multiculturalism and over

---

[52] Human Genetics Advisory Commission, n. 8, above, 6.1.

[53] *Ibid.*   [54] *Ibid.*

[55] As Valerie Hartouni has commented: 'among the more fervent responses to cloning is the charge that it entails the contrived replication and perpetuation into another generation of what already exists and, in (re)producing only sameness, robs the world of the rich hetero-geneity that nature—in this case the chance meeting of egg and sperm—would otherwise ensure', n. 51, above, 119.

the rights of and obligations to indigenous communities for example, are founded on a tension between recognition and respect for difference and the centripetal forces of the dominant culture. As Valerie Hartouni notes:

even a casual glance across the cultural landscape suggests that far from being richly appreciated, embraced, or encouraged, diversity and difference are often addressed as discrepancy or deviance and, in either case, as problems to be managed.[56]

It is useful to contrast the way that diversity is utilized in the cloning debates with its use in broader debates over genetics. One of the goals in the mapping of the human genome is to gain a better understanding of the genetic basis of certain diseases or conditions. The ultimate goal is, of course, not simply the identification of these conditions but the development of treatments that would effect a cure. With the identification of certain conditions as genetic in origin we are not only finding a physical source for these conditions, we are also identifying certain conditions as departures from the 'normal'. As Evelyn Fox Keller points out, the quest for genetic health leads us to look for the bases for 'genetic unhealth'. We are seeking freedom from 'disease-causing genes' in the quest for normality yet, as Keller points out, we can only define normality by the absence of these problem genes.[57]

Much has been written about the potential for discrimination based on genetic information. Not only are we identifying the genetic basis of conditions for those who are already ill, we are also now able to identify classes of the presymptomatically ill.[58] These are people who do not exhibit any symptoms but whose genome characterizes them as unhealthy. To the extent that we engage in genetic essentialism and see individuals as the products of their genes, it has been argued that the new genetics can lead to an impetus for the introduction and use of screening tests, 'creating a genetic underclass consisting of individuals whose genes have marked them for the "nowhere track" '.[59] The potential for discrimination in the areas of employment and insurance arising from genetic testing of individuals is very real. This is particularly so in the case of identification of presymptomatic conditions. We are, after all, still grappling with the significance of identification of presymptomatic genetic conditions. Would one, for example, wish to know that genetic testing revealed the presence of the gene for Huntington's Chorea, or the gene associated with breast cancer? What is the significance of that knowledge and how may it affect the life choices of an affected individual? A related issue is whether children should be tested for adult-onset conditions.[60]

---

[56] N. 51, above, 119.   [57] Keller n. 50, above, 298.
[58] Dreyfus and Nelkin n. 49, above.   [59] *Ibid*. 334.
[60] Cynthia B. Cohen, 'Wrestling With the Future: Should We Test Children for Adult-Onset Genetic Conditions?' (1998) 8(2) *Kennedy Institute of Ethics Journal* 111.

Yet it is not just diseases or conditions that are being geneticized. Increasingly, it is the very social nature of our being that is seen as genetically written. Intelligence, criminal behaviour, sexual preference,[61] and even infidelity[62] have all been analysed in recent years in terms of their possible genetic bases. In this context, individual agency and social and cultural influences fade into the background and biological coding takes on a new prominence. The identification of certain behaviour as genetic in origin further reinforces notions of genetic health and normality. The loaded nature of genetic information and social and legal consequences of that information are areas that the new genetics have opened up and that we are only now beginning to tackle.

In the debates over genetics, then, there are two different threads that can be identified. On the one hand we have debates about genetics and the identification of genetic disease which rely on an appeal to normality, even though the concept of normality itself remains rather elusive. These debates rest not on an appeal to diversity, but rather quite the opposite, for difference may be associated with a departure from genetic normality that is seen as undesirable. On the other hand, the debate over cloning rests on an appeal to diversity. In this sense the cloning debate really seems quite remarkable when viewed against other debates over genetics. Yet if we look closely at it, we can see that the concerns over genetic sameness evident in the cloning debate are not really a celebration of difference and diversity. In fact, the concept of diversity as utilized in cloning debates really serves to reinforce sameness. Valerie Hartouni notes:

What is curious about the argument from genetics . . . is that it appears to secure 'individual identity' at the expense of 'autonomy' and 'agency' and, thus, to displace what it aims primarily to rescue. While rendering us genetically distinct individuals, in other words, it also, in the end and rather ironically, renders us genetically determined.[63]

It is after all, the fact that we all have different DNA that makes us the same. Cloning would challenge that because, in a clonal world, some people would have naturally generated, different DNA, while others would have DNA that duplicates that of another.

In questioning the geneticization of identity I do not mean to suggest that genetics are irrelevant to identity. In fact I think it is highly relevant. Our sense of who we are and where we have come from is often determined, or at least influenced, by our family links, and our sense of self within a kinship structure. Knowledge of biological parentage is something

---

[61] For an analysis of biology and sexual preference see Janet E. Halley, 'Sexual Orientation and the Politics of Biology: A Critique of the Argument from Immutability' (1994) 46 *Stanford Law Review* 503.

[62] The cover of the 15 Aug. 1994 issue of *Time* magazine states 'Infidelity: It May be in Our Genes'. [63] Hartouni, n. 51, above, 118.

that is generally valued in our society and it is in this sense that genetic identity can be important. The significance that people can attach to knowledge of genetic 'roots' is apparent when debates over access to adoption information are considered. In recent years we have seen a freeing up of restrictions on access to information about biological parentage for adopted individuals. We are also now seeing a freeing up of access to information for individuals who have been conceived through the use of donated gametes or embryos in reproductive technology programmes. Of course it is not the biological nature of the genetic information, in and of itself, that is generally so important to us, but rather it is the social significance, the meanings of kinship, that attaches to that information.

Yet even while we recognize the cultural significance of genetic links between individuals it is also important to appreciate the normative component inherent in those links. Dorothy Roberts has pointed out the role of genetic ties in defining identity in terms of race and the 'indeterminacy of the legal and social meaning of the genetic tie'.[64] She argues that '[f]or example, the institution of slavery made the genetic tie to a slave mother critical to determining a child's social status, yet legally insignificant to the relationship between male slaveowners and their mulatto children.'[65] It is critical that we be aware of the ways that genetics can be used to ascribe certain characteristics and for these to be used as a means for ordering privilege.

There is a need, of course, a need to think beyond genetics and for a greater appreciation of kinship and family structures that are not founded on genetic links between family members. In the modern family where children may be conceived through assisted conception techniques using donated sperm and/or ova, where parents can divorce and remarry, where there may be only one parent, or where both partners may be of the same sex, it makes little sense for us to limit our understandings of family to a heterosexual couple and their two biological children. Nevertheless, even in the diversity of the modern family setting, knowledge of where one has come from, genetically speaking, whether that be from a resident parent or from a sperm donor, can still be an important element in one's identity. To deny the relevance of genetics for identity seems counter-intuitive. To overstate its relevance is also counter-intuitive.

A Framework for Law Reform

Clearly the new genetics have the potential to rewrite popular understandings of identity, of behaviour, and of health. As we seek critically to analyse the broad implications of the new genetics and to find an acceptable path for law reform there are three themes that should be borne in mind.

---

[64] Dorothy Roberts, 'The Genetic Tie' (1995) 62 *University of Chicago Law Review* 209, 210.   [65] *Ibid.*

The first theme rests on an appreciation of the nature of both scientific and legal reasoning. A large part of the appeal of science, and correspondingly of the new genetics, lies in the apparent objective and neutral nature of scientific reasoning. The notion that science is simply about discovery, the uncovering of new areas, or the provision of new, objective explanations for the world around us remains strong. Yet science does not exist in a social vacuum. Both the nature of the scientific enterprise and the use of scientific results are deeply embedded in and defined by cultural and historical specificities.[66] As Dreyfuss and Nelkin point out:

In fact, the history of science and numerous contemporary studies suggest that the choice of research topics, the nature of scientific theories, and the representation of research results are socially constructed, shaped by cultural forces, and defined to reflect the priorities and assumptions of particular societies at particular times. Furthermore, scientific information is interpreted and applied in a political context and is filtered through social lenses.[67]

While science appears as value-neutral in fact it cannot divorce itself from its social setting. As Dreyfuss and Nelkin point out, the fact that science is not value-neutral does not mean that scientific arguments should be rejected. They argue that it does however mean that 'science-based claims must be parsed with care before they are incorporated into the fabric of the law'.[68] Similar caution must be exercised with respect to science's appeal based on its ability to provide predictability or certainty.[69]

While it is important to be cautious about an uncritical acceptance of scientific explanations for human behaviour, it is equally important to be cautious about an uncritical acceptance of legal reasoning. Like science, law espouses the values of neutrality and objectivity. Like science, the reality of this objectivity has been questioned.[70] Feminist and critical scholars have been at pains to reveal the assumptions inherent in the processes of legal reasoning and to posit alternative interpretations and meanings. With the new genetics and the potential joining of scientific and legal reasoning, it is critically important to remember that neither discipline can exist outside its social setting.

The second theme to be borne in mind is that of multiple identities. There is a certain reductionism inherent in the new genetics, that provides universalized explanations for human behaviour and identity. Yet the notion of generic identity, and in particular its place within legal reason-

---

[66] See Sandra Harding, *The Science Question in Feminism* (Ithaca, NY, 1986).
[67] Dreyfuss and Nelkin, n. 49 above, 339.
[68] *Ibid.*, 341.   [69] *Ibid.*, 342–4.
[70] See, e.g., R. Graycar and J. Morgan, *The Hidden Gender of Law* (Sydney, 1990); M. J. Frug, *Postmodern Legal Feminism* (New York and London, 1992); P. J. Williams, *The Alchemy of Race and Rights* (London, 1993); N. Lacey, *Unspeakable Subjects; Feminist Essays in Legal and Social Theory* (Oxford, 1998); M. Thomson and S. Sheldon (eds.), *Feminist Perspectives on Health Care Law* (London, 1998).

ing, has been rejected. Feminist scholars and others have highlighted the multiple identities that each of us are comprised of. Identity is shaped by gender, race, ethnicity, disability, fertility, class, sexual preference, and a host of other factors that make us who we are.[71] Indeed it is the intersectionality and the layering of these multiple identities that go to making up our multi-dimensional selves. In this context, identity cannot be reduced simply to genetics.

There is undoubtedly a certain appeal in simple categories and biological explanations. They are, after all, so much easier than the shifting sands of cultural interpretation. Yet while the basic building blocks of our body (tissue, blood, skin, and organs) have changed little over time, the significance and meanings ascribed to that body have not proved immutable. Just as notions of gender, race, beauty, or other attributes of identity are culturally and historically specific, so too is our understanding of the basic biology of the human body. In seeking to formulate responses to the new genetics, it is important not to fall back on essentialist explanations of identity.

The third and final theme to be borne in mind when considering genetics and law reform is that of the impact of new technologies. It is important to consider the ways that the new genetics can impact on particular groups in society and whether particular steps are needed to respond to these impacts. For example, an analysis of the impact of genetics on women would have to include the impact of genetic information on prenatal testing, both in terms of the information available in the course of testing and the potential impacts of that information on the construction of reproductive choices during pregnancy.[72] It is also important to realize that reproductive choices that may be driven by genetic information may be constrained by other areas of the law, such as those regulating access to abortion services.[73] Given that women do all of the gestational work associated with having children and the bulk of the work in relation to child rearing, it is vital that the impact of any new developments on reproduction are evaluated critically in terms of their impact on women.

To conclude, advances in genetic science hold the promise of a bold and

[71] See Marlee Kline, 'Race, Racism and Feminist Legal Theory' (1980) 12 *Harvard Women's Law Journal* 115; Angela P. Harris, 'Race and Essentialism in Feminist Legal Theory' (1990) 42 *Stanford Law Review* 581; E. Spelman, *Inessential Woman: Problems of Exclusion in Feminist Thought* (Boston, Mass., 1988); Linda J. Lacey, ' "O Wind, Remind Him That I Have No Child"; Infertility and Feminist Jurisprudence' (1998) 5 *Michigan Journal of Gender and Law* 163; Anita Silvers, 'Reprising Women's Disability; Feminist Identity Strategy and Disability' (1998) 13 *Berkeley Women's Law Journal* 81.

[72] Abby Lippman, 'Prenatal Genetic Testing and Screening: Constructing Needs and Reinforcing Inequities' (1991) XVII *American Journal of Law and Medicine* 15; Mary B. Mahowald, Dana Levinson, Christine Cassel *et al.*, 'The New Genetics and Women' (1996) 74 *The Milbank Quarterly* 239.

[73] Ruth Schwartz Cohen, 'Genetic Technology and Reproductive Choice: An Ethics for Autonomy', in Kevles and Hood, n. 50, above, 244.

exciting future. In fifty years' time we may look back on this time as an age of discovery. But it is also possible that we will look back and see a time of tragic social wrongs and inadequate legal safeguards. The task for lawyers and others is to ensure that the processes of legal reform are informed by social as well as scientific versions of the future. When we consider the story told by the new genetics, it is important to remember that what is written in code is only the introduction. The rest of the story we write ourselves.

GENE THERAPY—CURE OR CHALLENGE?

Sheila A. M. McLean

The Report from the Human Genetics Advisory Commission and the Human Fertilization and Embryology Authority, *Cloning Issues in Reproduction, Science and Medicine*,[1] makes the following comment:

In our view, persons are more than their genes, their nature and character being substantially influenced by their nurture and life experiences. Personhood derives from a humanity that is expressed with others.[2]

Doubtless, this is an assertion that will be met with general agreement. However, it is also the case that people are becoming more and more identified with their genetic make-up, giving it an importance that might otherwise be missing. For example, perhaps as a result of intense media interest, people are more and more protective of their genetic make-up and more and more concerned about the possibility of having it changed or modified. Thus, whilst on the one hand eschewing the belief that genes are fundamental to what it is to be a person (as opposed to a collection of cells), we are simultaneously seduced into intense concentration on what they tell us about who and what they are. There exists, therefore, a fundamental fascination with advances in genetics—a fascination which may transcend concerns about reductionism, depending on what—if anything—the so-called genetics revolution has to offer. As Callahan says:

The most potent social impact of medical advancement is the way it reshapes our notions of what it is to have a life. . . . The greatest attraction of technological innovation is its promise of first breaking the barriers of natural, biological constraints, and then moving on to a dismantling of the cultural attitudes and institutions designed to live within these barriers.[3]

Thus although many approach the genetics revolution with some caution, it also seems to offer enormous hope for the future—not least the hope that our predisposition to certain diseases and disorders may be rectified or reduced by the possibility of gene therapy.

---

[1] London, Department of Trade and Industry, Dec. 1998.
[2] N. 1, above, 24, para. 6.1.
[3] D. Callahan, *What Kind of Life: The Limits of Medical Progress* (New York, 1990), 25.

Before considering the implications of gene therapy, therefore, it is important to unpick the mindset which lies behind responses to it, as in this way we might identify the source of these apparently conflicting approaches and identify whether or not their reconciliation is either possible or desirable. What is being suggested is that the public's attitude to genetics could loosely be described as schizophrenic. Arguments about ownership of genetic information, genetic privacy, and security reflect the importance of genes to individuals.[4] Even while resisting the impression that genes tell us everything about ourselves, we become more and more concerned to protect them, and the information they provide, from others—arguably a tacit emphasis (perhaps over-emphasis) on our genetic makeup.

To an extent, therefore, we both accept the perspective that 'genes are us' and reject it. And this will have important consequences, both for individuals and for communities. For example, rejecting the notion that we are merely a collection of cells, driven to fulfil their destiny and outside our control, may result in demands that the pace of the genetics revolution is slowed. On the other hand, too ready an acceptance of the importance of genes may lead to the shedding of responsibility for our actions and our health. In one US case[5], for example, it has already been (unsuccessfully) claimed that, since violent behaviour ran in the family, a 'genetic defence' should be available to criminal charges.[6]

Doubtless, the genetic revolution will affect the way in which we see humanity as a whole. Until the launch of the Human Genome Project it is probable that few people considered in any detail at all their genetic inheritance—beyond, that is, within those families who were aware of an inherited problem. The Genome Project has, however, stimulated general interest in each individual's genetic make-up, potentially leading to a revised perception of what it is to be human. As Callahan[7] hinted, we are both seduced by this and potentially empowered by it. The down side, however, is that we may also be disempowered, unless genes are kept in their place. As Rose et al. caution, '[h]umanity cannot be cut adrift from its own biology, but neither is it enchained by it'.[8] In addition, Charlesworth makes the following important point:

A theory of human nature should also provide some account of the relationship between the 'given' biological and physical constraints on human life and the

[4] See generally R. Brownsword, W. R. Cornish and M. Llewelyn (eds.), Law and Human Genetics: Regulating a Revolution (Oxford, 1998).

[5] Mobley v. The State 265 GA 292 (1995).

[6] For discussion, see M. Philpott, 'Not Guilty by Reason of Genetic Determinism' in T. Henry (ed.), Punishment, Excuses and Moral Development (Aldershot, 1996).

[7] Callahan, n. 3, above.

[8] S. Rose, L. Kamin, and R. Lewontin, Not in our Genes: Biology, Ideology and Human Nature (Harmondsworth, 1984) 10.

creative element which enables us to elaborate and transform biological dispositions and tendencies and inclinations and give them distinctly human meanings.[9]

Implicit in these statements is, of course, not only a caution against reductionism and resignation to our fate, but also more positively an acceptance that genes are not necessarily all that people are. Moreover, they may also be taken as a tentative permission to change the inheritance with which we are born—to liberate ourselves from the boundaries of genetic predisposition and actively to strive for change. As Engelhardt says, 'there is nothing sacrosanct about human nature . . . we persons are free to re-fashion it, as long as we do so prudently'.[10]

Gene Therapy

Yet the question remains; how is the good of genetics to be translated into practice? Although for the moment diagnostic capacity far exceeds therapeutic capacity, the hoped-for outcome of enhanced genetic knowledge is undoubtedly the capacity to provide treatment for such disorders. Indeed, in some cases, it has been suggested that:

Although most gene research aims to find the gene and gene product responsible for an illness and then to standardize tests for diagnosis and devise a therapy, there are instances in which diagnostic tests present ethical difficulties and therapy becomes the main, perhaps the only, goal.[11]

These situations would specifically include testing for late-onset disorders.[12]

If therapy for genetic conditions were to become available, many of its contentious aspects would disappear, or at least would be reduced. At the moment, for example, diagnosis of a genetic problem in a pre-implanted embryo or in the course of an established pregnancy generally has one outcome—namely the discarding of the embryo or the termination of the pregnancy. However, if gene therapy were available, neither of these options would be necessary. Equally, the decision whether or not to parent could be made safe in the knowledge that what for the moment appears to be the inevitability of genetic disorder can be obviated by therapy. Kand[13] suggests that the possibility of therapy could spare many women the

---

[9] M. Charlesworth, 'Human Genome Analysis and the Concept of Human Nature' in *Human Genetic Information: Science, Law and Ethics*, Ciba Foundation Symposium 149 (Chichester, 1990), 180.

[10] H. T. Engelhardt, *The Foundation of Bioethics* (New York, 1986), 381.

[11] A. Robinson, 'The Ethics of Gene Research' (1994) 150(5) *Canadian Medical Association Journal* 724.

[12] These are conditions which will not cause problems until later in life, such as Huntington's Chorea.

[13] A. S. F. Kand, 'The New Gene Technology and the Difference Between Getting Rid of Illness and Altering People' (1995) 1 *European Journal Gen. Soc.* 12.

'agonizing choice' of having an abortion or 'giving birth to a child facing a life, the length and quality of which would be affected by illness and suffering'.[14]

The toll of genetic disorder should not be underestimated, particularly when one considers disease which is partly as opposed to exclusively genetic in origin. In 1985, Kevles estimated that 'genetic disorders are now known to occur in between three and five percent of all live births. . . . The percentages may be small, but the absolute annual numbers suggest a wrenching magnitude of individual afflictions'.[15]

In fact, of course, we all carry 'defective' genes, although by and large we remain in ignorance of this. Thus, the true 'Holy Grail' of modern medicine seems likely to be the capacity to manipulate genes or to replace faulty genes with healthy ones. Simply put, gene therapy 'aims to introduce a normal gene to express the missing protein, but under regulation that is at least partly physiological'.[16] In this way, a major source of human suffering could be eliminated. Despite this, and despite the fact that gene therapy may hold out enormous potential, it nonetheless poses problems of its own. As Murray[17] says, '[t]he ethics of gene therapy have been discussed exhaustively. Indeed, there may be no other manifestation of modern genetics that has received such thorough ethical examination or that must pass through such extensive scientific and ethical review.'[18]

Gene therapy, however, has been hailed as the best hope for the future. Indeed, it has been suggested that:

Gene therapy will become the treatment of choice for several single gene disorders during the coming decade, particularly where the affected organs are accessible. . . . It won't happen immediately, but progress is occurring faster than anyone would have predicted even a decade ago.[19]

Thus, the future of medicine may well lie in gene therapy. However, and it is worth acknowledging this caveat, for the moment the great promise of gene therapy seems distant. Despite some claims, the following comment must be borne in mind:

Just a year ago, genetic therapy—treatment that works by rewriting bits of genetic code in patient's cells—was widely heralded as the next great champion of modern medicine. Then the champ hit an unexpected slump.[20]

---

[14] Kand, 'The New Gene Technology'.

[15] D. J. Kevles, *In the Name of Eugenics: Genetics and the Uses of Human Heredity* (Harmondsworth, 1985) 291.

[16] K. Davies and B. Williamson, 'Gene Therapy Begins' (1993) 306 *British Medical Journal* (BMJ) 1625.

[17] T. H. Murray, 'Ethical Issues in Human Genome Research' (1991) 5 *The FASEB Journal* 55.   [18] N. 17, above, 58.

[19] Davies and Williamson, n. 16, above, 1626.

[20] *Scientific American*, May–June 1999 (http://www.sciam.com.explorations. 10149 explorations html).

In evaluating the extent to which gene therapy holds out great hopes for cure, or simply poses more challenges, it is necessary to respond to some fundamental questions. Most importantly, as with all novel interventions, the nature of the treatment, as well as its form, must be explored. Thus, it is first necessary to address the question posed by Murray, namely, 'whether gene therapy is ethically distinctive from other forms of medical therapy'.[21]

Is Gene Therapy Different?

Gene therapy is variously described as therapy, manipulation, engineering, and enhancement. Each of these words conjures up different scenarios in the public mind, yet essentially they may contain no fundamental difference. The use of the word 'therapy' implies a medical or clinical event, generally presumed to have an underpinning 'good' or beneficent aim. 'Manipulation', on the other hand, connotes the assumption of power by one person or group over another. 'Engineering' suggests a scientific and creative project, whilst 'enhancement' seems to imply unwarranted or dubious interference into given characteristics, designed to give unfair advantage or to lead to the creation of 'designer babies'. Language alone, therefore, can significantly affect our perception of whether or not what is proposed is a 'good' thing.

However, it is not only the language used which is ultimately important, if we can unpick the different messages it seems to send. Rather, we should look behind the language to the intention of any act, and of course to its consequences. In the context of this paper, the language used will be that of gene therapy, which could include any or all of the terms outlined above. Indeed, it could even include enhancement (generally the most controversial aspect of therapy) as it might be argued that enhancement could be therapeutic, rather than simply being designed to gain unfair advantage over others or a eugenic push for 'desirable' genes. This, however, is a debate for elsewhere. What this paper is concerned with are the issues which arise from *changing* genes, and although the rationale for so doing is not irrelevant, a conclusion on its validity follows, rather than precedes, these arguments.

Of course, it must at the outset be acknowledged that for some there is no debate, nor need for it. Gene therapy for these people will always be anathema. For example, in a poll conducted in the USA for *Time/CNN* it is reported that '[m]ost people strongly oppose human genetic engineering for any purpose except to cure disease or grow more food. A substantial majority (58%) think altering genes is against the will of God'.[22]

---

[21] Murray, n. 17, above, 58.
[22] P. Elmer-Dewitt, 'The Genetic Revolution', *Time*, 17 Jan. 1994 no 334.

For others however, the picture is less clear. Debate over the ethics of gene therapy has raged for a number of years, despite its relative rarity and perhaps because of its current lack of success. Yet, although the technology differs, some might argue that gene therapy seeks to do no more than does conventional therapy—it tries to modify or remove whatever is causing the harm.[23]

However, as was noted at the beginning of this paper, the very fact that it is *genes* that are being tinkered with makes many anxious, given the importance which we currently place on our genetic make-up. Arguably, the seduction of the genetics revolution may serve to reduce rather than enhance public support for the therapies which it is hoped will flow from it. Yet, why should this kind of therapy be distinguished from any other?

The controversy surrounding gene therapy is based on a number of factors. First, as has already been noted, it might be argued that genes are so vital to what makes each of us human that they should not be tinkered with. Of course, this objection may be reduced or annihilated if and when gene therapy actually can do what it promises (although this may well depend on what characteristics we seek to change or modify). The toll of genetic disorder in the community is high and the capacity to reduce the mortality or morbidity associated with genes may well eventually convince doubters—altruistically or selfishly—that gene therapy is a 'good' thing. For the moment, however, this seems some way off as currently 'there remains a serious gap between disease characterization and treatment'.[24]

Nonetheless, hope remains high that the toll of genetic disorder may one day be reduced as the shortfall between diagnostic and therapeutic capacity is narrowed. Certainly the aim of correcting the genes which cause or contribute to disease is every bit as much the 'Holy Grail' of modern medicine as is the Genome Project itself. In 1994 it was suggested that '[m]ore than 40 trials are under way around the world, making gene therapy the hottest new area of medical research',[25] whilst others claimed that by 1993 the National Advisory Committee in the USA had approved 'about 50 separate protocols for gene therapy'.[26] This, the authors say, represents 'a clinical harvest from the human genome programme and the new genetics'.[27]

Kinderlerer and Longley[28] estimate the numbers involved in gene therapy at 2,300, and describe the kinds of conditions for which gene therapy has been attempted:

[23] Davies and Williamson, n. 16, above, 1625.

[24] T. Friedmann, 'Opinion: The Human Genome Project—Some Implications of Extensive "Reverse Genetic" Medicine' (1990) 46 *Am. J. Hum. Genet.*, 408, 411.

[25] Elmer-Dewitt, n. 22, above, 46.

[26] Davies and Williamson, n. 16, above.   [27] N. 16, above, 1625.

[28] J. Kinderlerer and D. Longley, 'Human Genetics: The New Panacea?' in Brownsword *et al.*, n. 4, above, 11.

For the first . . . patients where treatment has been attempted, only 10 per cent have been for a range of monogenic diseases, 60 per cent have been for cancer, and about 18 per cent for infectious diseases (primarily AIDS). At the beginning of 1998, approximately three hundred protocols had been approved, involving 2,293 patients. The vast majority of the patients have been in the USA (75 per cent . . .); 367 patients have been treated in the European Union and Switzerland, of whom 95 patients have been treated in the UK.[29]

Should the research which is going on in a number of countries prove successful, it is clear that gene therapy could have a significant impact on morbidity and mortality. For this reason alone, unless overwhelming clinical, social, or ethical problems are encountered, it surely must be welcomed. Indeed, given the unpleasant and sometimes dangerous side-effects of some existing treatments, and the paucity of help for certain conditions, gene therapy may come to be the preferred therapeutic option in the future. Presumably also, scientists are in the race to provide therapies for those conditions which are multifactorial in origin—those, for example, where correcting the genetic problem will reduce the impact of other factors on the individual, making the onset of certain conditions less likely, if not highly unlikely. In a real sense, arguably, gene therapy seeks to achieve exactly the same ends as does conventional therapy.

However, as was suggested earlier, the second reason for the intense scrutiny of gene therapy lies both in our current obsession with genes and the fact that gene therapy could—were it permitted—do more than merely affect individuals who are ill. Caplan,[30] for example, has noted a significant lack of debate about the concept of disease, a lack which is of particular significance when gene therapy is contemplated. It is widely accepted that a satisfactory definition of health eludes us, although generally speaking we do seem to recognize when we are not well. However, the tendency of genetics to go beyond traditional concepts (however badly defined) of health and disease, by linking other characteristics into the medical arena through the medium of genes, is one which he rightly suggests requires close scrutiny. As he says, '[t]he understanding that our society or others have of the concepts of health, disease and normality will play a key role in shaping the application of emerging knowledge about human genetics'.[31]

Thirdly, and relating to a point made earlier, the language of gene therapy is significant. As was noted, the use of the word 'therapy' appears to imply an established therapeutic act. Yet, the use of this language serves to confuse—perhaps even obfuscate—the reality of gene therapy. Unarguably, for the moment, it can best be described as research rather

---

[29] N. 28, above, 24.
[30] A. L. Caplan, 'If Gene Therapy is the Cure, What is the Disease?' in G. Annas and S. Elias (eds), *Gene Mapping* (Oxford, 1992) 128.   [31] N. 30, above, 128.

than therapy, presaging the need for additional standards of information
and a careful risk/benefits analysis. The Committee on the Ethics of Gene
Therapy[32] (Clothier Committee), apparently acknowledging the research
element of gene therapy, required that:

the therapy be useful for biomedical knowledge; that it be conducted in a way that
maintained ethical standards of practice, protected the subjects of research from
harm, and preserved the subject's rights and liberties. Moreover, reassurance had
to be provided to the professions, the public and Parliament that these standards
were being upheld.[33]

As Churchill et al.[34] point out, the very language itself leads to the blurring of the distinctions between research and therapy. This conflation of
the two may result in insufficient scrutiny being undertaken of attempted
genetic therapy, and undoubtedly raises problems about the quality of
consent offered by those who are the subject of experimental techniques.
Yet, the power of the term 'gene therapy' is great. The benefits which will
allegedly accrue from successful gene therapy undoubtedly inform the
scientific enthusiasm for progress in this area, and will doubtless influence
the public perception of its value. Gene therapy on one, common, view
'signifies revolutionary, almost miraculous, insight into the workings of
the human body'.[35] This perception, it is argued, 'gives gene therapy its
unique cultural appeal'.[36]

And there is no doubt that the appeal is there. Although within the
scientific community itself, knowledge of the failures of gene therapy is
widespread, few in the wider public will be aware of the extent to which
this much-vaunted technique has so far failed to live up to expectations.
Orkin and Motulsky, for example, claim that:

Expectations of current gene therapy have been over-sold. Overzealous representation of clinical gene therapy has obscured the exploratory nature of the initial studies, colored the manner in which findings are portrayed to the scientific press and
public, and led to the widely held, but mistaken, perception that clinical gene therapy is already highly successful.[37]

However unfortunate, and disappointing to pioneers in this area, as
Scientific American put it in 1999, '[g]ene therapy took a standing eight-
count last winter, after drug contenders sponsored by a host of biotechnology and drug companies failed to cure a single patient of disease'.[38] Yet,

---

[32] Cm 1788 (London, 1992).

[33] J. Black, 'Negotiating the Genetic Revolution', in Brownsword et al., n. 4, above, 29, 48.

[34] L. R. Churchill et al., 'Genetic Research as Therapy: Implications of "Gene Therapy"
for Informed Consent' (1998) 26 The Journal of Law, Medicine and Ethics 38.

[35] N. 34, above, 43.   [36] Ibid.

[37] S. H. Orkin and A. G. Motulsky, National Institutes of Health Ad Hoc Committee
Report, Report and Recommendations of the Panel to Assess the N.I.H. Investment in
Research on Gene Therapy (7 Dec. 1995) (http://www. nih.gov/od/orda/panelrep.html).

[38] Scientific American, n. 20, above.

despite its current shortcomings, '[i]n laboratories and on Wall Street, there are signs that gene therapy is starting to stage a comeback'.[39] Moreover, Churchill *et al.* report that, 'despite the fact that no therapeutic benefit has been clearly demonstrated for the more than 2,100 subjects enrolled in gene transfer research worldwide, enthusiasm for gene therapy persists unabated'.[40]

Finally, gene therapy could also affect future generations. The tentative conclusion that gene therapy may essentially be no different from other therapy would not necessarily stand in the face of the fact that:

The main ethically significant difference between gene therapy and other therapies is the potential for the changes wrought in an individual by gene therapy to be passed on to offspring of the treated person.[41]

The possibility of changing the genetic make-up of future generations by manipulation of reproductive rather than somatic cells is perhaps the more controversial aspect of gene therapy.

Somatic and Germline Therapy

Davis[42] makes the distinction between these clear:

The possibilities for altering genes in humans fall into two classes. Somatic gene therapy aims at correcting the defect in specific cells in patients already born with a hereditary disease, while intervention in a germline cell results in transmission of the desired gene to all the cells of the developing embryo and hence to all subsequent generations.[43]

Of course, somatic gene therapy could also be made available at the embryonic or foetal stage, and germline therapy could be conducted on someone already alive. The critical distinction is not the stage of the development of the human being but rather the nature of the cells affected. Somatic therapy, for obvious reasons, has been the beneficiary of by and large favourable comment, resembling most closely the kind of treatment to which we are used. Essentially, it heals a particular condition by targeting non-reproductive cells in the same way as more conventional treatment currently does. The techniques may differ but the intention and the outcome are similar.

In the United Kingdom, the Clothier Committee[44] felt that somatic gene therapy raised no new ethical issues, but that it required close regulation.[45] In addition, it recommended that gene therapy should be used only in the

---

[39] *Ibid.*   [40] Churchill *et al.*, n. 34, above, 38.
[41] Murray, n. 17, above, 58.
[42] B. D. Davis, 'Limits to Genetic Intervention in Humans: Somatic and Germline', in Ciba Foundation Symposium, n. 9, above, 81.
[43] *Ibid.*   [44] Clothier Committee, n. 32, above.
[45] Para. 4.8 and Part 6.

case of life-threatening disorders or those which cause serious handicap, or where there was no treatment, or the treatment available was unsatisfactory.[46] In 1982, the President's Commission for the Study of Ethical Problems[47] gave wholehearted endorsement to the development of somatic gene therapy, which aims for 'the correction of genes within somatic cells, cells other than ova, sperm cells and their precursors. It involves targeting cells in specific identifiable organs or tissues of individual patients'.[48]

Despite the enthusiasm and optimism surrounding it, somatic therapy has its limitations and 'can be expected to be beneficial in only a very limited range of hereditary diseases'.[49] Thus, even if gene therapy becomes of practical value, it will not necessarily prove to be a panacea.

It seems to be widely accepted, however, that if and when somatic gene therapy is tried, tested, and successful, it will present no real new dilemmas. This is in stark contrast to the alternative of germline therapy. However, the occasional cautionary voice can be heard even about somatic therapy. Billings, Hubbard, and Newman,[50] for example, have noted that '[u]nintended changes in DNA may occur when gametes are manipulated or stored. Inadvertent germline mutations, therefore, may have already occurred as a result of reproductive technologies in current use, such as artificial insemination and IVF.'[51] They urge that more research is needed into whether or not germline modifications are already occurring even where the therapy is intended only to be somatic.

Germline therapy, as has been noted. is generally frowned upon. The Clothier Committee recommended that germline therapy should not be permitted.[52] In the United States, as Davis reports:

The Presidential Commission strongly opposed the application of germline intervention in humans. Their main argument was that altering human genes in a heritable way would be taking human evolution into our hands—a Promethean undertaking that we should not initiate.[53]

The main criticisms of germline therapy are such as to distinguish it, apparently, from somatic therapy. Whereas somatic therapy, it is thought, affects only the treated individual, in germline therapy future offspring will carry the modified genetic blueprint through reproductive cells. Of course, this begs one important question—namely that it may be that in fact what we seek, or should be seeking, from genetic therapy *is* the eradication through the generations of a particular condition. On this view, it might seem strange to argue against germline therapy, since it would spare future

---

[46] *Splicing Life*, President's Commission for the Study of Ethical Problems (Washington, DC, 1982).   [47] Davis, n. 42, above, 82.
[48] *Ibid.*, 81.   [49] *Ibid.*, 82
[50] P. R. Billings, R. Hubbard, and S. A. Newman, 'Human Germline Modification; A Dissent' (1999) 353 *Lancet* 1873.
[51] Billings *et al.*, n. 50, above, 1873.   [52] Para 2.26 and Part 5.
[53] Davis, n. 42, above, 85.

children the requirement of therapy for a gene defect which perhaps could have been removed from their genotype before their birth.

However, this is as yet by no means a mainstream argument, and the conclusion of many commentators remains that germline therapy should not be accepted, whereas somatic therapy should be. The key argument against germline therapy may, therefore, lie in the uncertainty about just what intervention of this sort may ultimately do. Although it must be said that the impact of somatic therapy will also remain unclear until scientific progress has been made and gene therapy becomes a practical and relatively common reality, there is sufficient concern as to the possible outcomes of germline treatment for caution not to be inappropriate. As Kand says:

Because germ-line therapy is intended to cure not only the individual patient but future generations, it is fundamentally different from conventional treatment. Furthermore, while somatic therapy introduces new genetic information into cells in which only a small fraction of the individual's total genetic information is activated and utilised, germ-line therapy affects cells in which all or most of the individual's genetic information is yet to be activated and used. . . . Most genes are only 'switched on' as different cells differentiate and different tissues and organs assume different functions. Germ-line therapy, then, introduces a new element of uncertainty with unforeseeable risks to the future individual child. And even if the first-generation child is not itself affected, second or third generations might be.[54]

The future for germline therapy, therefore, looks bleak. However, as was noted in the Declaration of Inuyama (1990):

The modification of human germ cells for therapeutic or preventive purposes would be technically much more difficult than that of somatic cells and is not at present in prospect. Such therapy might, however, be the only means of treating certain conditions, so continued discussion of both its technical and its ethical aspects is essential. Before germ-line therapy is undertaken, its safety must be very well established, for changes in germ cells would affect the descendants of patients.[55]

The door may, therefore, be slightly ajar. Billings, Hubbard, and Newman[56] also suggest that, although germline therapy should continue to be outlawed at the moment, this may require reconsideration if it becomes more feasible or promises benefits.

Concern for the welfare of future generations is, of course, not misplaced. But it may pull in two distinct ways. On the one hand, The UNESCO Declaration of the Responsibilities of the Present Generations Towards Future Generations[57] maintains that '[t]he present generations

[54] Kand, n. 13, above, 14.
[55] Human Genome Mapping, Genetic Screening and Gene Therapy (Council for International Organization of Medical Sciences, 22–17 July 1990) Art. VI.
[56] N. 50, above.   [57] UNESCO Declaration (Paris, 1997).

have the responsibility of ensuring that the needs and interests of future generations are fully safeguarded'.[58] Article 6 also states that '[t]he human genome, in full respect of the dignity of the human person and human rights must be protected and biodiversity safeguarded. Scientific and technological progress should not in any way impair or compromise the preservation of the human and other species.' Arguably, these Articles may caution against intervention which affects future generations in the absence of knowledge of its consequences, but they surely could *not* be taken as a blanket prohibition on germline therapy should its potential turn out to be positive.

On the other hand, increasing credence is also given to the concept of intergenerational justice—a concept which may suggest that current genetic knowledge *should* be used in ways which enhance the health and well-being of children yet to be born. Macer,[59] for example, has this to say:

A common feature of many issues raised by the human genome project data is that we need to consider the effects of knowledge and technology on future generations. We have a responsibility to future generations. The beneficiaries and those at risk may not yet exist. In the sense of benefits and risks, it is their genome project more than ours. We have an obligation to the future based on the principle of justice.[60]

The genetic revolution has made it possible to take this obligation seriously, and, if this is done, it may yet be necessary to revisit the universal ban on germline therapy. As Fletcher and Wertz say:

The completion of the human genome project will provide a basis for acting on a moral obligation for *future* generations, a claim that has appeared weak in the past. A generation *with* such knowledge who neglected to use it to minimize the risks in reproduction could hardly be said to respect the requirements of intergenerational justice.[61]

Arguably, banning even research into the potential of germline therapy might conflict with this obligation and result in failing to allow children to be born without being genetically compromised.

For the moment, however, one final argument remains. Indeed, this may be seen as the single most telling argument against germline therapy—namely, that 'even if . . . medical risks could be overcome, there would still remain the consideration that germline therapy means treating tomorrow's children with today's techniques which may be deemed inferior in times to come'.[62]

---

[58] Art. 1.   [59] D. Macer, 'Whose Genome Project?' (1991) 5 *Bioethics* 183.
[60] Macer, n. 59, above, 209.
[61] J. C. Fletcher and D. C. Wertz, 'An International Code of Ethics in Medical Genetics Before the Human Genome is Mapped' in Z. Bankowski and A. Capron (eds.), *Genetics, Ethics and Human Values: Human Genome Mapping, Genetic Screening and Therapy* (xxiv CIOMS Round Table Conference, 1991) 97, 103.   [62] Kand, n. 13, above, 15.

However, this too begs questions. In reaching decisions about whether or not to screen for, and therefore screen out, certain genetic conditions (a practice already well accepted) we too deny these potential children the possibility of benefiting from future medical progress, particularly where the disorder being identified is late-onset. If the argument is to work against germline therapy, might it not also work here? Moreover, such an argument might have to be extended beyond germline and into somatic therapy also, thus bringing all, or much of, research into gene therapy to a halt. The possibility that even somatic therapy may have germline consequences has, for example, already been noted.

The debate, however, is probably not yet over. Indeed, some believe that it has not even been entered into thoroughly. Black,[63] for example, makes the following point:

Germ line therapy raises quite fundamental issues . . . which have not been aired by any of the current regulatory authorities . . . or by the Clothier Committee. These include whether germ line manipulation should be permitted as a matter of individual choice, with only manipulation which is deliberately intended to cause harm being prohibited; or whether manipulation should be seen as an act which directly affects another, and so limited to improving the health of that person . . .; how, if at all, germ line manipulation affects the dignity of another human being; the psychological effects of germ line manipulation on parents and children; and the broader implications for genetic diversity and variability.'[64]

What seems clear, therefore, is that gene therapy may offer great hope for the future but that its ramifications are less susceptible to the standard risks/benefits analysis used in conventional medicine. Whether somatic or germline, the consequences are, as yet, unknown and arguably unknowable. The ambivalence towards the application of genetics which was identified earlier is likely to make the decision whether or not to embrace progress in gene therapy more difficult. Time may, however, be on our side and on that of the geneticists involved. In fact, it has been suggested that the reported failures of gene therapy to date have led to 'geneticists . . . studying their failures and starting to develop a clearer picture of what they are up against. Many researchers are optimistic that the present retrenchment actually bodes well for the long-term success of genetic medicine.'[65]

However, it has already been suggested that public resistance to manipulation of genes stems from both an overestimate of the role played by genes in making us human and the concurrent, albeit somewhat paradoxical, desire to assert ourselves as free-thinking, free-willed individuals. Perhaps this apparent tension may be resolved by focusing not so much on the techniques which are or may be available to modify or manipulate our

---

[63] Black, n. 33, above.   [64] *Ibid.*, 49.
[65] *Scientific American*, n. 20, above.

genetic inheritance, but rather on the extent to which free will and reductionism may be tempered by control. Arguably, it is the fear of losing
control that results in much of the concern surrounding the future of gene
therapy.

Who Controls Technology?

It could be argued that the intense focus on genes, and what they may or
may not do, has skewed the debate. It has already been suggested that
people and communities may be focused—albeit understandably—on only
one part of the picture that is the genetics revolution. Current estimates
suggest that the Genome Project is ahead of time, and that we may learn
sooner rather than later the 'genetic blueprint of each of us'.[66] Academic
and other comment has rightly been concerned to explore not only the
genetic markers for disease, but also the rationale for their identification
and the possible uses to which genetic information might be put. It is
perhaps rather obvious, but necessary, to suggest that the knowledge gap
between the scientists involved in this venture and the general public is
considerably greater even than that which exists between diagnostic and
therapeutic capacity.

Public concern about the possible uses and misuses of genetic information is not misplaced, but it may be ill-informed on occasion. For this
reason, virtually every academic or other report on the new genetics
emphasizes the importance of public education about the consequences of
genetic research. The British Medical Association, for example, has said
that:

People's lack of knowledge about genetic modification has in the past given rise to
fear and to opposition to new developments . . . the scientific community, both in
academia and commerce has a duty to inform the general public of new developments in the application of genetic modification in a manner comprehensible to lay
people.[67]

Education has, of course, an important role to play both in clarifying
the potential for good and in elucidating the potential for harm that spring
from the genetics revolution. However, central to the argument in this
paper is the assertion that more than education is required. If, as has been
suggested, human beings are cautious, or outright anxious, about the
acquisition and use of genetic knowledge, in part it may not be just
because of the shortfall in understanding. It may also be because this

---

[66] Human Genome 1991–2 Program Report, United States Department of Energy, Office
of Energy Research Office of Environmental Research (Washington, DC, 1992), foreword,
p. iii.
[67] Our Genetic Future: The Science and Ethics of Genetic Technology (Oxford, 1992)
227–8.

shortfall leaves the power to use and manipulate the knowledge (and us) in the hands of faceless 'others'. Franklin puts this proposition starkly:

One of the important aspects of modern technological practice is that it allows the control of people in ways that make the control invisible. No longer does Big Brother blare out of loud speakers. Big Brother barely bleeps today. The invisibility of control ought to concern us very profoundly.[68]

Of course, some regulation is overt, albeit complex. Black, for example, says:

If you turn to ask what structures exist to regulate genetic technology . . . then you find a mass of legal regulations, non-legal rules, codes, circulars, practice notes, international conventions, and ethical codes. There exists an enormously complex set of advisory bodies, regulatory bodies, committees, professional bodies, and industry associations, operating at an international, national and sub-national level. In the UK, at the national level alone, there are over eleven different bodies involved in the regulation of some aspect of genetic technology.[69]

The major national organizations directly addressing the question of gene therapy are, however, considerably fewer. Following the report of the Clothier Committee in 1992, the Gene Therapy Advisory Committee (GTAC) was established in 1993. As Black notes, 'GTAC's remit is to consider the scientific merits and potential risks of gene therapy'.[70] However, she criticizes GTAC's approach, claiming that 'it has not appeared to see it to be necessary to consider itself the wider social or ethical implications of interfering with genetic make-up'.[71] If true, this would be unfortunate, as the Clothier Committee clearly recognized the need for careful regulation of gene therapy.

Little wonder that the genetics revolution causes anxiety—anxiety which will inevitably colour our approach to gene therapy. Given that the subtleties of such therapy may be lost on many, there is also the lurking suspicion about the nature of the entire enterprise. For some, science merely does things because it can, not because it should. Similar criticisms have, of course, been levelled at medicine's other revolution—that in assisted reproduction. What Ikenotos calls 'defaulting to science'[72] occurs when 'we assume that if the technology is there, we should use it, and then we act on this assumption without critical evaluation of the wisdom of acting'.[73] However, as with genetics, criticisms and critiques tend to arise after, rather than before, the event, in large part because science moves in mysterious (and unknown) ways. As Kass claims:

---

[68] U. Franklin, 'New Threats to Human Rights Through Science and Technology—The Need for Standards' in K. E. Mahoney and P. Mahoney (eds.), *Human Rights in the Twenty-First Century* (Dordrecht, 1993), 734. [69] Black, n. 33, above, 29.
[70] *Ibid.*, 48. [71] *Ibid.*
[72] L. C. Ikenotos, 'Code of Perfect Pregnancy' (1992) 53 *Ohio State Law Journal*, 1205, 1286. [73] *Ibid.*

Introduction of new technologies often appears to be the result of no decision whatsoever, or of the culmination of decisions too small or unconscious to be recognized as such. Fate seems to hold the reins; what can be done is done. But technological advance is not automatic. Someone is deciding on the basis of some notions of desirability, no matter how self-serving or altruistic.[74]

These comments would, I suggest, argue for a greater proactive concentration on the ethics of science itself, and by implication of gene therapy, than that which currently exists. Concentration on the uniqueness of individual genetic make-ups diverts attention from the real and critical question; namely, why are we searching for this information and who will control it? As the report from the Human Genetic Advisory Committee and the Human Fertilisation and Embryology Authority[75] says (in another context—that of cloning) 'the claim that each person is entitled to a unique genetic make-up is a . . . questionable assertion'.[76] Conceding this may lead to an acceptance that debate is better couched in terms of public control than in terms of private ownership of genetics.

And this may have an impact on how we seek to wrest control back into the hands of the public, rather than leaving it firmly in the hands of the scientist. Black argues that '[r]egulation has an important role to play in connecting the arguments of participants, in facilitating the integration of the wide range of views as to the appropriate course that the technology and its regulation should take'.[77]

Kinderlerer and Longley see a further benefit in regulation, arguing that:

By ensuring that controversial developments and the practices of scientists and clinicians are properly authorised and monitored a potent regulatory framework can assist public acceptance of 'cutting edge' techniques. . . . Besides being instrumental in the policy process law thus promotes legitimacy and accountability.[78]

Conclusion

In conclusion, let us return to the main strands of this discussion. First, it has been suggested that we are bigger than our genetic inheritance—that genes may predict some, but not all, of what we are. Yet contemporary obsession with genes and what they can tell us often leads to what the British Medical Association has called an 'incorrigibly reductionist'[79] view of what it is to be human. Concern about gene therapy—the capacity to change the mysterious make-up of individuals—is exacerbated by our growing obsession with ourselves as a conglomerate of genetic markers.

---

[74] L. R. Kass, *Towards a More Natural Science: Biology and Human Affairs* (New York, 1985), 25.   [75] N. 1, above.
[76] *Ibid.*, para 6.1.   [77] Black, n. 33, above, 29.   [78] Black, n. 28, above, 28.
[79] BMA, n. 67, above, 214.

Even if somatic therapy is little different from conventional therapy, any interference in genetic inheritance is, for the moment at least, greeted with considerable public anxiety. In effect, such anxiety falls directly into the trap of what it seeks to avoid. If we wish to declare ourselves bigger than our genes, we err by concentrating on them. The paradox is that the more our genetic inheritance is the focus of our interest, the more we may allow ourselves to be seen as little more than a collection of pre-programmed cells.

And the consequences of this relate to the second part of this discussion. To be sure, our genetic inheritance is of critical importance to how— perhaps even for how long—we live our lives. But investing it with an almost mystical symbolism, and forcing artificial constraints on how gene therapy may be developed, would be to cede control to others, precisely at the point at which we should be seeking empowerment. If we do this, we lose an important battle. To continue with the military analogy, Kass has said:

Thoughtful men have long known that the campaign for the technological conquest of nature, conducted under the banner of modern science, would some-day train its guns against the commanding officer, man himself.[80]

Understanding that the issues are bigger than our own fascination with our genes may presage the development of an informed and sophisticated set of principles with which to address gene therapy. And these we need. Whether it is cloning or genetic enhancement—the drive to improve characteristics rather than seeking to prevent or cure disease—we will be unable rationally to consider the rightness or wrongness of progress without them. We have always been in part the product of our genes—the genetics revolution merely makes this evident, it certainly does not change that truth. The fact that we can now show this does not alter the fundamentals of humanity—merely it provides another source of information about why we are as we are. Gene therapy is undoubtedly a challenge, but it may also lead to treatments hitherto unimagined. Caution in scientific advance is seldom misplaced, but decisions as to risks and benefits must be free from the taint of panic, or the threat of reductionism, which all too often characterize the contemporary obsession with genes. Genes are not us. Rather, as Charlesworth says, people are 'meaning-making animals who use their biological and genetic endowments for their own purposes'.[81]

There is no turning back from the genetic revolution, but, if we are to reap its benefits and minimize its potential for harm, we must not fall into the trap of re-evaluating ourselves and what it is to be human, simply because one more piece of scientific evidence is available. Certainly that

---

[80] Kass, n. 74, above, 43. [81] Charlesworth, n. 9, above, 188.

information is important, and equally certainly its acquisition may lead to therapeutic progress. But it, like other information about dysfunction in health, should not be taken as an unchangeable given. If we are bigger than our genes, then let us control rather than fear genetic information; let us recognize its potential without capitulating in the face of what it seems to say. If these pitfalls can be avoided, much of what currently concerns us (for example, gene therapy) will become less important than the truly vital question—who controls genetics and for what purpose?

Medicine and the Child

PROTECTING THE UNBORN CHILD FROM ITS DRUG OR ALCOHOL ABUSING MOTHER

Kenneth McK. Norrie

Introduction

Since the early 1990s, the starting point of any discussion of most aspects of child law has invariably been a reference to the United Nations Convention on the Rights of the Child.[1] One of the few areas in which the Convention is not normally discussed is in relation to the child before birth, for it does not extend its substantive rights to the unborn child.[2] Nevertheless the Convention does recognize, in its Preamble, that 'the child, by reason of his physical and mental immaturity, needs special safeguards and care, including appropriate legal protection, before as well as after birth'. It is the purpose of this paper to explore the special safeguards afforded the unborn child and to attempt to identify which forms of legal protection ought appropriately to be extended to such a child within the context of legal systems which accept that, in some circumstances at least, the unborn child may lawfully be aborted. There is no inconsistency between permitting abortion, even on very liberal grounds, and extending protection to the unborn child who is likely to be born alive because its mother has decided against abortion; rather there is simply a recognition that the legal regulation of abortion and its availability supersedes any other question.

In exploring the protections potentially available to the unborn child, this paper will adopt a relatively narrow focus, by concentrating on only one fact scenario—that of the pregnant drug or alcohol abuser. This example has been chosen not only because it illustrates well the various difficulties in reconciling the pregnant woman's rights with the state's interest[3] in

---

[1] Adopted on 29 Nov. 1989, ratified by the United Kingdom on 16 Dec. 1991. This has been one of the most widely accepted of all the UN conventions, having been ratified by all but two member states of the United Nations (the two being Somalia and the USA).
[2] Nor, indeed, is 'child' defined except as 'every human being below the age of 18 years' (Art. 1).
[3] And indeed obligation: see the UN Convention on the Rights of the Child, Art. 24.

enhancing children's health, but also because the scenario occurs very much more frequently than other situations in which the woman's rights and the state's interest clash.[4] The overarching question is always this: what is the appropriate legal response to the dangers that an unborn child is subjected to through its mother's drug or alcohol abuse? This question contains within it two separate but related issues: (i) what response is legally competent, and (ii) what response, if any, serves any socially useful purpose? Before exploring these questions, it is as well to remind ourselves that the proposed fact scenario seldom in real life involves a case of black and white. In *Winnipeg Child and Family Services* v. *G*,[5] a case which will be referred to frequently in the following pages, a woman addicted to glue-sniffing had given birth to three children, two of whom had sustained severe and permanent damage to their central nervous systems as a result of their mother's prenatal substance abuse. The case concerned the woman's fourth pregnancy and the state's attempt to protect the unborn child from the woman's actions. Yet she had sought treatment for her addiction in the early stages of her pregnancy and had been turned away due to lack of resources. The wise words of McLachlin J bear repeating:

This is not a story of heroes or villians. It is the more prosaic but all too common story of people struggling to do their best in the face of inadequate facilities and the ravages of addiction.[6]

Applicable Principles

LEGAL RECOGNITION OF THE UNBORN CHILD

The existence of an unborn child has been recognized by the law for many hundreds of years, though until very recently the consequences of that existence were limited. Roman law accepted the so-called *nasciturus* principle,[7] that is to say, '[a]n unborn child is taken care of just as much as if it were in existence, in any case in which the child's own advantage comes into question; though no-one else can derive any benefit through the child before its birth'.[8] It has been pointed out that the authors of the relevant passages in the *Digest* saw this proposition as no more than a rule of

---

[4] B. Furrow *et al.*, *Health Law: Cases and Materials* (3rd edn., St Paul, Minn., 1997) report at 998 that foetal alcohol syndrome is the single most common cause of mental retardation at birth in the USA. See A. Gilbody, 'Effects of Maternal Drug Addiction on the Fetus' (1991) 10 *Adverse Drug Reactions in Acute Toxicology Review* 77.
[5] (1997) 152 DLR (4th) 193.   [6] *Ibid.*, at 200.
[7] *Digest*: 1, v. 7: '*Qui in utero est, perinde ac si in rebus humanis esset, custoditur, quoties de commodis ipsius partus quaeritur; quanquam alii, antequam nascatur, nequaquam prosit*'. See also D. 1, v. 26.
[8] This translation of the passage was approved by the House of Lords in *Elliot* v. *Joicey*, 1935 SC(HL) 57 at 70.

succession[9] (so that, typically, a posthumous child could share in the estate of a father who had died before the child's birth[10]); nevertheless the principle has been applied rather more widely in modern times. So for example in *Montreal Tramways* v. *Leveille*[11] the *nasciturus* principle was used to justify an award of damages to a child who suffered prenatal injury as a result of the defendant's negligence,[12] and in *Cohen* v. *Shaw*[13] it was used to justify an award of damages to a child whose father had been negligently killed before the child's birth.

These are what one might call the traditional problems caused by the unborn child—succession claims, and claims for damages against third parties—and they have, by and large, been dealt with by applying traditional legal reasoning to the issues. This has been possible for two main reasons. First, the court has been able to give recognition to the unborn child's existence for these purposes without conferring upon it legal personality, by utilizing the concept of contingent rights; and, secondly, neither issue creates any clash between the child's contingent rights and the mother's personal freedoms. However, more recently the courts in various jurisdictions have been faced with a number of issues arising from the existence of the unborn child which both challenge the child's lack of legal personality and raise fears that the pregnant woman's rights and liberties may be unduly infringed. These issues include whether a pregnant woman can be prevented from aborting the child she is carrying,[14] whether a pregnant woman can be forced to undergo medical intervention, not for her own benefit, but for the benefit of her unborn child,[15] and whether she can be subjected to civil[16] or even criminal[17] liability for any harm she causes.

---

[9] Alan Rodger (now Lord Rodger of Earlsferry, Lord President of the Court of Session), 'Report of the Scottish Law Commission on Antenatal Injury' [1974] *Juridical Review* 83, 89–90.

[10] See *Villar* v. *Gilbey* [1907] AC 139; *Elliot* v. *Joicey*, 1935 SC(HL) 57; *V* v. *G* [1980] 2 NSWLR 366; *Cox's Tr* v. *Cox*, 1950 SC 117; *Jervey* v. *Watt* (1762) Mor. 8170. The Supreme Court of Tasmania took the matter rather further in *Re the Estate of K* (1996) 5 Tas. R 365 when they held that two embryos which had been created by IVF but which had not yet been implanted into a woman were entitled to benefit on the same terms as a foetus *en ventre sa mère*. S. 28(6)(b) of the Human Fertilization and Embryology Act 1990 would prevent the same result in the UK. [11] (1933) 4 DLR 337.

[12] Other courts have, it is true, reached the same result without resort to the civilian fiction: see, e.g., *Watt* v. *Rama* [1972] VR 353; *Duval et al.* v. *Sequin et al.* (1973) 40 DLR (4th) 666; *Burton* v. *Islington Health Authority, De Martell* v. *Merton & Sutton Health Authority* [1992] 3 All ER 833. [13] 1992 SLT 1022.

[14] *Paton* v. *Trustees of the British Pregnancy Advisory* Service [1978] 2 All ER 987; *C* v. *S* [1987] 2 WLR 1108; *Attorney General of Queensland, ex rel. Kerr* v. *T* (1983) 46 ALR 275; *Wall* v. *Livingstone* [1982] 1 NZLR 734; *Tremblay* v. *Daigle* (1990) 62 DLR (4th) 634; *Kelly* v. *Kelly*, 1997 SLT 896. See A. Grubb and D. Pearl, 'Protecting the Life of the Unborn Child' (1987) 103 *Law Quarterly Review* 340.

[15] *Re AC*, 573 A 2d 1235 (1990); *Re MB (Medical Treatment)* [1997] 2 FLR 426.

[16] *Lynch* v. *Lynch* (1991) 25 NSWLR 411; *Dobson* v. *Dobson* (1997) 148 DLR (4th) 332 (CA New Brunswick), 9 July 1999 (Sup. C. of Canada).

[17] *Johnson* v. *State*, 602 So. 2d 1288 (Fla. 1992).

Other than the first, all are relevant to the pregnant drug or alcohol abuser. The two most widely used arguments against resolving such conflicts in favour of the foetus are (i) that the unborn child lacks legal personality and (ii) that the woman's presently existing right to self-determination is necessarily stronger than the foetus's contingent rights. Neither of these arguments is, however, on its own, sufficient answer, though together they raise a formidable barrier to the recognition of foetal rights. Each will be examined separately before exploring the possible responses of the law to the ever more pressing social problem of the drug or alcohol addicted pregnant woman.

LEGAL PERSONALITY

That the unborn child has no legal personality is a proposition too well established, at least in Scots and English law, to be departed from by other than clear statutory provision.[18] Though its genesis may well lie in the rudimentary state of medical knowledge in times gone by,[19] the rule continues to dominate the law of pregnancy. It is sometimes attacked on the basis that there is no moral—or indeed biological—difference between a born child and an unborn child, but this misses the point that the unborn child's lack of legal personality is an artificial legal construct, not a matter of natural fact. The law requires to identify a factor which distinguishes between natural entities with legal personality and natural entities without legal personality, and it has chosen for pragmatic reasons (including, importantly, its certainty) the separation of the child from its mother as the point of this distinction. This is no more illogical than any other rule of law, such as, for example, that which states that adult competency does not exist the day before, but it suddenly comes into existence on the day of, a person's specified birthday. It would be just as rational—and at the same time just as illogical—to choose the moment (if

---

[18] 'A "person" denotes someone who is living, not someone who has yet to be born', *per* Woolf LJ in *D (A Minor)* v. *Berkshire County Council* [1987] 1 All ER 20, 30; '[i]n law a foetus is not yet a person, and is no more a person at [a] late stage than at any other stage from conception onwards', *per* Lord Prosser in *Hamilton* v. *Fife Health Board*, 1992 SLT 1026, 1030; '[a]n unborn person, or foetus, is not a person in the eyes of the law': *ibid.*, 1993 SLT 624, 629, *per* Lord McCluskey. In relation to English law, it was said by Baker P that this proposition 'permeates the whole of the civil law of this country': *Paton* v. *Trustees of the British Pregnancy Advisory Service* [1978] 2 All ER 987, 989. And in *Attorney General's Reference (No. 3 of 1994)* [1997] 3 WLR 421, 434G, Lord Mustill said '[i]t . . . is established beyond doubt for the criminal law, as for the civil law . . . that the child *en ventre sa mère* does not have a distinct human personality, whose extinguishment gives rise to any penalities or liabilities at common law'. This last-mentioned case is discussed by J. K. Mason in 'A Lord's Eye View of Fetal Status' (1999) 3 *Edinburgh Law Review* 246.

[19] See the dissenting judgment of Major J in the Supreme Court of Canada case of *Winnipeg Child and Family Services* v. *G* (1997) 152 DLR (4th) 193, 232–3.

such a moment could be determined with the requisite precision) the child acquires viability[20] or the moment of fertilization.

However, we must beware of making too much of the distinction and of investing the rule of the unborn child's lack of legal capacity with more import than it can bear. It is not, for example, true that lack of legal personality equals lack of legal protection. While accepting that the unborn child has no legal personality, it certainly does not follow that injury or death may be visited upon the unborn child with impunity (just as animals, who have no legal personality, cannot be subjected to acts of cruelty or neglect with impunity and just as a listed building, which has no legal personality, or a tree subject to a tree preservation order can be destroyed only with special permission).[21] Conversely, full legal personality does not guarantee full legal protection.[22] So lack of legal personality is not in itself sufficient to deny protection to a foetus from the noxious substances ingested by its mother. The law has, in fact, always protected the unborn child, notwithstanding its lack of legal personality, by prohibiting abortion except in certain specified circumstances.[23] It is suggested that there are only three propositions that flow from the unborn child's lack of legal personality: (i) it cannot own property nor be a party to court action or other juridical acts, (ii) any rights that may be retrospectively vindicated are entirely dependent on the child's subsequent live birth, so that if it dies before then no such right arises, and (iii) abortion is not homicide. This last proposition is far and away the most important and, in truth, is the primary reason we cling to the notion that the unborn child has no legal personality. However illogical in morals, biology, and law the rule is, any society that wishes to sustain the legality of abortion can do so with an easy conscience only when the unborn are characterized as something other than full human persons. But to repeat the important point—it is not lack of legal personality alone that qualifies the protections that the unborn child is entitled to receive.

---

[20] It is rational because this too is a moment that marks a change in the physical development of the foetus, and it is illogical because a child unable to survive without its mother arguably needs more protection from its mother than a child who is so able. Viability of course underpins the US Supreme Court's approach to abortion (see *Roe v. Wade*, 410 US 113 (1973)) and, legislatively, English law's concept of child destruction (see Infant Life (Preservation) Act 1929).

[21] 'Whatever else it may be, a 36-week-old foetus is not nothing; if viable it is not lifeless and it is certainly human': *per* Judge LJ in *St George's Hospital NHS Trust v. S* [1998] 3 All ER 673, 687.

[22] An air force pilot who drops bombs on Belgrade or Baghdad knowing that civilian casualities are possible is not guilty of homicide, nor are his superiors who ordered him to do so. For the protection of human life becomes highly qualified in times of war.

[23] A Scottish judge explained abortion in this way: 'abortion in the sense of the criminal law is held to be criminal because its successful accomplishment results in the destruction of potential human life': *per* Lord Anderson in *HM Adv. v. Anderson*, 1928 JC 1, 4.

PERSONAL LIBERTY

Though there are some rules regulating the conduct of every pregnancy (most particularly the rule against unlawful abortion) by and large the law adopts a hands-off approach to pregnancy, in the sense that it does not require the pregnant woman to follow any particular medical regime or require her to give up certain lifestyle activities. The principle of autonomy is often cited as the main reason for the law's diffidence in regulating pregnancy: a woman who becomes pregnant does not thereby become less of an individual human person who has all the rights and freedoms accorded other human persons.[24] While this is undoubtedly so, it does not follow that she is entirely at liberty to use her freedom to inflict harm, deliberately or even negligently, and for that reason the principle of autonomy is at best an incomplete answer to attempts to prevent pregnant women from acting as they wish.[25] While every human person has rights and freedoms, so too does he or she have responsibilities and duties and, so long as these responsibilities and duties serve some legitimate purpose, we do not regard them as an infringement of our personal autonomy. The parents of a child have the responsibility to safeguard and promote their child's health, development, and welfare, and to pay for its upkeep, and this is not regarded as any infringement of the parents' autonomy, although it does, of course, limit their freedom to act as they may wish. A parent of a young child cannot go out for an evening drinking, or go off to the south of Spain for a week's holiday, without making arrangements for the suitable care of the child. And if the parent has no family or friends to call upon for help and cannot afford a baby-sitter then she must simply stay at home and fulfil her parental duties. Society as a whole has no difficulty with this limitation of freedom. So the question with the pregnant woman is not so much what liberty she is entitled to but the nature and extent of the duties being pregnant imposes upon her.

At the very least, a woman who is pregnant is under a moral duty not to cause avoidable harm to another, by refraining from activities which,

---

[24] So, e.g., in *St George's Hospital NHS Trust* v. *S* [1998] 3 All ER 673 the Court of Appeal held that '[i]n our judgment while pregnancy increases the personal responsibilities of a woman it does not diminish her entitlement to decide whether or not to undergo medical treatment. Although human, and protected by the law in a number of different ways . . . an unborn child is not a separate person from its mother. Its need for medical assistance does not prevail over her rights. She is entitled not to be forced to submit to an invasion of her body against her will, whether her own life or that of her unborn child depends on it. Her right is not reduced or diminished merely because her decision to exercise it may appear morally repugnant', *per* Judge LJ at 692A–B. This reasoning strongly underpins the important decision of the Supreme Court of Canada in *Winnipeg Child and Family Services* v. *G* (1997) 152 DLR (4th) 193 and *Dobson* v. *Dobson*, 9 July 1999.

[25] So in *Dobson* v. *Dobson*, n. 24, above, the Supreme Court of Canada conceded that the application of strict tort principles would lead to maternal liability for injuring an unborn child and they were required to have recourse to public policy to deny liability.

foreseeably, may lead to such harm. And here we must remember that the unborn child can be—and is—regarded as an 'other' for these purposes, at least when foreseeably the child may become an 'other'. The child's lack of legal personality before it is born does not mean that there is no obligation to avoid inflicting injuries before birth, if it is foreseeable that a child will be born and may suffer as a result of these injuries. The law in fact has for long recognized this when the harm is caused by third parties, and prenatal injury has founded actions for damages on behalf of children who have been born suffering from the consequences of actions occurring before their birth.[26]

So, we are all subject to the duty not to harm others, and an unborn child may be an 'other' for these purposes, notwithstanding its lack of legal personality. Is the pregnant woman herself in any different deontological position? It is in the very nature of duties, moral and legal, that our liberties are qualified by the need to respect the rights and legitimate interests of both others and those who will become others, and in that sense are restricted. It follows that, as a moral proposition at least, the pregnant woman has a duty to change her behaviour if she can for the sake of her unborn child, notwithstanding the limitations on her freedom of action. The basis of this duty is neither that she is a woman, nor that she is pregnant, nor that the foetus has a right not to be injured, but that she, like everyone else, ought to avoid causing foreseeable pain and suffering to another person sometime in the future. We all have moral duties to modify our behaviour if we know that our behaviour is likely to harm others, and this is no less so in situations in which we did not intend to find ourselves.

The real question, however, is whether that moral duty can be enlarged into a legal duty. Now, the difference between a moral duty and a legal duty lies primarily in the sanction. The sanction for breach of a moral duty is diminution of respect—we do not like people who act against a generally accepted moral code.[27] The sanction for breach of a legal duty, on the other hand, is a state-enforced penalty, whether civil or criminal. A moral duty becomes a legal duty when society in general believes that diminution of respect is no longer an adequate response to its infringement. So the question becomes one of identifying the appropriate response to a pregnant woman's breach of her moral obligations. If a pregnant woman continues to take drugs or to abuse alcohol during her pregnancy, knowing of the risk of harm to her as yet unborn child, what *should* the law do?

---

[26] See, e.g., *Montreal Tramways v. Leveille* [1933] 4 DLR 337; *Womack v. Buchhorn* 187 NW 2d 218 (Mich. 1971); *Watt v. Rama* [1972] VR 353; *Duval et al. v. Seguin et al.* (1973) 40 DLR (3d) 666; *X v. Pal* (1991) 23 NSWLR 26; *Burton v. Islington Health Authority, De Martell v. Merton and Sutton Area Health Authority* [1992] 3 All ER 833. And see now, for English law, s. 1 of the Congenital Disabilities (Civil Liability) Act 1976.

[27] And while it cannot be denied that the concept of a 'generally accepted moral code' has far less breadth, and indeed far less validity today, than it once had, it is nevertheless submitted that most people would accept that it is 'wrong' to inflict avoidable harm on another.

There are various possibilities. It may incarcerate her as a means of preventing her from taking drugs, or subject her to legal liability, civil or criminal, for any harm that she causes, or it may remove the child, once born, from her, for its own protection. Whether these responses are competent and appropriate or not will be explored in the next section.

The Legal Response

DAMAGES AGAINST THE MOTHER

English law has, by statute, set its face against allowing a child to sue its own mother for injuries she caused it before birth.[28] Other jurisdictions do not have a statutory rule[29] and it has been left to the courts to decide whether one should be fashioned out of common law principles. In New South Wales in *Lynch* v. *Lynch*[30] a child successfully sued its mother for the injuries it received while *in utero* due to the mother's negligent car driving, though that decision was expressly limited to situations in which there is compulsory insurance.[31] On the other hand in *Dobson* v. *Dobson*[32] the Supreme Court of Canada held that for policy reasons there should be complete immunity from liability for actions done by a woman during her pregnancy.

Whether being given effect by statute or by common law, there are a number of reasons usually given to justify a rule of maternal immunity.[33] One is that if a child could sue his or her own mother this would disrupt family harmony and create an unwelcome adversarial atmosphere between

---

[28] Congenital Disabilities (Civil Liability) Act 1976, s. 2. The logic of the maternal exception has been challenged by M. Brazier, 'Parental Responsibilities, Foetal Welfare and Children's Health' in C. Bridge (ed.), *Family Law Towards the Millennium: Essays for PM Bromley* (London, 1997) 263–93 and by A. Whitfield, 'Common Law Duties to Unborn Children' (1993) 1 *Medical Law Review* 28.

[29] So, e.g., the 1976 Act was not extended to Scotland, the reason being that the main purpose of the 1976 Act was to provide recognition of the proposition that prenatal injury gave a cause of action—and this was assumed to be the law of Scotland in any case: see Scot. Law Com. No 30, *Liability for Antenatal Injury* (Edinburgh, 1973). So while the general rule applies in Scotland as in England the statutory exception—and the motor traffic exception to the exception—applies only in the latter jurisdiction.

[30] (1991) 25 NSWLR 411.

[31] It is, indeed, to be noted that as an exception to the maternal immunity rule in the 1976 Act, English law provides that a mother can be sued for prenatal injuries so long as those injuries were caused by her negligent driving of a motor vehicle: 1976 Act, s. 2. That maternal liability gives rise to unique difficulties is implicit in this exception since, generally speaking, the existence or otherwise of insurance is not permitted to influence a court's decision on liability. See J. Stapleton, 'Tort, Insurance and Ideology' (1995) 58 *Modern Law Review* 820, 823–4. The rule, however, is long gone that the court could not be informed that a defendant was insured: see *Smith* v. *Eric S. Bush (A Firm)* [1990] AC 831, 888, *per* Lord Griffiths.

[32] (1997) 148 DLR (4th) 332.

[33] See the English Law Commission's *Report on Injuries to Unborn Children*, Law Com. No. 60 (London, 1974).

the two.[34] This, however, is unconvincing, given that few legal systems today contain a restriction on the child's ability to sue either parent for injuries caused after birth. And in any case, in reality there will seldom be a truly adversarial relationship. The cases have mostly involved situations in which the child is seeking access to insurance funds through the mother's policy, and she is usually entirely supportive of this claim, being a defendant only in the sense of being the insurance company's nominee. Another argument is that the mother's freedom of action would be unduly restricted. There are two answers to this: first, as explained above, a restriction on the ability to inflict harm on another is not otherwise regarded as 'undue'; secondly, damages are a retrospective remedy—the woman is not prevented from acting as she wishes, but there is a cost to her actions.[35] A related argument is that the setting of the standard of care expected would be fraught with difficulty, requiring various policy distinctions to be made which the courts are ill-equipped to make and that, as a consequence, the woman's right to make so-called 'lifestyle choices' would be jeopardized.[36] However, it is not obvious that these difficulties would be any greater than those faced in other areas when the court is called upon to set the standard and to distinguish between those who can and those who cannot sue or be sued.[37] In any case, the lifestyle choices of a pregnant woman would be inhibited only to the extent that her choice could be shown (i) to be unreasonable, and (ii) to be the actual cause of the injury complained of. Adopting an unhealthy diet is not unreasonable if the woman cannot afford any better, and may not indeed be unreasonable in any circumstances in light of the importance of individual autonomy.[38] Smoking and drinking moderately may increase a risk of injury to

[34] This argument was used in an early American case, *Hewellette* v. *George* 68 Miss. 703 (1891) though that case involved a tort committed against a living child.

[35] In *Dobson* v. *Dobson* the Court of Appeal for New Brunswick (1997) 148 DLR (4th) 332 (and Major J for the minority in the Supreme Court) had attempted to answer this point by limiting their decision to circumstances in which the pregnant woman owed a general duty of care, such as to other road users, with the result that recognizing liability to her subsequently born child did not impose any duty beyond that to which she was already subject. The majority in the Supreme Court dismissed this, rather summarily, on the basis that the law of tort recognizes only specific and not general duties of care. This does not, however, address the underlying point that the limitation avoids the criticism that the pregnant woman's freedom of action is being interfered with.

[36] This argument particularly influenced the majority in the Supreme Court of Canada in *Dobson* v. *Dobson*, 9 July 1999.

[37] See, e.g., the 'nervous shock' cases and the economic loss cases in which the English courts have had to draw some overtly artificial distinctions between who can sue and who cannot.

[38] In the past two or three decades the major tort cases in many jurisdictions, and particularly in England, have concentrated on the existence of a duty of care and the policy reasons for denying that existence. In the process it seems to have been forgotten that liability can be denied in individual cases at other stages of the action, such as breach or standard of care, and causation. Accepting the existence of a duty of care does not deny the court the right to say that in the circumstances the defendant acted reasonably, or that any breach of duty was

an unborn child but it would be almost impossible to prove that either was the *causa causans* of a particular child's injury.[39] Foetal alcohol syndrome, on the other hand, may easily be traced to a pregnant woman's heavy drinking; drug damage to a newborn infant's central nervous system may similarly be traced to the mother's use of crack cocaine or heroin.[40] A rather different justification for maternal immunity is that the mother may be encouraged to avoid liability completely by seeking an abortion, but that argument suffers the flaw that in systems like the UK, where abortion is not a 'right' of the woman to obtain on demand, and in any case an identical argument was dismissed as unrealistic when it was raised as a reason not to recognize the actionability of wrongful birth.[41] Another argument is the fear that the pregnant woman may be discouraged from seeking medical attention when pregnant for fear of the consequences if her actions do not conform to medically expected norms, leading to an overall reduction in maternal and neonatal health. This is a much stronger argument than the others, and it is all the greater with drug-abusing women whose pregnancies may be expected to require even more medical intervention than normal.

Another argument which seems to underlie the decision in *Lynch* is the lack of good that recognizing liability would actually do when there is no insurance fund to call upon if the suit is successful. Suing drug addicts is likely in virtually all cases to be completely pointless due to their economic circumstances. Economic indigence carries with it a cloak of practical immunity from civil suit whether or not there is any statutory immunity. This, however, is a matter of practicality and is a poor argument against the very principle of maternal liability—it denies liability to all on the basis that those most likely to be found liable are least likely to be able to pay any damages. Nevertheless it is certainly true that the practicalities of pursuing the case will protect the economically vulnerable and so, if civil

not the *causa causans* of the injury complained of. It may be that the higher courts prefer to concentrate on duty of care, since that is more clearly a policy issue than the fact-influenced breach and causation elements of the claim, and to concentrate on the elements influenced by fact would involve a lessening of judicial control over the development of the law.

[39] Difficulties in proving causation is not normally sufficient reason to deny liability in principle: *Barrett* v. *London Borough of Enfield* [1999] 2 FLR 426. The point here, however, is that in practice the difficulties will minimize the potential limitations to the pregnant woman's lifestyle choices.

[40] These are not the only examples in which causation may be established. A parent may knowingly carry a deleterious gene and nevertheless reproduce in the fairly forlorn hope that the genetic defect will not be passed on. A child's claim in this case, however, would be one for wrongful life since there was no chance that he or she would be born whole (though some other child might). Such a claim is not competent at common law in either Scotland (see *P's Curator Bonis* v. *Criminal Injuries Compensation Board*, 1997 SLT 1180) or England (see *McKay* v. *Essex Health Authority* [1982] QB 1166) and is legislatively incompetent in England: Congenital Disabilities (Civil Liability) Act 1976, s. 1(4).

[41] See *Thake* v. *Maurice* [1986] QB 644 and *MacFarlane* v. *Tayside Health Board*, 1998 SLT 307.

liability in damages were held to be a competent remedy, it is unlikely ever to be one that would be utilized in practice and its efficacy in protecting unborn children would therefore be very low.

INJUNCTION OR INTERDICT

While there is much authority for the proposition that a pregnant woman cannot be interdicted from seeking and obtaining a lawful abortion,[42] very different considerations come into play when the wrong sought to be interdicted is injury rather than destruction, for that wrong does not prevent the very existence of the person on whose behalf the remedy is being sought. The Scottish court[43] put it thus:

> Whether it is an actionable wrong to an unborn foetus for an abortion to be performed depends entirely on whether Scots law confers on the foetus a right to continue to exist in the mother's womb. Our conclusion is that Scots law recognises no such right in the foetus. It follows that no person can invoke the power of the court to vindicate such a right.

Implicit in that statement is the supposition that the conclusion might be different if what was sought to be interdicted was an actionable wrong, and in that case there may well be a power vesting in a person representing the foetus to vindicate the right. The Court of Session had 'no difficulty in accepting the proposition that the remedy of interdict would be available at the instance of a person or that person's representative to prevent damage being deliberately caused to that person, being damage which, if it occurred, would sound in damages in favour of that person'. This passage might be interpreted as support for the recognition of the competency of granting an interdict to prevent damage being (at least *deliberately*[44]) caused to an unborn child if that damage would, if it were allowed to happen, found an action for damages. If a foetus has a right not to be injured then someone acting on its behalf could interdict the action that would cause the injury. There are, however, insuperable difficulties in applying this in practice where the threat comes from the mother, First, in English law the mother's activities would not found an action for damages and therefore would not justify an injunction. Secondly, even in other jurisdictions it will seldom happen that the pregnant woman is intending to injure the child she will give birth to. Most drug-abusing pregnant women have no control over their own lives, and are in the unhappy position of subsuming all their own desires and wishes to their narcotic needs. This is unlikely to be considered sufficient to create *animus injuriandi*.

---

[42] See n. 14, above.

[43] *Kelly* v. *Kelly*, 1997 SLT 896, 901E.

[44] The competency of injunction or interdict against a person acting negligently, that is to say without intent to injure, is, at the very least, questionable.

And, thirdly, injunction or interdict would be incompetent because it would be too late. The child once born may have a right not to have been injured but the foetus in the womb, being unable to hold any right, does not. An injunction issues only to prevent the infringement of rights but there is no right in the foetus until born, and by then the damage is done.[45] An injunction is not granted against harm that has already occurred.

FORCING MEDICAL TREATMENT OR KEEPING THE MOTHER SECURE

Pregnancy and childbirth are amongst the most heavily medicated and controlled of all the natural functions. It is not surprising, nor disturbing, that this should be so, given the great personal costs that women bear for the sake of reproduction, the sake, that is, of the species. Nevertheless, the increased ability to protect life and health, not only of the pregnant woman but of the child she is carrying, has brought with it an increased, and entirely understandable, desire on the part of the medical profession to perform such medical procedure as is predicted necessary for the achievement of the optimal outcome, being the safe (to the mother) delivery of a healthy child.[46]

The vast majority of pregnant women probably share that desire and many, indeed, would subvert their own wellbeing in the interests of delivering a healthy child. Very occasionally, however, that outcome is threatened, or at least is perceived to be threatened, by the failure or refusal of the pregnant woman to follow medical advice. An unhelpful, but it seems tempting, solution is to seek court authority to force advised treatment on an unco-operative pregnant woman. So in *Raleigh-Fitkin-Paul Morgan Memorial Hospital* v. *Anderson*[47] and *In Re Application of Jamaica Hospital*[48] hospitals were authorized to give blood transfusions to pregnant women against their will. And in a well-known case from the Supreme Court of Georgia, *Jefferson* v. *Griffin Spalding County Hospital Authority*,[49] the court ordered a woman who was thirty-nine weeks pregnant to undergo a caesarean section when the prognosis was that there was a 99 per cent chance of foetal death and a 50 per cent chance of maternal death if this procedure was not adopted.[50] In England, Sir

---

[45] See *Winnipeg Child and Family Services* v. *G* (1997) 152 DLR (4th) 193.

[46] See M. Fletcher, 'The Fetus as Patient: Ethical Issues' (1981) 246 *Journal of the American Medical Association* 772.   [47] 201 A 2d 535 (NJ 1964).

[48] 491 NYS (2d) 898 (NY 1985).   [49] 274 SE 2d 457 (1981).

[50] In fact (and not uniquely—which is one of the features that make these cases so unattractive) the mother, in defiance of the court order, gave birth naturally, with no ill-effects for either herself or her child. So did the mother in *Raleigh*, n. 47 above. These cases have faced almost universal academic hostility. Amongst the most trenchant criticisms is found in N. Rhoden, 'The Judge in the Delivery Room: The Emergence of Court Ordered Cesareans' (1986) 74 *California Law Review* 1951. It should be noted that most US jurisdictions reject the approach in *Jefferson*, and indeed it has in more recent cases been highly qualified. So the DC Court of Appeals in *Re AC* 573 A 2d 1235 (1990) held that 'in *virtually* all cases the

Stephen Brown P ordered a caesarean section be performed without the consent of a competent pregnant woman,[51] finding support for doing so in the ill-considered dictum of Lord Donaldon MR in *Re T (Adult: Refusal of Medical Treatment)*[52] to the effect that 'the only possible qualification [to the rule that an adult competent patient has an absolute right to choose his or her own medical intervention] is a case in which the choice may lead to the death of a viable foetus'. That dictum has since been disapproved,[53] though not before the English courts had followed Sir Stephen Brown P's lead on a number of occasions.[54] The Court of Appeal has now signalled strongly that in the case of a competent woman the court has no jurisdiction to order her to submit to any medical treatment for the benefit of her unborn child (and that for the incompetent woman, since it may be assumed that she would want the best for her child, treatment without consent could be authorized, though only on the basis that it was in the best interests of the patient—i.e. of the pregnant woman).[55] The Court of Appeal said this:

A competent woman who has the capacity to decide may, for religious reasons, other reasons, for rational or irrational reasons, or for no reason at all, choose not to have medical intervention, even though the consequences may be the death or serious handicap of the child she bears, or her own death. In that event the courts do not have the jurisdiction to declare medical intervention lawful and the question of her own best interests objectively considered does not arise.[56]

---

decision of the patient will control', but they still pointed out that 'we do not quite foreclose the possibility that a conflicting state interest may be so compelling that the patient's wishes must yield'.

[51] *Re S (Adult: Refusal of Medical Treatment)* [1992] 4 All ER 671.

[52] [1992] 4 All ER 649.

[53] *St George's NHS Trust v. S* [1998] 3 All ER 673; *Re MB* [1997] 2 FLR 426 at 444D. In *St George's*, Judge LJ said at 688D–E '[h]ow can a forced invasion of a competent adult's body against her will even for the most laudable of motives (the preservation of life) be ordered without irremediably damaging the principle of self-determination? . . . The autonomy of each individual requires continuing protection even, perhaps particularly, when the motive for interfering with it is readily understandable'. In *McFall v. Shimp* (1978) 10 Pa D&C 3d 90 (1978) 14 Flaherty J said '[o]ur society, contrary to many others, has as its first principle, the respect for the individual, and that society and government exist to protect the individual from being invaded and hurt by another. . . . For our law to *compel* the defendant to submit to an intrusion of his body [notwithstanding that, in the court's view, his refusal to do so is morally indefensible] would change every concept and principle upon which our society is founded. To do so would defeat the sanctity of the individual'.

[54] *Re S (Refusal of Medical Treatment)* [1992] 3 WLR 806; *Tameside and Glossop Acute Services Trust v. CH* [1996] 1 FLR 762; *Norfolk and Norwich Health Care (NHS) Trust v. W* [1996] 2 FLR 613; *Rochdale Healthcare (NHS) Trust v. C* [1997] 1 FCR 274.

[55] *Re MB (Medical Treatment)* [1997] 2 FLR 426.

[56] [1997] 2 FLR 426, 436–7. It is to be noted that an essential element of a woman's freedom from compulsory intervention is her competency. On that issue, see *Re C (Adult: Refusal of Medical Treatment)* [1994] 1 WLR 290 and *Re JT (Adult: Refusal of Medical Treatment)* [1998] 1 FLR 48. In *Re MB* the pregnant woman was held incompetent due to her irrational fear of needles which, the Court found, effectively 'froze' her ability to make decisions. It has, of course, been pointed out that her competency would never have been

This reasoning is based squarely on the civil liberties argument. The court has determined, as it did in *Re F (In Utero)*,[57] that society would simply not accept the limitations on a pregnant woman's freedom of action that would necessarily follow from the order sought. To put it another way, the state's interest in child health is outweighed by both the woman's interest in her own autonomy and the state's interest in preserving the individual autonomy of its citizens. Exactly the same reasoning applies when the pregnant woman abuses drugs and attempts are made to force the pregnant woman to undergo drug treatment or drug withdrawal. Courts in England and Canada have refused to make orders the effects of which would be to limit the pregnant woman's freedom of movement. In *Re F (In Utero)*[58] a woman 'dabbled' in drugs and her itinerant lifestyle was considered to pose a risk to her unborn child. Nevertheless the child-care authority was unable to control the pregnant woman's behaviour by an order making the foetus a ward of court. Primarily this decision was made on the basis that the wardship jurisdiction could be exercised only in respect of legal persons, which the foetus was not, but the Court of Appeal was also deeply troubled by the civil liberties implications. To ward a foetus would necessarily give priority to the interests of the unborn child over the interests of the mother, since the only way the order could be enforced would be to secure the mother. It may be taken from this judgment that the court has assessed that society would not wish the mother's moral obligation to be enlarged to a legal obligation if the consequences of that (or, to put it another way, the sanction) was a limitation on freedom of movement of pregnant women demanded of no-one else.

Similarly, in *Winnipeg Child and Family Services* v. *G*[59] a child-care agency had sought an order requiring a pregnant woman who was addicted to glue-sniffing to be committed to a place of safety where she would have no access to volatile substances for the remainder of her pregnancy. The Supreme Court of Canada (by a majority of seven to two) held that this was not possible for the same two reasons as the Court of Appeal in *Re F* had felt unable to ward a foetus: (i) there was no legal person on whose behalf the child-care agency could act, and (ii) the order would involve restrictions on the pregnant woman's liberty which only a legislature had the power to impose.[60] The only two ways in which the state

questioned had she been willing to follow medical advice. The result of the earlier English cases (see n. 54 above) suggested, C. Widdett and M. Thomson rather tartly remark, 'that women in labour (and perhaps earlier) may only have the capacity to withhold consent so long as they do not': (1997) 5 *Feminist Legal Studies* 77 at 86.

[57] Discussed below.
[58] [1988] 2 All ER 193. See also *In Re Dittrick Infant* 263 NW 2d 37 (Mich. 1977).
[59] (1997) 152 DLR (4th) 193.
[60] The dissenting judges, Major and Sopinka JJ, held that the rule that a foetus acquires no actionable right until live birth was an anachronism of the common law based on rudimentary medical knowledge, and that the courts should be able to act, in strictly limited circumstances, to prevent easily avoidable harm being done to a highly vulnerable individual.

could compulsorily detain a person was through criminal process or under the mental health legislation, and until Parliament created additional authority, the courts were powerless to do so, even if they were so inclined. There was, however, a strong dissenting judgment, in which the judge's frustration in not being able to act to prevent easily avoidable harm is apparent. Yet that frustration ought to be no more significant than the frustration felt when one living person refuses to sacrifice him or herself for the sake of another. For as Brazier put it,[61] 'demanding that a woman undergoes Caesarean section to protect the child is akin to demanding that a father donate a kidney to his child suffering from renal failure'. The law makes no such demands, for reasons that are entirely self-evident, however frustrating it is to watch the child die.[62] Parents do, of course, have responsibilities to their children, but their failure in these responsibilities seldom allows the court to make an order requiring them to act. Even the single mother with no support who wants to go on holiday to Spain (perhaps to give herself some respite from the demands of child-care) cannot be prevented from leaving the country, though her children may well face child-care and protection proceedings if she does so, and she herself may well face a criminal charge of neglect. But her personal autonomy and her freedom of movement are not unduly inhibited.

CARE PROCEEDINGS

Every developed legal system has procedures for removing a child from his or her parents in order to protect him or her from harm caused by the parents. While it is, of course, impossible to remove a child from dangerous parents before the child is born, it is both competent and appropriate for the court or other tribunal dealing with the case to take account of the parents' actions before the child's birth in order to predict the likelihood of continuing risk to the child once born. So in *D (A Minor)* v. *Berkshire County Council*[63] the House of Lords was asked whether a child born suffering from drug withdrawal symptons, directly attributable to the mother's drug addiction and continued drug-taking during pregnancy, came within the statutory definition of a child in need of care, even though the child had never been in the care of its mother at any time after its birth. The court had little difficulty in holding that it was entitled to look to past as well as present events in order to predict whether in the future the child would be subject to risk from his or her parents. Apart from a matter of statutory interpretation, the surprise is that this case proved so

---

[61] *Parental Responsibilities*, n. 28, above, 281.
[62] And however much the court regards the refusal to donate to be morally reprehensible: see the quotation from *McFall* v. *Shimp*, n. 53, above.
[63] [1987] 1 All ER 20. See J. Fortin, 'Legal Protection for the Unborn Child' (1988) 51 *MLR* 54.

contentious. The result is no different from taking account of the fact that a father, with whom the mother lives, has a long history of sexually abusing children in his care, though the abuse all took place at times before the birth of his child. The same result was reached by the Supreme Court of Canada in *Winnipeg Child and Family Services* v. *G*[64] where it was held that while the child could not be protected by state intervention before birth, the mother's pre-birth actions could justify state intervention thereafter. A New Zealand court went rather further on the question of when the state could intervene through the protective provisions contained in the New Zealand Children, Young Persons and their Families Act 1989. In *In the Matter of Baby P (An Unborn Child)*[65] a child was held to be a 'child in need of care and protection' even before it was born,[66] though the facts of the case were unusual. The declaration did not seek to limit the liberty of the pregnant woman, who consented to it, but to give both her and her unborn child injunctive protection from the violent father who had threatened to kill the child. There was, in other words, no clash between the interests of the unborn child and the rights of the pregnant woman.

If a drug addict were to give birth to a drug-damaged child, there would be little problem in bringing that child within the terms of most jurisdictions' child protection procedures, which may include removing the child from its mother, perhaps immediately after birth.[67] It is, however, important to remember the justification for this. Any child protection procedure is designed neither to punish parents for their harmful actions nor to deter others from doing so. Rather, its sole aim is to protect the child from further damage. So it would not necessarily follow that, just because a child has been born injured, it will necessarily be removed from the parent who injured it. Rather, the question is whether further harm is likely to occur if the child is not removed.[68] As Lord Goff of Chieveley put it in *D (A Minor)* v. *Berkshire County Council*:

[64] (1997) 152 DLR (4th) 193.

[65] [1995] NZFLR 577, commented upon at [1997] 5 *Medical Law Review* 143.

[66] At least if the foetus was so far developed that it could survive indepenently of its mother.

[67] US cases up to 1994 are collated together at 20 ALR 5th 534.

[68] So in the New York case of *In Re Fletcher* 533 NYS 2d 241 (1988), it was held that a woman's continued use of cocaine while she was pregnant was insufficient in itself to justify a finding of child neglect. In *In Re Williams* 533 A 2d 16 (Md. 1987), it was held that *mere* alcoholism was an insufficient ground to remove a child from its parental home, while in *In Re Dustin T*, 614 A 2d 999 (Md. 1992) the word 'mere' in that judgment was emphasized and the effect of prenatal drug abuse was held to be the factor that allowed the court to hold the child to be a 'child in need of assistance'. The drug use itself was relevant to (although not necessarily determinative of) the mother's ability to provide proper care for her child. The matter is quite different in jurisdictions whose statutory schemes permit state intervention whenever harm has been caused, regardless of whether it is likely to continue: see *In Re Baby X* 293 NW 2d 736 (Mich. 1980) in which a child born with drug withdrawal symptoms was held for that reason alone to come within the statutory definition of a 'neglected child' (though that merely granted the court jurisdiction and did not necessitate that the disposal would involve the child's removal from its mother).

It is not enough that something has avoidably been done or omitted to be done in relation to the child in the past which has, for example, impaired its health, and that the symptoms or effects still persist at the relevant time; for it cannot be said in such circumstances that, at the relevant time, the child's health is being avoidably impaired: all that can be said is that its health has been avoidably impaired in the past.[69]

This case was, of course, decided under legislation prior to the Children Act 1989 but it is likely that the same result would be reached today, on the basis that the threshold criterion contained in section 31(2)(a), that the child is likely to suffer significant harm, has been fulfilled.[70] There is nothing artificial in regarding prior drug use as a relevant indication of future parenting ability, for in every child-protection case past events are used to predict the level of risk to the child in the future.[71] But the point is that this response is one of protection for the child, not one of punishment of its mother. So in *In Re Valerie D*[72] while the mother's prenatal drug abuse justified the protective response of removing the child, once born, from the mother, it did not justify the further step of terminating permanently the parent–child relationship. For many jurisdictions, therefore, the utilization of child protection procedures is the most common—and often the only competent—response to a child harmed by his or her mother's prenatal drug use.

Some people see this as a frustratingly inadequate response. However, it is as well to remember that every aspect of child care and protection involves a balance of different rights and interests. The need to protect the vulnerable is balanced in both the Children Act 1989 and the Children (Scotland) Act 1995 with the principle of family autonomy, or the right of individuals not to be unwarrantably interfered with in their family lives.[73] The fact of the matter is that all child-protection measures are based on predictions—predictions of likely harm, of the effect of state interference on children, and of the good that is done by interference in contrast to the harm that is sought to be avoided. As such, there will always be occasions when the predictions are wrong—when children are not protected when

---

[69] [1987] 1 All ER 20, 44.

[70] See, however, C. Wagstaffe, 'Harming the Unborn Child: the Foetus and the Threshold Criteria' (1998) 28 *Fam L* 160, who doubts this.

[71] In the different context of a custody dispute the Court of Appeals of Maryland put it thus: '[w]e must look to the future welfare of this infant. In making our decisions we should not gamble about that future. We can only judge the future by the past' (*Miller* v. *Miller* 62 A 2d 293 (1948), 298) and in the child care context they said '[p]arents' [past] ability to care for the needs of one child is probative of their ability to care for other children in the family' (*In Re William B* 533 A 2d 16 (1987), 21).

[72] 613 A2d 748 (Conn. 1992).

[73] This is given statutory effect in the Scottish legislation with the so-called 'no-order presumption', whereby the court is prohibited from making any order unless persuaded that it would be better to do so than to make no order at all: Children (Scotland) Act 1995, s. 16(3).

they ought to be, and when children are 'protected' when there is no need for it. The only way to ensure that protection is provided in every case in which it is needed is to cast the net so widely that it captures children who, in the event, do not need protection.[74] As a society we are not willing to pay that price and so, inevitably, the net being cast rather less widely, we fail to protect some children who do need it. Some would say that by doing so we are sacrificing children at the altar of family autonomy. So too with the unborn child the question is one of what price, in terms of individual autonomy, society is willing to pay. Just as we are unwilling to do everything possible, at whatever cost, to protect the living child, so too are we unwilling to do everything possible, at whatever cost, to preserve the health of the unborn child. For otherwise mothers' lives and health would be but a secondary consideration and society currently gives preference to women's health. The courts in England and Canada have concluded that society is not willing to pay the price in terms of women's freedom either. Yet it should not be forgotten that a woman whose exercise of her freedom leads to an injured child will herself pay an emotional price, as well as the possibility of having her child removed. Her harmful actions are not, in other words, entirely without legal consequence.

CRIMINALIZING THE MOTHER

Possibly the most extreme response that the law might adopt to a child being harmed by its mother's prenatal drug abuse would be to criminalize the mother, that is to say to prosecute her for the harm she has caused. As with potential civil liability, it is easy to find a legal logic to this. If a mother deliberately took drugs (or a 'noxious thing') to kill her unborn child as a result of which she suffers a miscarriage then she could face a charge of unlawful abortion or child destruction;[75] if the child were born alive, only to expire sometime later as a result of its drug-induced injuries, then it could be argued that the woman would be guilty of criminal homicide.[76] And if this were so then her deliberate or reckless injuring but not

---

[74] So in the Cleveland case in the late 1980s, when a large number of children, suspected of being victims of sexual abuse, were removed from their parents there was a predictable—and surely justified—public outcry when only a minority of the children were, in fact, victims of abuse.

[75] Under, in English law, the Offences Against the Person Act 1861, s. 58 and the Infant Life (Preservation) Act 1929, s. 1(1). The difference in the two lies in the age of the foetus. The former deals with the unborn child who is not yet capable of being born alive; the latter deals with the unborn child who is.

[76] This result is predicated on the assumption that the deontological position of the mother in relation to the unborn child is no different from that of third parties, and that therefore the cases of *Attorney General's Reference (No. 3 of 1994)* [1997] 3 WLR 421, *McCluskey* v. *Her Majesty's Advocate*, 1989 SLT 175; and *R.* v. *F* (1996) 24 MVR 436 (Sup. C. of NSW) are in point. The correlation of position was, however, strenuously denied in the Supreme Court of Canada in the civil liability case of *Dobson* v. *Dobson*, 9 July 1999.

killing of the child would logically amount to an assault. In sociological terms, it has been suggested[77] that characterizing the pregnant drug abuser as a criminal actually makes it easier for society to identify the appropriate response. Society's feelings towards drug abusers are in the normal case highly ambivalent—we see the abuser as simultaneously criminal and victim. But when the abuser becomes pregnant she loses all claims to our sympathy and forfeits her right to be regarded as a victim. The legal response is therefore such as is appropriate to crime and is not clouded by notions of welfare (either of the abuser, the child, or the foetus).

To see the law's response in terms of the criminal law is, of course, too simplistic. On a practical level, prosecutions are unlikely to be successful. In large measure this is because of the difficulties in proving the necessary mens rea. Few drug abusers have the requisite intent to harm the children they are carrying, and even recklessness will seldom be appropriate given the lack of control over their own lives that characterises most addicts. A Canadian commentator put it thus: '[w]omen do not abuse drugs out of a lack of care for their foetuses. Drug abusing pregnant women, like other drug abusers, are addicts. People do not want to be drug addicts. In addition, a product of addiction is the inability to control in-take of the substance being abused'.[78] In the United States of America, some prosecutors have attempted to get around this difficulty by founding on statutes of strict liability, such as those prohibiting the 'supply' of drugs.[79] This approach is irredeemably artificial and, revealingly, these attempts have generally been unsuccessful in securing (or at least maintaining) a conviction.

And on a policy level prosecution simply does not serve any rational purpose. It is not undertaken for the good of the child (but then prosecution is not normally seen in terms of the good it does to the victim). If the purpose of prosecution is to benefit the mother then it is but a blunt and ineffective instrument (unless, perhaps, education, counselling, and medical help were an inherent part of the sentence). The aim might be deterrence. The American cases suggest a touching faith in the deterrent effect of criminalization. Yet deterrence, which is seldom a satisfactory explanation for punishment on its own, is even less satisfactory when dealing with women (or others) who have so lost control of their own lives that they can protect neither themselves nor those for whom they are responsible and who have not the ability, therefore, to make the cost-

---

[77] Note, (1990) 103 *Harvard Law Review* 1325, 1341–42.

[78] J. Hanigsberg, 'Power and Procreation: State Intervention in Pregnancy' (1991) 23 *Ottawa Law Review* 35, 53, quoted with approval in *Winnipeg Child and Family Services* at 212.

[79] See, e.g., *Johnson v. State* 602 So. 2d 1288 (Fla. 1992); *State v. Gray* 584 NE 2d 210 (Ohio 1992); *Commonwealth v. Welch* 864 SW 2d 280 (Ky 1993). See also the earlier Californian case of *Reyes v. State* 75 Cal. App. 3d 214 (1977).

benefit analysis that deterrence theory presumes. We are left with retribution: the primitive feeling that a person who has harmed another needs to
suffer harm him- or herself in order that the social balance can be restored.
That may well sometimes justify the law's response to criminality, but it
must be borne in mind that retribution carries a financial cost, both in
terms of court time and incarceration. In relation to drug misuse, this cost,
in social terms, would almost certainly be better spent in providing education, addiction counselling, and medical support for those seeking to
escape their drug misuse.

Conclusion

From the above it can be seen that in many jurisdictions the approach of
the law is to eschew actions which would involve requiring the pregnant
woman to act in particular ways, or to refrain from acting in particular
ways, but to permit some consequences to follow from any harm that the
child, once born, suffers. So while interdict is not available to protect the
unborn child from harm, damages can be awarded in at least some circumstances. While a woman cannot be forced to undergo medical treatment or
drug rehabilitation for the benefit of her unborn child, her failure to seek
proper medical care may well be held to be a wrongful act both in the law
of civil liability and, more practically, for the purposes of child care and
protection. The law is attempting to strike at the same time two balances.
The first is between personal liberty and individual responsibility. The law
strikes that balance by permitting the pregnant woman to act as she
pleases, without restraint, during her pregnancy but at the same time
recognizing that any harm the child suffers as a consequence may justify a
legal response after the child is born, in terms of care proceedings, civil
liability (in some jurisdictions), and even criminal liability. And the second
balance is between what is competent and what is appropriate as a legal
response to women harming their own children. In some situations a civil
claim or criminal charge may well be competently brought but, for the
reasons explored above, will seldom if ever be appropriate, leaving the
child protection procedures as the only practical response. It is likely that
the balances struck are generally acceptable, but they do illustrate the limitations on the legal process in protecting vulnerable individuals. If we test
the success of the law by the number of children born injured then the law
appears to have failed. Yet none of the responses examined above suggest
that a general, as opposed to individual, improvement is likely.
Recognizing civil liability will not ensure proper medical care for most
children injured; recognizing criminal liability will not deter those who are
beyond deterrence. This, however, is neither a counsel of despair nor a
case of sacrificing babies at the alter of autonomy. Rather it is society,
through the law, making a pragmatic choice about how best to respond to

a pressing social problem. The major response of the law in most jurisdictions mentioned in this paper is to avoid notions of force and of liability but instead to activate the child-protection procedures after birth. This will frequently result in the removal of the child from its mother, sometimes permanently. Those who seek punishment for the pregnant drug abuser may, in fact, already be achieving their aims.

STATUS OF THE EMBRYO IN THE LIGHT OF ISLAMIC JURISPRUDENCE

Abul Fadl Mohsin Ebrahim

Introduction

Whenever a woman becomes pregnant she is not looked upon as someone inflicted with an illness or a disease. Rather, people extend congratulations to her. This is because after conception a 'new life' is in the offing. This 'new life' is not referred to by the prospective parents as the embryo or the foetus, as men of science and doctors do, but as their child. For already they have great expectation that this 'new life' will be a person to grow up with them.[1] Here is where the problem arises and Daniel Ch. Overduin aptly alludes to this as follows:

The dilemma in the abortion debate has created a number of relevant questions to which a host of different answers are given. These questions may relate to the humanity of the unborn; the right of the unborn; the future of the unborn in terms of physical, mental and social health; the wishes, circumstances, and rights of the mother and father, people and their world.[2]

Definition of the Embryo

The word 'embryo', whose equivalent in the Arabic language is *janīn* (singular) and *ajinnah* (plural), literally stands for anything which is veiled or covered.[3] Hence, from this definition, the *janīn* or embryo would comprise anything that is in the offing from the time of conception until birth. There is at least one verse of the *Qur'ān* which makes mention of *ajinnah*. It is as follows: 'He (*Allāh*) knows you well when He brings you out of the earth, and when you are hidden (*ajinnah*) in your mothers' wombs'.[4]

While science maintains that embryo is the stage from eight weeks until

---

[1] The Church Assembly Board for Social Responsibility, *Abortion: an Ethical Discussion*, (London, 1968), 7.

[2] D Ch. Overdiun, 'The Ethics of Abortion' in T. W. Hilgers *et al.* (eds.), *New Perspectives on Human Abortion* (Frederick, Mld., 1981), 369.

[3] Edward Willliam Lane, *Arabic-English Lexicon* (New York, 1955), Bk 1, part 2, 463.

[4] *Qur'ān*, 53:32.

birth and that at that point in time (i.e. eight weeks) the embryo is in possession of all the necessary human characteristics,[5] Muslim jurists have basically three views on this issue. One view maintains that the embryo stands for that which is in the womb.[6] The other view is that of al-Shafi'i who holds that the least stage whereby that which is in the womb could be called an embryo is when the stages of *al-mudghah* (a chewed lump) and *al-'alaqah* (something that clings) have been differentiated; and it can clearly be made out to be of human generation, possessing such characteristics as finger, or nail, or eye, or anything else similar to that.[7] The third view is that of al-Nuwayri who says that the learned people use the word *janin* for that which exists in the womb after ensoulment has taken place.[8] Of the three views enumerated above, the Shafi'i interpretation seems to be the most plausible one. Imam Shafi'i was renowned to be a great linguist. Moreover, his definition of the embryo is closest to that of present-day scientific understanding.

Stages of Embryonic Development

It is to be noted that both the *Qur'an* and the *Hadith* (tradition of the Prophet Muhammad) have made references to the stages of embryonic development. The two main Qur'anic passages that refer to embryonic development are as follows:

(a) 'We created man from the quintessence of mud. Thereafter We cause him to remain as a drop of sperm (*nutfah*) in a firm lodging i.e. the womb. Thereafter We fashioned the sperm into something that clings (*'alaqah*), which We fashioned into a chewed lump (*mudghah*). The chewed lump is fashioned into bones which are covered with flesh. Then We nurse him into another act of creation. Blessed is *Allah* the Best of Creators'.[9]

(b) 'O men! If you are in doubt as to the resurrection, remember that, We have created every one of you out of dust, then out of a drop of semen (*nutfah*), then from something that clings (*'alaqah*), then from a chewed-like lump (*mudghah*) (complete in itself), and yet incomplete (*ghayr mukhallaqah*) which differentiates and either aborts or completes its growth. We rest whatever We want in the womb to the time We decide to bring you forth as infants.'[10]

[5] Ronald Munson, *Intervention and Reflection, Basic Issues in Medical Ethics* (2nd edn., Belmont, Cal., 1983), 41.

[6] Abū Faḍl Shihāb al-Dīn Sayyid Maḥmūd Al-Alūsī, *Rūḥ al-Ma'ānī*, 14 vols. (Beirut, n.d.), part 27, 64.

[7] Muḥammad Saʿīd Ramaḍān Al-Buṭī, *Taḥdīd al-Nasl* (Damascus, 1976), 197.

[8] Muḥammad Salām Madkūr, *Al-Janīn wa al-Aḥkām al-Muta'alliqah bihi fī al-Fiqh al-Islāmī* (Cairo, 1969), 32.

[9] *Qur'ān*, 23:13.   [10] *Ibid.*, 22:5.

There are at least two Prophetic traditions which make direct reference to embryonic development. They are:

(a) 'Each of you is constituted in your mother's womb for forty days as a *nutfah*, then it becomes an *'alaqah* for an equal period, then a *mudghah* for another equal period, then the angel is sent, and he breathes the soul into it.'[11]

(b) 'When forty-two nights have passed over the sperm drops, *Allāh* sends an angel to it, who shapes it and makes its ears, eyes, skin, flesh and bones. Then, he says, "O Lord! Is it a male or female?" And your Lord decides what He wishes and the angel records it.'[12]

The various stages as enumerated in the *Qur'ān* and *Ḥadīth* literature need to be elaborated upon. *Nutfah* literally means 'a drop of fluid'. Dr Maurice Bucaille emphasizes this point by stating that the *Qur'ān* makes it clear that the fertilizing capacity of the sperm does not depend on the volume of liquid 'poured out'.[13] *'Alaqah* literally means 'something that clings and adheres to the womb', clearly describing the implantation stage,[14] (i.e. of the fertilized ovule in the uterus[15]). *Mudghah* literally means 'a piece of flesh that has been chewed'. Dr al Bar says that the *Qur'ān* depicts this stage as if it was a piece of flesh or food that has been chewed.[16] It may be recapitulated here that in the *Ḥadīth* (a) above direct reference is made to the ensoulment of the foetus after 120 days from the time of fertilization. At the same time some of the exegetists of the *Qur'ān* hold that the words *khalqan 'ākhar* (i.e. 'another act of creation') in the Qur'anic passage (a) above signifies the ensoulment of the embryo;[17] and that the stage of *mudghah ghayr mukhallaqah* (i.e. the incomplete chewed-like lump) in the Qur'anic passage (b) above denotes the stages 'when no soul had yet been breathed into it'.[18] Furthermore, it is to be noted that *Ḥadīth* (b) above specifically mentions that forty-two nights after fertilization has taken place organ differentiation occurs.

Rights of the Embryo

In the Islamic juridical writings, the word embryo is used in its wider connotation, signifying anything that is in the offing after fertilization has taken place. Some of its rights are as follows:

---

[11] Muslim ibn al-Ḥajjāj Naysabūrī, *Ṣaḥīḥ Muslim*, (Cairo, n.d.), 'Kitāb al-Qadar', v, 496.
[12] *Ibid.*, 499–500.
[13] M. Bucaille, *What is the Origin of Man?* (9th edn., Paris, 1983), 183.
[14] Muḥammad 'Alī Al-Bār, 'Embryological Data in the Holy Qur'ān' in *Abstract of the Proceedings of the 8th Saudi Medical Conference* (Riyadh, 1983), 263.
[15] Bucaille, n. 13, above, 185.   [16] Al-Bār, n. 14, above, 264.
[17] Madkūr, n. 8, above, 84.
[18] Abū Ja'far Muḥammad Jarīr Al-Ṭabarī, *Tafsīr al-Ṭabarī*, (Beirut, n.d.), ix, 90.

RIGHT TO LIFE

Islamic law stipulates that the embryo has the right to life. This can be substantiated by the fact that all the schools of Islamic jurisprudence hold it necessary to postpone the carrying out of the death sentence on a pregnant woman until after she has given birth, and provisions have been made for the child to be suckled by a wet nurse.[19] Moreover, Ibn Qudāmah mentions that the Shāfiʿī School makes provision for the cutting of the belly of the dead pregnant mother so as to remove the embryo/foetus, if there is any sign that embryo/foetus is alive,[20] (today it would be in the form of the caesarean opeation).

RIGHT TO INHERITANCE

Islamic law maintains that as long as the embryo is still inside its mother's womb, it does not enjoy the right of inheritance as such. Hence, if the testator passes away while the embryo is unborn, then the division of the heritage/estate should be postponed until after its birth.[21] This is so because there is no real guarantee that it will be born alive. If it is stillborn then it has no right in the heritage/estate.[22] Likewise, under normal circumstances, it cannot be said whether the embryo will be born as a male or as a female—hence it is proper to await its birth before it is alloted its share from the heritage/estate, bearing in mind that there are special rules which govern the shares to be alloted to the males and females.

RIGHT TO BE BURIED

Islamic law states that the miscarried embryo or the stillborn embryo is to be buried. Ibn ʿĀbidin points out that the embryo that does not utter a sound at the moment of birth should be given the ceremonial bath (*al-ghusl*), named and placed in a piece of cloth (*kaffan*) and buried, but no prayer should be read over it. This, he maintains, applies to both the formed and unformed embryos/foetuses.[23]

From the above discussion, it is to be noted that Islamic law upholds the right to life of the embryo. The request that the division of the heritage/estate be postponed until after its birth shows that due consideration is taken of its existence. And the provision laid down for its burial after its life ceases denotes that its sanctity is fully recognized.

---

[19] Al-Shāfiʿī, Abū ʿAbd Allāh Muḥammad Idrīs (*Kitāb al-Umm*, Beirut (n.d.), 4 vols, ii, part 6, 136.
[20] Muḥammad ʿAbd Allāh bin Aḥmad bin Muḥammad Ibn Qudāmah, *Al-Mughnī* (Riyadh, n.d.), ii, 551.
[21] Madkūr, n. 8, above, 287–8.
[22] Muḥammad Amīn Ibn ʿĀbidīn, *Ḥāshiyat Radd al-Muḥtār* (Beirut, 1979), ii, 228.
[23] *Ibid.*

Aggression against the Embryo

Aggression against the embryo implies any action which leads to the termination of its existence or its separation from its mother's womb before the end of the normal period of pregnancy. Such an action may be undertaken by the pregnant woman herself or by someone other than herself. The aggression may take the form of a verbal rebuke or threat against the pregnant woman or in the way of direct or intentional action with the aim of expelling the embryo from the womb or by an indirect action, which may not be intended, but which results in a miscarriage. Examples of each of these forms may be enumerated as follows.

VERBAL REBUKE OR THREAT

Verbal rebuke or threat may be of such a nature that it creates within the pregnant woman a degree of fear which may cause her to have a miscarriage. For example, someone may threaten to kill her or hurt her in one way or another.[24]

DIRECT ACTION

Direct action in this regard is when the pregnant woman uses certain drugs with the aim of terminating the pregnancy[25] or visits a physician with the intention of undergoing an abortion. A direct action may also be the case when a person strikes the belly of a pregnant woman and as a result a miscarriage occurs and the embryo is separated dead from its mother's body.[26]

INDIRECT ACTION

Indirect action in this context is one that is not particularly aimed at terminating the pregnancy but, nevertheless, results in the termination. This may be effected by the pregnant woman in one of several ways, e.g., by starving herself, by fasting, or by smelling something pungent.[27]

Legal Consequences of Destroying the Embryo

Islamic law envisages the following consequences for terminating the life of the embryo.

---

[24] Abū Zakariyyā Yaḥyā bin Sharaf Al-Nawawī, *Mughnī al-Muḥtāj* (Cairo, 1908), iv, 103.
[25] *Ibid.*   [26] *Ibid.*   [27] *Ibid.*

AL-GHURRAH

Al-ghurrah literally means a whiteness on the forehead of a horse, above the size of a *dirham*. It also means the best of anything: the best or most precious and excellent of property; as, for instance, a horse, and an excellent camel, and a male slave and a female slave, or a clever female slave. Its application to a slave, male or female (among articles of property), is most common. Technically, however, it relates to compensation for the destroying of a child in the womb.[28] Reference to *al- ghurrah* is made in the *Aḥādīth* literature. For example, in *Ṣaḥīḥ al-Bukhārī*, Abū Hurayrah narrates that two women of the tribe of Hudhayl quarrelled. One of them threw a stone at the other, causing her to have a miscarriage. The Apostle of God gave his verdict that the *ghurrah* (compensation) be given in the form of manumitting a male or female slave.[29] It is on the basis of this tradition and other relevant *Aḥādīth* which make direct reference to *al-ghurrah* that Muslim jurists came to the conclusion that the payment of *al-ghurrah* is necessary for all the above-mentioned cases of aggression against the embryo.[30] However, there is a difference of opinion about whether it would be necessary to fulfil this obligation in the event that the embryo, upon which the aggression has been committed, separates from its mother's body while still in an unformed state. *Imām* Mālik holds that the *ghurrah* is to be paid although the embryo be in an unformed state.[31] *Imām* Abu Hanifah and *Imām* al-Shāfiʿī are of the opinion that it is to be paid as long as whatever comes out of the woman's body can be made out to be the beginning of human creation.[32] The Ḥanbalī school of jurisprudence is of the view that if any act to terminate the pregnancy (like the taking of certain medicines) be carried out before forty days after falling pregnant then the payment of *al-ghurrah* is not necessary.[33] *Al-ghurrah* therefore stands for compensation that is required to be paid for destroying that which is within the womb. The other issues that are related to *al-ghurrah* are its value, to whom it is due, and who benefits from it.

THE VALUE OF *AL-GHURRAH*

It is said that it is equivalent to *nisf ʿushr* (i.e., the twentieth part) of the

---

[28] Lane, n. 3, above, Bk 1, part 6, 2238.

[29] Muḥammad ibn Ismāʿīl Al-Bukhārī, *Ṣaḥīḥ al-Bukhārī* (Cairo, n.d.), iii, part 9, 14.

[30] Muḥammad Saʿīd Ramaḍān Al-Buṭī, *Taḥdīd al-Nasl* (Damascus, 1976), 199–200.

[31] Abū Walīd Muḥammad bin Aḥmad, bin Muḥammad bin Aḥmad Ibn Rushd, *Bidāyat al-Mujtahid* (Cairo, 1981), ii, 416.

[32] ʿAbd al-Qādir ʿAwdah, *Al-Tashrīʿ al-Jināʾī al-Islāmī al-Muqaranat bi al-Qānūn al-Waḍaʿī* (Cairo, n.d.), 295.

[33] Supreme Council of Islamic Affairs, *Mawsūʿat Jamāl ʿAbd al-Nāṣir fi al-Fiqh al-Islāmī* (Cairo, 1968), part 3, 161.

full *diyyah* or compensation.[34] It may take the form of either freeing a male or female slave of the best quality, as mentioned above, in the tradition of Abū Hurayrah as recorded in *Ṣaḥīḥ al-Bukhārī*.[35] Or its payment may be made in the form of 100 sheep, as recorded in the tradition of Abū Buraydah in *Sunan al-Nasāʾī*;[36] or in cash payment of 500 dirhams, as pointed out in the tradition of al-Shaʿbī in *Sunan Abī Dāʾūd*.[37] Sayyid Sābiq adds that its payment could also be made in the form of five camels.[38]

THE PERSON RESPONSIBLE TO PAYING *AL-GHURRAH*

It is important to note that aggression against the embryo may be committed by the pregnant woman herself or by someone else whose hostile action is directed at the pregnant woman but indirectly causes her to have a miscarriage. In the light of this the Ḥanafī and Shāfiʿī schools concur that the *ghurrah* should be paid by the family on the pregnant woman's father's side if she is found to be responsible for committing the aggression against the embryo or by the family of the other person who has, indirectly, caused the pregnant woman to have a miscarriage.[39] This ruling is based on the grounds that, first, it cannot be fully established that the miscarriage or death of the embryo took place as a result of the hostile action against the pregnant woman; secondly, the aggression did not directly aim at the embryo but, rather, was intended to hurt the pregnant woman.[40] The Ḥanbalī school, however, points out that if the embryo dies along with its mother and the aggression on the mother was a mistake or semi-intentional, then full compensation (for the dead mother) and the *ghurrah* are liable to be paid by the family (of the one guilty of committing the aggression). But in the event that the hostile action against the mother was deliberate or intentional, or if the embryo alone dies, the family of the aggressor is not responsible for paying anything and the onus is on the aggressor alone to pay the *ghurrah*.[41] The Mālikī school holds that the aggressor himself/herself is responsible for paying the *ghurrah* because the miscarriage of the embryo as a result of a blow to the pregnant woman's belly was not deliberate, but it (the aggression) was intentional as regards the pregnant woman, but a mistake as regards the embryo.[42]

---

[34] Ibn ʿĀbidīn, n. 22, above, vi, 588.
[35] Al-Bukhārī, n. 29, above, iii, part 9, 14.
[36] Abū ʿAbd al-Raḥmān Aḥmad ibn Shuʿayb Al-Nasāʾī, *Sunan al-Nasāʾī* (Cairo, 1938), part 8, 47.
[37] Abū Dāʾūd Al-Sijistānī, *Sunan Abī Dāʾūd* (Beirut, n.d.), part 4, ii, 193.
[38] Sayyid Sābiq, *Fiqh al-Sunnah* (5th edn., Kuwait, 1971), ii, 478.
[39] Ibn ʿĀbidīn, n. 22, above, vi, 589.   [40] Al-Būṭī, n. 7, above, 201.
[41] Ibn Qudāmah, n. 20, above, vii, 806.   [42] Ibn Rushd, n. 31, above, ii, 415.

THE BENEFICIARY

Al-Shāfiʿī and Abū Ḥanīfah are of the view that the heirs of the embryo should be the ones to benefit from *al-ghurrah*. The rule pertaining to *al-ghurrah* is the same as that which applies to *al-diyyah* (blood money) in that it is inherited. While there is another view, that of Rabīʿah and al-Layth, which holds that the sole beneficiary should be the mother of the aborted or miscarried embryo since it (the embryo) is part and parcel of its mother's body.[43] The discussion on *al-ghurrah* is summarized in *Mughnī al-Muḥtāj* in the following manner: there is no difference whether the aggressor (against the embryo) be a stranger or the pregnant woman herself. But if necessity calls upon her to use certain medicines then she is not to be held responsible for its result (i.e. the miscarriage). While Muslims are obligated to fast during the month of *Ramaḍān*, the pregnant woman is not required to keep the fast if she fears that a miscarriage may result while she is fasting. However, if she does fast and it results in her having a miscarriage then she is to be held responsible for that and she cannot inherit from the *ghurrah* for she is held as the 'destroyer' (of the embryo).'[44] Furthermore, a pregnant woman whose pregnancy is terminated as a result of taking a medication with the intention of terminating the pregnancy is liable to pay the *ghurrah*.[45]

Diyyah Kāmilah (Full Blood Money)

It may be recalled here that Muslim jurists hold that the embryo achieves a soul (ensoulment) after the fourth month of pregnancy on the basis of the tradition of the Prophet Muḥammad which makes direct reference to that. Hence, it follows that any act of aggression against the embryo after the fourth month is tantamount to taking the life of a human being. Thus the aggressor is liable to pay the *diyyah kāmilah* (the full blood money) in compensation, and not the *ghurrah*.[46] However, the Ḥanbalī school holds that only if the embryo is separated from its mother's body during the sixth month of pregnancy, will the *diyyah kāmilah* instead of the *ghurrah* be due. This school does not deny that ensoulment does take place after the fourth month of pregnancy. Its criterion for determining the time when the full blood money will be due as a result of aggression against the embryo is not the ensoulment, but rather the period during which the embryo is regarded as viable. This, it holds, can only be when the embryo is in its twenty-fourth week.[47] However, it is to be noted here that all four schools of Islamic jurisprudence concur that any aggression against the

[43] Ibn Rushd, n. 31, above 2, 416.
[44] *Mughnī al-Muḥtāj*, n. 24, above, iv, p. 103.
[45] Ibn Qudāmah, n. 20, above, vii, 816.
[46] Al-Būṭī, n. 7, above, 205.
[47] Ibn Qudāmah, n. 20, above, vii, 812.

embryo would be classified as semi-intentional if the aggressor deliberately intended the act, and a mistake if it was not deliberate.[48] The stipulation for paying the *diyyah kāmilah*is derived from the following verse from the *Qur'ān*: '[n]ever should a Believer kill a Believer, but (if it so happens) by mistake: if one so kills a Believer, it is ordained that he should free a believing slave and pay a compensation (*diyyah*) to the deceased's family'.[49]

Payment of *diyyah kāmilah* may be made to the deceased's family in the form of 100 camels, or 200 cattle, or 2,000 sheep, or 1,000 dinars, or 12,000 dirhams.[50] If the pregnant woman herself is the aggressor, then she will be liable to pay the full blood compensation to the heirs of the embryo, and she herself would not be entitled to have a share from the blood money.

Al-kaffārah

In the *Qur'anic* verse (4:92) it is explicitly stated that besides the compensation that one has to give to the family of the deceased as a result of having wrongfully killed another believing person, one has also to free a believing slave. This act is termed *kaffārah*, which means penance or atonement for a sin.[51] In the event that no slave be found then the *Qur'ān* stipulates that one should fast (instead) for two consecutive months.[52] The Shāfi'ī school and the Ḥanbalī school[53] hold that the *kaffarah* is necessary for any aggression against the embryo along with the payment of the *diyyah kāmilah*. The Hanafī school, however, says that only if the embryo is separated from its mother's body alive and then dies as a result of the aggression against it then only would the *kaffārah* become compulsory,[54] but it makes it a necessary obligation upon someone who has committed aggression against the embryo.[55] The *kaffārah* in our time would be fasting for two consecutive months, as stated earlier. This creates a problem: what would be the position of someone who has started to fast and falls ill before completing the required fasts? Or what would be the position of the woman since she menstruates once every month and menstruation in itself exempts one from keeping fasts according to Islamic law? Al-Jaṣṣāṣ solved this dilemma by suggesting that the one who falls ill during the two-month period should start all over again once he/she is well. Hence, the days

---

[48] 'Abd al-Qādir 'Awdah, n. 32, above, 298. [49] *Qur'ān*, 4:92.
[50] Sābiq, Sayyid, n. 38, above, ii, 466–7.
[51] Hans Wehr, *A Dictionary of Modern Written Arabic* (J. Milton Cowan (ed.), London, 1971), 833.
[52] *Qur'ān*, 4:92 also states: 'if one does not find the wealth with which to free a slave then one has to fast for two months consecutively'.
[53] Ibn Rushd, n. 31, above, ii, 416. [54] Ibn 'Ābidīn, n. 22, above, vi, 590.
[55] Ibn Rushd, n. 31, above, ii, 417.

already fasted would not be counted when the person concerned renewed his/her fast. This is so, he explains, because sickness in itself does not annul the fast and in the event that one does not fall ill it is possible to keep the fast for two months consecutively. However, the woman who misses some of the fasts as a result of menstruation can add the days fasted to those days that she would fast after the termination of the menstruation. Thus she does not have to start all over again, for it is a reality that any woman would normally menstruate each month (before she reaches the age of menopause). Al-Jaṣṣāṣ further explains that the reason for this is that menstruation necessarily annuls the fast (and much as a woman would like to continue with the fast she would not be able to do so). So, just as the night (wherein one cannot legally keep the fast) does not interrupt the consecutive days of the fasts, in the same way, menstruation would not interrupt the sequence of the consecutive fasts if the fasts missed as a result of the menstruation be made up immediately after the termination of the menstruation.[56] Dr 'Abd al-Qādir 'Awdah is of the opinion that all persons who are involved in aggression against the foetus should each share in the payment of the *diyyah*, and likewise each of them should engage in the *kaffārah*.[57]

The question which now arises is whether the Muslim doctor who may have been involved in carrying out an abortion be liable to share in the *diyyah* and engage himself/herself in the *kaffārah*? In trying to resolve this, it will be appropriate to find out whether a doctor, or a surgeon for that matter, is held accountable for any mistake that he/she may make while discharging his/her services. Ibn Rushd states that there is unanimity amongst Muslim jurists that a doctor ought to be held responsible for any mistake that he/she may make. But the *diyyah* or compensation for the mistake is to be paid off by the family on the paternal side of the doctor and not from the wealth of the doctor, for the mistake is to be regarded as unintentional.[58] Therefore, what may be deduced from this is that a Muslim doctor who participates in the act of abortion would make him- or herself responsible. However, it would not be regarded as a mistake on his/her part, if he/she took an active role in carrying out the abortion for non-therapeutic reasons, in view of the fact that abortion, as stated earlier, is considered a crime under Islamic law. So, if the abortion is carried out by him/her after the fourth month (after ensoulment has taken place) for non-therapeutic reasons he/she is liable to pay a share in the *diyyah kāmilah* and expected to atone for his/her role in it by fasting for two consecutive months (which would be regarded as his/her *kaffārah*). However, if he/she carries out the abortion for non-therapeutic reasons

---

[56] Abū Bakr Aḥmad bin 'Alī al-Rāzī Al-Jaṣṣāṣ, *Aḥkām al-Qur'ān* (Beirut, n.d.) ii, 246.
[57] 'Abd al-Qādir 'Awdah, n. 32, above, 302.
[58] Ibn Rushd, n. 31, above, ii, 418.

before the fourth month then he/she should pay the *ghurrah* in compensation.

Conclusion

From what has been discussed above, one can conclude that destroying the embryo is regarded as a crime in the light of Islamic jurisprudence. It is for this reason that Muslims in general do not opt for abortion once pregnancy has been established. In cases of what may be termed unwanted pregnancies, abortion can in no way be the acceptable solution. In order to curtail the crimes of illegitimate sex and rape, Islam lays emphasis on the purification of society from all temptations that could lead to indulgence in those crimes. Moreover, it prescribes severe punishment for the offenders which serves as a deterrent for such crimes. Opting for abortion for pregnancies which result from illegitimate sex or rape would be to advocate the killing of the innocent rather than punishing the guilty for their crimes.

In so far as the conceiving of deformed embryos is concerned, Islam stands for the taking of precautionary measures to avoid the conception of defective newborns rather than opting for their abortion. For the taking of the lives of these innocent creatures is not an act of true mercy; rather it is an act of oppression against them. Indeed with the advances being made in the field of biomedical technology one cannot overrule the possibility of prenatal treatment of certain embryonic deformities.

While it is true that *in vitro* fertilization may assist a woman to have children and thereby 'cure' her of her infertility, there are two issues involved in this procedure which makes its legality questionable. First, only a single fertilized ovum is selected for implantation while all the other fertilized ova are simply discarded. Secondly, it may happen that while monitoring the development of the fertilized ovum after implantation had taken place certain abnormalities may be detected which could tempt one to terminate the pregnancy. Discarding the fertilized ova and terminating the pregnancy on the grounds of abnormality would be questionable under Islamic law on the basis of what has been discussed under the section dealing with the legal consequences for destroying the embryo.

Abortion, according to Dr. al-Būṭī, a Syrian Islamic scholar, may be sanctioned in three cases before the onset of the fourth month of pregnancy: first, in the event that doctors fear that the mother's life is in danger as a result of the pregnancy; secondly, if it is feared that the pregnancy would lead to the appearance of a disease in the body of the mother; thirdly, in the event that the new pregnancy causes an upper limit on lactation and the pregnant woman has an existing infant who is absolutely dependent for his/her survival on her breastfeeding him/her.[59] On the

---

[59] Al-Būṭī, n. 7, above, 96-9.

other hand, it ought to be noted that if the mother's life is in danger after the fourth month of pregnancy then a serious situation arises, because after the 120-day period Muslim jurists hold that ensoulment occurs. Hence at that point in time the foetus has an equal right to life as its mother. But this dilemma is resolved by the general principle of the *Sharīʿah*—that of choosing the lesser of the two evils—the life of one should be given preference over that of the other instead of losing both. Shaykh Shalṭūt in his *al-Fatāwā* ruled that the mother's life in that case should be saved and the embryo be aborted and explains the reasons for this in the following manner: '[f]or the mother is the origin of the embryo; moreover, she is established in life, with duties and responsibilities, and she is also a pillar of the family. It is not possible to sacrifice her life for the life of the embryo which has not yet acquired a personality and which has no responsibilities or obligations to fulfil'.[60]

[60] Yūsuf Al-Qaradāwī, *Al-Ḥalāl wa al-Ḥarām fī al-Islām* (14th edn., Cairo, 1980), 202.

CAN WE LEAVE THE BEST INTERESTS OF VERY SICK CHILDREN TO THEIR PARENTS?

Michael Freeman

In October 1996 the Court of Appeal in England was confronted with a moral dilemma.[1] A baby of eighteen months (C) had at most a year to live unless he had a liver transplant. The parents (who were not married, so that only the mother had parental responsibility[2]) were health-care professionals and did not wish the operation to take place. The child had already undergone surgery which had caused him pain and distress. The unanimous clinical opinion of the consultants was that it was in the baby's best interests to undergo the operation as soon as a donor became available. Meanwhile, the parents had removed themselves and the child to a 'distant Commonwealth country'. There was no doubt that the parents' decision— in effect to condemn their child to death—was founded in love and care. They did not want to subject their baby to any further trauma. The inherent jurisdiction of the High Court was invoked and the Official Solicitor was appointed as guardian *ad litem*. Connell J held that it was in the best interests of the baby to undergo the surgery, though he did not appear to base his judgment on the welfare principle, but rather on his assessment that the mother's decision was unreasonable.[3] He gave permission to perform the operation, notwithstanding the mother's refusal to consent, and he ordered that the child be returned to the jurisdiction for the surgery.

The Court of Appeal found the case 'tragic and deeply worrying'[4] and 'desperately difficult'.[5] There was a strong presumption in favour of life, but prolonging life was not the court's sole objective. The judge, the Court of Appeal thought, had also erred in failing to have regard to other important considerations which should have been fed into the application of the welfare test. Butler-Sloss LJ stated that insufficient weight had been given to 'the enormous significance of the close attachment between the mother

---

[1] In *Re T* [1997] 1 FLR 502. I use this case as a hinge, but, of course, there are many other illustrations which could be chosen.

[2] Children Act 1989 s. 2(2)(a).   [3] His decision is not reported.

[4] *Per* Butler-Sloss LJ at 503.   [5] *Per* Roch LJ at 514.

and baby'[6] and 'whether it [was] in the best interests of C for [the] court in effect to direct the mother to take on this total commitment where she [did] not agree with the course proposed'.[7] Roch LJ thought the latter consideration had a clinical significance too, 'because in the absence of parental belief that a transplant [was] the right procedure for the child, the prospects of a successful outcome [were] diminished'.[8] To Butler-Sloss LJ the mother and child were 'one', and 'the decision of the court to consent to the operation jointly affects the mother and son as it also affects the father. The welfare of this child depends upon his mother'.[9] Unlike Re B[10] ('Baby Alexandra'), where a cure could be effected by a simple operation, the problems of C required 'complicated surgery and many years of special care from the mother'.[11]

It may be pertinent at this stage to ask whether C had any rights. Waite LJ addressed this issue, in a sort of oblique way. This was 'not an occasion —even in an age preoccupied with "rights"—to talk of the rights of a child, or the rights of a parent, or the rights of the court'.[12] And he expressed the opinion that in 'problematic' cases 'in the last analysis the best interests of every child include an expectation that difficult decisions affecting the length and quality of its life will be taken for it by the parent to whom its care has been entrusted by nature'.[13] Bainham is right to observe that '[t]his is surely not far removed from nineteenth-century notions of the natural rights of parents'.[14]

This is a heart-rending case. The court was confronted by a 'mortal choice',[15] and it decided that the life–death decision, which obviously could not be taken by the patient himself, should devolve upon those most intimate to his life, and not upon doctors or state institutions. It is true that the question in English law is what is in the best interests of the child[16]—the so-called paramountcy principle—and not whether the parent's decision is reasonable or not. It is my view that the Court of Appeal did not apply the paramountcy test wisely. It was over-influenced by parental wishes, taken in by their professional knowledge, over-emphasized the logistic problem of returning the child to the jurisdiction (even the most distant Commonwealth countries are only twenty-four hours away and, it should not be forgotten, have good health services!), and too little concerned with the interests of a very sick child. It is, I think, beyond doubt that this case, had it been presented to the Court of Appeal which

[6] N. 1, above, 512. [7] *Ibid.* [8] *Ibid.* 515.
[9] *Ibid.* 510. [10] [1981] 1 WLR 1421. [12] *Ibid.* 512.
[11] *Per* Butler-Sloss LJ, n. 1, above, 511.
[13] *Ibid.* 514.
[14] 'Do Babies Have Rights?' (1997) 56 *Cambridge Law Journal* 48.
[15] Cf Thomas Nagel, *Mortal Questions* (Cambridge, 1979); see also Ronald Dworkin, *Life's Dominion* (London, 1993).
[16] See Children Act 1989 s. 1(1).

decided 'Baby Alexandra' in 1981, would have been decided differently. The Court of Appeal turned the clock back. Its decision is a hangover from an era in which the unimpeachable parent held sway, when courts were convinced by the validity of such pseudo-scientific notions as the blood tie and judges could refer to parents' rights (more commonly fathers' rights) as sacrosanct.[17] I see the decision as pragmatic rather than principled, though it has to be said it is consonant with statutory, social work, and social policy developments of the 1990s, concepts like 'partnership'[18] and dispute mechanisms like the family group conference.[19]

Despite Waite LJ's denial, *Re T* endorses parental rights by allocating decision-making to them. This may accord also with what the medical profession wants. There is clear evidence, not least in *Re T* itself, that it is in practice heavily influenced by parental views. Indeed, one year after the decision the Royal College of Pædiatrics and Child Health, without alluding to *Re T*, in a new framework for practice, asserted that '[p]arents act for the child and in the best interests of the child'.[20] Nowhere did it confront the problem, of which *Re T* was paradigmatic, of what should happen where parents did not act in the best interests of the child. Thus, not surprisingly, one of the three hospital teams involved said it was not prepared to operate without the mother's consent. On the other hand, it has to be accepted that parents may be consciously or unconsciously guided by doctors.

Autonomy in Child-rearing

How important, then, is the parents' decision? Children need parents. All children have certain needs, physical and psychological. Sick and disabled children have greater needs. And parents do generally act in their children's best interests. The state is no substitute for flesh and blood parents. Goldstein, Freud, Goldstein, and Solnit in *The Best Interests of the Child* argue that 'the law does not have the capacity to supervise the fragile, complex interpersonal bonds between child and parent. . . . The legal system has neither the resources nor the sensitivity to respond to a growing child's ever-changing needs and demands. It does not have the capacity to deal on an individual basis with the consequences of its decisions, or to act with the speed that is required by a child's sense of time.'[21]

---

[17] See, e.g., *Re Thain* [1926] Ch. 676; *Re C(MA)* [1966] 1 All ER 838; *Re Agar-Ellis* [1883] 24 Ch.D 317.

[18] On which see June Thoburn *et al.*, *Paternalism or Partnership?* (London 1995).

[19] And see Department of Health, *Working Together To Safeguard Children* (London, 1999).

[20] *Withholding or Withdrawing Life Saving Treatment in Children: A Framework for Practice* (London, 1997), para. 2.5. Earlier in the report the RCPCH does say that parents should decide 'unless clearly acting against the best interests of the child' (para. 2.3.2.3).

[21] (New York, 1996), 91.

The costs of intervention may also be great. It may undermine family stability and harmony. It may even polarize the family. By intervention the state may achieve nothing valuable and may destroy that which is. It is accepted that child-rearing is a risk-taking enterprise.

Because parental autonomy is considered important, the argument for confining state intrusion into the family to cases of clear abuse is put frequently by legal, philosophical, and social welfare commentators, as well as by judges. Most famously, in the US Supreme Court Rutledge J said that 'it is cardinal with us that the custody, care and nurture of the child reside first in the parents, who primary function and freedom include preparation for obligations the state can neither supply nor hinder'.[22] There was, he argued, 'a private realm of family life which the state cannot enter'.[23] More recently, also in the US Supreme Court, Justice Burger spoke of '[t]he history and culture of western civilization [which] reflect a strong tradition of parental concern for the nurture and upbringing of their children'.[24] This case concerned the rights of a religious minority to withdraw its children from school. The remarks of another judge, Douglas J, are, therefore, especially pertinent: '[i]t is the student's judgment, not his parents', that is essential if we are to give full meaning to what we have said about the Bill of Rights and of the right of students to be masters of their own destiny'. And 'it is the future of the student, not the future of the parents, that is imperilled by today's decision'.[25]

It is against this background that the fullest, modern statement of minimum state intervention in parent–child relations was articulated, by Goldstein, Freud, Goldstein, and Solnit. They argue that:

> The child's need for security within the confines of the family must be met by law through its recognition of family privacy as the barrier to state intrusion upon parental autonomy. These rights—parental autonomy, a child's entitlement to autonomous parents, and privacy—are essential ingredients of family integrity.[26]

It will be noted the child's psychological need for security is conflated into a right—it is not clear whether this is a legal or moral right—without so much of a hint of justification. Their justification of minimum state interference is fourfold.

First, there is biology. To be a child is 'to be at risk', whereas to be an adult is 'to be perceived to take risk'. Children are 'incomplete beings'.[27]

Secondly, there is a justification sought within psychology, and in particular within Freudian psycho-analytic theory. These analyse 'complex and vital developments' that 'thrive in the protective enclave of family life under guardianship by parents who are autonomous'.[28] They argue:

---

[22] *Prince* v. *Massachusetts*, 321 US 158 (1944).   [23] *Ibid.*, 166.
[24] *Parham* v. *JR* 442 US 582 (1979).
[25] *Wisconsin* v. *Yoder* 406 US 205, 244–5 (1972).   [26] N. 20, above, 90.
[27] *Ibid.*, 89. They quote Bentham's *Theory of Legislation*.   [28] *Ibid.*, 90.

When family integrity is broken or weakened by state intrusion [the child's] needs are thwarted, and her belief that her parents are omniscient and all-powerful is shaken prematurely. The effect on the child's developmental progress is likely to be detrimental.[29]

Two purposes, they say, underlie the parents' right within the family to be free of state intrusion:

The first is to provide parents with an uninterrupted *opportunity* to meet the developing physical and emotional needs of their child in establishing the familial bonds critical to every child's health growth and development. The second . . . is to safeguard the continuing *maintenance* of these family ties—of psychological parent–child relationships. . . .[30]

This is presented as if it were uncontentious. Those who disagree—reference is made in end-notes to a number of 'behavioural' psychologists—are peremptorily dismissed (arguments about the resilience of cognitive functions are cast aside and those about social resilience are ignored).

Thirdly, they adduce a philosophical rationale. 'A policy of minimum intervention by the state . . . accords . . . with our firm belief as citizens in individual freedom and human dignity',[31] they state. This is, of course, to ignore the impact that the exercise of freedom can have on relationships where there is, as there is with parent–child relationships, an imbalance of power. Failure to intervene can, therefore, mean that a parent's will prevails over a child's legitimate interests and, even if some of these interests may seem relatively trivial, others may have profound effects on children's lives. The decision not to consent to life-saving treatment is the most egregious example.

The fourth strand in their rationale points to the dangers of state interference. Thus, they argue, 'by its intrusion' into the family 'the state may make a bad situation worse; indeed, it may turn a tolerable or even good institution into a bad one'.[32] There are dangers in state interference but there are also dangers in non-interference and in drawing the line for interference too conservatively.

It is accepted that intervention must not be excessive and it must be based on standards which are formulated as precisely as possible. Vague language invites unwarranted and arbitrary interventions. Further, where standards are insufficiently precise, decision-making can be left to the *ad hoc* analysis of welfare professionals, doctors, and judges. And vague standards can all too easily be employed to impose the standards of one section of the population on another, a problem which is, of course, accentuated in a multi-cultural setting. Standards, furthermore, should be as value-neutral as possible, for value-laden standards can impose unwarranted biases and intrude oppressively into parent–child relationships.

[29] *Ibid.*   [30] *Ibid.*   [31] *Ibid.*, 91.   [32] *Ibid.*, 92.

The doctrine of parental rights pervades the background of neonatal euthanasia discussion, though the argument for the doctrine is made with varying clarity and emphasis. The clearest, starkest example is in the writings of Goldstein, and subsequently in Goldstein, Freud, Goldstein, and Solnit. Goldstein would forbid the state to overturn parental medical decisions except where the medical procedure was 'proven'[33] and where 'its denial would mean *death* for a child who would otherwise have an opportunity for either a *life worth living* or a *life of relatively normal healthy growth* toward adulthood'.[34] He believes that outside a narrow central core of agreement, 'a life worth living' or 'a life of relatively normal healthy growth toward adulthood' are 'highly personal terms about which there is no societal consensus', so that 'it must be left to parents to decide, for example, whether their congenitally malformed newborn with an ascertainably neurologic deficiency and highly predictable mental retardation should be provided with treatment which may avoid death, but which offers no chance of a cure'.[35]

This is without doubt controversial. Adequate medical care is defined in as narrow a way as possible: the child must be faced with death and not, for example, with the prospect of blindness, deafness, or lameness. There must be medical consensus on the type of intervention, and on the fact that it is therapeutic, and the child must have a chance to live 'a normal life' or a life worth living (and clearly a consensual standard is assumed in relation to this).

Goldstein's test raises profound ethical, legal, medical, and social questions. His rationale, as it is articulated in *The Best Interests of the Child*, is to prevent the views of professionals (whether doctors, social workers, or judges) being substituted for those of parents. Professionals are thought to be no more capable—indeed probably less competent—to take decisions than parents. Decisions other than those over life or death are only reflections of a 'preference for one style of life over another'.[36] It is argued that 'the law cannot find in medicine (or, for that matter, in any science) the ethical, political or social values for evaluating health care choices'.[37] 'A prime function of law', they state, 'is to prevent one person's truth . . . from becoming another person's tyranny'.[38]

On this test, there is no problem with courts (or others) intervening when parents, for religious or other reasons, oppose medical care, for example, a blood transfusion, for an otherwise healthy child who without it would die. Parents who are Jehovah's Witnesses can thus be countered. But outside this relatively non-controversial area, there are cases which

---

[33] 'Medical Care For The Child At Risk: On State Supervision of Parental Autonomy' (1977) 86 *Yale Law Review* 645, 651.

[34] *Ibid.* The emphasis is in the original.   [35] *Ibid.*, 654, 655–6.

[36] N. 21 above, 129. There is an echo of this in *Re Phillip B*, 92 Cal. App. 3d 796, 801.

[37] *Ibid.*   [38] *Ibid.*

expose the limits of this thinking brutally. What is 'non-experimental' treatment? Is a procedure experimental because it challenges orthodox clinical opinion? What is a life worth living? How is quality of life to be judged? It is clearly an evaluative property. As Edward Keyserlinck put it, in a most helpful study written for the Law Reform Commission of Canada, it:

need not involve a comparison of *different human lives* as the basis for decisions to treat some and not others. Ideally, at the heart of quality of life concerns should be only a comparison of the qualities *this* patient now has with the qualities deemed by *this patient* . . . to be normative and desirable, and either still or no longer present actually or potentially.[39]

Of course, 'this patient' in our context will most often be incompetent and someone else will need to make the normative judgement. The parents of a child may be the obvious agents but concern about the nature of their decision-making (whether, for example, they can really put their child's interest first) necessitates surveillance and review.

The stipulation by Goldstein that intervention may be justifiable where refusal to authorize medical care would result in death *may* be sufficient to bring *Re T*, the case with which I started, within the test. I say 'may' because it is far from certain that the criterion 'normal, healthy growth or a life worth living' would be met. And it is particularly significant that the judgments of the Court of Appeal in *Re T* ooze with sentiments that could have been taken straight from Goldstein's article or from *The Best Interests of the Child*. Butler-Sloss LJ's characterization of the mother and the child as 'one',[40] and her conclusion that the 'best interests of this child require that his future treatment should be left in the hands of his devoted parents'[41] and Waite LJ's unfortunate dismissal of 'rights talk' and his conclusion that 'in the last analysis the best interests of every child include an expectation that difficult decisions affecting the length and quality of its life will be taken for it by the parent to whom its care has been entrusted by nature'[42] are not calculated to respect the integrity, individuality, or the citizenship of children.

It is clear where Goldstein and others who present the case for non-intervention derive this from, and where their error lies. Classic liberalism—its most obvious source is Mill's *On Liberty*[43]—believes that the state should stay out of our lives. Its paradigmatic conflict is between the citizen and the state. The state should stay out of the lives of citizens out of respect for their moral autonomy and human dignity. But the paradigmatic family conflict is not between the citizen and the state: it is between two

---

[39] 'Sanctity of Life or Quality of Life' (Ottawa, 1979), extracted in I. Kennedy and A. Grubb, *Medical Law* (London, 1994), 1244–7. The quotation is at 1245.
[40] N. 1, above, 510.   [41] *Ibid.*, 512.   [42] *Ibid.*, 512, 514.
[43] (London, 1859).

persons. And, where one of those persons is a child, the problem is accentuated because traditionally we have expected the parent to speak for the child, to represent the child's interests, in litigation literally to represent the child. Our discovery of child abuse in the 1960s, and, most graphically, the Maria Colwell case of 1973–4 demonstrated to us the inadequacy of such a conflation of interests. How could a parent accused of abuse or neglect represent that same child's interests? And, as a result, independent representation was born, and has expanded. The Official Solicitor always represents the child where life or death decisions are being taken regarding very sick children.

Why Parents have Rights

It is beyond the scope of this paper to investigate fully why parents should have parental rights. It is, of course, a subject of some importance, as the British government prepares to extend parental rights to unmarried fathers. And we cannot ignore it totally since it is at the root of the non-interventionists' case. Eekelaar had pointed out that behind the granting of parental responsibility (of which rights are a key element) lie both 'a factual recognition of a state of affairs, and also a normative granting of approval by the state to a given situation'.[44] He sees it as a status, which consists in, and is co-extensive with, practical action. But if this were true, its automatic assignment to married fathers and all mothers could not be justified. Why should parents on this test have rights if they have never actually looked after their children or do not now do so?

Different views have been expressed about why parents have rights. Many rest the case on biology. English law has never subscribed in a coherent way to this: it has always, by presuming legitimacy, granted parental status automatically to husbands of married women. The question remains why biology should confer rights. Some point to the unique biological relationship shared by parent and child. But, if genetic similarity alone were sufficient for ascription of parental rights, an identical twin would possess a greater claim than the parent, which looks odd, even absurd. At one time, the biological claim could seek support in property justifications. You owned, in John Locke's language,[45] that which you 'mixed your labour with'. The products of your body, like the products of your hands, were yours to do with as you pleased. But we have moved away from an exchange view of parenthood, where parental rights were based on an investment made by parents, to a more child-centred approach, where the interests of children are considered paramount. The

---

[44] 'Parental Responsibility: State of Nature or Nature of the State' [1991] *Journal of Social Welfare Law* 37.
[45] *Two Treaties of Government* (P. Laslett ed., London, 1960).

property rights argument is untenable today. Where support for it remains it tends to concentrate on the case for giving mothers parental rights. Thus, Katherine Bartlett points out that 'mothers have a kind of automatic responsibility for their children'.[46] She demonstrates this through decisions she takes during pregnancy (including whether she terminates). A third attempt to explain why parents have rights is the so-called 'intention theory'. Thus, according to Hill,[47] what is essential to parenthood is not the biological tie between parent and child, but the pre-conception intention to have a child accompanied by undertaking whatever action is necessary to bring the child into the world. But, if married, a parent acquires status irrespective of intention, and unmarried fathers who demonstrate an intention to be a social parent do not automatically have parental rights. At one time a further justification for parental rights, however unconvincing, was marriage. But, 'illegitimacy' has not just become increasingly common, with a third of children now born outside marriage, but it is also being perceived by many to be a 'legitimate' parenting option.

There is no totally satisfactory explanation of why parents have rights, any more than there is, for example, a convincing justification of the institution of private property. But, in both cases, we must begin somewhere and make some assumptions if we are to proceed at all. Let us grant, then, that parents have rights, whilst remembering the shaky foundations upon which the ascription rests.

And their Limits

Whatever their rationale, these rights are not absolute. They are not, for example, sufficient to authorize sterilization.[48] Certainly, where this is on non-therapeutic grounds,[49] the court's consent must be sought.[50] It must be the case with consent to medical treatment generally that the overriding criterion of the child's best interests is itself a limit on parental power. Even before legislation prohibited female circumcision,[51] it may be assumed that it did not lie within a parent's right to consent to a clitoridectomy on a daughter for religious or cultural reasons. They got away with it, and still do, because no one challenges them. Can it be supposed that a wardship court would agree to such mutilation? Or that a court would not

---

[46] 'Re-Expressing Parenthood' (1988) 98 *Yale Law Journal* 293.
[47] 'What does it Mean To Be A "Parent"? The Claims of Biology As A Basis for Parental Rights', (1991) 66 *New York University Law Review* 353.
[48] See *Re D* [1976] Fam 185.
[49] Although the House of Lords in *Re B* (n. 47 above) attempted to ridicule the therapeutic/non-therapeutic distinction, it has been assumed to exist by judges in later cases: *Re E* [1991] 2 FLR 585; *Re G F* [1992] 1 FLR 293.
[50] See *Re B* [1988] AC 199, *per* Lord Templeman.
[51] Prohibition of Female Circumcision Act 1985. That male circumcision is different is recognized in *Re J* [1999] 2 FLR 678.

regard it as 'significant harm'?[52] (I accept there might be a reluctance to make a care order[53].) And, where a child is at risk of suffering significant harm because of lack of treatment, a care order or emergency protection order can be made and the parent's refusal overridden.

And this is what happened in the first reported neonatal euthanasia case in this country. Said Templeman LJ in *Re B*[54] 'it devolves on this court . . . to decide whether the life of this child [a Down's syndrome baby with an intestinal blockage] is demonstrably going to be so awful that in effect [she] must be condemned to die'.[55] The Court of Appeal concluded that existence ('the life of a mongoloid child'[56]) was a better option than death. Dunn LJ explained that the court could not 'hide behind the decision of the parents or the decision of the doctors',[57] and that in making the decision the first and paramount consideration was the welfare of 'this unhappy little baby'.[58] In stating that there was no evidence that 'this child's short life is likely to be an intolerable one',[59] Dunn LJ introduced 'quality of life' arguments. And these must relate not to social worth or economic cost, but to the baby's potential for human contentment.

Quality of Life Decisions

There is clearly a distinction, to which attention was drawn in the United States President's Commission report *Deciding to Forego Life—Sustaining Treatment*,[60] between treatment that will clearly benefit the infant, the situation where all treatment is expected to be futile, and the situation where the benefits of treatment are ambiguous or uncertain (examples are given of a child with a debilitating and painful disease who might live with therapy, but only for a year or so, and of a respirator-dependent premature infant whose long-term prognosis becomes bleaker with each passing day).

Keyserlinck points out that quality of life comparisons need not be comparisons with others or a 'relativising of persons' lives'.[61] Nor, he says, 'need it be [*I* would say "should it be"] arbitrary or based upon how treatment or non-treatment will relieve or burden others or society'.[62] It is his view, and it is one with which I agree, that '[t]he norm can and must include whatever the value sciences, medicine and public policy agree upon

---

[52] A care order could thus be made: Children Act 1989 s. 31(2).
[53] Because of the minimal intervention principle in s. 1(5) of the Children Act.
[54] [1981] 1 WLR 1421.   [55] *Ibid.* 1424.   [56] *Ibid.*
[57] *Ibid.*
[58] *Ibid.* Since the Children Act 1989 it is the paramount consideration.
[59] *Ibid.* On the controversy sparked by the case see M.D.A. Freeman, *The Rights and Wrongs of Children* (London, 1983), 261.
[60] This is discussed in the report (Washington, DC, 1983) at pages 217–223 and is extracted in Kennedy and Grubb, n. 38 above, 1242–4.
[61] N. 39, above, 1245.   [62] *Ibid.*

concerning the essential quality or qualities of a human person; and the decision can and must be in the first instance by, and for the benefit of, the patient and no one else'.[63] We cannot be sure that parents have either the resources or the objectivity to take a decision using such criteria.

Quality of life decisions are not easy. But this does not justify us in refusing an attempt at a formulation. We can start with the presumption in favour of life: as Lord Donaldson MR said in *Re J* 'we all believe in and assert the sanctity of human life'.[64] But 'life' can mean more than one thing: it can refer to vital or metabolic processes alone and it can refer also to a level of life which goes beyond this to include at least a minimal capacity to experience or communicate. There is a difference, in other words, between being alive and living. 'Living' is itself a multi-layered concept, something which can be experienced on many levels, even by the same person at different stages in his life.[65] We need to look at life, not just from our perspective, whether we be parents, medical professionals or courts, but from the point of view of the patients, in our case the sick baby. To return to Lord Donaldson MR in *Re J* again, it is worth recalling his remark, immediately after his reference to the sanctity of human life, to 'the fact that even very severely handicapped people find a quality of life rewarding which to the unhandicapped may seem manifestly intolerable'.[66] He refers to the 'amazing adaptability'[67] of human beings. Taylor LJ, in the same case, sees the criteria as 'a matter of degree'.[68] In his view, the correct approach is 'for the court to judge the quality of life the child would have to endure if given the treatment and decide whether in all the circumstances such a life would be so afflicted as to be intolerable to that child'.[69] If this is an attempt to introduce a 'substituted judgment' test[70] (which English courts have rejected elsewhere[71]), it is out of place where the patient, as a baby, has never been competent to express a view or hold values. The decision cannot be the child's, but it could be what might be hypothesized as what that child would want, given his disabilities. In these terms, it could be hypothesized that the courts in *Re B* (where treatment was authorized) and in *Re J* (where approval was given to the cessation of invasive life-sustaining procedures at some time in the near future) were both right in coming to conclusions that our hypothetical child would want. And that the Court of Appeal in *Re T* came to the wrong decision.

---

[63] *Ibid.*   [64] [1991] Fam. 33, 46.
[65] And see R. Dworkin, n. 15, above, and Sanford Kadish, 'Letting Patients Die: Legal and Moral Reflections' (1992) 80 *California Law Review* 857.
[66] N. 64, above, 47.   [67] *Ibid.*   [68] *Ibid.* 55.
[69] *Ibid.*
[70] On which see Allen E. Buchanan and Dan W. Brock, *Deciding For Others: The Ethics of Decision Making* (Cambridge, 1989), 117 ff.
[71] See *Airedale NHS Trust* v. *Bland* [1993] AC 789, *per* Lords Goff at 771–2 and Mustill at 895 (who described it as 'a fiction'). But contrast *Re J*, n. 64, above, *per* Lord Donaldson.

There are those who are critical of 'quality of life' arguments. I accept it is an elusive concept and that it is too difficult to construct objective criteria. But it is an attempt at rational decision-making and must, I think, be preferable to leaving decisions to parents. The Royal College of Pædiatrics and Child Health stated unequivocally that '[t]he person we are responsible to is the child'.[72] For it 'we' is the medical profession, but I would generalize this to embrace 'society'. There must, as it concluded, 'always be respect for the child's life and a responsibility to relieve all suffering'.[73] This recognizes that sick children have the right to a rational determination of their future and that they are more likely to get this where the decision-making process is principled and reasoned.

---

[72] N. 20, above, para. 3.2.
[73] *Ibid.* Conclusions (at 27).

Reproductive Technology and the Law

THE CAESAREAN SECTION CASES AND THE SUPREMACY OF AUTONOMY

Jonathan Herring

Introduction

The rate of caesarean sections performed in Britain has increased dramatically over the past few decades.[1] Critics argue this does not reflect a higher level of care for pregnant women, but rather doctors' fear of litigation and hospitals' desire for administrative convenience. There is increasing concern that women's interests are not always the first priority in the medical treatment of childbirth. According to the Department of Health's Expert Maternity Group:

The woman must be the focus of maternity care. She should be able to feel that she is in control of what is happening to her and able to make decisions about her care, based on her needs, having discussed matters fully with the professionals involved.[2]

Few would disagree; but these are statements of ideal rather than of practice. The history of law and medicine is one in which women are not in control of their bodies, or are only in control to the extent that male-controlled law or medicine permit them to be.[3] Of course, in the vast majority of cases the pregnant woman will willingly accept the advice of experts and there will be no question about who is in charge of what happens during the pregnancy and labour.[4] Whether the woman is in truth

---

[1] In 1970 4.9% of births were by caesarean section. This had risen to 11.89% by 1989. See C. Wells, 'On the Outside Looking in: Perspectives on Enforced Caesareans' in S. Sheldon and M. Thomson, *Feminist Perspectives on Health Care Law* (London, 1998).

[2] Department of Health, *Changing Childbirth* (London, 1993), 9.

[3] See, e.g., M. Thomson, *Reproducing Narrative: Gender, Reproduction and the Law* (Great Yarmouth, 1998).

[4] For a layperson's guide to caesarean sections see National Childbirth Trust, *Caesarean Birth: Your Questions Answered* (London, 1996). For a professional guide see Royal College

in control of the birthing process is revealed when what the woman wants and what the doctors advise conflict.[5] The issue has come to a head in recent years with a number of cases in Britain where women have not consented to caesarean sections, even though the doctors warn that unless the operation is performed the woman and/or the foetus will die.[6]

To start, a brief outline of the law in England and Wales is necessary.

Summary of the Law and Moral Context

Following the Court of Appeal decisions in *St George's Healthcare NHS Trust* v. *S*[7] and *Re MB*[8] the legal position where a pregnant woman refuses to consent to a caesarean section is straightforward, deceptively so, and can be summarized in three points:[9]

(1) The doctor may lawfully operate on a competent woman if she voluntarily, with sufficient information about what is involved, consents to the caesarean section.

(2) If the woman is competent to make the decision and voluntarily refuses to consent to the operation then the doctor may not perform the caesarean section, even if the woman or her foetus may die if it is not carried out.[10] If the operation were performed in such circumstances then that act could be a crime and/or a tort.[11]

---

of Obstetrics and Gynæcologists, *A Consideration of the Law and Ethics in Relation to Court-Authorised Intervention* (London, 1996).

[5] V. Harpwood, *Legal Issues in Obstetrics* (Aldershot, 1996).

[6] For example, *St George's Healthcare NHS Trust* v. *S* [1998] 3 All ER 673 (hereafter *St George's* v. *S*); *Re MB (An Adult: Medical Treatment)* [1997] 8 Med. LR 217 (hereafter *Re MB*); *Re S (Adult: Refusal of Medical Treatment)* [1993] Fam. 123; *Re L (Patient: Non-consensual Treatment)* [1997] 2 FLR 837; *Norfolk and Norwich Healthcare (NHS) Trust* v. *W* [1997] 2 FLR 613; *Rochdale Healthcare (NHS Trust)* v. *C* [1997] 1 FCR 274; *Tameside and Glossop Acute Services Trust* v. *CH* [1996], 1 FCR 753. For a discussion of some of the American cases see N. Rhoden, 'The Judge in the Delivery Room: The Emergence of Court-authorised Caesareans' (1986), 74 *California Law Review* 1951.

[7] [1998] 3 All ER 673, discussed in R. Bailey-Harris, 'Pregnancy, Autonomy and Refusal of Medical Treatment' (1998) 114 *Law Quarterly Review* 550 and J. Herring, 'Caesarean Sections and the Right of Autonomy' [1998] *Cambridge Law Journal* 438.

[8] [1997] 8 Med. LR 217, discussed in S. Michalowski, 'Court-Authorised Caesarean Sections—The End of a Trend' (1999) 62 *MLR* 115; J. Herring 'Caesarean sections, Phobias and Foetal Rights' [1997] *Cambridge Law Journal* 509; M. Stauch, 'Court-authorised Caesareans and the Principle of Patient Autonomy' [1998] 15 *Nottingham Law Journal* 74; R. Francis, 'Compulsory Caesarean Sections: An English Perspective' [1998] 15 *Journal of Contemporary Health Law and Policy* 365; and S. Fovargue, 'Medical Law' [1998] 20 *Journal of Social Welfare and Family Law* 427.

[9] These statements represent the law in respect of all medical operations.

[10] *Re C (Adult: Refusal of Treatment)* [1994] 1 All ER 819. *Dicta* to the contrary in *Re S (Adult: Refusal of Medical Treatment)* [1993] Fam 123 and *Re T (Adult: Refusal of Medical Treatment)* [1993] Fam 95, 102 no longer represent the law. These cases are discussed in M. Thomson, 'After Re S' [1994] *Med. LRev.* 127 and K. Stern 'Court-ordered Caesarean Sections: In Whose Interests?' (1993) 56 *Modern Law Review* 238.

[11] e.g. *Re JT (Adult: Refusal of Treatment)* [1998] 1 FLR 48.

(3) If the mother is not competent to make the decision then the doctor may operate only if it is necessary and in the best interests of the woman. In reaching that decision the doctor should not consider the interests of the foetus.[12]

So at the heart of the law is the principle of self-determination.[13] The principle should be inviolate, Judge LJ in *St George's v. S* suggested:

How can a forced invasion of a competent adult's body against her will even for the most laudable of motives (the preservation of life) be ordered without irremediably damaging the principle of self-determination? When human life is at stake the pressure to provide an affirmative answer authorising unwanted medical treatment is very powerful. Nevertheless, the autonomy of each individual requires continuing protection even, perhaps particularly, when the motive for interfering with it is readily understandable . . .[14]

Hence, Judge LJ argued, 'S is entitled not to be forced to submit to an invasion of her body against her will, whether her own life or that of the unborn child depends on it. Her right is not reduced or diminished merely because her decision to exercise it may appear morally repugnant.'[15]

As a moral question—what ought a mother to do if a caesarean section is recommended?—there seems to be a strong case that she should consent, assuming there is only a minimal risk to her life.[16] One view is expressed by Kluge,[17] who argues:

By voluntarily allowing the fetus to become a person, possessed of a right to life, the mother has *de facto* accepted the conditions accompanying that action—which is to say, since she was aware of the dependent nature of the fetuses and children (or ought to have been thus aware) she had, through her action, voluntarily accepted the responsibilities attendant on the fact of such dependence and thereby has *de facto* subordinated her right to otherwise unhindered autonomy to the right to life of the fetus . . .

Such arguments may suggest that a woman who is seeking to follow the

---

[12] A doctor will not be forced by a court to perform an operation against her will: *Re C (A Minor)(Medical Treatment)* [1998] 1 FCR 1.

[13] For a similar approach taken by the Canadian Supreme Court in *Winnipeg Child and Family Services (Northwest Area) v. G* (1998) 152 DLR (4th) 193.

[14] *St George's v. S*, n. 6, above, 688.

[15] *Ibid.*, 692.

[16] A. Plummer, 'Judicially Enforced Caesareans and the Sanctity of Life' [1998] 27 *Anglo-American Law Review* 235; J. Bridgeman and S. Millns, *Feminist Perspectives on Law* (London, 1998), ch.. 6; and M. Brazier, 'Prenatal Responsibilities, Foetal Welfare, and Children's Health' in C. Bridge (ed.), *Family Law Towards the Millennium* (London, 1997) provide excellent starting points in discussing the issues. For a judicial perspective see Thorpe LJ, 'The Caesarean Section Debate' [1997] 27 *Family Law* 663.

[17] E.-H. Kluge, 'When Caesarean Section Operations Imposed by a Court are Justified' [1988] 14 *Journal of Medical Ethics* 205, 209–10. A similar argument is developed by H. Draper, 'Women, Forced Caesarean and Ante-natal Responsibilities' [1996] 22 *Journal of Medical Ethics* 327.

very highest moral standards *should* consent to a caesarean section, if her life is not thereby endangered. But they do not establish that the law should *compel* a woman to submit to the invasion of her body of the kind involved in such an operation.[18]

One leading philosopher, Judith Jarvis Thomson, has drawn a distinction between being a 'Good Samaritan' and being 'minimally decent'. The law, she argues, can require people to act in a minimally decent way but should not compel them to be Good Samaritans.[19] Indeed, the law traditionally is very reluctant to compel people to be injured against their will. Although the law does impose special obligations on parents to care for their children (and they can face criminal prosecution if they fail to meet these[20]), these duties do not extend to parents having to suffer serious physical harm themselves. This is probably in accord with most people's instincts. If a child was born and grew up in a healthy way but at the age of six developed an illness that required a bone-marrow transplant, few would countenance the mother or father being forced against his or her will to donate the marrow. Is not the situation with the mother refusing the caesarean section the same? Indeed, if anything, the justification for the compulsion may be less, given the debates over the correct moral and legal status of the unborn child.[21]

The remainder of this paper challenges the reasoning and approach of the courts and is divided into three sections. The first questions whether autonomy is accepted as an inviolate principle in the law generally. The second shows that using autonomy as an absolute principle throws up complexities in the law on consent that are not yet fully resolved. The third suggests that the law's general approach, based on autonomy, is flawed and offers an alternative approach.

Is the Right to Bodily Integrity Absolute?

At the heart of the law is one particular aspect of the principle of autonomy, namely the principle of bodily integrity—that your body should not be injured against your will. The impression given by the Court of Appeal in *St George's* v. *S* is that the law accepts the right to bodily integrity of competent people as an absolute right. However the law is not that simple. Although medical law has always treasured the right to bodily integrity,

---

[18] There are medical risks for the woman involved in a caesarean section; see the research noted in M. Field, 'Controlling the Woman to Protect the Fetus' [1989] 17 *Law, Medicine & Health Care* 114.

[19] J. J. Thomson, 'A Defense of Abortion' (1971) 1 *Philosophy and Public Affairs* 47. See also N. Rhode, 'Caesareans and Samaritans' [1987] 15 *Law, Medicine and Health Care* 118.

[20] *R.* v. *Senior* [1899] 1 QB 283.

[21] Indeed enforced caesarean sections sit uncomfortably with the fact that the law is not prepared to authorize automatically the taking of organs from cadavers in order to save lives.

outside medical law there is less squeamishness about breaching it. Three clear examples are section 55 of the Police and Criminal Evidence Act 1984 (permitting intimate searches without a suspect's consent); sections 35–36 of the Public Health (Control of Diseases) Act 1984 (authorizing tests to be carried out on people suspected of having certain infectious diseases[22]); and the defences of self-defence and prevention of crime in the criminal law.[23] It has also been suggested that force can be used to prevent a death, if the manner of death is particularly repellent to society's values,[24] although the authority for this is not strong.

So, in order to state that the principle of bodily integrity applies to women not consenting to a caesarean section it is necessary to consider these exceptions. Two are potentially relevant. First, self-defence. Under the common law A is entitled to use force against B if B is posing an unjust threat to A or another (C).[25] So could it be argued that the doctor (A) acts lawfully in carrying out the caesarean section in order to protect the foetus (C) from an unjust threat from the mother (B)? (I hasten to add that I engage in this analysis simply because this is what the present law requires. I will be arguing later that the present law's way of approaching these issues is flawed.) There are several reasons why this argument fails. The first is that the foetus is not regarded as a person in the eyes of the law, although as the foetus is protected by the criminal law in various ways this does not necessarily conclude the argument. The second is that the woman is failing to consent to the operation and that is an omission. The criminal law is generally reluctant to penalize omissions, and it is difficult to see how an omission could constitute a threat to or an attack on the foetus.[26] It could be argued that the foetus is dependent upon the woman for survival and a failure by her to do what is necessary to support the foetus is essentially a threat. However an obligation to require a person to undergo the serious injuries inherent within a caesarean section for the benefit of another is quite unlike any other obligation to act imposed by the law.[27]

A second possible exception to the principle of bodily integrity has been proposed by Marc Stauch, who argues that a person does not enjoy 'an

---

[22] M. Brazier and J. Harris, 'Public Health and Private Lives' (1996) 4 *Medical Law Review* 171 and *Malette* v. *Shulman* (1980) 67 DLR (4th) 321, 333.

[23] For completeness it should be added that there is no defence in criminal law simply based on the fact that one is committing the lesser of two evils—see *R.* v. *Pommel* [1995] 2 Cr.App.R 607.

[24] M. Stauch, 'Court-authorised Caesareans and the Principle of Patient Autonomy' [1998] *Nottingham Law Journal* 79.

[25] For a thorough discussion of the defence of self-defence see S. Uniacke, *Permissible Killing* (Cambridge, 1994).

[26] An analogy could be drawn with *Airedale National Health Service Trust* v. *Bland* [1993] AC 789, where it was stated that the withdrawal of ventilation by doctors was an omission.

[27] J. Eekelaar, 'Does a Mother have Legal Duties to her Unborn Child' in P. Byrne (ed.), *Medical Law and Ethics* (Oxford, 1988).

unlimited choice over the *manner* of their death, insofar as additional insult to the sanctity of life principle will be entailed'.[28] In relation to the caesarean section cases he suggests that the autonomy principle may not permit a woman and her foetus to be allowed to die as 'not only the woman but also her foetus, which (whatever its other attributes) is a potent symbol of life stands to die. . . . There is, perhaps, also the consideration that such deaths, if allowed, would take place in the maternity wards of hospitals.' Even if the exception to which he refers exists in law, it is hard to see why permitting the death of a symbol of life is a greater invasion of the sanctity of life principle than permitting the death of an actual life. Further, although death in a maternity ward would be traumatic to the other patients, perhaps more so would be a fellow patient being forced to the operating table against her will.[29]

So the issue is not quite as straightforward as the Court of Appeal would have us believe—the right of bodily integrity is not absolute in the law. However the invasion of a woman's rights by compelling a caesarean section would require a completely novel departure for the law by creating a unique obligation on a woman in pregnancy unlike any other legal obligation.

The Consequences of Having Autonomy at the Heart of the Law

The caesarean section cases have placed autonomy at the centre of the law. But to do so requires re-examination of three important questions relating to competence and consent.

Is the Test for Competence Too Strict?

Under the principle of autonomy a patient's refusal must be respected if a patient is competent. In English law to be competent a patient must be able to comprehend the information which is relevant to the decision, believe it, and be able to weigh it in the balance in reaching a decision.[30] Therefore the presumption of competence can be rebutted if, for example, 'some impairment or disturbance of mental functioning renders the person unable to make a decision whether to consent to or to refuse treatment' or that person is 'unable to comprehend and retain the information which is material to the decision, especially as to the likely consequences of having or not having the treatment in question' or 'the patient is unable to use the information and weigh it in the balance as part of the process of arriving at the decision'.[31]

---

[28] Stauch, n. 24, above, 84.

[29] J. Gallagher, 'Prenatal Invasions and Interventions: What is Wrong with Fetal Rights?' (1987) 10 *Harvard Women's Law Journal* 9.

[30] *Re C (An Adult: Refusal of Treatment)* [1994] 1 All ER 819.

[31] *Re MB*, n. 6, above, 224.

Professor Ian Kennedy has suggested that in *Re MB* the Court of Appeal applied the test for competency too strictly and that 'the court spoke the language of autonomy even as it practised the principle of paternalism'.[32] In other words, he suggested that although the court purported to uphold autonomy, by too readily finding MB incompetent it was able to permit the doctors to act in what they thought was the woman's best interests.

In considering whether the test for autonomy is too strict it is important to recall the basis of the principle of autonomy.[33] That is, that each person in society should be able to develop and live out her vision of how she wishes to live her life as long as that does not cause harm to other people. The principle therefore prohibits the state, or any third party, from forcing a person to do something against her wishes because that would be 'good' for her. Each person can decide for herself what is good. However, if the law is to say that if an operation cannot be performed on a competent patient without her consent even if the patient is to die, then it is understandable that the law would require a very high standard of competence. There are two reasons for this. The first is that if a person exercises her autonomy in choosing to die this will end all possible exercises of autonomy. The law will be allowing her to exercise her autonomy even though it destroys the very thing that the principle of autonomy most treasures—the ability to choose how to live. The second is that the choice to die is irrevocable, whereas a decision to live is not. In other words, if the patient truly wishes to die as part of her vision of the 'good life' then the fact that this is refused at one point in time does not deny her the opportunity to kill herself at a later time. It may be that a person's vision of the good life requires her to die at that particular moment or in that particular way, but these must be very rare cases. Therefore, it is understandable that the court needs to be absolutely sure that the choice is a deliberate and fully informed one. To abide by the request of a patient who was not fully competent to be allowed to die would be the ultimate *denial* of her autonomy.[34] The stricter the law is about upholding the inviolability of the self-determination principle, the stricter the law ought to be about the standard for an effective consent.

That said, the law on competence can justly be criticized for seeming to use a different standard for men than for pregnant women.[35] Indeed, in

---

[32] I. Kennedy, 'Commentary on *Re MB* [1997] *Medical Law Review* 317, 323. See also J. Harrington, 'Privileging the Medical Norm: Liberalism, Self-determination and Refusal of Treatment' [1996] 16 *Legal Studies* 348.

[33] See T. Beauchamp and J. Childress, *Principles of Biomedical Ethics* (4th edn., New York, 1994), ch. 3 and A. McCall Smith, 'Beyond Autonomy' [1992] 9 *Journal of Contemporary Health Law and Policy* 23.

[34] See G. Duval, 'Assisted Suicide and the Notion of Autonomy' [1995] *Ottawa Law Review* 1 for an application of this argument in relation to assisted suicide.

[35] C. Widdett and M. Thomson, 'Justifying Treatment and Other Stories' [1997] 5 *Feminist Legal Studies* 77.

only one of the recently reported caesarean section cases has the woman been found competent to refuse.[36] This may be explained by the kind of attitude expressed in *Rochdale NHST v. C.* [37] Here the pregnant woman stated during labour, 'I would rather die than have a Caesarean section again'. Johnson J, in deciding that the woman was incompetent, stated:

The patient was in the throes of labour with all that is involved in terms of pain and emotional stress. I conclude that a patient who could, in those circumstances, speak in terms which seemed to accept the inevitability of her own death, was not a patient who was able properly to weigh-up the considerations that arose so as to make any valid decision, about anything of even the most individual kind, surely still less one which involved her own life.[38]

It can be argued that the logical implication of this approach is that any pregnant woman in labour is automatically incompetent. By contrast in *Re C*[39] the court seemed to strive to find a confused paranoid schizophrenic man suffering from gangrene competent.

WHAT INFORMATION SHOULD A DOCTOR GIVE A PATIENT?

A second important consequence of making autonomy the supreme value in medical law is that the law should impose very strict rules governing the information with which a patient should be provided. If paramount importance is to be placed on autonomy and the choice of the patient, it is crucial that the patient is given as much relevant information to make that choice as is reasonable. It is a serious breach of the autonomy principle to operate on a patient whose consent has been obtained on inadequate or inaccurate information. So the present law on provision of information, that the patient need to be aware only of the broad nature of the treatment,[40] seems pitifully inadequate if autonomy is to be at the heart of the law.[41]

WHAT IF THE PATIENT'S WISHES CONFLICT?

The law must consider more carefully cases in which a patient has conflicting wishes. Of particular concern is the Court of Appeal's reasoning on competence is *Re MB*. It will be recalled that because of MB's needle-phobia

[36] Namely *St George's v. S*, n. 6, above.
[37] [1997] 1 FLR 274.
[38] A similar case is *Norfolk and Norwich Healthcare (NHS) Trust v. W* [1997] 1 FCR 269.
[39] *Re C (Adult: Refusal of Treatment)* [1994] 1 All ER 819.
[40] *Sidaway* v. *Governors of Bethlem Royal Hospital* [1985] AC 871.
[41] J. Katz, 'Informed Consent—Must it Remain a Fairy Tale?' [1994] 11 *Journal of Contemporary Health Law and Policy* 69. Making it possible to override consent may encourage doctors not to be too diligent in obtaining consent: J. Munby, 'Rhetoric and Reality: The Limitations of Patient Self-determination in Contemporary English Law' [1998] 15 *Journal of Contemporary Health Law and Policy* 315.

she objected to the injection necessary for the caesarean section although she wanted the operation to go ahead. The Court of Appeal found MB incompetent, but held that if the refusal to consent to the injection had been competent the doctors would not have been permitted to operate. It is submitted that this overlooks the role that consent is intended to play. The aim of autonomy is to place the patient in charge of the medical process and of what happens to her body. However in *Re MB* the patient wanted two contradictory things: to have the caesarean section but not to have the injection. It was not possible to comply with both of these choices. Of these two wishes—not to be injected, but to have the caesarean section performed—surely it was the latter which was the predominant wish, representing a far more important aspect of her personhood. The wish to have the child born alive was one far more closely aligned to her vision of what she wanted for her life than her desire to avoid the prick of a needle. It is submitted that therefore to perform the caesarean section would have been acting in accordance with her wishes, and there was no need to find her incompetent.

Maternal-Foetal Conflict: Reconceiving the Problem

How should the law analyse situations where women refuse to consent to caesarean sections?[42] I will first consider the approach of the present law, and then an alternative, and finally propose a better way of thinking about these cases.

THE PRESENT LAW

The present law is based on the right of autonomy of the woman, and this right trumps any interests of the foetus. Under the present law the status of the foetus is ambiguous.[43] In *St George's* v. *S* Judge LJ described the viable foetus as 'certainly human',[44] 'a unique organism',[45] and 'protected by the law in a number of different ways'.[46] But he stated that the foetus does not have any legal rights.[47]

The law's approach can be criticized on three fronts.

---

[42] C. MacIntosh 'Conceiving Fetal Abuse' [1998] *Canadian Family Law Review* 178.

[43] See J. Fortin, 'Legal Protection for the Unborn Child' (1988) 51 *Modern Law Review* 54.

[44] *St George's* v. *S*, n. 6 above, 687.

[45] *Attorney General's Reference (No 3 of 1994)* [1998] AC 245, 256.

[46] *St George's* v. *S*, n. 6 above, 687. Most notably through ss.58, 59 of the Offences Against the Person Act 1861, the Infant Life (Preservation) Act 1929, and the Abortion Act 1967.

[47] *C* v. *S* [1988] QB 135, 140. For a highly unusual example of a fœtus being recognized as a 'child' in the common law world see *In the Matter of Baby P (An Unborn Child)* [1995] New Zealand Family Law Reports 255.

Autonomy is Too Individualistic

Seeing autonomy as an absolute value can be challenged as being overly individualistic. As stated earlier, the aim of autonomy is to enable people to live their lives as they wish—developing their own version of the 'good life'.[48] However, the protection of community values may be important to other people's version of the good life. The values and structure of a society crucially affect the range of choices its members can make about how to live their lives.[49] To most people their relationships with others and their involvement with their community are of central importance to their view of the 'good life'. Could it then be argued that the infringement of a woman's autonomy in these circumstances is justifiable for upholding the value society places on the life of the foetus?[50] I would argue not, as the value society attaches to foetal life is insufficient to justify infringing the right to bodily integrity.[51] Even if it were there are real concerns that pregnant women might avoid medical assistance during pregnancy for fear of forced intervention, and this would be to the long-term detriment of foetuses. Indeed the value society should place on upholding and treasuring the relationship between mother and foetus militates against forced medical intervention.

The Best Interests Test is Too Individualistic

If the patient is not deemed competent then the doctor may perform an operation on the woman only if it is in her best interests.[52] Butler-Sloss LJ in *Re MB* specifically rejected the argument that the court should take into account the interests of the unborn child and balance them against the woman's interests. However the courts in these cases have been willing to order a caesarean section because it is in the medical interests of the mother, or because the mother wishes the child to be born and it would harm her psychologically[53] if the child were to die. The courts have also

---

[48] J. Smith, 'The Pre-eminence of Autonomy in Bioethics' in D. Oderberg and J. Laing, *Human Lives* (Basingstoke, 1997).

[49] R. A. McCall Smith, 'Beyond Autonomy' [1997] 14 *Journal of Contemporary Health Law and Policy* 23.

[50] For a discussion of the sanctity of life see J. Keown, 'Restoring Moral and Intellectual Shape to the Law after *Bland*' (1997) 113 *Law Quarterly Review* 481. See also H. Kuhse, *The Sanctity of Life Doctrine in Medicine* (Oxford, 1987) and W. Wilson 'Is Life Sacred?' [1995] 17 *Journal of Social Welfare and Family Law* 131.

[51] This is particularly so given that the burden of protecting foetal life would fall heavily on pregnant women and we live in a society which, in theory at least, puts a high value on sexual equality. See S. Sherwin, 'Feminism and Bioethics' in S. Wolf (ed.), *Feminism and Bioethics: Beyond Reproduction* (New York, 1996).

[52] *Airedale NHS Trust v. Bland* [1993] AC 789; *Re F (Mental Patient: Sterilization)* [1990] 2 AC 1. It may be in the patient's best interests not to provide treatment: *Re D (Medical Treatment: Mentally Disabled Person)* [1998] 2 FLR 22.

[53] In *Re MB*, n. 6, above, 225 it is clear that the court not only considered what was physically in the best interests of the woman but also psychologically in her interests.

mentioned the guilt that may be felt by the woman if the child were to die as an indication that it would therefore be in her interest to perform the operation.[54]

To use the best interests test as meaning that the only interests to be taken into account are the interests of the patient can be criticized. There are two particular arguments. The first is that it can be in our best interests to act altruistically. To live in a family or community where there is a degree of altruism can be to the benefit of all the members. Secondly, few people make decisions considering only their own interests. In particular, few pregnant woman make decisions relating to pregnancy without any consideration of their foetus. Pregnancy is usually about mutuality, sacrifice, and love, rather than self-interest. For the law to act on behalf of a patient using values alien to her seems clearly wrong. A better test may be to ask what would an ordinary pregnant woman want.[55] I doubt this would lead to the interests of mothers being the only relevant factor, or that the interests of the foetus would predominate.

The Law Perceives the Foetus and the Mother as in Conflict

The present law is couched in a way that sees these cases as requiring a balance between the rights and interests of the mother and the foetus.[56] This seems to place the mother and the foetus in competition with each other and is therefore alien to women's experience in pregnancy.[57] Judge LJ recognized that there was a 'profound physical and emotional bond between the unborn child and its mother'.[58] The law reflects no such bond, but rather represents a conflict between the two. As has been argued:

the legal analysis must shift from an assumption of conflict to an acknowledgement of the interdependence of the maternal-fetal relationship. . . . By characterizing the fetus as 'other,' this model of conflicting rights has undermined the development of effective policy alternatives.[59]

---

[54] *Norfolk and Norwich Health Care (NHS) Trust* v. *W* [1997] 1 FCR 269.

[55] There are however grave concerns that such a test could be used to promote an idealized vision of a pregnant woman. See A. Diduck, 'Legislating Ideologies of Motherhood' 2 [1993] *Social and Legal Studies* 461.

[56] B. Steinbock, *Life before Birth: The Moral and Legal Status of Embryos and Fetuses* (New York, 1992).

[57] This model could lead to extensive regulation and control of women during pregnancy. See S. Fovargue and J. Miola, 'Policing Pregnancy: Implications of the *Attorney General's Reference (No 3 of 1994)*' [1998] 6 *Med. LRev.* 265 and E. Pickworth, 'Substance Abuse in Pregnancy and the Child Born Alive' [1998] 27 *Anglo-American Law Review* 472.

[58] *St George's* v. *S*, n. 6 above, 695.

[59] Note, 'Rethinking [m]otherhood' (1990) 103 *Harvard Law Review* 1325, 1326. See also J. Mair, 'Maternal/Foetal Conflict: Defined or Defused?' in S. McLean (ed.), *Contemporary Issues in Law Medicine and Ethics* (Aldershot, 1996).

MOVING FROM CONFLICT TO UNITY?

An alternative approach that the law could take is to decide that the foetus and mother be regarded as a unity. The foetus could be seen as as much part of the mother as any other part of her body. A clear expression of this view is found in Lord Taylor's speech in *Attorney General's Reference (No 3 of 1994):*[60] 'the foetus is taken to be a part of the mother until it has an existence independent of the mother. Thus an intention to cause serious bodily injury to the foetus is an intention to cause serious bodily injury to a part of the mother just as an intention to injure her arm or leg would be so viewed'. However this approach was rejected in the House of Lords, and rightly so. It does not reflect the experience of pregnancy. As Mackinnon has written, the foetus is 'more than a body party but less than a person, where it is. From the standpoint of the pregnant woman it is both me and not me. It "is" the pregnant woman in the sense that it is in her and of her and is hers more than anyone's. It "is not" her in the sense that she is not all that is there.'[61] Nor does the unity argument acknowledge that a pregnant woman may have an independent interest in the well-being of her foetus, which should be protected in criminal and tort law.[62]

MOVING FROM CONFLICT TO RELATIONSHIP

As stated already there is a close physical and emotional bond between the woman and the unborn child which is not captured by the traditional legal tools of rights and duties. Dawson[63] writes 'there isn't language for fetuses that recognizes their integration with women: there isn't language for (pregnant) women which integrates their connection with the fetus'.

If the law is to move beyond conceiving the problem as one of conflict between the woman and the foetus, then the law must focus on the unique relationship between the foetus and the pregnant woman who are, at the same time, both two and one, physically and emotionally. In this relationship the woman, by the end of the pregnancy, has undergone enormous sacrifices for the foetus. There are two reasons why the law should not seek to impose legal duties at childbirth. First, the sacrifices and demands that pregnancy places on a woman are completely unlike any the law could, or would, compel. In the light of this relationship and the sacrifices

---

[60] [1996] 2 All ER 10, 18.

[61] C. MacKinnon, 'Reflecting on Sexual Equality under Law' (1991) 100 *Yale Law Journal* 1281, 1361.

[62] C. Wells and D. Morgan, 'Whose Foetus is it?' (1991) 18 *Journal of Law and Society* 431. See also L. Purdy, 'Are Pregnant Women Fetal Containers?' in L. Purdy, *Reproducing Persons* (New York, 1996).

[63] T. Brettel Dawson, 'A Feminist Response to "Unborn Child Abuse: Contemplating the Legal Solution" ' (1991) 9 *Canadian Journal of Family Law* 157, 168.

involved, the law cannot impose further legal duties. The woman has already given so much more than the law is entitled to require. Secondly, the language and tools of the law are inapplicable to pregnancy. Any attempt by the law to analyse pregnancy in terms of contract, crime, tort, or unjust enrichment shows the inappropriateness of legal intervention. The values that predominate in the relationship of pregnancy are ones of love and mutual sacrifice, not individualized autonomy and legally enforceable duties. The language of the law is not capable of capturing the kind of relationship in place.

There are two practical consequences of this relationship-based approach. First, the law would not impose legal duties on the woman—she and the foetus would have travelled too far together for that. If there can be no legal compulsion, the woman's voice would have to prevail, not because of the principle of autonomy, but because of the unsuitability of any legal obligations after all the sacrifices she has made. But, listening to her voice is not an easy matter. To suggest that a pregnant woman's answer to the dilemma posed by whether or not to have a caesarean section can be captured by a yes or no (consent or not consent), as the present law demands, is over simplistic.[64] In *Re MB,* MB was speaking with a variety of messages. She longed for the baby to be born. She was willing to undergo a caesarean section if necessary, but she could not face an injection. Indeed, at one time she consented to the injection but withdrew her consent to it when she saw the needle. What would really meet her desire here? It was argued earlier that the overall thrust of her wishes was to go ahead with the operation. By contrast in *St George's* v. *S* it seems that S had a strong view against medical intervention which she had held for quite some time. In the context of her life and pregnancy it seems clear that S did not want the caesarean section to take place. The court needs to hear a woman's wishes in the context of her pregnancy and life, not just at the moment before the operation. The listening process between the medical team and the woman should begin as early as possible in the pregnancy; 'birth plans' being one way of doing this. The wishes of the competent woman can then be heard and given effect.

The second practical consequence is more wide-ranging. The relationship-based approach recognizes that there is a state interest in upholding and supporting the relationship between the mother and the foetus, but not in a way that places legal duties on the mother. This has consequences in respect of, *inter alia,* state benefits for pregnant women; allocation of health resources for pregnant women; and protection for the woman and foetus from pollution.

---

[64] See the stimulating analysis of the case law by C. Wells, 'On the Outside Looking In: On Enforced Caesareans', n. 1, above.

Conclusion

This paper has shown that the caesarean section cases have presented a number of difficult issues for the law. The Court of Appeal has suggested the cases can be easily dealt with by referring to the supremacy of the principle of autonomy. However, it has been argued that the law does not generally accept autonomy as an absolute principle. Nor has the law developed sufficiently to enable the courts to make autonomy paramount. In particular, there is insufficient protection to ensure a patient receives all the information she needs for a decision, and the law has not yet sufficiently developed a way of dealing with a patient who has conflicting desires.

It has been argued that the vision of pregnancy that autonomy portrays—namely the rights of autonomy trumping the interests of the foetus—is a vision of conflict which is at odds with most women's experience of pregnancy. In the light of the enormous sacrifices in pregnancy and the mutual relationship between the woman and the foetus, the law has no basis for seeking to impose legal obligations on pregnant women. This leads us back to listening to the woman's voice about how her relationship with the foetus should continue through birth. Under the present legal structure it is hard enough for the woman's voice to be heard, yet alone decide what it is she is saying.

POLICING PREGNANCY: RIGHTS AND WRONGS

Meredith Blake

This paper explores and evaluates the idea that a pregnant woman should be the subject of legal regulation in order to protect the welfare of her unborn child. The concept of 'maternal–foetal conflict' has to date dominated legal discussion of maternal conduct which poses risks to the unborn child. This concept however can be unhelpful and damaging, and is ultimately unable to reflect the subtle ethical issues raised by pregnancy and the role of the medical profession in monitoring and intervening in pregnancy and childbirth.[1] The main focus of this discussion will be the impact that the new Human Rights Act 1998 may have on the current legal approach to situations in which the present and future welfare of the foetus is endangered as a result of the conduct of the pregnant woman. It is suggested that human rights jurisprudence may be better able to reflect the complexity of decision-making in pregnancy, and turn the spotlight away from the notion of conflict.

Although any academic venture into decision-making in pregnancy cannot justifiably exclude the issue of abortion, and probably contraception and assisted conception, the focus of this paper is on a pregnancy that exists and is *wanted*—that is, when the woman has conceived and has decided not to abort but to bring the child to full term. Although it is important that there is, in both ethics and law, consistency between the issues of conception, abortion, managing pregnancy, and childbirth, the decision to carry the foetus is a highly significant distinguishing factor in so far as any analysis is concerned.

It is within this more limited agenda that recent advances in obstetric medicine have been most intensely felt. These advances have enabled the physician to obtain information about the unborn child pertaining to its health and viability, such that these advances can now dramatically influence the course of pregnancy, including childbirth. Research has indicated the effects that maternal behaviour may have upon the unborn child, whilst technological developments allow the detection of foetal abnormalities, as well as indicate the general health and positioning of

[1] H. Draper 'Women, Forced Caesareans and Antenatal Responsibilities' (1996) 22 *Journal of Medical Ethics* 327.

the foetus.[2] Such knowledge and techniques have had two central implications for clinical practice. It has allowed increased access to the unborn child, to the extent that the physician may regard it as a 'second patient', and it has given increased opportunity for decision-making during the course of pregnancy.[3] Whilst this may appear to increase choice for the pregnant woman, it also increases the opportunity for the regulation of those choices, and therefore the reinforcement of paternalistic attitudes. Already this capacity for increased intervention has encouraged public debate and legal argument about the responsibilities of the pregnant woman.[4]

It is equally important, however, to recognize, that, despite the technology and the research, this area is still one in which medical prognosis is far from certain. Few would question the fairly extensive evidence of the connection between smoking in pregnancy and low birth weight, or between alcohol and drug addiction and babies born with substance addiction.[5] It is less certain, however, whether such factors as vigorous exercise and a stressful working environment have any deleterious effect upon the unborn child. It has recently been suggested that screening during pregnancy may have adverse effects upon the foetus, whilst debate about the benefits of caesarean sections to both baby and mother continues to exist.[6] There is therefore a significant degree of uncertainty about what constitutes a significant risk to the foetus, and it is appropriate that this factor should influence ethical and legal analysis on this issue.

The Moral Values at Stake

The intuitive response to intervene during the course of a problematic pregnancy is prompted by the belief that not to do so may result in needless loss of life; of the unborn child, and also the woman, where her welfare is threatened by her action or inaction. That most of us value human life is indisputable. The much more difficult question is *why* we value it. Much ethical debate on abortion presumes that the foetus represents the value of human life, but there is substantial force in the argument that human life is itself not valuable and that it is self-consciousness, or

[2] Such techniques include ultrasonogrophy, which can detect placenta previa and indicate whether the baby is in breech position, as well as foetal surgery and foetal heart monitors.
[3] N. Rhoden, 'The Judge in the Delivery Room', (1986) 74 *California Law Review* 1952.
[4] *The Guardian*, 18 Aug. 1998, 11 Mar. 1997; *Independent*, 19 Feb. 1997.
[5] E. Pickworth, 'Substance Abuse and the Child Born Alive' (1998) 27 *Anglo-American Law Review* 472. It has been claimed that even common tranquillisers may have adverse effects upon the foetus—the *Sunday Telegraph* (21 Sept. 1997).
[6] P. Foster, *Woman and the Health Care Industry: An Unhealthy Relationship?* (Buckingham: 1995), 131. Ultrasound has been linked to changes in body cells and low birthweight, whilst amniocentesis and chora villus testing have been linked with an increased risk of miscarriage. On the risks of caesarean sections see C. R. Leitch and J. J. Walker, 'The Rise in Caesarean Section Rate' (1998) 105 *British Journal of Obstetrics and Gynæcology* 621 and 15 Aug. 1998, (1998) 317 *The British Medical Journal* 462.

personhood, which is the source of our respect for human life.[7] In many moral theories, the very young foetus is not as 'valuable' as a self-conscious adult, although a gradualist approach would attribute value to the near-term, as opposed to the very young, foetus.[8]

Militating against the urge to intervene is the desire to respect the woman's autonomous choices about her conduct. Most ethical theories accept that autonomy is valuable in moral analysis, even if not intrinsically valuable.[9] In the present context, however, there are problems in defining and locating that value. Pregnancy poses unique challenges to the ordinary understanding of autonomy, especially where a decision has been made to continue with the pregnancy: is the autonomous decision to give birth to a healthy, viable child, or is it to satisfy the craving resulting from addiction? In the case of those who are substance addicted, or those acting on an uninformed basis, the decision may not be an autonomous one at all, and the value of autonomy not engaged. That is not to say that it is impossible or undesirable to promote any existing capacity for autonomy so that its value is engaged.[10]

An intuitive response based upon these two values encourages a picture of maternal–foetal conflict. However, it should be evident from the above that the situation is more complex than this suggests, and there exists good reason to question the assumption that these two values are even engaged at all by the situation, let alone necessarily at odds. If they are engaged, this does not necessarily mean the creation of an irresolvable conflict. A deontological approach based on rights and duties, for example, should admit that even if the foetus is capable of being a rights-bearer, it is not necessarily the case that it has a right to be born.[11] It may, however, possess other interests, such as an interest in being born free of avoidable harm, or an interest in not suffering pain or distress.[12] If that is the case, is there an obligation on others to act in order to secure that interest? In the situation where the woman has decided to continue with the pregnancy, it

---

[7] P. Singer, *Practical Ethics* (Cambridge, 1993), 83–110.

[8] N. Poplawski and G. Gillett, 'Ethics and Embryos' (1991) 17 *Journal of Medical Ethics* 62.

[9] J. Glover, *Causing Death and Saving Lives* (Harmondsworth, 1977); Singer, n. 7, above.

[10] T. L. Beauchamp and J. F. Childress, *Principles of Biomedical Ethics* (New York, 1991).

[11] M. Tooley, *Abortion and Infanticide* (Oxford, 1983). He maintains that in order to be a right-bearer the subject must possess the concept of a self as a continuing subject of experiences and other mental states, and believe that it is a continuing entity. His concept of what is valuable about human life is therefore reflected in his attribution of that particular right. For him, only persons have a right to life—because for him it is personhood that is intrinsically valuable. Also see J. Feinberg, 'Is there a Right to be Born?' in P. Foot (ed.), *The Problem of Abortion* (1980).

[12] I. Kennedy, 'A Woman and her Unborn Child' in P. Byrne (ed.), *Ethics and Care in Health Law and Research* (London, 1988) dismisses arguments based upon abortion as not necessarily relevant to the issue of regulation of pregnancy on the basis that we are not concerned in the latter case with the foetus's interest in being born, but with the issue of its being born free of avoidable harm.

is possible to conclude that, given the complete dependence of the foetus upon the woman (unlike a young child), there is a both a duty of non-interference and a positive duty of assistance upon the woman towards the foetus, based upon her assumption of responsibility for its safety.[13] The arguments for this become stronger the closer the child is to term, based on the more palpable assumption of responsibility. The more tenuous link between other agents (the clinician, the father of the child) and the foetus suggests that there is less mileage in any argument that the foetus is owed a duty at all by these other parties, and that the only duties they owe are to the pregnant woman.

The upshot of this deontological approach is that, in some cases, it is better to permit tragic consequences in order to avoid doing quite trivial wrongs. In the present context, this would mean that *if* the woman has made an autonomous choice as to her conduct during pregnancy and childbirth (bearing in mind the difficulties in ascertaining what the autonomous choice is), then it would be wrong for others to override that choice by interfering with her personal autonomy.

A utilitarian approach, in giving more weight to any good consequences, would perhaps be more likely to support the regulation of pregnant women where that would benefit the welfare of the unborn child. The uncertainty surrounding the risks, both short- and long-term, associated with substance abuse in pregnancy, ante-natal testing, and childbirth, however, means that there are inherent difficulties in calculating the most positive course of action. Moreover, although autonomy is not intrinsically valuable in utilitarian approaches, most utilitarians accept that ignoring autonomy is likely to have long-term deleterious side-effects, such as destroying pregnant women's trust in their physicians such they are reluctant to seek or continue with ante-natal care. Other sensitive and indirect considerations include the possibility that the relationship between the mother and child will be adversely affected, and the feminist rights debate which draws upon disturbing facts reflecting the social status and race of pregnant women whose choices against medical intervention are consistently overridden.[14] These side-effects are obviously more weighty where the woman's own welfare is not affected by her conduct and where the

---

[13] J. J. Thomson, 'A Defense of Abortion' in R. Dworkin (ed.), *The Philosophy of Law* (London, 1977) at 112, uses the analogy of a famous violinist to assert that abortion is justified on the basis of the woman's need to protect her bodily integrity or her property rights in her own body. However she accepts that that this argument does not hold with the same strength if the woman has voluntarily become pregnant and there are no self-defence arguments based on danger to her life or health to rest on.

[14] L. Ikemoto, 'Furthering the Inquiry: Race, Class and Culture in the Forced Medical Treatment of Pregnant Women' (1992) 59 *Tennessee Law Review* 487. This cites a 1987 US study of obstetricians revealing that of 21 petitions for court-ordered medical treatment of pregnant women, 17 were sought against black, Hispanic, or Asian women, and all of these women were receiving public assistance or using the public hospital system.

intervention involves a serious interference with her personal autonomy (for example, a forced detoxification programme or a caesarean section). Where the woman herself is at risk, the good consequences of an action that would save both woman and unborn child is more likely to outweigh such indirect considerations. Those good consequences are made up in part from the near certainty that a physician would much rather save lives and bring a healthy child into the world than watch needless decline and perhaps death.

The Current Legal Agenda

The above ethical analysis is useful in that it helps to isolate both the precise nature of the rights and duties that may be invoked by the sorts of situations with which we are concerned and the utilitarian considerations both supporting and rejecting intervention in the course of pregnancy and childbirth. The question that now has to be addressed is whether the current legal approach is able adequately to reflect the sorts of concerns that have emerged as important in moral theory. This does not amount to a claim that there should be legal regulation of the pregnant woman in the name of her unborn child. However, it is worth considering the present legal situation, and exploring the possibility that a different legal agenda may have the capacity to deal more appropriately with this difficult area.

As long ago as 1982, John Robertson painted a scene which suggested that legal regulation of the pregnant woman was an unstoppable beast which could justify significant invasions of her body:

[Pregnant women] may also be prohibited from using alcohol or other substances harmful to the fetus during pregnancy or be kept from the workplace because of toxic effects on the fetus. They could be ordered to take drugs, such as insulin for diabetes, medications for fetal deficiencies, or intra-uterine blood transfusion for Rh factor. Pregnant anorexic teenagers could be force-fed. Prenatal screening and diagnostic procedures, from amniocentesis to sonography or even fetoscopy could be made mandatory. And in utero surgery for the fetus to shunt cerebroventricular fluids from the brain to relieve hydrocephalus, or to relieve the urethral obstruction of bilateral hydronephrosis could also be ordered. Indeed, even extra-uterine fetal surgery, if it becomes an established procedure, could be ordered, if the risks to the mother were small and it were a last resort to save the life or prevent severe disability in a viable fetus.[15]

These predictions have not as yet materialized in English common law, which views the pregnant woman's resistance to medical or more general therapeutic intervention as a 'refusal of treatment' situation. The crimes and torts of assault and battery have dictated the approach of the courts to

---

[15] J. Robertson, 'The Right to Procreate and *in utero* Fetal Therapy' (1982) 3 *Journal of Legal Medicine* 333.

cases in which a person has refused medical treatment. Thus it is clear that competent adults can refuse medical treatment if that is their wish, even if this may have fatal consequences for them.[16] This has been expressed as an example of the principle of self-determination.[17] However, looking at the issue of *demands* for medical treatment (even in the situation where resource considerations would favour the honouring of those demands), it is clear that self-determination and respect for personal autonomy are not fully incorporated into the common law.[18] It is not the case, then, that the common law can claim to have a fully developed concept of self-determination.

Nonetheless, it is this concept which the court has recited in those cases where the pregnant woman's refusal of medical intervention has threatened the welfare of the unborn child. Although the foetus is protected in several respects under English law, both at common law and under statute, any protection appears to be suspended once there is a perceived 'conflict' between the woman and the foetus.[19] To date most of the English case law has concerned refusals of caesarean sections which have been perceived as necessary in the eyes of the medical profession in order to ensure the survival of the infant and, in some cases, the mother as well.

The most recent decision, in *St George's Healthcare NHS Trust* v. *S* (hereafter *St George's*), concerned the appeal of a woman who claimed that she had undergone a caesarean section against her express refusal, after her unlawful admission to and detention in a mental hospital.[20] That admission had occurred subsequently to the diagnosis of pre-eclampsia and advice that she needed to be admitted to hospital for an induced delivery. With respect to the question of the legality of non-consensual caesareans, Judge LJ's judgment resounds with the words of the House of Lords in *Airedale NHS Trust* v. *Bland*, upholding the right of every adult of sound mind to refuse medical treatment. The reasoning, therefore, follows *Re MB (Medical Treatment)*,[21] also a case concerning a refused caesarean section, in concluding that this right applies as equally to the pregnant woman as to any individual.[22]

If the situation with respect to decision-making in childbirth is now clear, it is less so with respect to decisions taken during the course of the

---

[16] *Re C (Adult: Refusal of Treatment)* [1994] 1 WLR 290.

[17] *Airedale National Health Service Trust* v. *Bland* [1993] 1 All ER 821.

[18] In *ibid*. The House of Lords rejected the contention that there was a 'right to die' based on autonomy arguments.

[19] The foetus is protected by the Abortion Act 1967, the Human Fertilization and Embryology Act 1990 (protection against genetic cloning), the Infant Life (Preservation) Act 1929, and the Congenital Disabilities (Civil Liability) Act 1976.

[20] [1998] 3 All ER 673.   [21] [1997] 2 FLR 424.

[22] Although Judge LJ did stress (at 687) that 'the interests of the foetus cannot simply be disregarded on the basis that in refusing treatment which would benefit the foetus a mother is simply refusing treatment for herself'.

pregnancy. It appears to have been assumed that if the pregnant woman's will could be overborne in childbirth, then this would open the door to the situation whereby pregnant women could be forced to do or refrain from doing activities during pregnancy which could affect the welfare of the foetus. Various comments in the caesarean cases give some insight into the court's thinking on this point. In both *St George's* and *Re MB*, direct reliance was placed upon the Canadian case of *Winnipeg Child and Family Services* v. *G*, in fact concerning the behaviour of a woman during pregnancy, and thus a decision taken in a different, 'non-emergency' context.[23] The woman in question was five months pregnant and addicted to glue sniffing. There was an attempt to detain her under the Mental Health Act 1987, the objective being the welfare of the unborn child. The Canadian Supreme Court confirmed the opinion of the Appeal Court in finding that the mother could not be detained, on the basis that it would be undesirable to recognize foetal rights which would infringe those of the mother, this being likely to generate resentment in the mother and therefore having detrimental effects on pre-natal care.

The decision in *Winnipeg* itself purported partially to rely upon an earlier decision of the English Court of Appeal. In *Re F (in utero)*, the local authority sought a declaration from the court that the unborn child be warded to it, and, after birth, that it have the care and control of the child, in view of its fears that the pregnant woman's conduct was posing risks to the foetus.[24] The court refused to extend the wardship jurisdiction in this way, basing its decision on the potentially damaging consequences of such an order, including the difficulties of reinforcement. In *Re P*, this approach was affirmed on the basis that 'there is no jurisdiction at the present time in the High Court to make an unborn child a ward of court'.[25]

The possibility of post-birth sanctioning of the woman for conduct during the pregnancy is specifically excluded by the Congenital Disabilities Act 1976, but is perhaps left open at common law under the recent decision in *Attorney-General's Reference (No. 3 of 1994)*. In that case the defendant (the pregnant woman's boyfriend and father of the child) was convicted of the unlawful and dangerous manslaughter of the child, which died after birth from injuries sustained whilst in the womb, a result of stab wounds to the woman's abdomen.[26] The reason for the former exception can be traced to the Law Commission's findings that there was a wide range of conduct during pregnancy through which a mother could cause injury to her child, and that it would add to the already stressful relationship between the

---

[23] 1997] 3 BHCR 611.   [24] 1988] 2 All ER 193.
[25] Unreported decision of Ewbank J, 28 Mar. 1988.
[26] [1997] 3 WLR 421. Also see *Grodin* v. *Grodin*, 301 NW 2d 869 (Mich. 1981) in which the court held admissible a claim for compensation by a child against his mother for allegedly using an antibiotic during pregnancy which was argued to have resulted in the child being born with discoloured teeth.

mother and the child were there to be tortious liability.[27] These comments were made, however, in the context of negligent actions by the woman—what if the mother were to do something *knowing* that it would endanger the life of the foetus?

Reading the case law and statute law together, it becomes evident that the concepts purportedly relied upon in resolving the situation where a pregnant woman's conduct and decisions threaten her unborn child's welfare are under-developed and misapplied. First, there is no analysis of the concept of autonomy. *If* it is to be the trump card, it is important that the law is able to recognize what is a truly autonomous decision or course of action. In the sorts of situations with which we are concerned, that is a challenging question to decide. For example, in *Re MB*, the woman refused the needle necessary for the carrying out of the caesarean section, but it was equally clear that she was prepared to have the operation and that she very much wanted the child born alive and well. By contrast, the woman in *St George's* was adamant from very early on that she did not want any medical intervention of this type, and her view was maintained in the face of significant pressure. It would seem wrong to equate these two decisions, and indeed in the former case it is arguable that truly to respect the autonomy of the woman would involve the administration of the injection and the carrying out of the caesarean section. Outside these sorts of emergency childbirth procedures, there is a need for a more robust analysis of the situation where the woman's conduct, fuelled by substance addiction, threatens the foetus, rather than a bland acceptance that this is simple question of respecting autonomy versus the child's welfare.

Secondly, even where a person has made an autonomous decision, it is apparent from other areas of the law that it is not always the case that this will be respected. Leaving aside those situations which demand action from the clinician, there are several examples in which autonomy has had to give way in the face of other demands. The Infectious Diseases (Notification) Act 1989 authorizes people to be held against their will if they are found to be suffering from an infectious disease, on the basis that this is in the public interest, as are bodily invasions under other criminal law statutes.[28] It has been said that the defence of necessity in medical law, justifying the treatment of incompetent patients, is based in the public interest, although it has also been termed a form of 'private defence', akin to the defence of self-defence in criminal law.[29]

It is also clear that both the criminal law and the civil law can require

---

[27] Law Commission, *Report on Injuries to Unborn Children* (London, 1974).

[28] e.g. under the Police and Criminal Evidence Act 1984, body searches in relation to drug offences.

[29] See *Re F (Mental Patient: Sterilisation)* [1990] 2 AC 1, *per* Lord Goff (although the House of Lords was concerned there with the incompetent patient who is unable to exercise a right to self-determination).

an individual to act against his or her will in certain circumstances, which, though they do not necessarily require an invasion of bodily integrity, are closely concerned with the scope of individual autonomy. These duties generally arise in situations where a person has created a dangerous situation or has assumed responsibility for the care of someone.[30] If the omission to act is negligent, civil liability may result; if the omission is reckless or intentional then criminal liability may ensue.

The Children and Young Persons Act 1933 is a clear example of this legal regime. By section 1(2), parents or legal guardians can be held criminally liable for neglect in relation to children and young persons under their care. These duties (to provide adequate food, clothing, medical aid, and lodging) are not founded on parental status *per se*, but result from assumption of responsibility and consequent reliance.[31] In *St George's*, Judge LJ indirectly referred to the idea of this parental duty, but framed it in the language of sacrifice:

If it has not already done so, medical science will no doubt advance to the stage when a very minor procedure undergone by an adult would save the life of his or her child, or perhaps the life of a complete stranger. If, however, the adult were compelled to agree, or rendered helpless to resist, the principle of autonomy would be extinguished.[32]

The earlier ethical analysis, however, indicated that it is arguably legitimate to draw a distinction between the born and unborn child based on the complete dependence of the latter upon the pregnant woman. This idea was canvassed by Twaddle J in the *Winnipeg* case. He considered the possibility of a tortious duty being owed to the unborn child, and that this might provide a lawful reason for restraining the pregnant woman's conduct through an injunction, in that it was seeking to prevent future harm. He held that for reasons of policy it could not, because it would create a 'conflict between the rights of the mother and those of the child'. With respect, this assertion rather begs the question—the point here is that the woman does have autonomy rights but that these may be restrained, not necessarily in the name of any specific 'right' of the unborn child, but rather in the public interest. His reference to a number of utilitarian reasons as militating against the duty was more consistent with this latter idea. He noted the difficulties in deciding what should be deemed unreasonable conduct and what should not, and concluded that to recognize such a tortious action might be detrimental to the future child:

A mother forced to quit a habit of her choice may grow resentful of the child whose existence in her womb brought about the restraint or the threat of it. This may seem insignificant in a case such as this where the mother's resentment of the

---

[30] R. v. *Miller* [1992] 2 WLR 937; R. v. *Stone and Robinson* [1977] QB 354.
[31] R. v. *Lowe* [1973] 2 WLR 481.   [32] *St George's*, n. 20, above at 687.

child would pale in comparison to the harm the child will likely suffer if she is not restrained. But, in the case of a mother with a less health-threatening habit (e.g. the occasional alcoholic drink), the mother's resentment may be more harmful to the child in the long run than her continuing to indulge her habit.[33]

Fourthly, he saw that such actions might have wider deleterious effects on the health of children—he thought it might drive pregnant women 'underground' in fear of state intervention if their conduct were known. There is, he stated, a 'public interest in having expectant mothers receive pre-natal care', and that this 'public interest militates against recognition of foetal rights'.[34]

It is submitted that this approach is helpful in that it draws the analysis away from the notion of 'conflict', instead based on the idea that autonomy can be lawfully restrained depending upon the strength of the more specific duty involved and more general utilitarian considerations.

The current legal approach does not appear to have really tackled the issue from this angle, instead preferring to emphasize the point that the woman's autonomy should be respected at all costs.[35] It is an 'all or nothing' approach, dictated by the fact that English common law attempts to protect autonomy through the rather blunt instruments of assault and battery. Once the situation is classified one of 'refusal of treatment', then it appears that there can be no amelioration so as to accommodate situations where there exist other interests which merit recognition. The pregnant woman's conduct is therefore currently regarded as a matter for moral, rather than legal, condemnation. The law as it stands is unable, or unwilling, to reflect the nuances of the issue for fear that 'all' autonomy will become 'nothing' autonomy.

A Human Rights Approach

The problems that the common law currently has in articulating a meaningful and complete concept of autonomy, and applying that concept to the particular context of a wanted pregnancy, may be rectified by the implementation of the Human Rights Act 1998. The following discussion is not necessarily advocating a change to the current position, but is rather an attempt to assess whether the Act will help to address these deficiencies.

At the outset it should be stated that human rights jurisprudence is not simply a question of asserting a right, and demanding that it respected. It is more widely concerned with balancing an individual's right against other societal interests—indeed this is said to be the aim of the European

---

[33] At 900.   [34] At 901–2.
[35] See n. 20, above, per Judge LJ—'while pregnancy increases the personal responsibilities of a woman it does not diminish her entitlement to decide whether or not to undergo medical treatment'.

Convention on Human Rights (ECHR). This process of balancing involves an identification of specific societal interests and generally requires that any interference with a right in the name of any wider interest is proportional to the aim that is sought to be achieved by the interference. It is thus clear that the human rights jurisprudence has a capacity to address both deontological and utilitarian concerns.

Although by section 2(1) of the Human Rights Act, ECHR case law must be taken into account by domestic courts and tribunals, it is less clear how relevant particular aspects of ECHR jurisprudence will be to the operation of the Human Rights Act. For example, the concept of the 'margin of appreciation' is a product of the fact that the ECHR machinery is subsidiary to the national systems safeguarding human rights, and that, in the absence of a European consensus on an issue, some leeway will be given to the established practice in particular states.[36] A domestic instrument has no immediate need for this sort of concept (although it is clearly possible that a similar doctrine will develop, affording the existing common law protection from intense review), and it is not unreasonable to suggest that the English courts may subject claims of violation to a level of scrutiny unseen in Convention jurisprudence. It is therefore relevant to consider the jurisprudence of those jurisdictions in which human rights are constitutionally guaranteed. Of particular relevance to the present context are those cases in the USA in which intervention with pregnant women has been the basis of a constitutional challenge.

Prior to 1991 there existed substantial authority to the effect that it was lawful under the American constitution to force a caesarean section, or a blood transfusion, upon a pregnant woman.[37] The Supreme Court's abortion ruling in *Roe* v. *Wade* was cited as support for this.[38] That case established the legality of abortion based on viability of the unborn child, a point set at the beginning of the third trimester, although it is lawful to regulate abortion after the first trimester. At the heart of the ruling was the finding that the state has an interest in not only maternal health and safety, but also as 'an important and legitimate interest in protecting the potentiality of human life'.[39] Earlier cases seemed also to recognize that

---

[36] e.g. in determining whether transsexuals have claims under the Convention—see *Rees* v. *UK* (1981) 3 EHRR 203; *X,Y,Z* v. *UK* [1997] 2 FLR 892.
[37] L. Haberfield, 'Pregnant Women: Judicial Intervention and the Right of Pregnant Women to Refuse Medical Treatment' (1995) 2 *JCULR* 1 at 24—a national US survey of cases published in 1987 indicated that there were 36 judicial attempts to override maternal refusals of proposed medical treatment. 15 of these were sought to authorize caesarean interventions, 13 of which were granted. In *North Cent. Bronx Hospital.* 1992–85 (NY Sup. Ct.) 1986, a court appointed the physician guardian *ad litem* for the foetus, with authority to consent to whatever diagnostic and therapeutic procedures were necessary for its protection.
[38] 410 US 113 (1973).
[39] However, it is equally clear that, even after viability, the mother's interest in her health prevails—the state cannot prohibit abortions where 'it is necessary to preserve the life or health of the mother'. In *Thornburgh* v. *American College of Obstetricians and*

the unborn child had a 'right to life'.[40] More recently, however, the courts
have questioned the legality of coercing or restraining pregnant women in
the name of the welfare of the unborn child.[41]

Generally speaking, the American case law is informative in view of the
Human Rights Act. Most of these cases have not admitted that the foetus
has a right to life, but have stressed that the right to privacy underlying the
woman's abortion rights is tempered by the state's power to restrict those
in pursuit of a legitimate state interest. The courts have identified four
state interests potentially relevant to the decision to accept or reject
medical treatment, they being preserving life, protecting third parties,
preventing suicide, and maintaining the ethical integrity of the medical
profession.[42] The latter two interests have only minimal, if any, relevance
to the issue in hand. However, the unborn child and any other existing
children have been recognized as third parties whom the state can act to
protect as *parens patriae*.[43] For example, in *In re Madyun*, the Supreme
Court of the District of Columbia ordered a caesarean in relation to a non-
consenting woman whose membranes had ruptured, thereby presenting a
risk of foetal blood poisoning to the unborn child, but no significant risk
to the mother.[44] The court identified the relevant state interest protecting
her privacy rights as that of both viability of the human life—*Roe* v.
Wade—and the interest that the state has in protecting third parties, here
the foetus. Inasmuch as the court appeared to be extending the protective
jurisdiction to the unborn, it is consistent with other authority in the USA
based on the premise that there was minimal risk to the pregnant woman
if the procedure were carried out, but a significant risk to the mother if it
was not.[45] The decision in *In re AC*, reversed this trend, but it is perhaps
significant in that case that the caesarean section was almost certain to
have a significant detrimental effect on the woman's health.

These cases therefore illustrate the inherent flexibility of the constitutional system, whereby the constitutional guarantee of life, liberty, and
property in the Fourteenth Amendment, and the protection of individuals

Gynaecologists 106 S. Ct. 2169, 2182–3 (1986) the court recognized the undesirability of
any 'trade-off' between the woman's health and additional points of foetal survival.

[40] *Jefferson* v. *Griffin Spalding County Hospital* 274 SE 2d 457 (1981) in which the court
weighed this right against the mother's right to practise her religion and refuse a blood transfusion—the former won out.

[41] In *Re AC* 573 A.2d 1235 (1990). Also see M. Field, 'Controlling the Woman to Protect
the Foetus' (1989) 17 *Law, Medicine and Health Care* 114.

[42] See *In re AC*, n. 41 above, and, in the context of 'right to die with dignity', *State of
Washington* v. *Glucksberg* 138 L Ed. 2d 777 (1997).

[43] *Raleigh Fitkin-Paul Memorial Hospital* v. *Anderson*; *Crouse Irving Memorial Hospital*
v. *Paddock* 485 NYS 2d 443 (1985)—based on the state's interest in protecting the health
and welfare of the unborn child.

[44] 114 Daily Wash. 1 Rep. 2233 (1986).

[45] *In re Dubreuil* 603 So 2d 528 (1992), in which a woman was given a blood transfusion
which she refused, on the basis that otherwise her four children would be abandoned.

from unreasonable searches and seizures under the Fourth Amendment have been seen to reflect a right to privacy encompassing the right to refuse medical treatment.[46] However, the caveat built within constitutional guarantees, allowing their restriction in order to protect certain state interests, gives the court the capacity to weigh the value of the viable foetus.[47] Under this structure a 'balancing approach' is permissible which may allow for forced treatment of pregnant women in those circumstances where the mother would not suffer substantial risk from the treatment, and where there exist no other alternatives to that treatment.

In light of the above it is worth considering which of those rights protected under the Convention, and now the Human Rights Act, may be relevant to the situation under consideration. Most of the cases which arose for consideration here resulted from petitions by hospitals seeking the court's permission for non-consensual treatment, or from third parties where there was disagreement between the pregnant woman and the physician. The main aim of the Convention, and the Act, is to prevent public authorities interfering with individual's rights. The Act states that courts are to be considered public authorities—therefore any action taken by an NHS hospital trust or clinic or any decision made by the court under common law must be in accordance with the provisions of the Act.[48]

The main issue for consideration is which, if any, of the rights protected under the Convention and the Act are relevant to litigation concerning the pregnant woman. Both the earlier discussion of ethics and the analysis of the US case law identified the protection of human life and personal autonomy as the two main values engaged by the question of deleterious effects of the conduct of pregnant women. That being the case, Articles 2 and 8 emerge as the most obvious candidates for consideration.

Article 2 concerns the protection of human life. It both prohibits the state from taking life and imposes a positive duty to safeguard life.[49] There have been no decisions directly concerning the applicability of Article 2 to the question of management of pregnancy or decision-making in childbirth, and so the most relevant cases are those concerning abortion. In *Paton* v. *UK*, this Article was invoked by a man seeking to restrain his wife from aborting their 10-week-old foetus.[50] The Commission found that Article 2 should not be construed as recognizing an absolute 'right to life'

---

[46] The right to privacy is therefore not specifically set out in the Constitution, but is said to emanate from these provisions and from the Bill of Rights. The Fourteenth Amendment has been used in 'right to die' litigation as including a right to privacy—see *State of Washington* v. *Glucksberg*, n. 42, above.

[47] The infringement must be in aid of legitimate governmental purposes of sufficient importance and the infringement must be sufficiently narrowly tailored to those purposes in order to be justified.

[48] Although there is an exception for primary legislation which is not deemed invalid even if incompatible with the Act.

[49] *X* v. *United Kingdom* (1978) 14 DR 31.   [50] *Paton* v. *UK* (1981) 3 EHRR 408.

for the foetus, being of the opinion that the life of the foetus cannot be regarded in isolation from that of the mother. The Commission thought that if an absolute protection were given to the foetus, that would be placing it above the value of a pregnant woman were her life to be threatened by the pregnancy, a conclusion thought to be against the object and purpose of the Convention. It did not, therefore, come to any conclusion on the question whether a later foetus (the foetus in question was only 10 weeks old) would be protected by Article 2.

Similarly, in a case in which two women challenged the restrictive abortion laws in Germany, the Commission did not find it necessary to come to a conclusion whether the foetus has rights within Article 2.[51]

In another case, in which an Irish group challenged the restriction on access to information on abortion, it was argued by the Irish government that the right to life under Article 2 was fundamental, and therefore justified infringement of Article 10 (the right to freedom of expression).[52] The Commission did not come to any view on whether Article 2 actually protected the unborn, but was clearly of the view that the right to life is no more 'fundamental' than any other right guaranteed under the Convention—the individual government's view on the value of unborn life did not preclude the court from reviewing the law in question.

The only other Article 2 case of significance to come before the Commission concerned a lawful abortion of a 14-week-old foetus for social reasons.[53] Although the Commission did not express an opinion on the scope of Article 2 in relation to the protection of the foetus, it did not rule out that in certain circumstances it would offer protection.

In *Re MB*, Butler-Sloss LJ considered the relevance of Article 2 in deciding the outcome of the health authority's application to perform a caesarean section. She concluded that there was nothing significant to be drawn from the case law:

It has not yet become necessary for the European Commission to make a decision about the application of Article 2 to the foetus at a stage later than 10 weeks. . . . We do not consider that this court can gain any assistance on this issue from the opinions of the Commission.

Although Butler-Sloss LJ concerned herself with Article 2 of the Convention, the abortion cases have in fact focused more upon Article 8, which concerns the protection of private and family life. It is suggested that this Article is clearly significant considering the role which the right to privacy has assumed in the comparative US case law. Unlike Article 2, this is not an 'absolute right' as the second paragraph of Article 8 provides that:

[51] *Bruggemann and Scheuten v. FRG* (1981) 3 EHRR 244.
[52] *Open Door Counselling Ltd and Dublin Well Woman Centre v. Ireland* (1993) 15 EHRR 112.
[53] *H v. Norway* (1990) (App. No 17004/90, unreported).

There shall be no interference by a public authority with the exercise of this right except such as in accordance with the law and necessary in a democratic society in the interests of national security, public safety or the economic well-being of the country, for the prevention of disorder or crime, for the protection of health or morals, or for the protection of the rights and freedoms of others.

Strictly speaking, the presence of this legitimate interference clause should allow for a broad interpretation of privacy. In *Bruggemann and Scheuten* v. *Federal Republic of Germany*, however, the Commission considered the scope of the right to privacy under Article 8 (in connection with the applicants' complaint concerning the restrictive abortion laws in Germany). It was of the opinion that pregnancy:

could not be said to pertain uniquely to the sphere of private life. Whenever a woman is pregnant her private life becomes closely connected with that of the developing foetus.[54]

In using the presence of the foetus to determine the scope of the woman's privacy rights, the Commission indirectly introduced the limitations set out in paragraph of Article 8. The effect of this approach is to make it more difficult to establish an initial violation of privacy were the woman's decisions overridden or her conduct forcibly controlled. Given that the woman is, however, able to establish that any such intervention constitutes a violation of her privacy rights, it is up to the state to establish that there is a 'legitimate aim' for the interference. If it cannot, then there is no need to proceed to the second question, which is resolved by asking whether the interference is 'necessary'—that is, whether it is in connection with a pressing social need and is proportionate to the aim pursued.[55]

In the present context, it is suggested that the most likely 'legitimate aim' to be invoked would be one based on the protection of morals. In *Open Door Counselling Ltd v. Ireland* and *Dublin Well Woman Centre* v. *Ireland*, the European Court of Human Rights accepted that the protection of morals was a legitimate aim for the ban on information on abortion (on the basis that the protection of the life of the unborn was an important moral belief in Irish society), but went on to find that the ban was not necessary to protect that aim.[56]

Apart from Articles 2 and 8, other protections provided by the Convention, and thus the Act, may be relevant to the question of the legality of the regulation of pregnant women. Article 3 protects the right to be free from torture or inhuman or degrading treatment or punishment. Non-consensual medical treatment could be regarded as degrading treatment, although to date this Article has been solely concerned with applications associated with punishment, rather than allegations associated with medical treatment.[57]

[54] (1981) 3 EHRR 244. [55] *Sunday Times* v. *UK* 2 EHRR 245 (1979).
[56] Judgment of 29 Oct. 1992, (1992) 15 EHRR 244.
[57] *Tyrer* v. *UK*, 2 EHRR 1 (1978); *Costello-Roberts* v. *UK*, 19 EHRR 112 (1993).

Article 9, which protects religious freedom, and Article 5, protecting the right to liberty and security of the person, are other provisions which have some relevance to the question under consideration, although there is little assistance to be gained from Convention case law on this point. In one American case, it was decided that the foetus's 'right to life' outweighed the pregnant woman's right to practise her religion and refuse a blood transfusion, but this case was before the present judicial trend which is less assertive of the foetus's rights.[58] The aim of Article 5 is to ensure that no-one is deprived of his or her liberty in an arbitrary fashion.[59] The Article lists six exceptions to the right to liberty and security of the person, one of which includes the lawful detention of persons of unsound mind, alcoholics, or drug addicts. Although the drug- or alcohol-addicted pregnant woman could potentially fit within this exception, it is suggested that there would need to be present other justifications, such as endangering others or oneself, for this exception to be legitimately invoked.[60]

It is suggested, however, that, apart from Articles 2 and 8, it is Article 14 which is most likely to be utilized in a petition or appeal to a court. This is not a general 'equal treatment' guarantee, but is a prohibition against discrimination with respect to the rights protected in the Convention. In this context it could be argued that any regulation, or restriction of choice, of the pregnant woman amounts to discrimination, in that other persons are not so restricted. Thus even if a court were to find that society's interest in the foetus were to override the woman's interest in her autonomy, or her privacy rights, the woman might well be in a position to assert that denial for those reasons represents an infringement of Article 14.

In some respects there is more scope for a discrimination claim under the European Convention, and therefore the Human Rights Act, than the American constitution. This is because the equal protection clause in the US constitution is widely regarded as creating an interest parasitic to another established under the constitution.[61] The jurisprudence of the Convention, however, maintains that an applicant can establish a violation of Article 14 even though she cannot show a violation of another Article, in that it is sufficient that an applicant's claim falls within the *ambit* of another Article.[62]

The essence of a successful Article 14 claim is the presence of differential treatment—that the applicant has been treated differently from someone in an analagous situation. A true application of Article 14 permits the

[58] *Jefferson v. Griffin Spalding County Hospital* 274 SE 2d 457 (1981).
[59] *Engel v. Netherlands* 1 EHRR 647 (1976).
[60] J. Wadham and H. Mountfield, *Blackstone's Guide to the Human Rights Act 1998* (1999).
[61] C. Sunstein, 'The Right to Die' (1997) 106 *Yale Law Review* 1123 at 1153.
[62] *Inze v. Austria* (1987) 10 EHRR 394, paras. 43–46.

question of discrimination to be kept separate from the question whether there is an 'objective and rational reason' for that discrimination. This involves the state establishing a 'legitimate aim' for the discrimination, whilst the applicant must 'clearly establish' a lack of proportionality between the aim and the discrimination. Under the Convention there was at this stage the possible concession to the margin of appreciation, but, as mentioned previously, this would not be relevant once the Human Rights Act is brought into force.

In the present context, the pregnant woman could argue that any other person is permitted to drink alcohol and smoke, and is entitled to refuse medical treatment. Certainly she could argue that detention against one's will is only otherwise possible under enacted laws. The 'badge' of discrimination must be identified, and the burden is on the applicant to show that this is the reason for the differential treatment. And whilst it is not necessary for the applicant to show a violation of another Article, she must have identified the Article under whose ambit the differential treatment falls. In the present context that 'badge' would be the fact that she is pregnant.

Even if there were an initial finding of differential treatment, the state may still argue that the treatment is for an 'objective and rational reason' or 'legitimate aim', that being the protection of unborn life. As with Article 8, the question of proportionality may arise in connection with the means used to pursue a legitimate aim. In the *Open Door* case discussed above, the Irish government's aim of protecting morals was accepted as a legitimate one, but a complete ban on information concerning abortion was found by the Commission to be a disproportionate way of pursuing that aim. By analogy, forced medical treatment or detention of pregnant women may be perceived as a disproportionate means of protecting the state's interest in unborn life.

Conclusion

It is evident from the above that, whilst the Commission has not accepted that the foetus may have any claim under Article 2, it has also not denied that possibility—no definitive conclusions have been reached on this point. It is suggested that the absolute nature of the right to life is responsible for this fence-sitting, and that the position is unlikely to change under the Human Rights Act. Secondly, the right to privacy in this context has clearly been interpreted to include the right of a pregnant woman to choose abortion in certain circumstances. There is every reason to suppose that Article 8 will be seen as protecting self-determination and therefore the right to refusal of medical treatment as currently protected in English law. It is therefore most likely that this Article will be the focus of legal argument concerning the regulation of pregnant women. Article 14, with its open-ended list of possible reasons for discrimination, may well prove equally relevant if the fact of pregnancy is used as a reason for forced treatment and detention.

Given the significance of these two Articles, the key point may well turn on how the English courts will utilize the concept of proportionality which, in word if not substance, has played a significant role in decisions of the Commission. It is evident from above that interference with Convention rights (those that are not 'absolute') is lawful only if for a legitimate reason *and* if that interference is proportionate to that aim. It is not difficult to assert that a pregnant woman's privacy rights are engaged by forced medical intervention or confinement. It is also conceivable that the protection of the unborn child or the protection of morals could constitute a legitimate aim for interference. The crunch question it seems is whether the sort of interference is proportionate. In this respect the door is open for regulation of pregnant women, albeit not in a form which would involve extreme invasions of personal autonomy. It is suggested that the courts may use the limited notion of proportionality in public law as a basis for a more expanded doctrine.[63]

The sort of balancing approach embraced by the Convention, and the Human Rights Act, allows a consideration of wider interests and principles, as is evident from the US cases. Whilst the documents are significantly different, the caveat which allows for the denial of a right in given circumstances is common to both, even if it is not a feature attached to all of the rights under the Convention and the Human Rights Act. To date, the English courts have resisted adopting true 'constitutional style' reasoning, but with the Convention incorporated as part of English law, this may no longer be an option.

So, it is possible that, depending upon the stage of the pregnancy, the risk to the pregnant woman posed by the forcible treatment, the availability of possible alternatives, and the risk to the unborn child, the outcome to a petition or appeal may be different— it will not be an automatic victory for autonomy. And it may be that this will result in a more accurate reflection of the true moral nuances of this issue; that society's 'moral interest' in unborn life may 'trump' the woman's interest in her autonomy in certain circumstances. Then again, the sorts of concerns that have already been raised by the courts in connection with the regulation of pregnancy may equally feature for consideration under the second limb. It may be that a court would be of the view that any forced intervention would be ultimately destructive of the maternal–foetal bond, and a deterrent to prenatal care.

Finally, it is submitted that the current emphasis upon the need to uphold autonomy is as dangerous as the previous emphasis upon the value

---

[63] R. v. *Cambridge HA, ex parte B* (1996) 25 BMLR 5, *per* Laws J; *Secretary of State v. Robb* [1996] 1 All ER 677.

of the unborn child. It deflects attention away from what is in reality a unique situation; a situation where there is a particular need to examine what is meant by autonomous choice, given that the woman has made a decision to continue with the pregnancy. What this suggests is that, in this context, as well as in others, there is a need to look carefully at a situation before blindly assuming that there is a conflict in existence, and that the principle of autonomy should triumph. In this respect the law can only benefit from ethical analysis.

THE GIFTS OF LIFE-DONATING GAMETES AND THE CONSEQUENCES

*Louis Waller and Debbie Mortimer**

Introduction

The following letter was published in *The Age*, Melbourne, Australia, on 7 June 1999:

The joys of giving

Years ago I was a semen donor at the old Prince Henry's Hospital. It was a pleasant experience.

Once a week I would go to the hospital, collect a small plastic container from staff, then enter a small but cosy room which was filled with dirty magazines and X-rated videos. One indulged in one's own pleasure, taking care not to spill the spoils. The product was then handed to the hospital staff. A few weeks later, the hospital would post a small cheque as a reward.

Alas, all good things have to end. After many years, I have fathered a total of nine children from my marriage and from the artificial insemination donors program. This is the maximum allowable number for my situation, to reduce the risk of accidental marriages between half-brothers and sisters.

The children from my marriage are a joy to me. I have no doubt that the artificially conceived children would also bring joy to their legal parents. I would like to thank these parents for raising the children. Raising children well is hard work.

The Victorian laws regarding artificial insemination seem to be very sensible, putting the interests of the children first. Once the children have reached adulthood, they can decide whether to trace their biological parents.

For my part, I would love to talk to them, as well as their legal parents. Having a few more friends does not hurt at all.

The writer does not herald, but rather echoes, the spirit of the times on the subject of gamete donors—nearly all, of course, sperm donors—and some of the most important consequences of their gifts of life.[1] Since 1976, 1,440 donors of sperm have been recorded in Victoria. Thousands of children have been born in Australia thanks to the use of donated sperm.[2]

---

* The views and comments are the authors', and not those of the Infertility Treatment Authority, Victoria.

[1] See The Committee to Consider the Social, Ethical and Legal Issues Arising from In Vitro Fertilization (Professor Louis Waller, Chair), *Report on the Disposition of Embryos Produced by In Vitro Fertilization* (Melbourne, 1984) ('Waller Committee').

[2] Information supplied by the Infertility Treatment Authority, Victoria.

Artificial insemination by donor, or AID, is now called donor insemination, or DI, and is one of the most successful methods of circumventing infertility. Since the development of *in vitro* fertilization, or IVF, donor sperm has been employed successfully in conjunction with oocyte collection and embryo formation. Oocyte donation and embryo donation have followed the development of IVF and its relations. The number of children born as a result of all these donations where assisted birth technologies of various kinds are used is already substantial. There is a very large community of families in which children born from donated gametes are growing up. Some DI children who have learned of their conception, and have spoken or written about it in public, are in their thirties. Many more have attained their majorities, and within the next decade thousands more will. A few—how many is not known—Australian children are growing up in families where their mothers did not bear them, but took them from the arms of a surrogate. In a very few cases, the surrogate bore a child to whom she had no genetic connection at all, beyond any possibly derived through nurturing the foetus and then giving birth. The most famous, and much publicized, instance in Australia is that of the Kirkman sisters.[3] The girl born as a result of the arrangement is now 11 years old, and knows the circumstances of her conception and birth.

Informing the Children

Whether or not a person pursues her or his origins, it should be possible for everyone to discover them. In this sense everyone has a strong interest in being able to discover some information about her or his origin.[4]

This is how the IVF Committee, appointed by the Government of Victoria, began that section of its *Report on Donor Gametes in IVF*,[5] published in August 1983, on recording, preserving, and releasing information in respect of children born through the successful use of donor gametes in IVF. The Committee's specific recommendations embodied the careful provision of information to the couples contemplating this course in the treatment of their infertility, sensitive counselling for them and for every donor, and meticulous recording by the hospitals providing infertility treatments of all relevant information about these procedures, including those items which identify a gamete donor, as well as those which relate to her or his medical, social, and educational history. But in addition to the recommendations about the obligations of hospitals to create and maintain records was the Committee's advice that a central register be established

---

[3] See generally M. Kirkman and L. Kirkman, *My Sister's Child: A Story of Full Surrogate Motherhood between Two Sisters Using In Vitro Fertilization* (London, 1988).
[4] Waller Committee, n. 1, above, para 3.30, 26.
[5] See Waller Committee, n. 1, above.

under the authority of the Health Commission (now the Department of Human Services), to which information about all donors whose gametes had been successfully used in establishing pregnancies should be sent. In 1983, the Committee envisaged that there was 'a substantial and growing view that the values of honesty and integrity are crucial to the creation of a happy family'.[6] It foresaw that many parents would tell their children who had been born through the use of donor gametes that their origins had involved one or other form 'of genetic variations in parenting'.[7] The Committee did not consider that parents could be compelled to tell, but it thought that as community views and attitudes developed many would, and that the existence of the central register would become more and more widely known. The Committee did not postulate how and in what exact circumstances access to that register might be permitted.

The pioneering Victorian legislation, the first of its kind, the Infertility (Medical Procedures) Act 1984 contained provisions to give effect to these recommendations.[8] The establishment of the central register, after the whole of the statute came into force on 1 July 1988, proved to be a protracted and delicate task. The Standing Review and Advisory Committee on Infertility (SRACI),[9] created by the Act, gave on-going advice about the formation of the register, and made sustained representations about its development. When SRACI completed its appraisal and review of the 1984 legislation, in its *Report* of October 1991, it recommended the preservation, and refinement, of the provisions dealing with information, and with the central register. SRACI went on to recommend that any person born as a result of the use of donor gametes should, upon reaching the age of 18, be permitted to obtain identifying information about the relevant gamete donor from the central register, but only after appropriate counselling. 'This recommendation', said SRACI in that *Report*, 'is based on the clear belief that the interests of such a person in discovering her or his genetic parent or parents should be accorded primacy'.[10]

This 1991 *Report* was the catalyst in engendering the complete revision and reformulation by the Government of Victoria of the Act of 1984. The enactment of the Infertility Treatment Act 1995 embodies many, indeed most, of the recommendations in the SRACI *Report*. The Act creates a clear-cut licensing system for centres and for doctors undertaking fertilization procedures for couples seeking treatment for infertility, or for couples seeking to avoid the birth of a child with a genetic abnormality or a

[6] *Ibid.*, para 3.30, 26.   [7] *Ibid.*, para 3.30, 26.

[8] See generally, R. Blank, 'Regulation of Donor Insemination' in K. Daniels and E. Haimes (eds.), *Donor Insemination. International Social Science Perspectives* (Cambridge, 1998), 131—50.

[9] See further *Standing Review and Advisory Committee on Infertility Annual Report 1996* (Melbourne, 1996).   [10] At 6.

disease transmissible as a result of pregnancy. The administration of this important arrangement is in the hands of an independent statutory entity, the Infertility Treatment Authority (ITA), which the Act creates.

The licensee of any centre licensed to perform fertilization procedures must maintain the most comprehensive records of such activities, including pregnancy outcomes. Doctors performing donor insemination have similar responsibilities. At six-monthly intervals, centres and doctors must give the ITA information about births and pregnancies resulting from donor treatment procedures. (In some cases, the ITA may seek information about donor treatment procedures even where the outcomes are not known by the centres.) That includes:

- all details of the babies born, including any particulars of any physical abnormality identified at birth;
- all details of the donor or donors, including any known physical abnormality; and
- all details of the women who had the donor treatment procedures, and their spouses, including details of any known physical abnormalities.

In addition, women who give birth after donor treatment procedures, or their husbands, must notify the ITA in writing of the details; or doctors or nurses who are aware of the circumstances and attend the birth of such babies must notify the ITA; or doctors who attend such women during pregnancy and know the circumstances of the births which ensue must notify the ITA. This obligation does not have to be met if one or other of these persons believes that the ITA already has the prescribed information.

The ITA now maintains the central register.[11] Access to it may be sought by any person over 18 about whom information is kept on the register. So may it be by the parents or guardians of someone under 18.

Information relating only to such a person who enquires—that is a child born, a donor, or a woman who had treatment, or her spouse—may be inspected in the register without any further formality. It is important to note those limits.

Information relating to donors which is sought by the children born from donor treatment procedures, or by the recipients of donor gametes or embryos, or by donors about the offspring born from their gametes may be provided in a variety of circumstances, spelled out in sections 71 to 82 of the Act. Non-identifying information—to use the well-established expression—must be provided by centres and doctors. The people concerned may seek this before donor treatment. If the donor has first consented, then identifying information may be provided (subject to any

---

[11] See Victoria, Infertility Treatment Authority, *Annual Report* (Melbourne, 1998), 15.

conditions imposed by that donor). Donors in their turn may ask for, and receive, non-identifying information about pregnancies and births resulting from the gifts of their gametes. Similarly, parents may request information about a donor from the central registrar. So may children born from donor treatment procedures. Donors may request information about a child born as a result, or about its parents. In all these Central Register cases there must have been an offer of counselling about the potential consequences of disclosure of such information.

If a donor gives her or his consent first, then identifying information in the register may be provided to a person in one of these categories. The ITA must make sure that such a consenting donor knows that the identifying information 'is about to be given'.[12]

There are important novel provisions in the Act. Clearly based on SRACI's recommendation in its 1991 *Report*, these are in sections 79 and 80. In short, the purpose of these provisions is to enable a child born as a result of a donor treatment procedure who is 18 or older to receive identifying information about the donor, even if there is no prior consent on the donor's part. There must be counselling for that enquirer. There must, on the part of the ITA, be reasonable efforts to inform the donor that the information is about to be released, with further advice that that donor may need counselling, and that information about specialist counsellors be available. It is important to emphasize that *descendants* of people born from donor treatment procedures are also empowered to apply, and to be given this information, under the same regime described above.

Section 184(4) of the Act provides that this new regime applies only to donor treatment procedures carried out after the Act of 1995 came into force, with regard to gamete and embryo donations made from that time onwards. The commencement date was 1 January 1998. Where donor treatment procedures have been, or are, undertaken after that date, using gametes or embryos donated before the provisions of the 1995 Act have come into effect, then, in short:

- only non-identifying information may be given without the donor's consent;
  or
- identifying information may be given *with the prior consent in writing of the donor*, and in accordance with any conditions or limitations the donor has imposed.

Licensed hospitals and clinics have, in some instances, obtained post-1998 consents from donors whose sperm was not used successfully before 1 January 1998.

In addition to the central register the ITA is obliged to establish *a*

---

[12] Infertility Treatment Act 1995 (Vic), s 80(2)(b).

Donor Treatment Procedure Information Register.[13] The new repository will record names and addresses of children born from these procedures, their descendants, the donors whose gametes have been used, the recipients of those gametes and embryos, and the relatives of all of these people, who request the ITA to record their particulars. In relation to each person registered, this register must record her or his wish in relation to obtaining information from it about another person in the register, and about another person in the register obtaining information about her or him. This separate register is to be developed and to be accessible only by request, and by consent. Section 82(3) obliges the ITA, from time to time, to publicize the establishment and the purposes of this register.

Changes of Mind in a Gamete Donor

THE JUDICIAL CONTEXT

Victorian courts—and Australian courts in general—are less familiar than some other jurisdictions with the exercise of judicial power in relation to medical treatment decisions.[14] There have of course been significant cases dealing with aspects of medical negligence. In *Rogers* v. *Whitaker* [15] the High Court of Australia firmly ruled that a surgeon owed a duty to warn his patients of material risks, and it was for the court to formulate for itself the appropriate standard of care. In a subsequent decision, in 1998, the High Court reaffirmed that conclusion.[16] In *Breen* v. *Williams*,[17] on the other hand, the High Court held that the ownership and control of most medical records were in the hands of the doctor who created them. There have been some significant decisions in the context of family law. In the area of assisted reproductive technology ('ART'), there has been litigation relating to the application of anti-discrimination laws and restricted access to ART. Exercises of judicial power, however, which have been increasingly familiar to British and American courts in relation to withdrawal of medical treatment and treatment decisions, have not touched Australia quite so much. The absence of such a body of judicial analysis makes our exercise a more speculative one.

THE LEGISLATIVE SCHEME

We have set out some of the legislative and policy background to the

---

[13] See Victoria, Infertility Treatment Authority, n. 11, above.

[14] See B. Bennett, 'Posthumous Reproduction and the Meanings of Autonomy' (1999) 23 *MULR* 286; R. v. *Human Fertilization and Embryology Authority, ex parte Blood* [1996] 3 WLR 1176 (QBD); and *Blood* [1999] 1 Fam. LR 151 (CA). For further discussion of *Blood* see D. Morgan and R. Lee, '"In the Name of the Father?" *Ex parte Blood*: Dealing with Novelty and Anomaly' (1997) 60 *MLR* 840. [15] (1992) 175 CLR 479.

[16] *Chappel* v. *Hart* (1998) 156 ALR 517. [17] (1996) 186 CLR 71.

statutory regime now in place in Victoria. For the purposes of the two issues now to be discussed, the following factors are important.

- Victoria has some of Australia's most energetic and dedicated medical scientists and doctors with a long-term commitment to, and investment (intellectual and practical) in, ART.[18]
- The first factor means Victoria has already a history of donated gametes in ART stretching back nearly thirty years, and a history of donated embryos stretching back at least fourteen or fifteen years. The passage of many years leaves more room for changes of mind and circumstances.
- The people of Victoria are aware of the availability, and the successes, of ART; it has been a high-profile media issue for a long time.
- Successive executive and parliamentary decision-makers have dealt with policy issues in a formal way, and have deliberately reformulated legislative schemes. Regulation is an historical fact of some fifteen years for ART in this state. In this context, the absence of litigation is surprising.[19]

Many communities are now familiar with the concept of organ donation, and in some communities its utility and ability to relieve suffering have led policy-makers to impose a presumption of donation on death, unless a person expresses his or her wishes to the contrary. Blood donation, too, is a familiar concept, and has become in some communities the subject of such demand that it has been commercialized. In Australia, and in many other countries, it remains in the realm of a free gift.[20]

With these kinds of donation, the donor contributes to the sustaining, and usually the improving, of the life of another human being.[21] Unlike donors of gametes, these donors do not contribute to the creation of a new life. The donation is frequently completed or 'spent' soon after it is made. A kidney is transplanted, blood is transfused, and a cornea is grafted. Gametes may be stored. Improvements in those storage procedures, combined with the decision-making process of a couple about when to conceive, mean gametes may be stored for more than a decade. Embryos formed from donor sperm may remain in storage for many years.

So the passage of time allows for second thoughts. So too the passage of time produces changes in a donor's circumstances, which may prompt

---

[18] See Waller Committee, n. 1 above; and a brief history of SRACI as found in *Standing Review and Advisory Committee on Infertility Annual Report 1996*, n. 9, above, 25–40.

[19] See L. Waller, 'Australia: The Law and Infertility—the Victorian Experience' in S. A. M. McLean (ed.), *Law Reform and Human Reproduction* (Dartmouth, 1992), 17–45.

[20] Human Tissue Act 1982 (Vic), s 38(1).

[21] See A. R. Schiff, 'Arising from the Dead: Challenges of Posthumous Procreation' (1997) 75 *NCL Rev.* 901.

second or third thoughts, where before there may have been none other than a feeling of altruistic satisfaction. Gamete and embryo donation is the donation of the potential even more than the actual, so that changes in a donor's life, or status—or beliefs—may cause a donor to wish to stop that potential being realized.

In Victoria, an ART clinic approached the Infertility Treatment Authority some time ago: one of its donors had contacted the clinic wanting to stop his sperm, and any stored embryos formed from his sperm, from being used any more.[22] He had donated well before the new regime introduced by the Infertility Treatment Act 1995. His donation came within the provisions of the Act of 1984. His change of heart and mind stemmed largely from his engagement to be married, and from the objections of his partner. The situation was especially complex, because this donor had both sperm and embryos formed from his sperm in storage. Some of those embryos were created for couples who had already successfully conceived from other embryos created from his sperm. So in storage were the biological brothers or sisters of children already born to infertile couples, couples who had planned, and hoped, to have more children using these embryos.

There were some statutory construction questions which arose because of the transition from one legislative regime to another. Donation and consent to use had occurred under the previous regime although the use, and the purported withdrawal of consent, occurred under the new regime.

A key issue of principle was also raised. Section 37 of the Infertility Treatment Act 1995 enables a donor to withdraw his or her consent 'at any time before the procedure or action consented to is carried out'. Putting to one side the exercise of statutory construction what, in this context, is the procedure or action consented to by the donor? What is the point of no return for the donor?

- Is it the collection of the sperm?[23]
- Is it the formation of an embryo?
  or
- Is it the implantation into the body of a woman of an embryo formed from that sperm, or the insemination of a woman with the sperm?[24]

In Victoria, the answer must be found predominantly in other parts of the Infertility Treatment Act 1995, particularly the sections dealing with the giving of consent. But on a more philosophical level, consider these propositions:

---

[22] See Victoria, Infertility Treatment Authority, n. 11, above.

[23] A parallel question could well be asked in relation to an oocyte donor.

[24] See the definitions of 'fertilisation procedure' and 'treatment procedure' in s. 3 of the Infertility Treatment Act 1995.

- We concede, and require, autonomy in the exercise of a free and informed choice whether to give gametes.
- It is the donation of the potential to create human life, being a life biologically connected to the donor.
- The donor gives to assist in creating a child, a child who, when she or he grows, will now have access to identifying information about her or his biological parent(s).
- If the giving of consent is such a meaningful and indeed portentous act, then any provision to withdraw that consent must also be meaningful.
- If the 'procedure' is the actual giving of the sperm or oocyte, then it may only be during the counselling stage that consent could be withdrawn.

Donors should be allowed to change their minds. Section 37 of the Act of 1995 recognizes such a right. Analogies with gift (and the inability to recall a gift) in property law are unattractive and smack of the commodification of humanity.[25] This is a gift with unique consequences. The law should treat it as such and recognize some autonomy in the donor in relation to the future use of his sperm or her oocyte.

However, once sperm, or oocyte, is used to create an embryo, then the interests change. There is a recipient couple connected with the embryo—often, but not always, biologically. There may be another donor, the ovum donor, who now also becomes a person affected. What the donor gave has been changed utterly by the application of medical technology. It is no longer something only of the donor: the donor's contribution is only half. There is one other actual interest, and several potential ones. In those circumstances, being able to recall the gift is inappropriate, and unjust to those other persons and their interests. This is not primarily because the recipient couple 'owns' or 'controls' the embryo to the exclusion of the donor. Rather it is because the formation of an embryo has welded together previously disparate interests and stakeholders in a way that demands compromise from each. The donor's compromise is that she or he will pass the point of no return in relation to the withdrawal of her or his consent when the gamete has been used in an ART procedure: the insemination of a woman; or the formation of an embryo, whether that embryo is immediately transferred, or stored for later transfer.

Making Babies after Death

There are probably less confrontational ways to describe this situation.[26]

---

[25] See D. Mortimer, 'Proprietary Rights in Body Parts: The Relevance of *Moore's Case* in Australia' (1993) 19 *Mon. LR* 217, 250–3.
[26] See Bennett, n. 14, above; and Schiff, n. 21, above.

But why should we be less confronting about it? At a time when people must cope with grieving over loss, medical technology has given them the opportunity to make a new life. No doubt the apparent opportunity to replace a lost life with a new one can become a form of coping with grief. In Victoria, a policy decision was made by the Parliament to proscribe the use of gametes from a person known to be dead: see section 43 of the Infertility Treatment Act 1995. It is consistent with the Act's policy that procedures are only available to married or *de facto* couples who are infertile, and that a child born as a result of the use of ART procedures shall be born into a family of mother and father. Another important rationale, however, is one based on bodily integrity, to which we refer below.

There is some inappropriateness in the use of the word 'donated' in this context. The word 'donation' implies a conscious and voluntary decision to give. By whatever method is used, and no matter how clear a person's wishes may have seemed prior to death, the taking of sperm from a dead man is not donation. It is extraction without his present consent. The question then is: does, and should, the law permit such an extraction? In Victoria, the question cannot readily be answered without recourse to the section of the Infertility Treatment Act 1995 which proscribes the use of gametes from a person known to be dead. Or so one might have thought.

In July 1998, a young man lost his life in Victoria as the result of a motor vehicle accident.[27] He and his wife resided in another part of Australia, but he was driving in Victoria. On hearing of her husband's death, the wife flew to Melbourne and that same afternoon made a request to the Coroner that all necessary medical and other arrangements be made so that sperm could be removed from her husband, for her subsequent use should she decide to attempt to conceive a child. In Victoria we may never know whether her request was the first in the state, and if not, how many have gone before. But in this case, someone was sufficiently unsure of the lawfulness of such a removal to seek an order from the Supreme Court of Victoria. The matter came on as a matter of urgency before a single judge. For some time after the hearing and judgment, the transcript and details of the case were suppressed. They have since been released, and it is Gillard J's judgment from which this account is taken.

Gillard J ordered that permission be given to a legally qualified medical practitioner to remove sperm and tissue from the dead man, and to store them in accordance with the Infertility Treatment Act 1995. He further ordered that the sperm and tissue so removed were not to be used for any purpose without an order from the court. He made this order clearly as an interim order, presumably to preserve the subject matter of the action so to speak. The matter has not come on for trial, so that the sperm and

---

[27] *A B* v. *A–G (Vic.)*, unreported, Supreme Court of Victoria, Gillard J, 21 July 1998.

tissue remain frozen awaiting the determination of the proceeding, such determination to rest in large part upon a decision about who has lawful possession and control of the sperm and tissue.[28]

The judge treated the matter as one that fell to be decided in terms of property law—who had a lawful right to possess the body and the tissue? This approach reflects a particular style of judicial thinking which may in part be explained by the absence of judicial experience in the areas to which we referred earlier. Issues which centre on the treatment of those involved as human beings—actual and potential—were not the first reference. Issues such as consent, autonomy, the question of assisting the creation of new life, and even the Delphic phrase 'best interests' were not considered. The legal principle which is first referred to in the judgment is '[t]here is no property in a corpse'.[29]

In fact this was not a case suitable for a division between interim and final relief. The interim relief is the final relief, in the important sense. Although the wife may be prevented by law from using the sperm in Victoria to achieve a pregnancy, the truly important aspect of the case is done with. The sperm has been removed and the legislative policy behind section 43 of the Act has been violated.

For the purposes of this paper, let us assume an opportunity to revisit this decision and reconsider it. What should be the starting point and the principles? We leave the conclusion open for consideration.

1. 'The fundamental principle, plain and incontestable, is that every person's body is inviolate . . . any touching of another person, however slight, may amount to a battery. . . . The breadth of the principle reflects the fundamental nature of the interest so protected.'[30]

2. 'Although the law's respect for the unique dignity of every person is the same, the protection of physical integrity which is required to preserve the dignity of one person may change from time to time and it may differ from the protection of physical integrity required to preserve the dignity of another . . . a donation of blood by a person of full age and understanding may enhance dignity, while the extraction

---

[28] See Bennett, n. 14 above.

[29] See *Doodeward* v. *Spence* (1908) 6 CLR 406, 421–2, *per* Higgins J (dissenting); and *R.* v. *Kelly* [1999] 2 WLR 384, 393 where it was stated by Rose LJ, giving judgment for the court, that:

'Furthermore, the common law does not stand still. It may be if, on some future occasion, the question arises, the courts will hold that human body parts are capable of being property for the purposes of section 4, even without the acquisition of different attributes, if they have a use or significance beyond their mere existence. This may be so if, for example, they are intended for use in organ transplant operation, for the extraction of DNA or, for that matter, as an exhibit in a trial.'

[30] *Collins* v. *Wilcock* [1984] 1 WLR 1172, 1177 *per* Robert Goff LJ giving judgment for the court.

of blood from a person who is incapable of consenting is an invasion of that person's physical integrity.'[31]

3. Violation of bodily integrity without consent should be the starting point. The dead man cannot consent. There is no statutory mechanism in Victoria which clearly removes the necessity for such consent, although section 26 of the Human Tissue Act 1982—which is the source of the statutory power to remove organs and tissue for transplantation—might be construed as extending this far.

4. It is possible that a guardian could be appointed to make the decision about removal. [32] In fact this has occurred in a second recent case in Victoria. The guardian so appointed was the Public Advocate, and he refused to consent to removal of the sperm from a man who was in a coma and unlikely to recover. However, the appropriateness of applying a guardianship regime intended to facilitate medical treatment decisions for legally incompetent people is questionable.

5. Extraction of sperm in this circumstance can have only one purpose and that is the creation of a child. Where in this complicated and emotional matrix are the interests of a child who might be born from such an extraction considered?[33]

6. The deliberate and premeditated creation of life out of death is an awesome exercise of power. It is not just an exercise of power by the medical profession, nor by a court asked to authorize it. Mostly, it is a considerable exercise of power by the partner of the dead man. Putting to one side the inconsistency of permitting such an exercise of power in a jurisdiction where there is a prohibition on the use of sperm in such circumstances, acquiescing in or sanctioning the exercise of such power diminishes the principle of bodily integrity, which is so firmly established in Anglo-Australian law. It is about much more than corpses, and any further judicial proceedings will it is hoped take place in circumstances conducive to a reasoned consideration of the issues.[34]

---

[31] *Secretary, Department of Health* v. *JWB (Marion's case)* (1992) 175 CLR 218, 266–7, *per* Brennan J. This case dealt with sterilization of an intellectually disabled young woman, who could not consent to that operation. Her parents sought it. The parallels, however, are powerful, for they challenge the basis for any removal of sperm from a dead man.

[32] Guardianship and Administration Board Act 1986 (Vic).

[33] See the Guiding Principles, in s. 5 of the Infertility Treatment Act 1995. In descending order of priority they are:
    (a) the welfare and interests of any person born or to be born as a result of a treatment procedure are paramount;
    (b) human life should be preserved and protected;
    (c) the interests of the family should be considered;
    (d) infertile couples should be assisted in fulfilling their desire to have children.

[34] See Bennett, n. 14, above, especially 302–7.

Beyond Victoria

Two other states, South Australia[35] and Western Australia,[36] have enacted legislation to regulate ART procedures. In addition, the National Health and Medical Research Council (NHMRC) has published revised *Ethical Guidelines on Assisted Reproductive Technology*, in December 1996. Whilst these do not have the force of statute, they are of high significance in terms of affecting practice in those states and territories which have not yet enacted legislation.

The NHMRC's Guidelines state that '[c]hildren born from the use of ART procedures are entitled to knowledge of their biological parents. Any person, and his or her spouse or partner, donating gametes and consenting to their use in an ART procedure where the intention is that a child may be born must, in addition to the information specified in this section, be informed that children may receive identifying information about them.'[37] South Australia's Reproductive Technology Act 1998 mandates the preservation of all information relating to the successful donations, but identifying information may only be given where the donor consents. Western Australia's Human Reproductive Technology Act 1991 provides for the establishment of registers of identity, containing identifying and non-identifying information. Only access to non-identifying information may be given.

Withdrawal of consent may be effective, in all regimes, only before an embryo is formed or an insemination is effected.

South Australia's *Code of Ethical Clinical Practice*, formulated under the authority of its statute, provides that stored embryos must be disposed—taken from storage—if a licensee becomes aware that 'the husband or wife has died'—unless specific directions have been given before storage is commenced. The Western Australia legislation may permit posthumous use of embryos, and is silent on the posthumous use of gametes. But directions made under the authority of that state's legislation provide that there shall be no posthumous use of gametes at all. The NHMRC Guidelines contains a list of prohibited practices. One of them is '[t]he use in ART treatment programs of gametes or embryos harvested from cadavers'.[38]

Conclusion

There are joys in giving. There are sorrows, disappointments, disasters,

---

[35] Reproductive Technology Act 1988 (SA).

[36] Human Reproductive Technology Act 1991 (WA).

[37] National Health and Medical Research Council, *Ethical Guidelines on Assisted Reproductive Technology* (Canberra, 1996), para 3.1.5, 6.

[38] *Ibid.*, para 11.11, 15.

and, sometimes, second thoughts. These observations about what we have called 'The Gifts of Life', are evoked by what the late Richard Titmuss wrote in his seminal book on blood donation, the complete title of which is *The Gift Relationship: From Human Blood to Social Policy*.[39] They are observations which may be made about other donations, in the ever-growing array of human tissue, given by one for the good of another. They have a unique force when the context is assisted human reproduction.

This paper has canvassed only several aspects of the subject. It has, we consider, underlined the importance of autonomy, of informed understanding, and of foresight in the process of considering, and deciding, to be a gamete donor. Autonomy, understanding, and foresight in deciding to accept the gifts of life are of the same moment.

[39] R. M. Titmuss, *The Gift Relationship: From Human Blood to Social Policy* (London, 1970).

CONSENT AND INTENT: THE LEGAL DIFFERENCES IN ASSISTED REPRODUCTIVE TREATMENTS

F. Shenfield

Introduction

In assisted reproduction treatments, consent in writing concerning licensed treatments, i.e. the techniques covered by the Human Fertilisation and Embryology Act 1990 (the HFE Act),[1] is mandatory. This involves gametes donation, either of sperm or oocyte (and hence embryo) donation and *in vitro* fertilization (IVF). By contrast treatment with thawed cryopreserved sperm is not covered by the Act unless it is also used *in vitro*, whilst the storing of the sperm in licensed units categorically is. Infertility specialists practise in one of the few fields where specific legislation has been deemed to be necessary by society, through a vote in Parliament and the enactment of legislation, binding patients and practitioners in a common endeavour. Not all assisted treatment for reproduction is covered by the Act if one takes the word 'assistance' in the largest sense, although the term has come specifically to indicate treatments which are indeed licensed.

This is in contrast to most other medical fields where written consent is not essential, and indeed all other current fertility treatments not covered by the Act arguably make a much bulkier contribution to the care of infertile patients in terms of daily practice. In unlicensed treatments it is generally assumed that patients' request for treatment is consensual to the care needed, that is the joint intention to provide a couple with a child. This is of course obtained without forgetting the necessary conditions for obtaining proper consent to the specific treatment(s) involved, as the patients' understanding of the information given by the carer(s), which includes any complications directly or indirectly linked to the proposed treatment.

The case of *R. v. Human Fertilisation and Embryology Authority, ex parte Diane Blood*[2] is used to illustrate the difference between intent and consent in assisted reproduction, in the context of the duty of care of the practitioner and the respect of the welfare of the child.

---

[1] Human Fertilization and Embryology Act 1990.
[2] *R. v. Human Fertilization and Embryology Authority, ex parte Diane Blood* [1997] 2 All ER 687.

Capacity and understanding are the main prerequisites of consent, but what is intent?A simple definition of intent may help delineate the argument: in law, intent is the will or purpose with which one acts; otherwise it also means implicit meaning, connotation.[3]

In ART, the end-point of the intent behind treatment is clear-cut indeed and the result obvious, not to be measured in molecules or nanomoles subject to laboratory assays and their variability, but by the birth of a child, whose 'welfare' English law requires us to take into account when offering licensed treatment[4]. The intention of the patient(s) is to have a child, not only to be offered treatment, and the fertility specialist's intention is assumed to be beneficent unless proved otherwise. Indeed, society at large recognizes the 'good' of having children, and this applies not only to English society, which is the focus of our discussion in this paper, but to many others, and in particular to the French, whose legislation[5] will also be described by way of comparison to English law. All this does not obviate in any way the need for information about the treatment especially concerning the possible complications, and its possible failure, so that the patient may make an informed decision of acceptance or refusal of proposed treatment. There is a disinclination to practise defensive medicine, and also to avoid being sued for battery and negligence, although the wish to establish good communication with one's patient(s) is more important. Happily, there is as yet no example of such suits concerning fertility treatments in the UK, although a well known case of refusal of treatment[6] involved the courts. This happened when a couple were refused IVF by a licensed centre in Manchester because they had not fulfilled the criteria for fostering. The unit was not found by the judge to be prejudiced or wrong in deciding that it was concerned about the welfare of the child to the extent of refusing them IVF treatment.

There is already a plethora of papers about the meaning of the welfare of the child, both as enjoined by the HFE Act,[7] and in general. A recent paper compared the interpretation of this matter in different countries worldwide:[8] this ranges from the requirement for couples to be married before treatment to the tolerance of the English legislation which does not forbid single women, women in lesbian couples, or widows to be treated (as French law does) and some apparently sexist decisions which permit sperm donation but forbid oocyte donation.

---

[3] *Collins Concise Dictionary* (revised third edn. London, 1995).

[4] HFE Act, s. 13(5).

[5] *Loi no 94–95 du 29 Juillet 1994, relative au don, assitance médicale à la procréation et diagnostic prénatal*, Journal Officiel, 30 July 1994.

[6] R. v. *Ethical Committee of St Mary's Hospital (Manchester)*, ex parte H [1988] 1 FLR 512.

[7] G. Pennings, 'The Welfare of the Child' (1999) 14 *Human Reprod*, 1146–50.

[8] *IFFS Surveillance* 98 (1999), *Fert and Ster*, Supplement 2, 71 no 59. 9. HFEA Code of Practice (revised Dec. 1995).

The recent case of Mrs Blood, which came to the attention of the court in England, raised an important point, namely the difference between the intent to have a child and the necessary consent particular to specific assisted reproduction treatments. Is it as simple as it seems when couples go through a lot of stress and hardship, sometimes financial as well as psychological, to equate intent and consent, at least in terms of what results are to be expected in the case of fertility treatments? We wish for a born child, preferably a singleton, a liveborn child indeed, rather than simply a clinical pregnancy. This desired end-result is worth analysing in the context of the compulsory Human Fertilisation and Embryology Authority (HFEA) collation of results of licensed treatments.[9] The HFEA was set up by the 1990 Act with a number of specific tasks including licensing of centres and establishment of a Code of Practice. This places specific demands onto the specialist, not matched in many other specialties, as he/she is expected to be judged by 'better than nature' success rate figures, in terms of 'take home baby'. In most fields the clinician is expected to amend the pathological state to the physiological ('healthy' rather than 'natural') state of for instance, a thyroid gland from hyper- or hypoactivity. We know that 'naturally' about 15–18 per cent of pregnancies miscarry at an early stage (early pregnancy loss). The patients' guide to licensed units in the UK published by the HFEA initially quoted only the live birth rate per cycle of treatment,[10] and only recently has mentioned pregnancy rate as well.[11] Understandably couples seek treatment to become parents and not just for the female partner to become pregnant, and thus although the consent obtained is consent to palliate or cure the infertile state of a couple (the treatment resulting in a pregnancy) the intent of all involved goes further than just the achievement of that pregnancy. Indeed outcome measurements may be measured by clinical pregnancy rates (a positive pregnancy test, then a foetal heart observed by ultrasound scan at six to seven weeks) or by the birth rate of live babies. Thus what counts for the patients is the tangible outcome of a live baby, a powerful human yearning, although in some cases the 'trying all is possible' in the face of practically unsurmountable obstacles is also of great therapeutic value, even if accompanied by final failure. This is particularly so if accompanied by the counselling, wisely advised in the HFE Act[12] and guidance of the Code of Practice.

But what if the intention is not matched by the consent of the parent(s) in a clear fashion? One of the aims of the 1990 Act is indeed to prevent such a decrepency by requiring written consent of both future parents to

[9] HFEA, *The Interim Patients' Guide to DI and IVF Clinics* (London, 1998).
[10] HFEA, *Fourth Annual Report* (London, 1995).
[11] HFEA, *Eighth Annual Report and Accounts* (London, 1999).
[12] HFE Act 1990, s. 13(6).

licensed treatments. This avoids, for instance, the difficulties encountered when divorced couples cannot agree about the fate of their cryopreserved embryos during treatment which preceded their divorce, as happened in the USA.[13] And arguably the intent of parents must be seen to be ratified by written consent in parallel to the arrangements made in the Children Act concerning parental responsibility, where only mothers and married fathers have such responsibility. Thus the written consent clause matches those set up at a similar time concerning the child in the Children Act 1989[14] where the spirit of legislation was changed to a pro-child stance from an adult's interest standpoint.

The Case of Diane Blood and Other Cases of Posthumous Treatment

The case of Mrs Diane Blood revolved around the distinction between consent and intent, since the sperm had been obtained by electroejaculation whilst Mr Blood was about to die in intensive care. It was indeed a case where intent was assumed to be present but consent in writing was not available. Not to have accepted intent would have been to deny the testimony of a young woman tragically widowed after her previously healthy young husband died of an infectious fulminating disease. The HFEA refusal to release the illegally obtained samples was upheld by the court, and export of the samples for treatment to another European country without legislation in this matter (in this case Belgium) was finally allowed after the appeal judge had confirmed the first instance judgment of refusal to release the samples to the widow. This had been suggested as a caring compromise. The judge made it clear, however, that this should not be considered a possible legal precedent. This dilemma must not overshadow the fact that each time the birth of a potential child is assisted posthumously, all parties have a responsibility to this child. With this in mind, the Code of Practice of the HFEA details several factors to be taken into account when considering the welfare of the child: this includes the parents' commitment to having and bringing up a child or children; their ability to provide a stable and supportive environment for any child produced as a result of treatment, their medical histories and the medical histories of their families, their age and future ability to look after or provide for a child's needs amongst others.

With the advent of successful cryopreservation of spermatozoa and embryos, the birth of a child whose genetic father was dead became technically available, after the usual period considered legally necessary for recognized paternity of the child (a posthumous child).

Posthumous treatment of a partner or widow is allowed in English law,

---

[13] *Davis v. Davis* (1992) 842 SW 2d 588 (Tenn. Sup. Ct.).
[14] Children Act 1989.

with prior consent of the man who preserves the sperm at the time of cryopreservation. In France, by contrast, posthumous treatment was forbidden by the Code of Practice of the Centre d'Etude et de Conservation des Oeufs et du Sperme Humain (CECOS) organization, a countrywide network of gametes banks created over twenty years ago and integrated in the French hospital system since the implementation of the French legislation of July 1994. This Code of Practice principle, not having the force of law, was contested several times in the courts, with different results in cases of both cryopreserved sperm and embryos.[15]

This legal time period is usually calculated on the assumption that the biological father is alive at the time of conception. The French Civil Code, as amended in 1977,[16] states that a child is presumed not to be of the husband if born more than 300 days after separation or divorce, and English common law enshrines a presumption of legitimacy. This confirms the spirit of the CECOS Code of Practice which had been put in place after the restitution of sperm samples from her late husband to a widow, Mme Parpalaix,[17] led the CECOS to add a special clause to their Code of Practice.[18]

The complexities of the decisions to be taken are exemplified by the analysis of cases of both posthumous embryo transfer and sperm insemination in France.

In June 1993, a tribunal delivered a judgment concerning a request for the transfer of two cryopreserved embryos by one of their parent donors, the widowed Mme Pires, whose husband had died in a car crash after seven failed attempts at *in vitro* fertilization (IVF) and embryo transfer.[19] As the CECOS Code of Practice 1986 forbids posthumous insemination or embryo transfer, the couple had in October 1990 signed a contract with the hospital stating the spouses' joint consent to cryopreservation, and the necessity of their joint presence for transfer of the thawed embryos, which would be destroyed in the case of the couple's relationship not surviving (the French term of 'dissolved' encompasses divorce, separation, and/or the ultimate separation through the death of a partner). In the proceedings the widow asserted that only the Tribunal de Grande Instance was competent to adjudicate in the realm of persons' rights, and that as an embryo was a potential person, the document allowing the destruction of such an entity was null and void.

---

[15] F. Shenfield, 'Filiation Problems in Assisted Reproduction: Potential Conflicts and Legal Implications' (1994) 9, *Human Reprod*, 1348–54.

[16] French Civil Code: *Code (Nouveau) de Procédure Civile Français*, 1977, arts. 315, 343, 1128, *Jurisprudence Dalloz*.

[17] *Parpalaix* v. CECOS, Tribunal de Grande Instance de Creteil, [1984] *Gaz Palais* 2.56018.

[18] Centre d'Etude et de Conservation des Œufs et du Sperme Humain (CECOS), *Code of Practice* (Paris, 1985).

[19] *Mme Veuve Pires* v. CECOS, Toulouse Tribunal de Grande Instance, 1993.

This first argument brings to the fore the complex notion of person-hood and whether it can apply to an embryo, an argument which has been particularly discussed in the context of the morality of abortion and embryo research.[20] Although Harris states that the real question is 'when does life begin to matter morally?', rather than 'what is a person?', the answer that a life is one which enjoys the quality endowed by 'a combination of rationality and self consciousness'[21] cannot apply to the embryo. In fact, the use of the term 'potential person' by Mme Pires to refer to the embryo follows the coining of this term by the French National Ethics Committee[22] and seems to fit best with most people's ideas regarding the status of this mass of cells resulting from human gametes, which should be given 'some protection in law'.[23]

Mme Pires' lawyers also alluded to the debate on the status of the embryo, stating that 'it is not a chattel to be inherited'. This precise point has been the subject of legal arguments in other jurisdictions, and in English law there is 'general reluctance to accept the property analysis'.[24] Interestingly, in the USA, and almost at the same time, the Supreme Court of Tennessee held that embryos could not be regarded as persons, nor as property, and used the same notion of potential; embryos were said to occupy an 'interim category that entitles them to special respect because of their potential for human life'. In French law, 'assisted reproduction treatments are solely to be used for a couple's parenting project' and 'the man and woman which constitute this couple, of a reproductive age, must be alive and give consent'.

The Toulouse Tribunal de Grande Instance's refusal of the transfer of two cryopreserved zygotes to Madame Pires, whose husband died in a car crash just after a failed IVF cycle, was made even more poignant by the fact that a month later a Tribunal in Rennes allowed the same procedure in a similar case, and that it happened at the time where legislation was not yet in place and when the French Comité Consultatif National d'Ethique pour les Sciences de la Vie et de la Santé (CCNE), having just published an *Avis* on this very question, had proposed that such embryos would be available to a widow after about nine months of reflection to allow the immediate grief reaction to be worked through. Interestingly, they also recommended that this would not be allowed for cryopreserved sperm after the death of the man who had stored it before a terminal

---

[20] F. Shenfield and C. Sureau, 'Embryo Research' in C. Sureau and F. Shenfield (eds.), *Ethical Dilemmas in Assisted Reproduction* (Canthorpe, 1997).

[21] J. Harris, *The Value of Life* (London, 1985).

[22] Comité Consultatif National d'Ethique pour les Sciences de la Vie et de la Santé, *Avis sur le Tranfert d'Embryons Après Décès du Conjoint (ou du Concubin)*, no 40.

[23] Warnock, *Report of the Committee of Inquiry into Human Fertilization and Embryology*, Cm 9314 (London, 1984).

[24] A. Grubb, 'The Legal Status of the Frozen Human Embryo' in *Challenges in Medical Care* (London, 1992), 69–87.

illness. The members of the CCNE made the point that the intention to become parents was necessarily stronger at the stage of embryos than at the stage of cryopreserved gametes, and thus deserved more respect from society at large by way of legislation. French legislators eventually decided otherwise.

To return to the the UK, posthumous treatment is allowed with explicit prior consent in writing and after the opportunity of counselling has been given to the gamete donor(s), neither of which happened with Mr Blood. The dilemma put to the courts, however interesting because of the unusual legal arguments centring mostly around the vows taken in church by the Bloods when they married, which involved a statement of their intention to have children, must not overshadow the fact that each time the birth of a potential child is assisted posthumously, all parties have a responsibility to this future child. As many media were supportive of the widow's plight, why was the decision taken by the courts one of refusal, and not one of acceptance of this request when all parties agreed to trust the plaintiff's assertions that she and her husband had discussed this very scenario whilst watching a television programme which showed the cryopreservation and use for his widow of the sperm of a man who died in intensive care in the USA? The report of Professor McLean clearly explains the rationale behind this decision, supports it strongly, and even concludes that 'the importance of the rule requiring consent cannot be underestimated and that no exceptions should be made beyond the current rules which take into account the situations of necessity or which authorise medical intervention where this is in the best interest of the person unable to consent at the time'.[25] It is noteworthy that the interest to reproduce was an argument used in court, but even a very loose interpretation of the European Convention on Human Rights (Article 12[26]), based on positive rather than negative rights (which is indeed not the spirit of such convention as analysed by Dworkin[27]), cannot give such rights to the clinically dead. The report goes even further by suggesting an even firmer control in licensed treatments where all such endeavours should require written consent. But with the logic for which she is well known, McLean suggests that if society by the symbolic representation of the law allows posthumous treatment 'consideration should be given to amending s28(6) of the Act which leaves the child thus created without a legal father', a point which has been described previously as perhaps symbolic of the ambivalence of our legislators at the time of the

---

[25] Report of Prof. Sheila A. M. McLean, *Review of the Common Law Provisions Relating to the Removal of Gametes and of the Consent Provisions in the Human Fertilization and Embryology Act 1990* (Glasgow, 1998) 4.

[26] Convention for the Protection of Human Rights and Dignity of the Human Being with Regard to the Application of Biology and Medicine: Convention on Human Rights and Biomedicine, Directorate of Legal Affairs, DIR/JUR (96)14, (Strasbourg, 1996).

[27] Ronald Dworkin, *Taking Rights Seriously* (London, 1977).

enactment. The fact that succession rights are not recommended is less important of course for married couples, but would be to partners unmarried at the time of their joint decision to reproduce even after the death of one of them. The following comments are not by a lawyer, but a clinician involved in the daily care of such couples (or, indeed rarely, widows or partners of deceased men who have cryopreserved their sperm), when they require treatment. It also seems logical that if a man is in a relationship at this very crucial and stressful time of preserving his reproductive ability in the face of a very serious threat to his life, that partner should be involved too as a matter of course in at least the counselling process. Whether legislation is needed to this effect is uncertain, but it certainly could be included in the recommendations of the Code of Practice, at least as a should, if not as a must, and an example of good practice.

Frozen Reproductive Tissues

Since the *Blood* case, the ensuing consultation document, and the McLean report, it falls to all of us to have some vision and to start reflecting on a major problem which can only loom larger and larger in the years to come. Furthermore, this problem is especially fraught with psychological components as it involves the cryopreservation of reproductive tissues in adolescents suffering from cancer, the treatment of which threatens their future reproductive capacity. This is especially sensitive, as reproduction is not a matter which they or their peers are accustomed to consider when they themselves are faced with the possibility of storing gametes or tissues. They are facing serious disease, if not possible death, are often under the age of consent to medical treatment although often Gillick competent,[28] but it is generally good practice to involve the parents in these sensitive decisions. A working party is at the moment about to address the issues with paediatric oncologists, lawyers, psychologists, ethicists, and patients' groups, but we are only now starting to address a problem which can only grow larger in view of the increased ability to store successfully testicular or ovarian tissue for future reproduction.[29] In this case too the intent, i.e. the conservation of the reproductive ability of children and adolescents, seems *prima facie* beneficent, but sometimes the intent is the young sufferer's parents' intent and not his or her own. This may indeed be biased by a desire one day to have a grandchild who might remind them of a beloved deceased child for instance, whatever the best interest of their child at the time. This may further be complicated by the fact that ovarian

---

[28] *Gillick* v. *West Norfolk and Wisbech Area Health Authority* [1986] AC 112.

[29] S. Golombok, R. Cook, A. Bish, and C. Murray, 'Families Created by the New Reproductive Technologies: Quality of Parenting and Social and Emotional Development of the Children', (1995) 66 *Child Development* 285–98.

biopsy may indeed be a fairly risky procedure in a relatively sick adolescent girl, much more so than sperm donation or testicular biopsy from a boy. Again we face a situation where the intent and the consent of the child or adolescent concerned may not be identical, where one could not be presumed to take the place of the other. Could a biopsy be taken, for instance, when the child is unable to consent because he/she is not deemed *Gillick* competent, or when he/she is so seriously ill that therapeutic privilege is invoked?

Conclusion

The main problem, however, remains: whether it is in the child's best interest to be born legally fatherless, or whether the positive symbolic value of a single loving parent outweighs the possible social burden and the psychological consequences entailed in his/her fatherless status. There is, for instance, a strong relationship between one-parent families and emotional or behavioural deprivation, but this was deemed to be probably due to social deprivation from poverty rather than to the absence of a father.[30]

The concern we must have for future generations, as recommended by Hans Jonas in his responsibility principle[31] is an important principle for us all in assisted reproduction and would indeed be better achieved by thus preparing the informed future parent(s) for this most awesome responsibility. It is the duty of society as a whole to see that we specialists do our best in the circumstances.

[30] A. Fagot-Largeault, 'Procréation responsable' in C. Sureau and F. Shenfield (eds.), n. 20, above.
[31] A. Fagot-Largeault, 'Procréation responsable' in C. Sureau and F. Shenfield (eds.), *Ethical Aspects of Human Reproduction* (Paris, 1995), 4.

SYMBOLIC HARM AND REPRODUCTIVE PRACTICES

Elisabeth Boetzkes

Introduction

Ethical and legal debate over our reproductive practices has been fascinating and broad, encompassing topics as diverse as the purpose of sexuality, the nature and significance of reproductive autonomy, the well-being of women and children, pronatalism and the significance of the genetic connection, the limits of commodification and commercialization, permissible uses of foetal and embryonic tissue, and genetic manipulation. Although recent argument over the ethics of reproduction has emphasized the *consequences* of particular practices or policies, nevertheless a number of arguments stand out as having a different logic. Thus, in an early discussion of the implications of contract pregnancy, George Annas alleged that by enforcing pregnancy contracts we are proclaiming that women are less important than the foetuses they are carrying,[1] and that, by requiring them to submit to invasive procedures 'for the sake of the foetus' and according to the terms of their gestational contracts, we violate sexual equality, since such restrictions can apply only to women.[2] Again, the Warnock Commission (notoriously) claimed 'it is inconsistent with human dignity that a woman should use her uterus for financial profit'.[3] Barbara Katz Rothman politicized this position, saying, 'I cannot ever believe that a woman is pregnant with someone else's baby. The idea is repugnant; it reduces a woman to a container ... for another, often more valued, person. In that sense, surrogacy is the *reductio ad absurdum* of technological, patriarchal capitalism.'[4] Lorraine Code presents a Marxist analysis. '[s]urrogate mothering', she says, 'is at the extreme end of the spectrum of alienated labour, since it requires a woman to renounce all the so-called "normal" love, pride, satisfaction, and attachment in, for, and to the product of her labour'.[5] Such alienation is not only threatening to a woman's

---

[1] G. Annas, 'Fairy Tales Surrogate Mothers Tell' in L. Gostin (ed.), *Surrogate Motherhood: Politics and Privacy* (Bloomington and Indianapolis, Ind., 1988) 51.
[2] G. Annas, 'Pregnant Women as Fetal Containers' (1986) 16 *Hastings Center Report* 13.
[3] M. Warnock, *A Question of Life: The Warnock Report on Human Fertilisation and Embryology* (Oxford, 1985) 45.
[4] B. Katz Rothman, *Recreating Motherhood: Ideology and Technology in a Patriarchal Society* (New York, 1989).
[5] L. Code, 'Commentary on "Surrogate Motherhood"' by Christine Overall,' cited in C. Overall, *Ethics and Human Reproduction* (London, 1987).

psychological and social health; it is an affront to her status as a moral being with a stake in personal integration. (Each of these claims, of course, can be, and has been, challenged. My purpose here, however, is not to evaluate the arguments but to identify their distinctive logic.)

Similar non-consequentialist objections are made to practices other than contract pregnancy. Speaking of the sale of embryos and gametes, Christine Overall says, '[i]n addition to these consequentialist considerations pertaining to the commodification of reproduction, there is also a further area of concern, less easy to delineate but important nevertheless. A person is not the kind of thing that may be bought or sold.'[6]

Sex selection, too, has invited censure on non-consequentialist grounds. While recognizing the complexity of consequentialist considerations relating to it, both Michael Bayles[7] and Tabitha Powlidge[8] assert that the practice is inherently sexist. A sexist practice, whatever its consequences, is *prima facie* open to moral disapproval because it pronounces persons inferior on the basis of sex.

This collection of deontological objections alleges that the denial of personhood, the downgrading of personhood based on group membership, and the systematic denigration of a style of personhood are harmful. It finds an echo in recent legal proposals and decisions.

For example, following its Royal Commission on New Reproductive Technologies, Canada's Ministry of Health has proposed a Human Reproductive and Genetic Technologies Act, to prohibit certain practices (including non-medical sex selection and commercial contract pregnancy) and to regulate through licensing and reporting others (such as *in vitro* fertilization and the use, handling, and storage of embryos and foetal tissues). Like the Royal Commission, the Ministry document recognizes the need to protect the dignity of vulnerable persons, to promote equality, and to secure the appropriate, respectful use of human reproductive material.[9] Although these concerns are identified as ethical principles, their role in justifying proposed legislation gives them unusual weight in a liberal legal framework which typically privileges consequentialist concerns.

Recent Canadian case law has flirted with such non-consequentialist reasoning also. Thus, in *R v. Keegstra*[10] (in which the section of the Canadian Criminal Code prohibiting wilful hate-mongering was upheld) the former Dickson CJ includes in his reasons the threat to the sense of self-worth and acceptance of members of target groups. Calling this the

---

[6] *Ibid.* 28.

[7] M. Bayles, *Reproductive Ethics* (Englewood Cliffs, NJ, 1984).

[8] T. Powlidge, 'Unnatural Selection: On Choosing Children's Sex' in H. B. Holmes, B. B. Hoskins, and M. Gross (eds.), *The Custom-Made Child? Women-Centred Perspectives* (Clifton, NY, 1981).

[9] Government of Canada: Ministry of Health, *New Reproductive and Genetic Technologies: Setting Boundaries, Enhancing Health* (Ottawa, 1996).

[10] *R. v. Keegstra* [1990] 3 SCR 697.

threat of 'psychological and social damage' Dickson anticipates that it may result in either avoidance of public activities or an attempt at assimilation, either of which 'bear[s] heavily in a nation that prides itself on tolerance and the fostering of human dignity through, among other things, respect for the many racial, religious, and cultural groups in our society'. Although Dickson's discussion of the harm to self-worth and acceptance classifies it under 'psychological and social consequences'—in principle reducible to customary interests of individuals—his treatment diverges substantially from the received view of such harms. An interest in psychological health has not traditionally been extended to avoiding discomfort, loss of dignity, or loss of self-esteem.[11] Nor has it been recognized as harmful to create an environment in which citizens are deterred from public participation or celebration of their group identity.

In *R. v. Butler*[12] the trend towards expanding the notion of harm is even clearer. In a decision upholding Canada's obscenity provision, former Justice Sopinka included in the 'undue exploitation of sex' (the actus reus of the crime) dehumanizing and degrading sexual representations. Such materials 'run against the principles of equality and dignity of all human beings' and are unacceptable 'not because [they] offend against morals but because [they are] perceived by public opinion to be harmful to society, particularly to women'.

These passages from recent case law, which reflects what has been called a 'harms-based equality approach', reveal the importation into the received notion of harm of the sort of deontological considerations identified earlier in the moral debate about our reproductive practices. Given the Canadian Charter's commitment to the values of equality and multiculturalism, such a broadening of legal reasoning is, perhaps, inevitable; yet stretching is clearly needed to accommodate such deontological concerns. For both rulings identify symbolism as a source of harm and the moral status of group members as its target.

Problems with Symbolic Harm

What is problematic about the incursion of deontological reasoning into the realm of legal argument? There are three broad areas of tension: the first conceptual, the second pragmatic, and the third jurisprudential.

The conceptual difficulty in recognizing symbolic denigration as a deontological harm has to do with the legal notion of harm itself. Within liberalism to be harmed is to suffer a wrongful setback of welfare or ulterior interests. By attacking your person or taking your things or even spreading malicious gossip about you, we can see how your capacity to flourish is

---

[11] J. Feinberg, *The Moral Limits of the Criminal Law* (Oxford and New York, 1984), v, 1.
[12] *R. v. Butler* [1992] 3 SCR 452.

compromised; but you may suffer an attack on dignity while material interests or significant aspirations remain untouched. Similarly, your equality and integration may be compromised while your interests are intact and you are functioning well.[13] Moreover, whereas the setback-to-interests model of harm recognizes only collective harms (such as pollution of public drinking water) as aggregative, a deontological affront may be mediated through your membership of a group. If deontological objections to our reproductive practices are weighty enough to invite legal censure, what conceptual revisions to the notion of harm are needed to accommodate them?

Furthermore, (and this is the pragmatic concern) how may *symbolic* harms be identified and weighed? Will all denigrative representation count as harmful? Off-the-cuff remarks at the pub? Ideological passion in the classroom? Lawyer jokes? Critics of viewing symbolism as harmful (even under the conventional model of harm) fear an intolerable expansion of liability and compromise of free-speech values, for questionable gains. And although there are persuasive arguments (for instance, by Frederick Schauer[14]) that speech can cause a wrongful setback of interests and thus may justifiably be limited, the deontological impact of symbolism cannot be measured in the same way. Furthermore, if we are claiming that practices have meanings which may be symbolically harmful, we must have satisfactory criteria for determining what practices are, what their meanings are, and when the harmfulness of such meanings is actionable.

Finally, there is the jurisprudential worry about the revisitation of legal moralism. For, notwithstanding the insistence of Canada's Supreme Court that its reasoning about hate speech and pornography was harm-based, looseness around the notion of harm has given rise to a scepticism about whether, by prohibiting such expression, we are in fact imposing a particular moral view.

John Robertson has been an outspoken critic of the deontological objections to our reproductive practices, which he sees as indefensibly illiberal. Thus, he dismisses George Annas's objections to contract pregnancy as 'moralistic or symbolic concerns that have no direct connection with actual harm to others. . . . The concern with paying donors for their gametes seems to be symbolic and moralistic. . . . Given the multiple meanings that can be found in paid surrogacy and the speculative nature of fears about the commodification of women and children, one particular moral-symbolic view of the transaction should not be sufficient to trump the fundamental procreative rights of infertile couples.'[15]

---

[13] Liberals who claim that expanding reproductive freedom is Pareto optimal because it improves the lot of some without making others worse off overlook this.

[14] F. Schauer, 'The Phenomenology of Speech and Harm' (1993) 103 *Ethics* 635.

[15] J. A. Robertson, 'Procreative Liberty and the State's Burden of Proof in Regulating Noncoital Reproduction' in L. Gostin (ed.), n. 1, above, 42. See also J. A. Robertson, *Children of Choice: Freedom and the New Reproductive Technologies* (Princeton, NJ, 1994.)

Are critics like Robertson correct when they charge that meanings are subjective and speculative, and ought not to weigh against reproductive freedom? Is the call for legal remedies to denigrative symbolism just the revival of legal moralism? To answer these questions we must consider the conceptual, pragmatic, and jurisprudential objections I have outlined.

Conceptual Concerns

The conceptual challenge requires us to provide criteria for settling the meaning of a practice, to suggest a mechanism for immediate harm and to provide a relevant taxonomy.

THE MEANING OF A PRACTICE

Can there be an objective meaning to a practice like contract pregnancy, and how would we discover it? Melinda Vadas, addressing the issue of women's subordination in the context of the pornography debates, gives the following definition of a practice:

A practice is a socially established, socially orchestrated human activity that aims at certain goals or internal goods. Ideologies provide the conceptual support for practices, and institutions are the arenas in which practices are manifested and which materially support those practices.[16]

Acts, events, and objects within practices—practice constituents—gain their identity from their role in the practice, and that identity can be traced 'backward to its generation by the practice's ideology and forward to a manifestation in the practice's supporting institution'. Thus, 'the practice-informed identity of practice constituents is nonsubjective and determinate'. Object as we may, we cannot by our individual decision alter the identity of a practice constituent. As Vadas says, in baseball, a baseball bat is a baseball bat (not 'really' a piece of wood); and the qualities needed to be a good bat or a good batter are similarly non-subjective practice-functions. Where the practice-meaning of an event, act, or object is in dispute, we may scrutinize both the context and the relation between the governing ideology and its outcomes for a plausible interpretation. Is a raised arm a salute or a request to speak? If the context is a political rally, the former is more plausible; furthermore, if the determining ideology (which should settle the meaning of the practice) is educational rather than political, why does hand-raising result in mass chanting?

What is the most plausible interpretation of the meaning of contract pregnancy and sex selection, then? According to Annas, contract preg-

[16] M. Vadas, 'A First Look at the Pornography/Civil Rights Ordinance: Could Pornography Be the Subordination of Women?' [1987] *Journal of Philosophy* 487.

nancy pronounces the gestational woman a foetal container, and commod-
ifies her. According to Powlidge (and others), sex selection declares
females of lesser worth than males. Robertson, by contrast, (notwithstanding his contention that meanings are subjective) consistently presents the
meaning of assisted reproduction practices as providing help to the involuntarily childless, and enhancing reproductive and contractual freedom.
Who is right? Vadas' analysis suggests a way of settling the dispute non-
subjectively, by looking at the goals and values driving the practices, and
the consistency between these and their outcomes. Where outcomes are
discontinuous with the alleged goals, bizarre with respect to them, we
rightly suspect a co-optation of meaning and a dissimulation.

A thorough discussion of the competing interpretations is not possible
here; however, let me cast sceptical doubt upon Robertson's position by
pointing out the paradoxical results of contract pregnancy if we agree with
Robertson in taking as its goal the expansion of procreative opportunity
and reproductive and contractual choice. Aiding the involuntarily childless
is limited in practice to a small wealthy minority—those who can afford
the services involved. And because wealth is in large measure distributed
along racial lines, the distribution is not just classist but also racist, both in
terms of offering reproductive opportunities and in terms of the division
between gestational workers and beneficiaries. Further, whereas offering
gestational services to buyers expands their contractual options, it is highly
doubtful whether even the basic conditions for autonomous choice are met
for the gestating woman.[17] Forfeiting decisional and parental privileges
which would otherwise accompany pregnancy jeopardizes the exercise of
autonomous choice. There is therefore such a serious dissonance between
the assertion that contract pregnancy is a vehicle of reproductive fulfilment
and choice and the actual decisional status of contract gestators that
Robertson's description of the practice is quite implausible. That of Annas,
however, faces no such discontinuity.[18]

With sex selection a similar analysis can be provided. Whereas there is
no injured or demeaned individual (at least in preconception sex selection),
in the social context of patriarchal preference for males and (in some

[17] E. Boetzkes, 'Equality, Autonomy and Feminist Bioethics' in A. Donchin and L. M.
Purdy (eds.), *Embodying Bioethics: Recent Feminist Advances* (Oxford, 1999).

[18] I acknowledge that there are other competitors for 'the right' description of the relevant
practices, and degrees of dissonance amongst respective descriptions need to be measured to
settle on the most reasonable interpretation. That investigation necessarily goes beyond the
scope of this paper. However, see C. Overall, *Ethics and Human Reproduction: A Feminist
Analysis* (Winchester, Mass., 1987); C. Overall, *Human Reproduction: Principles, Practices,
Policies* (Toronto, 1993); B. Katz Rothman, *Recreating Motherhood: Ideology and
Technology in a Patriarchal Society* (New York, 1989); G. Corea, *The Mother Machine:
Reproductive Technologies from Artificial Insemination to Artificial Wombs* (New York,
1985); S. Sherwin, *No Longer Patient: Feminist Ethics and Health Care* (Philadelphia, Penn.,
1992).

places) neglect, persecution, and murder of females, presenting sex selection as an enhanced reproductive choice is, again, implausible.[19]

THE IMMEDIATE HARMFULNESS OF MEANINGS

Having in hand a model for determining the meaning of a practice, we may now ask how meanings can immediately harm? One approach is to utilize the illocutionary accounts of harmful speech developed by Catherine McKinnon[20] and Rae Langton[21] in the context of the pornography debates. Appealing to Austin's speech act theory,[22] Langton argues as follows. When uttered authoritatively and within certain conventions, speech acts may accomplish results without causal mediation. Thus, in the paradigm case, the judge, in sentencing you, brings about your being sentenced rather than simply predicting or ordering it. Complying with institutional convention and bearing the requisite authority, the judge's utterance has power to bring about the result immediately. Observers, understanding the conventions and witnessing the utterance, provide 'uptake', that is, they recognize that a person has been sentenced and, where appropriate, act accordingly (providing the perlocutionary outcome). Deviations from the paradigm do not necessarily bring about a complete misfire of the illocutionary act. For example, illocutionary acts can be unintentional but nevertheless have force. In asking '[w]here's my dinner?' the traditional husband may indeed simply be asking a question. Nevertheless, in taking the query as an order to get busy in the kitchen his wife quite reasonably takes her husband to have performed an illocution, and here the context (the conventional distribution of domestic labour) determines the uptake, notwithstanding the husband's lack of intent.

Combining the theory of illocutionary effectiveness with the analysis of the meaning of contract pregnancy and sex selection given above, we can claim that these practices are symbolically harmful. For in revealing the classist, racist, and sexist elements in both practices we have already anticipated the conditions for illocutionary force, and identified the dominant groups whose 'voice', actions, choices, preferences carry authority.

---

[19] See H. B. Holmes and B. B. Hoskins, 'Prenatal and Preconception Sex Choice Technologies: A Path to Femicide?', and M. Kishwar,'The Continuing Deficit of Women in India and the Impact of Amniocentesis,' in Corea *et al.* (eds.), *Man-Made Women: How New Reproductive Technologies Affect Women* (London,1985). Canada's Royal Commission on New Reproductive Technologies was sceptical about the need to regulate sex selection technology in Canada, but see E. Boetzkes, 'Sex Selection and the Charter,' (1994) VII *Canadian Journal of Law and Jurisprudence* 173; and Boetzkes, n. 17, above.
[20] C. McKinnon, *Feminism Unmodified* (Cambridge, Mass., 1987); and *Only Words* (Cambridge, Mass.,1993).
[21] Rae Langton, 'Speech Acts and Unspeakable Acts' (1993) 22 *Philosophy and Public Affairs* 293.
[22] J. L. Austin, *How To Do Things With Words* (New York, 1962).

Whether intended or not, the pursuit of this sort of reproductive assistance or preference can reasonably be taken as the (further) demeaning of the women whose 'assistance' is sought, and the women whose sex is disparaged. Just as pornography may subordinate, so contract pregnancy and sex selection may demean.

A RELEVANT TAXONOMY

But what is it symbolically to demean? Can we provide a taxonomy of symbolic harm? Above we identified three objectionable 'messages' about persons as deontological affronts: attacks on dignity, equality, and integration. What exactly is the moral affront of these messages? An initial classification of symbolic harms includes: the denial of personhood, the devaluing of personhood, and an attack on a style of personhood.

Denial of Personhood

Consider the analysis of moral equality given by Bernard Williams in his essay 'The Idea of Equality'.[23] Searching for a non-trivial and politically significant meaning for moral equality, Williams examines the implications of recognizing the moral status of others. Rejecting as either empirically false or vacuous the notion of equal moral agency, he asks what might support the notion that respect is owed to all persons. In a move we see echoed in current debates over euthanasia, he concludes that by virtue of having a life, being the subject of projects, goals, aspirations, and engagements, each person is deserving of identification and understanding. 'Objective' attitudes (based on social standing, titles, labels) will not suffice. And, since some individuals fail to have self-respect because of social exploitation or degradation, our obligation to identify is not just a matter of viewing them as they view themselves. We must work to provide conditions in which our respect *for* them engenders self-respect *in* them.

Following Williams, we could say that one ingredient of symbolic harm is failing to view and represent persons as persons, as having (or deserving to have) a life that renders functional descriptions of them seriously incomplete. Thus, when contract pregnancy proclaims women foetal containers, it is a symbolic harm of this sort, violating dignity, equality, and the stake in personal integration that persons have as subjects of their own lives.

Devaluing of Personhood

But the denial of personhood cannot be the only symbolic harm. Denigrating one's personhood also harms. Thus, when hate propoganda insinuates that its target group is inordinately covetous, cowardly, schem-

---

[23] Bernard Williams, 'The Idea of Equality' in H. Bedau (ed.), *Justice and Equality* (Englewood Cliffs, NJ, 1971) 116.

ing, promiscuous, lazy, irrational—rather than denying personhood, its insinuation devalues persons by group stereotyping.

Now, as Lorraine Code argues in *What Can She Know*,[24] there cannot be a language of particulars. Using categories, and thus generalizing, is unavoidable and epistemically profitable. Much generalizing, though logically suspect, is relatively morally harmless. When is it harmful then? Part of the answer lies in the type of human collective over which the generalization scopes. Arguably, generalizing is morally problematic when it scopes, not over aggregates or associations, but over groups. In her account of oppression, Iris Marion Young[25] claims that what distinguishes groups is that membership of a group contributes to one's identity, whereas being part of an aggregate or association does not. Being lumped together with other green-eyed people does not symbolically harm me; being called a stupid bitch, however, does.

But scoping over groups, even with negative labelling, is not, by itself, morally problematic. It becomes so when the claim made is reductionist and essentializing. As Code argues, denigrative stereotyping essentializes the allegedly dominant feature and also resists revision.[26] That is, counter-evidence is ignored or explained away, as when we characterize gays as promiscuous or women as irrational.

Downgrading the personal status of women through such essentializing attends both contract pregnancy and sex selection. In the case of sex selection, the very arbitrariness of preferring males reveals the belief that women as a group are inferior. And the support of contract pregnancy, with the implicit acceptance of the natural role of women as 'breeders', embedded as it is in a dualistic and exclusionary contrast between mind and body/nature, dowgrades women as persons.

Attack on a Style of Personhood

Finally, persons may be symbolically harmed when their style of personhood is devalued. It may be acknowledged that they are persons, and that they are distinctive, but their primary and defining commitments may be disparaged. Calling a female healer a witch or a civil-rights worker a nigger-lover condemns a vocation; 'better dead than Red', and 'Indian-giver' condemn a way of life. By contrast, '[n]o sex please, we're British' lovingly approves one. Whether we view the denigration of one's vocation

---

[24] L. Code, *What Can She Know: Feminist Theory and the Construction of Knowledge* (Ithaca, NJ, and London, 1991) 188.
[25] I. Marion Young, 'Psychological Oppression' in her *Throwing Like A Girl and Other Essays in Feminist Philosophy and Social Theory* (Bloomington, Ind., 1990).
[26] Those familiar with discussions of the logic of domination will recognize this essentializing as part of the process of creating hierarchies and justifying patterns of domination. For a sophisticated analysis of the logic of domination see V. Plumwood, *Feminism and the Mastery of Nature* (London and New York, 1993).

as a denial of dignity, moral equality, or integration, and hence as a symbolic harm, will depend upon our view of the metaphysics of persons. That is, if we see persons as separable from their central projects, disparagement of these projects will not compromise their moral status. If, by contrast, we see selves as constituted by their commitments, attacking a style of personhood will count as a third sort of symbolic harm. This third sort (if it is one) will have little bearing on the debate over sex selection; but in the debate over contract pregnancy it is likely to be presented *in support of* the reproductive choices of both contracting men (or couples) and gestators, in so far as their choices will be presented as life-options worthy of respect. Whether this view can be sustained will depend upon our assessment of the meaning of the acts and events within the overall practice, and, as I have argued, viewing the practice as autonomy-enhancing is highly debatable.

Pragmatic Concerns

When introducing the notion of symbolic harm, I recognized that we would need criteria for identifying and weighing harm. Principally the pragmatic concern is one of limiting liability. How broadly do we want to penalize symbolic harm?

I believe that a substantive theory of equality is necessary to ground and limit the scope of liability for symbolic harm. Rather than countenancing all disparaging representation as harmful, a substantive account of equality would be sensitive to historical patterns of group disadvantage and to the differential impact of attacks on personhood.

Kathleen Mahoney, writing in response to *R. v. Keegstra*, recommends adopting such a contextualized approach as a way of limiting liability for hate speech.[27] She argues that, like racial segregation or harassment, hate speech (and, we may add, other forms of symbolic harm) should be viewed as an element within a violent practice which undermines equality. To promote group hatred is to practise discrimination.[28] By locating hate speech within a discriminatory practice, Mahoney, like Vadas, is providing it with a practice-identity. And by recognizing its immediate as well as its instrumental power to injure, she is acknowledging the reality of symbolic harm.

But how is liability limited, on this view? Here also Mahoney takes a contextual approach, arguing that liability can be limited by protecting only certain groups. She claims that by appealing to the thick wording of section 15 of the Canadian Charter of Rights and Freedoms (which

---

[27] K. Mahoney, 'The Canadian Constitutional Approach to Freedom of Expression in Hate Propaganda and Porgnography' (1992) 55 *Law and Contemporary Problems* 77.
[28] *Ibid.*, 82.

permits differential treatment based on group disadvantage), and by avail-
ing ourselves of current equality jurisprudence (and especially its substantive interpretation in *Andrews* v. *The Law Society of BC*[29]) we can identify
vulnerable groups and thus distinguish permissible from impermissible
representation. She says:

Constitutional equality as interpreted in Andrews . . . is essentially designed to
protect the groups that suffer social, political, and legal disadvantage. If hate
propoganda were directed against historically dominant group members, a contextual approach would constitutionally protect it, even in the section 1 balance. . . . If
the groups were equal, presumably any special protection would be removed.[30]

Mahoney's contextualized approach is important for integrating the
notion of symbolic harm into an acceptable policy objective (that of equality) while both containing liability and permitting dissident speech by
members of subordinate groups.[31] On the contextualized view, liability
would attach to symbolic harms which are practice-constituents in a practice of inequality. A practice of inequality targets members of a particular
group, and renders them disadvantaged, or perpetuates their disadvantage.
Thus, the asymmetry between groups (which can be determined by examining historical discrimination or current status, or a combination of the
two) provides the boundaries of liability for symbolic harm.

If, as I have argued above, the messages of contract pregnancy and sex
selection are symbolically harmful to women, it is clear that such harm can
play a role in the justification of legal restrictions. Thus, proponents of
these practices render themselves liable for their role in the perpetuation of
disadvantage, something which, in Canadian law at least, is a legitimate
target for remedial measures.[32]

Jurisprudential Concerns

Finally, how may the proposal to impose liability for symbolic harm resist
the charge of legal moralism? Robertson, as we have seen, objects to the
involvement of the state in regulating meanings, and he is representative of

---

[29] [1989] 1 SCR 143, 154. This case concerned whether non-citizens were entitled to practise law in Canada. In its decision, the Supreme Court identified non-citizens as a vulnerable
group, and gave substantive content to the constitutional guarantee of equal protection and
benefit before and under the law.

[30] Mahoney, n. 27, above, 88.

[31] For an interesting challenge to attempts to regulate speech, see J. Butler, *Excitable
Speech: A Politics of the Performative* (New York and London, 1997). Butler argues that
legal liability for hate speech silences dissident speech and misplaces liability on individual
agents, thus concealing the true sites of power.

[32] Like many other Canadian feminists, I propose legal measures in the spirit of protecting
the disadvantaged. Thus, I support targeting third parties—brokers, corporate providers,
lawyers, procurers, rather than those solicited for reproductive services or pregnant women
seeking reproductive help.

much liberal thought. However, I have argued, such resistance cannot plausibly be based on a scepticism about uncovering the meaning or the message of the practices in question. Meanings and symbolic pronouncements, though deeply embedded, can be uncovered.

A more plausible objection to state involvement in regulating representation—and one which is particularly sensitive to the social context of representation—is that of Joseph Raz. In his 'Free Expression and Personal Identification'[33] he recognizes that acts of expression often display a way of life, validating it as an option, and facilitating its adoption by members of the community. Thus, he renders a 'public goods' argument in favour of free expression.

When expression of this sort is censored, argues Raz, not only is the merit of validation removed; censorship also insults those whose way of life it is, as well as those who are implicitly denied the opportunity to assess and embrace or reject the life in question. Censorship is thus powerful beyond the restriction it places on particular acts; it is taken as a symbolic denunciation. Permission, by contrast, argues Raz, is not approval; it does not carry the same symbolic weight.

If Raz is right, even if we recognize the symbolic force of acts as revelatory of undignified ways of life and the inegalitarian values driving them, we may not be justified in prohibiting them. For utilizing the censorious symbolism of legal pronouncements and postures may be inadmissible.

But I believe Raz is mistaken about both the uptake that attaches to certain prohibitions, and the asymmetry of meaning between permission and prohibition. For, first, the choice to rule out certain novel practices (such as those employing new reproductive technology) may be seen simply as cautious and preventative, rather than insulting.[34] In Canada we have made many preventative policy decisions, and some have symbolic as well as consequentialist justifications. For instance, we have decided not to permit the sale of blood or body parts, and this is not simply out of fear of coercion or exploitation; it is also in virtue of a resistance to the commodification of human bodies. Precluding certain novel practices in the interests of promoting equality and affirming the value of vulnerable members of the community need not be viewed as insulting or paternalistic.

Secondly, if we adopt Mahoney's contextualized approach, we cannot assume, as Raz does, that persons are equally well placed to exercise rationality and shape their environments according to their choices. Where serious inequalities exist, the silence of the state over expressions may well be taken as complicity, and its intervention welcomed as expressing, not withholding, respect. Under such conditions permission, not prohibition, is the

---

[33] J. Raz, 'Free Expression and Personal Identification' (1991) 11 *Oxford Journal of Legal Studies* 303.

[34] C. Overall, *Human Reproduction: Principles, Practices, Policies* (Toronto, 1993), 131.

insult. For instance, in *Native Women's Association of Canada* v. *Canada*,[35] a case was successfully made that failure to provide funds for aboriginal women to participate in discussions over the constitution violated their freedom of expression. Thus an inequalities approach gave rise to a positive state obligation which cast state inaction as discriminatory.

Appealing, as I have done, to the inequalities approach to challenge Raz's characterization of state interference in symbolic representation, I have provided a defence that is available in jurisdictions like Canada. However, a broader defence can be given of recognizing symbolic harm, one which is not limited to the Canadian legal context but can be appealed to within any liberal polity that recognizes the embeddedness of persons in a world of public meaning with a history of discrimination. This is the account given by Drucilla Cornell in her book, *The Imaginary Domain*.[36] There, notwithstanding a hearty endorsement of the importance of free expression to both women and men, Cornell has recently argued for what she calls the 'degradation prohibition', a restriction on speech deriving from deontological concerns such as those I have been discussing. Making a case that is neither moralistic nor offence-based, Cornell argues that the state has a responsibility to protect 'the imaginary domain' by prohibiting degrading representation. The obligation derives from the role of the state in offering citizens equal protection, in particular protection of the opportunity to become persons.

On Cornell's view, the project of personhood requires bodily integrity, access to the means to develop linguistic skills, and participation in the symbolic realm, in which our imaginative self-projections are acknowledged by symbolic others. Since the symbolic realm (which also provides models of personhood from which we derive a personal self-image) contains downgraded gendered images of the feminine, women are systematically disadvantaged in the personhood project.[37] Cornell calls for the state, which is also a symbolic Other in so far as it affirms or denies the equivalent value of persons, to remove such downgraded images from the public imaginary and to create space within it for the equivalent opportunity for individuation and the construction of personhood.

Combining Cornell's proposal that the state monitor representations and prohibit degradation with my analysis of symbolic harm, we can provide a more general justification for the involvement of the state in protecting the realm of meaning. For if symbolic representation is harmful whenever it denies or devalues the personhood or style of personhood of a disadvantaged group, and if adequate images are necessary for the

---

[35] [1992] SCR 192.
[36] D. Cornell, *The Imaginary Domain* (New York and London, 1995).
[37] Diana T. Meyers argues the same point without appealing to psychoanalytic developmental theories. See her *Self, Society and Personal Choice* (New York, 1989).

equivalent opportunity to develop as persons, and if the state has a responsibility to provide such an equal opportunity, there is a non-moralistic justification for state involvement in symbolic representation. Furthermore, if reproductive practices such as contract pregnancy and sex selection exacerbate the already downgraded images of women, as of inferior worth, or as reducible to reproductive commodities, there is a *prima facie* case within liberalism for limiting those practices.[38]

I am not arguing that symbolic representation alone or always is sufficient to justify the curtailing of representations, actions, or practices. As always, the argument for such limitations must be weighed against arguments in favour of permission. However, since it is doubtful whether there is a positive right to reproductive assistance or to accessing practices that contribute to discrimination, the demand for such 'reproductive alternatives' as contract pregnancy and sex selection technology probably cannot outweigh the (now expanded) objections to them.

Conclusion

In this paper I have attempted to outline a logic, taxonomy, and justification for the notion of symbolic harm as legal harm, and to apply it to the practices of contract pregnancy and sex selection. Both these practices (and others, for instance, the retrieval of germ cells from aborted female foetuses for *in vitro* fertilization) stimulate consequentialist objections and raise worries about the interests of women. However, once the dust settles around such debates, there is a deontological residue which has yet to be captured and analysed within our legal framework. Although symbolic harm alone may not 'trump', it is important to recognize its role as sometimes a symptom, sometimes a constituent, and sometimes a herald of harmful practices. Where practices are novel, developing swiftly, and supported by significant economic interests, it is important and appropriate to consider the impact of such practices upon the project of achieving the good of personhood. And if we view the state as having a responsibility to depict and respond to its members in morally appropriate ways, it must pay attention to both the symbolic meanings attaching to social practices and the symbolism of its own pronouncements and silences.

---

[38] I develop this argument in more detail in my 'Equality, Autonomy and Feminist Bioethics,' n. 17, above.

VIAGRA IS COMING! THE RHETORIC OF CHOICE AND NEED

Hazel Biggs and Robin Mackenzie

The rhetoric of choice and need is well established where the allocation of scarce resources is in question. In England, where the National Health Service (NHS) system purports to offer free health care for all on the basis of individual need, we look to the law to adjudicate on these issues: effectively, to police the boundary between choice and need. In this context it is arguable, however, that the law itself can be informed by rhetoric and be instrumental in the generation of rhetoric. This paper seeks to explore the discursive construction of choice and need by examining the rhetoric which represents them as competing bipolar opposites and simultaneously informs consumers, providers, and the law. It will do so by reviewing the law's engagement with the rationing debate before embarking upon a multi-layered analysis of the rhetorical strategies of the interest groups concerned, drawing upon the competing representations of Viagra in relation to health care resources and the notion of recognised clinical need.

Law and the Rhetoric of Choice and Need

A raft of legislation[1] dictates the level of resources available to the NHS and responsibility for their allocation and provision. Within that framework the Secretary of State for Health comes under a duty to:

continue the promotion in England and Wales of a *comprehensive* health service designed to secure improvement [a] in the physical and mental health of the people . . . [b] in the prevention, diagnosis and treatment of illness . . . to provide or secure the effective provision of services (emphasis added).[2]

The term 'comprehensive' is regarded as meaning available to all and encompassing all necessary forms of health care.[3] However, as Christopher Newdick reports, since its inception the NHS has struggled to meet this standard and prescription charges were being introduced as early

---

[1] *Inter alia*, the National Health Service Act 1977, the NHS Community Care Act 1990, the NHS (Primary Care) Act 1997, and the Health Act 1999.

[2] National Health Service Act 1977, s. 1.

[3] See the White Paper of 1944, entitled *A National Health Service*, Cmd. 6502 (London, 1944).

as 1951.[4] In 1999 the scope of the NHS extends far beyond what could be envisaged in 1944, not least because of statutory political and economic change within and outside the NHS. The kinds of treatment available today are costly beyond belief by comparison with fifty years ago, and the mechanisms set up then to secure resources to provide them through the NHS cannot hope to keep pace. The increasing longevity of the population, therapeutic and diagnostic developments, and the demands of a society whose expectations have been raised by its awareness of technological advancement and the art of the possible, all contribute to the escalating expense of modern medical care. Inevitably this has led to questions about how the provision and different therapies might be prioritized. What forms of health care are 'necessary' and for whom?

Various methods have been suggested for prioritizing between potential recipients. Examples include the ubiquitous quality adjusted life year (QALY), triage, and competitive lottery. Many health-care professionals are happy to confess that in day-to-day practice random allocation is the norm and, at the micro level, they tend to treat patients in the order in which they present and according to their individual clinical needs. Decisions about the level of funds each Trust, hospital department, or general practice should allocate for each facet of the service are taken at a level once removed from the clinical setting. It is here that mechanisms have developed to distinguish between the cost efficiency of different treatment methods. Concepts such as 'evidence based medicine' and institutions such as the internal market and fund-holding general practices[5] have been devised as a result. Central to policy decisions is the requirement to balance clinical integrity with financial and managerial considerations.[6] It is when the balance seems to tip too far in favour of fiscal constraints that disputes arise which call for legal resolution.

The courts have grappled with questions of how much should be made available, to whom, and for what.[7] Despite an evident unease on the part of the judges concerned to participate in the rationing process, many of these judgments now provide benchmarks for distributing funds and the bases upon which allocations may be made.

R. v. Secretary of State, ex parte Hinks[8] concerned the provision of treatment to four patients who were awaiting orthopaedic surgery. At issue was the interpretation and scope of section 3 of the National Health

---

[4] C. Newdick, *Who Should We Treat? Law, Patients and Resources in the NHS* (Oxford, 1996), 1.

[5] Now defunct under the Health Act 1999, s. 1.

[6] A range of policy documents can be viewed on the Department of Health Website at http://www.doh.gov.uk.

[7] See, e.g., *R. v. Secretary of State, ex parte Hinks* [1992] 1 BMLR 93, decided in 1980; *R. v. Secretary of State, ex parte Walker* [1992] 3 BMLR 32, decided in 1987; *R. v. Cambridge HA, ex parte B* [1995] 2 All ER 129 (CA).

[8] N. 7, above.

Service Act (NHS Act) 1977 since the patients in question claimed that the 'general duties' of the Secretary of State described here included a legal duty to provide services that met their needs. In the Court of Appeal Lord Denning held that the only duty was 'to meet all reasonable requirements such as can be provided within the resources available'.[9] While Bridge LJ concluded that the level of resources provided 'must be determined in the light of current Government economic policy'. In short the court declined to find that the Act imposed an absolute duty, this despite Bridge LJ's assertion that:

the health service currently falls short of what everyone would regard as the optimum desirable standard. This is very largely a situation brought about by lack of resources, lack of suitable equipment, lack of suitably qualified personnel, and above all lack of adequate finance.[10]

Similar arguments were rehearsed in *R. v. Secretary of State, ex parte Walker*,[11] where a mother alleged that her baby had been denied a heart operation, even though the health authority acknowledged that the child needed the surgery. The proposed operation had been scheduled and postponed five times due to shortages of skilled nursing staff. Macpherson J stated that in the absence of illegality, procedural defect, or unreasonableness, the court could not interfere in the decision-making process. Questions about the allocation of scarce resources should, in his opinion, 'be raised, answered and dealt with outside this court'.[12] His comments were reiterated in the subsequent cases of *R. v. Central Birmingham HA, ex parte Collier*,[13] which involved the same Health Authority. Only if the decision itself was *Wednesbury* unreasonable, that is to say so unreasonable that no reasonable authority could have made it, would it fall within the jurisdiction of the court.

Yet cases concerning resource allocation decisions continue to exercise the courts and demand that models be developed to answer them. One such case is *R. v. Cambridge HA, ex parte B.*[14] Here the health authority steadfastly refused to discuss its decision to withhold treatment in terms of the potential costs of the therapy. Instead it opted to define the issue as one of clinical need emphasized by its assessment of child B's 'best interests'. Child B, later identified as Jaymee Bowen, was 10 years old and had suffered from lymphoma and leukaemia since she was five. The case arose when the health authority declined to provide further treatment to the child who had already undergone two courses of chemotherapy, a bone marrow transplant, and whole body irradiation. The complexities of the analysis of her chances of survival, her expected quality of life during what

[9] *R. v. Secretary of State, ex parte Hinks* n. 7, above, at 95.
[10] *Ibid.* 96.   [11] [1992] 3 BMLR 32, decided in 1987.
[12] *R. v. Secretary of State, ex parte Walker* n. 7, above, at 34.
[13] 6 Jan. 1988, unreported.   [14] [1995] 2 All ER 129 (CA).

were considered to be potentially her last weeks of life, and the characterization of the proposed treatment as experimental, all contributed to the decision to deny access to her treatment of last resort. Jaymee Bowen was expected to survive no more than six to eight weeks in the absence of further treatment. However, her father had obtained opinions from America that she had an 18 per cent chance of a complete cure following further therapy. He sought a judicial review of the decision.

Evidence was presented by the health authority that the proposed treatment would be likely to be distressing and that local doctors considered the child's chances of being cured as between 10 and 2.5 per cent. Given the child's medical history this could not, it argued, be regarded as being in the child's 'best interests'. The potential £75,000 cost of the procedure, which would have to be performed in the private sector, was described as an inefficient use of limited resources and raised as a supplementary reason for the decision not to treat her.

At first instance Laws J ordered that the authority reconsider its decision on the basis of the child's 'right to life'. However, the Court of Appeal upheld previous judicial decisions and sentiments regarding the limited role for the courts in these cases and overturned the order. The insistence of the health authority that the decision had been based on an assessment of Jaymee Bowen's clinical need as defined by an analysis of her 'best interests' failed to avoid its portrayal in the media as being solely financially orientated. These comments by Sir Thomas Bingham MR in the Court of Appeal must have encouraged speculation that the case turned on the allocation of scarce NHS resources rather than the needs of the individual patient:

I have no doubt that in a perfect world any treatment which a patient . . . sought would be provided if doctors were willing to give it, no matter how much it cost . . . It would, however, be shutting ones eyes to the real world if the court were to proceed on the basis that we do live in such a world.[15]

Ultimately the financial intervention of a private benefactor ensured that Jaymee Bowen received the treatment, but sadly the eventual outcome was only delayed. She died fourteen months after having the treatment.

The health authority in Jaymee Bowen's case claimed that the decision not to treat her was based on clinical need; but how is such a need assessed? The existence of a need relates to an individual's particular circumstances and/or characteristics. Surely, therefore, needs, whether clinical, social, or financial, exist regardless of whether the resources are available to meet them? Jaymee Bowen's need for treatment was an objective reality arising from her medical condition. Perhaps the incidental effects of

[15] R. v. Cambridge HA, ex parte B (1995) 23 BMLR 1 (CA), per Sir Thomas Bingham MR at 8–9.

performing the therapy were less desirable and could be considered to outweigh the potential benefits, but the costs of providing the treatment could not extinguish the underlying need. Lord Lloyd's dissenting judgement in *R. v. Gloucestershire CC, ex parte Barry*[16] graphically illustrates this point:

How can resources help to measure . . . need? . . . His needs remain exactly the same. They cannot be affected by the local authority's inability to meet those needs.[17]

Similarly, in *R. v. East Sussex CC, ex parte Tandy*,[18] Lord Browne-Wilkinson attempted to define needs when discussing the duty to provide suitable education under the Education Act 1993:

it is difficult to talk about the lack of a radio or a holiday or a recreational activity as giving rise to a need: they may be desirable but they are not in the ordinary sense necessities.[19]

Following on from this however, he declared that resource considerations were/are not relevant to the question of what constitutes 'suitable education' and went on to state that Parliament had, in this situation, imposed a statutory duty, i.e. to provide suitable education. That is not the same as a power which would permit the authority to exercise discretion and would accordingly allow the courts little control over how that discretion was exercised. In the case of a statutory duty Parliament required an authority to perform in a particular way and the courts should be cautious about downgrading the duty to a discretionary control.

Andrew Grubb has suggested that *Tandy* may be read as implying that this duty is absolute, in the context of prescribing for patients' needs in primary care.[20] The nature, i.e. the definition of need, however, still remains inconclusive. Thus need, and clinical need, have been recognized as a foundation upon which resources should properly be allocated but the definition of need, as will be seen in relation to Viagra, is fluid and often inherently political. Recent controversies over Viagra and other so-called lifestyle drugs have, like the judgments in *Barry* and *Tandy*, introduced an additional factor in the equation, that of choice or desire. Rather than being necessary for life these preparations are perceived as recreational and simply improving quality of life. Their users can consequently be regarded as choosing an enhanced lifestyle rather than requiring a medicinal remedy for a genuine ailment.

---

[16] (1997) 36 BMLR 69, (HL).
[17] *R. v. Gloucestershire CC, ex parte Barry* (1997) 36 BMLR 69, (HL) at 96.
[18] [1998] 2 All ER 769.
[19] *R. v. East Sussex CC, ex parte Tandy* [1998] 2 All ER 769, at 776.
[20] A. Grubb, *Principles of Medical Law (First Supplement)* (Oxford, 1998), 5.

Contested Concepts in Health Care: Broken Hearts v. Broken Legs

Choice too is a flexible concept, particularly where it is regarded as responsible for generating a health-care need, as where a woman chooses to wait until her mid-thirties or later before attempting to conceive a child.[21] In a climate of limited availability and rationing her choice may effectively deny her access to NHS fertility treatment should she need it. Of course she may need it only because she has apparently chosen to delay until her natural fertility is declining, but she may also have been constrained by career, personal, or financial considerations and effectively denied the opportunity to exercise a choice. Such realities are masked by judicial recourse to the compelling notions of limited resources and inevitable scarcity in the NHS, and the depiction of the body as a complex machine susceptible to disease.

In many cases it is clearly appropriate to apply the disease model and to represent the body as a complex machine; setting a broken leg is, after all, not too far removed from mending a puncture, and both need to be remedied before the machine can function adequately. But where the need is founded on psychological precursors, as might be the case with fertility treatment, to perhaps body modification, and certainly erectile dysfunction, the justification for regarding those concerned as suffering from a medical condition becomes increasingly tenuous and uncomfortably close to consumer choice. This may be regarded as the ghost in the machine: resulting in emotional heartbreak rather than physical breakdown. Dr Steve Lamm has described sexual dysfunction as 'devastating to men and devastating to couples and devastating to relationships'.[22] The debate surrounding the introduction of Viagra, the only orally administered drug presently licensed to treat erectile dysfunction, exemplifies the close associations between need and physical suffering and choice and psychological pain. Here the rhetoric of choice and need has been pervasive in Parliamentary debate,[23] Department of Health press releases, and prescribing guidelines,[24] documentation provided by Viagra's producers,[25] media reporting, and public perceptions, as considered in depth below.

On Friday, 26 June 1998 the Department of Health issued a press

---

[21] See R. v. Ethical Committee of St Mary's Hospital (Manchester), ex parte H [1988] 1 FLR 512, and R. v. Sheffield HA, ex parte Seale (1994) 25 BMLR 1.

[22] J. Donovan and T. Koppel, 'Viagra: a New Sexual Revolution?' http://virilitysolution.com/nightline.html (consulted 1 July 1999).

[23] See comments from Alan Milburn, Minister of State for Health in the House of Commons, 14 July 1998.

[24] See NHS Executive Press Release Briefing Notes, BN: 02/99, NHS Prescription Proposals on Viagra, 21 Jan. 1999, and NHS Executive Health Service Circular HSC 1999/115, Treatment for Impotence, 7 May 1999.

[25] Pfizer publish a fact sheet on Viagra and its operation in conjunction with background information on erectile dysfunction.

release concerning Viagra.[26] The press release took the form of a statement from the Medicines Control Agency purporting to clarify 'the legal position on the sale and supply of Viagra (Sildenafil)'. Viagra was at the time unlicensed in the UK and Europe but was licensed and widely available in the USA,[27] where it had been portrayed in the media as a recreational drug capable of enhancing sexual performance as well as countering erectile dysfunction. The cost of the drug,[28] and the projected level of demand based on evidence from America, led commentators to suggest that the state-funded NHS would have inadequate resources to cope. Mechanisms would therefore be required to limit its impact on the overburdened NHS.

Unlicensed pharmaceutical products can be obtained in the UK only by prescription. There must be an identified clinical need and the prescribing doctor is personally responsible for supplying the drug. The publicity from the USA surrounding Viagra's performance had apparently encouraged potential beneficiaries to seek supplies through mail order and internet shopping. The DoH press release stressed the fact that Viagra could be prescribed only on the basis of clinical need and emphasized the criminal penalties for supplying unlicensed drugs in contravention of the Medicines Act 1968. It described Viagra as a 'powerful medicinal product' which should not be used except under medical supervision and stated that '[p]eople run very real risks with their health if they obtain it . . . and take it without the direction of a doctor. We strongly recommend against buying Viagra this way'. Essentially, Viagra could exceptionally be made available to those who needed it but people who chose to obtain it for themselves would be exposed to unspecified risks and criminal sanction. The rhetoric of choice and need is clear to see.

Authorization for Viagra to be marketed throughout Europe was received from the European Medicines Evaluation Agency on 15 September 1998 but access to it for NHS patients remained restricted. An investigation into Viagra's potential impact on the NHS by the Standing Medical Advisory Committee (SMAC)[29] was already under way and a circular providing interim guidance to doctors was issued by the Department of Health on 16 September 1998.[30] SMAC's initial recommendations that doctors should not prescribe the drug and health authorities should not

---

[26] DoH 98/257, *Viagra Sale—Statement by Medicines Control Agency.*

[27] Following the authorization of Viagra's US marketing licence in Mar. 1998 and a favourable report by the European regulatory body in May 1998 it was inevitable that UK marketing authorization would be granted.

[28] Then estimated by the Department of Health at £10 per tablet and potentially costing the NHS between £125,000 and £200,000 *per* 100,000 population *per annum.*

[29] A body of medical experts set up under the National Health Service Act 1977, as amended, with duties 'to advise the Secretary of State (a) upon such matters relating to services with which the Committee are concerned . . . and, (b) upon questions referred to them by the Secretary of State relating to those services' s. 6(5).

[30] Department of Health Circular, No. 1998/158.

support its provision except in (undefined) exceptional circumstances were included in the guidance even though the Committee had not finalized its advice. Ordinarily doctors may, and should, according to their terms and conditions of service, prescribe medications as clinically indicated unless they are included in the lists contained in Schedules 10 and 11 to the National Health Service Act 1977. The Act does not specifically empower the Secretary of State to issue directions that will effectively prevent doctors prescribing particular drugs. The kinds of drugs typically included in these lists are those that have no greater benefit than other cheaper, usually generic, substances. As there is no equally effective competitor for Viagra, its eventual inclusion in Schedule 10 could, according to counsel in the High Court case, not be justified. An amendment to Schedule 11 to include Viagra might however be justifiable because of the resource implications of permitting it to be prescribed without restriction. The lawfulness of Circular No. 1998/158 was therefore uncertain and it became the subject of a successful legal challenge. It was held that the Circular's 'purpose and effect was to ban or restrict the prescribing of Viagra to such an extent as to prevent GPs from carrying out their statutory obligations',[31] and that in European law it breached Directive 89/105/EEC, the Transparency Directive.

In the meantime, on 21 January 1999 the Department of Health launched a six-week public consultation on new policy proposals concerning the NHS prescription of Viagra and other treatments for impotence.[32] Figures cited in the document estimated that two million UK men suffer from complete impotence and eight million are affected by partial impotence, out of a total population of approximately fifty million. Of these, only men suffering from specific medical conditions might be prescribed NHS treatment. The designated conditions were spinal cord injury, radical pelvic surgery (including prostatectomy), diabetes, multiple sclerosis, and single gene neurological disorder. Viagra therefore would be available from GPs for men with an appropriate medical history. Only 180,000 of the estimated eight million impotence sufferers fall into the disease categories described, and of these between 25,000 and 30,000 were expected to seek treatment. Men experiencing severe distress due to impotence caused by other conditions or of unknown aetiology might receive treatment for impotence on the NHS 'in exceptional circumstances only after specialist assessment in a hospital'.[33] By implication these were the men with a recognized clinical need.

On completion of the consultation process[34] the categories for which

---

[31] R. v. Secretary of State for Health, ex parte Pfizer Ltd, [1999] Lloyds Rep Med 25.

[32] Interestingly all impotence treatments were included in the guidelines, even those to which access had not previously been restricted.

[33] BN: 02/99, NHS Prescription Proposals on Viagra, 21 Jan. 1999.

[34] The process eventually took in excess of 15 weeks instead of the promised 6.

treatment may be prescribed on the NHS had been extended to include men who have poliomyelitis, spina bifida, and Parkinson's disease alongside those who have received treatment other than surgery for prostate cancer.[35] Representations from doctors' groups and patients' advocates were largely responsible for the extended definition of clinical need. However, those men whose impotence was iatrogenic or the result of depression were still excluded, and even where NHS prescription was permitted residual concerns about excessive demand led to further rationing, in that doctors may prescribe only four pills per patient per month.

Viagra as Theatre

How did this come about? An examination of the public debate over the proper allocation of health-care resources of NHS funding of Viagra reveals a reliance upon three justifications for drawing fine bright boundary lines: arguments based upon the necessity of rationing resources, a focus on risk, and the making of normative judgements which hinge upon classifying claimants as either deserving or undeserving. In order to enable a multi-layered analysis in considering these discursive productions of the rhetoric of choice and need, the figuration of the theatre of representation will be drawn upon. This strategy has been used by N. Katherine Hayles in her studies of the production of meaning as constituted by metaphoric networks.[36] Hayles defines the theatre of representation here as the public space within which significant actors present their own and each others' views in interdependent and mutually constituting sets of discursive strategies. These political and rhetorical negotiations result in rich collections of images which contribute to the public meanings of culturally significant products and processes. Jose van Dijck has considered popular images of genetics from this theoretical basis.[37] She has refined it further to distinguish between three perspectives within the figuration: those of performance, production, and context. These enable a complex representation of the contests over the semantic and symbolic territories of meaning as follows:

Viewed as a performance, we can dissect the 'theatre of genetics' as a drama in which nothing less than a hegemonic definition of genetics is at stake. Various special interest groups—actors on the stage—propel images and imagination in competition, not in contemplation. From the perspective of production, a theatre involves a number of professional groups engaged in the scripting, staging and

---

[35] NHS Executive Health Service Circular, n. 24 above.
[36] N. K. Hayles, 'Constrained Constructivism: Locating Scientific Inquiry in the Theatre of Representation' in G. Levine (ed.), *Realism and Representation* (Madison, Wis., 1993) 27.
[37] J. van Dijck, *Imagenation: Popular Images of Genetics* (London, 1998).

setting of a performance, such as script writers, reviewers, public relations managers, producers and others. Translated to the 'theatre' of genetics, popular images and imaginations are equally generated by scientists, public relations managers, journalists and fiction writers, and the dynamics between these groups are inherently part of their meaning production. A third possible angle is to look at how a performance or production is embedded in its larger social, historical and cultural context. Popular images of genetics are always struck against a backdrop of general historical developments, social concerns and cultural developments.[38]

What, then, of the theatre of Viagra and the rhetoric of choice and need? It is immediately apparent that hegemonic definitions of Viagra and, by implication, other prescription drugs such as Seroxat and Xenecal are indeed being contested. Special interest groups here include the Department of Health, the medical profession, the pharmaceutical industry, and consumers. A prime strategy adopted by these groups is equally clearly that of image production: they, along with public relations officials and the media, promulgate narratives of choice and need populated by cultural icons in order to affect resource allocations decisions. Finally, the theatre of Viagra is without doubt embedded in a socio-economic and historical context within which specific cultural preoccupations such as self-interrogation over sexual performance deeply influence the forms and outcomes of the rhetorical representations of what is at stake. This theoretical model will now be applied to the discursive productions of the current debate over Viagra. As space constraints prevent each interest group's rhetorical strategies being considered in detail as performance, production, and in context, the analytical focus will be upon those which appear most illuminating within each category.

Viagra as Performance

Van Dijck subdivides performance into the three elements of characters, plots, and metaphors. Applying this to representations of Viagra promulgated by the special interest groups listed above, the strategies of those who purport to be acting on behalf of the groups certainly include engaging in image management. Performance here thus includes not only their putting themselves forward as performing starring roles but also their constructing narratives wherein characters, plots, and metaphors are manipulated in order to persuade. The primary competing performative narratives here were those of the NHS and the medical profession. Both constructed salvation stories wherein they sought to save the British populace from the scourges of, respectively, profligacy and an unjustly imposed lack of sexual pleasure.

The struggle over who should monopolize the high moral ground over

[38] J. van Dijck, *Imagenation: Popular Images of Genetics* at 16–17.

who should be entitled to Viagra on the NHS exemplifies this process, as well as illustrating the unlikely alliances which may eventuate during such strategic manœuvres. Health Secretary Frank Dobson, whose responsibility it was to decide on who should be able to claim NHS prescribed Viagra, and how often, was portrayed in the media as restricting, for the first time, a drug of proven effectiveness in treating a recognized clinical need on straightforward economic grounds of probable costs to the NHS.[39] Dobson's rhetorical strategies here began with simple resource-speak: delays in the availability of prescription guidelines and the severity of their eventual restrictiveness were justified in terms of demand otherwise bankrupting the NHS, taking 'money away from paying doctors and nurses, dealing with cancer and people who have accidents'.[40] This monetarist approach was married with risk discourse and the division of those wishing to obtain Viagra on the NHS as the deserving few and the undeserving majority. The risks to the NHS posed by the undeserving were highlighted, along with the risks associated with the taking of the drug itself.[41] Figures of over a billion pounds per year, as opposed to a frugal fourteen million, were used to bolster the figuration of the ultimate icon of the undeserving: selfish men brandishing NHS-funded erections on nightclub dance floors.[42] This construction of Viagra as legitimate clinical treatment for the deserving few as opposed to lifestyle drug of choice for the undeserving frivolous majority was echoed by media commentators who might in other circumstances be regarded as strange bedfellows. Claire Rayner, the agony aunt, concerned that 'the over ambitious, old and greedy' should not 'drain the NHS coffers', did not see why 'the hard-pressed NHS should fund the sexual desires of the elderly, who are very likely to regard this pill as a fountain of youth, nor should it be freely provided to those whose lifestyle—too much work, too much alcohol and not enough common sense—make them liable to flop'.[43] In similar vein, Germaine Greer stated categorically that 'Viagra is a recreational drug. Ask the gay guys who keep Trade's club floor jumping and fill the pages of Attitude. They should know—they've been using it for months. And health is the least of their concerns'.[44]

[39] BBC News, 'UK Moves Towards National Policy on NHS Drugs' hhtp://194.130.56.40/hi/english/specia...t/1998/viagra/newsid_171000/171750.stm (consulted 4 July 1999).

[40] BBC News, 'Doctors rebel against "cruel" Viagra rules', http://news.bbc.co.uk/hi/english/speci...t/1998/viagra/newsid_259000/259331.stm (consulted 11 May 1999).

[41] BBC News, 'UK Moves Towards National Policy on NHS Drugs' http://194.130.56.40/hi/english/specia...t/1998/viagra/newsid_171000/17150.stm (consulted 4 July 1999).

[42] BBC News, 'More Men to get NHS Viagra' http://news.bbc.co.uk/hi/english/speci...t/1998/viagra/newsid_337000/337851.stm (consulted 11 May 1999); 'Viagra', *Independent*, 19 Sept. 1998.

[43] C. Rayner, 'Should Viagra be free on the NHS?', *BMA News Review*, 10 Oct. 1998, 41.

[44] G. Greer, 'Viagra', *Observer*, 24 Jan. 1999.

Doctors resisted this framing of the debate. While the legal obligation to prescribe according to recognized clinical need, or run the risk of being sued, formed an important subtext of the ensuing rhetorical contest, doctors' compassionate wish to relieve the suffering undergone by impotent patients and their partners formed the primary narrative upon which their arguments centred.[45] Dr Michael Fitzpatrick attacked the images of the undeserving promulgated by Frank Dobson and Clare Rayner in the following terms:

By contrast with the popular image of lusty swingers demanding enhanced 'recreational' sex, all but one of the men requesting Viagra in my surgery was over sixty and most were over seventy. The younger man had become impotent as a result of a surgical procedure that went badly wrong. Most of these men have significant medical problems—diabetes, high blood pressure, coronary heart disease. . . . The quest for Viagra, in my patients at least, expresses an admirable determination to achieve pleasure and an equally admirable aspiration to give pleasure. . . . Agony aunt Clare Rayner has characterised protests at the ban of Viagra as 'childish howls of frustration from a menacing mob of elderly but immature blokes who want to recapture an illusory lost youth'. This is not just nonsense, but offensive too. My patients just want to have sex with somebody. What is childish or immature about that?[46]

Similarly, Dr David Pickersgill asks:

Is it reasonable to deny patients access to what appears to be a very effective treatment for a distressing condition? . . . erectile dysfunction . . . is a condition that causes a great deal of unhappiness and misery, broken marriages, clinical depression and even suicide. Not all patients with erectile dysfunction are elderly. Many are younger men with conditions such as diabetes and various neurological disorders. Despite perfectly normal feelings of sexual arousal, they are unable to obtain an erection and, as a result, experience considerable emotional and sexual frustration, problems that will also be felt by their wives or partners.[47]

Doctors' storyline wherein the deserving pair-bonded couple achieve happiness through Viagra, prescribed according to recognized clinical need has been assisted by redefinitions of the clinical need in question. Whereas this was once medically perceived as being impotence, defined as 'an inability to achieve or maintain an erection sufficient for sexual intercourse', impotence is now seen as a subset of a new medical condition, erectile dysfunction, defined by the US National Institute of Health as 'the inability to get an erection adequate for satisfactory sexual performance'.[48]

---

[45] Questions of doctors' terms of service, conflicting interpretations of government guidelines on the part of health authorities and the BMA have led to difficulties for individual GPs: see BBC News, 'Viagra Patients Could Sue, Says Doctor', http://news.bbc.co.uk/hi/english/speci. . .t/1998/viagra/newsid_262000/262590.stm (consulted 11 May 1999).

[46] M. Fitzpatrick, 'Viagra and the Staff of Life' (1998) 115 *LM* 41.

[47] D. Pickersgill, 'Needy or Greedy?', *BMA News Review*, 10 Oct. 1998, 40.

[48] D. Nolan, 'Stiffening up' (1998) 111 *LM* 8.

Whereas impotence affected only one in ten men, erectile dysfunction can affect more than 50 per cent of men at any time.[49] The symbolic meaning of doctors' rescue mission here is thus endowed with extra force. As the more than 50 per cent of men, within this plot or narrative frame, are characterized as attached to more than 50 per cent of women suffering from the lack of their partners' sexual attention, more than half of the population of Britain may be seen as possessing a claim to NHS resources on medical grounds.

Only once this narrative of Viagra established as the preserver of happy heterosexual partnerships[50] has been established do doctors venture into resource-speak. Doctors portray themselves here as wishing to initiate an informed public debate on NHS funding, resource allocation, and rationing criteria which would lead to the promulgation of medically and ethically sound standards. The British Medical Association has consistently attacked Frank Dobson, both for delays over issuing guidelines for the prescribing of Viagra since his statement in September 1998 that 'seeking further expert guidance' would lead to definitive advice in a few weeks, and for the content of the preliminary guidelines once they were issued in January 1999, together with that of the definitive guidelines of June 1999. A typical condemnation here is that of the chairman of the BMA's GP committee, Dr John Chisholm, who characterized the January guidelines as flouting the founding principles of the NHS and as ignoring sensible measures of clinical effectiveness, since it was 'wholly unethical to discriminate against patients with equal clinical need':

Patients deserve better of the NHS than this. This is a cruel and unethical decision that is making totally unjustifiable distinctions between good and bad, deserving and undeserving causes of impotence. Doctors are there to respond to their patient's needs and as far as the patient is concerned they all deserve treatment that is available and effective.[51]

Dr Chisholm criticized the guidance issued as ignoring clinical evidence since 'the eligible categories of patients had been selected without regard to evidence of cost effectiveness, equity or social values', adding that in future rationing decisions should be made with more care.[52]

Doctors' programme of establishing Viagra as a drug to be prescribed in response to a recognized clinical need, as opposed to one to be purchased as a recreational consumer choice has been supported by a judicious use of risk rhetoric. Dr Ian Banks, chair of the Men's Health Forum and a

---

[49] BBC News, 'The Science of Desire', http://news.bbc.co.uk/hi/english/speci. . .t/1998/viagra/newsid_168000/168737.stm (consulted 11 May 1999).
[50] Apart from the quotation from Germaine Greer, n. 44, above, there has been a surprising presumption that Viagra is of interest to heterosexuals rather than homosexuals.
[51] BBC News, n. 40, above.
[52] BBC News, 'Give Impotent Men Viagra', http://194.130.56.40/low/english/speci. . . t/1998/viagra/newsid_302000/3026124.stm (consulted 4 July 1999).

spokesperson for the BMA, made a persuasive attempt to disempower
Frank Dobson's combination of the spectre of the risk of NHS funds posed
by undeserving men waving NHS-funded erections at nightclubs by
reframing this as an issue of professional competence:

The government has an unwarranted concern that men with normal sexual function will seek to enhance their potency, with the availability of new, more effective
and convenient management options. Yet, GPs are perfectly capable of diagnosing
those patients who are genuinely suffering from impotence.[53]

Medical opinion has also been mustered to promote the contention that
recreational use brings risks without benefits. A consultant urologist,
Roger Kirby, warned those proposing to take Viagra for recreational
purposes that they risked impotence through damage to the muscle that
produces an erection, as well as the possibility of developing a medical
condition known as priapism, a persistent and painful erection, or indeed
risked a fatal heart attack or stroke where Viagra was taken as part of a
drugs cocktail. 'Sildenafil has little to offer normally potent men and usage
by them carries inherent risks. The message is, don't take it if you have not
got erectile dysfunction. It is not a good recreational drug'.[54]

Viagra as Stage Production

Whereas performances may be considered simply in terms of constructed
images, characters, and plots competing in the public arena, analysing
discourse pluralism as a stage production adds the element of professional
orchestration of a rhetorical campaign. Van Dijck here proposes a
triparate image-producing process made up of scripting, staging, and
setting. This public relations orientation is clearly most suited to the efforts
of the pharmaceutical industry to persuade the NHS, the medical profession, the media, and the public that Viagra was a prescription medicine
which would relieve suffering rather than a designer drug which would
enhance pleasure. Marketing and promotion strategies depended initially
upon scripts, which were created to be delivered by scientists who would
establish Viagra as the definitive treatment for erectile dysfunction.
Settings chosen for these staged performances included prestigious scientific and medical gatherings in order to silence any overtones of recreational use. Gill Samuels, the director of early clinical research into Viagra,
issued statements designed to establish scientific respectability by margin-
alizing issues of pleasure to focus upon measurement instead. A scientific
device, the rigascan, combined with weights, enabled estimates of the
length and rigidity of Viagra erections to be released: for most men on

[53] BBC News, 'Give Impotent Men Viagra'.
[54] BBC News, 'Viagra Impotence Warning', http://news.bbc.co.uk/hi/english/speci. . .t/
1998/viagra/newsid_263000/263971.stm (consulted 11 May 1999).

Viagra, there was 80 per cent rigidity for ten minutes. Dr Samuels described the Pfizer team's attitude to the research in wholly scientific terms: '[w]e felt like we were right on the cutting edge of science'.[55]

Research data on the efficacy of Viagra administered to men suffering from erectile dysfunction, compared to that of placebos, was accompanied by a framing of Viagra as a medical treatment rather than simply a drug designed to enhance pleasure. The suffering of affected men and their partners was used to promote the clinical efficacy and respectability of Viagra. At the annual meeting of the American Association of Urologists in 1996, George M. Milne, the president of Pfizer Central Research, stated that 'impotence has a major, sometimes devastating, psychological and social impact on patients and their partners. Effective drugs currently available involve injections and for that reason have not been widely accepted. Viagra, because it is a pill and enhances the normal sexual response, offers advantages to these patients in terms of both convenience and safety'.[56] Similar sentiments were expressed by Dr Osterloh, one of the primary researchers, on behalf of Pfizer. 'This is not a "superstud drug". It is a serious medication for a serious disease. It is not intended for healthy, functioning men. Sensational news coverage has given the false impression that Viagra is for "regular guys" who want a little extra performance'.[57]

Once this platform of scientific and clinical credibility had been established, Pfizer were able to engage in resource-speak and risk rhetoric from a position of strength.[58] While Pfizer was happy to acknowledge Viagra's status as the most successful drug ever launched in America, where its sales reached £332 million in the first six months, it was promoted as a means whereby not only could suffering be relieved but money could be saved.[59] Whereas Viagra's cost to the NHS would be £4.84 per 50 mg pill, and Pfizer expected that in five years it would cost the NHS around £50 million annually, Andy Burrowes, Pfizer's head of marketing in the United Kingdom, asserted that Viagra would save the NHS money in the long term. The basis for this claim was that Viagra would encourage men with impotence to report the condition, and that since impotence was often

[55] BBC News, 'The Science of Desire', http://news.bbc.co.uk/hi/english/speci. . .t/1998/viagra/newsid_168000/168737.stm (consulted 11 May 1999).

[56] PSL Group, 'Safety and Efficacy data Presented on Pfizer Oral Drug For Impotence', http://pslgroup.com/dg837e.htm (consulted 11 May 1999).

[57] Healthwatcher, 'Viagra Falls: The Ups and Downs of the World's First Supercolossal Impotence Drug', http://www.healthwatcher.net/Viagra/viagra_falls.html (consulted 11 May 1999).

[58] The third rhetorical focus isolated in this analysis, the imposition of normative standards in order to justify dividing those eligible for Viagra on the NHS into the deserving and undeserving, will not be considered here as this has taken place, above, in the analysis of the case brought by Pfizers against the NHS.

[59] BBC News, 'Viagra Attracts 338 Million Pounds in Six Months', http://194.130.56.40/hi/english/specia. . .t/1998/viagra/newsid_194000/194029.stm (consulted 4 July 1999).

caused by other conditions such as heart disease or diabetes, which a patient might not realize he had, doctors would be enabled to diagnose these underlying conditions earlier than might otherwise have been possible. 'Doctors will be able to get the conditions under control, which will provide savings and benefits in the long run'.[60]

Pfizer's use of risk rhetoric was similarly directed towards establishing Viagra as a prescription drug appropriately available for defined clinical conditions, and safe within these. While the media and those who opposed Viagra's being widely available on the NHS laid stress upon the number of deaths attributed to Viagra, Pfizer has consistently maintained that Viagra is safe provided that it is taken 'only by men suffering from erectile dysfunction and only on advice from a doctor, following medical assessment'.[61] In an interview with the BBC, granted in response to a report in the *Lancet* claiming that the collapse of a 65-year-old Dutch man could be attributed to his taking Viagra, Dr Gill Samuels of Pfizer accused the *Lancet* of publicity seeking. She denied that Viagra, when properly prescribed, could be regarded as risky:

Unfortunately a number of men have died after taking Viagra. Any death is a tragedy, and we are always concerned when there are reports of serious adverse events associated with the use of any of our pharmaceuticals. But to my knowledge none of these deaths have been directly attributable to Viagra. One thing that we have to remember is that we are talking about approximately 130 deaths among 3,000,000 men who have received Viagra. Many of them are older and often have another disease such as heart disease, kidney disease or diabetes. When you resume sexual activity that can actually place a strain on the heart. It is exercise and it does increase cardiac workload.[62]

Context

The full value of the figuration of the theatre in considering the cultural constitution of public knowledge becomes clear once the dimension of context is added. Once the rhetorical strategies, scripts, and set pieces set out above are placed within their socio-economic and cultural contest, a new dimension enables them to be understood in more complex ways. In relation to her study of the means by which contemporary Euro-American societies have become geneticized, Van Dijck has described 'theatre' as providing 'a critical, self-reflexive tool for figuring out what is being said by first figuring out who is saying what to whom for what reasons. It offers a multi-layered viewpoint that accounts for both the production and [re]presentation of science in the public domain, while acknowledging its

---

[60] BBC News, 'Viagra Attracts 338 Million Pounds in Six Months'.

[61] Pfizers, 'Viagra™ (Sildenafil Citrate) Fact Sheet' 1999.

[62] BBC News, 'Viagra Risks Unproven', http://news.bbc.co.uk/hi/english/speci. . .t/1998/viagra/newsid_259000/259/737.stm (consulted 11 May 1999).

intrinsic embeddedness in society and culture'.[63] Placing the players considered above, the NHS, the medical profession, and the pharmaceutical manufacturers in the context of current negotiations over health-care resources thus allows insights into their rhetorical strategies which are otherwise unobtainable.

The NHS entered the debate over Viagra from a position wherein ministers from both parties had denied that it engaged in rationing, but it was nonetheless subject to financial constraints. Funded by taxes, the NHS spends more than £42 billion every year, but this sum has been proving increasingly insufficient.[64] A report by the National Audit Office demonstrated that in 1996–7 the combined financial deficit of the almost 50 per cent of health authorities experiencing 'serious financial difficulties' was £238 million, in addition to the £553 million deficit carried forward from previous years. The passing on of these problems to the NHS Trusts which ran the hospitals led to nearly 20 per cent of these being equally financially constrained, with others balancing their books only via severe cuts in services. The report predicted that the NHS would be likely to be forced to pay out £2.3 billion as a result of actions for medical negligence.[65]

Although Frank Dobson had resolutely refused to admit that NHS resources were subject to rationing, he had been trenchantly criticized for doing so by the shadow health secretary, Ann Widdicombe, who said 'I know it's almost too incredible to believe, but Labour's White Paper actually said "we don't find the arguments in favour of rationing to be convincing". Astonishing, isn't it? But you've got to feel a little bit sorry for Frank. . . . He doesn't seem to realise that he is making rationing decisions every day. You can't get operations for varicose veins, lipomas, or sebaceous cysts any more in our health service on a national basis'.[66] The independent health-care watchdog, the King's Fund, has also been calling for transparent, credible guidelines on NHS rationing which take account of public opinion and medical expertise. Professor Rudolf Klein, of the King's Fund, called for politicians to acknowledge that priorities in health-care must be set, and that this must be seen as a political process. Advocating the establishment of a National Council for Health Care Priorities as a forum and a focus for a rationing debate including politicians, professionals, and the public, he argued that principles must be developed in order to reconcile conflicting values and competing claims. Viewing current rationing disagreements about whether specific treatments

---

[63] Van Dijck, n. 37, above, 29.

[64] BBC News, 'Rationing Care From Limited Funds' http://news.bbc.co.uk/hi/english/speci. . .nhs_in_crisis/newsid_251000/251988.stm (consulted 11 May 1999).

[65] BBC News, 'Mounting NHS Cuts Could Eat Up Extra Cash', http://news.bbc.co.uk/hi/english/health/newsid_136000/136153.stm (consulted 11 May 1999).

[66] BBC News, 'Dobson "Must Accept NHS Rationing"', http://news.bbc.co.uk/hi/english/health/newsid_189000/189095.stm (consulted 11 May 1999).

should be limited or banned as ignoring fundamental issues of procedure, he condemned contemporaneous covert rationing decisions which involved diluting services, reducing time doctors spent with patients, and cutting the number and quality of nurses on wards.[67]

The BMA has consistently demanded more input into decisions on health-care resources which its members perceive as being made on bases which sideline medical expertise, as in its suggestion that waiting list targets be set not merely in terms of numbers but according to criteria which incorporate measures of clinical need.[68] Hence the BMA has echoed the call for informed public debate on health-care rationing, reflecting the anxiety of GPs over the consequences of the devolution of NHS funding decisions to primary care groups. GPs as a group have been demonstrated to be most concerned about rationing. A survey of nearly 3,000 doctors by *Doctor* and *Hospital Doctor* reported that 20 per cent of doctors knew patients who had suffered harm as a result of rationing, while more than 5 per cent knew of patients who had died as a result of being denied treatment on the NHS. 82 per cent thought GPs would be held personally responsible for rationing decisions, nearly 80 per cent thought it would cause friction in the doctor–patient relationship, 75 per cent feared that rationing would increase complaints against them, 70 per cent had been asked not to prescribe certain drugs, and nearly 50 per cent asked not to refer patients for particular procedures.[69] BMA GP negotiator, Dr Hamish Meldrum, favoured input being sought from the public so that choices could be made and priorities set in a principled way, reforming the present unco-ordinated approach.[70] Another BMA spokeswoman stressed the need for rationing decisions to be made at a national level rather than in a consulting room, so that doctors could refuse treatment to patients who fell outside nationally imposed categories 'with a clear conscience'.[71]

Politicians' wish to avoid acknowledging rationing on the NHS in order to avoid making unpopular decisions open to the public scrutiny of voters is easily understood, as is the desire of doctors for a clear conscience and a lack of litigation. Pharmaceutical companies, the third main interest group, have equally accessible motivations. Since their sales depend primarily on ethical drugs, or those that are prescribed, establishing the clinical respectability of the drugs concerned is an obvious priority. Another is to fit within the apparatus within which these sales take place. As health-care institutions in the USA and the UK move towards prioritizing financial

[67] BBC News, 'Dobson "Must Accept NHS Rationing" '.

[68] BBC News, 'Doctors Say How Long We Should Wait', http://news.bbc.co.uk/hi/english/health/newsid_178000/178334.stm (consulted 11 May 1999).

[69] *Ibid.*   [70] *Ibid.*

[71] BBC News, 'UK Moves Towards National Policy on NHS Drugs', http://194.130.56.40/hi/english/specia...t/1998/viagra/newsid_171000/171750.stm (consulted 4 July 1999).

efficiency in health-care in environments resembling HMOs (Health Management Organizations), pharmaceutical companies are being forced to justify the costs of their drugs. These are increasingly being promoted as the most cost-effective component within the health-care budget: while pharmaceuticals account for 7 per cent of health-care spending in the USA, they allegedly keep patients from draining the other 93 per cent spent on hospitals, doctors' surgeries, and so forth.[72] As managed care becomes a more popular health-care option, its share of the retail pharmaceutical market grows: from a 30 per cent share in the USA in 1990 to an estimated 90 per cent by the millennium. This growth puts pressure on pharmaceutical companies, in that managed care providers typically insist upon using low-cost generic drugs wherever possible. Hence there is a great incentive for maximizing brand recognition and use of new drugs before their patent protection expires (typically, in eight to ten years) and generic drugs deplete their profitability by up to 90 per cent.

Pharmaceutical companies are subject to other pressures. Research and development costs have risen exponentially, while only one in 5,000 compounds discovered ever reaches the pharmacy shelves, and fewer than one third of these achieve enough commercial success to cover research costs. Developing a new drug takes from ten to fifteen years and costs more than US$500,000,000. Predictions for the market share of prescribed drugs of generic drugs are that this will rise from 22 per cent in 1985 and 42 per cent in 1996 to nearly 75 per cent by 2000. Strategies adopted by pharmaceutical companies are to promote specific drugs in the mass media direct to consumer advertising to maximize brand recognition and to convert branded products from ethical to over-the-counter status.[73] While there is still demand for new pharmaceuticals, fuelled by advances in disease prediction and prevention, demographic changes, niche market products, and borderline lifestyle drugs such as cosmeceuticals, the requisite new technologies involved in genomics, combinatorial chemistry, and high throughput screening are costly, and satisfactory returns on investment are decreasing in likelihood. A strategy recommended here has been that pharmaceutical companies increase their lead time and adopt the IT industry procedure of conducting phase III trials, or the smaller refinements, post launch.[74]

Thus, while Pfizer must promote Viagra's respectability as a drug developed to treat a recognized clinical need, it is in their interests that media

[72] A. Zisson and R. J. Olan, 'Emerging Pharmaceutical Industry Overview', http://www.hamquist.com/research/exerpts/pharma_961218.html (consulted 24 June 1999).

[73] Orion, 'Pharmaceutical Industry', http://orion.neiu.edu/lagkanali/ACTG450/ Pharma.html (consulted 24 June 1999).

[74] S. Arlington and S. Hughes, 'The Pharmaceutical Industry 2005: A Window on the Future', http://www.pwc.co.za/gx/eng/about/ind/pharm/phissue_2005.html (consulted 24 June 1999).

360   *H. Biggs and R. Mackenzie*

publicity enable as much brand recognition as possible, in order to maximize lead time before generic versions swallow up the market. It is also sensible for them to define the recognized clinical need as widely as possible, and to expect further refinements to be made once Viagra I has established a market: hence Lady Viagra and the discovery of female sexual dysfunction.[75] Son of Viagra will no doubt address the needs of men and women who do not suffer from sexual dysfunction but wish to enhance their sexual enjoyment: evidence suggests that clubbers are treating Viagra in this light with undoubted success.[76] While Pfizer presented expert medical evidence in their High Court action that Viagra I was not an aphrodisiac and could not enhance a man's libido if he did not suffer from erectile dysfunction, they did not produce the results of clinical trials as evidence of this.[77] Since Viagra I's effect on the penis was discovered during clinical trials which were being carried out for conditions other than erectile dysfunction, when the subjects reportedly refused to give back the surplus pills, the High Court portrayal of Viagra I may well not represent the truth, the whole truth, and nothing but the truth. Pfizer's opposition to mail shots to pensioners[78] and to sales of Viagra on the internet, as well as to impotence 'cures' which may be seen as attempting to pass off, such as Vigorex, Vaegra, and Viagro, may thus be interpreted as protecting future markets.[79] The media hype over Viagra, along with the omnipresent Viagra jokes, serve to embed Son of Viagra in the not too distant future, as Viagra I passes to generic or over-the-counter status.

Conclusion

How much audience participation in this theatre of Viagra should we, the health-care consumers, want or need? The informed public debate wherein our opinions might contribute towards transparent rationing procedures open to public scrutiny would be of undoubted value. However, Frank Dobson's so-called public consultation exercise, which resulted in guidelines which still exclude 83 per cent of those suffering from erectile dysfunction upon grounds which cannot be justified, in terms of either efficiency or clinical need, does not augur well here. Condemned as 'arbitrary' by the BMA, 'still unfair, discriminatory and arbitrary' by Pfizer, and as

[75] BBC News, 'Women Can Benefit From Viagra' http://news.bbc.co.uk/hi/english/health/newsid_334000/334636.stm (consulted 11 May 1999).
[76] BBC News, 'Clubbers Taking Viagra', http://194.130.56.40/hi/english/specia. . .t/1998/viagra/newsid_258000/258629.stm (consulted 4 July 1999).
[77] R. v. *Secretary of State for Health, ex parte Pfizer Ltd*, 26 May 1999 (QBD), draft transcript 12, see http://www.casetrack.co./ct/Casetrack.
[78] BBC News, 'Stop Viagra Mail Shots' http://194.130.56.40/hi/english/specia. . .t/1998/viagra/newsid_281000/281521.stm (consulted 4 July 1999).
[79] BBC News, 'Drug Wars Over Potency Pill', http://news.bbc.co.uk/hi/english/speci. . .t/1998/viagra/newsid_167000/167249.stm (consulted 11 May 1999).

'discriminatory and restrictive' by the Impotence Association, the guidelines fail to take into account the group which is most affected by impotence, those suffering from cardiovascular problems, who are among the poorest in Britain.[80] At present this approach to resource allocation and the choice versus need dichotomy inevitably mean that 'the criteria for NHS provision is now perceived as unfair and unprincipled'.[81] Without procedures which ensure informed public input into future decision-making, salient issues such as the prevalence of iatrogenic erectile dysfunction are glossed over rather than confronted. When eight out of ten of the most frequently prescribed drugs induce erectile dysfunction, i.e. those which treat blood pressure, depression, high cholesterol, and stomach acid, it is surely unconscionable to suggest that men suffering in this way, along with their partners, may be seen as undeserving or as without a recognizable clinical need.[82]

Who, then, is to define what constitutes a recognizable clinical need which deserves NHS-funded treatment? A summary of the theatrical performance of Viagra would certainly include ithyphalloi, but the most comic aspect might well be the politicians and the professionals tossing about the hot potato of accountability. Politicians do not wish to lose votes, and the doctors do not wish to lose the respect and trust of their patients. Transparent health-care rationing principles and procedures open to public scrutiny put both at risk.

---

[80] BBC News, 'Keep On Prescribing Viagra, Doctors Told', http://news.bbc.co.uk/hi/english/speci. . .t/1998/viagra/newsid_337000/337930.stm (consulted 11 May 1999).

[81] N. Whitty, ' "In a Perfect World": Feminism and Health Care Resource Allocation' in S. Sheldon and M. Thomson (eds.), *Feminist Perspectives on Health Care Law* (London, 1998), 137.

[82] J. Donovan and T. Koppel, 'Viagra: a New Sexual Revolution?', http://virilitysolution.com/nightline.html (consulted 1 July 1999).

THE POLITICS OF PATERNITY: FOETAL RISKS AND REPRODUCTIVE HARM

Cynthia Daniels and Janet Golden

When men drink, women and children suffer, explained nineteenth-century temperance advocate J. H. Beadle in 1874:

From half a million women a wail of anguish is wafted over an otherwise happy land; and over the graves of forty thousand drunkards, annually, goes up the mourning cry of the widow and the orphan. The chief evils of the traffic in ardent spirits have fallen on women . . .[1]

In the nineteenth century, science, policy, and law combined to make the subject of male-mediated harm one of intense public interest and, ultimately, of political action. Concerns about men's drinking focused not just on the social harm done to their families (and the nation's economy) by alcohol consumption, but on the foetal damage wrought by deformed male germ cells. Such concerns animated a politically powerful temperance movement. After efforts to secure voluntary abstinence failed, American temperance advocates turned from blaming the drinker to blaming the drink. They secured state and municipal prohibition measures and ultimately triumphed with the passage in 1919 of the Eighteenth Amendment to the United States Constitution outlawing the manufacture, sale, or transportation of intoxicating liquors. This effort proved to be a brief experiment in what the Women's Christian Temperance Union called 'home protection'—an effort to restore moral order and defend society from a menace that, as one historian termed it, 'ruined lives, destroyed families, caused diseases, created poverty and robbed the economy of productive work'.[2]

---

[1] J. H. Beadle, *The Woman's War on Whiskey: Its History, Theory, and Prospects* (Cincinnati, Ohio, 1874), 9, cited in B. L. Epstein, *The Politics of Domesticity: Women, Evangelism, and Temperance in Nineteenth Century America* (Middletown, Conn., 1981), 101.

[2] G. D. Moss, *America in the Twentieth Century* (3rd edn, Saddle River, NJ, 1997), 58. In this particular instance, however, the victory was short-lived—in part because the loss of liquor taxes had the effect of raising the tax rates of the well-to-do, and in part because the broad sweep of prohibition had the effect of turning large numbers of citizens into outlaws. Nevertheless, before its repeal in 1933, prohibition did result in lowering drinking rates in a

Now at the end of the twentieth century in the United States, concern about the destruction wrought by alcohol on offspring is almost exclusively focused on the behaviour of pregnant women. While lacking the political power to generate an amendment to the United States Constitution, the tenor and pitch of the movement to protect foetuses from maternal harm is as intense as that of the earlier temperance movement. 'Home protection' has been recast as an effort to protect foetuses, first by warning women against misbehaviour in pregnancy and then by threatening those who disobey with imprisonment. Every American who purchases a bottled alcoholic beverage reads an official government label warning that 'according to the Surgeon General women should not drink alcoholic beverages during pregnancy because of the risk of birth defects'.[3] Several states and municipalities mandate additional warnings in establishments dispensing alcoholic beverages.[4] More importantly, state prosecutors have arrested and sanctioned pregnant women who drink alcohol for a variety of criminal offences, such as 'endangering the life of the fetus', or even the 'attempted murder of a foetus', through alcohol consumption.[5]

Targeting has also expanded to include drug use by pregnant women, with the most extreme conservative advocates arguing that a 'bio-underclass' of drug-addicted pregnant women should be confined to 'colonies' throughout their pregnancies.[6] Law enforcement officials, meanwhile, have succeeded in using local laws in order to arrest and imprison women

large portion of the country. After repeal, another cultural shift occurred and alcohol abuse was again reframed. The locus of concern shifted back, from the drink to the drinker. 'Inebriates' became 'alcoholics'—a label that suggested they suffered from a disease rather than from moral weakness—although the condition was never completely destigmatized.

[3] The complete warning reads: 'GOVERNMENT WARNING: (1) ACCORDING TO THE SURGEON GENERAL WOMEN SHOULD NOT DRINK ALCOHOLIC BEVERAGES DURING PREGNANCY BECAUSE OF THE RISK OF BIRTH DEFECTS. (2) CONSUMPTION OF ALCOHOLIC BEVERAGES IMPAIRS YOUR ABILITY TO DRIVE A CAR OR OPERATE MACHINERY AND MAY CAUSE HEALTH PROBLEMS'.

[4] In 1983 New York City enacted the first municipal law mandating the following sign be posted in establishments selling alcohol: 'Warning: Drinking alcoholic beverages during pregnancy can cause birth defects': Michael Goodwin, 'Council Bill Warns on Drinking During Pregnancy', New York Times 16 Nov. 1983.

[5] The most prominent alcohol-related arrests include the cases of Rosemarie Tourigny in New Hampshire (in 1996) and Deborah J. Zimmerman in Racine, Wisconsin (1996). Details of cases can be documented through the Center for Reproductive Law and Policy, New York City, New York. See also news stories in: Doreen Vigue, 'Pregnant Woman Booked for Drinking', Boston Globe, 15 Aug. 1996, B1; Anne Marie O'Neill, L. Eskin, and L. Satter, 'Under the Influence' People, 9 Sept. 1996, 53–5.

[6] In a 1989 article in the Washington Post conservative writer Charles Krauthammer described the menace of the 'bio-underclass, a generation of physically damaged cocaine babies whose biological inferiority is stamped at birth'. Writing during the peak of a moral panic over crack cocaine, Krauthammer proposed the creation of colonies for substance-abusing mothers: '[w]e can either do nothing, or we can pass laws saying that any pregnant woman who takes cocaine during pregnancy will be sent until delivery to some not uncomfortable, secure location (boot camp, county jail, house arrest—the details are a purely technical matter) where she will be allowed everything except the liberty to leave or to take drugs': Charles Krauthammer, 'Children of Cocaine,' Washington Post, 20 July 1989.

who abuse drugs while pregnant. More profoundly, an emerging national discourse has defined substance abuse by pregnant women, particularly women of colour, as a grave social threat.[7] Where once men stood at the heart of the social, political and medical storm, pregnant women are now caught in the maelström of social concern over foetal harm. Men have, as a result, been rendered virtually invisible as either victims or vectors of harm.

This paper highlights the paradigms of gender, medicine, and law that served first to expose and then to obscure the link between paternal behaviour and foetal harm. In asking about men we are not attempting to refute the serious problem of foetal alcohol syndrome (FAS) and issues of female-mediated harm; rather, we are asking how harm produced by and through men has historically shifted from the visible to the invisible. Taking the issue of alcohol and offspring as a starting point, we ask several questions. How is it that the idea of risk, as linked to alcohol consumption, shifted from a nineteenth-century crusade to control the behaviour of men to a twentieth-century crusade to control the behaviour of pregnant women? What happened to the fears that men were drinking up the family wage and, if drunk during the act of conception, were begetting children who, it had been believed since ancient times, were 'dull, stupid or diseased'?[8] Why was medical evidence about the effects of maternal alcohol abuse on foetal development ignored for much of the nineteenth and twentieth centuries? Why has medical evidence about the effects of paternal alcohol abuse on sperm been ignored for much of the late twentieth century?

The answers, we assert, reside in the gendered assumptions which help to construct paradigms of vulnerability and risk in medicine and law. They lie, as well, in the politics of ethnicity, race and national identity—in nineteenth-century temperance campaigns to control the 'undisciplined' behaviour of immigrant men and in twentieth-century campaigns to curb the reproductive behaviour, primarily, of Native American and African American women.

Science, Temperance, and the Politics of Paternity

The parallels between the nineteenth-century crusade against male drinking

---

[7] For a recent discussion about jailing women who abuse drugs in pregnancy see Abagail Trafford, 'Should Women Who Use Drugs While Pregnant Be Locked Up?' Washington Post, 18 Aug. 1998. The reasons such laws have not been enacted are discussed in L. E. Gomez, Misconceiving Mothers: Legislators, Prosecutors, and the Politics of Prenatal Drug Exposure (Philadelphia, Penn., 1997). For an analysis of the crack panic and the role of medicine, the media, and the criminal justice system in stigmatizing pregnant addicts see D. Humphries, Crack Mothers: Pregnancy, Drugs and the Media (Columbus, Ohio, 1999).

[8] J. B. DeLee, Principles and Practice of Obstetrics (2nd edn., rev Philadelphia, Penn., 1915), 228–9. In discussing the effects of alcohol DeLee cites the ancient Diogenes on its effects on men who conceived while drunk.

and the twentieth-century campaign against female substance abuse exist not in the specific catalogue of foetal harms disclosed in each era, but in the ways in which medical science served and was used by those who sought to control the drinking behaviour of each group. As the nineteenth-century drive to control male inebriety shifted from moral persuasion and male-led efforts to a campaign by female moral reformers to compel abstinence, growing numbers of physicians added fuel to the temperance fires. In the name of 'scientific temperance' they examined the pathology of inebriety, including its effects on offspring. In the late nineteenth century Auguste-Henri Forel, a leading Swiss psychiatrist and influential temperance advocate, claimed that 'from about one-half to three-quarters of the idiots and epileptics can be shown to spring from alcoholic parents or at least fathers'.[9]

The science of habitual drunkenness (as alcoholism was termed in the nineteenth century) crossed national boundaries and disciplinary domains.[10] In addition to cataloguing the effects of alcohol on the mind and body of the drinker, scientists endeavoured to explain the hereditary effects of alcohol and located three types. First, there were cases in which the 'morbid taste for alcohol' passed from parent to child. Secondly, there were cases in which the physical or mental deterioration of the parent was passed along as a congenital anomaly in the child, resulting in reduced vitality and degeneration—ranging from criminality to feeble-mindedness to insanity. Finally, there were cases in which the intoxication of the parent at the time of conception resulted in a child who exhibited poor health.[11] Degeneration posed the greatest threat. Its leading proponent, French psychiatrist Benedict Auguste Morel argued in his classic and influential work *Traité des Dégénérescences Physiques, Intellectuelles et Moral de L'Espèce Humaine* that physical, moral, and intellectual degeneration resulted from hereditary weakness and ultimately threatened social vitality.[12] Morel and other nineteenth-century social theorists conflated the effects of maternal and paternal drinking and reviewed scientific literature of various types that purported to show how alcohol damaged 'germ cells'. Yet, since drinking was largely perceived as a male

---

[9] A. Forel, *Hygiene of Nerves and Mind in Health and Disease* (H. A. Aikins (trans.), 2nd German edn., New York, 1907) 192, 211. See also August Forel, 'The Effect of Alcoholic Intoxication Upon the Human Brain and Its Relation to Theories of Heredity and Evolution' (1893) 12 *Quarterly Journal of Inebriety* 203–21. For a later example of how experts focused on parental or paternal effects despite reviewing data that discussed the effects of drinking during pregnancy see G. P. Frets, *Alcohol and Other Germ Poisons* (The Hague, 1931).

[10] William F. Bynum, 'Chronic Alcoholism in the First Half of the 19th Century' (1986) 42 *Bulletin of the History of Medicine* 160–85.

[11] William F. Bynum, 'Alcoholism and Degeneration in 19th Century European Medicine and Psychiatry' (1984) 79 *British Journal of Addiction* 59–70.

[12] B. A. Morel, *Traité des Dégénérescences Physiques, Intellectuelles et Morales de l'Espèce Humaine* (Paris, 1857), 114.

vice, most of the examples offered were of the degenerate offspring of male drunkards and it was male drinking that aroused the ire of temperance-minded physicians.

The concern with male drinking that drove the nineteenth- and early twentieth-century temperance movement cast a shadow over evidence demonstrating that maternal drinking during pregnancy caused foetal harm. In the late nineteenth century, William C. Sullivan, a Deputy Medical Officer of Parkhurst Prison, confirmed through a series of elegant studies that maternal alcoholism was, in his words, 'an agent of race degeneracy'. The offspring of female inebriates confined in Liverpool prison, he showed, had significantly higher mortality and morbidity rates than the children born to their sober sisters. Furthermore, when female inebriates were forced into sobriety by imprisonment, the children they bore were healthier than those delivered during the periods when they could drink freely.[13] With this evidence in hand, Sullivan wrote his defining work, *Alcoholism: A Chapter in Social Pathology*, in 1906. In it, he argued against parental rather than maternal inebriety, and elsewhere he crusaded against industrial drunkenness and the late opening of public houses—where men congregated to drink.[14] In sum, the compelling evidence about the effects of maternal drinking was diluted—watered down by being part of a larger tract about the evils of drink. The drumbeat of protest against the drinking of urban, working-class men harmonized with scientific research on the problems of paternal or parental alcohol abuse, but as a result it muffled the findings regarding the negative effects of maternal drinking.

By the twentieth century, the unquestioned leader of the medical temperance crusade was Thomas Davison Crothers (1842–1918) editor of the *Journal of Inebriety*, leader within the American Medical Association, and author of numerous articles on alcohol and health and of *Inebriety: A Clinical Treatise on the Etiology, Symptomology, Neurosis, Psychosis and Treatment and the Medico-Legal Relations*. Like medical men before him, Crothers attempted to shift inebriety from its stigmatized status as a 'voluntary vice and moral evil' to a disease, and thus he catalogued its many physiological and psychological sequelae. In reviewing the influence of heredity on inebriety, he concentrated for the most part on parental (rather than maternal) influences. In one example he described five children born to an inebriate father and a temperate mother. All were feeble in childhood and only two achieved sobriety in adulthood. Citing numerous nineteenth-century scientists who discoursed on the inheritance of acquired characteristics, Crothers charted the lines of descent that led generations

---

[13] W. C. Sullivan, 'A Note on the Influence of Maternal Inebriety on the Offspring' (1899) 45 *Journal of Mental Science* 489–503.

[14] W. C. Sullivan, *Alcoholism: A Chapter in Social Pathology* (London, 1906) and W. C. Sullivan, 'Industry and Alcoholism,' (1906) 52 *Journal of Mental Science* 505–14.

spiralling downward into extinction, unless their path was interrupted by intermarriage with those of more vigorous, temperate stock.

In the ensuing decades, biologists tested this claim by examining the progeny of alcoholized laboratory animals. As historian Philip J. Pauly has eloquently described, their efforts resulted in a consensus that the question of the effects of alcohol on reproduction was 'scientifically uninteresting'. Veering from claims that alcohol harmed offspring to claims that it offered a eugenic benefit by eliminating the unfit, those who argued that alcohol had an effect on reproduction were ultimately checkmated by a scientist who 'proved' it had no effect whatsoever.[15]

While bench scientists gave up on alcohol research, eugenicists continued to label alcohol a beneficial agent. It attacked the germ cell, they claimed, and eliminated the weak before birth, led them to produce fewer children, or simply took them out of the breeding pool because of their early deaths.[16] As late as 1935, college students would learn from the *Applied Eugenics* text by Paul Popenoe and Roswell Hill Johnson that '[t]hose who "drink themselves to death," therefore, represent persons with weak nervous systems, and alcohol represents a powerful agent of natural selection'. Rejecting the obvious implications, which might call for taverns on every corner or the provision of alcohol to youths, the authors were quick to note there were better 'discriminating, socially controlled measures' at hand that caused fewer social and economic losses.[17]

As arguments supporting the inheritance of acquired characteristics lost scientific credence, as biological findings about alcohol having no effect on reproduction became widely accepted and as Prohibition dampened research in alcohol science, the problem of the effects on offspring of male (and female) drinking evaporated. By the second half of the twentieth century alcohol scientists declared that any data purporting to show that alcohol damaged offspring were simply biased and wrong—an artifact of a failed political crusade. Thus, in their classic work, *Alcohol Explored*, Yale researchers Howard M. Haggard and E. M. Jellinek—the leaders of the modern alcoholism movement—termed the belief in alcoholic inebriety 'entirely obsolete' and the notion that alcohol harmed germ cells lacking in 'acceptable evidence'.[18] And, when a Yale researcher later studied the offspring of alcoholic parents reared in foster homes and found they had

---

[15] Philip J. Pauly, 'How Did the Effects of Alcohol on Reproduction Become Scientifically Uninteresting?' (1996) 29 *Journal of the History of Biology* 1–29.

[16] M. A. Aldrich *et al., Eugenics: Twelve University Lectures* (New York, 1914).

[17] P. Popenoe and R. H. Johnson, *Applied Eugenics* (rev edn., New York, 1935), 28–9. See also Bartlett C. Jones, 'Prohibition and Eugenics, 1920–1933' (1963) 18 *Journal of the History of Medicine* 158–172. Jones notes, as does Pauly, that anti-prohibitionists pointed out the eugenic benefits of alcohol as it improved the race by eliminating the unfit, this compelled those who supported temperance to argue that alcohol had no effect on offspring.

[18] H. W. Haggard and E. M. Jellinek, *Alcohol Explored* (Garden City, NJ, 1942) 145, 207.

lower intelligence than the controls, she quickly explained this as 'not caused by the alcoholism of the parents'.[19] This new scientific orthodoxy would blind a generation of researchers, much as the old orthodoxy had done.

The paradigm of non-effect would remain dominant until the 'discovery' of FAS—a pattern of birth defects—in 1973. FAS is caused by heavy maternal alcohol use in pregnancy and is characterized by a spectrum of physical and behavioural defects; it is the most common cause of mental retardation in the United States.[20] William Sullivan saw and described what later researchers would term FAS in 1899. He discussed the 'toxic influence' of alcohol on the developing embryo, noting how female inebriets gave birth to children who, 'if they survive' were 'a burden or a danger to society'.[21] But only in the late twentieth century, when researchers rediscovered Sullivan's work, would they understand its full import.

Female Mediated Harm: From Foetal Alcohol Syndrome to Crack Babies

What made FAS visible in the late twentieth century? Several things. Heightened public awareness of the vulnerability of the foetus in the wake of the thalidomide disaster of the 1960s and a subsequent rubella epidemic made it easier to grasp the argument that alcohol could inflict damage on an unborn child. The feminist demand for greater attention to issues of women's health and reproduction helped make both pregnancy and female alcoholism subjects of growing concern. Finally, the legalization of abortion made it easy to conceptualize FAS as a medical problem with a medical solution, while also stimulating a very public debate over the rights of pregnant women and of foetuses. Together, these elements made the politics of pregnancy and alcohol use a high-profile subject (until the politics of pregnancy and crack overshadowed it), while casting a shadow over the science and politics of paternal/foetal harm.

A moral panic over 'crack babies' followed close on the heels of the 'discovery' of FAS. In 1988 Ira Chasnoff, director of the newly-formed National Association for Perinatal Addiction Research and Education (NAPARE), released a report stating that 375,000 babies were born every year 'exposed to illicit drugs in the womb'.[22] The press immediately reported and exaggerated these findings, broadcasting claims that

---

[19] Anne Roe, 'Children of Alcoholic Parents Raised in Foster Homes' [1945] *Quarterly Journal of Studies on Alcohol* 115–27.
[20] W. M. Barron, M. D. Lindheimer, and J. M. Davison (eds.), *Medical Disorders During Pregnancy* (2nd edn., St. Louis, Miss., 1995), 467.
[21] Sullivan, n. 13, above, 498–9.
[22] Ira Chasnoff, 'Drug Use and Women: Establishing a Standard of Care' (1989) 562 *Annals of the New York Academy of Science* 208–10.

one out of every ten children were born 'addicted to crack cocaine' or damaged by women's use of drugs. By 1993, nine influential daily newspapers had run more than 197 stories on pregnancy and cocaine addiction alone.[23]

Chasnoff's study suffered from fundamental flaws—none of which were reported by the press. The sample surveyed public inner-city hospitals and made no distinction between a single use of illegal drugs and chronic drug addiction during pregnancy. Neither did the study document the actual effects of drug use on newborn infants. Nevertheless, the alarm created by the media coverage encouraged physicians, nurses, social workers, and teachers to attribute a wide range of problems experienced by infants at birth to the use of drugs or alcohol by the child's birth mother, particularly in low-income, inner-city neighbourhoods.[24]

The sense of social distress created by media images of babies wired to tubes in hospital incubators stimulated efforts criminally to prosecute pregnant women suspected of drug and alcohol abuse. While only one state has successfully enacted a law criminalizing prenatal conduct, prosecutors have used existing statutes to charge women with prenatal neglect or abuse of children. At least 200 women have been criminally prosecuted for suspected drug use during pregnancy, although almost all of these cases have been overturned on appeal. However, in 1998, the South Carolina Supreme Court upheld the prosecution of a woman for child abuse—for smoking cocaine during pregnancy—and forced her to serve her sentence of five years' imprisonment.[25]

Public campaigns to stem the tide of crack babies have been clearly racialized, primarily targeting women of colour in low-income neighbourhoods. In similar fashion, FAS has been racialized as a 'Native American problem'. Scientific research has supported the racialization of the pregnancy and substance abuse debate by focusing research heavily on poor communities and on substances used most often by low-income women. Simultaneously, public health warnings have targeted racial minorities. The subject of pregnancy and addiction thus tapped into broader political concerns and effectively argued that low income, minority women were abandoning their commitment to 'selfless motherhood'. In this cultural context, particular kinds of scientific research and political action gained public credibility, funding, and support while research on men went unnoticed or undone.

---

[23] C. R. Daniels, *At Women's Expense: State Power and the Politics of Foetal Rights* (Cambridge, Mass., 1993).

[24] Daniels, n. 23, above, ch. 4.

[25] Over a dozen states have attempted to pass laws allowing for civil detention of women suspected of abusing drugs or alcohol during pregnancy, although most of these legislative efforts have failed. A newly enacted law in Wisconsin is the first successful effort.

Rediscovering Male-mediated Harm

For nearly fifty years, research on men disappeared into the scientific backwaters. Assumptions that male alcohol consumption was benign and that earlier research on paternal harm was politically tainted erased both social and scientific concerns about paternal/foetal risks.[26] Gone were arguments advanced by prohibitionists that 'the germ plasm itself—that vital spark which continues on thru [sic] countless centuries—is so affected by alcohol that the children for generations to come suffer from the sins of the fathers'.[27]

A number of social and political events in the 1970s and 1980s triggered renewed concern over the potential connections between fathers and foetal harm. In the early 1970s, Vietnam veterans returning from the war who fathered children with birth defects and childhood diseases suspected war-time exposure to Agent Orange (TCDD/Dioxin) as the cause. In 1977, men exposed to Dibromochloropropane (DBCP) in a chemical plant in California noticed a pattern of sterility and high rates of miscarriages among their wives. National media accounts of such clusters began to spur new research into damage to male reproduction wrought by chemical exposure and to stimulate new studies of the transmission of harm to children fathered by exposed men.[28] Further alarms were raised when, in 1979, a study in Florida documented a 40 per cent overall drop in sperm counts over the previous fifty years.[29]

In the 1980s, it was once again men's wartime exposure that focused attention on the connection between fathers and foetal harm. Soldiers returning from the Gulf War complained not only of strange ailments (dubbed 'Gulf War Syndrome' in the press) but also reported fathering babies with unexplained health defects including rare blood disorders, underdeveloped lungs, missing or fused fingers, and club feet. Also reported were deaths of children from rare disorders, among them liver cancer, heart defects, and lack of a spleen.

Until such public events forced a rethinking of biological damage and processes of conception, most of the scientific community assumed that defective sperm were not capable of fertilizing eggs. Framed by a conceptual

---

[26] For a more complete discussion of the science and politics of male reproductive hazards see Cynthia R. Daniels, 'Between Fathers and Fetuses: The Social Construction of Male Reproduction and the Politics of Fetal Harm' (1997) 22(3) *Signs* 579–616.

[27] Quoted from a US National Educational Association poster, in Brian S. Katcher, 'The Post-Repeal Eclipse in Knowledge About the Harmful effects of Alcohol' (1993) 88 *Addiction* 729–44.

[28] Christine F. Colie, 'Male Mediated Teratogenesis' (1993) 7 *Reproductive Toxicology* 6.

[29] Elisabeth Carlsen, Aleksander Giwercman, Miels Keiding, and Miels E. Skakkebaek, 'Evidence for Decreasing Quality of Semen during Past Fifty Years' (1992) 305 *British Medical Journal* 609–12. Subsequent studies also reported declines and noted an association between increases in testicular cancer in key countries and substantial sperm count declines.

dichotomy between virile and vulnerable sperm, men were assumed to be either immune from toxicity or rendered completely infertile by their particular vulnerability to risk. Yet anecdotal associations between paternal exposures and child health problems suggested just the opposite— throwing into question the validity of the 'all or nothing' theory. Researchers soon found proof that this thinking was flawed, and began to consider the possibility that sperm might be even more susceptible to toxins than eggs because cells that are continuously dividing, like sperm, are more vulnerable to toxins than cells that are fully developed and at rest, like eggs.

During the 1980s and 1990s, suspected associations generated scores of new studies on paternal transmission of foetal harm. Research has since suggested that male reproductive exposures are linked not only to fertility problems but also to miscarriages, low birth weight, congenital abnormalities, cancer, neurological problems, and other childhood health problems.[30] Dozens of studies have analysed the effects of various occupational exposures. Toluene, xylene, benzene, TCE, vinyl chloride, lead, and mercury have all been associated with childhood leukaemia and childhood brain tumours.[31] Analyses have been done both on exposures to specific substances and of the correlations between specific occupations and foetal health problems.[32] Painters and workers exposed to hydrocarbons, for example, have been shown to have higher rates of children with childhood leukaemia and brain cancer.[33]

Studies addressing occupational and environmental exposures suffer from a number of methodological problems. It is difficult to specify the nature and duration of men's exposures to toxic substances, particularly at work or in war. It is difficult also to get a sample size large enough to yield conclusive results, especially when the outcome measure is a rare childhood condition. Finally, as with all epidemiological studies, it is difficult to control for confounding factors, such as the effects of multiple chemical exposures and alcohol and drug use.

There is a critical distinction between the pattern of research on female-mediated foetal harm and that for male-mediated harm. Research on men is focused almost exclusively on what might be termed 'unintentional'

---

[30] D. L. Davis, Debra Lee, Gladys Fiedler, Donald Madison, and Robert Morris, 'Male–Mediated Teratogenesis and Other Reproductive Effects: Biological and Epidemiologic Findings and a Plea For Clinical Research' (1992) 6 *Reproductive Toxicology* 289–92; Andrew F. Olshan and Elaine M. Faustman, 'Male-Mediated Developmental Toxicity' (1993) 7 *Reproductive Toxicology* 191–202; Christine F. Colie, 'Male Mediated Teratogenesis'(1993) 7 *Reproductive Toxicology* 3–9.

[31] Olshan and Faustman, n. 30, above, 196.

[32] More than 30 studies have examined the relationship between paternal occupation and childhood cancer. See D. Savitz and J. Chen, 'Parental Occupation and Childhood Cancer: Review of Epidemiological Studies' (1990) 88 *Environmental Health Perspectives* 325–37.

[33] See Savitz and Chen, n. 32, above, and Olshan and Faustman, n. 30, above.

occupational and environmental exposures, while research on women has focused on 'voluntary' exposures to drugs, alcohol, and cigarettes. The connections between these 'lifestyle' behaviours in men and their effects on offspring have been surprisingly under-investigated. Yet, as early as the 1970s animal studies on illicit drugs found birth defects and behavioural abnormalities linked to opiate exposure.[34]

Recently, male-mediated harm linked to illicit drug use and smoking has received more scientific attention. The findings suggest that men using hashish, opium, heroin, and cocaine can have resulting structural defects in their sperm.[35] In a 1991 clinical study, Ricardo Yazigi, Randall Odem, and Kenneth Polakoski found that cocaine could bind to or 'piggyback' on sperm and be directly transmitted to the egg during fertilization—although controversy persists over the potential effects of such transmission.[36] Similarly, researchers have found associations between paternal smoking and various birth defects, including cleft lip, cleft palate, and hydrocephalus.[37] Significant associations have also been shown for paternal smoking and low birth weight.[38] Additionally, laboratory stories have shown that cotinine, a metabolite of nicotine, has been found in seminal fluid, although researchers are uncertain about any possible effect on foetal health.[39]

Echoing nineteenth-century concerns about the damaging effects of alcohol, modern researchers have begun to document associations between drinking and reproductive health. Research has long shown that excessive alcohol consumption can cause sterility in men and that chronic alcoholism can reduce sperm motility and increase morphological abnormalities in sperm. Indeed, the concentration of alcohol in sperm is almost identical to that in blood. The epidemiology of alcohol abuse is critical to

---

[34] See Gladys Fiedler, 'Effects of Limited Paternal Exposure to Xenobiotic Agents on the Development of Progeny' (1985) 7 *Neurobehavioural Toxicology and Teratology* 739–43 and Gladys Fiedler and Howard S. Wheeling, 'Behavioural Effects in Offspring of Male Mice Injected with Opioids Prior to Mating' in *Protracted Effects of Perinatal Drug Dependence* Vol. II, Pharmacology, Biochemistry and Behaviour (Fayetteville, NY, 1979).

[35] Zenab El-Gothamy and May El-Samahy, 'Ultrastructure Sperm Defects in Addicts' (1992) 57 *Fertility and Sterility* 699–702.

[36] M. B. Brachen, B. Eshenazi, K. Sachse, J. E. McSharry et al., 'Association of Cocaine Use with Sperm Concentration, Motility and Morphology' (1990) 53 *Fertility and Sterility* 315–22 and Ricardo A. Yazigi, Randall R. Odem, and Kenneth L. Polakoski, 'Demonstration of Specific Binding of Cocaine to Human Spermatozoa' (1991) 266 *Journal of the American Medical Association* 1956–9.

[37] D. Savitz, P. J. Schwingle, and M. A. Keels, 'Influence of Paternal Age, Smoking and Alcohol Consumption on Congenital Anomalies' (1991) 44 *Teratology* 429–40.

[38] Jun Zhang and Jennifer Ratcliffe 'Paternal Smoking and Birthweight in Shanghai' (1993) 83(2) *American Journal of Public Health* 207–10; Fernando D. Martinez, Anne L. Wright, Lynn M. Taussig, and the Group Health Medical Associates, 'The Effect of Paternal Smoking on the Birthweight of Newborns Whose Mothers Did Not Smoke' (1994) 84(9) *American Journal of Public Health* 1489–91.

[39] Davis *et al.*, n. 30, above, 290; Devra Lee Davis, 'Paternal Smoking and Foetal Health', (1991) 337 *Lancet* 123.

interpreting the ramifications of these findings. Men, as a class, are more than three times as likely as women to be heavy drinkers (defined as two or more drinks per day). Additionally, alcoholic women are highly likely to be married to alcoholic men, more so than alcoholic men are to be married to alcoholic women.[40] Given these patterns, it would seem that paternal alcohol use should be of major concern to those studying the potential foetal effects of alcohol.

Recent research conducted in the 1980s and 1990s underlines the need for attention to the problem of excessive paternal alcohol use and foetal harm. Studies have correlated paternal alcoholism with low birth weight and an increased risk of birth defects. Savitz and others found a twofold increase in risk of ventricular septal defect in the children of men who consumed more than five drinks per week, but the same study found that paternal alcohol consumption reduced the risk of other birth defects. Yet to be determined is whether alcohol offers some kind of protective effect, whether the conceptus carrying defects from male alcohol consumption might be at increased risk of foetal loss or whether other cofactors are at work.[41] Case reports suggest an association between paternal drinking and 'malformations and cognitive deficiencies' in children of alcoholic men, while animal studies have linked paternal alcohol exposure to behavioural abnormalities and higher foetal mortality. Other, confounding reports have found no adverse associations for animals exposed to alcohol. Clearly there is much research that needs to be undertaken and a number of methodological problems to be solved.[42]

Acknowledging the need for more and better research should not obscure the way in which gender has shaped the application of standards of scientific scrutiny. Studies on men are criticized for lack of control for maternal exposures; studies on women virtually never control for, or even acknowledge, the need to control for, paternal exposures. Studies of men's occupational and environmental exposures are criticized for rarely control-ling for men's use of drugs or alcohol and, likewise, studies of male 'lifestyle' factors are criticized for failing to control for workplace expo-sures. When women are the subjects, however, these critiques are often absent. Investigations of women's alcohol and drug use, for example, rarely control for women's occupational or environmental exposures, and are not criticized for this scientific lapse. Except for particular cases in

[40] Ernest L. Abel, 'Paternal Exposure to Alcohol' in T. B. Sonderegger, *Perinatal Substance Abuse* (Baltimore, Mld., 1992),132–60.

[41] Savitz, Schwingl, and Keels, n. 37, above.

[42] See Colie, n. 30 above; Theodore J. Cicero, Bruce Nock, Lynn H. O'Connor, Bryan N. Sewing, Michael L. Adams, and E. Robert Meyer, 'Acute Paternal Alcohol Exposure Impairs Fertility and Foetal Outcome' (1994) 55 *Life Sciences* 33–6; D. Savitz, Jun Zhang, Pamela Schwingl, and Esther M. John, 'Association of Paternal Alcohol Use With Gestational Age and Birth Weight' (1992) 46 *Teratology* 465–71.

which women are exposed to substances such as thalidomide which cause severe visible deformities and are clear markers for exposure, questions of causality are as complicated for women as they are for men. Nevertheless, in the late twentieth century, assumptions about the distance of men from foetal harm make the scientific findings more tentative in their conclusions and less powerful in terms of public discourse.

The Public Response

Public responses to findings of male-mediated reproductive harm contrast sharply with the response to evidence of maternal/foetal damage. Popular magazines, for example, often cast both sperm and men as victims of toxic exposures, even then it is men's voluntary use of alcohol or drugs that is being recounted. *Health* magazine ran a story in 1991 entitled 'Sperm Under Siege' with images of bottles of chemicals and alcohol pointed threateningly at a group of sperm circling around a centre target.[43] A story in *Parenting* magazine presented an image of a man and his sperm huddled under an umbrella as chemical bottles, beer cans, and martini glasses rained down upon them.[44] By conflating exposure to alcohol with exposure to chemicals the images suggested men were not responsible for the assaults on their sperm. Stories about women's exposure relied on entirely different images and language—many of them pointing the finger of blame exclusively at pregnant women.

Evidence of paternal–foetal harm has generated virtual silence from both public health authorities and the courts. In *Reproductive Toxicology* editor Anthony Scialli argued that the impulse to link paternal exposures with foetal effects is not based upon scientific findings but upon 'political correctness'—defined as the mistaken impulse to establish equality of risk (and fault) between men and women for foetal harm.[45] In making such an assertion Scialli is overlooking data published in this same journal and case reports, laboratory studies, animal experiments, and human epidemiological surveys that all throw into question his assertion.

Even researchers who accept the validity of the evidence regarding male-mediated foetal risks construct responses that demonstrate the prevailing role of gender ideology. Researcher Bruce Ames of the University of California found evidence that smoking depressed levels of Vitamin C and that men with low levels of the vitamin experienced twice the oxidation damage to DNA in their sperm. Rather than suggesting public health initiatives to inform men and get them to change their

[43] Anne Merewood, 'Sperm under Siege', *Health*, Apr. 1991, 53–76.
[44] Rosemary Black and Peter Moore, 'The Myth of the Macho Sperm' (1992) 6(7) *Parenting* 29–31.
[45] Anthony Scialli, 'Paternally Mediated Effects and Political Correctness' (1993) 7 *Reproductive Toxicology* 189–90.

behaviour or proposing the addition of warning labels on tobacco products—tactics that had been employed for female-mediated harms, Ames
recommended that the US government raise the standard for minimum
daily requirements for Vitamin C for all Americans to counteract the
reproductive effects of paternal smoking.[46] The reluctance to recommend
restrictions on men as a class can be seen in other areas of male reproduction. Controversy still exists, for instance, over whether men who are
undergoing chemotherapy should abstain from procreation during treatment.[47]

Conclusion

Clearly, it is the population targeted, not the nature of the risk, that determines both the public and the scientific response to evidence of foetal risk.
There has been no movement to post signs or print labels warning men of
the risk of testicular atrophy, increased rates of miscarriage, and the possibility of genetic damage that can arise from their consumption of alcohol.
Such warnings have been given to women alone. One might attribute the
lack of public health measures aimed at men to the limitations of pater-
nal/foetal research, but this is not a sufficient explanation. The rush to
judgement as regards the problems of 'crack babies' despite a lack of reliable scientific evidence, and the virtual silence which has greeted research
on men point to the role of gender in shaping this response.

Historically, cultural assumptions about maternity and paternity, feminin-
ity and masculinity, race, and gender have had a profound effect on both the
science and politics of foetal risk. New research on men and reproduction
makes it clear that paternal exposures can significantly influence men's
reproductive health and the health of the children they father. Anthony
Scialli, who so adamantly criticized research on paternally-mediated foetal

---

[46] Karen F. Schmidt, 'The Dark Legacy of Fatherhood' *US News and World Report*, 14
Dec. 1992, 92; Brett Wright, 'Smokers' Sperm Spell Trouble for Future Generations', *New
Scientist*, 6 Mar. 1993, 10.

[47] Cyclophosphamide, used during chemotherapeutic treatment, is a known female reproductive hazard, and rodent studies indicate it might cause miscarriage, birth defects, and
childhood tumours in the children conceived by men during treatment. Yet at the first major
medical meeting on male-mediated developmental toxins at the University of Pittsburgh in
1992, men were given 'conflicting advice' about whether to postpone procreation during
cancer treatment (or 'bank' sperm before treatment). In addition, in 1992 the journal *Human
Reproduction* published a recommendation stating that sperm saved in the early stages of
chemotherapy was safe 'based on the belief that since the drugs did not kill sperm ... the
sperm were healthy'. Yet others argued that sperm that survive therapy may be more likely to
carry genetic defects. One researcher simply recommended that men use condoms to protect
their partners during treatment. But other scientists at the conference were wary of 'confusing
the public with the results of animal studies that may not apply directly to humans'.
'Speculation tends to get us into trouble', stated Jan Friedman, a clinical geneticist and
specialist in birth defects. See Susan Katz Miller, 'Can Children Be Damaged by Fathers'
Cancer Therapy?' (1992) 135 *New Scientist* 5.

risks as politically motivated warned in another editorial (in defence of animal research on maternally-mediated risks) of the need to take seriously the early warning signs produced by animal studies: '[w]ithout taking away from the importance of surveillance of human populations . . . it would be preferable to perform a detailed evaluation in nonhuman systems than to wait until there are malformed children to be counted'.[48] Why then would it not be a perilous error to fail to heed the growing body of animal and epidemiological studies that demonstrate male-mediated risks?

Without asserting that male and female mediated risks are identical or even equal in weight, we can expect that each area of risk deserves investigation and an appropriate public health response. Current research acknowledges that because women carry the foetus to term, gestation provides avenues for the transmission of harm that are unlike men's. By the same token, men can inflict particular forms of harm on maternal and foetal health. Researchers have argued that drug or alcohol abuse can be a coping mechanism for dealing with the trauma of sexual abuse or rape.[49] Other researchers have described drug and alcohol use by pregnant women as an attempt to self-medicate the pain of physical or psychological abuse by husbands, fathers, or boyfriends.[50] Or male partners may simply encourage or pressure pregnant women into continuing their drug and alcohol abuse. Significantly, pregnant women are much more likely to be battered by their partners than non-pregnant women, and the physical abuse that occurs during pregnancy is often more frequent and more severe than that which occurs at other times and can result in high rates of adverse birth outcomes.[51] Male-mediated foetal harm, these data suggest, need not be measured only in laboratories, and is ignored only at great social risk.

In the nineteenth century, the temperance crusade was part of a larger cultural enterprise—an on-going effort to contain working-class, immigrant, urban, ethnic men and to enshrine in law and practice the bourgeois

---

[48] Anthony Scialli, 'Animal Studies and Human Risk' (1993) 7 *Reproductive Toxicology* 533–4.

[49] L. Nelson-Zlupco, E. Kaufman, and M. M. Dore, 'Gender Differences in Drug Addiction and Treatment: Implications for Social Work Intervention with Substance Abusing Women' (1995) 40 *Social Work* 45–54; M. O. Marcenko and M. Spence, 'Social and Psychological Correlates of Substance Abuse among Pregnant Women' (1995) 19 *Social Work Research* 103–9.

[50] Lynn Paltrow, *Criminal Prosecutions against Pregnant Women: National Update and Overview* (New York, 1992); Dorothy Roberts, 'Punishing Drug Addicts Who Have Babies: Women of Colour, Equality and the Right to Privacy' (1991) 104 *Harvard Law Review* 1419–82.

[51] Richard J. Gelles, 'Violence and Pregnancy: Are Pregnant Women at Greater Risk of Abuse?' (1988) 50 *Journal of Marriage and Family* 841–7; Judith McFarlane, Barbara Parker, Karen Soeken, and Linda Bullock, 'Assessing for Abuse During Pregnancy' (1992) 267(23) *Journal of the American Medical Association* 3176–8; Jean Reith Schroedel and Paul Peretz, 'A Gender Analysis of Policy Formation: The Case of Foetal Abuse' (1994) 19 *Journal of Health Politics, Policy and Law* 335–60.

values and behaviours that made industrial capitalism run smoothly and profitably. In the late twentieth century, concerns about social disorder now focus on the 'undisiciplined' reproductive behaviour of women, particularly women of colour, in the United States. The science and politics of foetal harm are, in part, driven by concerns about women's drift from 'proper motherhood'. Social and political conditions which cast women as the source of disruption make women more 'targetable' for blame than men. This shift from men in the nineteenth to women in the twentieth century is also racialized, with ethnic men the focus of many temperance advocates and women of colour the focus of foetal protectionism now.

In the twentieth, as in the nineteenth, century it is clear both literally and metaphorically that, 'when men drink, women and children suffer'. Yet until our gender blinkers are fully removed—blinkers which skewed law and medicine in the nineteenth century in the direction of blaming men and now in the twentieth century in the direction of blaming women—we will have no clear view of the roots of foetal harm.

Issues of Research

RESEARCH ON HUMAN SUBJECTS, EXPLOITATION, AND GLOBAL PRINCIPLES OF ETHICS

John Harris[*]

Introduction

In 1997 5.8 million people became infected with HIV, 30.6 million people are living with HIV/AIDS, and infection is running at about 16,000 new infections a day, of which more than 90 per cent are in low-income countries. If current transmission rates continue, there will be more than forty million people infected with HIV by the millennium.[1]

Against this background the urgency and importance of the fight against HIV/AIDS can scarcely be exaggerated. While a cure for AIDS remains elusive, research to discover more effective treatment and possible vaccines is vital. It is at this crucial moment that moral criticism has emerged of some of the most promising research towards treatments and vaccines for HIV/AIDS. This criticism has focused on, and purports to be justified by, the major current international principles and protocols on the ethics of research on human subjects. If this criticism is valid and no better ways of prosecuting successful research on AIDS can be found, the consequences, as the figures above indicate, are truly bleak.

This paper will attempt to provide an appropriate framework for assessing the ethics of research on human subjects generally, and in doing so will assess the relevance and force of the major ethical criticisms that have been levelled at current research on human subjects in the context of HIV/AIDS therapy and vaccines.

[*] This paper arose from work done as a consultant to the Joint World Health Organization and United Nations programme on HIV/AIDS (UNAIDS) in 1997–8. I would like to record a considerable debt to UNAIDS. Thanks are due to Robert Levine, Reidar Lie, and Ruth Macklin for detailed comments on earlier work presented to that programme and to Justine Burley for her trenchant comments on an earlier draft of this paper. I must also thank the European Commission (DGXII) for its stimulus and support. I have attempted to apply some of these arguments in the very different context of genetics research. See my 'Ethical Genetic Research' in (1999) 40 *Jurimetrics: The Journal of Law Science and Policy*.

[1] Source: UNAIDS and WHO Global HIV/AIDS and STD Surveillance, *Report on the Global HIV/AIDS Epidemic* (Geneva, 1997), 1–2.

Background

Recent commentators on the ethics of clinical trials in low-income countries have talked about 'the retreat from ethical principles'[2] and have drawn parallels with the notorious Tuskegee Study of Untreated Syphilis.[3] A retreat from ethical principles is not of course necessarily the same as a retreat from ethics. This is because some of the most widely held and frequently cited 'ethical principles' may, as we shall see, be highly problematic from the point of view of their ethics. The controversy about whether or not existing and proposed trials in the context of treatments and vaccines for HIV/AIDS do constitute a retreat from ethical principles is vital, not least because of the emergency that the HIV pandemic represents. If existing ethical principles mean that research on vaccines and treatments for HIV/AIDS cannot be undertaken in low-income countries this is in itself a global catastrophe.[4] It is therefore vital to see to what extent this may be true.

The AIDS pandemic signals the urgency and the moral importance of the ethics of research on human subjects. This is a clear case in which philosophical medical ethics, as distinct from globalized medical ethics, can not only contribute to theory but also do palpable good.

The Globalization of Ethics

The globalization of ethics, as I am using the term, is the phenomenon whereby the ethical agenda is increasingly set, not by religious, cultural, and indeed ethical traditions, nor by competition in the market-place of ideas, nor by community leaders, exceptional sages, or 'saints', nor indeed moral philosophers; but rather this agenda is set by national and international ethics committees, conventions, protocols, and the like.

Three features of this phenomenon are particularly important.

The first is that the standard of ethical argument where it exists is often poor. Too often indeed argument is excluded from the reports altogether. The second feature that should be noticed is that it is these conventions and protocols that are cited in ethical justification, not only of personal conduct but of national legislation. In other words it is these reports that are fast becoming the reference points for ethical decision-making. This is disturbing because, even where the reports are well argued, the argument

---

[2] See Marcia Angell, Editorial: 'The Ethics of Clinical Research in the Third World' (1997) 337 (12) *The New England Journal of Medicine* 844. See also the symposium on HIV/AIDS Vaccines in (1998) 12 *Bioethics* 286–334.

[3] 'Twenty Years After: The Legacy of the Tuskegee Syphilis Study' (1992) 22 *Hastings Center Report* 339–42.

[4] Barry R. Bloom, 'The Highest Attainable Standard: Vexed Ethical Issues in AIDS Vaccines' (1998) 279 *Science* 186–8.

is necessarily brief and itself dependant upon other sources. We are in danger of seeing an increasing marginalization of serious work in bioethics and an increasing use of, and reliance on, reports and other relatively brief public statements of various sorts.

The final telling feature of the globalization of ethics concerns the ways in which these international conventions are arrived at.

Classically, they are the products of high-level meetings, so they should be of course, but such meetings must achieve consensus, and consensus can often only be marshalled around high-minded, resonant, and increasingly abstract principles. Too little attention is paid to the consequences of these principles, when applied to particular circumstances and to the ways in which they are often incongruous with other equally widely held and respected principles that have escaped formal articulation in international conventions.

Very often also they involve so-called 'consultation exercises' through which attempts are made to find out what the public feels about the issues or would do about them by way of legislation. This is fine, because it is important to know where we are starting from, so to speak. All too often however, the results of a consultation exercise are taken as powerful indicators of where we ought to end up. And where the consultation exercise has been undertaken by a body reporting to a national government or other elected body, these results cannot help but be taken as indicators of what the voters want and therefore what it would be 'good' to deliver by way of any resulting legislation or regulation.

The only point in assembling committees of those whom we tend to call in Britain 'the great and the good' is that such great and good people should give a lead on the great issues of the day. All too frequently, however, they feel constrained by political prudence and the need to achieve consensus, to follow rather than lead public opinion.

This tendency towards conservatism is often thought to be consistent with prudence and with the so-called 'precautionary principle' which, while vague, is generally interpreted as requiring, not unreasonably, that we always proceed responsibly, exposing communities and one another to the least danger. However, the line of 'safety' is not always co-extensive with a policy of minimum change. Very often the failure to take radical steps is the policy that costs us most, both in the short and in the long term.

Of course, whether this is true and the extent to which it may be true in any particular case is just what we want committees of the great and the good to assess for us. In this paper we shall be concerned with various international ethics protocols purporting to regulate research.[5] Here, as we

---

[5] For other examples of this phenomenon and its problematic consequences see John Harris, 'Goodbye Dolly: The Ethics of Human Cloning' (1997) 23 *The Journal of Medical*

shall see, the road to safety, let alone to ethical conduct, is far from clearly that indicated in such protocols.

In this paper we will start in sharp focus, concentrating on two different areas of research on human subjects in the context of HIV/AIDS that are currently under consideration. One concerns proposals for Phase III clinical HIV vaccine trials, the second, the possibility of conducting trials of dose-sparing anti-retroviral therapy.[6] The lessons to be learned from such highly applied research are of very general application and of the greatest importance. They will, as we shall see, involve the radical revision of currently accepted international protocols and generally agreed principles and will necessitate a complete re-examination of the ethics of research on human subjects. Before beginning the process of this re-examination we must first briefly describe what is proposed and the issues that such proposals raise.

Two Proposals for HIV/AIDS Research

Phase III HIV Vaccine Trials in Low-income Countries

What, in research terms, is of benefit about conducting Phase III Clinical HIV vaccine trials in parts of the low-income world? To answer this question it will be useful to distinguish between the 'primary endpoint' or objective of a vaccine trial, namely the prevention of infection, and its 'secondary endpoint(s)', the delay or prevention of disease post-infection. Most people believe that vaccines operate like a coat of armour, which the infection cannot penetrate. However, the HIV vaccines presently being developed most probably will not prevent infection. They will not achieve what we have called their primary endpoint. However, should we, for that reason, abandon the idea of the trials entirely?

It is thought that the danger of HIV developing into AIDS depends upon the amount of active virus in the body, the 'viral load'. This viral load appears to vary throughout the period of infection. The best current treatment for HIV (as this is generally understood in the United States) involves the administration of anti-retroviral combination therapy (ACT) including a protease inhibitor (PI), a cocktail of different drugs which has

---

Ethics 353–60; John Harris, 'Cloning and Human Dignity' (1998) 7 Cambridge Quarterly of Healthcare Ethics 163–8; and John Harris, 'Genes, Clones and Human Rights' in Justine C. Burley (ed.), The Genetic Revolution and Human Rights: The Amnesty Lectures 1998 (Oxford, 1999).

[6] A third contentious type of clinical research on HIV concerns 'the ethics of ongoing trials in the Third World of regimens to prevent the vertical transmission of . . . HIV infection. All except one of the trials employ placebo-treated control groups, despite the fact that Zidovudine has already been clearly shown to cut the rate of vertical transmission greatly': Angell, n. 2 above. The ethics of this sort of trial raise different issues with which we will not here be directly concerned.

the collective effect of reducing viral load.[7] Note that the efficacy of ACT is measured in terms of its ability to prevent or delay the onset of disease, that is, by its *secondary endpoints*. The reduction of viral load following infection with HIV is also the likely effect of the HIV vaccine in its current state of development. Hence it makes sense to measure the potential medical benefits of the vaccine trials not in terms of *primary endpoints* (prevention of infection), but in terms of their *secondary endpoints* (either delay of onset or prevention of disease).

Once it is recognized that the medical benefits of an HIV vaccine are best measured in terms of secondary endpoints it is easier to see why conducting Phase III clinical HIV vaccine trials in parts of the low-income world might be indicated. If people in a Phase III trial of a vaccine for HIV become infected with HIV and they receive the best current treatment (again, as this is generally understood in the United States), this will reduce their viral load and may therefore mask any viral load reducing effect of the vaccine. Hence if the vaccine trial were to be held in a country where most infected people would receive the viral load lowering antiretroviral combination therapy (e.g. the United States or Brazil) or in a population which could afford and would be likely to obtain such antiretroviral combination therapy, even if such therapy were not usual or accepted treatment in that country, then it is likely that the secondary endpoints could not be measured because the viral load lowering effect of the anti-retroviral treatment would mask the viral load lowering effect of the vaccine. If, on the other hand, the vaccine were to be tested in a country or in a population that could not afford the treatment or would not for what-ever reason use it, then the trial could measure secondary endpoints. The countries in Africa where HIV/AIDS is most widespread, for example, fit this description, as do parts of south east Asia. Thus, it will almost certainly be necessary to conduct HIV vaccine trials in parts of the low-income world if it is to be undertaken at all.

Recent thinking[8] indicates that it may be possible to measure the 'secondary endpoints' of HIV/AIDS vaccines even if ACT is administered to anyone infected during the course of a trial. This is however as yet by no means certain. Other factors will require that such trials will still need to be held in low-income countries where it will not be certain that thera-pies provided during a trial can be continued indefinitely thereafter.[9] For

---

[7] This treatment is by no means indicated in all cases of HIV infection. In the UK, e.g., in cases in which CD4 count remains high and viral load is low, antiretroviral combination ther-apy is not routinely offered.

[8] Oral evidence given at a meeting of the working party for the joint United Nations programme on HIV/AIDS (UNAIDS) Geneva, 25–26 June 1998.

[9] e.g. different clades (varieties) of the virus may be dominant in different regions of the world and it may not be possible to guarantee that the infrastructure which could deliver complicated and expensive therapy during a trial that would be maintained (or be maintain-

these reasons the ethics of conducting the trials we have been describing will continue to be pertinent.

Since the Nuremberg Trials following World War II, international protocols have emerged designed to protect human subjects from the atrocities of medical experimentation that were literally routine under the Nazis. The most influential of these, the World Medical Association Declaration of Helsinki, states: '[c]oncern for the interests of the subject must always prevail over the interests of science and society'[10] and '[i]n any medical study, every patient, including those of a control group, if any—should be assured of the best proven diagnostic and therapeutic method'.[11] We will return to these and other international protocols later. For the moment we must note that if they are to be strictly observed, research of the sort just described and also that we are about to consider will be impossible. This is because the 'best proven therapeutic method' will mask the effects of the vaccine to be tested and hence vitiate the trial.

TRIALS OF AFFORDABLE DOSE SPARING ANTIRETROVIRAL (ARV) THERAPY

As we have seen, in most of the high-income world, standard treatment for HIV/AIDS is now ACT therapy including a protease inhibitor (PI). While this dramatically improves survival rates for those with HIV it is extremely expensive and technically complex to monitor. The drugs cost in excess of US$12,000 annually and require laboratory investigation of viral loads and other investigations which add another US$1000 to the annual cost. This puts such therapy well beyond the reach of countries, such as Uganda, where the annual *per capita* expenditure on health is about £6.

One possible line of research to find therapies that will be financially viable in low-income countries is to 'to find ways to use existing (tried, tested and licensed) Anti-Retroviral drugs (ARV) in new combinations that retain effectiveness and safety but are cheap. ARV therapy will then be more generally accessible (can be used with minimal monitoring in most areas of Uganda), affordable to many (less than $3–500 per annum drug costs) and can potentially be bought by individuals and households (as opposed to provided free by the state). Finally, they are unlikely to harm the individual or the public health by spreading drug resistance'.[12] Like the HIV phase III vaccine trials we considered above, the proposal here is to

---

able) thereafter. See Harold Varmus and David Satcher, 'Ethical Complexities of Conducting Research in Developing Countries' (1997) 337 *The New England Journal of Medicine*.

[10] The World Medical Association Declaration of Helsinki as amended by 48th General Assembly, Somerset West, Republic of South Africa, Oct. 1996. Art. 1, para. 5.

[11] *Ibid.* Art. II, para. 3.

[12] Charles Gilks, Benon Biryawaho, Janet Darbyshire, Neil French, Elly Katabira, Pontiano Kaleebu, Jonathan Weber, Jimmy Whitworth, Draft proposal May 1998, unpublished private communication. I have drawn on this proposal at a number of points in this paper.

provide cheaper, and possibly less effective, therapies than those currently available in high-income countries, but which will be more likely to be actually of benefit to the people of those countries. This is a crucial point because 'ethical' guidelines and protocols which have the effect of exacerbating inequalities in health and leaving the most vulnerable populations unprotected are clearly to this extent radically defective.

False Parallels

It is worthwhile insisting that sensible debate about the ethics of current research requires that we not muddy the waters by drawing false parallels between such research and notorious cases like the Tuskegee Study of Untreated Syphilis.[13] In that study 412 poor African-American men were deliberately left untreated from 1932–72 so that the natural history of syphilis could be determined.[14] Even when penicillin became known to be effective against syphilis they were left untreated. The principal and material ethical problem with the Tuskegee study was that the subjects were not informed about the study or its purposes and did not consent to any of it. Initially they were not informed that there were therapies available (which admittedly were not very effective ones before antibiotics became available), then they were not informed when penicillin became a highly effective and inexpensive treatment, and they were not informed that their health was being compromised by omission of effective antibiotic therapy. Moreover, the subjects were told deliberate lies about the purposes of some of the procedures. For example, the spinal taps designed to monitor protein levels were described to the subjects as a special new form of treatment. The subjects were deliberately and cynically denied the most basic of information and the opportunity to consent or object to their participation. Moreover, the Tuskegee Study, despite claims to the contrary,[15] did not, in fact, rely on the ethics of guaranteeing local standards of care. Indeed, the immorality of the study depended in part on participants being consistently denied what were accepted local standards of care, since even poor African Americans might reasonably have expected to receive penicillin, not, even in its early days, a massively expensive intervention.[16] Finally, of course, the Tuskegee study was of doubtful scientific validity or interest and, once antibiotics became available, ceased to have any remaining purpose that could have justified its continuance.

Thus, while it is clear that Phase III clinical HIV vaccine trials do pose ethical problems, it is simply not the case, as some critics have suggested, that these problems are, in any meaningful sense, analogous to the ones presented by the Tuskegee Study. While it is true that some of the

---

[13] See Angell, n. 2, above.   [14] N. 3, above, 29–40.   [15] *Ibid.*
[16] Here, as elsewhere, I am grateful for the expert advice of Søren Holm.

justifications used to support the Tuskegee study have a formal similarity with some of those which may also be features of the trials we are considering. They share the fact that the Tuskegee study did not, in one sense at least, make the subjects worse off than they would have been had there been no study. But this just shows that this is inappropriate as a justificatory criterion.

The fact that a (possibly) good study and a clearly unethical one share a feature does not show that they are equally unethical unless it is the existence of that feature that makes them so. It is like raising questions about the ethics of a rail system characterized by the punctuality of its trains, and suggesting that such a system is wicked because the Nazis (allegedly) made the trains run on time (this being sometimes cited in mitigation of fascism.)[17]

The proposed studies on HIV vaccines and therapy that we have examined and many others currently in train raise important issues about the acceptability and indeed the ethical status of a number of the most widely used and cited international ethical guidelines and principles. It is to these that we must now turn.

Global Ethics Protocols

The World Medical Association Declaration of Helsinki, as we have noted above, states: '[c]oncern for the interests of the subject must always prevail over the interests of science and society'[18] and '[i]n any medical study, every patient, including those of a control group, if any—should be assured of the best proven diagnostic and therapeutic method'.[19] The International ethical guidelines for biomedical research involving human subjects[20] (commonly referred to as the CIOMS guidelines) quote Article II.3 of the Declaration of Helsinki and are widely interpreted as requiring that human subjects of research in low-income communities 'receive protection at least equivalent to that in the sponsoring country'.[21] And CIOMS guideline 4 says that if inducements to subjects are offered 'the payments should not be so large or the medical services so extensive as to induce prospective subjects to participate in the research against their better judgement (undue inducement)'.

All of these guidelines raise fundamental questions, which turn on the concept of justice in one sense or another. It is also important to see that slavish adherence to the letter of such guidelines can lead to real and palpable harms.

---

[17] This is effectively the invocation of a principle definitively lampooned by F. M. Cornford in 1908. 'The principle is that a few bad reasons for doing something neutralise all the good reasons for doing it': F. M. Cornford, *Microcosmographia Academica* (Cambridge 1908), ch. VIII.   [18] N. 10 above, Art. 1, para. 5.
[19] *Ibid.*, Art. II para. 3.   [20] Geneva, 1993.   [21] See Angell, n. 2, above.

Let us look at each of these guidelines in turn and assess whether the HIV vaccine and ARV therapy trials would transgress them and, if they would, what importance we should accord to those transgressions.

'CONCERN FOR THE INTERESTS OF THE SUBJECT MUST ALWAYS PREVAIL OVER THE INTERESTS OF SCIENCE AND SOCIETY' (DECLARATION OF HELSINKI)

Let us first examine *de novo* the idea of what is or is not in someone's interests.[22] Here we will neither follow nor consider what other commentators have made of this idea but attempt a rigorous analysis of the meaning of the concepts involved. We should note at the outset that what is or is not in a particular individual's interests is an objective matter. While subjects have a special role to play in determining this, we know that human beings are apt to act against their own interests. Indeed, the idea of respect for persons which underpins this guideline has two clear and sometimes incompatible elements, namely, concern for welfare and respect for autonomy. Because people often have self-harming preferences (smoking, drug abuse, selfless altruism, etc.) they sometimes are bad judges of their interests, although they can never, of course, be bad judges of their wishes. Leaving aside the problematic case of unconscious wishes, of their own preferences humans may be said to have infallible awareness.

There are dangers in being too conservative about what does or does not benefit someone or in defining someone's interests too narrowly. Everyone benefits from living in a society, and, indeed, in a world in which medical research is carried out and which utilizes the benefits of past research. It is both of benefit to patients and research subjects and in their interests to be in a society which pursues and actively accepts the benefits of research and where research and its fruits are given a high priority. We all also benefit from the knowledge that research is ongoing into diseases or conditions from which we do not currently suffer but to which we may succumb. It makes us feel more secure and gives us hope for the future, for ourselves, and our descendants, and others for whom we care. If this is right, then I have a strong general interest that there be research, and in all well-founded research; not excluding but not exclusively, research on me and on my condition or on conditions which are likely to affect me and mine. All such research is also of clear benefit to me. A narrow interpretation of the requirement that research be of benefit to the subject of the research is therefore perverse.[23]

In addition, and despite the implication in the words of the Declaration

---

[22] Here the argument echoes my 'Ethical Genetic Research on Human Subjects' in *Jurimetrics*.

[23] See, e.g., John Harris, 'The Ethics of Clinical Research with Cognitively Impaired Subjects' (1997) 18 *The Italian Journal of Neurological Sciences* 9–15.

of Helsinki, the interests of the subject *cannot* be paramount. Being or becoming a research subject is not the sort of thing that could conceivably augment either someone's moral claims or, for that matter, her rights. *All* people are morally important and, with respect to one another, each has a claim to equal consideration. No one has a claim to overriding or prevailing consideration. To say that the interests of the subject must prevail over those of others, if it means anything, must be understood as a way of re-asserting that a researcher's narrowly conceived professional interests must not have primacy over the human rights of research subjects. Moreover, while acknowledging that health professionals and researchers may have special professional and even contractual or quasi-contractual obligations to their research subjects this does not mean that societies or even the world community must always (or ever) privilege research subjects over others.

We will return to this point when we discuss the obligation to partici-pate in public goods below, but for the moment we may observe that, as a general remark about the obligations of the research community, the health-care system, or of society or indeed of the world community, it is not sustainable.[24]

This is not of course to say that human rights are vulnerable to the interests of society whenever these can be demonstrated to be greater. On the contrary, it is to say that the rights and interests of research subjects are just the rights and interests of persons and must be balanced against comparable rights and interests of other persons. There may, of course, be cases where we want to protect particularly vulnerable groups by privileg-ing their rights or interests, not because these are more important than those of others but specifically in order to secure equality of concern, respect, and protection. However, these will be rare and special cases, and we should be reluctant to accept such claims to privilege in the absence of compelling evidence and argument. It is one of the claims of this paper that such evidence and argument as there is does not make even a *prima facie* case for privileging research subjects over those who might benefit from the research. They should be considered as one, potentially vulner-able, group to be sure, but their vulnerability is, on the face of it, no greater than the vulnerability of the group which may be defined as those who stand to benefit from successful research. I suggest that it is not only unjustifiable, but also self-defeating to privilege the protections afforded to research subjects as opposed to this other vulnerable sector of the popula-tion.

Finally, although what is or is not in someone's interests is an objective matter about which the subject him- (or her-) self may be mistaken, it is

---

[24] I wish to acknowledge explicitly that this paper does not examine certain pertinent ques-tions of detail concerning the kind of information that ought to be given to any subject participating in the research.

usually the best policy to let people define and determine 'their own interests'. While it is if course possible that people will misunderstand their own interests and even act against them, it is surely more likely that people will understand their own interests best. It is of course also more respectful of research subjects for us to assume that this is the case unless there are powerful reasons for not so doing.[25]

'IN ANY MEDICAL STUDY, EVERY PATIENT, INCLUDING THOSE OF A CONTROL GROUP, IF ANY—SHOULD BE ASSURED OF THE BEST PROVEN DIAGNOSTIC AND THERAPEUTIC METHOD' (DECLARATION OF HELSINKI)

Are there treatment regimens that should be assured by an investigator to participants in preventive HIV vaccine or in ARV therapy trials? Is there a rationale for considering such trials to have no obligation to assure provision of therapy to those infected during the trial?

What then should be the obligations of researchers to their subjects? As I argue at length below, the obligations to research subjects are derived from a more general obligation to refrain from harming others (the obligation of non-malifience which is the obverse of the obligation of beneficence).[26] Such obligations are no more stringent to research subjects than they are to anyone in similar need. That said, it will look like special pleading to reject the requirements of the Declaration of Helsinki which provide that all research subjects 'be assured of the best proven diagnostic and therapeutic method'. In the face of the scale and the urgency of the AIDS pandemic, special pleading is not of course out of the question, but it should clearly be a last resort and be carefully argued and justified.

Barry Bloom has produced a *reductio ad absurdum* of the standard of care we are discussing. He points out[27] that: '[f]ew, if any, clinical trials have been carried out in low-income countries to evaluate whether simple, inexpensive interventions, such as aspirin or β-blockers, will reduce mortality from heart attacks and strokes as they do in the industrialised world. . . . Were the standard of "best proven therapeutic method" literally invoked, in such a trial, many study subjects suffering heart attacks would have to be provided with either angioplasty or coronary artery bypass surgery, hardly "reasonably available" in countries where per capita expenditure for health are $10 per year or less.'

---

[25] e.g. in cases of research on young children, mental patients, and others who it is reasonable to assume may not be adequately competent.
[26] This is generally acknowledged as one of the major principles of bioethics if not of ethics more generally. See John Harris, *Violence & Responsibility* (London, 1980) and Tom L. Beauchamp and James F. Childress, *Principles of Biomedical Ethics* (4th edn.) (New York, 1994).
[27] Barry R. Bloom, 'The Highest Attainable Standard: Vexed Ethical Issues in AIDS Vaccines' (1998) 279 *Science* 186–8.

While Bloom's reminder is important, it cannot follow from the fact that we cannot do everything that we are permitted to do nothing. The question must be what standard of care is appropriate, given all the circumstances of the study, including all the costs involved? We cannot simply move from the impossibility of providing anything or everything that may reasonably be interpreted as 'best proven diagnostic and thera-peutic method' to the conclusion that the only alternative is 'local stand-ards of care'. However, Bloom's *reductio* argument does at least show that the provisions of the Declaration of Helsinki cannot, as written, be univer-sally applied.

Because of the symmetry between acts and omissions[28] it is not, other things being equal, justifiable to let people suffer when we could protect them, nor is it normally ethical to leave people with poorer standards of care than could reasonably be provided for them. However, we need to look more closely at the equality of other things and how we may reason-ably assess 'what could reasonably be provided'.

The moral argument that requires that we try to ensure that others are not made unduly worse off applies to *all others*, not simply the subjects of any trial. Therefore, when we are considering the others whom we must try not to make unduly worse off we must also include those who may benefit from the results of the trial. Thus the argument that supports the best standard of care for those in the trial also supports the best standard of care *for those who would benefit from the trial*. No one would be made worse off by such a policy; some will be made better off. Other things being equal, we should maximize the number of the better off. The other things that must be equal here of course include the stipulation of minimal risk of participation in the research and adequate safeguards against exploitation.[29]

It merits insistence that leaving people no worse off than they would have been had no trial taken place is a minimum standard of care. The *relevant* question is not, surely, will the participants be no worse off than they would have been? Rather it is what obligations do we have towards people to protect them from avoidable harm?[30] We will try to answer this question in dealing with the following interpretation of the Declaration of Helsinki but before doing so it is worth noting that the CIOMS guidelines are not entirely supportive of this particular article of the Declaration of Helsinki.

---

[28] Here I assume that this symmetry is self-evident. I argued for it in my 'The Marxist Conception of Violence' (1974) 3 *Philosophy & Public Affairs* 192–221 and in my *Violence & Responsibility*, n. 26, above.
[29] See the discussion of undue influence below and my discussion of the concept of exploitation in *Wonderwoman and Superman: The Ethics of Human Biotechnology* (Oxford, 1992).
[30] See *Violence & Responsibility*, n. 26, above.

HUMAN SUBJECTS OF RESEARCH IN LOW-INCOME COMMUNITIES MUST 'RECEIVE PROTECTION AT LEAST EQUIVALENT TO THAT IN THE SPONSORING COUNTRY' (CIOMS GUIDELINES)

What are the obligations of investigators to those who enter a drug or vaccine trial? These are of course in part determined by what we judge participants to be entitled to by way of protection. I shall consider obligations of two kinds: those arising from any adverse consequences to the individual as a result of being involved in the trial; and the obligations of those conducting the trial to provide therapy to participants who become infected or otherwise injured during the trial.[31]

Where I benefit from research but refuse to participate in it I am clearly acting unfairly in some sense. I am free-riding on the back of the contribution of others. Where people volunteer to participate in research they are doing what any reasonable decent person should be willing to do if they wish and expect to receive the benefits of research, at least where the risks and dangers to research subjects are minimal. The level of protection required to render the risks of participation minimal are then a question of fact or at least of judgement in each case. It is not obvious that these must be 'equivalent to that in the sponsoring country'.

It should be clear that I am not here invoking the so-called 'principle of fairness' developed by Herbert Hart and later used by John Rawls.[32] That principle may be interpreted as saying 'those who have submitted to . . . restrictions have a right to similar aquiescence on the part of those who have benefited from their submission'.[33] Here I do not suggest any obligation to participate, nor any entitlement to enforce participation, based on fairness. The obligation to participate derives from the importance of the research and the extent to which it is of both personal and public benefit and utility,[34] not from the unfairness of being a free rider, although being a free rider is unfair and we all have moral reasons not to act unfairly. I will suggest later that we should neither presume that people would wish to act unfairly, nor institutionalize mechanisms which encourage this.

Moreover, it is widely recognized that there is clearly sometimes an obligation to make sacrifices for the community or an entitlement of the community to go so far as to deny autonomy and even violate bodily integrity in the public interest, and this obligation is recognized in a

---

[31] I note here that I have omitted discussion of whether or not issuing free condoms to participants should be part of the obligation to protect subjects.
[32] See H. L. A. Hart 'Are There any Natural Rights?' [1955] *Philosophical Review* and John Rawls, *A Theory of Justice* (Cambridge, 1972).
[33] This formulation of the principle dervies from Robert Nozick, *Anarchy, State and Utopia* (Oxford, 1974), 90.
[34] As I argue at greater length later in this paper.

number of ways.[35] The following areas in which this is already recognized and accepted to some extent will serve as a reminder: control of dangerous drugs, control of road traffic, compulsory vaccination, screening tests, blood donation, quarantine for communicable disease, compulsory military service, detention under Mental Health Acts, safety guidelines for certain professional activities of HIV positive people, and compulsory attendance for jury service at criminal trials. All these involve some denial of autonomy, some imposition of public standards even where compliance is not based on the competent consent of individuals. However, these are clearly exceptional cases where overriding moral considerations take precedence over autonomy. To what extent is the case of HIV vaccine trials analogous?

MANDATORY AND VOLUNTARY PARTICIPATION IN THE PUBLIC GOOD[36]

Let us look more closely at two familiar cases, those of jury service and blood donation.

All British citizens between 18 and 70[37] are liable for jury service. They may be called and, unless excused by the court, must serve. This may involve a minimum of ten days but sometimes months of daily confinement in a jury box or room, whether they consent or not. However, although all are liable for service only some are actually called. If someone is called and fails to appear she may be fined. Most people will never be called, but some must be if the system of justice is not to break down. Participation in or facilitation of this public good is mandatory.

Blood donation is an example of participation in a non-mandatory public good. It is not compulsory, but we all rely on some people being willing to volunteer. We (that is society) would be justified in compulsorily drafting blood donors in an emergency. We almost never need to because there are enough volunteers. However, when people give blood, we do not assume that elaborate consent or education is necessary. This is because it is ethically unproblematic. Blood donation is a public good and the presumption is that those donating blood do so willingly, just because it is a public good. Even, as in the USA, where payment is made, there is, for example, *no presumption that the payment is coercive.*

There are many senses in which participation in HIV vaccine trials involve features relevantly analogous to jury service or blood donation. All involve inconvenience and the giving of certain amounts of time. Blood donation involves minimal risk and some invasion of bodily integrity. All

---

[35] See John Harris, 'Ethical Issues in Geriatric Medicine' in R. C. Tallis, J. C. Brockelhurst, and Howard Fillett (eds.), *Textbook of Geriatric Medicine and Gerontology* (5th edn., London, 1998).

[36] I use this term in a non-technical sense.

[37] Those over 65 may be excused if they wish.

are important public goods. It is this latter feature that is particularly important.

If I am right in thinking that vaccine trials are a public good then a number of things may be said to follow:

- It should not simply be assumed that people would not wish to act in the public interest, at least where the costs and risks involved are minimal. In the absence of specific evidence to the contrary, if any assumptions are made, they should be that people are public-spirited and would wish to participate.

- It may be reasonable to presume that people would not consent (unless misinformed or coerced) to do things contrary to their own and to the public interest. The reverse is true when (as with vaccine trials) participation is in both personal and public interest.

- If it is right to claim that there is a general obligation to act in the public interest, then there is less reason to challenge consent and little reason to regard participation as actually or potentially exploitative. We do not usually say 'are you quite sure you want to' when people fulfil their moral and civic obligations. We do not usually insist on informed consent in such cases; we are usually content that they *merely* consent or simply acquiesce. When for example I am called for jury service no one says, 'only attend if you fully understand the role of trial by jury, due process, etc. in our constitution and the civil liberties that fair trials guarantee'.[38]

Let us now take together the two requirements of the Declaration of Helsinki that we have been considering, namely that 'concern for the interests of the subject must always prevail over the interests of science and society'[39] and 'in any medical study, every patient, including those of a control group, if any—should be assured of the best proven diagnostic and therapeutic method'.[40] We suggested above that a narrow interpretation of the first requirement is unwarranted and that, in the case of research, a clear distinction between the interests of the subject and the interests of other people equally entitled to our concern, respect, and protection cannot be sustained. We have seen that the same arguments, the same ethical standards that require us to assure the best proven standards to those *in* a study also require that they be assured to *all who stand in need of them*.

It would surely be irrational to sacrifice the many who would benefit from the development of a vaccine to the interests of the few who

---

[38] If these suggestions are broadly acceptable and an obligation to participate in research is established, this may well become one of the ways in which research comes to be funded in the future.

[39] N. 11, above, Art. 1, para. 5.   [40] *Ibid.*, Art. II, para. 3.

participate in the trials. Equally irrational would be to sacrifice the participants in the trial to the needs of the many who wait upon its result. But
there has never been the remotest suggestion of any such sacrifice of
research subjects. What then would be reasonable and ethical?

The answer to this question must be that we must weigh carefully and
compassionately what it is reasonable to put to potential participants in a
trial for their free and unfettered consideration. However, provided potential research subjects are given full information, and are free to participate
or not as they choose, then the only remaining question is whether it is
reasonable to permit people freely to choose to participate, given the risks
and the sorts of likely gains. Is it reasonable to ask people to run whatever
degree of risk is involved, to put up with the inconvenience and intrusion
of the study, and so on in all the circumstances of the case? These circumstances will include both the benefits to them personally of participating in
the study and the benefits that will flow from the study to other persons,
persons who are of course equally entitled to our concern, respect, and
protection.[41] Putting the question in this way makes it clear that the standards of care and levels of protection to be accorded to research subjects
who have full information must be, to a certain extent, study relative.

It is crucial that the powerful moral reasons for conducting HIV vaccine
and ARV therapy trials are not drowned by the powerful reasons we have
for protecting research subjects. There is a balance to be struck here, but it
is not a balance that must always and inevitably be loaded in favour of the
protection of research subjects. They are entitled to our concern, respect,
and protection to be sure, but they are no more entitled to it than are the
people whom HIV/AIDS is threatening and killing on a daily basis.[42]

It is surely unethical to stand by and watch 2.3 million people die this
year and avoid taking steps to prevent this level of loss. Steps which will
not put lives at risk and which are taken only with the fully informed
consent of those who participate. Fully informed consent is the best guarantor of the interests of research subjects. While not foolproof, residual
dangers must be balanced against the dangers of not conducting the trial,
which include the massive loss of life that AIDS causes.[43]

The Declaration of Helsinki is clearly deficient. Article 4 of the
Declaration of Helsinki states: '[b]iomedical research involving human
subjects cannot legitimately be carried out unless the importance of the

---

[41] If any are.

[42] Of course the historical explanation of the Declaration of Helsinki and its concerns lies
in the Nuremberg Trials and the legacy of Nazi atrocities. However, we are, I believe, in real
danger of allowing fear of repeating one set of atrocities lead us into committing other new
atrocities.

[43] These residual dangers include the difficulties of constructing suitable consent protocols
and supervising their administration in rural and isolated communities and in populations
which may have low levels of formal education.

objective is in proportion to the inherent risk to the subject'. A principle which is the correlate of this would state:

> Biomedical research involving human subjects cannot legitimately be neglected, and is therefore permissible, where the importance of the objective is great and the risks to and the possibility of exploitation of fully informed and consenting subjects is small.[44]

Thus, while fully informed consent and the continuing provision to research subjects of relevant information does not eliminate all possibility of exploitation,[45] it does reduce it to the point at which it could no longer be ethical to neglect the claims and the interests of those who may benefit from the research. It should be noted that it is fully informed consent, and the concern and respect for the individual that it signals which severs all connection with the Nazi experiments and the concerns of Nuremberg and which rebuts spurious comparisons with the Tuskegee study. It is this recognition of the obligation to show equal concern and respect for all persons which is the defining characteristic of justice.[46] The recognition that the obligation to do justice applies not only to research subjects but also to those who will benefit from the research must constitute an advance in thinking about international standards of research ethics.

IF INDUCEMENTS TO SUBJECTS ARE OFFERED '[T]HE PAYMENTS SHOULD NOT BE SO LARGE OR THE MEDICAL SERVICES SO EXTENSIVE AS TO INDUCE PROSPECTIVE SUBJECTS TO PARTICIPATE IN THE RESEARCH AGAINST THEIR BETTER JUDGEMENT (UNDUE INDUCEMENT)' (CIOMS GUIDELINES)

CIOMS guideline 4 prohibits the offering of inducements to participate in research. However, it permits payments in cash or kind but states 'the payments should not be so large or the medical services so extensive as to induce prospective subjects to participate in the research against their better judgement (undue inducement)'. However, the CIOMS document also states '[s]omeone without access to medical care may be unduly influenced to participate in research simply to receive such care'.[47] What is it then that might make an inducement *undue*? If inducement is undue when it undermines 'better judgement', then it cannot simply be the level of the inducement nor the fact that it is the inducement that makes the difference between participation and non-participation that is crucial. If this were so, all attractive employment would constitute 'undue' inducement.[48]

---

[44] For a version of this principle applied in the context of genetics see my 'Ethical Genetic Research on Human Subjects', n. 23, above.

[45] As Marcia Angell rightly points out in her editorial, n. 2, above.

[46] See Ronald Dworkin, *Taking Rights Seriously* (London, 1977).

[47] CIOMS Guidelines 18–19.

[48] The CIOMS gloss on their own guideline creates a kind of Catch 22 which is surely

We might begin to regard inducement as undue if the trial was so obnoxious that only coercive inducement would tempt someone to participate. If the study were contrary to public morals or against the public interest there might be a legitimate presumption of undue influence.

However, where a vaccine trial is well founded scientifically, has important objectives which will advance knowledge, and may prove the efficacy of a vaccine, where the subjects are at minimal risk, and where the inconvenience and so on of participation is not onerous, then surely it is not only in everyone's best interests that *some* people participate but also in the interests of those who do. *Better judgement* surely will not indicate that any particular person should not participate. Of course someone consulting personal interest and convenience might not participate. However, removing the force of *these sorts of objections* with incentives is not undermining *better judgement* any more than is making employment attractive.[49]

Conclusions

A number of important conclusions flow from our discussion:

1. There is no justification for confining the definition of the interests of the research subject narrowly to include only personal and selfish interests. All people, including research subjects, have a substantial and real interest in ongoing medical research.
2. Becoming a research subject does not augment anyone's rights and/or moral claims. Therefore the interests of the research subject cannot be paramount. *All* individuals are entitled to be treated with equal concern and respect.
3. Adequate informed consent remains the best guarantor of the interests of research subjects. While informed consent is not foolproof, residual dangers must be balanced against the dangers of not conducting research. It is fully informed consent and the continuing provision to research subjects of all relevant information that marks all ethical research and distinguishes it from the concerns of Nuremberg and the taint of Tuskegee.
4. While research protocols should retain the ideal of providing the 'best proven diagnostic and therapeutic method', this is not simply a

unreasonable and unwarranted. Wherever the best proven diagnostic and therapeutic methods are guaranteed by a study in a context or for a population which would not normally expect to receive them, this guideline would be broken. CIOMS guideline 4 therefore surely contradicts and violates not only the Declaration of Helsinki but also its own later guideline 14.

[49] See also M. Wilkinson and A. Moore, 'Inducement in Research' and P. McNeill, 'Paying People to Participate in Research: Why Not?' both (1997) 11 *Bioethics* 373, 390. And the discussion of commercial exploitation in Harris, n. 29, above, 373–97, ch. 6.

function of what is practically available in each country, but rather of what may reasonably be provided as part of the research protocol given all the circumstances.

5. The provision of inducements to research subjects is neither coercive nor otherwise unethical or inappropriate so long as the research is well-founded and in the public interest.

GOVERNMENT PRIORITIES FOR BIOMEDICAL RESEARCH: WHAT DOES JUSTICE REQUIRE?

Rebecca Dresser

During the 1990s, US government priorities for biomedical research funding became the focus of heated debate. Some members of Congress joined with organizations advocating on behalf of persons with various health problems to raise questions concerning how funds are allocated at the National Institutes of Health (NIH), the major government agency supporting biomedical research. Certain critics charged that the agency was devoting disproportionately high amounts to research on specific diseases while neglecting other significant health problems. Others charged that NIH officials and scientists had been insufficiently responsive to members of the public and their elected representatives seeking clarification of and a voice in the priority-setting process. In turn, NIH officials produced a document setting forth the substantive criteria used to determine funding allocation. The agency also took steps to increase opportunities for members of the public to provide input on funding priorities. Yet the underlying debate remains unsettled.

Differing conceptions of distributive and procedural justice underlie the controversy over priority setting. The debate over funding for particular health conditions reflects different views of what constitutes a fair share of public funds for various health problems. Officials at NIH have stated that they consider the following criteria in allocating agency funds: (1) public health needs; (2) scientific merit of research proposals; (3) level of scientific promise in different clinical and basic science areas; (4) breadth and diversity across the full research portfolio; and (5) training and infrastructure needs. Public health needs are evaluated according to these considerations:

The number of people who have a particular disease.
The number of deaths produced by a disease.
The degree of disability produced by a disease.
The degree of which a disease cuts short a normal, productive, comfortable lifetime.
The economic and social costs of a disease.
The need to act rapidly to control the spread of a disease.[1]

[1] NIH Working Group on Priority Setting, Setting Research Priorities, and the National Institute of Health, NIH Pub. No. 97–4265 (Sept. 1997).

The agency has not, however, indicated how these criteria are weighed and balanced; nor has it presented examples in which certain research efforts were ranked high and others low, based on application of the above considerations.

The debate over NIH priority-setting also reflects different views of who can make legitimate contributions to the ranking process. This dispute pits scientific experts against public advocates and elected representatives seeking a greater role in determining which research topics ought to be assigned high significance. Although the NIH is in the process of establishing mechanisms to elicit increased public input, the proper role of public representatives in agency priority-setting has yet to be clarified.

In this presentation I will analyse distributive and procedural justice issues raised by research priority setting, with the goal of clarifying the values, choices, and trade-offs at stake in this policy context. I will also examine difficulties inherent in assigning priorities based on factors such as disease incidence, disease severity, prevention versus treatment, and age, gender, and ethnicity of affected populations. Lastly, I will consider the potential roles of laypersons and experts in establishing priorities for publicly-funded health research.

Each year in the USA, a congressional subcommittee hears testimony in a place unofficially known as 'Mother Teresa's Waiting Room'. In April 1999, a *New York Times* reporter described the scene:

Here, for three days this week and two days next week, the sick and afflicted and their lobbyists are gathering in an annual telethon of sorts: the competition for research financing to cure disease. Hundreds of ailments are represented, from the most common cancer to the rarest genetic disorder. Even erectile dysfunction received a mention.

So many people asked to testify before the subcommittee that holds the purse strings to the National Institutes of Health that two-thirds of them were turned down. The rest were selected by lottery for the privilege of delivering a five-minute talk. . . .[2]

The speakers sought to influence members of the House Appropriations Subcommittee on Labor, Health and Human Services, Education, and Related Agencies. This is one of four congressional subcommittees that determine funding for the twenty-five institutes and centres comprising the National Institutes of Health (NIH). Congress influences biomedical research priorities by awarding designated amounts to the institutes and centres, each of which is dedicated to the study of specific health problems

[2] Sheryl Gay Stolberg, 'In "Mother Teresa's Waiting Room", Optimism', *New York Times*, 14 Apr. 1999, A16.

(e.g. the National Cancer Institute and National Institute of Mental Health), organ systems (e.g. the National Eye Institute), or clinical fields (e.g. the National Institute of Nursing Research). At times, Congress directs or strongly encourages NIH to devote a certain sum to a particular disease or other health concern—hence, the high demand for time in Mother Teresa's Waiting Room.

Although Congress directs special funding to some research areas every year, NIH officials also have substantial control over the areas and types of research that receive government support. Institute and centre officials work with the NIH director to determine the appropriate emphasis for their research programmes. Researchers and members of other interest groups influence this decision-making as well.

For many decades, this process attracted little public notice. During the 1990s, however, research-funding decisions gained a higher public profile. Activists from the HIV/AIDS and breast cancer communities drew media attention to the importance of research funding for their causes. When these groups achieved success in their quest for increased funding, advocates representing persons affected by other health problems and populations with specific health needs adopted their lobbying tactics. Some advocates began to complain that their constituents had been short-changed in the funding process, and a competitive environment emerged.[3]

Other developments intensified the public focus on research funding. Debate over access to health care led to charges that much of the medical technology produced through research was expensive and marginally beneficial.[4] Cost-cutting measures by health insurers reduced private funds available for clinical studies, which produced requests for the government to increase support for this form of research.[5] Biomedical research participation came to be seen as a means of obtaining cutting-edge therapy for medical problems; general demands for increased research in specific areas accompanied this new perception of biomedical science.[6]

By the late 1990s, government officials had begun to respond to the heightened public scrutiny. Congress held hearings on setting priorities for health research.[7] The Institute of Medicine, an advisory organization to the federal government, issued a report on the strengths and weaknesses of the government's approach to research priority setting.[8] An NIH working

---

[3] Institute of Medicine, *Scientific Opportunities and Public Needs* (Washington, DC, 1998), 56–7.

[4] Peter Neumann and Eileen Sandberg, 'Trends in Health Care R & D and Technology Innovation' (1998) 17 *Health Affairs* 111. [5] *Ibid.*

[6] Robert Levine, 'The Impact of HIV Infection on Society's Perception of Clinical Trials' (1994) 4 *Kennedy Institute of Ethics Journal* 93.

[7] Rebecca Dresser, 'Setting Priorities for Science Support' (1998) 28 *Hastings Center Report* 21.

[8] Institute of Medicine, n. 3, above.

group published 'Setting Research Priorities at the National Institutes of
Health', which described in ordinary language the criteria and process
used to allocate research funds.[9]

Yet the debate over research priority setting remains unsettled. Mother
Teresa's Waiting Room is overcrowded because advocates believe personal
pleas are necessary to protect their constituents' interests in adequate
research funding. Members of Congress seek favoured treatment for afflictions that have touched them in personal ways. Scientists perceive threats
to their autonomy from government and public pressure for concrete
health-care advances.

The controversy illuminates a neglected question in health-care ethics:
What is a just allocation of resources for biomedical research? Although
justice in allocating health-care resources is widely analysed, just allocation in the research context has been for the most part ignored.
Philosopher Daniel Callahan thinks the omission is in part explained by a
pervasive attitude that 'we like what [NIH] is doing, we trust its leadership to make good priority decisions, and we see no good reason to shake
the faith of the Congress or the general public about the way NIH goes
about carrying out its mission'.[10] Neglect of this issue may also be due to
another common perception, here expressed by law professor Roger
Dworkin:

The questions of how much money to spend on research and what kinds of
research to support are, quite properly, political questions. We elect representatives
to decide questions that have no inherently right answers, like . . . how much to
spend on basic and how much on applied research; and how much to spend on
each of an almost infinite number of worthy ends—cure versus prevention, AIDS
versus birth defects, and so forth.[11]

In this paper, I take a different view. The increased activity addressing
research priority setting indicates that at least a vocal minority questions
the existing system. Moreover, though biomedical research priority setting
is inevitably a political process, it presents significant moral dimensions
and values trade-offs that should at minimum be openly acknowledged.
Important distributive and procedural justice issues are raised by research
priority setting. The remainder of this paper discusses: (1) existing substantive criteria and procedural mechanisms for funding allocation, (2) criticisms of the existing approach, (3) distributive justice considerations,
(4) procedural justice considerations, and (5) future policy directions.

---

[9] NIH Working Group on Priority Setting, *Setting Research Priorities at the National
Institutes of Health* NIH Publication No. 97–4265 (Washington, DC, Sept. 1997).

[10] Daniel Callahan, 'Shaping Biomedical Research Priorities: The Case of the National
Institutes of Health' (1999), 7 *Health Policy Analysis* 115–29.

[11] R. B. Dworkin, *Limits: The Role of the Law in Bioethical Decision Making*
(Bloomington, Ind., 1996), 146–7.

The Existing Approach to Priority Setting

As noted above, US biomedical research priorities are established at two levels. Building on budget proposals from the President that incorporate recommendations from NIH and other agency officials, Congress determines (1) the percentage of the federal budget that will be devoted to biomedical research[12] and (2) how the total sum will be divided among NIH institutes and centres. (A few other federal agencies receive funds to support biomedical research, but most of the money goes to NIH.)

When members believe that the budget proposal gives inadequate attention to particular health problems, Congress exercises its authority to designate specific amounts for research on those problems or encourages NIH to give heightened attention to them. Congressional priority setting appears to rely on factors normally influential in the political process, including constituents' personal interests and the economic welfare of the senators' and representatives' home districts. Observers also claim that 'politicians frequently support additional investments in research on a particular disease after a grandchild or spouse has contracted it'.[13]

In recognition of their foibles, a number of House and Senate leaders are working to reduce the incidence of specific congressional directives on the use of biomedical research funds. Advocates of reduced congressional interference see increased NIH accountability as an avenue to this goal. The theory is that if NIH officials offer the public clearer explanations of their funding decisions and more opportunities to participate in priority setting, there will be less pressure from advocates in Mother Teresa's Waiting Room and elsewhere for Congress to intervene. As a result of this view, NIH priority setting is undergoing close examination.

According to 'Setting Research Priorities', NIH officials evaluate public health needs using the following criteria:

> The number of people who have a particular disease.
> The number of deaths produced by a disease.
> The degree of disability produced by a disease.
> The degree to which a disease cuts short a normal, productive, comfortable lifetime.
> The economic and social costs of a disease.
> The need to act rapidly to control the spread of a disease.[14]

The report notes that exclusive reliance on any one of these criteria would

---

[12] Although significant justice issues are raised by this component of allocation, I do not address it in this paper. For discussion of these issues, see Rebecca Dresser, 'Public Advocacy and Allocation of Federal Funds for Biomedical Research' (1999) 77 *Milbank Quarterly* 257.

[13] James Fallows, 'The Political Scientist' *New Yorker* 7 June 1999, 66, 68. See also John F. Lauerman, 'Turning the Tables', *Harvard Magazine* July–Aug. 1998, 26, 27.

[14] Working Group on Priority Setting, n. 9, above, 8.

produce dramatically different priorities; for example, '[f]unding according to the number of deaths would neglect chronic diseases that produce long-term disabilities and high costs to society'.[15]

Further complexity comes with the additional factors that influence NIH priority setting. Besides public health needs, the agency allocates its resources based on the following considerations: (1) scientific merit of research proposals, (2) level of scientific opportunity in different areas (i.e. whether important breakthroughs appear imminent), (3) breadth and diversity of topics and approaches ('[b]ecause we cannot predict discoveries or anticipate the opportunities fresh discoveries will produce'), and (4) training and infrastructure necessary to support current and future research demands.[16]

'Setting Research Priorities' presents explicit criteria affecting NIH priority setting. Priorities may be affected by other criteria as well. Current NIH Director Harold Varmus notes that funding decisions may also reflect desires to (1) preserve the nation's leadership position in science, (2) contribute to economic activities in the private sector, and (3) elevate the public image of science. He even suggests that targeted research funding can promote international relations:

I offer as one example the effort that the NIH has made through the National Cancer Institute to promote a Middle East Cancer Consortium. This effort provides one of the few vehicles that allow representatives of the states of the Middle East to sit down at a common table and talk about common interests.[17]

Citing the negative impact of disease on a country's political stability, he also asserts that US-sponsored research can improve the political and economic health of developing nations.

The NIH applies its substantive priority setting criteria through a lengthy and intricate process. After consulting with institute and centre directors (who have previously met with scientists and other interest groups), the NIH director submits budget recommendations to the President. Once Congress establishes the final budget figures, officials at the institutes and centres determine how their funds will be divided. Most of the funds are used to support proposals from scientists at NIH and at academic and other research institutions. The remaining funds are used primarily for training, administration, and infrastructure support. In most years, a little more than half the agency's research resources support basic research (defined as 'systematic study directed toward greater knowledge or understanding of the fundamental aspects of phenomena and of observable facts without specific applications towards processes or products in mind'[18]). The rest of the research

---

[15] Working Group on Priority Setting, n. 9, above, 9.   [16] *Ibid.* 4.

[17] H. E. Varmus, 'The View from the National Institutes of Health' in C. E. Barfield and B. L. R. Smith (eds.), *The Future of Biomedical Research* (Washington, DC, 1997), 9, 15.

[18] Institute of Medicine, n. 3, above, 20.

budget supports applied research proposals focused on specific health problems and development proposals intended to produce materials or methods addressing specific health or research needs.[19] Most research proposals involve single projects, but some are for interdisciplinary programmes and centres in which several investigators conduct research on different dimensions of a health or research problem.

Proposals are selected for funding according to their merit, which is assessed by review panels composed of scientific (and sometimes lay advocate) experts in the relevant field. Merit is judged in part according to the importance of the problem or question the proposal addresses, a judgement that may incorporate health as well as scientific significance.[20] Funding choices also are made by a second group, the advisory council of each institute and centre. Advisory councils are usually composed of two-thirds scientist and one-third public members. In consultation with their advisory councils, institute and centre directors are authorized to fund proposals with lower merit scores when the research is deemed particularly promising and important.[21]

The above process gives scientists submitting and reviewing proposals a substantial role in determining the direction of biomedical research, thus affecting the government's research priorities. NIH officials also have mechanisms to guide the types of proposals they receive, however. Officials engage in activities to keep them in touch with the areas and problems scientists, clinicians, and patient-interest groups deem significant. Some institutes and centres hold meetings at which researchers, clinicians, and advocacy groups are asked to discuss areas they perceive as underfunded. Based on this information, NIH officials decide when affirmative steps are needed to encourage research interest in a particular area. Agency officials may then sponsor a conference or issue requests for proposals on that area. Two or more institutes and centres may act together to encourage research proposals in a neglected area relevant to more than one of their missions. Finally, the NIH director is authorized to take certain actions to fund studies or areas deemed especially important.[22]

Criticisms of the Existing Approach to Priority Setting

The increased focus on NIH priority setting has brought challenges to the agency's substantive allocation criteria as well as to its allocation procedures. One common criticism is that the articulated priority setting criteria are so general and vague that NIH officials have almost total freedom in their allocation choices.[23] As a result, it is claimed, the curiosity and career

---

[19] *Ibid.*   [20] Working Group on Priority Setting, n. 9, above, 11.
[21] *Ibid.*   [22] *Ibid.*, 11–13, 15.
[23] Institute of Medicine, n. 3, above, 27; Callahan, n. 10 above.

interests of the agency's scientist-administrators and their academic research colleagues assume the highest priority in funding decisions. For example, at a Senate hearing on setting health-research priorities, a representative of the Parkinson's Action Network said NIH had adopted a '*laissez faire*' approach that allowed scientific imagination to be the dominant force in shaping research.[24] In her view, this approach had led to relatively low levels of funding for research into Parkinson's disease, even though the disorder would merit substantially higher amounts if the formal NIH criteria were strictly applied.

The same witness voiced another common perception of NIH allocation choices. This is the view that NIH officials have steered disproportionately large sums to disorders represented by highly visible and sophisticated advocacy groups.[25] As a congressional analyst reported, critics believe 'NIH spending often follows current politics and political correctness' rather than the articulated morbidity and mortality considerations.[26]

The NIH is criticized as well for its lack of 'a systematic process for collecting and analyzing data on the full range of [the nation's] health indicators'.[27] The absence of good data on national health needs, together with the extreme flexibility of the NIH criteria, make it difficult to evaluate how well the agency's funding choices conform to the nation's health needs. A related point is that the agency does not do enough to determine what it spends on research addressing different health problems.

NIH officials admit that their data on spending by disease are incomplete and inaccurate. Critics suspect that the lack of good data provides a convenient excuse when officials are charged with failing to allocate sufficient funds to specific disease areas. Although they acknowledge that it is impossible to know the precise applications of basic and even some applied studies, critics think the NIH could do a much better job classifying funded research according to its relevance to particular health problems. Improvements in the quality of these data and in estimates of the burdens different diseases impose on the nation's population would allow Congress and NIH officials to establish funding priorities that better address the nation's health needs. Such improvements would also permit the public and its representatives to evaluate retrospectively whether the agency's actual allocation choices conformed to those needs.[28]

More formidable challenges come from those who disagree with the

---

[24] *Biomedical Research Priorities: Who Should Decide? Hearing Before the Subcomm. on Public Safety of the Comm. on Labor and Human Resources*, 105th Cong. 1st Sess. 76–8 (1997).   [25] *Ibid.*

[26] Judith A. Johnson, 'Disease Funding and NIH Priority Setting', *Congressional Research Service Report*, No. 97–917 (Washington, DC, 26 Mar. 1998), 5.

[27] Institute of Medicine, n. 3, above, 33.

[28] Tammy O. Tengs, 'Planning for Serendipity: A New Strategy to Prosper from Health Research', *Progressive Policy Institute Health Priorities Project*, Policy Report No. 2 (Washington, DC, July 1998), 13–20.

current priority setting criteria. For example, analyst Tammy Tengs argues that 'Congress and the Administration should revise NIH's mission statement to clarify that its primary goal should be to produce the greatest possible reduction in the future burden of disease and injury'.[29] She believes that NIH institutes and centres should receive sums tied to the predicted future burden of disease in their mission areas; furthermore, the agency should abandon its passive stance of reacting to fortuitous breakthroughs and instead actively create scientific opportunity by channelling funds to research relevant to the most burdensome health problems.[30] Others believe the agency should more explicitly recognize the importance of funding to investigate the behaviours and environments that contribute to numerous health problems.[31] Additional criticism comes from Daniel Callahan, who thinks the existing criteria implicitly envisage 'progress without end in the improvement of health'. He would like to see them replaced with more precise and realistic goals, such as 'relief of pain, suffering and disability to the level that the majority of those liable to suffer from them are able to function effectively as persons, citizens, and workers'.[32]

The other primary target of criticism is the agency's funding process. Most frequently raised are problems with the agency's procedures for obtaining public input. Many say the opportunities for public input are inadequately publicized. Consequently, advocacy groups with the highest political awareness and skills participate, while other groups are left out. Another complaint is that patients and their advocates are insufficiently represented among the public members of advisory councils and other NIH committees. According to the critics, this lack of representation is due to the agency's inadequate outreach and recruitment efforts.[33] Finally, patients and advocates seek a meaningful role in priority setting and funding allocation. As one congressional witness noted, '[s]ome patient groups believe the decision-making process at the NIH is basically a closed process where patient organizations are only consulted at the later stages, when decisions in fact have already been made'.[34] At another meeting on priority setting, an advocate reported that public participants, 'though politely received, often come away feeling patronized'.[35]

Additional process concerns focus on NIH accountability. Critics think the NIH should be required to show how its budget recommendations to Congress are justified by its stated research priorities. They also want NIH officials to furnish periodic reports to Congress and the public demonstrating that spending was consistent with the agency's articulated priorities.

---

[29] *Ibid.*, 3. [30] *Ibid.*, 2, 9.
[31] Institute of Medicine, n. 2, above, 31; Judith Randal, 'How to Divvy Up NIH's Research Pie Sparks Debate' (1999) 91 *Journal of the National Cancer Institute* 410, 411.
[32] Callahan, n. 10, above. [33] Institute of Medicine, n. 3, above, 63.
[34] *Biomedical Research Priorities*, n. 24, above, 42. [35] Randal, n. 31, above, 411.

The public discussion over NIH priority setting has produced some changes in NIH policy, which are discussed below. To date, however, the distributive justice issues raised by priority setting have not been systematically analysed. Moreover, although the NIH is moving to publicize and expand opportunities for public participation, no clear or formal procedure exists for incorporating public input into agency decisions. In the next two sections of this paper, I examine distributive and procedural justice concepts relevant to biomedical research priority setting.

Distributive Justice Considerations

Distributive justice theories seek to establish criteria that will lead to a fair distribution of benefits and burdens among persons. Distributive justice considerations are at the heart of the debate over NIH priority setting. The debate addresses whether certain health and scientific areas receive a disproportionately high level of funding, while other areas receive disproportionately low levels of funding. Of course, what is 'disproportionate' depends on one's view of the appropriate criteria for allocating research funds.

The criteria on public health needs presented in 'Setting Research Priorities' strongly resemble criteria used to determine priorities for funding health-care services: the degree of benefit offered (in terms of preventing death and disability), the number of persons who could benefit, and the potential for reducing financial and social costs associated with various conditions. As discussions of justice in allocation of health-care resources frequently point out, however, use of these criteria cannot resolve several significant allocation dilemmas.

One such dilemma concerns the appropriate priority to assign to the 'worst off' individuals—those most in need of improved health.[36] This dilemma raises numerous questions in the context of research allocation decisions. Should the NIH assign highest priority to research on disorders and injuries that cause death or significant disability? If so, how much priority? Should the agency give less to research on such conditions so that it can support research addressing less serious health problems? If so, what would be a fair proportion to direct to the less serious problems? How should funding be affected by scientists' predictions that the chances of a research 'breakthrough' are low for a lethal or seriously debilitating disease? What if studies addressing a less serious condition are believed to have a high likelihood of significantly benefiting persons at risk for that condition?

---

[36] Norman Daniels and James Sabin, 'Limits to Health Care: Fair Procedures, Democratic Deliberation, and the Legitimacy Problem for Insurers' (1997) 26 *Philosophy and Public Affairs* 303, 319.

A second unresolved distributive justice conflict arises when there is a choice between distributing a limited resource to all who may benefit or reserving it for those with the greatest chance of benefit (the 'fair chances/best outcomes' problem[37]). In the research funding context, this problem arises when officials must decide whether to allocate relatively significant sums to areas in which research is deemed to have the greatest promise of significant advancement. In doing so, they reduce the funds available for distribution across all areas, which in turn reduces the possibilities for unexpected breakthroughs in the low-priority areas.

A third distributive justice conflict is posed by the 'aggregation problem'.[38] This problem arises when funds must be divided among studies deemed likely to help many individuals with less serious health problems (e.g. research on a cure for the common cold) and studies likely to advance treatment of more serious conditions affecting relatively few persons.

A fourth point of contention concerns whether and, if so, in what situations, past neglect requires compensatory justice—in other words, an 'affirmative action' approach to research funding. For example, in the early 1990s women's health advocates called for remedial NIH funding to increase enrolment of women in clinical trials and to support research on health concerns specific to women.[39] The shift in priorities was justified, they argued, by the agency's prior failure to allocate sufficient funds to these research needs. In turn, some commentators disagreed with this position, arguing that the data were unclear on whether women were underrepresented in clinical studies and that research on diseases affecting primarily women actually received more than its 'fair share' of funds.[40]

With respect to the above issues, the research priorities debate raises distributive justice problems similar to those encountered in health-care funding decisions. But certain distributive justice problems are intensified in the research context because of the greater uncertainty characterizing predictions of benefit. Research is necessary because it is unknown whether particular lines of inquiry will lead to health benefits. Some research funds must be expended on studies that find certain approaches unlikely to yield such benefits. In these situations, research funds are not wasted, even though they fail to produce health improvements. Further uncertainty is introduced by the many factors that affect whether research knowledge is translated into practical health interventions and how any health benefits that emerge are distributed among those in need. Although research funding decisions ought to incorporate evidence-based predictions that a proposed study's results will produce knowledge relevant to

[37] *Ibid.*, 321.   [38] *Ibid.*
[39] Marcia Angell, 'Caring for Women's Health—What is the Problem?' (1993) 329 *New England Journal of Medicine* 271.
[40] Ace Allen, 'Women's Health' (1993) 329 *New England Journal of Medicine* 1816.

improvements in health care, the link between funding and health benefits will always be more tenuous in the research context than it is in decisions on health-care priorities.[41]

Resource allocation in the research context also is more challenging because it requires trade-offs between benefits to persons who will experience the burdens of disease in the near future and persons expected to suffer health problems in the more distant future (for example, a choice between funding a clinical trial of a new medication and funding a gene sequencing project whose health benefits will not materialize for many years). Additional complexity is introduced by foundation and industry funding for research. The presence of other funding sources requires government officials to take into account the extent to which particular research areas are and will be addressed by the private sector.[42]

The moral and practical complexities of applying distributive justice criteria to research allocation decisions are revealed by data from an empirical study of NIH disease-specific funding.[43] In the study, health policy analysts compared six measures commonly used to represent the burden of disease with NIH estimates on disease-specific funding. For three such measures—the total number of persons with the disease, the number of new cases, and the number of days persons with the disease were hospitalized—the analysts found no relation between severity of disease burden and amount of NIH funding. There was a weak association between level of funding and number of deaths caused by the disease; funding levels also were weakly associated with years of life lost from the disease. NIH funding was strongly associated with another measure of disease burden known as the disability-adjusted life-year. This measure is based on the number of years of healthy life lost due to disability or death from illness or injury.

When the study authors used the three latter measures of disease burden to predict the level of research funding specific diseases should receive, they found that research on AIDS, breast cancer, dementia, and diabetes received higher amounts than would be justified by the burdens imposed. Other conditions, including chronic obstructive pulmonary disease, perinatal conditions, and peptic ulcers, were under-funded according to these measures. For some diseases, judgements on the appropriateness of NIH funding varied with the criterion used to measure disease burden. For example, when the number of lives lost or the number of years of life lost was applied, schizophrenia and depression received more than the expected level of funding. But when number of disability-adjusted life-

---

[41] Newman and Sandberg, n. 4, above, 117–18.

[42] Institute of Medicine, n. 3, above, 33.

[43] Cary P. Gross, Gerard F. Anderson, and Neil R. Powe, 'The Relation Between Funding by the National Institutes of Health and the Burden of Disease' (1999) 340 *New England Journal of Medicine* 1881.

years was the basis for evaluating disease burden, these conditions received less than they should have.

What should we make of these findings? Do they indicate that NIH distributes its resources unfairly? The findings do raise questions about the fairness of NIH resource allocation decisions. Why was NIH funding strongly related to only one disease burden measure? Why did perinatal conditions—disorders affecting the very young—and chronic obstructive pulmonary disease—a common and seriously debilitating condition— receive less funding than would be predicted by their disability-adjusted life-years scores? Do the findings on AIDS and breast cancer funding verify the claim that NIH funding reflects public advocacy efforts?

It would be a mistake, however, to cite this study as strong evidence of unfair allocation. First, the available data on disease burdens and NIH funding by disease are partial and of debatable quality. Secondly, some of the apparent unfairness may be adequately explained by other factors, such as scientific opportunity and past NIH funding levels 'since diseases that have been underfunded in earlier years may deserve additional funding'.[44] For example, these factors might provide reasonable justification for the higher levels of funding received by studies on AIDS and breast cancer. Thirdly, some of the apparently problematic disparities may disappear if the contributions of other funding sources are taken into account. For example, research on pneumonia received less NIH funding than would be justified by disease burden, but this illness has been extensively studied by drug companies seeking to develop new antibiotics.[45] Fourthly, and most significant, different disease burden measures incorporate different value judgements, with some reflecting the view that 'all lives are equal in importance', some that avoiding premature death is more important, and some that providing improved quality of life can be as important as preventing death.[46] Thus, one's position on the fairness of NIH allocation will to some degree reflect one's position on these values issues.

In sum, like the debate over allocating health-care resources, the debate over research priority setting cannot be settled solely by reference to distributive justice considerations. Though broad allocation criteria may be devised to exclude funding decisions that few people would defend, they will leave numerous funding questions unresolved.[47] A statement on health-care priority setting by the American Medical Association's Council on Ethical and Judicial Affairs applies equally to the research context: '[d]isagreements about these choices are to be expected because of the

---

[44] *Ibid.*, 1886.   [45] *Ibid.*, 1885.   [46] *Ibid.*

[47] According to Daniels and Sabin, members of some European national commissions asked to set health-care priorities report that the consensus-based abstract principles they initially adopted were too vague to provide meaningful or acceptable resolutions when applied in practice. The groups are now focused on devising fair procedures to govern specific decisions. Daniels and Sabin, n. 36, above, 349.

diversity of moral, religious, and cultural traditions in this country and the complexity of the task'.[48] And, as Norman Daniels and James Sabin observe:

The weightings that different people give to different moral concerns, such as helping the worst off versus not sacrificing achievable medical benefits, probably depend on how these moral concerns fit between wider moral conceptions people hold. If so there is good reason to think these disagreements will be a persistent feature of the situation.[49]

According to these and other commentators, the best strategy in such a situation is to create a fair process for making controversial allocation decisions. In the next section, I discuss the possible features of such a process.

Procedural Justice Considerations

When modern democracies encounter values conflicts in establishing and applying public policies, fair procedures are seen as the best way to resolve the disagreements. In the words of US Supreme Court Chief Justice Rehnquist, '[a]greed-upon procedures for airing substantive divisions must be the hallmark' of public deliberative bodies.[50] The research funding process requires officials to weigh, balance, and trade off different and sometimes incompatible values as they allocate limited public resources to a subset of those who could benefit from them. Much of the debate over NIH funding allocation addresses perceived inadequacies in the existing priority setting process. In this section, I discuss empirical and conceptual work on the characteristics of fair allocation systems.

During the late 1980s, psychologist Tom Tyler conducted an extensive empirical inquiry into public perceptions of procedural justice.[51] Though Tyler's study focused on how fairly citizens thought they had been treated by police officers and judges, he also collected data on and reviewed studies of fairness in other policy contexts, including government distribution of scarce resources. One of Tyler's major findings was that achieving a favourable outcome was *not* the most important factor affecting citizens' evaluations of the fairness of public officials' decisions. Nor were their evaluations most affected by how much they were able to influence officials' decisions.

Instead, Tyler found that seven characteristics of official decision-making procedures had significant and independent effects on citizens'

---

[48] Council on Ethical and Judicial Affairs, American Medical Association, 'Ethical Issues in Health Care System Reform' (1994) 272 *Journal of the American Medical Association* 1059.

[49] Daniels and Sabin, n. 36, above, 321.

[50] 'Rehnquist Speaks', ABCNEWS.com. (12 Feb. 1999).

[51] T. R. Tyler, *Why People Obey the Law* (New Haven, Conn., 1990).

fairness evaluations: (1) authorities' effort to be fair, (2) authorities' honesty, (3) authorities' neutrality, (4) authorities' 'ethicality'—defined as politeness and concern for citizens' rights, (5) citizens' opportunities for representation, (6) the quality of officials' decisions—defined as whether authorities 'had gotten the information they needed to make good decisions' and 'had tried to bring the problem into the open so that it could be solved', and (7) citizens' opportunity to correct errors.[52] Tyler summarized his findings as follows:

> People believe that decisions should be made by neutral, unbiased decision-makers, and they expect the decision-makers to be honest and to make their decisions based on objective information about the issues.
>
> . . . People also feel that procedures are fairer when they believe they have had some control in the decision-making procedure. Such control includes having the opportunity to present one's arguments, being listened to, and having one's views considered.[53]

Tyler also determined that when decisions were made through a process with these characteristics, most people accepted the results, including personally unfavourable outcomes.[54]

Additional guidance on fairness in research priority setting comes from Norman Daniels's and James Sabin's analysis of fair procedures for allocating health-care resources—specifically, for insurers' decisions whether to cover particular health-care interventions. These authors believe that affected persons are more likely to regard decision-makers as trustworthy, legitimate, and fair if an allocation system has four features. First, decisions and their supporting rationales must be publicly accessible. Daniels and Sabin suggest that decision-makers develop a written, publicly available 'case law' to encourage 'more efficient, coherent, and fairer decisions over time, . . . strengthen broader public deliberation and contribute to the perceived legitimacy of the decision-makers'.[55] In their view, because the case-law approach creates pressure to produce an articulated and thoughtful explanation for a resource allocation choice, the approach will contribute to higher-quality decisions over time.

The second feature of a fair allocation system, according to Daniels and Sabin, is that the rationales for decisions supply 'reasons those affected by the decisions can recognize as relevant and appropriate for the purpose of justifying decisions to all who are affected by them'.[56] For example, they write, it is reasonable to exclude coverage for a health-care service if research shows that it is less beneficial than a currently available alternative. Daniels and Sabin think that public articulation of the reasons for allocation decisions can promote a deliberative process in which decision-makers and affected persons can determine what count as acceptable

[52] *Ibid.*, 137. [53] *Ibid.* [54] *Ibid.*, 107.
[55] Daniels and Sabin, n. 36, above, 327. [56] *Ibid.*, 330.

reasons. Perceptions of fairness, legitimacy, and trustworthiness will be enhanced, they believe, if persons disadvantaged in the allocation process accept that the unfavourable decision was based on an appropriate reason.

Thirdly, a fair allocation system will include a dispute resolution procedure that allows '[P]articipants that may have been excluded from the decision-making process and whose views may not have been clearly heard or understood find a voice . . .'.[57] According to Daniels and Sabin, such a mechanism will enhance perceptions of fairness and also decision-makers' ability to correct erroneous findings, thus improving the quality of allocation choices. They propose that the fourth feature of a fair allocation system is 'voluntary or public regulation of the process to ensure that conditions 1–3 are met'.[58]

The existing NIH allocation process fails to include many of the above features. These omissions may account for some of the controversy over research priority setting. In the concluding section of this paper, I describe ways the NIH allocation process could be altered to take procedural justice features into account.

Toward a More Just Priority Setting System

Government priority setting for biomedical research raises difficult distributive and procedural justice issues. Besides presenting controversial values questions, the funding allocation process is complex and multi-faceted. Its political and emotional dimensions add to the difficulties of reforming the process. Allocation choices inevitably disadvantage some persons, with serious consequences to them—a classic 'tragic choice' situation. Indeed, the desire to keep such painful trade-offs from public view may account for some of the vagueness and generality characterizing the existing NIH allocation system. But the increasingly heated debate over the system's fairness indicates that such an approach is no longer feasible or acceptable.[59]

To address the shortcomings of the existing system, officials should take several actions. First, the existing NIH priority setting criteria should be evaluated by persons inside and outside the agency. The evaluation should consider whether the existing criteria should be reordered to clarify that the paramount criterion is reduction of disease burden and that the remaining criteria (scientific merit, scientific opportunity, breadth of

---

[57] Daniels and Sabin, n. 36, above, 340.

[58] Ibid. 323. As Daniels and Sabin note, the features they deem important to a fair allocation system resemble principles promoting deliberative democratic decision-making proposed by Amy Gutmann and Dennis Thompson. According to Gutmann and Thompson, the deliberative process should be governed by publicity, reciprocity, and accountability: A. Gutmann and D. Thompson, Democracy and Disagreement (Cambridge, Mass., 1996).

[59] Daniels and Sabin, n. 36, above, 313–14.

research portfolio, and infrastructure needs) are relevant only to the extent that they contribute to reduction of disease burden.[60] Another factor to be considered is the extent to which US research funding should incorporate the goal of reducing disease burdens of persons in developing countries. The inquiry should also consider whether factors such as maintenance of national science leadership and promoting international relations are appropriate objectives for biomedical research funding.

The inquiry into priority setting criteria should explicitly address the values elements of different disease burden measures.[61] The goal should be to establish an ethically defensible measure of disease burden for NIH use—most likely, one that assigns value to both extending life and improving its quality. The discussion should also include the possibility of adopting functional measures that would represent benchmarks of success in addressing specific disease burdens. Strategies for improving the quality and scope of data on the burdens of health problems should be addressed as well.

Such an inquiry will be opposed by persons who believe that systematic planning is inappropriate in science. A common refrain is that scientists must have substantial freedom in conducting research if society is to gain the significant benefits conferred by unexpected discoveries. But the claim that this approach produces greater health gains is speculative; moreover, 'serendipity can happen anywhere—including in the context of goal-related research'.[62] Scientists themselves have recognized that research planning can be workable and acceptable. For example, in commenting on the resistance to establishing goals and planning for research funding, the editor of the journal *Science* asked, '[d]oes it make sense to be scientific about everything in our universe except the future course of science?'[63] Similarly, a 1999 report by a joint panel of the National Academy of Scientists, National Academy of Engineering, and Institute of Medicine concluded that federal agencies conducting and supporting research can meaningfully evaluate the outcomes of basic and applied research on a yearly basis. The report rejected what it called the 'widespread myth' that the value of basic and other forms of research cannot be assessed in the short term. It also took issue with the claim that science would be harmed by a more systematic approach. The committee issuing the report instead asserted, 'more effective and objective assessments of research programmes can only benefit the national research enterprise, both by focusing resources on the most vital fields, and by allocating those resources more effectively'.[64]

---

[60] Tengs, n. 28, above, 2.

[61] Paul Menzel, Marthe R. Gold, Erik Nord, Jose-Louis Pinto-Prades, Jeff Richardson, and Peter Ubel, 'Toward a Broader View of Values in Cost-Effectiveness Analysis of Health', (1999) 29 *Hastings Center Report* 7.   [62] Tengs, n. 28, above, 2.

[63] Floyd E. Bloom, 'Priority Setting Quixotic or Essential?' (1998) 282 *Science* 1641.

[64] Philip A. Griffiths, Public Briefing (17 Feb. 1999) www.nas.edu/new/, 3. The panel was discussing research agency compliance with the Government Performance and Results Act,

The evaluation of NIH priority setting criteria should aim to produce an enriched and revised version of 'Setting Research Priorities'. Unlike the initial version, the revised document should incorporate input from patient interest groups and others outside the agency. A draft version should be widely distributed and public comment elicited for consideration in preparing the final draft.

Congress and NIH officials should use the revised priority setting document to guide their budget decisions. The document should also be used as a mechanism to increase NIH accountability. It should serve as the basis of a planning and reporting system resembling the one Institute of Medicine President Kenneth Shine proposed in his Senate Hearing testimony:

We ought to hold the scientific leadership of the NIH . . . to a process in which they periodically review their research plans with intramural and extramural scientists as well as other important stakeholders in research and explicitly demonstrate to Congress and the public that they have considered [the agreed-upon funding principles] in generating their recommendations to the Congress with regard to the budget. . . .

I would urge that the various voluntary health agencies, advocacy groups, and interested parties express their views to Congress with regard to funding in a particular area based upon these principles, and that their views form a part of the periodic planning activities for the health science research enterprise. As a corollary to these recommendations, Congress should hold the leadership of the institutes and agencies responsible [for demonstrating] that the level of research investment in the various disease areas and specific problems is consistent with this set of principles. . . .[65]

As Shine asserted, NIH should be accountable to Congress and the public for showing how its actual funding decisions incorporated the agency's stated priorities. The agency's strategic plans, annual targets, and retrospective reports should contain more than simple descriptions of research areas and announcements of progress (NIH's traditional approach). Instead, the documents should indicate how the objectives and funding decisions are related to the goal of improved public health. The plans and reports should explain the public health justification for elevating certain areas above others. Furthermore, the reports should directly address the suspicion that scientific curiosity underlies many funding choices. Accordingly, when scientific opportunity is the claimed justifica-

which states that all federal agencies must provide to Congress: (1) a strategic plan by 1997, (2) a performance plan with specific annual targets by 1998, and (3) a report on success in meeting those targets by 2000. After that, strategic plans must be revised every three years and the performance plans and reports submitted every year. Though not directly aimed at NIH priority setting, this new law will require NIH to engage in a more systematic approach to funding allocation: Committee on Science, Engineering, and Public Policy, National Academy of Sciences, *Evaluating Federal Research Programs: Research and the Government Performance and Results Act* (Washington, DC, 1999).

[65] *Biomedical Research Priorities*, n. 24, above, 85.

tion for assigning higher priority to certain areas, detailed support for this judgement should be provided. Plans should state which potential funding areas have been assigned lower priority and give reasons for this choice. Reports should include information on areas that received less funding because others were deemed more important to support. When low merit scores on submitted proposals led officials to award a lower-than-expected amount to a high-priority area, the reports should include plans for encouraging higher-quality proposals in the future.

Elements of the above process should be incorporated into allocation decision-making at the institutes and centres as well. Institute and centre officials should apply the revised priority setting document to develop specific objectives for research in their mission areas. They should also provide well-publicized opportunities for patient representatives and other interested persons to provide input on the needs and problems most significant from their perspectives.[66] Institutes and centres should prepare and widely distribute annual reports describing how funding decisions advanced their research objectives.

The above changes would add several fairness elements to the NIH funding allocation process. A good faith effort by NIH officials to provide this information to Congress and the public would enhance perceptions of decision-makers' efforts to be fair, their honesty, and their respect for the interests of those providing the funds supporting biomedical research. Enriched accounts of research plans and actual funding decisions with clear reference to public health objectives and the ethical dimensions of those objectives would give the public and their representatives more confidence in the quality of the agency's choices, as well as an opportunity to respond and seek altered decisions in the future. In short, these documents would serve the case-law function Daniels and Sabin discuss in their account of fair allocation procedures, and would incorporate many of the features Tyler found important to public perceptions of fairness.

Further progress in establishing a fair system will require the NIH to revise its approach to obtaining and incorporating public perspectives on funding allocation. Based on recommendations from the Institute of Medicine, NIH officials have taken two actions to increase the breadth and depth of public input. First, they have created a new advisory body to the NIH director, the Council of Public Representatives (COPR). This group is composed primarily of persons from the lay advocate community, although it also includes several individuals with research of clinical training. Its twenty members were chosen from among 250 persons submitting

---

[66] In a 1999 statement to Congress, NIH Director Varmus said that public representatives would participate in preparation of the institute's and centre's strategic plans and review of the specific targets for the year: Harold E. Varmus, 'Fiscal Year 2000 President's Budget Request for the National Institutes of Health', www.nih.gov/welcome/director (22 Feb. 1999), 5.

applications (after a widely-publicized call for nominations). The rest of the applicants will become 'COPR Associates'; they will be enlisted to provide input on COPR activities and participate in other NIH activities. According to an NIH announcement, COPR will be a 'forum for discussing issues affecting the broad development of NIH policy, programs, and research goals and will advise the NIH Director on these matters'.[67]

The second initiative is to establish in the NIH director's office and in each institute and centre a public liaison office that will increase opportunities for interaction with agency officials. Beginning in spring 1999, the NIH had on its web site contact information on public liaison offices for the director and each institute and centre.[68] The offices are intended to publicize and improve opportunities for public communication with NIH staff about research priorities and results. According to the Institute of Medicine report, staff responsibilities should include collecting information on priorities from 'a broader range of constituencies' than had input in the past, arranging the information 'in a way that can be informative in priority setting', and ensuring that the agency's leaders obtain and reply to the information.[69]

The NIH also is moving to expand participation by public representatives in merit review of research proposals.[70] It remains to be seen, however, whether these initiatives will increase public influence on NIH priority setting. The major question is whether agency officials will provide opportunities for meaningful lay participation. Past attempts to integrate public representatives into science policy decision-making often failed to disturb expert control. What happened instead was that 'significant decisions remained largely within the hands of the scientific community, the public representatives consistently found that they were unable to exercise any significant leverage . . .'.[71]

Several conditions must be met for public participation in NIH funding decisions to have a different result. Meaningful participation in research priority setting will require NIH officials to see public representatives as possessing legitimate knowledge relevant to the task. Public participants will need to acquire sufficient understanding of the funding system and the complex policy considerations relevant to priority setting. They also will have to develop their roles as public advocates rather than advocates for particular populations or illness groups. Officials and public representatives will have to join in devising approaches that enable lay participants to express their views on the values relevant to priority setting and the trade-offs they would find most acceptable.[72]

Unless NIH officials are perceived as sincere and unbiased in their

[67] NIH News Alert (5 Apr. 1999), www.nih.gov/news/par/apr99.
[68] www.nih.gov/welcome.   [69] Institute of Medicine, n. 3, above, 62–3.
[70] Varmus, n. 66, above, 4.
[71] D. Dickson, *The New Politics of Science* (Chicago, Ill., 1988) 256.
[72] Dresser, n. 12, above.

efforts to incorporate public views on research priorities, public perceptions of fairness in NIH location are unlikely to change. Moreover, perceptions are unlikely to change unless officials provide the public and its congressional representatives with reports demonstrating that public input was considered and presenting reasons for the ultimate funding choices. Without such a response, dissatisfaction with NIH decisions is likely to persist, and Mother Teresa's Waiting Room will remain overcrowded. For ethical as well as political reasons, NIH officials and researchers should work with the public to create a more just system for determining how limited research resources can best serve humankind.

HEALTH RESEARCH WITH CHILDREN: THE NEW ZEALAND EXPERIENCE

Nicola Peart*

Introduction

In 1996 researchers at the University of Otago in New Zealand were awarded a grant by the Health Research Council of New Zealand to investigate the physiological causes of Sudden Infant Death Syndrome or cot death (SIDS). SIDS is still a significant problem in New Zealand, though the number of deaths has dropped substantially since likely hazards were identified in 1987.[1]

The 1996 study sought to monitor the responses of babies, aged one to four weeks and at risk of SIDS, to normal environmental stresses by mimicking common events such as re-breathing their own breath or a sudden drop in blood pressure. The researchers wished to ascertain whether these babies were at risk of SIDS because of a poor response to such events. Participating babies were attached to several sensors to monitor their heart rate, breathing, and oxygen levels. They were then strapped into a 'jolly jumper' harness and placed in a basinet to go to sleep. Once asleep, the level of carbon dioxide was raised gradually from the usual 0.04 per cent to 5 per cent while the oxygen level was lowered from its normal level of 21 per cent to 14 per cent or 13 per cent to mimic a common re-breathing event. After recording the baby's responses for about 500 heart beats, the baby was tilted to an angle of 60 degrees to

* I am grateful to Associate Professor David Holdaway of the Department of Paediatrics and Child Health, University of Otago, for his assistance with an earlier paper on this topic published in (1998) 2 (2) *ChildreNZ Issues Journal* 42. I am also indebted to Professor Barry Taylor, Dr Barbara Galland, Rachel Sayers, and Rebecca Hayman of the Department of Paediatrics and Child Health, University of Otago, for their generous assistance in preparing this paper. Jane Ashby, the Law Faculty's research assistant in 1999, spent many hours perusing the literature which proved to be invaluable in the preparation of this paper. Finally, I acknowledge with gratitude the very helpful comments of my colleagues, Professor Peter Skegg and Professor Mark Henaghan, on an earlier draft of this paper.
[1] E. A. Mitchell, J. M. Brunt and C. Everard, 'Reduction in Mortality from Sudden Infant Death Syndrome in New Zealand: 1986–92' (1994) 70 *Archives of Disease in Childhood* 291; R. Gilbert, 'The Changing Epidemiology of SIDS' (1994) 70 *Archives of Disease in Childhood* 445. 109 babies died as a result of SIDS in New Zealand in 1996 and 81 in 1997, according to the Ministry of Health, *Otago Daily Times,* 19 June 1999.

drop the blood pressure and measure the heart rate in response to this change. These tests were repeated during the various sleep stages and in several sleep positions, on their backs or sides as well as on their fronts. The babies were very closely monitored throughout and if there was any sign of distress the tests were stopped.

The study proposal was reviewed by the Health Research Council and received ethical approval from the Otago Ethics Committee. This committee, which comprises an equal number of health professionals and non-health professionals, is responsible for providing independent ethical appraisal of health research in the Otago province.[2]

The study was publicly attacked by Dr Jim Sprott, a forensic scientist with his own theory on cot death.[3] He claimed that the experiments were potentially dangerous and that parents therefore did not have the right to consent to their babies' participation in the study.[4] The Health Research Council referred his concerns to six overseas experts in pædiatrics and respiratory medicine for review. They were unanimous in their view that the study was safe and appropriate.[5] The risk was not significantly greater than many infants experienced naturally and the reviewers accordingly supported the Ethics Committee's approval of the study. Dr Sprott nonetheless continued his objections by writing to all parents of newborn babies about his concerns.

This case elicited a great deal of media attention in New Zealand. It also raised concerns in the minds of politicians and child-welfare organizations that the involvement of children in health research had not been fully considered in New Zealand.[6] There are no regulations or guidelines in

---

[2] Its composition is governed by the National Standard for Ethics Committees, promulgated by the Associate Minister of Health in 1996. The Otago Ethics Committee is accredited by the Health Research Council of New Zealand, which enables the Committee to comply with statutory requirements for ethical approval of health research such as those laid down by the Accident Insurance Act 1998 and its predecessor, the Accident Rehabilitation Compensation and Insurance Act 1992. The membership of the Otago Ethics Committee at the time was as follows: a lawyer, chair (me), bio-statistician, deputy chair, six health professionals (surgeon, physician, general practitioner, nurse, psychiatrist, and pharmacologist) and five non-health professionals (priest, bio-ethicist, patient advocate, and two Maori lay members).

[3] In his view cot death results from toxic gasses produced from antimony, a fire retardant used in mattresses and advocates wrapping them in a special plastic: J. Sprott, *The Cot Death Cover-Up?* (Auckland, 1996). This theory was discredited by C. Dezateux, H. Trevor Delves, J. Stacks, A. Wade, L. Pilgrim, and K. Costeloe, 'Urinary Antimony in Infancy' (1997) 76 *Archives of Disease in Childhood* 432–6.

[4] Sprott's press release was published in all the national newspapers, including the *Otago Daily Times*, 20 Feb. 1997.

[5] 'Cot Death Research Study Vindicated' (1997) 21 *Health Research Council Newsletter* 10.

[6] The then Commissioner for Children, the late Laurie Reilly, expressed his concerns to the researchers in a letter, dated 27 Feb. 1997 and undertook to consider the involvement of children in health research. Phillida Bunkle, MP, who was one of the persons responsible for

New Zealand which adequately deal with the conduct of health research with children. The National Standard for Ethics Committees is incomplete and vague in regard to children as research participants.[7] The Ministry of Health is currently reviewing the National Standard and may include more appropriate guidelines for health research with children.

In the meantime researchers and ethics committees depend on foreign and international guidelines to assess the appropriateness of involving children in research projects.[8] These guidelines are also vague, incomplete, and in some important respects inconsistent. For example, they appear to set different limits on the degree of risk to which children may be exposed if the research is not intended to provide a therapeutic benefit to the participating children, as was the case in the SIDS study described above.

There appear to be three fundamental issues in the conduct of health research with children. The first is whether children should be involved in health research.[9] Part one of this paper will show that there appears to be general agreement nowadays that their involvement is not merely desirable but necessary for the promotion of their health and well being.

The second issue is whether parents have the right to consent to their child's participation in research and, if so, under what conditions. The degree of permissible risk and the justification for proxy consent will be considered in this part. Section 10 of the New Zealand Bill of Rights Act 1990 poses a particular problem because it appears to prohibit parents from consenting to their children's participation in medical or scientific experimentation.

Part three will deal with the third issue: the child's right to consent or refuse participation. The law is mostly concerned with the child's capacity to consent to medical treatment. Whether a child of 15 or 16 has the capacity to give legally effective consent to participate in health research is unclear and the various guidelines are inconsistent. The paper will conclude by considering what changes New Zealand should make to correct the current deficiencies in the National Standard and ensure that health research with children is conducted in an ethically appropriate manner.

bringing into the open in 1987 the unethical cervical cancer study at Auckland's National Women's hospital, which subsequently gave rise to an enquiry chaired by the then Chief Family Court Judge Sylvia Cartwright, raised Dr Sprott's concerns in Parliament and sought information under the Official Information Act 1982: correspondence to the Southern Regional Health Authority on 26 Mar. 1997.

[7] N. 2, above. The National Standard was developed as one of the responses to the findings of the 1988 Cervical Cancer Inquiry. See for a summary of this inquiry, its findings, and recommendations: C. Paul, 'The New Zealand Cervical Cancer Study: Could it Happen Again?' (1988) 297 *British Medical Journal* 533–9.

[8] The term 'guidelines' will henceforth be deemed to include statutes as well as international conventions, unless the context indicates otherwise.

[9] Genetic research is excluded from this paper as it raises additional issues which deserve separate consideration.

Should Children be Involved in Health Research?

The answer to this question is now unequivocally in the affirmative. But that is a relatively recent phenomenon. The desire to prevent a repetition of the inhumane experiments conducted by the Nazis on non-consenting prisoners during World War II led to the adoption of very strict guidelines for the conduct of medical research in the Nuremberg Code of 1947. Clause 1 provided:

The voluntary consent of the human subject is absolutely essential. This means that the person involved should have legal capacity to give consent.

Children were thus excluded from participating in health research because of their inability to give legally effective consent.

Article 7 of the International Covenant on Civil and Political Rights could be viewed as an endorsement of this stance:

No one shall be subjected to torture or to cruel, inhuman or degrading treatment or punishment. In particular, no one shall be subjected without his free consent to medical or scientific experimentation.[10]

Yet Article 12 of the International Covenant on Economic, Social, and Cultural Rights, adopted at the same time, seems to give implicit support to the conduct of research with children.[11] It requires signatories to take steps to ensure that everyone enjoys the highest attainable standard of physical and mental health, *inter alia* by providing for the reduction of stillbirths, infant mortality, and the healthy development of the child as well as preventing, treating, and controlling epidemic and other diseases. This goal cannot be achieved without research. As the Explanatory Report to the recently adopted European Convention on Human Rights and Biomedicine explains:

Diagnostic and therapeutic progress for the benefit of sick children depends to a large extent on new knowledge and insight regarding the normal biology of the human organism and calls for research on the age-related functions and development of normal children before it can be applied in the treatment of sick children. Moreover, paediatric research concerns not only the diagnosis and treatment of serious pathological conditions but also the maintenance and improvement of the state of health of children who are not ill, or who are only slightly ill.[12]

The two United Nations Covenants followed shortly after the adoption

[10] GA Res. 2200 (XXI), 1966, in force on 23 Mar. 1976.

[11] GA Res. 2200 (XXI), 1966, in force on 3 Jan. 1976.

[12] Directorate of Legal Affairs, Council of Europe, *Explanatory Report to the Convention for the Protection of Human Rights and Dignity of the Human Being with Regard to the Application of Biology and Medicine* (*Explanatory Report*), 1997, 24. See also the *International Ethical Guidelines for Biomedical Research Involving Human Subjects*, prepared by The Council for International Organizations of Medical Sciences in collaboration with the World Health Organization (*CIOMS Guidelines*), 1993, 11.

by the World Medical Assembly of the Declaration of Helsinki in 1964.[13] This Declaration explicitly permitted children to participate in biomedical research, whether in combination with clinical treatment or not, provided proxy consent and, where possible, the child's consent was obtained.[14] No other special conditions were imposed in respect of children.

Health research with children nonetheless remained subject to severe restrictions. In the United Kingdom, for instance, it was thought that children could not participate in health research which was not intended to benefit them and carried some risk of harm.[15] As almost all medical procedures carry some risk of harm, this view effectively precluded all research which had no intended therapeutic benefit for the child participants.

It has since become apparent that excluding children from participating in such health research also excluded them from its benefits. The American Academy of Pediatrics noted that 81 per cent of drugs listed in the 1991 Physicians' Desk Reference, a widely used drug formulary in the United States, included a disclaimer for use with children or lacked appropriate dose information.[16] The studies required to produce this sort of information had not been done, leaving the prescriber with the unenviable choice of either denying the child potentially beneficial treatment or risking an unforeseen toxic effect due to the different physiology of childhood.[17] Treatments which are safe in adults are not necessarily safe in children, because their disease processes are often peculiar to their age groups. Their anatomy, physiology, metabolism, responses, and reactions are different from those of adults.[18] Children's unique interests were thus endangered by the very mechanisms set up to protect them.

This realization resulted in the development of new national and international guidelines.[19] New Zealand's National Standard for Ethics

---

[13] As amended in 1975, 1983, 1989, and most recently by the 48th General Assembly of the World Medical Association in 1996.

[14] N. 13 above, II.1 and III.3a in the 1964 Declaration; Basic Principle 11 in the most recent version.

[15] Medical Research Council, 'Responsibility in Investigations on Human Subjects', *Report of the Medical Research Council for the Year 1962–63* (London, 1964), 21–5 as cited in R. H. Nicholson (ed.), *Medical Research with Children: Ethics, Law, and Practice* (Oxford, 1986), 6. See also P. Ramsey, 'The Enforcement of Morals: Non-therapeutic Research on Children' (1976) 6(4) *Hastings Center Report* 21–30.

[16] R. E. Kauffman *et al.*, 'Guidelines for the Ethical Conduct of Studies to Evaluate Drugs in Pediatric Populations' (1995) 95(2) *Pediatrics* 258. See also J. P. Walsh, C. M. Dayan, and M. J. Potts, 'Prescribing Medicines for Children' (1999) 319 *British Medical Journal* 70.

[17] Prescribing to children medicines not evaluated for use in their age group is condemned by the Committee for Proprietary Medicinal Products, *Note for Guidance on Clinical Investigation of Medicinal Products in Children* (CPMP Guidelines), CPMP/EWP/462/95, 1.11.

[18] The CPMP Guidelines argue that these differences are the scientific justification for conducting drug trials with children: *ibid.* 2/11.

[19] CIOMS Guidelines, n. 12 above; Council of Europe, Convention for the Protection of Human Rights and Dignity of the Human Being with Regard to the Application of Biology and Medicine (European Convention on Human Rights and Biomedicine) 1996; United States

Committees, adopted by the Associate Minister of Health in 1996, is the principal guide for New Zealand's ethics committees. It follows the overseas guidelines in permitting both therapeutic and non-therapeutic research with children.[20] Therapeutic research is intended to provide therapeutic benefit to the research participants, whereas non-therapeutic research has no such aim. The purpose of the latter is to contribute to generalizable scientific knowledge. The SIDS study described in the introduction is an obvious example of non-therapeutic research. Its purpose was not to benefit the babies who participated, but to generate knowledge about babies' arousal patterns which could assist in the prevention of SIDS in the future.

There appears to be a consensus that the involvement of children in both forms of research is not only desirable, but necessary if their health and wellbeing are to be promoted.[21] As the World Health Organization and the Council for International Organizations of Medical Sciences (CIOMS) noted in their Guidelines:

The participation of children is indispensable for research into diseases of childhood and conditions to which children are particularly susceptible.[22]

Further support for this view may be found in the United Nations Convention on the Rights of the Child to which New Zealand, like almost every country in the world, is a party.[23] Article 6 requires States Parties to ensure the survival and development of the child, while Article 24 requires

of America: Code of Federal Regulations (US Code) Title 45, 1991; National Institute of Health Policy and Guidelines on the Inclusion of Children as Participants in Research Involving Human Subjects (NIH Policy) 1998; United Kingdom: Medical Research Council, *The Ethical Conduct of Research on Children* (MRC Report), 1991 and British Paediatric Association, *Guidelines for the Ethical Conduct of Medical Research Involving Children* (BPA Guidelines) 1992; South African Medical Research Council, *Guidelines on Ethics for Medical Research* (South African Guidelines) 1993; Australia: Australian College of Paediatrics, *Policy Statement on Ethics of Research in Children* (Australian College Statement) 1998 and National Health and Medical Research Council, *National Statement on Ethical Conduct in Research Involving Humans* (NHMRC Statement) 1999; New Zealand: *National Standard for Ethics Committees*, 1999.

[20] CIOMS Guidelines, n. 12 above, 20; European Convention on Human Rights and Biomedicine, n. 19, above, Art. 17(2); CPMP, n. 17, above, 1.11; BPA Guidelines, n. 19, above, 4 and 7; MRC Report, n. 19, above, 6.2 and 6.3; South African Guidelines, n. 19, above, 1.4.1 and 6.2.2.

[21] The US House of Representatives and Senate were sufficiently concerned by the lack of information on treatments in regular use with children that they urged the National Institute of Health to establish priorities for paediatric research. The NIH issued a Policy and Guidelines to increase the participation of children in research on 6 Mar. 1998: NIH Policy, n. 19, above. CIOMS Guidelines, n. 12, above, Guideline 5; European Convention on Human Rights and Biomedicine, n. 19, above, Art. 17; US Code, n. 19, above, 46.405 and 46.406; MRC Report, n. 19, above, 6.2; BPA Guidelines, n. 19, above, 7; South African Guidelines, n. 19, above, 1.4; Australian College Statement, n. 19, above, 3.2; NHMRC Statement, n. 19, above, 4.1.

[22] CIOMS Guidelines, n. 12, above, 20 and 24. See also the Explanatory Report on Art. 17(2) of the European Convention on Human Rights and Biomedicine, n. 12, above, 22.

[23] GA Res 44/25, 1989. New Zealand ratified the Convention in 1993.

States Parties to recognize the right of the child to the enjoyment of the highest attainable standard of health and to facilities for the treatment of illness and rehabilitation of health. Article 24(2)(a) is particularly apposite to SIDS research because it requires States Parties to take appropriate measures to diminish infant and child mortality.[24] If states are to comply with these obligations, therapeutic as well as non-therapeutic research with children will be essential.

There is thus good scientific justification for involving children in health research. The question is whether there is a legal and ethical justification for doing so. The normal justification for participation in health research is the participant's free and informed consent.[25] As children often lack legal capacity the answer to this question depends on the right of parents to consent on their children's behalf. This issue will be considered in the next section.

Parents' Right to Consent to their Children's Participation in Health Research

The Declaration of Helsinki is widely regarded as establishing the basic principles for the conduct of biomedical research involving humans.[26] Fundamental to all health research are the principles that concern for the interests of the participants must always prevail over the interests of science and society and that the importance of the objective must always be in proportion to the inherent risk to the subject.[27] Provided the conditions expected of all research are met, the Declaration permits parents to consent to their children's participation.[28]

More recent guidelines have added a number of other conditions specifically designed to protect children. They may participate only if the research cannot equally well be done on adults and the purpose of the research is to obtain knowledge relevant to the health needs of children.[29] Some guidelines recommend that older children be used before younger

---

[24] G. Van Bueren, *The International Law on the Rights of the Child*, International Studies in Human Rights, (Dordrecht, 1995), xxxv, 293–302.

[25] International Covenant on Civil and Political Rights, n. 10, above, Art. 7; New Zealand Bill of Rights Act, 1990, s.10. Declaration of Helsinki, n. 13, above, Basic Principle 9; CIOMS Guidelines, n. 12, above, 13; European Convention on Human Rights and Biomedicine, n. 19, above, Art. 5; National Standard, n. 2, above, 5.1.2 and 5.1.3.

[26] The CIOMS Guidelines, n. 12, above, National Standard, n. 2, above, MRC Report, n. 19, above and BPA Guidelines, n. 19, above, all refer to the Declaration of Helsinki in these terms.

[27] N. 13, above, Basic Principles 4 and 5. See also European Convention on Human Rights and Biomedicine, n. 19, above, Art. 16.

[28] N. 13, above, Basic Principle 11.

[29] European Convention on Human Rights and Biomedicine, n. 19, above, Art.17; CIOMS Guidelines, n. 12, above, 20; National Standard, n. 2, above, 5.1.4; NHMRC Statement, n. 19, above, 4.1.

ones.[30] One or two have added such sensible criteria as: the research must be designed and carried out by people experienced in doing research with children and only the number of participants must be used that is scientifically and clinically essential.[31]

RISK

The crucial issue in relation to health research with children is the risk of harm to which children may be exposed. 'Risk' has a number of meanings. It refers both to the probability and the magnitude of harm which may result from participating in a research project. 'Harm' includes the physical, psychological, and emotional hazards to the child and to the child's family. Children's perceptions of and responses to harm tend to change as they mature, so that generalizations about risk will alter with age. Yet, most guidelines fail to address these variables adequately.

In describing the risk of harm to which children may be exposed in research, most guidelines distinguish between therapeutic and non-therapeutic research. If the research has no intended therapeutic benefit for the children participating, the degree of risk is set at a very low level, though there is some variation between the different guidelines. The English Medical Research Council (MRC) Report, for instance, stipulates that the risk should be 'negligible' at most. This means:

that the risks of harm anticipated in the proposed research are not greater, considering the probability and magnitude of physiological or psychological harm or discomfort, than those ordinarily encountered in daily life or during the performance of routine physical or psychological examination or tests.[32]

Examples include non-invasive observations and assessments, physical examinations, changes in diet, and obtaining blood and urine specimens.

In therapeutic research, by contrast, no attempt is made to set a fixed limit on the degree of the risk. Therapeutic research is generally seen as a form of medical treatment, and the degree of permissible risk is thus dependent on the anticipated benefits to the patients who are participating.[33] The principle applicable to health research with adults applies equally to children in this type of research: the likely benefits of the research must (clearly) outweigh the possible risk of harm to the participants.[34] The CIOMS Guidelines also require the therapeutic interventions to be at least as advantageous to the child as any available alternative.[35]

---

[30] CIOMS Guidelines, n. 12, above, 20; BPA Guidelines, n. 19, above, 6.

[31] CPMP Guidelines, n. 17, above, 5.2. In adult health research there is more likely to be a minimum number of participants, rather than a maximum.   [32] N. 19, above, 6.3.3.

[33] Ibid.; South African Guidelines, n. 19, above, 6.2.2.1; MRC Report, n. 19, above, 3.3.1; NHMRC Statement, n. 19, above, 1.6.

[34] MRC Report, n. 19, above, 6.2; South African Guidelines, n. 19, above, 1.4.3.ii; CIOMS Guidelines, n. 12, above, 20.   [35] N. 12, above, 20.

The classification into therapeutic and non-therapeutic research poses a problem, however, because 'therapeutic research' is seldom wholly for the participant's benefit. Most projects classified as such include non-therapeutic interventions which the participant would not undergo but for the research. Two examples may help to clarify this point. A clinical trial comparing the effectiveness of two registered drugs designed to treat a particular disease from which all the research participants are suffering will be classified as therapeutic research, even though it will probably include interventions, such as the collection of blood samples by venepuncture, solely for the purposes of the research. These interventions are not therapeutic and do carry some risk. Most guidelines nonetheless permit the taking of venepunctures in this situation.[36]

The classification problem becomes even more acute if, instead of comparing two registered drugs, the researchers propose to compare a new drug with a placebo.[37] Participants are normally randomly allocated to the treatment group or the placebo group of the trial. Neither the participants nor the researchers will know to which group each participant has been allocated. This is done to ensure no bias creeps into the results. Leaving aside the possible benefits of placebos (which are well described), that group is not intended to benefit. It is included to provide a standard against which the new drug may be compared. To classify such a trial as therapeutic is clearly misleading. Only one group is intended to benefit and its membership is unknown. Nor is it non-therapeutic, because one group is receiving treatment. What then is the degree of permissible risk?

This classification problem has been overcome in some guidelines by linking risk to the therapeutic or non-therapeutic purpose of the individual interventions, rather than the research project as a whole. The CIOMS Guidelines, for example, provide that:

the risk of interventions that are not intended to be of direct benefit to the child-subject . . . should be minimal—that is, no more likely and not greater than the risk attached to routine medical or psychological examination of such children. When an ethical review committee is persuaded that the object of the research is sufficiently important, slight increases above minimal risk may be permitted.[38]

---

[36] The Explanatory Report on Art.17(2) of the European Convention on Human Rights and Biomedicine explains that venepunctures are permitted: n. 12, above. See also the MRC Report and the South African Guidelines, n. 19, above.

[37] A placebo is a non-active substance. The CPMP Guidelines set strict limits on the use of placebos in clinical trials of medicinal products: n. 17, above, 5.2.1.1.

[38] N. 12 above, 21. See also the NHMRC Statement, n. 19 above, app. 3. A decision of a New York court prohibited the participation of incompetent people in any research which contains even a single non-therapeutic component that carries more than minimal risk. A slight increase over minimal risk would be illegal. *TD* v. *New York State Office of Mental Health and Department of Health*, 228 AD 2d 95 (App. Div., First Dept., 5 Dec. 1996), as cited and discussed by S. Haimowitz, S. J. Delano, and J. M. Oldham, 'Uninformed Decisionmaking: The Case of Surrogate Research Consent' (1997) 27 (6) *Hastings Center Report* 9.

This approach has the advantage of focusing on the potentially harmful interventions, but the guidelines are still far from precise. How much is a slight increase above minimal risk? What are routine medical examinations? Is it the severity of harm or the probability of it occurring which should be minimal, or both? And what about formulations which include as a norm 'the risks encountered in daily life', as in the MRC Report quoted above?[39] Their measure fluctuates depending on the society in which the children live. The more violent the society, the greater the risk to which a child is allowed to be exposed, presumably. This is unlikely to have been the intention, even if it is the logical consequence of the chosen words. The South African Medical Research Council was obviously conscious of this problem and amended the wording of its risk definition to the 'daily lives of people in a stable society'.[40] That still begs the question: what is a stable society?

New Zealand's National Standard for Ethics Committees is even more uncertain. It distinguishes between therapeutic and non-therapeutic research, but the degree of permissible risk to which a child participant may be exposed is the same for both. It provides that proxy consent cannot authorize research which carries 'significantly greater risk to the child than normal clinical treatment' would pose.[41] Not only is it unclear what significantly greater than normal risk means, the norm against which this comparison has to be made is also unclear. Some 'normal clinical treatments' carry very significant risks and in the context of non-therapeutic research there is no normal clinical treatment against which the necessary comparison can be made.

Such imprecise measures are unhelpful guides and may result in unacceptable risks being taken. Workable, value-neutral definitions which provide some certainty as to the degree of permissible risk are an indispensable aid to the task of assessing whether the study meets ethical requirements.[42]

The British Paediatric Association Guidelines go a long way towards meeting this requirement. Instead of a vague general definition of risk, they list the procedures which are permissible in non-therapeutic research:

Minimal (the least possible) risk describes procedures such as questioning, observing and measuring children, provided that procedures are carried out in a sensitive way, and that consent has been given. Procedures with minimal risk include collecting a single urine sample (but not by aspiration), or using blood from a sample that has been taken as part of treatment.

---

[39] See text accompanying n. 32, above. See also the definition of minimal risk in the NHMRC Statement, n. 19, above, app. 3.

[40] N. 19, above, 5.4.3.1.   [41] N. 2, above, 5.1.4.

[42] M. Freeman, 'Childrearing: Private Matter or Public Concern?' in J. Pousson-Petit (ed.), *Liber Amicorum Marie-Thérèse Meulders-Klein* (Brussels, 1998), 255, 265–6.

Not only is this list quite precise, it is also, somewhat unusually, drawn up from the child's perspective rather than a medical perspective. Venepunctures are excluded because of children's fear of needles.[43] None of the listed procedures are likely to hurt or disturb children. Some might say that they carry no risk at all. The disadvantage of this list is its inflexibility. It applies to all children, irrespective of age. Fear of needles may be a valid reason for excluding infants and young children, but it is less convincing in older children and teenagers. Even if these older children have not overcome their fear of needles, they are old enough to voice their objections and to understand that the pain can be avoided by the use of a topical anaesthetic, such as Emla cream.

Not surprisingly, the blanket prohibition on venepunctures in non-therapeutic research has been criticized, because it precludes potentially valuable research.[44] Worse still, ethics committees may be persuaded to ignore this prohibition and grant approval to invasive procedures, thus rendering the guideline worthless. Given the paucity of information on childhood diseases and treatments, guidelines should be more attuned to the needs of paediatric research and the varying circumstances of potential child participants.

JUSTIFICATION FOR PROXY CONSENT

No matter how precise the definitions, the question still remains: what is the justification for proxy consent? The Nuremberg Code prohibited proxy consent, but the more recent guidelines permit it, though they admit that the legal basis for doing so is unclear.[45] Proxy consent for medical treatment is normally justified as being in the best interests of the child, because its purpose is to provide therapeutic benefit to the child. That justification cannot apply in the context of most research. Even in so-called therapeutic research, not all interventions are usually intended to be of direct benefit to the participants. Besides, as McLean notes, the uncertainty inherent in research precludes an accurate assessment of the risks and benefits so that it is also impossible to predict that participation is in the best interests of the child.[46]

The English Medical Research Council argued in its report that proxy consent is justified if participation is not clearly against the child's interests.[47] The European Convention on Human Rights and Biomedicine appears to have adopted a similar stance, albeit cautiously. The

---

[43] D. Hull's Commentary on the BPA Guidelines, n. 19, above, 3.

[44] See, e.g., Walsh *et al.*, n. 16, above.   [45] MRC Report, n. 19, above, 7.2.7.

[46] S. McLean, 'Medical Experimentation with Children' (1992) 6 *International Journal of Law and the Family* 173, 183–5.

[47] MRC report, n. 19 above, 11. See also the discussion of this issue in Nicholson, n. 15, above, 135.

Explanatory Report on the Convention provides that children may take part in research which is of no direct benefit to them, but only in exceptional circumstances.[48] It justifies their participation in such research on a broad view of benefit: the possibility of indirect or future benefit to participants. However, it does not preclude research which has no hope of ever personally benefiting the participants. The 'highly protective conditions' under which such research may take place are aimed at avoiding harm.[49] It appears therefore that this Convention also justifies children's participation in research on the basis that it is not against their interests.[50]

Parents are not required to act in the best interests of their children all the time. As Skegg points out, society assumes that parents have the authority to permit a wide range of activities which are not for the child's benefit and may expose their children to some risk of harm. He argues that, when a minor is incapable of consenting, a parent can give legally effective consent to any procedure to which a 'reasonable parent' would consent.[51] He refers to a decision of the House of Lords concerning blood tests for forensic purposes, in which Lord Reid held that a reasonable parent would consent to a blood test on a child, which was in the public interest rather than the child's interest, unless he or she thought that the test would clearly be against the child's interests.[52] Though this decision cannot be relied on as authority for proxy consent to non-therapeutic research procedures, it does reflect an approach to proxy consent that now appears to be quite widely accepted.[53]

The European Convention on Human Rights and Biomedicine brings some much-needed clarity to the issue of proxy consent for health research with children, at least in Europe. For those states that are not a party to this Convention, such as New Zealand, the legal status of proxy consent remains somewhat uncertain. New Zealand's Guardianship Act provides that parents have the right to control the upbringing of their child, which includes all the rights, powers, and duties in respect of the child's person.[54] Whether this provision encompasses the right to authorize a child's participation in health research is unclear. Section 10 of the New Zealand Bill of Rights Act 1990 suggests that it does not:

Every person has the right not to be subjected to medical or scientific experimentation without *that person's* consent.[55]

---

[48] N. 12, above, 22.   [49] N. 12, above, 24.

[50] The proposed provision relating to medical experimentation in the UN Convention on the Rights of the Child provided a similar justification, but it was omitted because there was insufficient time to debate it fully: Van Bueren, n. 24, above, 311–2.

[51] P. D. G. Skegg, *Law, Ethics and Medicine* (Oxford, 1984), 66. The MRC has adopted this test in its Report, n. 19, above, 7.2.10.

[52] *S* v. *McC; W* v. *W* [1972] AC 44, 45; Skegg, n. 51, above, 67.

[53] NHMRC Statement, n. 19, above, 4.3.   [54] Guardianship Act 1968, s. 3.

[55] My emphasis. The Bill of Rights applies to acts done by persons in the performance of

This right is taken from Article 7 of the International Covenant on Civil and Political Rights, but unlike that Article, section 10 is not part of the larger right to freedom from cruel, inhuman, or degrading treatment.[56] Section 10 thus has the potential to be wider in scope. Section 5 of the New Zealand Bill of Rights Act permits such reasonable limits on the rights contained in the Act as can be demonstrably justified in a free and democratic society, but only if prescribed by law. The New Zealand National Standard arguably meets this requirement, because it acquired the force of law indirectly through the Code of Health and Disability Consumers' Rights, which was set out in the Schedule to Regulations made in 1996 under the Health and Disability Commissioner Act 1994. Though this Code was drafted for purposes of health service delivery, Right 9 extends the rights listed in the Code to research and teaching. Right 4(2) provides: 'every consumer has the right to have services provided that comply with legal, professional, ethical and other relevant standards'. The National Standard undoubtedly comes within the scope of this provision. The National Standard thus having the force of law, it could be viewed as a justified limitation on section 10 of the Bill of Rights Act.[57]

Even if parents in New Zealand have the right to consent to their children's participation in health research, they are not permitted to do so if it would harm their child. If they did, the care and protection proceedings outlined in the Children, Young Persons, and Their Families Act could be activated.[58] The limits imposed on the degree of permissible risk and the other conditions referred to earlier in this part of the paper are aimed at avoiding harm to the child. Compliance with those conditions would ensure that participation is not against the child's interests, and parental consent in these circumstances would satisfy Lord Reid's test.

The parents' motivation in granting consent is also an important factor, though it is seldom mentioned. Parents may be induced to consent for a variety of inappropriate reasons, such as financial gain, and so may expose their children to an unacceptable risk of harm. A poor community is easily exploited by an offer of payment. The CIOMS Guidelines accordingly provide that parents should be compensated only for their expenses and

any public function, power, or duty. As most health research is conducted in public hospitals for which a licence under the Hospitals Act 1957 is required, the conduct of that research will come within the purview of the Bill of Rights Act. See further A. Nunns, *Drug Trials Involving Children: Section 10 of the New Zealand Bill of Rights Act and the Law of Consent,* unpublished LLB Hons. dissertation, University of Otago, 1998.

[56] It was appreciated by the drafters that by separating medical experimentation from the larger right s. 10 might prevent legitimate research, but they saw no good reason to limit the s.: Department of Justice, *A Bill of Rights for New Zealand—a White Paper* (Wellington, 1985) 10.164.

[57] An alternative argument justifying proxy consent is provided elsewhere: N. S. Peart and D. Holdaway, 'Legal and Ethical Issues in Health Research with Children' (1998) 2(2) *ChildreNZ Issues Journal* 42, 45.

[58] Children, Young Persons and Their Families Act 1989, part II.

should receive no remuneration if their children participate in a research project.[59]

This was not an issue in the SIDS study, since no payment was involved. Nor were the children or the parents intended to benefit in any other way from participating in the study. So what did motivate them to participate? This was the question posed in a subsequent survey of all parents who were invited to enrol their babies in the SIDS study.[60]

86 per cent of the respondent parents who consented to their babies' participation did so to benefit medical science and to prevent SIDS. All understood the purpose of the study and most realized that it would not benefit their children.[61] Though 26 per cent had initial concerns about the safety of the tests, principally as a result of Dr Sprott's campaign, they nonetheless agreed to take part and none had any residual concerns after the tests had been completed. The principal reason for declining to participate in the study was inconvenience. Only 29.3 per cent refused because of concerns for the safety of their children, which may have been induced by the unfounded objections of Dr Sprott. Given the very small risk of any harm resulting from the investigations and the conditions under which the study took place, it seems that the parents who decided to take part met Lord Reid's test. They acted reasonably, because participation was not against their babies' interests. Proxy consent in such circumstances is in my view permissible.

Children's Right to Consent to their Participation in Health Research

Children in New Zealand attain majority at the age of 20.[62] From that age onwards such competence as a child may have lacked solely by virtue of age ceases. But even before they attain the age of majority children have the capacity to give legally effective consent to a wide range of activities. Section 25 of the Guardianship Act, for instance, provides that:

the consent of a child of or over the age of 16 years to any donation of blood by him, or to any medical, surgical or dental procedure to be carried out on him *for his benefit* by a person professionally qualified to carry it out, shall have the same effect as if he were of full age.[63]

---

[59] N. 12, above, 19; South African Guidelines, n. 19, above, 6.2.2.2.

[60] R. Hayman, B. J. Taylor, N. S. Peart, B. C. Galland, R. M. Sayers, 'Participation in Research: Informed Consent, Motivation and Influence', presented at the European Society for the Prevention of Infantile Apnoea and Sudden Death: the verge of the millennium, Jerusalem, June 1999. 101 parents consented to their babies' participation in the SIDS study and 104 declined. 69% of the consenting parents and 42% of the declining parents responded to the questionnaire.

[61] Some thought the study would reveal whether their babies was safe from SIDS, even though this was not one of the stated objectives of the study. However, parents of babies who responded poorly to the tests were given additional advice and a monitor.

[62] Age of Majority Act. 1970, s. 4. The UN Convention on the Rights of the Child defines a child as a human being below the age of 18: Art. 1.   [63] My emphasis.

As therapeutic research is regarded as a form of medical treatment, it is generally argued that a child over the age of 16 has the legal capacity to consent to participate in such research. However, this section cannot be relied on if the research is not intended to be of benefit to the participants, since one of the essential conditions of the section cannot be satisfied.

The common law, by contrast, does not make capacity age specific. The famous ruling of the House of Lords in *Gillick v. West Norfolk and Wisbech Area Health Authority*, recognizes that capacity evolves gradually as children mature, and that children below the age of 16 may be legally competent to consent.[64] This view has yet to be formally adopted in New Zealand. One High Court judge held that section 25 of the Guardianship Act implied that a child below the age of 16 was not competent to consent to medical treatment.[65] However, the Court of Appeal has since noted the *Gillick* reasoning with approval.[66] Even if *Gillick* is part of New Zealand law, it is not clear how it may apply to health research as the dictum was made in the context of medical treatment which in the view of the doctor was in the best interests of the child.

The various guidelines regulating the conduct of health research all stipulate that the child's consent should be sought wherever possible.[67] Most add that a child's refusal ought to be respected.[68] Children are thus accorded a voice in the consent process. Their involvement in this process is not dependent on their formal legal capacity, but on their ability to understand, at least in broad terms, what the research involves. It is clearly envisaged that even very young children should participate in the consent process. They are entitled to an explanation in language that they understand and to have their views taken seriously, though in that case it is more appropriate to speak of the child's assent or willing co-operation.[69] Whatever the terminology used, it expresses the same principle: the child's point of view is crucial and should not be dismissed without due cause. The tendency to ignore this requirement because of time constraints or a presumed inability of the children to understand should not be countenanced and is a serious breach of all the guidelines.[70]

[64] [1986] AC 112.

[65] *Auckland Health Services* v. *Liu*, unreported, High Court Auckland, 1996, M812/96.

[66] *Re J* [1996] 2 NZLR 134. Right 7 of the Code of Health and Disability Services Consumers' Rights appears to endorse the principle that children may consent if they are competent.   [67] e.g. Declaration of Helsinki, n. 13, above, Basic Principle 11.

[68] e.g. NHMRC Statement, n. 19, above, 4.4.

[69] MRC Report, n. 19 above, 6.1.4. While it may not be possible to explain a research study to infants, they are likely to indicate their unwillingness by crying or not co-operating. One or two babies in the SIDS study were excluded for this reason. J. H. Pearn, 'The Child and Clinical Research' (1984) 2(1) *The Lancet* 510–12, suggests that children over the age of 10 should be approached for informed consent. The Institute of Medical Ethics recommends that children's assent should be sought from the age of 7, but not below that age: Nicholson, n. 15, above, 144–51.

[70] G. Lansdown, 'Children's Rights' in B. Mayall (ed.), *Children's Childhoods: Observed and Experienced* (London, 1994), 33, 35. M. Freeman, *The Moral Status of Children— Essays on the Rights of the Child* (The Hague, 1997), 37.

The requirement to seek the child's consent or assent accords with Article 12 of the UN Convention on the Rights of the Child:

States Parties shall assure to the child who is capable of forming his or her own views the right to express those views freely in all matters affecting the child, the views of the child being given due weight in accordance with the age and maturity of the child.[71]

Yet, a closer examination of the guidelines reveals some ambiguity about the child's rights in this regard. It appears that both the child's consent and refusal may be overridden by the parents, though the various guidelines are far from consistent as to when parents may trump their children's decisions.[72] The CIOMS Guidelines, for instance, provide that the child's refusal to participate in research will be respected unless the child would receive therapy for a condition for which there is no medically acceptable alternative.[73] The parent's view is apparently decisive even if the child understands the consequences of refusing to participate. It seems that even a competent child is merely accorded a voice, not a veto.[74]

Nor is the consent of a mature and competent child always effective, *Gillick* and the Convention on the Rights of the Child notwithstanding. Most guidelines suggest that a child's consent is insufficient without proxy consent, thus giving parents a power of veto, in some cases until the age of majority.[75] The US Federal Code even requires the consent of both parents as well as the child's if the child is to participate in non-therapeutic research which carries a minor increase over minimal risk.[76]

This raises the fundamental question of the balance between children's rights and parents' rights. At what point should parental autonomy give way to child autonomy? The line is not easily drawn and may not be drawn in the same place for every child or for every activity in which the child is involved. While parents have the right to control the upbringing of

---

[71] See also Art. 5 where the States Parties undertake to respect the responsibilities, rights, and duties of parents to provide, in a manner consistent with the evolving capacities of the child, appropriate direction and guidance in the exercise by the child of the rights recognized in the Convention.

[72] The Institute of Medical Ethics, for instance, is of the view that parental consent is required for all children below the age of 16, even though children over the age of 14 have been found to be as competent as adults: Nicholson, n. 15 above, 151. The English Department of Health's guidelines, *Local Research Ethics Committees* (London, 1991), para. 4, require parental consent even for 16 and 17-year-olds, unless it would be against the child's interests to comply with this requirement.

[73] N. 12, above, 20.

[74] The European Convention is a notable exception: Explanatory Report, n. 12, above, 22 para. 106.

[75] See n. 72, above; NHMRC Statement, n. 19, above, 4.2; CIOMS, n. 12, above, 21 even though children of 13 and above are deemed to be capable of informed consent. The South African Guidelines provide a limited exception in 8.4.3: with ethics committee approval parental consent need not be obtained if the child is of sufficient maturity and the obtaining of parental consent might impede the research.

[76] US Code, n. 19, above, 46.408.

their children, this right dwindles as children mature and develop the necessary capacity to make their own decisions.[77] It is a gradual process and depends on the nature of the decision and the child's level of understanding.

Though *Gillick* was decided in the context of medical treatment, it is widely seen as having much broader application.[78] It would be difficult to argue against its application to health research, given the overlap with medical treatment. The issues and concerns will be similar. If anything, decisions to participate in health research will be less onerous than decisions about medical treatment. The conditions imposed on all paediatric research and the limitations on the risk of harm in non-therapeutic procedures provide additional safeguards for research participants which are not normally present in medical treatment. So, a child who is competent to consent to medical treatment in terms of the *Gillick* test should be at least as competent to consent to research of a similar nature. Proxy consent should not be required in that case.

Whether a competent child's refusal will always be accorded the same respect is questionable. There can be little doubt that it should be binding if the child is not intended to derive therapeutic benefit from participation, but the CIOMS Guidelines and case law suggest that a competent child's refusal of therapeutic treatment may be ignored.[79] That approach may not be followed in New Zealand because section 11 of the New Zealand Bill of Rights Act gives '[e]veryone . . . the right to refuse to undergo any medical treatment'. Whether competent children will fully enjoy this right has yet to be decided. The only case in which this section has been considered held that 'everyone' meant 'every person who is competent to consent'.[80] This interpretation suggests that if children understand the consequences of their decision, there is no legal justification for overriding that decision, as distressing as it may be. To hold otherwise is to ignore a child's autonomy solely because of its status as a minor.[81]

The fundamental question in relation to the child's role in the decision-making process is, therefore, whether they have the necessary competence to make their own decisions. Do they have the maturity and intelligence to understand the nature, purpose, risk, and benefits of the research project, and do they fully appreciate the consequences of their decision? Their

---

[77] *Gillick*, n. 64, above.

[78] G. Austin, 'Righting a Child's to Refuse Medical Treatment' (1992) 7(4) *Otago Law Review* 578, 586.

[79] Text accompanying n. 73 above: *Re W* [1992] 3 WLR 758 in which the refusal of medical treatment by a competent 16-year-old was overridden by the Court of Appeal. See also J. V. McHale's discussion of this issue in 'Guidelines for Medical Research—Some Ethical and Legal Problems' (1993) 1 *Medical Law Review* 160, 174.

[80] *Re S* [1992] 1 NZLR 363, 374, in which a committed psychiatric patient who wished to refuse medication for his mental illness was found to be outside ambit of the section.

[81] Austin, n. 78, above, 587–95.

competence will vary depending on the nature of the research. The less intrusive the research, the younger the age at which they are likely to be competent. If they have the necessary competence, their consent or their refusal should be respected and acted on. Parents should not have the right to override their decisions.

Proxy consent should be used only where the child lacks the necessary competence. Even then, the child's assent or willing co-operation should be sought and his or her refusal respected unless the child will receive treatment for a condition for which no other medically acceptable therapy is available. To accord parents a greater right violates the United Nations Convention on the Rights of the Child.[82]

Central to the requirement of consent is that it must be freely given, without pressure or influence. Payment to participants is frowned upon as it may induce people to take undue risks. This is particularly important if the participants are children. They are easily persuaded to consent to a major research study on the promise of a burger! Inducements in paediatric research are not well addressed in most guidelines and they are not mentioned in New Zealand's National Standard.

Conclusion

The approach to health research with children has changed considerably since the days of the Nuremberg Code. From outright prohibition we have moved to cautious acceptance that both therapeutic and non-therapeutic research with children is necessary for the promotion of their health and well-being. Their unique needs and interests are now widely recognized as deserving special attention.

While the need for paediatric research is acknowledged, there is no agreement on the conditions under which such research is ethically and legally permissible. A plethora of guidelines has attempted to regulate the conduct of health research with children, but they are vague, inconsistent, and incomplete on several crucial points. The risk formulations are imprecisely worded and do not take account of the changing responses of children as they mature. The justification for proxy consent is often not addressed and the respect accorded to children's views is generally ambiguous.

New Zealand's National Standard for Ethics Committees is particularly deficient and requires urgent attention. The Standard is currently under review, and it is hoped that it will incorporate detailed and clearly formulated guidelines for research with children. A general risk formulation is

---

[82] In *Tavita* v. *Minister of Immigration* [1994] NZFLR 97 the New Zealand Court of Appeal held that the UN Convention should be considered even when domestic law is silent as to its application.

best avoided. A list of permissible procedures for various age groups is preferable. Proxy consent should be required only when the child is not competent to consent and is justified if participation, in the view of the reasonable parent, is not against the child's interests.

If a child understands the nature, purpose, risks, and benefits of the research, his or her consent or refusal should be respected and acted on without the need for a proxy decision. Children who lack this competence are nonetheless entitled to be informed about the research in language that they understand and their assent should be sought. If they are too young to understand even the simplest explanation, as the participants in the SIDS study were, they may participate with proxy consent as long as it does not distress them. If incompetent children object or refuse to participate their views should be respected in all but the most exceptional circumstances. Such a circumstance will arise if the child is suffering from a disease or condition for which there is no medically acceptable therapy other than the treatment offered as part of the research. Parents and health professionals will have to be satisfied that the reason for overriding the child's refusal is the child's lack of competence, not the child's minority status.

While it is no doubt possible to devise very clear conditions which provide certainty for paediatric research, that certainty may well be at the expense of flexibility and prevent valuable research. If flexibility is considered desirable, some degree of uncertainty is bound to remain. Children's interests need not be jeopardized by this uncertainty if there is a robust system of ethical review. The system currently in place in New Zealand was designed to safeguard the interests of research participants, but its focus was on adults. Given the special needs and interests of children, the inclusion on ethics committees of an independent paediatrician is in my view essential.

If these changes were made to the National Standard for Ethics Committees, children's rights would be appropriately safeguarded. Moreover, unlike most other countries, they would be readily enforceable in New Zealand, as they would have the force of law through the Code of Health and Disability Services Consumers' Rights.[83] Children would have access to the Health and Disability Commissioner's complaints procedure and the right to seek remedies for any breach of their rights.[84]

---

[83] See the text following n. 56, above.
[84] Part IV of the Health and Disability Commissioner Act 1994.

Privacy and Confidentiality

MEDICAL DATA, NEW INFORMA-TION TECHNOLOGIES, AND THE NEED FOR NORMATIVE PRINCIPLES OTHER THAN PRIVACY RULES

Anton Vedder *

Introduction

Recent technological developments invite us to reconsider our traditional conceptions of privacy and to extend the normative framework for the moral and legal assessment of new information technologies. I will propose a new account of the conceptualization of privacy and I will introduce some additional normative principles, which—taken together—are more fit to capture the social problems relating to certain technologies. The technologies on which I will focus are those of profiling through data mining, especially profiling through data mining in epidemiology.

In the years to come, profiling through data mining will become an important and powerful set of techniques in the hands of epidemiologists and policy-makers in the field of health care. The techniques of data mining will enable them to predict the developments in the health condition and health risks of populations more accurately and, more importantly, much easier than ever before. Applying the techniques results in generalizations about groups of persons, rather than about individuals. For this reason, existing privacy norms do not apply. Nevertheless, some of the ways in which these generalizations are used or can be used may lead to serious social and moral problems. In this paper, I will first present some preliminaries about profiling through data mining. Next, I will explain in

* The research for this paper was partially funded by the Netherlands Organization for Scientific Research. Thanks are due to Peter Blok and Eric Schreuders of Tilburg University for their constructive suggestions and criticisms.

some detail why current conceptions of privacy, as they occur in law, legal theory, and ethics, are too weak in their normative and descriptive evaluation and distinction potential to capture the problems relating to profiling through data mining. Subsequently, I will propose a new conceptual scheme for the privacy notion. This approach equips us with a better understanding of the descriptive core and the basic points of the value notion. In addition, it enables us to understand and articulate the problems arising in relation to profiling through data mining that cannot be adequately and completely formulated in terms of other evaluative notions and principles. Nevertheless, invoking these additional principles and values is necessary. I will expound the ones needed to extend the normative framework for assessing information technologies. Finally, I will put forward and discuss some practical solutions to the problems at issue.

Profiling through Data Mining

'Data mining' is the term I use to refer to the whole set of techniques certain experts call 'knowledge discovery in databases (KDD)'. This set of techniques is applied in a process that is traditionally divided into three phases, i.e. the data-warehousing phase, the data-mining phase proper, and the interpretation phase. In the data-warehousing phase, data are collected, enriched, checked, and coded. The data are analysed in what the aforementioned experts call the data-mining phase in the strict sense. Finally, the results are interpreted. During these phases, a search hypothesis is used to guide the process.[1] In this paper, I will use the perhaps somewhat sloppy language that has become customary, and *not* restrict the use of 'data mining' to refer to the middle phase of the KDD process only.

The basic aims and greatest opportunities of data mining are description and prediction through the discovery of significant patterns in the relationships of whatever kind between data.[2] By 'profiling through data mining', I refer to those data-mining processes that result in profiles of groups of persons, i.e. characterizations of groups that can be assigned to those groups and to the members of those groups. The process of profiling through data mining aims at tracking down significant relationships between characteristics that define and identify a group of persons on the one hand and whatever properties or characteristics on the other.

[1] Cf. U. Fayyad, G. Piatetsky-Shapiro, and P. Smyth, 'Knowledge Discovery and Data Mining: Towards a Unifying Framework' in E. Simoudis, J. Hian, and U. Fayyad (eds.), *Proceedings of the Second International Conference on Knowledge Discovery & Data Mining* (Menlo Park, Cal., 1996); W.J. Frawley, G. Piatetsky-Shapiro, and C. J. Matheus, 'Knowledge Discovery in Databases: An Overview' in G. Piatetsky-Shapiro and W. J. Frawley (eds.), *Knowledge Discovery in Databases* (Menlo Park, Cal./Cambridge, Mass./London, 1991).

[2] Of course, the significance of patterns is determined by contextual factors such as the aims of the analyst, the analyst's superiors' aims, their institutional environment, social and political situation, natural predicament, etc.

In recent years, profiling through data mining has been acknowledged as an important set of techniques in analysing data for purposes such as direct marketing and credit scoring. Other applications include checking for patterns in criminal behaviour for forensic and judicial purposes and defining high-risk groups for tax evasion in order to improve rateability. A very inviting and—at least from the perspectives of public interest and public health—very useful utilization is analysing medical data or data about the use of medical services in combination with demographic data for epidemiological purposes. So, for instance, data about the use of medical services in the files and databases of health-insurance companies, or data from medical files or electronic care records maintained by health-care providers, could be merged and analysed. These analyses can result in the description and prediction of the incidence and prevalence of diseases. They also enable epidemiologists to ascertain and find high-risk groups, and to determine relations between chances of recovery from diseases and other—until now as yet unknown—influencing factors, etc.

It is primarily the utilization for epidemiological or public health purposes I will be concerned with here. I will not go into the details of these specific applications. Much of what I will say equally applies to profiling through data mining for other purposes—be they fiscal, judicial, or commercial. One of the reasons to select data mining and profiling for epidemiological purposes is that it is a salient example of applying the techniques for undoubtedly good and legitimate primary purposes, while many of the secondary uses of the resulting profiles may turn out to be highly questionable.

Throughout this paper, I will treat profiling and data mining only in so far as they involve the use of personal medical data in the so-called 'warehousing phase'. Personal medical data are personal data directly or indirectly—e.g. *via* data concerning the use of medical services and medication—referring to health condition and health prospects. Of course, I will include profiling through data mining in so far as it involves the use of medical personal data *in combination with* other data, be they personal or of another kind. I will, however, not address profiling through data mining involving no personal data at all.

Current Conceptions of Privacy

For an understanding of present-day conceptions of privacy, some acquaintance with the legal notion of privacy is necessary, especially with what might be called the legal conception of informational privacy. Over the last decades, informational privacy has become more and more important in law and regulation. Informational privacy in law and regulation is mostly interpreted as data protection. There is one kind of data that is considered exclusively eligible for protection by privacy law and regulation: personal data. Personal data are commonly defined as data and information relating to an identified or identifiable person. A clear illustration of this rather narrow starting point can be found in the highly influential European Directive 95/46/EC[3] of the European Parliament and of the European Council of 24 October 1995 'on the protection of individuals with regard to the processing of personal data and on the free movement of such data'. The Directive poses some basic principles with regard to the processing of personal data. As may be expected from the definition of 'personal data', most of these principles lean heavily on the idea that there is some kind of direct connection between a particular person and his or her data.

First, there are some principles regarding data quality. Personal data should only be collected for specified, explicit, legitimate purposes and should not be further processed in a way incompatible with these purposes. No excessive amounts of data should be collected, relative to the purpose for which the data are collected. Moreover, the data should be accurate and, if applicable, kept up to date. It must be guaranteed that inaccurate or incomplete data are either rectified or erased. Also, personal data should be kept in a form which permits identification of data subjects for no longer than is necessary for the purpose for which the data were collected.

Secondly, some principles apply to the processing of personal data. Data processing is legitimate if an individual has unambiguously given his or her consent. Furthermore, processing may be legitimate if it is needed for compliance with a legal obligation, for the protection of vital interests of the data subject, for some public interests, or for some legitimate interests pursued by the data controller or by third parties to whom the data are disclosed.

Thirdly, the data subject has some specific rights with regard to 'his or her' personal data. Among these rights are the right of knowing what data are being stored and whether the data relating to the data subject are being processed, the right of rectification, the right to know to whom the data have been disclosed, and the right to object to the processing of data relating to the data subject.

The definitions and principles formulated in the European Directive are implemented in the national privacy laws and regulations of the European Union Member States. For this reason, the impact of the Directive's definition and principles should not be underestimated.

The conceptual and normative individualism of the Directive reflects ideas about informational privacy currently held amongst legal and ethical theorists.[4] Sometimes, these ideas on informational privacy are not much

---

[3] [1995] OJ 6281/31.

[4] Anita Allen and Helen Nissenbaum have also drawn attention to the problem of restricting data protection to the protection of personal data, though from other perspectives: A. Allen, *Uneasy Access* (Totowa, NJ, 1988); H. Nissenbaum, 'Protecting Privacy in an Information Age: The Problem of Privacy in Public' (1998) 17 *Law and Philosophy* 559–96.

more than implicit assumptions. However, things are different where theorists define privacy as being in control over (the accessibility of) personal information, or where they indicate some kind of personal freedom, such as the preference freedom in the vein of John Stuart Mill's individuality, as the ultimate point and key value behind privacy.[5] These theorists consider privacy to be mainly concerned with information relating to individual persons. They also tend to advocate protective measures in terms of safeguarding an individual's control and consent *vis-à-vis* certain dispositions of personal information.

Applying the narrow definition of personal data and protective measures such as the Directive's and some philosophers' to the profiles discussed here is problematic. As long as the process involves personal data in the strict sense of data relating to an identified or identifiable individual, the definition and the principles apply without reservation. This will mainly concern some of the source material in the so-called warehousing phase of data mining. However, as soon as the data have ceased to be personal data in the strict sense, it is not at all clear how the principles should be applied. For instance, the right of rectification applies to the personal data in the strict sense; it does not apply to information derived from these data. The same goes for the requirement of consent. Once the data have become anonymous, or have been processed and generalized, an individual cannot exert any influence on the processing of the data at all. In sum, the definition and the rights and requirements—at least as they are traditionally formulated and interpreted—make no sense regarding anonymous data and group profiles.

Before I can elaborate further on this problem, it seems advisable to take a closer look at current conceptions of privacy in the legal and ethical debate over recent decades. Doing so will enable us to be more accurate when dealing more specifically with the normative and descriptive evaluation and distinction potential of the notion of privacy.

In recent decades, there has been ample discussion on the subject of privacy, particularly on the descriptive and normative aspects of the notion. One line of discussion has focused on the normative political problem of the (right to) privacy of citizens versus the duty of government or those same citizens to serve the public interest or the common good.[6] The conception of privacy that played a part in this environment could perhaps be best characterized as a conception of *decisional* privacy. The debate

[5] See, for instance, W. A. Parent, 'Recent Work on the Concept of Privacy' (1983) 20 *American Philosophical Quarterly* 341–56; S. I. Benn, *A Theory of Freedom* (Cambridge, 1988), 264–305; J. L. Johnson, 'Privacy, Liberty and Integrity' (1989) 3 *Public Affairs Quarterly* 15–34.

[6] See, e.g., P. Devlin, *The Enforcement of Morals* (Oxford, 1959); H. L. A. Hart, *Law, Liberty and Morality* (London, 1963); A. MacIntyre, 'The Privatization of the Good, An Inaugural Lecture' (1990) 52 *The Review of Politics* 344–61; and, more recently, A. Etzioni, *The Limits of Privacy* (New York, 1999).

concentrated on the political question of how much liberty should be granted to an individual regarding his or her intimate personal domain, particularly concerning his or her sexual orientation, the use of contraceptives, abortion, etc. In this approach, privacy boils down to a kind of personal freedom within a restricted area.

Other discussions ran along the borders of the partially overlapping fields of semantics, epistemology, and value theory. So, for instance, there has been discussion on the role of conventions, traditions, and the total network of social practices in a given culture regarding the identification of spheres of life or aspects of persons which are called private or personal.[7] Other debates have been concerned with the question whether the right to privacy could be derived from the autonomy of individual persons or be better interpreted as protective of certain kinds of interests of individuals. There have been debates about the question whether privacy was concerned with the inaccessibility of personal spheres as such or rather with an individual's control over access to his or her personal sphere. Again, others have been about the question whether privacy is just about physical accessibility of personal spheres or about access to information about an individual's personal sphere as well. In this debate, the information approach, with a conception of privacy as informational privacy in its wake, remained dominant.[8]

Furthermore, important work has been done explicitly on the normative point of privacy. Fried and Rachels emphasized the importance of privacy norms for the ability of individuals to establish and maintain different kinds of relationships with different persons. According to them, the character of a relationship does not so much determine the kind of information that is exchanged within that relationship. It is rather the other way round. By communicating different kinds of information to different persons, we differentiate our relationships with others. By enabling individuals to control the dissemination of information about their personal spheres, privacy norms contribute to the possibilities of individuals to establish and maintain social relationships at their own discretion.[9] In addition to this, Deborah Johnson emphasized privacy's empowering role. Privacy as control over personal information is an important instrument to strengthen the position of citizens and consumers *vis-à-vis* governmental institutions and private organizations.[10] Stanley Benn and Jeffrey Johnson highlighted the possibilities, offered by privacy norms, to be immune from

---

[7] J. J. Thomson, 'The Right to Privacy' [1975] 4 *Philosophy and Public Affairs* 295–315; T. M. Scanlon, 'Thomson on Privacy' [1975] 4 *Philosophy and Public Affairs* 315–22.

[8] W. A. Parent, n. 5, above.

[9] C. Fried, *An Anatomy of Values* (Cambridge, Mass., 1971); J. Rachels, 'Why Privacy is Important' [1975] 4 *Philosophy and Public Affairs* 323–33.

[10] D. Johnson, *Computers and Privacy* (Upper Saddle River, NJ, 1994) 81–102.

the judgement of others and to be respected as a (now and then erring and failing) plan-making and plan-implementing being, instead of an object without will, ready to be fixed and pinned down in the judgement of others.[11]

Privacy: A Contextual-functional Approach

Although privacy is an often and easily used notion, its precise meaning is far from clear, and liable to stimulate controversies.[12] In order to avoid digressions, I will stipulate an account of the meaning of privacy. This account serves two purposes. First, it indicates a defensible unifying core concept that is common to most of the conceptions of privacy currently used. Together with some broader considerations concerning the contextuality and functionality of meaning in the account, the core concept enables us to clarify and systematize the seemingly diffuse and chaotic family of privacy conceptions. Secondly, the account of privacy put forward will help us to understand and articulate the problems in relation to profiling and data mining that cannot be formulated adequately and completely in terms of other evaluative notions and principles.[13]

My account of privacy leans heavily on Jeffrey Johnson's conception of privacy as 'immunity from the judgements of others'. I think that Johnson is right in assuming that the idea of immunity from the judgement of others is in some way or other the *trait d'union* between all the instantiations of privacy. The way in which it performs the function of this unifying feature is important. Unfortunately, Johnson is not very clear about this. I would say that we are in fact talking about two levels: the level of the phenomena in which privacy is instantiated and the level of language in which these instantiations are articulated. I claim that apart from all other characteristics that may be present, common to most of the phenomena in which privacy is instantiated is the feature of an individual's immunity from the judgement of others (as being present or as being absent). At the level of linguistic articulations or propositional renderings of instantiations of privacy, I would say that the absence or presence of immunity from the judgement of others is the basic description frame common to the correct

---

[11] J. L. Johnson, 'Privacy and the Judgement of Others' (1989) 23 *Journal of Value Inquiry* 157–68; 'Privacy, Liberty and Integrity' n. 5, above; 'A Theory of the Nature and Value of Privacy' (1992) 6 *Public Affairs Quarterly* 271–88; S. I. Benn, n. 5, above, 264–305.

[12] One should not say that privacy is an essentially contested concept. Gallie's idea of essential contestedness ultimately tends to suggest that essentially contested concepts are nonsense; W. B. Gallie, 'Essentially Contested Concepts' (1955–6) 56 *Proceedings of the Aristotelian Society* 167–98.

[13] For some methodology regarding the ways I expound and defend the conceptual scheme of privacy, see: A. Vedder, 'Considered Judgements: Meaning, Community and Tradition' in W. van der Burg and Th. van Willigenburg (eds.), *Reflective Equilibrium* (Dordrecht, 1998) 55–72.

articulations of all possible instantiations of privacy. By calling the individual's immunity from the judgement of others a basic description frame, I mean that in the articulations of instantiations of privacy somehow a positive or negative account of a description of this immunity to the judgement of others is present, or at least presupposed.

The feature of immunity to the judgement of others can be found in most instantiations of privacy—with the important exception of decisional privacy, but to this issue I will return later. Privacy is often rightly considered as the condition of an individual in which others do not have access to his or her personal sphere as such or without the individual's permission. 'Having access', however, should be understood as being near to or present in an individual's personal sphere. This nearness or presence may be physical (with one's body) or instrumental (by bugging, using binoculars, etc.), or by apprehending information that has already been abstracted by oneself or by others from one's personal sphere. A common feature of all these variations of access is that another person or other persons become *informed* about certain aspects of the individual's personal sphere. Through this information, others are enabled to judge and evaluate the person in some respect. A person's privacy is being directly infringed when others have physical or instrumental access to his or her personal sphere, thereby gathering information without permission. A journalist infringes the privacy of a person, for instance, if he or she intrudes uninvitedly into the person's home and takes a picture of this person while he or she is asleep. Furthermore, the journalist infringes this person's privacy indirectly by publishing the photograph in a newspaper to inform the readers about the person's personal sphere. The readers who are thus informed infringe this person's privacy directly, albeit possibly non-voluntarily.

This articulates sufficiently the basic description frame of privacy. The basic description frame is the common denominator of privacy conceptions. The normative point for (the importance of) articulating problems and problematic situations in terms of privacy and for valuing privacy is a different subject. It is to be found in a complex amalgam and interplay of contextual elements and different values, and not only, as Johnson would have it, in conventions, on the one hand, and freedom or autonomy, on the other.

Why is it important to protect or to safeguard the immunity of persons from the judgement of others? Why is infringing privacy, why is compromising this immunity, a serious thing to do? Many writers have suggested that there is one value or one set of some familiar values at issue for which the value of privacy is instrumental or constitutive. This single value or small set of familiar values is thought to underlie all instantiations of privacy. Johnson has suggested that personal freedom is behind privacy. Benn suggested that we are dealing with specific kinds of freedom: the freedom of self-presentation and moral autonomy. Again, others have put forward other connected values. Interestingly enough, they all seek the unifying factor of the apparent diversity of privacy conceptions in a single or in some familiar values that are thought to be behind privacy. A possible reason for this is that they have all been trying to find the conceptual link between decisional privacy and privacy in terms of access or information *via* some common underlying value that was supposed to bridge the gap between these notions.

The unity of privacy, however, is not to be sought in the value(s) behind privacy, but precisely in what I have called the basic description-frame. This should not lead us to underestimate the importance of all the different values associated with privacy. Let me start to clarify this point by commenting on Jeffrey Johnson's view that conventions determine what is to be considered the personal sphere, the domain supposed to be protected by privacy:

Privacy is a conventional concept. What is considered private is socially or culturally defined. It varies from context to context, it is dynamic, and it is quite possible that no single example can be found of something which is considered private in every culture. Nevertheless, all examples of privacy have a single common feature. They are aspects of a person's life which are culturally recognised as being immune from the judgement of others. . . . The function of privacy, therefore, is to isolate certain limited and culturally defined aspects of the individual's life as being morally and legally protected from the evaluative judgement of others.[14]

By an individual's personal sphere we usually mean the domain of a person, consisting of his mind and body, possessions, letters, home, certain activities, etc. It should be kept in mind that the notion of personal sphere is originally a metaphor. It should not be interpreted exclusively in terms of spatial dimensions or territory. The personal sphere also includes *aspects* and *dimensions* of persons, lives, and actions, as seen from certain perspectives. Jeffrey Johnson is right in claiming that what is considered to belong to the personal sphere is in several respects defined by the conventions and traditions of one's culture and community. One should not, however, feel tempted to equate conventions and traditions too hastily with either arbitrary tendencies or purely contingent social arrangements. In many cases, conventions are only part of the story. The rationale for including certain elements in the personal sphere (e.g. nudity of the body, the performance of certain biological functions) in a Western community nowadays seems sometimes hard to find. Nevertheless, for some of these there certainly has been a reason and for most of the others there certainly have been good reasons to count them as belonging to the personal sphere.

Conventions also play a part in combination with the prevention of harm and offence, or some conception of individual well-being. The point

---

[14] J. L. Johnson, 'Privacy and the Judgement of Others' n. 11, above, 157.

of defining certain items or aspects of persons as 'personal' often lies in the fact that persons with respect to these items and aspects just tend to be vulnerable, and are therefore in need of protection. Conventions and traditions are important in the definition of the personal sphere to the extent that they themselves or the social arrangements accompanying them create or keep up the conditions and occasions for special kinds of harm or offence. So, for instance, one's medical condition and prospects are rightfully considered to belong to the personal sphere. There is a certain tradition, convention, or at least a seemingly ineradicable tendency in Western societies towards harmful discrimination and stigmatization of and scorn for the ill and the suffering. Although this tendency is mostly suppressed, it sometimes comes to a head in the rejection of persons with certain diseases. Recent examples are AIDS and other communicable diseases.

Conventional aspects of privacy like these are unfortunately rarely acknowledged by contemporary scholars, impressed as they are by the apparent irrationality of some conventions designating certain features as belonging to the personal domain. The scholars who do have an open eye for conventions are a little fuzzy about the precise role of conventions. So, for instance, it is not in the least clear whether Jeffrey Johnson, when talking about the conventional aspects of privacy, envisages the delineation of the personal sphere. He may as well be making a statement about the development of the value of privacy in the traditions of a community when he wrote the passage quoted above.

Both these interpretations are important to privacy, but they should not be confused. They explain part of the constitution of the personal sphere and part of the constitution of the value of privacy. Conventions determine in part under which aspect or from which perspective the disclosure of a feature of a person or a person's life may hurt or harm this person. These features—and these not necessarily *per se* but under a certain aspect or in a certain perspective—are part of the personal sphere. They explain indirectly why such disclosure would be bad: the person would be hurt or harmed because of the stigma, taboo, prejudice, or (social) exclusion that is in the normal course of events in a society or culture like the one involved attached to such disclosure. The value which in such situations is to be protected ultimately is the well-being of individuals. It is protected by avoiding the possibility of disclosure of information about persons that might harm them by exposing them to prejudice, stigmatization, and exclusion, etc.

Conventions are not the whole story about the personal sphere. Neither are they—in combination with some ideal conception of personal well-being—the whole normative point of privacy. Economic and social arrangements and technical and technological developments play their role as well, as do important values other than that of individual well-being.

Certain social, economic, and technical arrangements—themselves partially based on conventions and traditions—provide the opportunity, and sometimes even the institutional necessity, to harm persons on the grounds of features of their personal sphere, such as their medical condition and prospects. They do so, for instance, by hindering access to insurance, credit facilities, jobs, and offices, some of the few social institutions in which discrimination on the grounds of health aspects of persons is still accepted in Western societies and cultures. Here, disclosing information about the health condition and prospects of persons is reckoned to be private or belonging to the personal sphere because people may be harmed by it, in that they are excluded from certain social provisions and amenities. Again, an ideal of individual well-being is the normative point behind protecting the privacy of individuals in this respect.

Other values also play their part. Fried and Rachels have shown that privacy enables individuals to control the spread of information about their personal spheres. Fried certainly has a case in claiming that privacy is constitutive of friendship and instrumental to veracity. Rachels understands the control over the dissemination of personal information as an important constituent of autonomy, enabling persons themselves to define the character of relationships which they (choose to) establish or maintain with other individuals and institutions. Jeffrey Johnson considers privacy to be a guarantee against the undesired evaluative judgement of others and therefore as a constituent of freedom. Benn shows the further point of such immunity: abstaining from judgements about an individual's personal sphere allows him, at least in a certain area, to be respected as a person. 'The value of privacy', says Benn, 'hinges on a person's interest in forms of self-presentation, as part of his self-awareness as a maker of projects, without which the individual is depersonified, reduced to an object. . . . The ends of privacy rights are derived from the needs of human beings to be safe from persecution, to develop intimate personal relations, etc.'[15]

The unity in the family of privacy conceptions lies hidden in a common description frame, and not in some value or values underlying privacy. There are many values behind privacy. For which value privacy exactly functions as an instrument depends on the context of social, economic, and technical circumstances and conventions. This is why the meaning of privacy is determined by context and function.

A potential objection against this account of privacy could be that immunity to the judgement of others can be discovered in all instantiations of privacy, with the exception of instantiations of decisional privacy. The main thesis of my account is, however, that all privacy *conceptions* have the common feature of using one basic description frame. There is a difference between the instantiations of privacy in the phenomena and the linguistic articulations of such instantiations of privacy. Immunity to the

---

[15] S. I. Benn, n. 11, above, 264, 305.

judgement of others is a common basic description frame for all articulations of instantiations of privacy; it is *not* a common feature of all instantiations of privacy in concrete cases. In other words, although the immunity to the judgement of others is in some way or another always referred to in conceptualizations of privacy, it is not always part of the ways in which privacy materializes in reality. I would say that instantiations of 'decisional privacy' as they occur in the phenomena do not share this characteristic. There are other reasons for talking about these cases in terms of privacy. The domain of life and actions which decisional privacy covers—in the sense that it requires respect for or forbids interference with decisions and actions in this domain—is essentially part of the sphere or the domain in which persons normally are thought to have immunity from the judgement of others. In addition to this, there seem to have been strategic and practical reasons to bring the kind of decisions that decisional privacy actually protects under the label of privacy. The idea of decisional privacy is strongly associated with a certain interpretation of some of the amendments to the American Constitution. The notion of privacy—as relating to physical access and information about persons—already played some role in the interpretation of these. It lay in the natural course of events that the defenders of what I have labelled 'decisional privacy' would turn to the privacy vocabulary. A more appropriate juridical linguistic framework just seems to have been missing. Apparently, other constitutional starting points were not at hand. Finally, although there may be better ways of formulating the instantiations and the general values of decisional privacy, convention and custom have kept us from abandoning the conception in favour of a better one. Needless to say, although immunity to the judgement of others is not a feature of instantiations of decisional privacy, it is a basic description frame of articulations of instantiations of decisional privacy because the idea of immunity from the judgement of others is conceptually, *indirectly,* presupposed by the articulation. To put it differently: the conception of decisional privacy feeds on the conception of privacy that generally articulates instantiations of privacy in which immunity to the judgement of others is at issue.

In sum, privacy is a servant of many master values. In addition to the values that have been brought to the fore there are still others, such as individuality, fairness in judgement and treatment, etc. In the next section, I will show how these values are active behind instantiations of privacy. In this section, I have put forward an account of privacy in which the basic description frame of 'immunity to the judgement of others' is the unifying factor in the family of privacy conceptions. The variety, which I labelled decisional privacy, stands somewhat apart from the other varieties because it is only indirectly connected to the basic description frame. I have also explained that privacy should not be considered to be derived somehow from just one value or from some familiar values. Behind different instantiations of privacy, in different contexts, different values may be active, mostly in combination with certain conventions, traditions, and technical, economic, and social-institutional arrangements.

Categorical Privacy, Individuality, Fairness, and Justice

Most conceptions of individual informational privacy currently put forward in law, regulation, and ethical debate have one feature in common which is important to my point. Not only do they assume that the personal data with which privacy is concerned, *originally* consist of statements about states of affairs or aspects accompanied by indicators of individual natural persons, they also assume that the data during processing *continue* to contain those identifiers of individual natural persons. This feature of many current privacy conceptions has two significant consequences: it makes it difficult to label the problematic aspects of using data abstracted from personal data and producing and applying group profiles and generalizations; it also makes it difficult to fathom the seriousness of these problems in practice.

It should be observed that group profiles and generalizations may occasionally be incompatible with respect for individual privacy and laws and regulations regarding the protection of personal data, as it is traditionally conceived of. In order to understand this, we must distinguish between distributive profiles and non-distributive profiles. Distributive profiles assign certain properties to a data or information subject, consisting of a group of persons however defined, in such a way that these properties are actually and unconditionally manifested by all members of that group. Distributive generalizations and profiles are put in the form of down-to-earth, matter-of-fact statements. As opposed to this, *non*-distributive profiles are framed in terms of probabilities and averages and medians, significant deviancies from other groups, etc. They are based on comparisons of members of the group with each other and/or on comparisons of one particular group with other groups. Non-distributive profiles are, therefore, significantly different from distributive profiles. The properties in non-distributive generalizations apply to individuals as members of the reference group, whereas these individuals taken as such need not in reality exhibit these properties. For instance, an applicant may be refused a life insurance on the basis of a non-distributive generalization of certain health risks of the group (e.g. defined by a postal code) to which he happens to belong, whereas he or she is a clear exception to the average risks of his or her group. In all such cases, the individual is primarily judged and treated on the basis of belonging to a group or category of persons and not on his or her own merits and characteristics.

Distributive generalizations and profiles may sometimes rightfully be thought of as infringements of (individual) privacy when the individuals involved can easily be identified through a combination with other information available to the recipient or through spontaneous recognition. In the case of non-distributive profiles, the information remains attached to an information subject constituted by a group. It cannot be traced back to individual persons in any straightforward sense. The groups which are the information subjects of non-distributive profiles can often only be identified by those who defined them for a special purpose. From the perspectives of people other than the producers and certain users of the profiles and generalizations, the definition of the information subject will remain hidden because people who are neither producers nor users do not know the specific purposes of the definition. When accidentally discovered by the people in the reference group, they will probably think of the definition as being arbitrarily chosen. Most importantly, however, the information contained in the profile envisages individuals as members of groups; it does not envisage individuals as such. Supposing for the sake of argument that the profile has been produced in a methodically sound and reliable way, it only tells us some truth about individual members of those groups in a very qualified, conditional manner. Therefore, privacy rules, as they are traditionally conceived of, do not apply. The information in non-distributive profiles cannot be traced back to individual persons.

One might think that perhaps we could be saved by some notion of collective privacy. However, collective privacy will not do the job properly. The notion of collective privacy is too easily associated with the concept of collective rights. The subjects of collective rights are groups or communities. In order to make sense of the idea of collective rights, these subjects are often treated as beings analogous to persons or moral agents, or at least as conglomerates having certain characteristics which cannot ultimately and exhaustively be explained by the input of the individual members. Furthermore, they are often thought to be structured or organized in some way so as to be able to exercise their rights or let their rights be advocated by vicarious agents.[16] All these properties do not apply to the reference groups of the profiles we are considering. From the perspective of their members, these groups are mostly randomly defined. Their members do not have any special ties of loyalty to each other. Nor do they have organizational structures. Therefore, they are not able to take decisions or to act as collectivities.

In order to remove the deficiencies of current conceptions of privacy as regards analytical and distinctive evaluative potential, we would be better off utilizing a concept which I have elsewhere labelled 'categorical

[16] M. Hartney, 'Some Confusions Concerning Collective Rights' (1991) 4 *Canadian Journal of Law and Jurisprudence*, 293–314.

privacy'.[17] I suggest that we conceive of categorical privacy, not as an independent concept, but as a dimension of privacy. This dimension relates to data or information to which the following conditions apply. (1) The information was originally taken from the personal sphere of individuals, and—after aggregation and processing according to statistical methods—is no longer accompanied by identifiers of individual natural persons, but, instead, by identifiers of groups of persons. (2) When attached to identifiers of groups and when disclosed, the information is apt to carry with it the same kind of negative consequences for the members of those groups as it would for an individual natural person if the information were accompanied by identifiers of that individual.

Categorical privacy is strongly connected with individual privacy. It uses the same basic description frame as individual privacy, i.e. immunity from the judgement of others. The values which—in combination with contextual factors such as conventions and social arrangements—oppose infringements on individual privacy, such as individual well-being, personal autonomy, individuality, and certain social interests, equally oppose infringements of categorical privacy. But there are more values at issue, such as fair judgement and treatment, and respect for the individuality, i.e. the individual merits and characteristics, of persons. Unlike collective privacy, categorical privacy is directed towards respecting and protecting the individual rather than respecting and protecting some group to which the individual belongs. Furthermore, the conception of categorical privacy presented here—just like many current conceptions of individual privacy—builds on a conception of the personal sphere that is partially predefined by conventions and social, economic, and technical arrangements. Categorical privacy, however, is different from its individual counterpart in that it draws attention to the attribution of generalized properties to members of groups, which may result in the same effects as the attribution of particularized properties to individuals as such. In this respect, infringements of categorical privacy resemble stereotyping and wrongful discrimination on the basis of stereotypes.

We began reconsidering privacy norms by questioning the possibilities of profiling through data mining for epidemiological purposes. In the second part, I emphasized that many of these applications are undoubtedly very useful. Earlier on, I also stated that it might be difficult to come to understand precisely the darker side of these applications, the current conceptions of privacy in law, regulation, and ethical theory standing in the way. By now, things may be a little less complex. Problems accompanying distributive profiles may at least in part be articulated in terms of

---

[17] A. Vedder, 'Privatization, Information Technology and Privacy: Reconsidering the Social Responsibilities of Organizations' in Geoff Moore (ed.), *Business Ethics: Principles and Practice* (Sunderland, 1997), 215–26.

a traditional privacy conception. Problems related to non-distributive profiles can be partially articulated in terms of the notion of categorical privacy. It is important to see, however, that the significance or seriousness of these drawbacks depends heavily on the context in which the profiles are used. Suppose that the profiles are produced and used only and strictly for epidemiological purposes, in such a way that there are guarantees that access to them is permitted to some researchers only who do not pass the information on to others. Against this background the privacy objections have a seriousness that is of a rather academic kind. Things are different, however, as soon as the guarantees mentioned are absent. Then the information in the profiles may become available to others and thus become part of the body of public knowledge in society, or the information may be used for completely different purposes, such as selection procedures for jobs, insurance, loans, etc. Of course, if the latter happens, then not only is privacy at stake, but also values of social justice and fairness. Social justice is at stake where the distribution of provisions and amenities in society is based on health criteria. Fairness is at stake where non-distributive profiles as such are used. When such profiles are applied, an individual is judged and treated on the basis of characteristics he or she did not acquire voluntarily, such as a bad health condition or a bad health prospect. More importantly, however, an individual as such will often not exhibit the characteristic at all, since such a characteristic is one of the group and not necessarily also of the individual.

Medical profiles may have yet another problem. Through data mining and profiling, information may be produced about an individual which is unknown to this individual. For instance, one may think of a profile indicating a health risk of a group of persons, without these persons knowing the risk. In such a case, disclosure of the profile to the members of the group may confront these individuals with medical information about themselves which they have not sought freely. It may even confront them with information about a risk which they as a matter of fact do not have. Of course, in situations like these much depends on the ways in which people are confronted with the information. Are they, for instance, informed about the methodical and methodological aspects of the profiles and risks indicated, so that they may conclude that they do not necessarily run the risk? Is it clear to those involved what kind of disease the risk is about? Nevertheless, in certain cases divulging profiles about health condition and health risk may confront persons with information that they have no desire to have.

From the Protection of Privacy to the Protection of Persons: Practical Solutions

The problems surrounding profiling through data mining cannot be dealt with in ways similar to those in which individuals are protected against possible infringements of individual informational privacy. The application of principles and rights of, for instance, rectification and consent to potential infringements on categorical privacy is to a large extent impossible. Even if it were possible, it would nevertheless be unacceptable for obvious reasons. First, as has been explained above, the reference group of the profile will only rarely be able to reach and enact collective decisions because of its lack of organizational structure and personal or social ties. Secondly, if one were to turn from the group as such to the individual members of the group, then an individual's possibility of refusal or of opting out could be harmful. It would be harmful to other members of the reference group as well as to the very person refusing to allow personal information to be used in producing the profile. For actual refusal will reduce the reliability of the profile or generalization. Nevertheless, all members of the reference group, including the individual who opted out, are at risk of being judged and treated on the basis of just this profile with reduced reliability. Of course, the possibility of opting out may also, in some respects, benefit the members of the reference group. If, in the case of application in selection procedures, only people with bad risks actually refuse the use of their information, this may turn out to be rather advantageous for the healthy. In spite of such advantages for some individuals, there still remains wrongfulness or unfairness in the fact that they are judged and treated on the basis of group properties, rather than on the basis of their own individual properties.

Perhaps then the only way to protect individuals against the possible negative consequences of the use of generalizations and profiles based on personal information in the broad sense lies in a careful case-by-case assessment of the ways in which the group profiles are in fact used and can be used. By meticulously investigating and evaluating these applications one may hope to find starting points for restrictions of the purposes for which the profiles are produced and applied. An elaborate proposal concerning such acceptable and unacceptable purposes cannot be provided here. It is important, however, to keep in mind that solutions will not be found only in forbidding the production and application of profiles for certain purposes. In many cases, it may be more appropriate to reconsider those purposes themselves. Sometimes it may be easier or even morally more desirable to do something about social and economic arrangements that induce wrongful applications of information technologies than abolishing those applications. This is the case especially where, for instance, profiles can be used for desirable purposes and for undesirable purposes at the same time. Also, in such situations where there is a possibility of good use and bad use of the same newly produced information, doubtless some help is to be expected from encryption and authentication techniques. It may turn out to be possible, for instance, to protect databases against certain types of queries, or to make certain information accessible only to certain persons for certain purposes. Together with agreements in the legal or contractual sphere, through which the behaviour of these persons is bound and can be controlled, technical solutions may turn out to be the best practicable solutions to the problems mentioned.

Touching on practical solutions, it should be noted that data mining can in some way complicate even further the problems that have so far been discussed. Data mining gives us the opportunity of producing profiles more easily, more quickly, and in greater numbers than was possible before the technique, called data mining, came to hand. It also enables us to discover many more correlations between phenomena, such as characteristics of individuals and groups, than were known hitherto. For instance, data mining may show correlations between characteristics that are trivial in a certain context and characteristics that are significant in that same context. It may be possible to establish a statistical relationship between the ownership of a certain type of car, on the one hand, and a certain health risk, on the other (without there necessarily being any natural causal relationship between the two). If this were the case, then the use of the health-risk profile could be hidden, as it were, 'behind' the use of the profile of car owners. This is especially complicating in situations where we would not have other possibilities of controlling what people in a certain institution or enterprise were doing with profiles than to wait until an individual consumer or patient discovered what was happening and started to complain. The possibility of linking significant, potentially harmful, profiles to trivial ones makes it difficult to uncover dubious applications.[18]

Conclusion

Our current moral and legal vocabularies and conceptual frameworks for dealing with information technologies should be revised and extended in order to adjust them to the problems that arise. Regarding problems relating to data mining and profiling for epidemiological purposes, I have suggested a reconceptualization of privacy. In my account, the basic description frame of 'immunity to the judgement of others' is the unifying factor in the family of privacy conceptions, while the importance of privacy in different situations depends on contextual factors such as conventions, social and economic arrangements, and technical developments on the one hand and a large set of diverging values, ranging from individual well-being and personal autonomy to fairness and individuality, on the other. Practical problems relating to new technologies such as those

---

[18] J. Harvey, 'Stereotypes and Group-Claims: Epistemological and Moral Issues and Their Implications for Multiculturalism in Education' (1991) 24 *Journal of Philosophy and Education* 39–50.

lying at the heart of data mining require the moral and legal assessment of information technologies to be no longer exclusively focused on privacy norms and related norms such as those of confidentiality. Instead, the scope of privacy norms should be interpreted more broadly, so as to cover a wider range of personal data than data relating to identifiable individual persons only. In addition, the criteria for assessing the technologies in the field of medical information should also include norms of social justice, fairness, and respect for the individuality of persons. Only by making these adjustments will we be able to understand the significance of the problems occurring and will we be in a position to solve conflicts between public-health interests and the protection of individuals and groups against stigmatization, discrimination, and violations of their dignity.

PRE-EMPLOYMENT HEALTH SCREENING

Diana Kloss

It is common for employers to require prospective employees to undergo health screening before making the decision to offer them a job. In most cases, this is in order to screen out employees who may constitute an unacceptable risk, because they are likely to need long periods of sickness absence, or early retirement through ill-health (a particularly common occurrence in the public services). It is also a legal obligation on all employers under the Management of Health and Safety at Work Regulations 1992 to undertake a risk assessment, which includes identifying individuals who are at increased risk to their health, for example individuals who are sensitive to particular substances and therefore likely to contract asthma or dermatitis, or those who because of a physical disability are more likely to be the victims of accidental harm.

Employers engage occupational health (OH) staff, who may be doctors or nurses, to undertake this pre-employment screening. These OH personnel may be directly employed, but increasingly are self-employed independent contractors. The most common method of pre-employment screening is the standard questionnaire, but in some cases (e.g. High Court judges) there will be a full medical examination by a doctor. The interest of the employer may conflict with that of the prospective employee. The employer needs employees who are fit and healthy, and likely to remain so. The prospective employee needs the job. The OH practitioner is engaged by the employer, and owes contractual duties to him. How far does he also owe duties to the job applicant?

There are ethical dilemmas for OH professionals engaged in pre-employment screening.[1] Where biological testing is involved, it is important that only reliable methods are employed. Tests must be both sensitive (giving positive results in the presence of the effect) and specific (giving negative results in the absence of the effect). The methods of assessment must not in themselves create a hazard to the worker which outweighs their preventive value (e.g. unnecessary x-rays). Personnel must be

---

[1] *Guidance on Ethics for Occupational Physicians*, Faculty of Occupational Medicine (5th edn., London, 1999); *Health Surveillance in Great Britain*, HSE Contract Research Report No 121/1996.

adequately trained to conduct and interpret the results of physiological or biological tests. Health professionals should only be involved in screening which is scientifically justified. Job applicants should not be rejected on the basis of prejudice. Epileptics are competent to undertake most jobs as long as their epilepsy is controlled. HIV-positive workers do not constitute a risk to others except in a narrow range of jobs. The Nuffield Council on Bioethics in its report on ethical issues relating to genetic screening suggests that, in the context of workforce screening, genetic tests should be confined to instances where there is strong evidence of a clear connection between the working environment and the development of the condition for which the screening is conducted, the condition is serious and is one for which the dangers cannot be eliminated or significantly reduced by reasonable measures taken by the employer to modify or respond to environmental risks.[2]

The Human Genetics Advisory Commission has produced a report on the use of genetic testing in employment. The report finds that genetic testing is not being used systematically in the United Kingdom and recommends that it be used only in very restricted circumstances. These should be:

(i)   to detect any condition which may put the employee or others at risk in the workplace; or

(ii) to assess whether a specific variation in the employee's genetic constitution affects his or her susceptibility to specific features of a particular type of employment, which represent no hazard to most employees.

It should never be used to provide information about a condition or a predisposition to a condition which might lead to raised levels of sickness absence.[3]

When it comes to legal duties it is clear that the employer owes a duty of care to the employee *in employment*. The employer is liable under the criminal law (principally the Health and Safety at Work Act 1974) and the civil law of tort. In the civil law, the employer is vicariously liable for the negligence of OH professionals to whom he has delegated his duty of caring for the workers. Thus, in *Stokes* v. *Guest, Keen, Nettlefold*,[4] an employed OH physician who did not fully advise management or the workers of the dangers of scrotal cancer to male employees arising from leaning over oily machines was held to be negligent, and his employers therefore liable to an employee who had contracted scrotal cancer. This

---

[2] Nuffield Council on Bioethics, Genetic Screening: Ethical Issues (London, 1993); K. van Damme and L. Casteleyn, *Genetic Screening in the European Context*, (1998) 89 *La Medicina del Lavoro*, Suppl. 1.

[3] *The Implications of Genetic Testing for Employment*, Human Genetics Advisory Commission, (London, 1999).   [4] [1981] 1 WLR 1776.

case is an illustration that knowledge by OH personnel of work-related dangers is imputed to the employer, and puts the employer under a duty of care to guard against them. Another recent example is *Armstrong* v. *British Coal*[5] where the employer was held to know of the risk of vibration white finger through a report by Dr Milne, deputy area medical officer for North Yorkshire.

Is there a legal duty of care to the job applicant? The employer has no such duty until the applicant is accepted into employment (other than general duties arising from, for example, the law of occupier's liability). Does the OH professional owe a job applicant a duty of care? There are, in fact, two areas of possible damage arising from pre-employment screening. The first is *physical* damage. It is generally accepted that where the OH professional causes physical damage by negligence in the course of pre-employment screening he will be liable. For example, if a blood sample is taken for screening purposes and an infected needle is used, the doctor or nurse is liable for any infection thereby transmitted.

More controversial is the scenario where the OH professional either discovers or ought to have discovered a medical condition in the course of the examination but does not alert the job applicant to the need to seek further medical advice. Is there a legal or ethical duty on the OH professional to advise the job applicant that there is cause for concern and that he should consult his GP? Most health professionals would consider that they have an ethical duty to inform those with whom they come into contact on a professional basis of any health problems which they discover. This is not a 'Good Samaritan' situation where the health professional comes upon the patient lying injured at the side of the road. However, it seems that there is doubt about whether there is a legal obligation in such cases. In *X* v. *Bedfordshire County Council*, Lord Browne-Wilkinson said,[6] that a doctor engaged by a third party, whether insurance company, prospective employer, or whatever, owed only the limited duty not to injure the claimant while examining him. He cited no authority. The facts in the relevant case related to a psychiatrist examining a child at the behest of the local authority in order to investigate suspected sexual abuse. In such a situation there are strong policy reasons why the psychiatrist should not owe a duty of care to the child or its mother. The local authority is charged with statutory duties, the purpose of which is the protection of vulnerable children. Decisions may have to be made swiftly on the basis of evidence from an immature witness. Psychiatrists are usually advising in connection with potential court proceedings, and therefore can claim the immunity of an expert witness.[7] These policy reasons, it is submitted, do not apply in the case of an insurance examiner or an occupational physician. In

---

[5] [1997] Med. LR 259.
[7] *Watson* v. *M'Ewan* [1905] AC 480.

[6] [1995] 2 AC 633, 753.

addition, there is a conflict between the duty owed to the local authority and that to the child which does not exist in the case of the insurance examiner or the occupational physician.[8] It is in the interests of both that an adverse medical condition is identified.

In *R. v. Croydon Health Authority*[9] counsel for the defendant conceded that a radiologist who negligently failed to spot a serious medical condition (primary pulmonary hypertension) revealed by a pre-employment x-ray was liable for the extra distress and anxiety caused to the claimant who discovered her condition only during her pregnancy. Had she been told of her condition before, she would have not have conceived a child. However, the child was healthy, and the claimant's condition was not aggravated by the pregnancy and childbirth. Damages were denied by the Court of Appeal for the costs of bringing up the child, mainly because of lack of causation. There was insufficient connection between the pregnancy and the radiologist's negligence. The obligations assumed by the radiologist did not extend to the claimant's private life:

He [the radiologist] would no doubt have accepted that insofar as he failed to observe an abnormality which could have affected her fitness for work as an employee of the health authority in the immediate future, that was something for which he should be held accountable, but her domestic circumstances were not his affair.[10]

Authorities from the United States are conflicting. In *Beadling* v. *Sirotta*[11] the New Jersey Supreme Court held that the absence of a therapeutic relationship excludes the full duty of care, but in *Green* v. *Walker*[12] a doctor carrying out annual health checks for the employer was held liable for negligently failing to detect lung cancer in an employee. In *Betesh* v. *United States*[13] a recruit underwent a military pre-induction physical examination by a doctor who was held liable for negligently failing to diagnose cancer which should have been suspected because of an abnormality on an x-ray.

The second kind of potential harm which may be caused by the OH professional is *economic*. It is, of course more difficult in English law to establish a duty of care to protect against pure economic loss than against physical harm. Where the negligence of the doctor or nurse leads to the job applicant not being appointed to the job can liability be established? The principle of *Hedley Byrne* v. *Heller*[14] permits the employer who hires an unreliable employee—say a Beverley Allitt or a Nick Leeson—on the faith of a negligent reference to sue the referee in tort. The OH professional will

---

[8] I. Kennedy and A. Grubb, *Principles of Medical Law* (Oxford, 1998), 332.
[9] [1998] Lloyd's Rep. Med. 44 (CA).
[10] [1998] Lloyd's Rep. Med. 58, *per* Kennedy LJ.   [11] (1964) 197 A 2d 857.
[12] (1990) F 2d 291 (5th Cir).   [13] (1974) 400 F Supp. 238 (DC Dist Ct).
[14] [1964] AC 465.

also be liable to the employer in such circumstances for a negligent breach of contract. Yet the doctor or nurse makes no statement to the *job applicant* on which he or she relies.

The *Hedley Byrne* principle was extended in *White* v. *Jones*.[15] A special relationship giving rise to a duty of care may exist where the defendant (in that case a solicitor) assumes responsibility for providing services knowing and accepting that the future welfare of a third party (in that case potential beneficiaries under a will) is dependent on his careful execution of the task. Two other decisions of the House of Lords have confirmed this principle, *Henderson* v. *Merrett Syndicates Limited*[16] and *Williams* v. *Natural Life Limited*.[17] In the *Williams* case, Lord Steyn stated that once there is established a special relationship between the parties there is no need to embark on a further inquiry as to whether it is fair, just, and reasonable to impose liability for economic loss.

The High Court in *Baker* v. *Kaye*[18] applied this principle to an OH physician conducting a pre-employment medical examination who advised the potential employer that the job applicant was unfit for the job because blood tests in his opinion demonstrated over-indulgence in alcohol. It was held that the physician owed a duty of care, though he was not negligent on the facts. He had assumed a responsibility to the job applicant as well as to the potential employer. However, in *Kapfunde* v. *Abbey National*[19] the Court of Appeal held that an occupational physician reviewing pre-employment questionnaires (who never saw the job applicants) was not under any duty to the job applicant. Her only duty was to the employer who engaged her. Reliance was placed on the authority of *X* v. *Bedfordshire County Council*.[20] In my view, the policy underlying the *X* case does not apply in this situation, and the arguments in *Baker* v. *Kaye* are to be preferred. Of course, the claimant will have to show causation, that on the balance of probabilities he would have got the job had the medical report been favourable. On the facts, Baker would find this easier than Mrs Kapfunde since he had already been offered the job 'subject to a medical'. Millett LJ in the Court of Appeal refused to make a distinction between a physical examination and a review of a questionnaire; in neither case, he held, was there a duty of care. Kennedy LJ did make this distinction. In addition, both judges emphasized that the case concerned a claim for economic loss and not one for personal injury.

It is submitted that the decision of the House of Lords in *Spring* v. *Guardian Assurance Plc*[21] supports the view that there is a duty of care, though in that case the plaintiff had been employed by Guardian Assurance and was not in a pre-employment situation. The House of Lords held

---

[15] [1995] 2 AC 207.   [16] [1995] 2 AC 145.   [17] [1998] 2 All ER 577.
[18] [1997] IRLR 219.   [19] [1998] IRLR 583.   [20] N. 6, above.
[21] [1995] 2 AC 296; *Bartholomew* v. *London Borough of Hackney* [1999] IRLR 246.

the employer liable both in tort and contract for a negligently written reference relating to the employee's honesty and reliability. Without a reasonable reference, the plaintiff would find it impossible to get another job in an industry subject to financial regulation. It is submitted that there is no difference in principle between a negligent reference and a negligent medical report, or between a medical report written pre-employment and one written for an existing employee, given that the duty of care in tort is independent of any contractual duty. The Court of Appeal in *Kapfunde* disagreed; the *Spring* case was distinguished as applying only to those who were in employment, or who had recently been employed, and not to job applicants pre-employment.

Confidentiality and Privacy

The presence of a therapeutic relationship is not essential to the existence of a duty to maintain confidence. Anyone who receives information of a confidential nature has a duty not to reveal it to third parties without consent. Doctors and nurses are further constrained by the ethical rules of their professions. In the course of occupational health practice the health professional will acquire confidential clinical information. She will not convey this to management without the worker's consent, unless public interest dictates that the rights of third parties must take precedence. One example is knowledge that a health professional who is HIV-positive is continuing to perform exposure-prone procedures and ignoring advice.

In the pre-employment situation, the job applicant will usually be told that there will be a report by the doctor or nurse on fitness for work, without clinical information being revealed. The General Medical Council advises that a doctor, when assessing a patient on behalf of a third party, must obtain the patient's written consent to undergoing the assessment, and his acceptance that this may necessitate the disclosure of personal information.[22] Employers need to know whether a prospective employee is especially vulnerable, because this is part of the risk assessment which must be performed by virtue of the Management of Health and Safety at Work Regulations 1992. In addition, there may be a need to make suitable adjustments to the premises or to working practices in order to comply with the Disability Discrimination Act 1995.

Where an employee or agent has knowledge of a particular fact, that knowledge is imputed to the employer or principal. Otherwise, management would be able to deny that it knew, for example, that one of its employees was suffering from stress, because the employee's line manager, who might be causing the stress, had not reported it to senior management. Where the employer knows about a particular vulnerability, he has a

---

[22] *Guidance from the General Medical Council on Confidentiality* (London, 1995) 9.

higher duty of care.[23] It follows that, if this general principle applies to occupational health, the employer has imputed knowledge of all the clinical details in the occupational health files, despite the legal and ethical rules of confidentiality:

Normally, the informed written consent of the individual is required before access to clinical information may be granted to others, whoever they may be and whether professionally qualified or not, e.g. solicitiors, insurers, managers, trade union representatives, HSE staff, etc.[24]

Thus, if a counsellor working in the employer's occupational health department is giving confidential counselling to an employee for stress-related illness, the employer notionally knows the details, though I trust that they will never in reality be revealed to him without the employee's consent.

This extremely illogical conclusion creates particular problems in the law of disability discrimination. The Code of Practice,[25] paragraph 4.62, advises that if an occupational health officer knows in that capacity of an employee's disability, the employer cannot claim that he does not know of it. 'This will be the case even if the disabled person specifically asked for such information to be kept confidential.' In no other area of medicine is a third party deemed to be in possession of confidential information which the doctor holding the information is ethically constrained from revealing to him without the consent of the patient.

Would it not be possible to argue that confidential medical information, because of its special nature, is not automatically imputed to the employer when it is given to the OH professional? It will then be for the OH professional to pursuade the employee or job applicant to reveal it to the employer. The employee will have to choose between keeping the information secret and losing any special protection which might otherwise be conferred, or revealing the information and risking rejection by the employer (in the case of disability employers of fifteen or more workers will now have to justify that rejection under the Disability Discrimination Act 1995).

A further problem which arises is that employers increasingly try to expand the medical questionnaires and tests which they require occupational health to administer. Drugs testing is becoming popular (recently introduced by the Metropolitan Police) and genetic testing is being proposed. The anti-discrimination legislation provides some restraint.

---

[23] *Paris* v. *Stepney Borough Council* [1951] AC 367; *Walker* v. *Northumberland County Council* [1995] 1 All ER 737.
[24] Faculty of Occupational Medicine, *Guidance on Ethics for Occupational Physicians* (5th edn., London, 1999).
[25] *Code of Practice for the Elimination of Discrimination in the Field of Employment against Disabled Persons or Persons who have had a Disability* (London, 1996).

Employers are not permitted to discriminate against a job applicant on the ground of sex.[26] Certain medical problems will be confined to members of one sex (pre-menstrual syndrome, prostate problems). Others will be suffered more by members of one sex than another (most HIV-positive individuals are male, more women are diagnosed as suffering from clinical depression than men). Thus, to exclude sufferers from these conditions is indirect sex discrimination because the requirement or condition that job applicants be free of them is one with which members of one sex find it substantially more difficult to comply. The employer must justify indirect discrimination by showing that the health condition makes it impossible or inadvisable for the employee to be engaged. For example, HIV-positive individuals should not be employed as health-care workers on exposure-prone procedures, and are barred by immigration controls from working in some countries abroad. It is interesting to note here that the National Health Service has introduced universal immunization for Hepatitis B of health-care workers in training and those involved in exposure-prone procedures. There is no vaccine for HIV, the HIV test is unreliable in the first months of infection, and can provide only a 'snapshot' of the individual's HIV status on the day of the test. Thus, hitherto, compulsory testing for HIV has been rejected. Nevertheless, now that drugs are available to treat AIDS-related conditions, and now that the shortage of nurses from the UK is leading to recruitment in some African countries where an AIDS epidemic is raging, there may be increased pressure to introduce some HIV testing for health-care workers.

The Race Relations Act 1976 makes it unlawful for an employer to discriminate against employees or job applicants on grounds of colour, race, or ethnic or national origins. Certain health problems are more prevalent in some races than in others. Hepatitis B is far more common in Asia and in sub-Saharan Africa than in Europe. Sickle cell anaemia is also infrequently found in those of Caucasian race. Thus, the exclusion of health-care workers who are carriers of Hepatitis B from renal units has to be justified by evidence that they constitute a risk to patients and other workers. If genetic testing is shown to be linked to racial group, it will have to be similarly justified.

The Disability Discrimination Act 1995 makes it unlawful for an employer of fifteen or more employees to discriminate against a disabled person for a reason which relates to that person's disability. A disabled person is one who has a physical or mental impairment which has a substantial and long-term adverse effect on his ability to carry out normal day-to-day activities, or which did so in the past, though the person has now recovered. The employer who knows of a disability may reject a job applicant where he can show that the disability is a material and substantial

---

[26] Sex Discrimination Acts 1975 and 1986.

reason why he should not be employed. However, before he does this he should explore whether a reasonable adjustment to the physical environment or working practices would enable the disabled job applicant to undertake employment.

Apart from the anti-discrimination legislation there are virtually no legal controls over the pre-employment screening process. The job applicant has the choice either of refusing to co-operate, when he will not get the job, or of lying on the questionnaire, when he may be dismissed for dishonesty if he is found out.[27] Should OH personnel therefore agree with any policy which the employer wishes to adopt? The ethics of occupational health demand that the protection of the life and health of the worker and of his human dignity are their primary responsibility. One controversial area is that of mental illness. In 1991 there was a series of unexpected events on the children's ward of the Grantham and Kesteven Hospital, which eventually led to a nurse on the ward, Beverley Allitt, being convicted of four murders, nine attempted murders, and nine cases of grievous bodily harm, all to children on the ward. It was shown that in training she had had considerable periods of sickness absence. These were due to a series of unrelated health problems. An inquiry chaired by Sir Cecil Clothier reported in 1994.[28] It recommended that no candidate for nursing in whom there is evidence of a major personality disorder should be employed in the nursing profession. The problem is to identify such candidates:

We have sought to discover if there is any way in which a serious personality disorder could be detected at a pre-employment screening interview. It has been suggested that some kind of psychological questionnaire might be used, but the evidence we heard suggests that such questionnaires cannot be relied on to detect personality disorder and furthermore they tend to be lengthy and to require interpretation by psychologists.

Another suggestion was that it might be made a condition of employment in certain occupations, like nursing, that candidates must themselves grant full access to all their medical history. However, the Faculty of Occupational Medicine in its guidance on ethics advises that this can never be justified, though it may be necessary to seek specific information from a GP (or a consultant) for a specific purpose.[29]

In the later case of Amanda Jenkinson, a nurse convicted of tinkering

---

[27] *O'Brien v. Prudential Assurance Co Limited* [1979] IRLR 140.

[28] *Report of the Allitt Inquiry* (London, 1994); *Guidelines on Occupational Health Services for NHS Staff,* HSG (94) 51.

[29] Faculty of Occupation Medicine, n. 24, above, para 3.10; the Access to Health Records Act 1990 renders void any term or condition of a contract which purports to require an individual to supply any other person with a copy of his health record. It is extended by ss. 56, 57 of the Data Protection Act 1998 to demands by the employer to produce medical records pre-employment.

with life-support machinery in order to discredit a colleague, the Bullock report commissioned by the North Nottinghamshire Health Authority (1997) was critical of OH personnel who 'should be reminded of their duty not only to the employee or potential employee to whom they render professional services, but also to that employee's patients or colleagues'.

The need for the occupational health department to stand firm and not yield to every request for information from the employer is threatened by two considerations. The first is that occupational health is subject to the financial control of management. The second is that OH personnel, like most doctors and nurses these days, are afraid of accusations of negligence and potential litigation. If they remain silent, they may be blamed either for not protecting third parties, as in the Allitt and Jenkinson cases, or for not protecting the worker who claims that he should never have been allowed to work in a job which did damage to his health. The Clothier Report suggests that occupational health should declare an applicant for nursing as unfit where he or she has had excessive sickness absence, excessive use of counselling or medical facilities, or self-harming behaviour such as attempted suicide, self-laceration or an eating disorder, until he or she has shown an ability to live an independent life without professional support and has been in stable employment for at least two years.

It should also be noted that the Police Act 1997, when it is fully in force, will permit employers to demand the criminal records of prospective employees, even details of spent convictions and cautions where the employee will work with children, in the health professions, pharmacy, and law, or in senior management in banking and financial services. The trend is towards compelling disclosure of 'skeletons in the cupboard'.

On the other hand, the Data Protection Act 1998, when it comes into force, will give more protection to employees in respect of the processing by the employer of sensitive data, including information about the employee's health.

There is considerable doubt about the effect, if any, of the Human Rights Act 1998 when it eventually comes into force. Article 8 provides that everyone has the right to respect for his private and family life, his home, and his correspondence. Will this lead courts to be restrictive in sanctioning employers' requests for medical information from prospective employees by confining employers to those areas where medical conditions are directly relevant to the job which is sought (e.g. eczema in a job involving physical contact with irritant chemicals)?

In *A* v. *EC Commission*[30] the Court of First Instance of the European Communities held that the requirement of the staff regulations that every person should undergo a medical examination prior to being recruited as a

---

[30] Case T–10/93 [1994] ECR II–179; see also Case C-404/92 *X* v. *EC Commission* [1994] ECR I–4780.

Community official is in no way contrary to the fundamental principle of respect for private life set out in Article 8 of the European Convention on Human Rights. In this case the applicant voluntarily told the medical officer that he was HIV-positive and agreed to undergo an HIV test. He was rejected because the tests showed that he was symptomatic, and because the job in question would take him to developing countries, where the medical infrastructures were deficient. The medical officer's decision was upheld by the Court.[31]

A Canadian case, *Re Canadian Pacific Limited and United Transportation Union*,[32] applying the right to privacy in the Canadian Charter of Rights and Freedoms, illustrates the potential of the Human Rights Act. There, an employer's policy of random drug testing was held to be in breach of the Convention. It may be argued that our courts should uphold such testing only where it can be demonstrated that there is a real risk to other workers or the general public, that employees have been made aware of the policy, that tests are properly carried out by trained personnel, and that there is a right of appeal.

The development of a human rights dimension in this area will prevent employers from invading privacy at will. Until that occurs, the existing law fails adequately to restrain the employer who seeks to appoint a 'master race' of perfect human beings who will never have accidents or take long-term sick leave. Much depends, therefore, on the professionalism and integrity of the occupational health profession.

---

[31] It should be noted that asymptomatic HIV infection is not included within the definition of disability in the Disability Discrimination Act, but becomes a disability once symptoms, however slight, start to appear.

[32] (1987) 31 LAC (3rd) 179; reference should also be made to the Universal Declaration on the Human Genome and Human Rights, (Paris, 1997); Convention for the Protection of Human Rights and Dignity of the Human Being with regard to the Application of Biology and Medicine (Ovied., 1997); J. D. R. Craig, *Privacy and Employment Law* (Oxford, 1999).

Life and Death Issues

HUMAN ORGAN TRANSPLANT ORDINANCE: FACILITATING ADULT LIVE DONOR TRANSPLANTS?

Athena Liu *

Introduction

Organ transplant raises difficult legal and ethical issues. Organs may come from a live or dead donor, and a donor may be an adult or a minor. This paper deals with only live[1] adult (i.e. over 18[2]) donors and recipients. In Hong Kong, there are currently two categories of live transplant: kidneys, which are relatively well established,[3] and livers, which are still in their infancy.[4]   Live transplant is mainly governed by the Human Organ Transplant Ordinance (HOTO) which has two main objectives: first, to prevent organ trading, which can take two forms: commercial agencies acting as intermediaries between donors and recipients, and recipients buying organs by paying potential donors as a means of inducing a donation which would not otherwise have taken place. The other objective of the HOTO is to protect the right to self-determination of both donors and recipients. This is likely to be compromised if the donor's consent is not free or voluntary because of the presence of financial or other coercion or inducement to donate. Additionally, self-determination of both donor and recipient is likely to be undermined if either of them fails to understand the

---

* The author would like to thank Nigel Bruce, Laurence Goldstein and David Price for their comments on the earlier drafts.

[1] For cadaveric donation, see Medical (Therapy, Education and Research) Ordinance.

[2] HOTO excludes minor donors, even though such a donor may be *Gillick*-competent: see *Gillick* v. *West Norfolk and Wisbech AHA* [1986] AC 112. In other jurisdictions, donations by minors are also not permitted: see the Human Tissues Act 1982 (Victoria, Australia); the Transplantation and Anatomy Act 1979 (Queensland, Australia).

[3] Approximately 250,000 kidney transplants have been performed worldwide and one quarter have come from living donors: see EC Commission, *Questioning Attitudes to Living Donors Transplantation*, Commission of the EC Commission (Luxembourg, 1997), 1.

[4] The first live liver transplant was performed in England in 1993 and up to 1998 there had been in total 18 such transplants. In Hong Kong, the first live liver transplant was also performed in 1993. See also Appendix A.

nature of the procedure and the risk involved prior to consenting to a transplant. This paper focuses on self-determination, which inevitably is also linked to organ trading.

To achieve the two objectives (preventing organ trading and protecting self-determination), the HOTO employs the simple mechanism of distinguishing between 'related' and 'unrelated' donors. A related donation is allowed to proceed subject to certain preconditions, but an unrelated donation is prohibited unless the Human Organ Transplant Board (HOTB) approves it.

This paper first examines the scope of the HOTO by reference to the meaning of 'organ' and 'payment prohibited'. Parts II and III examine the legal structure for related and unrelated donations and the extent to which the objectives of the HOTO are achieved. Part IV examines the position of adult comatose recipients. In a recent Hong Kong case, such a patient died as a result of not being able to have a liver transplant.[5] This paper discusses the position of such a patient under a recent amendment to the HOTO and examines one of its implications.

1. Organ and Prohibited Payment

In the late 1980s and early 1990s, rumours were rife that Hong Kong residents had transplants in the People's Republic of China using organs procured in the People's Republic of China.[6] Responding to rumours that this was facilitated by Hong Kong doctors, the Hong Kong Medical Association adopted guidelines against the practice of buying and selling human organs for purposes of transplant, deeming that it was both unethical and morally repugnant.[7] The controversy over organ trading led to the Human Organ Transplant Bill, which was modelled on the English Human Organ Transplants Act 1989. The Bill was gazetted on 27 March 1992 and enacted on 23 February 1995, but it did not come into operation until 1 April 1998. It prohibits commercial dealing in organs and restricts the transplanting of organs between unrelated persons. [8]

ORGAN

According to section 2 of the HOTO, an 'organ' means:

any part of the human body consisting of a structured arrangement of tissues which, if wholly removed, cannot be regenerated by the body, and includes part of an organ.

---

[5] The case of Mr Chow Yam-fun who became unconscious as a result of an acute liver cirrhosis: *see South China Morning Post* (SCMP) 10 Nov. 1998; *Apple Daily* 9–10 Nov. 1998; *SCMP*, 20 Nov 1998; *SCMP*, 24 Nov. 1998; *SCMP*, 9 Mar. 1999.

[6] *South China Morning Post*, 25 July 1993.

[7] Hong Kong *Hansard*, 8 Apr. 1992, 2546.   [8] See the long title to the HOTO.

The term 'organ' is used as a term of art rather than in its medical sense. A cornea, for example, is not an organ in a medical sense, but is now included in this definition. Crucial to this definition is the idea that certain organs/tissues, once removed, are not regenerated; hence the removal represents a permanent loss to a donor. Thus, unlike gametes, blood, and bone marrow which are replaced by the body, the heart, kidney, pancreas, and lung, once removed, are non-regenerative. The definition captures not only these non-regenerative organs when they are wholly removed, but it also covers the partial removal of some organs, e.g. a live liver transplant entails the removal of a lobe of a liver;[9] after the transplant, the donor's liver will grow back, as will the transplanted proportion.[10]

PAYMENT PROHIBITED

Payment in Hong Kong for the supply, or offer to supply, for payment of an organ, whether the payment is made before or after the organ is removed, is now an offence.[11] This prohibition covers activities such as advertisement, brokerage, and private transaction.

> Example 1: X, through word of mouth gets to know that Mr Lee, a wealthy tycoon, needs a kidney for transplant, and receives payment (in Hong Kong) from Mr Lee for his kidney to be removed, with a view that it be transplanted to Mr Lee. Both X and Mr Lee commit an offence.

> Example 2: Mr A seeks (in Hong Kong) a kidney for sale for his wife (B). Mr A and any donor (e.g. C) who receives payment commit an offence.

Section 2 provides that 'payment' means:

payment in money or money's worth but does not include any payment for defraying or reimbursing—
(a) the cost of removing, transporting or preserving the organ to be supplied; or
(b) any expenses or loss of earnings incurred by a person and attributable to his supplying an organ from his body.

In short, not all payment is prohibited, and if X or C receives payment which is limited to medical expenses or loss of earnings incurred for supplying the organ, and does not take a profit over and above recovery of out-of-pocket expenses, no offence is committed.

> Example 3: Dr D receives payment for removing a kidney from a

---

[9] See also lung-lobe transplant: see Unrelated Live Transplant Regulatory Authority (ULTRA), *Report 1995–8* (London, 1998) (hereafter cited as ULTRA's Report).
[10] I. Kennedy and A. Grubb, *Medical Law: Text with Materials* (2nd edn., London, 1994), 1094.   [11] S. 4(1).

donor and transplanting it into a recipient in Hong Kong. Dr D commits no offence.

This is because the word 'removing' in section 2 means 'excising' of an organ.[12] As the cost of removing an organ is not payment, fees received by a transplanting doctor are also lawful. As such, doctors are not considered 'suppliers'.[13] Similarly, payment to an organ bank for transporting or preserving an organ is not prohibited so long as such operation is not commercial in nature.

2. Related Donors: Doctors as Clinicians, Psychologists, and Quasi-policemen

The HOTO assumes that where the parties are related (or have a close status relationship) they will be motivated to act altruistically and commercialization is unlikely.[14] The people who are considered related by the HOTO ('HOTO-related') are those who have certain genetic/blood relationships and certain married couples. In the case of the genetically related, it means parent–child; brother–sister (of whole or half blood); uncle/aunt–nephew/niece (of whole or half blood); and cousins (of whole or half blood). Those whose marriages have subsisted for not less than three years are also included,[15] although they are not genetically related.

Where the donor and recipient are HOTO-related, *a removing doctor may lawfully remove* the organ for transplant provided he is satisfied that certain conditions have been fulfilled.[16] According to section 5(4) of the HOTO, he must satisfy himself that:

(b) the donor has reached the age of 18 years or 16 years and is married;
(c) another registered medical practitioner, who is not the medical practitioner who will remove the organ or transplant the organ, has explained to the donor and the recipient, and each has understood
  (i) the procedure;
  (ii) the risk involved; and
  (iii) his entitlement to withdraw consent at any time;
(d) the donor has given his consent to removal of the organ without coercion or the offer of inducement and has not subsequently withdrawn his consent; and
(e) no payment prohibited has been, or is intended to be, made.[17]

---

[12] See ss. 4, 5 of the HOTO and the reference to the removing/excising doctor; see also the rule of construction against repetition and surplusage.

[13] Kennedy and Grubb, n. 10, above, 1094.

[14] B. Dickens, 'Donation and Transplantation of Organs and Tissues' in I. Kennedy and A. Grubb (eds.), *Principles of Medical Law* (Oxford, 1999), at 832.

[15] S. 5(1).   [16] S. 5(6).

[17] At one time, there was uncertainty whether failure to comply with any of the conditions would render a removing doctor liable to an offence (s. 5(7)). An amendment makes it clear that no offence is committed.

A removing doctor is responsible for determining (i) the alleged status of the donor and recipient, (ii) their comprehension of the procedure and risk involved in a transplant operation, (iii) whether there is any coercion or offer of inducement, and (iv) whether payment prohibited has been or is intended to be made. Arguably task (i) is the responsibility of an administrator, task (ii) requires clinical judgement, task (iii) is for a psychologist to determine, and task (iv) is for a policeman to investigate, but they are now all the responsibility of a removing doctor.

STATUS

The responsibility of determining whether the parties are HOTO-related rests with the removing doctor.[18] The Human Organ Transplant Regulations[19] provide that the fact of a genetic relationship shall be established by means of certain identity documents. Where a removing doctor is not satisfied that the parties are HOTO-related (e.g. in a case involving documents from other jurisdictions such as the People's Republic of China), it would be safe to treat the parties as HOTO-unrelated.[20] Marital status must have 'subsisted' for not less than 3 years. Arguably, 'subsisting' means not only in 'name' but also in 'substance', and hence excludes a marriage of convenience (or sham marriage). However, it is now provided that marital status shall be established by means of marriage documents or a statutory declaration by either party to the effect that the marriage has subsisted for not less than three years. When in doubt, the safest course of action, again, is to treat the parties as if their marital relationship has not been established.[21]

This categorization of the HOTO-related and the HOTO-unrelated is bound to be crude. Those who are HOTO-related may act as donors for reasons other than love and affection, whereas those who are HOTO-unrelated, e.g. grandparent–grandchild, cohabiting couples, the newly-weds, to-be-wed, close friends, or priest and church member, may be acting altruistically.

COMPREHENSION OF RISKS AND BENEFIT

Unlike other medical treatment where a patient may consent to undergo a risky procedure for a cure, organ transplant is unique for two reasons. First, it is an operation of the last resort for the recipient and, secondly, a healthy donor is required to undergo a surgical operation from which he

---

[18] S. 5(6).
[19] r2 as amended by the Human Organ Transplant (Amendment) (No 2) Reg. 1999 (LN 168 of 1999).
[20] S. 5(1), and see mistake of fact as a defence.
[21] The Human Organ Transplant (Amendment) (No 2) Reg. 1999 (LN 168 of 1999).

derives no medical benefit. The unique nature of an organ transplant means that both donor and recipient must understand the nature of the procedure and the risk involved. Thus, section 5(4)(c) especially requires that an explanation be given on the nature of the procedure and the risks involved to both donor and recipient, and that they both understand the information. This requirement reflects the idea of self-determination and in practice differs significantly from other medical treatment in two ways: (i) the general rule governing consent to medical treatment and (ii) duty of a doctor to disclose risks.

The law on consent to medical treatment in Hong Kong is concerned with a real (and valid) consent. This is not the same as what is sometimes called 'the doctrine of informed consent'. For there to be a valid consent, what a doctor needs to do is to inform the patient 'in broad terms of the nature of a procedure'[22] intended. If a patient consents after being so informed, the consent is real, and the doctor will not be liable for battery.[23] This is to be distinguished from the law of negligence which imposes a duty on a doctor to inform a patient of certain risks associated with a particular treatment or procedure. The standard of disclosure adopted by the court is sometimes called 'the doctrine of informed consent'[24] which refers to an objective standard (as opposed to clinical judgement).[25] In reality, both the law on consent to medical treatment and the duty of disclosing risk have to be distinguished from the requirement of understanding which is closest to the idea of an informed decision/choice or self-determination. Cardozo J in *Schloendorff* v. *Society of New York Hospital* has provided the classic expression of the concept of self-determination as:

Every human being of adult years and sound mind has a right to determine what shall be done with his own body; and a surgeon who performs an operation without his patient's consent commits an assault.[26]

Not only is there a conceptual gap between the law on consent to medical treatment (the primary function of which is to protect doctor from the civil liability of battery)[27] and the duty of risk disclosure, on the one hand, there is a further conceptual gap between the duty of risk disclosure as opposed to actual understanding of a patient, and hence a patient's right

---

[22] *Chatterton* v. *Gerson* [1981] 1 QB 432, *per* Bristow J at 443.   [23] *Ibid.*
[24] Which sometimes carries a connotation as to the nature/quality of the consent, see *Reibl* v. *Hughes* (1980) 114 DLR (3d) 1.
[25] *Bolam* v. *Friern HMC* [1957] 2 All ER 118; *Sidaway* v. *Bethlem Royal Hospital* [1985] 1 All ER 643; *Canterbury* v. *Spence* 464 F 2d 772 (1972); *Rogers* v. *Whitaker* (1992) 109 ALR 625; A. Grubb, 'Consent to Treatment: the Competent Patient' in Kennedy and Grubb, n. 14, above, 109.
[26] (1914) 211 NY 125 at 126.
[27] *Re W (a minor) (medical treatment: court's jurisdiction)* [1992] 3 WLR 758 at 765 *per* Lord Donaldson MR.

to self-determination, on the other hand.[28] In practice, the latter gap is resolved by a presumption of fact; an adult of sound mind is presumed to have the ability to understand and, in most cases, is assumed actually to understand.[29] Thus, in an action for battery, it is for the plaintiff-patient to prove that he did not in fact understand when he consented to the treatment or procedure, and consequently that his consent was not valid. However, there is increasingly more discussion about the gap between information provision (on the part of the doctor) and the cognitive process/comprehension on the part of the patient.[30]

Live donors and recipients are not only protected by the law on consent to medical treatment and disclosure of risk, but they are also required to have actually understood the explanation given regarding the 'procedure and the risk involved'. This is because, unlike with most medical treatment, a healthy donor undertakes a risky and harmful procedure for the sake of another,[31] hence a more stringent measure to protect him from a potentially harmful decision is considered justifiable. Similarly, although a recipient may have no other option apart from a transplant to prolong life or have an improved quality of life, transplant involves medical as well as non-medical considerations. Thus, it was said that:

From a purely clinical standpoint, the physician may feel strongly that the proposed intervention is the 'best decision'. However, it is the patient's legal and moral right to be afforded an opportunity to make a decision based upon his or her own personal values, knowledge and beliefs . . . The physician is in no position to weigh all of the intensely personal factors that may be of extreme importance to the patient: will the pain be worth the procedure when the chance of survival is uncertain? Will a slower, probably more peaceful death be preferable to undergoing trauma of major surgery and a large risk of later death by organ rejection or infection? Will financial and emotional burdens on the patient and the patient's family be justifiable in light of the risks?'[32]

[28] P. Dawes and P. Davison, 'Informed Consent: What do Patients Want to Know?' (1994) 13 *Monach Bioethics Review* 20; S. Harth and Y. Thong, 'Parental Perceptions and Attitudes About Informed Consent in Clinical Research Involving Children' (1995) 41 *Soc.Sci Med.* 1647: D. Tribe and G. Korgaonkar, 'The Impact of Litigation on Patient Care: An Enquiry into Defensive Medical Practices' [1991] *Professional Negligence* 2; Gerald Roberston, 'Informed Consent Ten Years Later: The Impact of *Reibl* v. *Hughes*' (1991) 70 *Can.Bar Review* 423.

[29] Except in cases involving people whose competence is questionable, e.g. a minor and mentally incapacitated person, or where a person refuses to undergo treatment or procedure, see M. Jones and K. Keywood, 'Assessing the Patient's Competence to Consent to Medical Treatment' (1996) 2 *Medical Law International* 107; J. Wong *et al.*, 'Capacity to Make Health Care Decisions: its Importance in Clinical Practice' (1999) 29 *Psychological Medicine* 437.

[30] *Re C (adult: refusal of treatment)* [1994] 1 WLR 290. The three-stage test of competence is comprehension and retention of the information which is material to the decision, use of the information and weighing it in the balance as part of the process of arriving at the decision.

[31] For an exception, see 'domino' transplant in ULTRA's Report, n. 9, above.

[32] T. Overcast, 'Legal Aspects of Death and Informed Consent in Organ Transplant' in D. Cowan (ed.), *Human Organ Transplantation: Societal, Medical-Legal, Regulatory and Reimbursement Issues* (Ann Arbor, Mich., 1987).

Today, live donation involves mainly kidney and liver transplants.[33] As a healthy donor is placed at some risk, full disclosure of risk and benefit to the donor[34] is needed with the view to allowing him to make an informed decision. The donor needs to be informed of the risks and benefit to himself; risks include mortality, perisurgical complications (major or minor),[35] and long-term side effects.[36]

'Benefit' to a donor includes psychological benefit, and it is for the donor to decide what amounts to benefit and whether such benefit is commensurate with the risks involved. The court has interpreted benefit widely, notably in a recent case involving bone marrow transplant which it considered to be relatively unintrusive, with no long-term consequence to the donor. Thus, in *Re Y (mental incapacity: bone marrow transplant)*[37] a 25-year-old leukaemia patient, a mother of a young child, faced death if a bone marrow transplant was not done. The only suitable donor was her 35-year-old incompetent sister who was severely physically and mentally handicapped from birth. The sisters' mother was 62 years old and was in ill-health. The relationship between the sisters was not close but they belonged to a close and supportive family. The incompetent sister had a close relationship with her mother who visited her frequently in the institution where she lived. The patient sought a declaration that tests could be done on her incompetent sister to ascertain her suitability as a donor. It was held that tests could only be done if it would be in the incompetent sister's best interests. Taking a broad approach to the best interests of the incompetent sister, it was concluded that, should the patient die, it would adversely affect the mother's health. Furthermore, the mother would need to look after her young grandchild and this would reduce the incompetent sister's contact with her mother. Consequently, it was to the emotional, psychological, and social benefit of the incompetent sister to act as donor.

Another relevant aspect for the donor's consideration is the medical condition of the recipient, his chance of survival and quality of life post-transplant, in that the recipient's health status may impact on the donor's psychological well-being. [38]

---

[33] See ULTRA's Report, n. 9, above, as well as Hong Kong figures in Appendix A.

[34] On recipients, see Dickens, n. 14, above, and Overcast, n. 37, above.

[35] General figures (given by Professor Fan, Department of Surgery, University of Hong Kong) for liver transplant, are in terms of mortality, are 6% for recipient and 1% for donor; for perisurgical complication 30–40% for recipient and 10% for donor.

[36] C. Henderson, 'Complications in 100 Living Liver Donors' *Transplant Weekly* 21 Sept. 1998; P. Whitington, 'Living Donor Liver Transplantation: Ethical Considerations' (1996) 24 *Journal of Hepatology* 625; D. Simmons, 'Risk of Diabetic Nephropathy in Potential Living Related Kidney Donors' (1998) 316 *BMJ* 896; J. Najarian, '20 Years or More of Follow-up of Living Kidney Donors' (1992) 340 *The Lancet* 807, F. Rosner 'Is Living Kidney Donation Still Justifiable?', *Chest* August 1994; P. Singer, 'Ethics of Liver Transplantation with Living Donors' (1989) 321 *New Eng. J of Med* 620.   [37] [1996] 2 FLR 787.

[38] D. Wolcott, 'Psychological Adjustment of Adult Bone Marrow Transplant Donors Whose Recipient Survives' (1986) 41 *Transplantation* 484.

Section 5(4)(c) envisages that a registered medical practitioner, who is not the removing or transplanting doctor, explains the risks and benefit to the parties. This removes the appearance of conflict of interest— that of a removing or transplanting doctor understating the risks and overstating the benefit to the detriment of the parties. The tendency and the danger of this can be seen in the context of the first human heart transplant:

> When Christiaan Barnard performed the first human heart transplant on Louis Washkansky, he considerably overstated the probability of success, leading Mr Washkansky to believe that the procedure had an 80 percent chance of success, even though that figure applied only to the chance of living through the operation itself. Dr Barnard's justification was:
>
> > 'He had not asked for odds or any details . . . he was at the end of the line . . . For a dying man it was not a difficult decision . . . [I]f a lion chases you to a bank of a river filled with crocodiles, you will leap into the water convinced you have a chance to swim to the other side, but you never would accept such odds if there were no lion.'

Dickens categorizes this problem differently:

> when a trusted informant significantly downplays chances of transplantation failure or factors likely to compromise the recipient's survival, the inducement to donate may become undue, and vitiate a potential donor's capacity to exercise choice voluntarily. Coercion negates consent, and non-consensual removal of tissues may constitute battery or criminal assault to which those who use pressure or deception are parties.[39]

Christiaan Barnard told his patient a white lie, and it could not be said to be coercion, but it was intended to, and probably did, dispose the patient to move favourably towards the transplant. Although section 5(4)(c) guards against this possible, or the appearance of, conflict of interest, it does not prohibit an explanation to be provided by a doctor who is a member of the same transplant team. Furthermore, if a form of transplant is in its infancy, how can a doctor accurately explain the risks to the parties?

FREE OR VOLUNTARY CONSENT?

Consent obtained as a result of coercion or inducement is not free and voluntary.[40] Coercion may be moral, psychological, or familial (especially in a Chinese society where family ties are strong). The pressure is greatest where the donor is the only rescuer who could save the life of the recipient

---

[39] Dickens, n. 14 above, 823.
[40] For a definition in the context of marriage, see *Szechter* v. *Szechter* [1970] 2 All ER 905; *Singh* v. *Singh* [1971] 2 WLR 963; *Hirani* v. *Hirani* [1983] 4 FLR 232.

or improve the recipient's quality of life. Thus, in *Urbanski* v. *Patel*[41] a mother-wife patient underwent a sterilization operation and had her only kidney mistakenly removed. Failing to find a suitable donor, her father volunteered one of his kidneys to his daughter with the hope of improving her life-style, and giving her a better chance of survival. What he did was more than understandable. However, it was stated later by one commentator that the father's 'parental feelings towards his daughter, coupled with an understandable sense of moral obligation, left him without any real choice in the matter'.[42] As such, the father was overcome by the plight of his daughter's distress and he had no 'real' choice but to act as a donor.

Coercion may be covert or overt. One example of overt pressure in its most aggressive kind comes in the form of seeking an order compelling that person to be a donor. Thus, in the case of *McFall* v. *Shimp*[43] the plaintiff suffered from a rare bone marrow disease and the survival prognosis was very slim unless he received a bone marrow transplant (BMT) from a compatible donor. Such a donor was limited to close relatives. After certain tests, it was determined that only the defendant was a suitable donor. The defendant refused to submit to transplant and the plaintiff sought to compel him to submit to further tests and eventually to the BMT.[44] It was argued that the need to save life justifies the court infringing upon the defendant's right to bodily security. It was rightly held that the decision whether to act as a donor rested with the defendant. However, the court itself endorsed a form of covert pressure, commenting that the defendant's failure to assist was 'morally indefensible'. As such, the defendant was likely to be ostracized by relatives and friends should he refuse to co-operate with a view to acting as a donor.

Coercion may be in the form of payment. Although it is presumed that a related donor is unlikely to be motivated by monetary consideration, such a possibility cannot be dismissed altogether, especially where the emotional bonding of the parties is tenuous. The HOTO prohibits payment over and above out-of-pocket expenses arising out of the donation, made or to be made. Enforcing this prohibition is likely to be difficult, if not impossible, even with the commitment of investigative resources. How is payment to be detected if a recipient agrees that he will take out a life insurance policy on the donor for the benefit of his dependant family? Given the health risk of acting as a donor, what if a recipient

[41] (1978) 84 DLR (3d) 650. Similarly, in *Sirianni* v. *Anna* (1967) 285 NYS 2d 709 an exploratory operation to see if an acute infection which set in after a routine hernia repair was caused by a wound abscess or by appendicitis resulted in the patient's only kidney being removed. The patient's mother offered to donate one of her kidneys; see also *Moore* v. *Shah* (1982) 458 NYS 2d 33.

[42] G. Roberston, 'A New Application of the Rescue Principle' (1980) 96 *LQR* 19.

[43] (1978) 10 Pa. D & C (3d) 90.

[44] W. Curran, 'Beyond the Best Interests of a Child; Bone Marrow Transplanting Among Half-Siblings' (1991) 324 *New Engl. J Med.* 1818.

agrees to buy the donor health-care insurance (which is a contingent and deferred payment)? What if the donor owes a third party money and the recipient agrees to repay it for him? What if the recipient agrees to allow his apartment to be used by the donor and his family for as long as they wish? Even if there is no payment in money or money's worth, what about payment in kind?[45] What if there is an understanding that the recipient would assist the donor's family members in need, e.g. with better job security, promotion opportunity?[46] How may these forms of transactions be policed?[47]

The HOTO requires only that *a removing doctor* be satisfied that no prohibited payment has been or is intended to be made. It is an offence for *a doctor to remove or transplant* an organ where he either knows or ought, after reasonable inquiry, to have known that a payment was, or was to be, made for the supply of an organ.[48] Transplant doctors are expected to act as quasi-policemen, but as the parties are unlikely to volunteer information about any payment when the doctor makes his reasonable inquiry, this provision serves no more than a symbolic function. Although coercion, especially familial, can be real, there is no clear provision that a potential donor should be interviewed by a psychologist whose task would be to ensure that s/he has not been coerced to act as a donor. In sum, it is commendable that the HOTO provides for an independent explanation of risk and benefit and the requirement of understanding. Doctors, however, cannot be expected to act as psychologists and quasi-policemen. As such, there appears to be little effective enforcement machinery against coercion within the family context or the making of 'payment prohibited'. As will be seen in the next section, the safeguards against these dangers are no more effective where the parties are HOTO-unrelated.

3. Unrelated Donor and the HOTB

Where the parties are HOTO-unrelated, the HOTB is expected to perform independent scrutiny beyond that performed by *a removing or transplanting doctor*. Thus, apart from the conditions described above (which apply), the HOTB itself has to be satisfied with those conditions prior to granting an approval. In determining an application which is to be made by a doctor who has clinical responsibility for a donor, the HOTB is not limited to the evidence presented to it by the applicant, and it may receive

---

[45] A needs a kidney and B needs a liver. A gives B a lobe of liver and B gives A one of his kidneys.

[46] See ULTRA's Report, n. 9 above, on preferential medical treatment given to a family member. See also R. Titmuss, *The Gift Relationship: from Human Blood to Social Policy* (London, 1970).

[47] Dickens, n. 14, above, 833. [48] S.4(5)–(7).

information from a variety of sources, including interviewing the donor and recipient. Such an investigative function has resource implications and may cause delay to a proposed transplant. To assist it in discharging its function, the HOTB may rely on a report compiled by a suitably qualified person on the explanation (and comprehension) of the nature of the procedure and the risk involved, the absence or presence of coercion or inducement, but not on whether payment prohibited has been or is intended to be made.[49]

However, given the assumption that a HOTO-unrelated transplant is financially driven, how could the HOTB be satisfied that 'no payment prohibited has been or is intended to be made'? The Administrative Guidelines envisage that an application consists of the filling in of standard forms, one of which involves a declaration by the applicant doctor that 'to the best of his knowledge, no payment prohibited has been, or is intended to be made'.[50] Indeed, it seems that an application may be determined on the basis of these standard forms which contain no information such as the relationship between the parties, their respective financial positions, reasons for desiring to donate and the donor's family background (such as whether the donor is married with children). In the absence of such information, it is difficult to see how the HOTB may assess whether payment prohibited has been, or is intended to be, made.[51]

What if the donor and recipient (who are strangers[52]—the donor coming from an economically deprived background and the recipient wealthy) declare that no payment prohibited has been, or is intended to be, made? Would such a donation, nonetheless, appear to be suspicious, and in the absence of a good reason, would it be tempting to believe that there was an understanding between the parties that the recipient would reciprocate some benefit/advantage to the donor or the donor's designate in return for the donor's generosity?

In light of the scanty information which is required to accompany (in writing) an application, the machinery for ensuring the donor's free and voluntary consent is largely ineffective. Prior to the HOTO, because transplantation was beset by legal/ethical difficulties and uncertainties, doctors had to negotiate it with extreme caution. Although the objectives of the HOTO are to prevent organ trading and protecting self-determination, the HOTO, by providing a clear procedure for both HOTO-related and HOTO-unrelated donations, has removed many of these uncertainties. However, it has done so without putting in place a system of effective safeguards. Consequently, the HOTO has indirectly legitimized and facilitated live transplants.

---

[49] Administrative Guidelines, Annex D.
[50] Administrative Guidelines, Annex A
[51] Cf ULTRA's *Guidance to Clinicians* (London, 1993).
[52] 'Stranger's Gift of Transplant Came Too Late', *SCMP* 22 March 1999.

4. Incompetent Recipient

Under the HOTO, the requirement of understanding for both a donor and a recipient can never be fulfilled in the case of an incompetent patient. Consequently, where the parties are HOTO-related, a *removing doctor could not lawfully remove* an organ, and where the parties are HOTO-unrelated, the *HOTB could not approve a transplant*. In a recent Hong Kong case, a comatose adult patient died as a result of not being able to have a liver transplant.[53] This raised the question whether the requirement of understanding needed to be amended. Two issues arise from this. First, how would this legal obstacle be compatible with *a transplanting doctor's* ethical duty to save life?[54] Secondly, and assuming that the legal obstacle was removed, to what extent would the best interest of the patient require a transplant? In the following section, I shall discuss the legislative amendment made following the death of the comatose patient and one of its implications.

TRANSPLANTING DOCTOR'S ETHICAL DUTY

Assuming an organ is available, it could be argued that a transplanting doctor confronted with such a legal obstacle is placed in a difficult dilemma; if he acts in accordance with his ethical duty to save life, he compromises his legal position.[55] Arguably, in an emergency this dilemma may be resolved by acting in the best interests of the patient. Indeed, the House of Lords in *Re F (Mental Patient: Sterilization)*[56] had held that, at common law, a doctor could lawfully treat an adult incompetent patient without consent provided that the treatment was in the best interests of the patient. Treatment would be in the best interests of the patient if, and only if, it was carried out in order to save life or to ensure improvement or prevent deterioration in physical or mental health.[57] Whether a proposed treatment was in the best interests of the patient was to be determined by what would be accepted as appropriate treatment by a responsible body of medical opinion skilled in that form of treatment. The justification for the principle in *Re F (Mental Patient: Sterilization)* was the doctrine of necessity and what was in the best interests of a patient was to be determined by clinical judgement.

---

[53] See n. 5 above.

[54] K. Norrie, 'Human Tissue Transplants: Legal Liability in Different Jurisdictions' [1985] 34 *ICLQ* 442.

[55] Indeed, the International Code of Medical Ethics adopted by the Hong Kong Medical Council as part of its code of conduct for doctors provides that a doctor 'shall owe his patients complete loyalty and all the resources of his science'.

[56] [1990] 2 AC 1.

[57] Some judges went further to say that there was a duty to treat.

SELF-DETERMINATION OR BEST INTERESTS OF THE PATIENT

The rationale for requiring understanding of both donor and recipient is that, from the donor's point of view, he undergoes a procedure which brings him no medical benefit. From the point of view of the recipient, although he is the sole medical beneficiary of the transplant, transplantation is the most invasive procedure for a 'catastrophic' disease (of the last resort). Given the involvement of a healthy donor, a decision to undergo a transplant or not entails medical as well as non-medical considerations, and the latter must be for the recipient to decide, and not a matter of clinical judgement. Consequently, most literature only emphasizes how crucial it is that a recipient is given all the relevant information (risks and benefit) before making an informed decision.[58] Thus, it is not unimaginable that a recipient would not want his only son to risk his life by acting as a donor:

Informed patients for whom transplantation is proposed are free to reject the option. They may prefer not to take the risks of surgery or infection, not want relatives to take the risks of live donation, not want dead person's materials in their bodies or, for instance, not want to receive transgenically prepared animals' organs. They may enquire (if they are not informed) whether organs they may receive come from members of races different from their own, from other countries, or from involuntary 'donors', and may be made aware of organ recovery, for instance, from executed prisoners. Their decisions on whether or not to accept transplantation at all or from particular sources can give expression to their philosophical, social, religious, cultural or other convictions.[59]

This partly explains why the English Human Organ Transplants Act 1989 and the HOTO are silent on the incompetent recipient. Complicating the issue is the fact that some forms of transplant (e.g. liver or other forms of new transplants) belong to 'innovative therapy'—involving an element of unknown risk where, arguably, there is little room for the application of the best interests of the patient test which should be restricted in its application to 'standard medical practice'.[60]

LEGISLATIVE AMENDMENT

Given that the common law position in *Re F (Mental Patient: Sterilization)* was not preserved by the HOTO,[61] one simple option would be to amend

---

[58] Dickens, n. 14, above and Overcast, n. 32 above.

[59] Dickens, n. 14, above, 837.

[60] D. Cowan, 'Regulation of Medical Practice' in D. Cowan (ed.), *Human Organ Transplantation: Societal, Medical-Legal, Regulatory and Reimbursement Issues* (Ann Arbor, Mich., 1987).

[61] By a saving provision stating, for instance, that 'nothing in this Ordinance shall be construed as rendering unlawful any transplantation which would have been lawful if this Ordinance had not be enacted.' See, for instance, s. 6 of the Medical (Therapy, Education and Research) Ordinance.

the HOTO so as to preserve the principle in *Re F (Mental Patient: Sterilization).* Another option is to introduce some form of advance directives or proxy decision-making by relatives or next-of-kin.

The amendment adopted by the Human Organ Transplant (Amendment) Ordinance[62] was neither; rather it was an enlarged form of the common law principle in *Re F (Mental Patient: Sterilization).* The amendment permits the dispensing with understanding in relation to certain incompetent recipients. They are in four categories: those who, by reason of suffering from any illness, being minors, or being mentally incapacitated persons or suffering from an impaired state of consciousness, are incapable of understanding the procedure and the risk involved. The effect of the amendment is that the *HOTB may approve a proposed transplant*, and where approval is not required, the *removing doctor may remove* an organ intended to be transplanted, providing that a doctor certifies that the recipient falls within one of the four categories and that it would not be in the best interests of the patient to wait until he is capable of understanding the explanation required in section 5(4)(c). The exemption from understanding covers anyone who is incompetent (e.g. a minor or anyone who is severely mentally handicapped) or becomes incompetent because of any illness or condition. Hence, the exemption would cover a person who suffered a liver failure as a result of an overdose of paracetamol or a person whose organ had been severely damaged after a traffic accident and hence required a new organ. The amendment dispenses with understanding (and consequently consent), and replaces it with clinical judgement.

The amendment, however, is much wider than the principle in *Re F (Mental Patient: Sterilization).* Minors as recipients are now catered for in the HOTO. Although this brings the law up to date with current transplant practice, parental consent for a minor to receive an organ is no longer necessary. Consequently, parental objection to an organ transplant raises only an ethical dilemma for a transplanting doctor, and a transplant may lawfully be performed if it is in the best interests of the minor. This position may be compared with a recent English cases of *Re T (wardship: medical treatment)*[63] where the court was unwilling to override the informed parents' decision not to proceed with a liver transplant for their infant. There a 1-year-old boy was suffering from a life-threatening liver defect. His parents were both health-care professionals experienced in the care of sick children. The unanimous opinion of medical consultants were that the baby should undergo transplant surgery since the prospects of success were good. Without transplantation, the expectation of life was just over two years. The parents refused to consent to the transplant. The father found a job overseas and, against medical advice, the mother travelled with the boy

---

[62] No 7 of 1999, in force on 19 Feb. 1999.
[63] [1997] 1 FLR 502.

to visit him. The doctor formed the view that the mother was not acting in the best interests of the child. At first instance, the judge found that the mother's refusal to consent to the transplant was unreasonable. The judge directed that the mother return with the child to the jurisdiction within twenty-one days. In the Court of Appeal, it was held that there was a strong presumption in favour of a course of action which would prolong life, but to prolong life was not the sole objective of the court, and to require that at the expense of other considerations might not be in the child's best interests. In this case, the court had to consider not only the advantages and disadvantages of the medical procedure, but also the child's post-operative care and development. The Court of Appeal held that such care and development would be affected if his day-to-day care depended on the commitment of a mother who had suffered the turmoil of having her child being compelled to undergo a major operation. Consequently, the best interests of the child required that future treatment be left for the parents to decide.

However, not all minors are incapable of understanding the procedure and the risk involved.[64] The amendment, however, means that capacity to understand is unlikely to be issue for the court as happened in a recent English High Court decision where the court authorized a heart transplant on a 15-year-old girl despite her refusal to undergo the transplant. The court held that the girl lacked the capacity to make an informed decision and that the surgeons were allowed to treat her in accordance with their clinical judgement.[65]

In the case of a mentally incapacitated person (as defined by the Mental Health Ordinance), the amendment derogates from the law governing consent to medical treatment and special treatment under Part IVC of the Mental Health Ordinance. More importantly, the amendment takes away the right of an adult to refuse an organ transplant by means of an anticipatory refusal or advance directive.

During the passage of the Human Organ Transplant (Amendment) Bill, the right of a patient to self-determination was stressed and the inroads into such right was a matter of concerns to some legislators. Thus, Mr Ronald Arculli said:

If a patient has expressly indicated that he will not receive an organ from a specific live donor, the medical practitioner cannot act against his wish even if the patient has become unconscious. However, if a patient has not made any advance directives regarding his wish, the medical practitioner can act in accordance with his clinical judgment of what is in the patient's best interests. *To facilitate the work of the medical practitioners, members have suggested that a new section be added to the form for doctors to sign stating whether the patient has made any directives in this regard.*[66]

---

[64] See *Gillick* v. *West Norfolk and Wisbech AHA* [1986] AC 112.
[65] *BMJ*, 24 July 1999, 209.
[66] Hong Kong *Hansard*, 10 Feb. 1999, 81 (author's italics).

Similarly, Mrs Sophie Leung, Chair of the HOTB said:

The medical practitioner can state in writing that the patient has not previously issued any specific directive against or raised any objection to receiving an organ transplant. If such a written statement can be put before the Board and confirmed by the medical practitioner making it, the wishes of patients will be more nearly taken into account and the scope of their treatment can be widened. In addition, *the Board will be more secured under the law when it approves a transplant for a comatose patient, and the medical practitioner performing the transplant can proceed without the threat of legal action hanging over him.*[67]

Today, a doctor needs to confirm that an incompetent patient has not made any directives or raised any objection to receiving an organ transplant, and this enables the HOTB's approval as well as a transplantation to proceed.

Prior to the amendment, parental consent (in the case of a minor) and consent of a guardian or the court (in the case of a mentally incapacitated person) arguably would be required. Today, these people have no *locus standi* to participate in making a decision as to whether there be an organ transplant. Consequently, it is questionable to what extent non-medical factors form part of a decision whether there should be a transplant. Clinical judgement on what amounts to the best medical interests of the patient may suggest that non-medical factors are irrelevant, and this appears to be the position of the HOTO. As mentioned earlier, the effect of the amendment is that the *HOTB may approve a proposed transplant* and, where approval is not required, the *removing doctor may remove* an organ intended to be transplanted, providing that the recipient falls within one of the four categories and a transplant would be in the best interests of the patient. There is no point in removing an organ if it is not intended to be transplanted; indeed, to do so would be negligent. Once an organ is available and may lawfully be removed, it should be transplanted. In other words, if there is any non-medical reservation about transplanting an organ, the amendment appears to render it insignificant by reference to the best interests of the patient. If best interests of the patient requires dispensing with consent, and hence permitting removal, best interests of the patient also requires a transplant.[68] Transplantation is now solely a medical decision and is fully endorsed and facilitated by the HOTO, although facilitating transplantation was not an objective of the HOTO at the time when it came into operation on 1 April 1998.

CONCLUSION

The HOTO attempts to capture a complex and sophisticated area of medicine which brings with it concomitant legal, moral, and social implications.

---

[67] Hong Kong *Hansard*, 10 Feb. 1999, 85 (author's italics).
[68] *Re F (Mental Patient: Sterilization)* [1990] 2 AC 1.

Transplantation is a fast-advancing area and the law finds itself lagging behind and that catching up is no easy task. The objectives of the HOTO are difficult, if not impossible, to achieve; appointing doctors as psychologists and quasi-policemen does not assist in achieving these objectives. Consequently, the HOTO performs a largely symbolic function, indirectly facilitating organ transplants between the related as well as the unrelated. By exempting the incompetent recipient from the requirement of understanding, replacing it with clinical judgement, the HOTO has made substantial inroads into the law governing consent to medical treatment and the concept of self-determination. As can be seen from the debates during the passage of the Human Organ Transplant (Amendment) Bill, the amendment was framed with a view to facilitating transplants.

Appendix A below shows the figures of live liver transplants in the United Kingdom and in Hong Kong. It can be seen that the total number of live liver transplants in the United Kingdom in 1993–8 was eighteen, whereas the total number for the same period in Hong Kong is fifty-eight. One explanation for this is that there is a good supply for cadeveric donation in the United Kingdom and the same is under-supplied in Hong Kong. Consequently, Hong Kong relies more on live donation. The HOTO may now be instrumental to live transplants and it may act as a bridge between an innovative therapy (e.g. live liver transplants and other form of new transplants) and the standardization of such therapy to medical practice in Hong Kong.

The transplantation debate, however, has only just begun. Apart from the positions of an incompetent patient and the risk and benefits assessment, it was recently disclosed that each liver transplant cost HK$1.2 million, and it is six times the cost of a kidney transplant. Further, the immuno-suppression drug (FK506) costs a hospital a sum of money representing 13 per cent of the total drug budget of its surgery department. This is not all the 'costs': other transaction costs include that sixty patients at a hospital had operations postponed at the last minute to make way for the twelve liver transplants done.[69] An open and thorough debate on resource allocation and selection of patients is needed to inform decision-making process in this area of medicine.

[69] SCMP, 17 May 1999.

Appendix A

Table 5: *Live transplants in the United Kingdom by year and organ**

Year	Kidney	Liver
1989	118	0
1990	101	0
1991	88	0
1992	98	0
1993	142	1
1994	136	7
1995	155	1
1996	183	3
1997	174	4
1998	246	2

*figures supplied by the United Kingdom National Health Service.

Table 6: *Total number of live and cadeveric (kidney and liver) donations in Hong Kong hospitals***

Organ/Tissue	1991	1992	1993	1994	1995	1996	1997	1998	Waiting
Kidney									
Living	20	24	20	16	19	28	23	37	1,000
Cadaveric	30	34	31	44	44	58	47	33	
Liver									
Living	0	0	5	4	11	15	1	12	100
Cadaveric	3	2	4	8	12	12	14	15	

**figures supplied by the Hong Kong Hospital Authority.

THRIFT-EUTHANASIA, IN THEORY AND IN PRACTICE: A CRITIQUE OF NON-HEART-BEATING ORGAN HARVESTING

Howard M. Ducharme*

The irresistible utilitarian appeal of organ transplantation has us hell-bent on increasing the donor pool . . . Are we headed for the utilitarian utopia espoused by Jack Kevorkian, where organ retrieval and scientific experimentation are options in every planned death, be it mercy killing or execution?'

> Robert M. Arnold and Stuart J. Youngner, 'The Dead Donor Rule: Should We Stretch It, Bend It, or Abandon It?' in R. M. Arnold *et al.* (eds.), *Procuring Organs for Transplant* (1995), 227–8.

Dr Robert D. Truog, of Harvard Medical School, consideration of 'the view that killing may sometimes be a justifiable necessity for procuring organs.'

> R. D. Truog, 'Is It Time to Abandon Brain Death?' [1997]
> *Hastings Center Report*

Introduction

The modern mind is in moral confusion on the status of the traditional ethical principle, 'do not kill an innocent person', and simultaneously engaged in soul-searching debates on the individual's right to forgo life-sustaining treatment and euthanasia. Indeed, the general public reconsideration of euthanasia, fuelled by numerous academic attacks on the traditional ethic against legalization of euthanasia (E) and physician-assisted suicide (PAS), are stark evidence of the social collapse of the traditional ethic.[1] While these issues are debated, other life-and-death procedures go on, in particular, organ harvesting and organ transplantation. Here we are ever pressed

* I would like to thank several people who have read various drafts of this paper, offering criticism, comments and encouragement: Ruth and George Kirchhausen, Edmund Pellegrino, Robert Veatch, and Stuart Youngner.

[1] See Peter Singer, *Rethinking Life and Death: The Collapse of the Traditional Ethics* (New York, 1994).

by less than acceptable supplies of organs. It is the co-existence of PAS, E, organ harvesting, and transplantation in modern society that sets the stage for the co-joining of these practices. The argument of this paper is that they are in fact co-joined, in both theory and practice, in what is called thrift-euthanasia.

In *Procuring Organs for Transplant*, Robert M. Arnold and Stuart J. Youngner hint that a connection may exist between the utilitarian utopia of Jack Kevorkian's 'medicide'[2] and the actual procurement of organs harvested via the Non-Heart-Beating Cadaver Donor Protocol (NHBCDP).[3] They do not develop this idea, noting that many would immediately dismiss it as being 'outlandish and inflammatory'.[4] This paper investigates the outlandish connection. What is uncovered is that thrift-euthanasia is not only advocated in theory, but is also conducted today on a national and international scale with impunity.

Definition of Euthanasia and Thrift-euthanasia

There is not one, simple, unarguable definition of euthanasia. The principal definitions prominent in the literature are: (1) painless inducement of death; (2) killing with a certain kind of motive or reason, e.g. beneficence, kindness, pity, compassion; (3) homicide that is in the best interest of the deceased; (4) intentional termination of life upon request; and (5) allowing a person to die, commonly called passive euthanasia.[5] Difficulties over an acceptable definition of euthanasia arise in large part due to the compound, complex nature of the issues involved. Both the descriptive and normative content that must go into such a definition are controversial. A Venn diagram of the complexity here would show euthanasia being that act which occurs in the over-lapping area of four concerns—two overlapping circles representing the major competitors for the descriptive nature of the act would be those of 'killing' and 'allowing to die'. Two additional overlapping circles representing the major competitors for the normative nature of the act would be those of 'beneficence' and 'do not kill'.

The working definition of euthanasia adopted here emphasizes the descriptive nature of the act, leaving open as much as possible the norma-

---

[2] Jack Kevorkian, *Prescription: Medicide—The Goodness of Planned Death* (New York, 1991), 202, 221–30.

[3] See Robert M. Arnold and Stuart J. Youngner, 'The Dead Donor Rule: Should We Stretch It, Bend It, or Abandon It?' in Robert M. Arnold, Stuart J. Youngner, Renie Schapiro, and Carol Mason Spicer (eds.), *Procuring Organs for Transplant: The Debate over Non-Heart-Beating Cadaver Protocols* (Baltimore, Mld., 1995) 219, 227–8.

[4] Arnold and Youngner note that some 'will argue that this scenario is outlandish and inflammatory': see *ibid.* 227–8, 231 n. 17.

[5] *Encyclopedia of Bioethics* (New York, 1995), s.v. Harold Y. Vanderpool, 'Death and Dying: Euthanasia and Sustaining Life'; Philip E. Devine, *Ethics of Homicide* (Notre Dame, Ind., 1990), 167–9.

tive elements and ethical evaluation for subsequent discussion. Thus, *euthanasia is an intentional act of one or more individuals that directly causes or knowingly contributes to the death of another.* The normative elements enter into the definition with virtually any qualification that might be added. For example, is it still E if a voluntary request, terminal illness, unbearable pain, or suffering is not present, say in the case of a persistent vegetative state patient who has left no living will? Is it still E if a physician acts upon the voluntary request of a patient to end his or her life, but the physician does not act upon a motive of beneficence when the act is performed? Because of these and numerous other debatable conditions on normative elements of E, normative conditions are left out of the working descriptive definition above. This definition also accommodates those acts of assisted suicide that fall into the grey zone between suicide and euthanasia.

The complexities in the definition of euthanasia are multiplied by the standardized short-list of species of euthanasia. These species of euthanasia are voluntary, non-voluntary, involuntary, active, and passive euthanasia, together with all of the logical combinations of the same.

These species each pick out an ethically relevant and debated feature in certain acts of E. No definitions of these species are offered here. Rather, my argument is that this recognized short-list of the forms of euthanasia is too short. It is too short because there are in fact other forms of euthanasia, in both theory and in practice, that are not recognized even though they are practised. My principal claim is that the official short-list must be expanded to include another species, if not another genus, of euthanasia. In the spirit of simplicity and readily accessible terminology, it is thrift-euthanasia that must be added to the contemporary bioethical agenda.

The definition and concept of thrift-euthanasia will have no fewer complexes than euthanasia. It is a form of euthanasia done for an explicit reason, one that necessarily carries normative content with it. *Thrift-euthanasia is an intentional act of one or more individuals that directly causes, or knowingly contributes to, the death of another in a manner conducive to the benefit of others,* as in terminal live-organ harvesting and/or terminal vivisection experimentation. This type of act may be considered a *specie* of euthanasia because it looks like another variant that could be added to the official short-list of species. However, as is shown below, acts of thrift-euthanasia are uncovered that possess all of the recognized species of euthanasia *per se*, e.g. involuntary active thrift-euthanasia, non-voluntary passive thrift-euthanasia, etc. Therefore, it is appears thrift-euthanasia is best recognized as a distinct *genus* of euthanasia. Either way, whether *specie* or *genus*, thrift-euthanasia must be recognized so that substantive evaluation of it can occur—in the general public as well as in medicine, law, ethics, and religious traditions.

A Short History of the Practice of Thrift-euthanasia

Thrift-euthanasia is historically not a new form of terminating life, even if it is newly recognized. Minimally, it is a new way of looking at an array of deeds, a new perspective that can produce fresh insight and enhance our ethical clarity. As shown below, it is uncovered in the past and in the present, in the termination of the lives of animals and of human beings.

Thrift-euthanasia of animals in vivisection experimentation has a long history and is still conducted today, even if it is now under closer scrutiny than at other times.[6] Much of this animal experimentation was done for the reason of gaining information and knowledge of the workings of the human body. Some of it was done to learn more about animals themselves. In both cases, the life of an animal was intentionally terminated in a manner conducive to benefit others, e.g. by adding to the body of scientific knowledge of how the circulatory system works.

Thrift-euthanasia of animals via live organ harvesting also has its own history. In 1984, the heart of Goobers the baboon was harvested and transplanted into an infant known as Baby Fae, who was dying of hypoplastic left heart syndrome. Baby Fae survived the xenograft some three weeks.[7] Here the life of one was intentionally sacrificed for the presumed benefit of another. To be sure, there is basic normative content that is added to such cross-species life-taking and life-saving procedures. It is this content that is the source of controversy between the traditional ethic and some versions of animal rights. Both sides in these debates, however, agree on the descriptive nature of such procedures, i.e. thrift-euthanasia. It *is* thrift-euthanasia *and* it calls for considered ethical discussion. Innumerable variations on this type of procedure, e.g. genetically engineered pigs, as a source of kidneys for human transplantation, are likely in the very near future. My point is simply that thrift-euthanasia has been and continues to be done. It is not, however, restricted to the termination of the life of non-human animals for the benefit of humans. It is also conducted on various categorizations of human beings for the benefit of other human beings.

There is a long and continuous history of thrift-euthanasia conducted on human beings—on capital criminals, political prisoners, prisoners of war, demeaned ethnic groups, as well as mentally and physically compromised individuals—in the form of terminal human vivisection experimentation. Many of these instances of thrift-euthanasia fall under a broad

---

[6] Brian Luke writes, '[a]nd at least one theorist, R. G. Frey, has publicly advocated allowing the vivisection of 'marginal' humans as a means of preserving the vivisection of animals on a consistent, rationalized basis': see Brian Luke, 'Review of *Taking Animals Seriously*, by David DeGrazia (Cambridge, 1996)' (1998) 107 *The Philosophical Review* 301.

[7] Gregory E. Pence, *Classic Cases in Medical Ethics* (New York, 1990; 2nd edn., New York, 1995), 314–27.

categorization of utilitarian decision-making. For instance, given that certain individuals are going to be killed anyway, or that they are going to die soon, it is deemed better to exploit significant benefits for others rather than simply allow these deaths to be wasted. Most of these deaths are further categorized as instances of active non-voluntary thrift-euthanasia conducted for the benefit of others and/or for the advance of medical knowledge in general. They have been historically followed up with and without legal impunity. A brief sketch of some instances is offered below.

There is historical evidence that some doctors in ancient Hellenistic Alexandria and medieval Cilician Armenia conducted terminal vivisection experimentation on individuals. Herophilos of Chalcedon (*c.*330–260 BC), the father of anatomy, and Erasistratos of Cos (*c.*330–255 BC), the father of physiology, performed medical experiments on living human beings with impunity.

Both Herophilos and Erasistratos, according to Celsus [around AD 40], 'dissected such criminals alive, as were delivered over to them from the prisons by royal sanction; carefully observing before they had ceased to breathe, those parts which are by nature concealed.' This charge of human vivisection has been believed by some medical historians, doubted by more.[8]

Lois N. Magner considers this 'a brief and rare' practice, but does not find the historical claim difficult to believe:

Most important, for a brief and rare interval, the practice of human dissection was not only tolerated, but actively encouraged ... The vivisection question remains unanswered because the writings of the Hellenistic anatomists have not survived ... but there is no particular reason to believe that the authorities would have prohibited this form of death and dissection, especially if the victims were criminals or prisoners of war.[9]

Given the concept of thrift-euthanasia, this 'brief and rare' practice regularly occurs around times of war. For example, it occurred *en masse* prior to and during World War II, conducted by doctors on medically compromised individuals and despised ethnic groups in Nazi Germany, and on prisoners of war in special camps run by Japanese doctors. These examples (described below) are cases of active involuntary thrift-euthanasia conducted by doctors for the benefits of medicine, for nationalistic (military) interests, for reasons of economic frugality, and/or for ethnic gains.

The racial politics of Hitler fuelled some ongoing medical practices and produced the so-called 'mercy deaths' and 'euthanasia by starvation' at numerous mental hospitals. Between:

---

[8] R. H. Major, *A History of Medicine* (Springfield, Ill., 1954), i, 145. L. W. Conrad, M. Neve, V. Nutton, R. Porter, and A. Wear, *The Western Medical Tradition: 800 BC to AD 1800* (Cambridge, 1995), 33, add that Tertullian also makes reference to this point.
[9] Lois N. Magner, *A History of Medicine* (New York, 1992), 77–8.

January 1940 and September 1942, 70,723 mental patients were gassed, chosen from those whose 'lives were not worthy living,' drawn up by nine leading professors of psychiatry and thirty-nine top physicians ... Some of the victims were selected so that German medical scientists could conduct programmes of human experimentation. Camp doctors used inmates to study the effects of mustard gas, gangrene, freezing, and typhus and other fatal diseases. Children were injected with petrol, frozen to death, drowned or simply slain for dissection purposes.[10]

Thrift-euthanasia was also conducted by medical personnel on thousands of POWs captured by the Japanese military:

Doctors also played a key role in the pursuit of human experimentation in Japan. In 1936 ... Hundreds of doctors, scientists and technicians led by Dr Shiro Ishii were set up in the small town of Pingfan in northern Manchuria, then under Japanese occupation, to pioneer bacterial warfare research, producing enough lethal microbes—anthrax, dysentery, typhoid, cholera and, especially, bubonic plague ... Disease bombs were tested in raids on China. Dr Ishii also developed facilities for experimenting on human guinea pigs or *marutas* (the word means 'logs'). Investigating plague and other lethal diseases, he used some 3000 *marutas* to investigate infection patterns and to ascertain the quantity of lethal bacteria necessary to ensure epidemics. Other experimental victims were shot in ballistic tests, were frozen to death to investigate frostbite, were electrocuted, boiled alive, exposed to lethal radiation or vivisected ... At the end of the war ... Dr Ishii and his team did a deal with the American authorities, trading their research to avoid prosecution as war criminals. The American government chose to keep these atrocities secret.[11]

Josef Mengele conducted the most infamous atrocities of medicalized thrift-euthanasia. At Auschwitz, he participated in the death of some 400,000 victims, doing lethal experiments on thousands. Mengele managed to escape to Brazil and Paraguay, where he lived for forty years:

Later, in conversations with his grown son Rolf, Mengele never expressed any regret for his actions or even any consciousness of having done wrong. *He reasoned that it was not his fault that Jews were to be killed at Auschwitz, and since they were to die anyway, why not use them first to advance medical knowledge, Nazi programs, and his own chance of a professorship?*[12]

During the Cold War, the AMA conducted US government-sponsored research on human subjects in the Tuskegee Syphilis Study in Nature (1930–72) and extensive medical research was conducted by the government in innumerable US Radiation Tests and experimentation done on the general population, military personnel, and infants (1940s–1970s).[13] Since these experiments were not immediately lethal, they can be grouped under the species of passive involuntary thrift-euthanasia for the benefit of medicine, the national interest, and/or worldwide democracy.

---

[10] Roy Porter, *The Greatest Benefit to Mankind: A Medical History of Humanity from Antiquity to the Present* (London, 1997), 649.   [11] *Ibid.*, 649–50.
[12] Pence, n. 7, above, 228, emphasis added.   [13] *Ibid.*, 231–51, 251–2.

Another instance of large-scale thrift-euthanasia—actions that intentionally terminate one life for the benefit or interests of another—is the fervently contested territory of legalized abortion that has gone on for at least twenty-five years. Here the complexities found in the abortion debates, as to the moral or amoral status of a person and a human foetus; if and when a substantial soul (or person) comes into being in the developing body; the nature, presence, and/or absence of a woman's and a foetus' right to life; and the legal right of choice to abortion, constitute part of the normative domain of the abortion debates. Relatively independent of the preceding (but overlapping) ethical issues engaged by abortion, given the minimal biological point that an embryo or foetus is alive and that abortion is an intentional act, then at least some percentage of abortions would be instances of thrift-euthanasia. Also, further refinements and species of thrift-euthanasia would be discernable here, e.g. legal, socially accepted, active, voluntary thrift-euthanasia; parents coercing a pregnant teenage daughter to have an abortion may be an instance of active involuntary or non-voluntary thrift-euthanasia, etc.

There are other instances of thrift-euthanasia via live organ harvesting for the benefit of transplantation in others. There was an apparent locus of such activity recently reported to have occurred in Egypt. In March 1999, the Associated Press carried a story that an orphanage may have sold children for their organs. In a town thirty miles north of Cairo, Egypt, an orphanage for handicapped children reportedly sold some thirty-two children for up to $30,000 each to major hospitals that cater to wealthy Gulf Arabs. Twenty-five of these children died within three months, with forged death certificates, allegedly having been sold for their organs. Ten Parliament members demanded that the state launch an investigation into the allegations. The head of the orphanage and his wife had been removed in late 1998 after an investigation found financial irregularities and problems with the care being provided. No charges had been filed, however, at the time of the article.[14]

In Japan there currently exists a situation that lends itself to thrift-euthanasia, if it does not in fact encourage and promote it. Brain death is directly connected with organ donation. Japanese law:

> refuses to recognize as brain dead anyone but organ donors . . . [F]amilies cannot choose to allow their tube-supported, respirated relative to die naturally unless they agree to organ donation . . . The only time the machines can be stopped is if everyone concerned agrees to organ donation, which produces even more money for the hospital [than maintaining the patient indefinitely].[15]

---

[14] Associated Press, 'Orphanage Allegedly Sold Organs: Egyptian Legislators say 25 Children Died' *Akron Beacon Journal* (19 Mar. 1999).

[15] Carl Becker, 'Money Talks, Money Kills—The Economics of Transplantation in Japan and China' (1999) 13 *Bioethics* 238.

This 'opens the door to legal organ transplantation from warm pulsating cadavers'. The law 'provides no legal safeguards against the Japanese fears that donors may be prematurely pronounced brain-dead'.[16]

In China, a situation exists that is much more alarming than in Japan. It appears that a virtual governmental machine has executed thousands of individuals ('prisoners') in order to procure viable organs for transplantation in to senior party officials, their family connections, military personnel, and their families, as well as for wealthy clients from Hong Kong, Singapore, and surrounding countries.[17]

China has a 'Strike Hard' campaign to fight crime that applies the death penalty to common criminals, for example producing more than 6,100 death sentences in 1996. There are more than seventy crimes that can invoke capital punishment, including possession of politically incorrect manuscripts, hooliganism, bribery, and political deviance. David Rothman gives an example of these activities:

[A] young lady teaching middle school in Jiangxi in the 1970s was found guilty of possessing politically incorrect manuscripts written by a colleague. Her blood type was determined, she was condemned and shot in the head twice, but even before she died, her kidneys were removed and transplanted to the son of the military officer who arranged the operation.[18]

China has no brain death law. This allows for a normal removal of organs to be done while the individual is technically alive (not meeting brain death definitions of death), if not in fact alive, with some level of consciousness.[19] China does, however, have legal 'Rules Concerning the Utilization of Corpses or Organs from Corpses from Executed Criminals'. Here it is specified that organs can be procured from any prisoner who consents to organ harvesting. The obvious question is: can such a prisoner in such a system give anything approaching a meaningful consent, let alone really be allowed free refusal? This current situation and these activities are evidence of various forms of thrift-euthanasia, e.g. active voluntary (?) and involuntary thrift-euthanasia, occurring on a large scale with impunity.

Various elements of the practice of thrift-euthanasia are seen in the

---

[16] Carl Becker, 'Money Talks, Money Kills'.

[17] David Rothman, 'Body Shop: China's Booming Trade in Organs for Transplant' (1997) 37 *Science* 17; Asia Watch Committee, Human Rights Watch, 'China: Organ Procurement and Judicial Execution in China' (1994) C609 *Human Rights Watch* 42; Barbara Basler, 'Kidney Transplants in China Raise Concern About Source' *New York Times*, 3 June 1991, A1; Paul Lewis, 'China Executes Dissidents in Secret (Amnesty International Reports)', *New York Times*, 31 Aug. 1989, A3; Dmitry Balburov, 'China's Chechnya', *Moscow News*, 22 May 1997; Stacy Mosher, 'Ultimate Response (Execution of Smugglers in China)' (1992) 155 *Far Eastern Economic Review* 9; in Becker, n. 15, above, 240–1.

[18] Rothman, n. 17, above, quoted from Becker, n. 15, above, 240–1.

[19] David P. Hamilton, 'China Uses Prisoners for Transplants (Human Rights Watch Asia Report)', *Wall Street Journal*, 29 Aug. 1994, A6–A7.

numerous examples given above. Some of its elements are seen more or less clearly and some practices of it are covered over in ambiguities. There is, however, one further, widespread practice of thrift-euthanasia to discuss here. It is one that is very carefully constructed upon ambiguities in law, medicine, and definitions of death, with deft use of ethical principles. Constructed as it is for professional level discussion (but carried out on the general populace), it is only known by its exclusionist label—the controlled non-heart-beating cadaver donor protocol (NHBCDP). I suggest it be called thrift-euthanasia. Such a term can help remove the erudite secrecy that sustains this practice. It can also allow the general public access to understand it, so as to be able to evaluate it.

The NHBCDP: The *de facto* Practice of Thrift-euthanasia

Thrift-euthanasia is not simply the pipedream of fringe radicals, as shown in the numerous examples listed above. It is, arguably, already practised at established medical centres in the United States,[20] and in various medical establishments around the world, but is virtually unknown to the general public. It is embedded in a specific type of theory-laden, organ-harvesting protocol.[21] It is practised under a protocol formally called controlled or planned death under the Non-Heart-Beating Cadaver Donor Protocol (NHBCDP).[22] This source of organs is distinguishable from the normal source, namely, brain-dead (but heart-beating) donors. In this section, the specific protocol employed at the University of Pittsburgh Medical Center since 1992 is carefully reviewed,[23] even though other institutions also

---

[20] Although the Pittsburgh Protocol is the particular thrift-euthanasia protocol reviewed here, other possible *de facto* practices of it include the following. (1) the Regional Organ Bank of Illinois policy that allows the injection of preservation fluid into freshly deceased patients who failed resuscitation after cardiac arrest, without obtaining consent, so as to improve viability of organs if and when harvesting is done. The notion of *presumed consent* was invoked after 35 of 35 families *declined* to give consent for insertion of catheters for *in situ* cold preservation of organs; (2) heart-beating donors who 'died in the operating room because they could not survive the removal of cardio-pulmonary bypass after open heart procedures', who in 1962 became kidney donors 'prior to discontinuing bypass'. These donors 'were not dead before kidney removal', but they were 'certain to die when cardiopulmonary bypass was stopped'. See Michael A. DeVita, James V. Snyder, and Ake Grenvik, 'History of Organ Donation by Patients with Cardiac Death' in Arnold *et al.* (eds.), n. 4, above, 26, 19, respectively.
[21] The controlled death NHBCDP is the specific type of organ-harvesting that is described and evaluated in this paper as being an instance of thrift-euthanasia. Criticisms offered apply to it alone and not to brain-death organ harvesting, nor necessarily to uncontrolled NHB donation. These latter types of organ harvesting are not instances of thrift-euthanasia because the *dead donor rule* requirements are met. These latter types can be acknowledged as making 'use of a corpse for the gain of the living', but such use is ethically permissible because it is distinguishable from thrift-euthanasia. See *ibid.*, 22.
[22] There are also three categories of 'non-controlled' NHB organ donation that can be distinguished. These non-controlled types are not discussed here.
[23] It is interchangeably referred to as the Pittsburgh Protocol or as the NHBCDP. However, as there is no uniform national policy on NHB protocols in the USA, and since

employ this protocol. The University of Wisconsin has used such a policy to procure organs ever since 1974.[24] Most significantly, the NHBCDP already enjoys national stature, seen in the fact that at least thirty-four of the sixty-three organ procurement organizations (OPOs) in the USA either have NHB protocols or are in the process of developing them.[25] Although NHBCDs account for a small percentage of organ donors at present, this percentage could quickly increase. Given the large number of potential NHBCDs in hospital beds, one estimate is that there could be 14,000–25,000 NHBCDs annually.[26] Robert Truog estimates that 'at least two-thirds of all hospital deaths currently occur after the withholding or withdrawal of life-sustaining treatment', which is a great waste of human organs that could save the lives of others, wasted because of our cultural taboo against killing.[27]

Success in organ transplantation techniques has increased the demand for viable organs, which has outpaced the supply of viable organs.[28] The objective of the NHBCDP is to help supply the needs of potential recipients by increasing the supply of viable organs:

Non-heart-beating organ donation was discontinued because of poor survival rates more than because of questions regarding whether it was ethical. It is being reintroduced because of need, donor requests, and because the practical problems appear to have been overcome by medical advances . . .[29]

At the same time, however, an 'unofficial moratorium on organ donation from non-heart-beating cadavers persists in most of the world'.[30] The moratorium exists, at least in part, due to ethical limits on organ harvesting

significant variations exist between NHBCD protocols in use in different institutions, there is properly speaking no one protocol that is *the* NHBCDP. Nonetheless, the Pittsburgh Protocol is the only one that has made itself open to scholarly review in the literature and therefore it is taken as the best known representative of the NHBCDP. Indeed, Dr Robert Arnold, chair of the committee that developed the NHBCDP at Pittsburgh is the exemplar here. He stresses that his aim is not simple public trust in the protocol, but to be 'really deserving of it by thoroughly examining all of the areas of possible conflict of interest or appearance of impropriety': see Roger Herdman and John T. Potts, *Non-Heart-Beating Organ Transplantation: Medical and Ethical Issues in Procurement* (Washington, DC, 1997), 85.   [24] *Ibid.* 84.

[25] *Ibid.* 3. As early as Nov. of 1994, 11 of 40 Organ Procurement Organizations (OPOs) had protocols in place for the permissibility of using organs procured from non-heart-beating donors. The same report notes that 17 of 40 OPOs had already procured organs from non-heart-beating donors. See (Nov. 1994) *UNOS Update* 4, and Robert M. Arnold, Stuart J. Youngner, Renie Schapiro, Carol Mason Spicer, 'Introduction: Back to the Future: Obtaining Organs from Non-Heart-Beating Cadaver Donors' in Arnold *et al.* (eds.), n. 4, above, 3.

[26] Herdman and Potts, n. 23 above, 82.

[27] Robert D. Truog, 'Letters', (1999) 29 *Hastings Center Report* 4.

[28] DeVita *et al.*, n. 20, above, 25–6: 'success bred demand, and this demand has outpaced the supply. In 1991, more than 16,000 major organ transplantations were performed in the United States. At the end of March 1993, however, the UNOS waiting list included more than 30,000 potential recipients, and on average six to seven per day died awaiting organs.'

[29] *Ibid.*, 26.

[30] *Ibid.*, 25. Use of non-heart-beating donors has been reported in Japan, Latvia, Spain, The Netherlands, New Zealand (Auckland), England (reports of non-controlled NHBCD at Leicester and Newcastle upon Tyne) and the USA.

imposed by the *dead donor rule*—an *a priori* rule that the donor be a corpse before organ-harvesting begins. The principal formulators of the NHB protocol acknowledge that it was written with the understanding that we have a 'shifting social and legal environment, and an increasingly inadequate organ supply'.[31] The utilitarian needs of growing numbers of potential recipients, rather than adherence to the confines of the non-utilitarian *dead donor rule*, takes precedence.

If Diethelm's prediction that increasing demand will fuel searches for new sources continues to bear out, we will need to reassess prior ethical, legal, and social rationales for excluding certain types of patients from donating organs.[32]

Thus, from this broad, external, sociological perspective, the NHBCDP shares the same utilitarian drives that are so starkly present in Kevorkianism. However, the NHBCDP must be evaluated internally—on its own stipulated conditions and justifications.

The protocol procures paired and non-paired organs from donors who are labelled, pre-*mortum*, as NHBCDs. A defender of morality of the policy describes a case of harvesting organs via the NHBCDP:

The patient is wheeled down the hospital corridors on what all know will be a one-way trip to the operating room. In the OR, physicians remove the respirator that the patient depends upon for life. Drugs are administered. Soon the patient is unconscious. The patient is draped for surgery. The heartbeat becomes irregular, then the heart fibrillates. A physician begins timing. After two minutes of fibrillation, death is pronounced and the organ transplant team begins its work.[33]

The pre-*mortum* patient will be declared dead—a cadaver donor, at the mark of two minutes of pulselessness.[34] In the words of the protocol:

The pulse pressure must be zero, or by definition the heart is beating. In addition to pulselessness (as defined here), the patient must be apneic and unresponsive to verbal stimuli. Given the above, any one of the following electrocardiographic criteria will be sufficient for certification of death . . .:

- 2 minutes of ventricular fibrillation
- 2 minutes of electrical asystole (i.e. no complexes, agonal baseline drift only)
- 2 minutes of electromechanical dissociation.[35]

---

[31] DeVita *et al.*, n. 20, above, 28.

[32] *Ibid.* Diethelm's prediction is that the ever-growing felt utilitarian need for organs will drive the ethical decisions here, rather than the reverse: see Arnold Diethelm, 'Presidential Address: Ethical Decisions in the History of Organ Transplantation' (1990) 211 *Annals of Surgery* 505–20.

[33] David Cole, 'Statutory Definitions of Death and the Management of Terminally Ill Patients Who May Become Organ Donors after Death' in Arnold *et al.* (eds.), n. 4 above, 69.

[34] Other NHBCDPs 'do not require any elapsed time, and some leave the definition to the attending physician's discretion. Others prescribe intervals of 1, 2, or 5 minutes or yet other timing': see Herdman and Potts, n. 23, above, 58.

[35] 'University of Pittsburgh Medical Center Policy and Procedure Manual, Subject: Management of Terminally Ill Patients Who Become Organ Donors After Death', Appendix, n. 4, above, 240.

NHBCD patients are declared 'cadavers' according to medical criteria different from those used for the determination of death for virtually all other patients in hospital.[36] NHBCDs become 'cadavers' by stipulation, for they do not meet the brain death criterion of death.[37] These two-minute-cadavers will be unresponsive to verbal stimuli, but they may have brain activity (data that are available but intentionally ignored by the protocol), as well as twitching hearts (ventricular fibrillation).[38] Stipulating death (without testing for irreversibility) creates a theory-laden, question begging, definition. It is, however, a theory-laden definition of death compatible with utilitarian concerns.[39] The longer the wait, the lower the viability of each organ, the lower the number of total organs available to save the lives of others in need.

IS THE DONOR A CADAVER AT THE ONSET OF ORGAN HARVESTING?

To be sure, the NHBCDP expressly asserts that, '[n]o organs may be procured until death has been certified'.[40] But, it must be asked, are two-minute-cadavers, 'with their warm bodies, quivering hearts, and possibly quite healthy brains',[41] really dead? (In 1997, the Institute of Medicine favourably reviewed the practice of NHB organ transplantation in 1997; it found that 0 to five minute agonal periods are used at different

[36] It may be objected that the NHB criterion of death simply returns to an ancient concept of irreversible loss of heart function. But (1) this claim fallaciously begs the question at issue: is 2 minutes of asystole empirically equivalent to the irreversible loss of heart function? (2) When the ancient criterion was employed, it was not used as a justification for immediate organ harvesting, as is the case of the NHBCDP. It is argued below that this additional factor is ethically relevant. (3) We do not live in ancient times. As it is unethical to do surgery today as the ancients did—in non-sanitary, non-sterile conditions, using sharpened stones for scalpels. So too is it unethical to forego modern means at our disposal to determine whether a patient is alive or dead, especially when immediate, irreversible loss of organs is countenanced.

[37] It may be objected that no law requires that brain death occur before death can be declared. This objection is considered in more detail below, but here it is replied that the law does require that patients who are declared dead actually be dead, the clear entailment of the dead donor rule.

[38] In an attempt to explain these complexities to the general public, recent articles speak of the donors as gravely sick people whose 'hearts have stopped, [but whose] brains work': see Associated Press story by Alice Ann Love, 'Standards proposed to increase donors', *Akron Beacon Journal* (19 Dec. 1997); and by Eileen Smith, 'Group urges quicker organ harvests', *USA Today* (19 Dec. 1997).

[39] The arguments that support this controversial claim are given below. Some might argue that if the Pittsburgh Protocol only changed its 2-minute asystole criteria to 15 minutes, then all utilitarian-laden objections to it would be removed. The reply is that a 15-minute criterion would remove most of its violation of the dead donor rule, but a 15-minute criterion would also dismantle the NHBCDP. The argument given in the following sections is that undeclared utilitarian reasoning drives this protocol in numerous places, not just in the choice of a 2-minute criterion.

[40] 'University of Pittsburgh Medical Center Policy and Procedure Manual', iii, R, in Arnold *et al.* (eds.), n. 4, above, 240.

[41] Cole, n. 33, above, 70.

hospitals.[42]) The affirmative answer to this question is the crux assumption of the protocol. Its answer is taken to be that given by DeVita and Snyder:

since no attempt would be made to resuscitate patients who had forgone treatment, the ad hoc committee concluded that death, the *irreversible* cessation of cardiac function, may be *declared* when it is determined that auto-resuscitation will not occur. Based upon the little scientific evidence available, a group of intensivists with clinical and research expertise in resuscitation selected *two minutes as the duration of pulselessness required for determining death, i.e., the duration after which the likelihood of auto-resuscitation is vanishingly small.*[43]

There is a compound assertion here, composed of empirical claims and dubious moral assumptions. A few questions asked of the protocol bring out these points. Are unresponsiveness to verbal stimuli, together with two minutes of zero blood pressure, sufficient criteria to determine that a patient is a cadaver? If auto-resuscitation of a sedated individual does not occur after 120 seconds, is it true that it will not occur? Is a warm body with zero pulse, a quivering heart, and possibly a healthy brain a cadaver ready for burial? On straightforward empirical grounds, Dr Joanne Lynn supplies the accepted medical answer to these questions:

No one would claim that two minutes of anoxia is sufficient evidence that the brain will have irreversibly ceased to function. The number of counterexamples refuting this claim would be legion. Thus, death cannot be declared by cardiopulmonary criteria and cannot be declared by neurologic criteria until the periods of observation ordinarily required have passed.[44]

Herdman and Potts note the same fact: '[i]n the Pittsburgh protocol, the standard is 2 minutes without cardiac function, and this defines the cessation as "irreversible." There are few, if any, empirical data that indicate when autoresuscitation of cardiac function is no longer possible.'[45]

Put another way, if the heart of a NHBCD can be restarted in another person, why would it not be restartable in the original owner's chest?[46] If

---

[42] Its survey of hospital protocols found that 'some controlled NHBD protocols take into account the manner of death, allowing a shorter interval after a longer agonal period. Some do not require any elapsed time, and some leave the definition to the attending physician's discretion. Others prescribe intervals of 1, 2, or 5 minutes or yet other timing': see Herdman and Potts, n. 23, above, 58.

[43] Michael A. DeVita and James V. Snyder, 'Development of the University of Pittsburgh Medical Center Policy for the Care of Terminally Ill Patients Who May Become Organ Donors after Death Following the Removal of Life Support' in Arnold *et al.* (eds.), n. 4, above, 63, emphasis added.

[44] Joanne Lynn, 'Are the Patients Who Become Organ Donors under the Pittsburgh Protocol Really Dead?' *ibid.* 99. Herdman and Potts also take this statement by Lynn as sufficient to report that '2 minutes are not supported by any experimental data on the probability of autoresuscitation and are too short to support a determination of brain death due to circulatory arrest': see Herdman and Potts, n. 23, above, 59.   [45] *Ibid.*, 86.

[46] See Albert Rosenfeld, 'Heart Transplant: Search for an Ethic' (1968), 64 *Life* 75, cited from DeVita *et al.*, n. 20, above, 23.

the heart is restartable and the brain is not dead, most people find it counter-intuitive to perceive that the patient is a corpse. On empirical grounds alone, the answer to each of the preceding questions is negative. But the NHBCDP's answer to these same questions is affirmative. It follows that its definition of death is false and its stipulation of death is a *de facto* cover for volitional commitments to planned death/organ harvesting. Upon analysis, both of these claims are shown (below) to exist in the protocol itself, although present in its characteristic subtle manner.

The NHBCDP definition of death is false because it does not meet the accepted medical and legal criteria of *irreversible loss of heart/lung function* (overlooking for the moment the presence or absence of brain activity). Since *irreversible* loss of heart/lung function ≠ a *low probability* of auto-resuscitation, the protocol criterion of death is a fallacious, question-begging definition of death. To assert that these two conditions are equivalent is the same as asserting that my little red sports car *cannot run any more*, because its old *starter has a low probability* of igniting. The assertion that the patient is dead before being opened for organ harvesting is, as a straightforward empirical claim, false.

It may be objected that irreversibility = low probability, because we can never prove an impossibility and all death pronouncements are based on vanishingly small probabilities. The reply is that an effort to restart the heart could be made—so that it could be known whether the cardiac function is present or irreversibly lost. If cardiac arrest occurs anywhere else in the hospital, will the patient be declared dead because there is a low probability of resuscitation? What is the medical textbook and legal definition of low probability? The point is obvious: an acceptable verification of death can be obtained here, but it is just such data that are intentionally evaded because of their disutility in procuring viable organs. Dr Arnold acknowledges the contingent, non-empirical basis of the definition of death in the NHBCDP:

the 2 minute definition assumes that even if the cessation could be reversed, it can be defined as irreversible *because a decision has been made* not to resuscitate. It is important to remember that *these patients have decided, or their families have decided*, that they will forgo life-sustaining treatment.[47]

Here the determining element of the purported medical condition of death is clearly exposed—a volitional decree by the patient, and/or the patient's family, together with the volitional commitment of the medical personnel involved. The criticism is obvious. Appendicitis is not determined by volitional decree of a patient and/or his or her family. Kidney failure is not determined by volitional decree of a patient and/or his or her family. Brain death is not determined by volitional decree of a patient

---

[47] Herdman and Potts, n. 23, above, 86, emphasis added.

and/or his or her family. Neither is irreversible loss of heart/lung function determined by volitional decree of a patient and/or his or her family. The presence or absence of a medical condition is an empirical matter. Volitional decisions to forgo life-sustaining treatment (FLST) are ethical decisions. The criticism here is that the Pittsburgh protocol ultimately exchanges the former for the latter. Thus the objection that the two-minute criterion is a medical determination of death is invalid, deceptive, and repugnant. David Cole, a defender of the morality of the protocol, comments on this issue:

> As an interpretation of what it means for a state to be *irreversible*, this [NHBCDP] seems to me to be perverse. It is clear that the attending physicians could, in fact, resuscitate at least some of these patients under the circumstances described in the protocol, *after* death has been certified.[48]

The protocol is shown here to be a seedy, *de facto* protocol for thrift-euthanasia. In an effort to avoid the daunting ethical problems of pre-*mortum* organ harvesting, the protocol explains that *these organ donors are declared* to be corpses before harvesting can begin. This has now been shown to be a fallacious truth-by-stipulation. It employs a charade declaration of death, employing a medical designation to stand for a volitional commitment to planned cardiac death and organ harvesting.[49] Empirically, it rests upon inferential probabilities ('the little scientific evidence available' that 'the likelihood of auto-resuscitation is vanishingly small'), rather than verification by simple, readily available empirical tests, e.g. waiting fifteen minutes and/or attempting CPR to confirm irreversible loss of cardiac capacities.

It may be objected here that doing CPR would violate the patient's DNR (do not resuscitate) order. There are two replies, either of which can show this objection fails. First, if the patient is dead, as the protocol asserts, it is not necessarily a violation of the patient's DNR to attempt CPR on his or her corpse, if it truly is a corpse. The DNR order is a pre-*mortum* order. If the objector insists that CPR cannot be done without violating the DNR, then it is an acknowledgment that the patient is not yet dead at the onset of organ harvesting. It is a patent acknowledgement that irreversibility ≠ low probability.

Secondly, if the protocol wishes to meet the empirical requirements of the *dead donor rule*, then it could request permission of the patient ahead of time to do CPR for the purposes of verifying death, so that organ harvesting could proceed without waiting, say, fifteen minutes. If the patient is medically dead at two minutes, as the protocol asserts, then CPR on a cadaver will not turn a cadaver into a living human being. Thus both

---

[48] Cole, n. 33, above, 73.
[49] This volitional commitment, when acted upon, is also an illegal act of euthanasia.

paths that this objection can take are dead ends that only reinforce the utilitarian commitments to thrift-euthanasia in the NHBCDP.

One question still festers deep within this protocol. Why would an attending physician stipulate that his or her patient is dead upon such inferential probabilities? Could an attending physician act on the NHBCDP without premeditated commitment to the utilitarian motives, means, and objective of thrift-euthanasia? Consider the following list of just some of the voluntary, intentional acts and omissions of an attending physician who follows the protocol. There is wilful commitment and/or compliance to:

- usher patients who are about to die away from loved ones at the scheduled OR time;
- declare death at the location most advantageous for organ harvesting;
- allow pre-*mortum*, physical preparations of the patient's body for organ harvesting (skin preparation and draping for surgery);[50]
- a special procedure of FLST not used elsewhere in hospital;
- a value-laden criterion of death (zero pulse for 120 seconds and unresponsive to verbal stimuli);
- forgo empirical verification of death (not doing CPR to verify that cardiac function is irreversibly lost);
- turn the patient/two-minute-cadaver over to the organ harvesting team for immediate removal of organs;
- action by the surgical team to open up a patient who does not empirically meet the *dead donor rule*;
- surgically open up a sedated patient who may be unconscious, revivable, and not yet a corpse;
- harvest organs from their patient, early enough to retain viability, for the benefit of numerous other individuals.

It is not necessary for my argument to posit all possible objections that might be raised to this list, most of which have already been covered. It is sufficient for my purpose if this list shows any additional evidence that *de facto* utilitarian commitments are required in carrying out the protocol. The only objection calling for a reply is the assertion that all concepts of death are value-laden, and this one is no different. My reply is that that is exactly my point. Not only is the NHBCDP value laden, but also it is value laden with utilitarian values of life and death. We are ethically obliged to be open about such values, especially in organ harvesting protocols that include illegal acts of euthanasia. Hence my argument stands.

---

[50] See n. 40, above, 240: '[t]o keep warm ischemia time to a minimum, all other appropriate preparations for the procurement operation may take place prior to death but never before the patient has become totally unconscious and unresponsive to noxious or painful stimuli. Skin preparation and draping may be performed by the staff of the Center for Organ Recovery and Education ('CORE').'

Since each element of the NHBCDP entails volitional conditions necessary to the protocol, it is thereby shown that the NHBCDP is essentially
laden with, and driven by, deep utilitarian commitments. It is anything but
a mere empirical, value-neutral protocol. The two-minute countdown from
personhood to cadaverhood is fundamentally driven by utilitarian commitments. Thus, the NHBCDP is shown to meet the all of the fundamental
conditions of the definition of thrift-euthanasia

The utilitarian driving force of this protocol, demonstrated above, can
also be seen in unsuccessful NHBCDP cases. According to the protocol:

If organ ischemia is prolonged (e.g. beyond two hours), it may not be possible to
utilize organs designated for donation and procurement may not be performed.
The decision to cancel organ procurement because of prolonged ischemia rests with
the responsible transplantation surgeon. Under these circumstances, the designated
ICU physician may also decide to return the patient to the ICU.[51]

Thus, a living, competent patient who consents to the NHBCDP is taken
to the OR and has her respirator removed. But it may be that a 120-
second gap between heartbeats over a two-hour waiting period does not
occur. Warm ischemia will ruin the viability of the organs during an
extended wait. After a two-hour wait, the transplant surgeon is to give a
consultation as to the usefulness of the patient's organs for harvesting. If
the patient's organs are now found to be non-usable, the patient will be
returned to the ICU. The patient who was conscious and competent two
hours earlier will now likely suffer from irreversible brain damage as a
result of a failed NHBCDP. If the implicit, *de facto* utilitarianism of the
protocol were expressly acknowledged, as it is by Kevorkian, then a utilitarian appeal to the argument from mercy[52] would propose active
euthanasia here. Since the NHBCDP does not openly commend euthanasia, it returns the non-usable patient, now in a more tragic condition, to
the ICU.[53] The protocol offers the formal appearance of being committed

---

[51] *Ibid.*
[52] See James Rachels, *The End of Life: Euthanasia and Morality* (Oxford, 1987), 152–8.
[53] It may be objected that the Pittsburgh Protocol is not a utilitarian protocol, for if it were
it would not invoke all these complexities. It would overtly disregard the dead donor rule and
proceed directly to organ harvesting. The reply is that Kevorkian presents just such a crude
utilitarian argument for thrift-euthanasia. My argument is that the NHBCDP is shown to be
an undeclared, refined, not fully consistent, utilitarian protocol. That is why it is called a *de
facto* utilitarian justification for thrift-euthanasia. Put another way, a sensitive utilitarian
calculation would take into consideration the emotional factors that breaking the dead donor
rule (i.e. do not break the traditional ethic of do not kill an innocent person) produces in the
lives of anti-utilitarians in society. But if a utilitarian end can be achieved by convincing the
anti-utilitarians in society that no violation of the basic moral principle has occurred, then
happiness has been extended all the further. Thus the objection is important but not demon-
strative. The protocol was fundamentally driven by the teleological aim of finding more
organs to save more lives. The objection is not that this is an unethical or objectionable end.
Rather, the criticism is that this good end is procured by a means that *de facto* violates the
traditional ethic and the dead donor rule, a means that logically requires commitment to utilitarianism.

to *do not kill* and the *dead donor rule*, while simultaneously carrying out thrift-euthanasia. Here actions speak louder than words.

It follows that the non-empirical elements (the utilitarian values) of the NHBCDP's definition of death do the real work in the protocol. The protocol has not made a new discovery about death. Neither has it returned to an old criterion of death, because the old criterion does not presume the context of immediate organ harvesting. Rather, this protocol has an agenda, one that is at odds with traditional morality and the *dead donor rule*, namely, thrift-euthanasia. As most defenders of the NHBCDP will likely refuse to acknowledge the policy as advocating thrift-euthanasia, the NHBCDP is a *de facto* practice of thrift-euthanasia. It has been shown that there is no essential moral difference between the NHBCDP and the definition of thrift-euthanasia. Just how fully committed the protocol is to thrift-euthanasia can be seen in its position on the issue of respect for self-determination.

RESPECT FOR SELF-DETERMINATION: A SUFFICIENT BUT NON-ESSENTIAL CONDITION

As in Kevorkianism, the Pittsburgh Protocol overtly asserts that personal autonomy, self-determination, and the conditions of informed consent are non-negotiable moral requirements for organ harvesting. However, a closer look at the policy reveals that this is not a necessary requirement in the protocol. First, the relevant statement in the policy itself is carefully qualified:

> The UPMC policy is *based substantially* on patient autonomy in medical decision making. The ad hoc committee concluded that as long as the medical decision to forgo therapy is made *without disproportionate influence* regarding organ donation, it is both permissible and laudable that organ donation occur *provided informed consent is obtained*. Whether a patient is pronounced dead by cardiac or neurologic criteria is ethically unimportant.[54]

Secondly, the evidence that patient autonomy is not a necessary requirement of the policy is seen in the policy's concept of patient autonomy and patient consent. According to the policy, *patient consent is equated with surrogate consent*: '[i]n this policy . . . the term "patient" includes the surrogate of a patient who lacks decision making capacity'.[55] In the Pittsburgh protocol, if a patient is incompetent, a surrogate can make the decisions to FLST on the patient. He or she can also make the decisions to donate organs via the NHBCDP, for the patient to be declared dead at 120 seconds of asystole, and for the patient to have organs immediately removed.

[54] DeVita and Snyder, n. 45, above, 65, emphasis added.
[55] N. 40, above, 236.

Obviously, a conscious, competent patient may, as a matter of fact, request the termination of life-sustaining treatment and volunteer for organ donation. Patient autonomy would then meet the sufficient legal conditions to FLST and, after the empirical conditions of death have occurred, for organ donation to proceed. But according to the policy, a surrogate's decision can replace a patient's request, particularly where a patient 'lacks decision making capacity'. The criticism of this claim reduces to a matter of fact. The fact is that the protocol does not recognize that patient consent is logically and ethically distinct from surrogate request and consent. The separateness is obvious in the fact that if and when a surrogate decides that a patient will become a NHBCD, the patient will die and be harvested. The surrogate will not die nor have any of his or her organs harvested. He or she will go home intact. If the protocol held to personal autonomy as a necessary moral requirement, then without a first-person request, it simply would not be done. As the protocol asserts, however, if the patient cannot consent, then a surrogate can consent in his or her place.

This criticism is likely to be labelled outlandish. It will be objected that surrogate decision-making to FLST is now widely accepted and it is even deemed necessary for organ donation. My criticism does not doubt this socio-medical state of affairs. Rather it points out a potential cultural blindspot, one that the Dutch are known to level at our *status quo* methodology. The legal permissibility of euthanasia in Holland is esteemed as resting upon individual freedom and personal autonomy. One retort the Dutch make to Americans abhorred by active euthanasia is to point out that Americans typically act upon surrogate decisions to FLST as if these were the patients' decisions. Therefore, these decisions result in the death of individuals without autonomous request. The Dutch draw a bright line between autonomous and surrogate decisions. This is the objection made here against the Pittsburgh protocol. It may proceed without patient request or consent. Therefore patient autonomy is not a necessary condition in the protocol. American pragmatism, of just getting consent from some responsible party, potentially abuses and turns a blind eye to the depth of what a more considered view of personal autonomy requires.

In addition to the fact that a first-person end-of-life decision is non-identical to a third-person decision, there is the additional problem of conflict of interest. When a surrogate is considering whether or not to request this protocol, it is impossible to eliminate from the surrogate's mind the conflict between the patient's interests and the interests of others in the patient's organs. The state of Pennsylvania now offers a $300 incentive (funeral benefit) to families of those who donate organs for transplantation after they die.[56] The ambiguity exploited here is that the 'plan

---

[56] For a brief discussion on this see, Editor, '$300 incentive doesn't taint gift,' and George Annas, 'Organs are Not Commodities' in *USA Today* (2 June 1999) 14A. There is research

doesn't violate federal law barring payment for organs because no money goes directly to the donor, supporters say'.[57] Hence a classic conflict of interests scenario, innate to the protocol, is produced. The protocol does not recognize this surrogate decision-maker problem or, if it does, it deems it to be non-problematic.

It is interesting, by contrast, to see that the protocol recognizes that a conflict of interest can arise for the donor's physician. If the donor's physician is also an organ transplant surgeon, or has another patient in need of an organ transplant, then a potential conflict of interest may occur. The protocol does view this as significant enough to add a special requirement—that the physician who declares death cannot be the surgeon who harvests the organs. The parallel conflict of interest for a surrogate is not, however, recognized. The surrogate, charged with decisions for the patient's wellbeing, is also the *de facto* decision-maker for all potential transplant recipients. The interests of the individual patient are thereby exploitable in principle, if not in fact.

Thus, in the NHBCDP, utilitarian decisions about wasting a potential donor's viable organs can procure organs even where patient consent is impossible. In such cases, the act would be an act of *non-voluntary thrift-euthanasia*. Hence, there is no *potential* slippery slope criticism to be made here, because the protocol itself *actually* permits voluntary and non-voluntary thrift-euthanasia.

The only rejoinder left for the protocol to make is to claim that a moral equivalence exists on decisions to FLST and decisions to employ the NHBCDP. This final rejoinder is considered below.

DOES BRAIN DEATH + FLST + ORGAN HARVEST = FLST + NHBCDP ORGAN HARVEST?

Defenders of the NHBCDP assert that there is no moral difference between FLST on a brain dead patient followed by organ harvesting, and FLST on a conscious, competent patient who makes a request to be a NHB donor. DeVita and Snyder claim that there is *only a sequential difference* of events in these two protocols:

In cases of 'brain death': (1) a patient is pronounced dead, (2) some appropriate person consents to organ donation, and (3) organs are procured. The sequence of the first two steps, which is reversed for non-heart-beating donors, was considered logistically but not ethically important.[58]

This is a fallacious assertion.

which shows that $100 has an influence of doctors' decisions, e.g. gifts from pharmaceutical companies, on decision-making.

[57] Associated Press, 'Pennsylvania organ donors to receive money for funeral', *Akron Beacon Journal*, 15 Apr. 1999.

[58] DeVita and Snyder, n. 43, above, 56–7. See also, 'Whether a patient is pronounced dead by cardiac or neurologic criteria is ethically unimportant': *ibid.*, 65.

This assertion begs the crucial medical and metaphysical question at issue. If and when a physician pronounces a patient dead, it is presupposed that the patient is medically and metaphysically dead. The declaration is an official and symbolic recognition of the fact that the individual is dead. The declaration does not make anyone dead, because simply saying so does not make it so. To pronounce a patient dead means that the individual is dead. It is true that a declaration of death is a verbalization made over a patient in both protocols. However, as shown above, pronouncing a patient dead based upon empirical evidence that the entire brain has suffered irreversible loss of function *is not* medically or ethically the same as pronouncing a patient dead who is sedated, who may have a healthy brain, who has just had a two-minute pause between heartbeats. Simply put, brain death + presence of heartbeat ≠ live brain + 120-second heartbeat gap. Brain death (the irreversible loss of total brain function) ≠ 120-second heartbeat pause (a potentially reversible loss of cardiopulmonary cessation). Therefore the claim of the NHBCDP that the donor is a corpse is false. This also shows that FLST on a NHB donor *is not* medically, metaphysically or ethically, equivalent to FLST on a brain-dead patient. Appealing to distinctions between direct and indirect intentions, e.g. the direct intention is to remove the ventilator and the indirect intention is to procure organs, cannot overcome this problem. Respect for the proper use of the PDE entails much more than mere stipulations of direct and indirect intentions and effects, as noted earlier.[59]

Finally, it must be asked of the protocol just how indirect is the death of the donor. While in the operating room, how indirect is the intention to harvest organs when a femoral arterial line is hooked up to facilitate preservation of the organs after death is declared? How indirect is the intention of the attending physician to harvest organs when a surgical team is not only scrubbed, ready and waiting, but when it actually comes into the operating room while the patient is still alive (but anaesthetized) and do skin preparation and draping to facilitate organ harvest? How indirect is the intention to do no more than provide comfort to the patient when a NHBCD's respiratory rate climbs above 24 per minute and morphine IV is increased to prevent the patient from regaining consciousness? How indirect is the intention to harvest organs when *only* in this operating room is 120 seconds of pulselessness employed as the sufficient criterion of death?[60] The answer to all of these questions is that it takes a grand naïveté on our part to believe that intentional termination of a patient's life is not being conducted. The aim and purpose of the NHBCDP

---

[59] See the section below on 'The Goal of Kevorkianism'.

[60] The specifics in these questions are taken from the Protocol, III, L,1; III, L, 4; III, N; III, R and Addendum 1, 3.4, n. 40, above, 235–49.

is primarily the procurement of organs for transplantation, i.e. thrift-euthanasia. The aim and purpose of FLST is not organ-harvesting.

Thrift-euthanasia in Theory: Unhindered Utilitarianism

Thrift-euthanasia is in theory a utilitarian utopia, as suggested by Arnold and Youngner. It is logically consistent with and *prima facie* required by, unhindered utilitarianism. James Rachels lays out the generic utilitarian argument for euthanasia:[61]

(1) Any action is morally right if it serves to *increase the amount of happiness in the world* or to decrease the amount of misery . . .

(2) Killing a hopelessly ill patient, who is in great pain, at his own request, would decrease the amount of misery in the world.

(3) Therefore, such an action would be morally right.

Given (this form of) utilitarianism, euthanasia is 'morally right', i.e. it is justified because it increases the amount of happiness in the world by decreasing the amount of suffering in the world. The logical entailment is that thrift-euthanasia is 'morally right', i.e. it is justified because it simultaneously decreases the amount of suffering in the world and significantly increases the amount of happiness in the world.

(4) *Therefore, given utilitarianism, if euthanasia is morally right and good, then thrift-euthanasia is morally superior and obligatory.*

Rachels also provides a more refined form of the utilitarian argument for euthanasia. It shows that euthanasia is morally acceptable in at least some cases and, logically, it shows that thrift-euthanasia must be morally acceptable in most cases. It entails that thrift-euthanasia is *prima facie* an obligatory (opt-out) method of death for all members of society.[62]

(5) If an action *promotes the best interests of everyone concerned*, then that action is morally acceptable.

(6) In at least some cases, euthanasia promotes the best interests of everyone concerned.

(7) Therefore, in at least some cases euthanasia is morally acceptable.

This refined utilitarian argument for euthanasia not only entails the justification of thrift-euthanasia—it positively requires thrift-euthanasia. It requires thrift-euthanasia because the interests of *numerous others* whose lives can be saved by organ harvesting readily promote the summary interests of everyone concerned, the interests of the suffering individual donor, and the interests of the numerous suffering recipients. Comparatively,

---

[61] Rachels, n. 52, above, 154–5, emphasis added.
[62] *Ibid.*, 156–7, emphasis added.

thrift-euthanasia multiplies the presumed goodness of death and saving of lives, whereas euthanasia merely works with addition and/or subtraction factors of one life and death.

To be sure, utilitarianism is not an unqualified warrant for killing, even though it does not object to killing in principle (in contrast to duty-based and some rights-based theories). As Jonathan Glover explains, the morality and immorality of killing are determined by the *contingent side-effect* consequences to others, together with the *contingent direct objection* to killing—the contingency of whether or not a happy life exists in the potential subject. He writes:

Utilitarianism is the belief that we ought to live in such a way as to promote the greatest happiness. For a utilitarian, killing is wrong to the extent that it reduces happiness or creates misery. The 'side-effect' objections to killing . . . endorsed by a utilitarian, and his direct objection to killing is that it is *wrong to shorten a happy life*.[63]

Thus, for utilitarianism, the morality and immorality of killing by thrift-euthanasia is determined by the contingent side-effects. Clearly, thrift-euthanasia increases the overall amount of happiness in the world, i.e. it promotes the best interests of everyone concerned, *per* (1) and (5) above. Also, ethical killing should not 'shorten a happy life', but shortening an unhappy or misery-filled life can be a utilitarian imperative. Put another way, a serious disutility (utilitarian wrongdoing) occurs whenever individuals die intact, with organs that could otherwise save the lives of numerous others.

(8) Thus, utilitarianism is necessarily committed to some acts of euthanasia and to most acts of thrift-euthanasia.

An illustration of the logical entailment of thrift-euthanasia in a utilitarian theory can be seen in Singer's *Rethinking Life and Death*. The Princeton bioethicist argues that the traditional ethic (do not kill) has collapsed and that accepted acts of killing occur in our hospital practices of FLST, ATD, and late-term abortion. These practices violate the traditional ethic and are evidence it is a 'transparent fiction no-one can really believe'.[64] It is an ethic that should have been replaced a century ago.

Traditional belief in the intrinsic value of persons is a myth disproven by Charles Darwin. It is an idea left over from 'the Hebrew myth of creation' and belief that we are made in the image of God.[65] This is the 'fiction' at the heart of the traditional ethic that is now collapsed and overdue for burial. It should be replaced with a coherent set of utilitarian values, values that are humbly stipulated as 'New Commandments'. The

---

[63] Jonathan Glover, *Causing Death and Saving Lives* (Harmondsworth, 1981), 62, emphasis added.
[64] Singer, n. 1, above, 4.   [65] *Ibid.*, 171.

traditional ethic holds that persons have an irreducible, intrinsic moral value that is an essential property of persons. Orthodox utilitarianism does not allow the existence of such Platonic or deontological moral values. Only utilitarian values exist. Hence the *'First New Commandment: Recognize that the worth of human life varies'*.[66] Given only a variable, instrumental worth of individuals, responsible utilitarian justification of killing is permissible and obligatory. Such killing is justifiable when guided by the *'Second New Commandment: Take responsibility for the consequences of your decisions'*.[67] The new commandments move acts of killing out of the closet and identify them for what they are. Singer argues that FLST, ATD, abortion, PAS, and E are justifiable utilitarian acts of killing. Therefore it is logically entailed that thrift-euthanasia is a justifiable practice. The only requirement is orthodox faith in the ultimate authority of the Principle of Utility.

Kevorkianism: An Explicit Argument for Thrift-euthanasia

> *The aim [of medicine] should extend far beyond a mere 'good' death toward a superlative ideal . . . or best death. And that calls for the legalization of obitiatry [thrift-euthanasia] which can exploit the full potential of altruism and extract all possible good from the purposeful and morally justified termination of human life: for the individual, for his or her family and friends, and now especially for all humankind.*
>
> Jack Kevorkian, 'The Last Fearsome Taboo: Medical Aspects of Planned Death' (1988) 7 *Medicine and Law* 12.

An explicit argument for thrift-euthanasia is put forward by Jack Kevorkian. Kevorkian is both famous and infamous. He is the single name most often associated with physician-assisted suicide (PAS) and euthanasia (E). He is widely disregarded within the medical profession and by bioethicists. Since very little academic attention is given to Kevorkian's publications, it is not surprising that he is incorrectly perceived to be crusading for PAS, when he aims to accomplish much more.

If one reads any of Kevorkian's published works, wherein he clearly explains his true objective (medicide), it is patently clear that PAS is merely the first, calculated, stepping-stone to his real objective. He employs numerous homemade terms to express his ultimate goal, e.g. medicide, positive medicide, positive euthanasia, obitiatry, planned death, eutatosthanasia, and thanatiatrics.[68] The objective of this 'prescription' for

---

[66] Singer, n. 1, above, 190, his emphasis.   [67] *Ibid.*, 195, his emphasis.

[68] Thrift-euthanasia is used as a synonym to cover all of these obtuse Kevorkianisms. The differences between most of them are secondary distinctions about thrift-euthanasia. For instance, medicide is an individual act of thrift-euthanasia and obitiatry is the proposed medical specialty that would procure thrift-euthanasia. Thus, for purposes of clarity and the concerns of this paper, thrift-euthanasia is employed as a generic term that includes all of these variants.

society is, however, one and the same as thrift-euthanasia. It aims to produce as much benefit as possible for others, in situations where the inevitable death of an individual is foreseen. He argues that medicide (thrift-euthanasia) turns an otherwise negative event, the intact death and burial of an individual, into an act of life-saving proportions for many otherwise doomed individuals. The elements of Kevorkian's justification of thrift-euthanasia are identified below.

THE GOAL OF KEVORKIANISM: GETTING 'LIFE BACK FROM DEATH' VIA THRIFT-EUTHANASIA

Kevorkian describes his 'righteous crusade' and 'self-imposed mission'[69] as one characterized by 'the highest regard for the value of human life in the most emphatic sense'.[70] He could be called a pro-lifer:

That's the biggest misunderstanding about me, that I'm obsessed with death. I'm really pro-life. My writings are all about trying to get medical benefits from death. Life back from death.[71]

The practice of medicine ought to extend beyond mere PAS and E, to the 'goodness of planned death' (the subtitle of Kevorkian's book), wherein altruistic concern for all humankind would exploit the otherwise negative ends of PAS and E.

The aim [of medicine] should extend far beyond a mere 'good' death [euthanasia] toward a superlative ideal . . . or *best* death. And that calls for the legalization of obitiatry [thrift-euthanasia] which can exploit the full potential of altruism and extract all possible good from the purposeful and morally justified termination of human life: for the individual, for his or her family and friends, and now especially for all humankind.[72]

Acts of PAS and E are not as inclusively planned as they ought to be. They exclude the utilitarian needs of the suffering that are left behind.[73] PAS, E, terminating a pregnancy ('feticide'), and capital punishment can, with a bit more advance planning, exploit benefits for others from the life, body and organs of the terminated subject.

Planned death is a very broad concept, which includes capital punishment, suicide (obligatory and optional), euthanasia, and feticide. *Physician involvement should extend far beyond mere termination of life to permit exploitation . . . of organs for transplantation and the performance of daring and otherwise impossible*

---

[69] Kevorkian, n. 2, above, 27.
[70] *Ibid.*, 163.
[71] Michael Betzold, *Appointment with Doctor Death* (Troy, Mich., 1993), 337.
[72] Kevorkian, 'The Last Fearsome Taboo: Medical Aspects of Planned Death' (1988) 7 *Medicine and Law* 12.
[73] Such acts of planned death must 'extract something of value from an otherwise totally nihilistic act': see Kevorkian, n. 2, above, 114.

human experiments under irreversible general anaesthesia. Criticism of this proposal cannot withstand rational analysis. The growing pressure of human need will soon overcome the intimidation exercised by this last, most fearsome taboo compelling our civilized society to callously ignore what is surely inevitable.[74]

Organ harvesting has an obvious 'immediate utility'[75] that everyone can see. But Kevorkian adds that thrift-euthanasia via terminal vivisection medical experimentation will potentially produce the greatest of all benefits, because such experimentation can produce long-range benefits for all humanity. The types of terminal experiments that he foresees include maintaining surgical depth anaesthesia for four days to carry out drug research, practising chimpanzee liver implantation, and drug research on women with breast cancer who have otherwise chosen E, PAS, or suicide.[76]

Thrift-euthanasia is not immoral, argues Kevorkian. It is not immoral because it is not murder, nor (he sometimes argues, is it) even a homicide, an act of killing.[77] The determining factors of the morality and immorality of such acts, we are told, are located in the 'intent' of the actor and the 'consequences' of the action.[78] Thrift-euthanasia, properly carried out, will not violate either of these conditions. There will be no malicious intent and there will be beneficent consequences. What is clearly violated, however, is the ancient taboo against acts of killing:

The fear of being seen as killers intimidates doctors. Some mistakenly try to equate with murder the act of executing a peacetime death sentence. But how can that be? The law defines murder as 'criminal homicide . . . committed with malice afore-thought, either express or implied, and committed recklessly under circumstances manifesting extreme indifference to the value of human life.' It is obvious that this

---

[74] Kevorkian, n. 72, above, emphasis added.

[75] Kevorkian, n. 2, above, 132.

[76] Betzold, n. 71, above, 32. Vivisection experimentation is the subject of a lengthy chapter in Kevorkian, n. 2, above. 'Nothing New Under the Sun', 135–58. Kevorkian's book is also dedicated to the vivisectionists of ancient Hellenistic Alexandria and medieval Cilician Armenia. 'They dared to do what is right': see Kevorkian, n. 2 above, 5.

[77] Kevorkian, n. 2, above, 115, argues that death of a patient during vivisection experimentation would not be an act of killing any more than death of a patient during therapeutic surgery: '[t]he primary, in fact, the only, aim is to probe and to discover, not to kill. If the subject dies in the process, it would be accidental and no more intentional killing than would be the case with inadvertent death during routine curative surgery in hospitals'. Live-organ harvesting would not be murder, he argues, because taking organs from a willing subject would not be 'committed with malice aforethought', a necessary condition of the legal definition of murder or criminal homicide: *ibid.* 162–3. Here Kevorkian's good motive plus good consequence formula is presupposed. Its ethical ineptness allows the following as non-homicidal acts: 'I value life so much that I will do consensual, irreversible vivisection brain surgery on you, "hitherto limited to animals," to help save the lives of people suffering from Alzheimer's. If you do not happen to die during this experiment or the two-day observation period, then I will remove your kidneys, heart and lungs, according to your wish. In none of these acts, however, do I have any wish for you to die, and certainly no malicious intention toward you': see Kevorkian, n. 72, above, 9.

[78] Kevorkian, n. 2, above, 78.

cannot apply to a doctor who has been permitted to experiment on, or take organs from, a willing criminal being executed [or a patient whose death is foreseen and/or planned]. In fact, the doctor's act would manifest the highest regard for the value of human life in the most emphatic sense.[79]

The practitioner of thrift-euthanasia acts with the intention of '*uncompromising* benevolence', a '*disciplined* dedication to serving any and all medical needs of humanity'.[80] Furthermore, Kevorkian appeals to (a sophomoric misunderstanding of) the Principle of Double Effect (PDE), arguing that death by medicide can be viewed as an indirect result of thrift-euthanasia and not as a direct act of killing.

The primary, in fact, the only, aim is to probe and to discover, not to kill. If the subject dies in the process, it would be accidental and no more intentional killing than would be the case with inadvertent death during routine curative surgery in hospitals.[81]

Kevorkian also asserts and assumes that no essential ethical difference exists between acts of allowing a patient to die (ATD) and acts of killing (K). His assumption is that forgoing life-sustaining treatment (FLST) on a patient is an act of ATD, and that this is ethically equivalent to an act of K. The presumed equation is FLST = ATD = K. These supposed equivalences obtain solely because the consequences of the actions are effectively the same: a patient dies. This is, however, a disingenuous appeal to the PDE.

Proper application of the PDE (disregarding the important fact that it is a deontologist's, but not a utilitarian's tool) requires that several conditions be met. One condition is that the unintended effect cannot be the means of accomplishing the intended effect. But when the intended effect is to harvest two kidneys, a heart, and liver, the unintended effect (death) is the means to the intended effect. So Kevorkian's use of the PDE is fallacious. He is ill informed to think it is a relative and unconstrained ethical concept.[82]

Kevorkian correctly identifies his opposition, i.e. the traditional ethic, which is also the official position of the AMA. This position holds that FLST may be viewed as an instance of ATD and that it may be ethically permissible (within restricted conditions), but acceptable cases of FLST are not equivalent to acts of killing; intentional acts of killing are *prima facie*

---

[79] *Ibid.*, 162–3.   [80] *Ibid.*, 176, his emphasis.

[81] *Ibid.*, 115. As blatant and crude as this may appear, the same basic defence is found in refined form in the Pittsburgh protocol, where it is argued that a patient is taken to surgery to FLST and to see if their heart happens to stop beating.

[82] A suggestion on how the PDE might be exploited by the NHBCDP is offered by Dr Arnold. 'Dr. Arnold noted that this principle could be extended to viewing the preservation of donor organs as the family's good objective and accepting certain measures that further this objective even if they may pose the unintended risk of hastening death': in Herdman and Potts, n. 23, above, 87.

wrong. Kevorkian argues against the traditional view, by enlisting examples that its proponents' claims and actions are contradictory. He argues that doctors that assert the traditional ethic are self-righteous to object to thrift-euthanasia because they already kill:

[C]ontrary to their self-righteous objections, doctors do indeed kill—they kill condemned fetuses, infants without brains, and living patients with dead brains . . . doctors themselves arbitrarily decide when to take hearts, lungs, and livers, from comatose, brain-dead, but otherwise living subjects. They therefore kill innocent and gravely ill humans who are comatose *persons* . . .[83]

This argument works only if the presence of a person is assumed in all of these varied conditions, and only if acts of killing are expressly denied in all the cases listed.

First, Kevorkian is mistaken to believe that FLST on brain-dead foetuses, brain-dead infants, and brain dead respirator dependent patents, are acts of killing. Killing is an act of intentionally ending the life of an innocent person. The immoral act of killing cannot be done to entities that are not persons (snakes, mosquitoes), nor to entities that are just human bodies or human organs (corpses, hearts, kidneys). The traditional ethic against killing a person assumes the traditional metaphysical concept of death—death is separation of soul (or person) from body. Thus, FLST on a brain-dead human body maintained via respirator and feeding tube is not an act of killing because it is not presumed to be an embodied person. It is an act of allowing a non-ensouled body (where no soul or person is present in the body) to die. This fits easily within the medical and legal criteria of death—the irreversible loss of heart/lung function, and/or the irreversible loss of total brain function. Hence FLST in such cases is neither a homicide nor an act of a killing, for no person is present. Thus no contradiction occurs and Kevorkian's criticism fails.

Secondly, a reasonable and consistent application of the traditional metaphysical concept of death employed to justify FLST in cases of brain death logically includes the conditions of correctly diagnosed PVS and anencephalic. Defended elsewhere,[84] the reasoning is that no person is inferred present in the condition of brain death, not because there is irreversible loss of lower brain or brain stem function, but because there is irreversible loss of upper brain activity. Upper brain (neocortical) function is deemed necessary to sustain the embodied activities of persons. Given this criterion, the correctly diagnosed conditions of PVS and anencephalic newborns entail that no person is inferred present in either type of case.

---

[83] Kevorkian, n. 2, above, 166, his emphasis. Peter Singer similarly argues that doctors already kill, as does Kevorkian, in FLST on PVS patients, etc. See Singer, n. 1 above, 57–80.

[84] Howard M. Ducharme, 'The Metaphysics of Defining Death' in William L. Craig and Mark S. McLeod (eds.), *The Logic of Rational Theism: Exploratory Essays* (Lewiston, NY, 1990), 211–26.

Hence FLSTs when such conditions obtain are neither homicides nor acts of killing, for no persons are present.[85] So Kevorkian is mistaken to claim an ethical contradiction occurs here.[86]

Thirdly, the controversial issue of abortion brought into this argument by Kevorkian commits the fallacy of diversion, of throwing a red herring into the fray. The problem is that both those who argue against abortion, as well as many that argue for its permissibility, acknowledge it to be an act of killing. Opponents argue it is unjustified killing and proponents argue it is justifiable killing (for other competing reasons). Thus, Kevorkian's unqualified appeal to the fact that abortions are performed does not demonstrate the claim that FLST is an act of killing an innocent person. So again, Kevorkian's argument fails. Hence he has not produced any valid criticism against the traditional ethic of Do not kill.

THRIFT-EUTHANASIA JUSTIFIED VIA SITUATION ETHICS/ACT UTILITARIANISM

Is Kevorkian's justification of medicide based upon utilitarianism? His short answer is that he is expressly committed to the '*situation ethics*'[87] of Joseph Fletcher. The medical profession in particular and society at large, Kevorkian argues, need situation ethics. In both of these social arenas, we must be set free from traditional morality, from rule-based and duty-based ethics. Such old, traditional methods of ethical reasoning are inflexible to the pressing needs of humanity. Furthermore, the secularization[88] of the *mores* of modern society and the adoption of situation ethics are long overdue. Kevorkian calls for:

> wrenching the profession entirely free of so-called *rule ethics*. According to philosopher-theologian Joseph Fletcher, rule ethics mandates *a priori* what one must do 'according to some predetermined precept or categorical imperative.' It is a coercive, nondiscriminatory, 'doctrinaire or ideological method of deciding what is right.' On the other hand, *situation ethics* is *a posteriori*, 'relative, flexible, and changeable according to variables (from which) the moral agent, the decision maker, judges what is best in the circumstances and in the view of foreseeable consequences'.[89]

---

[85] Not all instances of diagnosing PVS (e.g. a child who has fallen into an icy lake versus a patient who has been in Stage III Alzheimer's) have the same clinical certainty of correctly diagnosed brain death. Only where irreversible loss of upper brain function can be confirmed is this concept of death properly applied.

[86] It can also be argued here that traditional ethics can properly apply the PDE in such conditions and indirectly allow death to occur without committing mercy killing.

[87] Kevorkian, n. 2, above, 171, his emphasis. Kevorkian also interprets Albert Einstein as a situation ethicist/utilitarian: '[a]s Albert Einstein himself said: "When life and death are at stake, rules and obligations go by the board" ': *Ibid.*, 174.

[88] 'In our modern world, medicine and religion should be *completely* divorced from one another': Kevorkian, n. 2, above, 170, his emphasis.

[89] *Ibid.*, 171–2, his emphasis. Kevorkian is quoting from Joseph Fletcher.

So, Kevorkian expressly acknowledges commitment to situation ethics. In categories of the classic moral theories, situation ethics is a version of act utilitarianism. Fletcher acknowledges that his agapeistic calculus (the love calculus) is a theological imitation of Jeremy Bentham's utilitarianism.[90] If one presses Fletcher to provide an academic heritage and a classic source of situation ethics, then '[s]ituation ethics is . . . [i]n their arcane journals [what] philosophers call *act* ethics'.[91] In contrast with traditional, rule-based ethics, '[w]e agree with Jeremy Bentham: "If any act can with propriety be termed pernicious, it must be so by virtue of some events which are its consequences . . . no act, strictly speaking, can be evil in itself" '.[92] Thus, the justification of Kevorkian's thrift-euthanasia is grounded in situation ethics, which is a species of Bentham's act utilitarianism.

RESPECT FOR SELF-DETERMINATION: A SUFFICIENT BUT NON-ESSENTIAL CONDITION FOR THRIFT-EUTHANASIA

There is one final question to ask of the situation ethics of Kevorkianism. Since individuals' acts of S, PAS, E, and thrift-euthanasia are permissible, justifiable, good, and obligatory, are we correct to assume that *respect for personal autonomy* is a non-negotiable moral value? Are we correct to assume that *respect for personal autonomy* reigns supreme here?

The answer given by Kevorkian is that there is 'one essential principle' that must remain 'uppermost and permanently honored in the mind of every doctor: the highest respect for the personal *autonomy or self-determination of every patient*—for what the patient deems best for his or her own earthly existence'.[93] However, situation ethics/act utilitarianism eschews moral decision-making via *a priori* moral principles. Therefore appeal to the principle of *do not kill* does not determine the morality of euthanasia. However, the rejection of all moral principles (except the principle of utility, of course) necessarily includes the principle of *respect for personal autonomy*. It is the utilitarian estimation of the consequences of the situation that determines what ought to be done, not any *a priori*, predetermined rule, moral principle, or categorical imperative.[94] So here Kevorkian appears confused. He asserts that consent is 'the only stipulation of all extant codes which is equally indispensable' *and* that the 'matter of competency is irrelevant' in the thrift-euthanasia of condemned

---

[90] See Joseph Fletcher, *Situation Ethics* (London, 1966) 95. For an evaluation of this theological ethic, see David Brown, *Choices: Ethics and the Christian* (Oxford, 1983), 6–16.

[91] Joseph Fletcher, *Humanhood: Essays in Biomedical Ethics* (Buffalo, New York, 1979), 3.   [92] *Ibid.*, 83–4.

[93] Kevorkian, n. 2, above, 175, his emphasis.

[94] There is a serious contradiction in Fletcher's and Kevorkian's moral theory: that *no a priori* precept can be morally authoritative (e.g. do not kill) *and* that *one a priori* precept is authoritative in any and every situation (e.g. maximize happiness for all effected).

criminals, the senile, the insane, foetuses, and children.[95] Is this a contradiction, or is this a rhetorical way to win support from advocates of personal autonomy without clearly informing them that the principle of autonomy and self-determination can be trumped by utilitarian benefits to all? The best interpretation of Kevorkian is that respect for autonomy (or the principle of self-determination) is a sufficient basis for conducting thrift-euthanasia, but it is not a necessary requirement.

Kevorkian gives formal lip service to the principle of self-determination. He says that 'personal *autonomy or self-determination of every patient*' is the 'one essential principle' that must remain uppermost 'in the mind of every doctor'.[96] (The general public understanding of the numerous cases of PAS that Kevorkian has presided over assumes that he regards the autonomy of the individual terminated to be an absolute requirement.) However, within Kevorkian's situation ethics, an autonomous request for termination is only a sufficient criterion for termination; it is *not* a necessary condition for termination. This can be seen in Kevorkian's long list of prospective subjects for thrift-euthanasia.

The extensive, logically consistent list of potential candidates for thrift-euthanasia includes not only individuals who make autonomous requests for termination. It includes all types of non-voluntary and involuntary terminations as well. It includes justly and unjustly condemned criminals,[97] patients at the 'end stage of incurable disease,' 'hopelessly ill' individuals, people with 'crippling deformity', people with 'intense anxiety or psychic torture inflicted by self or others', cases of 'severe trauma', 'politicians during and after revolutions', designated victims of 'gangland-style executions', 'some random murders', religious martyrs like those of ancient Masada or recent mass suicides like those of the Jim Jones cult, 'persons who are in no way afflicted by illness but who have arbitrarily and irrevocably decided that they must die', and all subjects who would die in instances of FLST 'by the decision and action of another, of foetuses, infants, minor children, and every human being incapable of giving direct or informed consent.'[98] To be sure, if the subjects of thrift-euthanasia can include the 'comatose, mentally incompetent, or otherwise completely uncommunicative individuals',[99] the senile, children, infants, and foetuses, then it includes those who can not possibly exercise self-determination and make autonomous decisions.[100] Kevorkian summarizes his list of potential

---

[95] Kevorkian, 'A Comprehensive Bioethical Code for Medical Exploitation of Humans Facing Imminent and Unavoidable Death,' (1986) 5 *Medicine and Law* 189–90.

[96] Kevorkian, n. 2, above, 175, his emphasis.

[97] *Ibid.*, 33.   [98] *Ibid.*, 195–200.

[99] *Ibid.*, 255. The quotation is from Kevorkian's suggested legal code for 'medicide', i.e. thrift-euthanasia.

[100] Kevorkian, n. 72, above, 3. See also Jack Kevorkian, 'Marketing of Human Organs and Tissues Is Justified and Necessary' (1989) 7 *Medicine and Law* 557–65.

subjects for thrift-euthanasia and gives his logically consistent, utilitarian justification:

I believe that death in every category discussed can be merciful and at the same time yield something of real value to the suffering humanity left behind.[101]

So thrift-euthanasia is consistently (and immoderately) defended in Kevorkianism. Furthermore, it produces no mere medical protocol for a few patients. It produces an all-encompassing social policy of the grandest magnitude.[102]

According to Kevorkianism, the only necessary criterion needed to justify thrift-euthanasia is that an individual be 'unavoidably condemned to death'.[103] Since an individual can be unavoidably condemned to death, either by one's own will or that of another,[104] autonomous consent of the subject is not necessarily required. If death is inevitable, then the alternatives are to allow the death without producing any positive benefits for humanity or to perform thrift-euthanasia and thereby produce positive benefits for humanity. The alternatives amount to the difference between being wasteful versus being thrifty with scarce resources. To be condemned to death is to be a 'doomed human being',[105] where one is 'inextricably trapped in circumstances mandating certain death'.[106] Thus, the *uncompromising* benevolence'[107] of Kevorkianism calls for thrift-euthanasia in all situations where the death of a doomed individual can be exploited. That is to say, personal autonomy of the one is trumped by the utilitarian needs of the many.

Conclusion

It has been shown that an oft-chilling form of taking life, thrift-euthanasia, must be added to the contemporary topics of FLST, PAS, E, the concepts of brain death and cadaver, together with the practices of organ harvesting

---

[101] Kevorkian, n. 2, above, 200–1.

[102] Singer, n. 1, above, similarly calls for a full-scale, social revolution on the ethics of life and death—to abandon the old, traditional ethics of duty-based lineage, and embrace the new commandments of utilitarian heritage. Truog's suggestion is also one that requires widespread social changes, in law, medicine, and traditional ethics. Thus other proponents of thrift-euthanasia share Kevorkian's grand vision.

[103] Kevorkian, n. 2, above, 33.

[104] Although this sounds ruthless, to proceed with thrift-euthanasia on the basis of the *will of another*, the Pittsburgh Protocol proceeds to harvest organs based upon the *will* of the attending physician who declares the patient dead after 120 seconds of pulselessness. The patient is thereby asserted to meet the criteria of irreversible loss of heart/lung function because of the attending physician's *will* not to attempt a restart, nor to wait until the medical and legal criteria of death are met, for then warm ischemia will have rendered the organs less viable.

[105] Kevorkian, n. 2, above, 210.

[106] *Ibid.*, 195.

[107] *Ibid.*, 176.

and organ transplantation. Sociologically, if our historical situation is one where the traditional ethic has collapsed and various utilitarian theories are the chief replacements, then the NHBCDP is just the leading edge of thrift-euthanasia as a radical, modern social policy. Lastly, it has been shown that if E and the NHBCDP are justified, then thrift-euthanasia is necessarily justified; that if thrift-euthanasia is unjustified, then the NHBCDP and E are unjustified. So it is that uncovering the practice and the theoretical commitment to thrift-euthanasia entails a circumspect review of a great range of practices, policies, laws, and basic ethical commitments.

THE COMATOSE PREGNANT WOMAN: ABORTION AND THE SUBSTITUTED-JUDGEMENT APPROACH

Erwin Bernat

An Austrian Case of First Impression

On 11 November 1997 the Austrian Supreme Court (OGH)[1] had—for the first time—to answer the question whether abortion may be carried out lawfully if the pregnant woman is permanently incompetent to make her own decision.[2]

The facts of the case are simple. In September 1997 Christina, a woman in her twenties, was involved in a car accident. She suffered severe brain injuries and fell into a deep coma. At the time when the OGH had to decide her case her medical state had not improved significantly and it seemed at that time that her coma might turn into a persistent vegetative state. Because of the concrete medical diagnosis it was clear that Christina was not—and never would be—able to give informed consent to any kind of medical interventions. The car accident deprived her completely of consciousness.

If Christina had to be regarded as a 'regular' patient, although incompetent to decide, her case certainly would not have attracted jurisprudence and the courts. She would just have received medical treatment on the basis of the best interests or the substituted judgement approach. As in the United States of America[3] these two approaches govern the Austrian physician's obligation to treat the incompetent patient.[4] There is an additional requirement to be obeyed in Austria if the treatment is required for the benefit of an incompetent patient: the patient's legal guardian has to give consent.[5] If the incompetent patient did not have—before losing

---

[1] Oberster Gerichtshof.

[2] The OGH's decision is reprinted in (1998) 120 Juristische Blätter (JBl) 443–6; for English law cf. *T* v. *T and another* [1988] 1 All ER 613 (Fam. Div., Wood J).

[3] Cf., e.g., A. E. Buchanan and D. W. Brock, *Deciding for Others: The Ethics of Surrogate Decision Making* (Cambridge, Mass., 1989).

[4] See O. Edlbacher, 'Körperliche, besonders ärztliche, Eingriffe an Minderjährigen aus zivilrechtlicher Sicht', (1982) 37 *Österreichische Juristen-Zeitung* 365–76.

[5] S. 8(3) sentence 1 of the *Krankenanstaltengesetz* (*KAG*) (Federal Act on Hospitals) [1957] Official Gazette No. 1 as amended.

capacity—a (legal) proxy, the doctor may administer treatment only after a legal guardian has been appointed by the court.[6] These rules do not, of course, apply if the patient's life or health is suddenly endangered and emergency treatment is required. In such a case, the physician is generally obliged to treat the sick or injured party.[7]

After Christina received medical treatment in order to save her life, the physicians established that she was pregnant. Neither Christina's mother nor her cohabitant was aware of this fact before she was involved in the car accident. Sonography carried out on 15 October 1997 showed that the foetus was already 12 to 13 weeks old; in other words, Christina was in the second trimester of pregnancy at that time. Christina's cohabitant and her family were probably shocked when they were informed of her pregnancy. Her medical prognosis was in any case poor. What could be said with certainty was that she would always be too retarded mentally to take care of a child. On 21 October 1997 the guardianship court appointed Christina's mother as her legal guardian. She, as her daughter's proxy, then applied for judicial approval of the decision to let her daughter have an abortion.

The first instance court issued its decision on 28 October 1997;[8] it dismissed the application. The court of appeal confirmed that judgment on 3 November 1997.[9] And finally, only eight days after the court of appeal's ruling, the OGH delivered its decision on 11 November 1997.[10] It modified the court of first instance's and the court of appeal's order, in that it generally approved of the proxy decision to let Christina have an abortion.

What is the legal framework of this case? First of all, we have to be aware of the fact that this is a case within the jurisdiction over non-contentious matters. It is not a case decided by a criminal court. To put it differently, it is—seen from a procedural viewpoint—a case within the jurisdiction of a court that is generally in charge of dealing with matters of private law. How can that be true? Is not the question whether abortion is permissible a question which is dealt with in criminal law? According to Austrian law the answer is yes. And consequently, if the abortion had been carried out, our case could have been a case for the criminal court if our basic question, '[i]s abortion allowed for the benefit of an incompetent woman?' is to be answered in the negative. In other words, the criminal

---

[6] S. 8(3) sentence 2 *KAG* as amended.

[7] S. 95 of the Austrian Penal Code imposes criminal liability on the so-called 'bad samaritan'; cf. J. Feinberg, 'The Moral and Legal Responsibility of the Bad Samaritan' in J. Feinberg, *Freedom & Fulfillment* Philosophical Essays (Princeton, NJ, 1992), 175–96. If a doctor has taken over the responsibility for the care of a patient he can even be charged with murder if he fails to carry out the appropriate treatment so that his patient dies; see ss. 2, 75 of the Austrian Penal Code: murder by omission.

[8] Trial Court (Bezirksgericht) Klagenfurt, 28 Oct. 1997, 3 P 151/97i (unpublished).

[9] Court of Appeal (Landesgericht) Klagenfurt, 3 Nov. 1997—4 R 463/97y (slip opinion).

[10] OGH (1998) 120 JBl 443.

court would be responsible for answering the basic question only if there were facts established which were to be regarded as a violation of criminal law. This did not happen in our case, where Christina's physicians and relatives wanted to know *ex ante* whether they would violate the criminal law if abortion were to be carried out. They had the moral feeling that abortion should be permissible in their particular case, but they wanted to be sure that this feeling was in accordance with current Austrian law.

This is why the case of Christina finally turned out to become a case within the jurisdiction over non-contentious matters. The application aspired only to seek *declaratory relief*. This is very similar to so-called right-to-die cases decided in the United States[11] and in England,[12] where the applicant wants to know whether withdrawing life-sustaining treatment is permissible or whether it would constitute a criminal offence.

The Austrian Law on Abortion

The Austrian law on abortion is part of the Austrian Penal Code (1974).[13] Sections 96 and 98(1) of the Austrian Penal Code prohibit the practice of abortion generally. However, sections 97 and 98(2) establish so-called grounds of justification, which are far-reaching exceptions to criminal liability. If a doctor carries out abortion within the first three months after the establishment of pregnancy he does not violate the law if the woman has given informed consent after appropriate counselling.[14] This is what legal scholars call the lawfulness of abortion on request or on demand. It is an approach that favours the woman's right of privacy and self-determination.[15] Although still controversial in current discussions, the Austrian Constitutional Court held as early as 1974 that this approach does not infringe upon the alleged foetus's right to life.[16] Like the US Supreme Court's ruling in *Roe* v. *Wade*[17] the Austrian Constitutional Court denied a constitutionally granted right of the foetus to live.

---

[11] Cf. A. Meisel, 'The "Right to Die": A Case Study in American Lawmaking' (1996) 3 *European Journal of Health Law* 49–74.

[12] Cf. the House of Lords' case of first impression, *Airedale NHS Trust* v. *Bland* [1993] 1 All ER 821, [1993] AC 789. However, the main distinction between Christina's case and *Bland* is the fact that Christina was represented by a legal guardian whereas Anthony Bland was a ward of the court; for further details cf. E. Bernat, 'Der persistent vegetative state als ethisches und rechtliches Problem: Weist das House of Lords den richtigen Weg?' in E. Bernat and W. Kröll (eds.), *Intensivmedizin als Herausforderung für Recht und Ethik* (Vienna, 1999), 47–63.

[13] [1974] Official Gazette No. 60 as amended.

[14] S. 97(1) para. 1 of the Austrian Penal Code.

[15] Cf., e.g., J. J. Thomson, 'A Defense of Abortion' (1971) 1 *Philosophy & Public Affairs* 47–66.

[16] Austrian Constitutional Court (Verfassungsgerichtshof—VfGH) 11 Oct. 1974 in Sammlung der Erkenntnisse und wichtigsten Beschlüsse des Verfassungsgerichtshofes (VfSlg.) 7.400.

[17] 410 US 113 (1973).

After the completion of the first trimester of pregnancy abortion is permissible when good cause is shown. What constitutes good cause is exclusively enumerated in section 97(1) paragraph 2, which lists three cases. The first case describes what could be labelled medical indication: abortion is permissible if the pregnant woman's life or physical or mental health is severely endangered and if abortion proves to be the last resort. The second case is called embryopathic indication. There must be a preponderance of evidence that indicates a severe mental or physical handicap of the child-to-be. The third case is—as far as I know—an Austrian peculiarity: a female under 14 who becomes pregnant. In all three cases abortion may lawfully be performed beyond the first trimester. There is no time limit. The only restriction to these three cases is the birth of the child.

Finally section 98(2) states that abortion is not punishable if a pregnant woman is incompetent and if abortion proves to be the last resort in order to save her life. If that is established, an abortion may be performed legally. No one's consent is then necessary. Section 98(2) is nothing but a codification of the abovementioned substituted-judgement standard.[18] The legislature is of the opinion that if a pregnant woman were competent to give free and informed consent to abortion in a life-threatening situation she presumably would do so. This valuation seems convincing. The average pregnant woman probably would choose to have her foetus aborted instead of losing her own life.

The Austrian Supreme Court's Judgment

What is now the law concerning our case? Was the Austrian Supreme Court right to approve of the proxy consent or is it a crime to carry out an abortion without the free and informed consent of the pregnant woman? The latter could be inferred from section 98(1) of the Austrian Penal Code: whereas illegal abortion, with the woman's consent, is at the very most punishable by imprisonment of up to three years, illegal abortion without the woman's consent can be punished by imprisonment of up to five years. What does the law's phrase 'without the woman's consent' mean? Does it include proxy consent where the pregnant woman is incompetent to give free and informed consent?

According to the OGH a legal guardian is generally allowed to give consent to abortion on behalf of a ward. The guardian's right to substitute the incompetent pregnant woman's consent is a matter of justice and fairness.[19] According to the Supreme Court there are two factual decisions one could make. One choice would be to bring the baby to term. The

---

[18] See O. Triffterer, *Österreichisches Strafrecht*, Allgemeiner Teil (2nd edn., Vienna–New York, 1994), 244, 245.
[19] OGH (1998) 120 JBl. 445.

other choice would be abortion. However, both of these decisions would have far-reaching effects on Christina's life situation. According to the OGH a general denial of the right of abortion would therefore mean burdening Christina with the birth of a child. The Supreme Court is of the opinion that such a result should be seen as inconsistent.

However, the OGH did not give an opinion on whether abortion on demand within the first trimester of pregnancy would be a lawful option in the case at issue; as we know, Christina's pregnancy was already in the second trimester. Therefore the Supreme Court had to decide the question of lawful abortion only on good cause shown. The OGH expressed the opinion that the legal guardian could lawfully give proxy consent in every single case that is a ground of justification if the pregnant woman herself gave free and informed consent. In other words, if the physicians *had certified* either a medical or an embryopathic indication in the case of Christina, then the Supreme Court's judgment would have served as quasi-declaratory relief. I emphasize 'would have served'. The facts as established by the trial court were not meaningful enough to confirm the existence of either a medical or an embryopathic indication. Therefore the OGH seemed to be in a dilemma. There were two choices: either to remit the case to the trial court in order to establish those facts that were necessary for the decision-making process or to decide the case on its merits. Favouring the first choice would probably have decreased Christina's chances of having an abortion. There is a high probability that, if the case had to be retried, nature would have decided it pro-life. To put it slightly differently, a second judgment of the trial court would probably not have been issued before the natural delivery of the child. This is why the Supreme Court gave *declaratory relief*. But its judgment was a conditional one. The OGH's judgment read: '[w]e confirm Christina's mother's proxy consent if it turns out after our judgment that abortion could be performed on good cause shown; viz. on the ground of either a medical or an embryopathic indication'.[20] How did the case actually turn out? According to the newspapers Christina gave birth to a healthy baby in April 1998.[21] The delivery itself also had no negative impact on Christina's health. That is to say the physicians had rightly decided not to end Christina's pregnancy. One could say all's well that ends well. However, we are not relieved of asking the question whether the Supreme Court's judgment was based on a sound interpretation of the law of abortion.

Proxy Consent and Free and Informed Consent

Therefore, the basic question is still open for further consideration: is it

[20] *Ibid.* 446.
[21] Cf., e.g., *Kleine Zeitung*, 15 Apr. 1998, 28.

true—as is the opinion of the OGH—that a proxy consent stands on the same footing with free and informed consent?

To understand this question and its consequences we have first and foremost to clarify the function of what is called the principle of free and informed consent. This principle governs the whole physician–patient relationship, *if* the patient is able to make competent decisions. According to widespread opinion, competence of the patient means nothing but the ability to form rational judgements.[22] If the patient is competent, *he* decides whether he wants to be treated and to what extent. He also decides when the doctor ought to stop treatment. The ability to form rational judgements does not mean that the patient must necessarily come to a conclusion that is overwhelmingly preferred in society. If the patient is competent, he also has the right to make unreasonable decisions.[23] In the words of an American judge, '[i]ndividual choice is determined not by the vote of the majority but by the complexities of the singular situation viewed from the unique perspective of the person called on to make the decision'.[24] The theory of free and informed consent therefore protects the citizen's right of autonomy that is—in the context at issue—his right of self-determination. What follows from that for decisions to be made for the benefit of incompetent patients? First, it seems to me arbitrary to assume that the proxy's consent—acting on behalf of the incompetent ward—stands on the same footing as the free and informed consent of a competent patient.[25] Whereas the latter is autonomous and can therefore come to decisions that seem to be—at least for the little man on the Clapham omnibus—unreasonable, the proxy's consent must never deviate from what could be called a reasonableness standard.[26] Under what circumstances does the proxy's consent meet this standard? First, I would guess that the proxy's consent meets the reasonableness standard if there is a medical indication—or at least a medico-social necessity—to perform a medical intervention. Medical interventions that prove to be neutral or even harmful are illegitimate;[27] they do not further the best interests of the incompetent patient. This is also the position of the Austrian and English judiciary. Let me just give the example of non-voluntary sterilization of

---

[22] See G. J. Annas and J. E. Densberger, 'Competence to Refuse Medical Treatment: Autonomy vs Paternalism' (1984) 15 *Univ. Toledo L Rev.* 561.

[23] Cf. E. Bernat, 'Behandlungsabbruch und (mutmaßlicher) Patientenwille' (1995) 2 *Recht der Medizin* 51–61.

[24] *Superintendent of Belchertown State School et al. v. Joseph Saikewicz*, 370 NE2d 417, 428 (Mass. 1977).

[25] See A. E. Buchanan, 'The Limits of Proxy Decisionmaking for Incompetents' (1981) 29 *Univ. of California Los Angeles L Rev.* 386–408.

[26] Cf. R. M. Veatch, 'Limits of Guardian Treatment Refusal: A Reasonableness Standard' (1984) 9 *American Journal of Law & Medicine* 427–68.

[27] See B.-R. Kern, 'Fremdbestimmung bei der Einwilligung in ärztliche Eingriffe' (1994) 47 *Neue Juristische Wochenschrift* 753, 758.

mentally retarded women.[28] According to the Austrian Supreme Court such intervention is permissible if the best-interests approach is met.[29] That is the case if the incompetent woman does not realize the possible consequences of sexual intercourse and if she would not be able to take care of a child. The OGH requires also that there be at least an abstract danger of her becoming the victim of sexual intercourse and that an improvement in the mental-health status of the woman can be ruled out.[30] If these facts are established the performance of non-voluntary sterilization seems to be a lesser evil in comparison to involuntary pregnancy and child-birth. Performing non-voluntary sterilization in such a case is therefore legally justified by necessity. In other words, the incompetent woman's corporal integrity (that is violated by performing sterilization) is of lesser value as compared with her best interest in not becoming pregnant.

One could be tempted to draw an analogy between the case of legitimate non-voluntary sterilization and Christina's case. But I doubt that analogy is appropriate.[31] Non-voluntary sterilization serves the best interests of the woman if she is in danger of becoming pregnant. In Christina's case it is questionable whether it better serves her interests to have an abortion or whether abortion and child-delivery are—from the perspective of *her* best interests—not one and the same procedure: late abortion and (spontaneous) child delivery are probably equally burdensome to her. There is just the physical aspect to be taken into account. Christina would neither have understood what was being done to her if an abortion had been carried out, nor have realized the wonder of childbirth. Due to her mental retardation she understands neither the one nor the other; she understands nothing. There is a second argument that favours the conclusion that non-voluntary sterilization and non-voluntary abortion do not stand on the same moral and legal footing. In the former case there is just the woman's corporal integrity that is at stake. In the latter case it is her corporal integrity *and* the life of the foetus that are at stake. And killing the foetus is—according to Austrian law—only permissible on grounds of necessity in the broadest sense of the word; is abortion justified on simple request of the woman or is it justified alone or additionally on good cause

---

[28] For English law cf. *F. v. West Berkshire Health Authority and another (Mental Health Act Commission intervening)* [1989] 2 All ER 545, 546 (HL): '[a]t common law a doctor can lawfully operate or give other treatment on adult patients who are incapable of consenting to his doing so, provided that the operation or treatment is in the best interests of such patients. The operation or treatment will be in their best interests only if it is carried out in order either to save their lives or to ensure improvement or prevent deterioration in their physical or mental health'.

[29] OGH (1992) 24 Der Österreichische Amtsvormund 89; OGH (1979) 1 *International Journal of Medicine and Law* 371.

[30] *Ibid.*

[31] See Th. Lenckner, 'Einwilligung in Schwangerschaftsabbruch und Sterilisation' in A. Eser and H. J. Hirsch (eds.), *Sterilisation und Schwangerschaftsabbruch* (Stuttgart, 1980), 173, 174.

shown, the assumption underlying all these cases is that the pregnant woman suffers from a troublesome situation and that abortion is held to be a justified means of eliminating her difficulties.[32] This interpretation does not necessarily require us to assume a right to life of the unborn child. On the contrary, the more explicitly the jurisdiction approves of the unborn's right to life, the less abortion seems to be legitimate.[33] Even if the legal order denies that right, the foetus is not seen just as an object but as an entity that is a symbol of a future person.[34] As far as international law is concerned, the Austrian Constitutional Court denied the existence of a right to life of the foetus that could be derived from Article 2 of the European Convention on Human Rights.[35] However, section 22 of the Austrian General Civil Code[36] reads unambiguously: '[u]nborn children are protected by law from the time of their conception. Insofar as concerns their individual rights . . . they are to be considered as born.' Therefore the foetus seems to be a legal subject under Austrian law.[37] Non-voluntary abortion on the basis of a best-interests approach is therefore problematic, because the woman's sphere of objective interests cannot be improved by performing an abortion, whereas the foetus is deprived of a high-ranking right: the right to life. Of course, the legislative solution to permit abortions on the one hand and to grant a right to life to the unborn on the other might be seen as not free of inconsistencies, at least from a moral and theoretical viewpoint. But we have to live with these inconsistencies.[38]

One argument favouring the Supreme Court's approval of proxy consent could be framed as follows. The legal guardian must not only act in the best interests of the ward but—as far as possible—also has to take into account value-judgements that were part of the formerly competent person's life. To put it in other words: the guardian has to ask and answer the question what the putative preferences of her ward would be. That means to ask and answer the question what Christina would be likely to want regarding abortion if she were competent and able to speak for herself.

According to the facts as established by the trial court Christina seemed

---

[32] This has been explicitly emphasized by the legislator; cf. the report of the judiciary committee, reprinted at 959 of the appendices to the shorthand records of the National Council (i.e. the federal legislative assembly), 13th legislative period, 20.

[33] See N. Hoerster, *Abtreibung im säkularen Staat*, Argumente gegen den s. 218 (2nd edn., Frankfurt/Main, 1995), 163–96.

[34] See J. Feinberg, 'Abortion' in T. Regan (ed.), *Matters of Life and Death*, New Introductory Essays in Moral Philosophy, (2nd edn., New York, 1986), 256–93.

[35] VfGH in VfSlg. 7.400.

[36] Official Gazette 1811 No. 946.

[37] See W. Selb, *Rechtsordnung und künstliche Reproduktion des Menschen* (Tübingen, 1987), 42–51.

[38] Cf. E. Bernat, 'The Interaction of Rationality and Freedom of Conscience in Legislation on Controversial Bioethical Issues' in D. Evans (ed.), *Creating the Child, The Ethics, Law and Practice of Assisted Reproduction* (The Hague, 1996), 167–73.

to have a negative attitude towards children and had always emphasized that she herself did not want to end up having children. Do these facts suffice to assume with high probability that Christina would approve of abortion if she could be asked? I do not think so. Many—probably most—women who have a negative attitude towards children and who persistently emphasize that they do not want to become mothers change their views radically once they are pregnant. Therefore a substituted-judgement approach does indeed not favour non-voluntary abortion.[39] Incidentally, the relevant question that would have to be asked more specifically is: would Christina now approve of abortion knowing that her pregnancy would not result in any conflict between her interests and the foetus's normatively alleged interest? As we know, Christina has permanently lost consciousness and is able to experience neither pleasure nor pain. For her, pregnancy does not cause this particular *event of conflict* that was the legislative motive for decriminalizing abortions. From a slightly different perspective one could say a subject, who at t_1 assumes that she will have an abortion if she becomes pregnant at t_2, gives herself the idea that there will be an *event of conflict* at t_2. However, if the subject at t_2 does not suffer from a conflict, then the value-judgement expressed at t_1 is not a sufficient basis for the assumption of a putative preference to have an abortion at t_2.

Whose Interests Deserve Legal Protection?

If one takes these arguments seriously, then the conclusion is obvious that—at least in general—abortion may be carried out only in cases of free and informed consent given by the pregnant woman. If a pregnant woman is incompetent to decide, her legal guardian is not allowed to give proxy consent. To assume (in such a case) the pregnant woman's putative consent proves to be fiction rather than presumption. Therefore abortion in Christina's case would have constituted—contrary to what the OGH held—a criminal offence.[40]

This conclusion could also be inferred from the written law in a somewhat more 'legalistic' way of reasoning. Section 98(2) of the Austrian Penal Code justifies the performance of abortion if there is an immediate threat to the life of the incompetent pregnant woman and abortion is the last resort. This is—one can assume—the *only* case in which the legislature was of the opinion that the mere putative will of the pregnant woman suffices to abort the foetus. If only her health is endangered or if only the foetus is presumed to be afflicted with disease, there is no 'green light' to

---

[39] Cf. E. Bernat, 'Schwangerschaftsabbruch ohne Einwilligung der Schwangeren?' (1998) 120 *JBl.* 464, 467.
[40] S. 98(1) of the Austrian Penal Code.

abortion if the woman herself cannot give free and informed consent. This may be seen to be a very strict interpretation of the law; however, if one is inclined to take section 22 of the Austrian General Civil Code seriously, then this interpretation is more in touch with the spirit of the law than is the OGH.

Christina's case leaves the reader with the slightly bitter taste that the OGH wanted to protect Christina's relatives more than Christina herself could be protected by having an abortion. The relatives—be it the grandparents or the father of the child-to-be—are not protected by the current law of abortion. They have no right to force the pregnant woman to undergo an abortion. Of course, in regular cases this follows from the pregnant woman's right of self-determination. She must never be under pressure and must be allowed to bring the baby to term if she herself objects to abortion. In the case of a permanently incompetent pregnant woman there are just the (alleged) interests of the foetus and the interests of the relatives that can be weighed against each other. The woman herself is not a factor in the decision-making process. However, under current law, the cases of justified abortion are exclusively enumerated by the legislator. There is no room for taking the interests of those parties into account who will take over social and financial responsibility for the child due to the mother's incapacity. This is especially true for a jurisdiction that treats the unborn as if he were already born.[41] The relatives' conflict of interests is, by the way, somewhat different from the conflict of interests between mother and foetus in regular cases: they are not exposed to pregnancy and childbirth. One has to confess, though, that on a utilitarian basis this kind of difference may not be decisive. Within a utilitarian calculus the major question would probably be whether it is basically justified to assume individual rights of the child-to-be. But this is a question beyond the objectives of this paper.[42]

---

[41] Cf. s. 22 of the Austrian General Civil Code.

[42] For an overview of consequentialist pro-choice arguments cf. R. Macklin, 'Abortion—Contemporary Ethical Perspectives' in W. Th. Reich (ed.), *Encyclopedia of Bioethics* (2nd edn., New York, 1995), i, 6–15.

Mental Health and
the Law

THE MENTAL HEALTH ACT:
TAKING STOCK OF THE CURRENT
POSITION AND THINKING ABOUT
THE FUTURE

Peter Bartlett*

We are in a period where much of mental health law is under legislative review. The Law Commission's proposals on mental incapacity were published in 1995, triggering a government response the following year,[1] and it was finally announced by the Lord Chancellor's Department in October 1999 that most of those proposals would in fact be implemented.[2] In September 1998, a 'Scoping Review Team' chaired by Professor Genevra Richardson was created by the government to advise on the future of the Mental Health Act itself. The team's report was presented to the government in July 1999, and published the following November.[3] Coincident with its publication, the government published a green paper

* An earlier version of this paper was presented to the symposium on Law and Medicine at University College London, in July 1999, and thus well before publication of the Richardson Report, the green paper on the future of the Mental Health Act, and the Lord Chancellor's position paper on the future of legislation on mental incapacity. While it has been possible to indicate some points of contact with those policy documents, and while the issues raised in the chapter remain relevant to a critical understanding of those documents, this chapter does not purport to be a commentary on those policies. My thanks go to Oliver Lewis and Robert Dingwall for commenting on a draft of this chapter.

[1] Law Commission (England), *Mental Incapacity,* Law Com. No. 231 (London: 1995); Lord Chancellor's Department, *Who Decides? Making Decisions on Behalf of Mentally Incapacitated Adults,* Cm 3803 (London, 1995).

[2] Lord Chancellor's Department, *Making Decisions: The Goverment's Proposals for Making Decisions on Behalf of Mentally Incapacitated Adults,* Cm 4465 (London, 1999).

[3] Department of Health and Welsh Office, Expert Committee, *Review of the Mental Health Act 1983* (G. Richardson, chair) (London, 1999).

on the subject.[4] While this green paper calls for further consultation, it is clear that the scope of civil control of people with mental health problems, and the legal responses to those controls, are likely to change in the near future. Finally, the Home Office and Department of Health have issued a green paper on increased control over persons who are perceived to be dangerous and suffer from severe personality disorder.[5] We are at a time when everything in mental health law seems open to re-appraisal.

The public debate surrounding the Mental Health Act reforms leaves me with a peculiar sense of unease. There has been much discussion of detail, with little discussion of broader principles. The situation also has something of a sense of urgency about it: everyone agrees that there are problems and has a view on how those problems ought to be solved. The longer view of how the current situation relates to the historical picture seems to have been lost in the immediacy of the present presumed crisis. The object of this paper is to provide a start at some of that broader debate. It concerns a reformed Mental Health Act only; it is assumed following the October announcement that incapacity legislation in a form broadly similar to that proposed by the Law Commission will be introduced. It will further focus on matters of civil regulation, since people found to be insane in a criminal context raise rather different issues. At issue will be the broader pictures: how did we get to our current legal and political position regarding mental health, and in particular how novel are the problems we face; and what sort of a Mental Health Act do we want? On the latter point, the premise, deliberately provocative to promote discussion, will be that consistently with the developing law and politics of human rights, legislation should not inappropriately discriminate on the basis of mental disability.

A Historical Sketch: Where are we Now?

The statutory roots of the current Mental Health Act can be understood as the consolidation of five streams of law. The first and oldest concerns the Royal Prerogative powers, originally codified in approximately 1324.[6] Flowing from feudal practice, this power vested authority over 'idiots' and 'lunatics' in the King. From relatively early times, this authority was delegated, generally, to the Lord Chancellor. A series of nineteenth-century statutes regularized the exercise of this power, as for example by further delegating the finding of a Commission in Lunacy to Commissioners unless a jury was required, in which case to a superior court judge.

---

[4] Department of Health and Welsh Office, *Reform of the Mental Health Act 1983: Proposals for Consultation*, Cm 4480 (London, 1999).
[5] Home Office and Department of Health, *Managing Dangerous People with Severe Personality Disorder—Proposals for Policy Development* (London, 1999).
[6] 17 Edward II, stat. I.

The first legislation relating to the regulation of public asylums was the County Asylums Act 1808,[7] which allowed Quarter Sessions to construct asylums for their insane poor and pay for them out of the county rate. Once again, a plethora of statutes amended this early legislation, but the consistency over the course of the nineteenth century is perhaps more revealing than the development. Admission was throughout effectively restricted to paupers, although a somewhat loose definition of that term might sometimes be adopted. County asylums remained under the control of Quarter Sessions until 1888, when, along with the bench's other poor law administrative functions, they were removed to local government administration.[8] Throughout the century and well into the twentieth century, applications for admission were made by poor law officers (overseers until the passage of the Poor Law Amendment Act in 1834, relieving officers thereafter), and required the sanction of a Justice of the Peace. From very early on, certification by a medical professional was also necessary, a duty performed almost exclusively by the local poor law medical officer after 1853. The roots of these statutes are to be understood in terms of nineteenth-century poor law administration, and the politics of local government.[9]

Criminal lunacy was originally subjected to legislation in 1800,[10] following *Hadfield's Case*.[11] After 1808, this area was for a time subsumed into the county asylum statutes, reflecting both the practicalities of relatively few criminal lunatics in the system in absolute terms, and perhaps also some of the early Victorian social confusion between poverty and criminality. With the construction of Broadmoor in the early 1860s (it eventually opened in 1863), criminal lunatics increasingly were subjected to separate legislation, commencing with the Criminal Lunatics Act 1860.[12]

Private asylums were subject to yet another legal régime. Ineffective eighteenth-century legislation was comprehensively redrafted in 1828,[13] introducing licensing of the facilities by Justices of the Peace, and routine inspections by a specialized set of commissioners in London, and by Justices of the Peace elsewhere. In 1845, the Lunacy Commission's jurisdiction in this regard was extended to all of England and Wales. In addition, the 1828 Act established procedures for admission, which once again

---

[7] 48 George III, c. 96.

[8] See Local Government Act 1888, ss. 3(vi), 86, 111.

[9] For a detailed discussion of these poor law roots, see P. Bartlett, *The Poor Law of Lunacy* (London, 1999); P. Bartlett, 'The Asylum and the Poor Law: The Productive Alliance' in J. Melling and W. Forsythe (eds.), *Insanity, Institutions and Society, 1800–1914* (London, 1999); W. Forsythe, J. Melling and R. Adair, 'The New Poor Law and the County Pauper Lunatic Asylum—The Devon Experience 1834–1884' (1996) 9 *Social History of Medicine* 335.

[10] 39–40 Geo. III, c. 99.

[11] 27 Howell's St. Tr. 1281.

[12] 24–5 Victoria, c. 75.

[13] 9 George IV, c. 41.

remained largely unchanged through the century: an application by a family member, supported by certificates of two medical practitioners. Commencing in 1890, these applications further required the approval of a Justice of the Peace.

These four strands were consolidated, but not integrated, in the Lunacy Act 1890.[14] This is clearest regarding criminal lunacy and the Chancery jurisdiction, which remained as separate and largely independent parts of the Act, a scheme reflected to a considerable degree in the modern Mental Health Act. The continuity represented by the 1890 Act is also clear for civil admissions. Certainly, there were amendments in detail. For the first time, for example, private patients could be admitted only upon the authority of a Justice of the Peace, a system used for paupers from the first County Asylum Act in 1808. Nonetheless, the fundamental differences between pauper and private patients remained, and for the paupers, who represented the vast bulk of those in the system, the 1890 Act made little difference. In so far as Jones is correct in describing the 1890 Act as a 'triumph of legalism',[15] the change was brought about not so much by legislative amendment as by a change in the perceived role of Justices of the Peace, away from local administrators, toward a more exclusive role as low-level judicial officers. Thus in *Hodson* v. *Pare*[16] lunacy duties were held to be part of the Justices' judicial, not administrative, role. This is significant not merely because of the result, but also because it was only in 1899 that the question arose, re-enforcing the re-articulation of the role of the Justice into these more clearly defined compartments at this time.

The first half of the twentieth century offered two significant alterations. The first was to add yet another strand of legislation, the Mental Deficiency Acts.[17] The previous legislation had always had persons with developmental disabilities, as we would now call them, under its remit, but in the final quarter of the nineteenth century, a separate set of statutes began to focus on this class of person. The Idiots Act 1886[18] was the first of this stream, but was largely ineffective. Not so the Mental Deficiency Acts of 1913 and 1927. By the Second World War, roughly 150,000 people were cared for pursuant to this legislation in England and Wales. This legislation has been given short shrift by legislative historians of insanity. That is inappropriate. Not only did it provide the basis of the current guardianship provisions of the current Mental Health Act; it also provided the legislative framework for some early care in the community. Here again, the legislation was a product of its period. In this case, the

---

[14] 53 Victoria, c. 5.
[15] K. Jones, *Asylums and After: A Revised History of the Mental Health Services from the Eighteenth Century to the 1990s* (London, 1993).
[16] [1899] 1 QB 455.
[17] 3–4 George V, c. 28 and 17–18 George 5, c. 33.
[18] 49 Victoria, c. 25.

control mechanisms had to do with new strategies of social policing growing from the perceived fear of spreading degeneracy—the soft (and sometimes not so soft) side of the eugenics movement.[19]

Secondly, the Mental Treatment Act 1930[20] introduced informal admissions for the first time—perhaps the most significant alteration in mental health law ever. Previously, all persons under lunacy or mental deficiency legislation were subjected to the coercive power of the law. While there might be procedural safeguards provided, in theory their choice was irrelevant to the imposition of services. The Mental Treatment Act changed that, and anyone who was 'desirous of voluntarily submitting himself to treatment for mental illness'[21] could be admitted without a formal reception order signed by a Justice.

The creation of the National Health Service in 1948 largely removed the distinction between public and private facilities, with the incorporation of charitable hospitals into the public sector and the introduction of state funding regardless of the patient's means. Pauperism was at an end, and the old legislative distinctions made less and less sense. It is in this legislative context that we must understand the Mental Health Act 1959.[22] Where the 1890 Act had left the distinctions largely untouched, but included all legislative strands in one statute, the 1959 Act made a greater effort to consolidate the divergent strands into one, at least as regards civil admission. The solution of the 1959 Act was largely to ram the different processes together. Where compulsory admission up to that time would be in the hands of poor law/social service officials if the patient was poor and the family if the patient was able to afford private care, for example, under the new system all compulsory admissions required both family and social services involvement.[23] Guardianship was adopted from the Mental Deficiency Acts, but made available to everyone with a mental disorder, not merely to 'mental defectives'.[24]

There were, of course, some changes in 1959. Restricting some of the excesses of the mental deficiency legislation, for example, and reflecting the fall from grace of the eugenics movement following the war, the new Act provided that promiscuity or immoral conduct *simpliciter* would be insufficient to bring an individual within the remit of the Act.[25] Review

[19] Regarding the Mental Deficiency Acts, eugenics, and community care, see J. Walmsley, D. Atkinson, and S. Rolph, 'Community Care and Mental Deficiency 1913 to 1945' in P. Bartlett and D. Wright (eds.), *Outside the Walls of the Asylum: The History of Care in the Community 1750–2000* (London, 1999), 181; M. Thomson, 'Family, Community, and State: The Micro-politics of Mental Deficiency' in D. Wright and A. Digby (eds.), *From Idiocy to Mental Deficiency: Historical Perspectives on People with Learning Disabilities* (London, 1996), 231; M. Thomson, 'Community Care and the Control of Mental Defectives in Interwar Britain' in P. Horden and R. Smith (eds.), *The Locus of Care: Families, Communities, Institutions and the Provision of Welfare since Antiquity* (London, 1998), 198.

[20] 20–1 George V, c. 23, s. 1.   [21] Mental Treatment Act 1930, s. 1.
[22] 7–8 Elizabeth II, c. 72.   [23] Mental Health Act 1959, s. 27.
[24] *Ibid.*, s. 33.   [25] *Ibid.*, s. 4(5).

tribunals were provided for the first time, allowing patients to challenge their confinement or placement under guardianship.[26] Justices of the Peace were removed from the civil admission process. How much this had been a real protection in the previous decades is open to question. Forsythe, Melling, and Adair note that as early as 1911 Justices of the Peace in Barnstaple Union had been signing sheaves of blank admission orders, with the particulars to be completed subsequently by social service officials on an *ad hoc* basis, thus completely avoiding the due process protections of the 1890 Act.[27] This, along with the introduction of informal status under the Mental Treatment Act, suggests that psychiatric facilities were no longer places which were understood to require an intrusive system of judicial controls. By implication, power could be entrusted to the hospital management in general, and the doctors in particular.

The 1983 amendments reflect a period where patient rights were taken more seriously. The 1983 Act made alterations to the scope of guardianship, of significant relevance for the history of incapacity legislation, but not relevance for the current discussion. Much more important for present purposes, the 1959 Act had not regulated treatment directly, leaving doubt about patient rights to consent. The 1983 amendments introduced specific rules. A few treatments were subject to particular safeguards,[28] but most treatment of civilly confined patients was allowed without consent for the first three months, and thereafter either upon consent or with a second medical opinion attesting that the treatment in question 'ought' to be given.[29] The extension of these general rules to involuntary patients only meant that common law was taken to apply to informal patients. This is significant because it gave these patients, if competent, a right to refuse treatments for the first time, but it is also significant for breaking any perceived automatic equation between psychiatric hospitalization and treatment: it was now quite possible that persons would be appropriately in hospital, in a situation where the law would not allow them to be treated owing to their own refusal of treatment.

Some retreat was made from this rights-based approach, it seems largely as a reaction to high-profile cases in the media, with the introduction in 1995 of aftercare under supervision.[30] While enforced treatment in the community has not been allowed by law (although it may be, following the proposed legislative revisions in the near future), closer surveillance was mentioned by the 1995 legislation.

[26] Mental Health Act 1959, s. 3, 123.

[27] W. Forsythe, J. Melling, and R. Adair, 'Politics of Lunacy: Central State Regulation and the Devon Pauper Lunatic Asylum, 1845–1914' in Melling and Forsythe (eds.), n. 5 above, 68, 83.

[28] Mental Health Act 1983, s. 57. Unlike the general rules contained in ss. 58 and 63, these restrictions applied to informal and involuntary patients alike.

[29] Mental Health Action 1983, ss. 58, 63.

[30] Aftercare under supervision was introduced by the Mental Health (Patients in the Community) Act 1995.

Reading the History

What does this history mean to us now? How are we to read it in terms of assessing our current situation regarding mental health law?

We may begin with a point which is mundane, but no less important for that. The current Act bears the detritus of almost 200 years of statutory drafting. The result is an Act which borders on the incomprehensible. As an example, the 1959 amendments attempted to introduce a standard of confinement by amending sections which until that time had been largely procedural, without appropriately altering the nineteenth-century substantive standards contained elsewhere. The phrase 'health or safety of the patient or the protection of others' was incorporated into what are now sections 2 and 3 of the 1983 Act.[31] Using proper rules of statutory interpretation, 'health' should be read in the context of the other two terms, suggesting that quite a significant impairment of health would be necessary to justify confinement. Yet how are we to understand this, given an express dangerousness standard in section 25? Is there a difference between 'safety' and 'protection' in sections 2 and 3, and 'dangerous' in section 25? The argument would be that, notwithstanding their fairly clear language, the earlier sections cannot really mean 'dangerous', since the legislature has used the word elsewhere, and is therefore deemed to have meant something different in sections 2 and 3;[32] yet if 'safety' and 'protection' are not about dangerousness, what can they possibly mean?

The historical answer is that section 25 grows out of the nineteenth-century statutes, which provided families with a general right to remove a patient from a county asylum on the undertaking that he or she would no longer be chargeable as a pauper (thus a scheme to save public funds), or from a private madhouse on the basis that they wished not to pay for the care any longer. That authority was in turn circumscribed in cases where the patient was dangerous, when continued detention would be required notwithstanding the financial ramifications for the poor law or to the family, as the case might be. Section 25 now exists entirely outside its original context, where safety was balanced against rights flowing from financial obligations. It may now be questioned whether there is now any justification for the section, given the standard of admission contained elsewhere in the statute; but certainly it is questionable whether it ought to be used to colour the modern reading of sections 2 and 3.

The people administering mental health law at first instance are not going to be lawyers, but instead doctors (often general practitioners), social workers, police officers, and similar professionals. If society wants

---

[31] Mental Health Act 1959, ss. 25(2), 26(2).
[32] This argument is made, e.g., in B. Hoggett, *Mental Health Law* (4th edn., London, 1996), 44.

them to administer the Act properly, they have a reasonable expectation that they will be given an Act they have a reasonable chance of being able to understand. Without that level of drafting clarity, content will count for nought. Whatever the result of the review processes now underway, a comprehensive rewriting of the statute rather than yet another series of amendments is in order.

The history also allows us to place some of the current debates in mental health law in perspective. The current debate on mental health takes place in a climate of moral panic. 'Community care' is perceived as a failure, leaving the public at risk. Greater controls upon those living in the community are perceived as vital. The point was made by Health Minister Paul Boateng in the press release announcing the formation of the Richardson Committee:

We are determined to develop comprehensive mental health services that are safe, sound and supportive. They must protect the public, and provide safe and effective care for mentally ill people. New legislation is needed to support our new policies, for example to provide extra powers to treat patients in a range of clinical settings, including, where necessary, in the community, and to ensure a proper balance between the interests of the public and the rights of the individual.[33]

The pressure toward such controls relies upon a specific account of historical change. According to that account, the rise of asylum in the nineteenth century resulted in large-scale and long-term confinement of the insane, a pattern which continued through much of the twentieth century. At the end of the twentieth century, as institutions close, and there has been inadequate co-ordination with social services in the community, people have been left on the streets, falling through social security nets. Ex-patients cease taking their medications; homicidal maniacs roam the streets. Society is unsafe, and existing law has been insufficient to provide an adequate response. Stronger powers are therefore required, the account concludes, to control people in the community.

This account is problematic, on almost all its counts. Yes, asylums have closed; but psychiatric in-patient admissions have nonetheless continued to rise. In 1976, 178,841 people with mental illness were admitted as in-patients to psychiatric facilities in England. By 1986, this number had risen to 197,251, and by 1993–4 to 219,270. Since that time, admissions have continued to rise, from 4.2 per thousand population in 1991–2 to 4.4 per thousand population in 1996–7.[34] The bulk of these have been informal admissions, but civil confinements have also risen, from 14,780 in 1986 to 24,191 in 1996–7, a rise of 64 per cent. In the same period, criminal

---

[33] DOH press release, 22 Sept. 1998.

[34] Department of Health, *Health and Personal Social Service Statistics* (London, 1990, 1995, and 1998). Hospital admissions of persons with developmental disabilities have in the last 5 years remained relatively stable, at 1.1 per thousand population.

confinements experienced a much more moderate growth, from 1,521 to 1,883, a rise of 24 per cent.[35] While length of individual stays has dropped dramatically, intervention has clearly not been abandoned.

Certainly, many people classed as homeless have problems of mental illness, but the calculation of the prevalence is difficult. Gill *et al.* interviewed people resident in hostels, private-sector short-leased accommodation, and nightshelters, along with those sleeping rough, identified through their use of day centres.[36] Certainly, the overall findings make for eye-catching reading. Roughly half of those in hostels and private-sector short-leased accommodation, and closer to 60 per cent of those in nightshelters and sleeping rough, had psychiatric difficulties, or were believed so to have based on the interviews with the researchers. The overall picture is misleading, however. For those in hostels and short-term private accommodation, most of the cases were neuroses such as inability to sleep or irritability, relatively harmless to others. The prevalence of psychoses in these groups was much less—8 and 2 per cent respectively. For those in nightshelters and sleeping rough, alcohol dependency was diagnosed in roughly 40 per cent of the sample, and drug dependency in 46 per cent and 37 per cent of the sample respectively, matters where greater legal controls are not obviously appropriate, given the availability already of an intensive and coercive legal regime. More severe psychiatric problems in these groups cannot be discounted, but as the authors of the study acknowledge, the data are not entirely reliable. Thus 43 per cent of the nightshelter population were suspected to suffer from psychoses from their answers to a questionnaire, but in only 10 per cent could such a diagnosis be confirmed, due to practical difficulties of the study. For those sleeping rough, 47 per cent were suspected to suffer from psychoses but, for the same reason, only 4 per cent could be confirmed.

Even with these limitations, hesitation is appropriate in approaching the statistics. The homeless may well be a population whose needs are not being met, and in a comprehensive health care system, services should be available even for mental illnesses which are merely troubling. That is not an argument for compulsory powers. The presence of psychosis does not equate to dangerousness, and the authors of the study make no attempt to assess the latter. And in any event, these are not obviously people who would previously have been confined in asylums. The homeless, and particularly the itinerant homeless, have always been the most difficult for social service networks to oversee and cope with. It is impossible to tell whether the prevalence of mental illness in this group is getting greater or less; reliable historical data do not exist.

[35] Confinement statistics from Department of Health, *Statistical Bulletin*, bulletin 1998/01 (Leeds, 1998).
[36] B. Gill, H. Meltzer, K. Hinds, M. Petticrew, *Psychiatric Morbidity among Homeless People*, OPCS Surveys of Psychiatric Morbidity in Great Britain Report 7 (London, 1996).

There have clearly always been ex-patients in the community. Roughly two thirds of the inmates of Victorian asylums were discharged within two years. While this is admittedly considerably longer than current average stays, most people were released.[37] Those not released tended to be persons physically unable to live outside the asylum—the sort of people now quite effectively dealt with by group homes and other community facilities. Many of the former maniacs and depressives, the sorts now causing concern, were released. Other people with psychiatric difficulties were never admitted. It is simplistic to the point of misleading to suggest that asylums superceded community care in the nineteenth and early twentieth centuries. Thus in 1871, the census reported a total of 69,019 'lunatics, idiots or imbeciles' in England and Wales, of which only 39,743 were in a hospital, public asylum, or other place licensed under legislation,[38] and the Census Commissioners believed the former number to be under-reported by as much as a half.[39] Of the almost 150,000 persons cared for under the Mental Incapacity Acts in the late 1930s, about two thirds were cared for in community settings.[40] People with mental health difficulties have clearly been living in the community throughout the last 200 years, and no doubt before. This is simply not a new situation.[41]

Even if the demise of the traditional asylum is creating new difficulties, the traditional account does not explain why those difficulties are surfacing only now. The project of decarceration began, not in the mid-1980s, but by the mid-1950s. In 1955, there were 143,000 psychiatric hospital beds in England; by 1975, that figure had dropped to 87,000; by 1986 to 60,000, and by 1996–7, to under 46,000.[42] With the introduction of new psychiatric medications in the mid-1990s lengths of stay began to fall. The current hospital admission criteria have remained largely unchanged since 1959, and apparently for years proved quite able to cope with the problems created by this allegedly new class of persons with psychiatric difficulties in the community. Structural change and inadequate law are thus unconvincing as reasons why community care is perceived as a problem of regulation at the end of the 1990s.

[37] For a discussion of the release statistics in the Victorian period, see D. Wright, 'Getting Out of the Asylum: Understanding the Confinement of the Insane in the Nineteenth Century' (1997) 10 *Social History of Medicine* 137, 143.

[38] *Twenty-eighth Report of the Commissioners in Lunacy*, PP (1874) xxvii, 34.

[39] E. Higgs, *Making Sense of the Census: The Manuscript Returns for England and Wales, 1801–1901* (London, 1989), 74–6.

[40] Thomson, n. 14, above, 201. The number cared for in the community includes both those under formal control of statutory supervision and guardianship orders, as well as those under voluntary supervision.

[41] Regarding the history of care in the community, see P. Bartlett and D. Wright (eds.), *Outside the Walls of the Asylum: The History of Care in the Community 1750–2000* (London, 1999), and the sources cited therein.

[42] Figures for 1955, 1975, and 1986 from P. Bean and P. Mounser, *Discharged from Mental Hospitals* (Basingstoke, 1993), 20. Figure for 1996–7 from *Health and Personal Social Services Statistics*, n. 27, above (1998 edition).

Similarly, the difficulty of integrating health and social services programmes is not new. Running parallel to the old lunacy and mental deficiency laws was the poor law, substantially reformed in 1834 and remaining, albeit in an increasingly amended form, until the formation of the welfare state after the Second World War. The poor law offered a variety of programmes relating to insanity, including workhouse provision, infirmaries, schools for 'feeble-minded' children, and outdoor relief (a system of doles to allow people to live in the community). The Victorian system in theory had poor-law medical officers off combing the shires in search of lunatics; but that was never the reality. In practice, families caring for those with mental health problems approached poor law officials, the nineteenth-century social services network, when things got too difficult at home.[43] Then, as now, police became involved only in crisis situations. Then, as now, those who were homeless or living on their own were, no doubt, at particular risk of 'falling through the net', to use the modern expression, since they lacked the family surveillance network which would invoke official intervention when required.

The final point to stress is that whatever the papers may say, the streets are simply not full of homicidal maniacs. The number of homicides related to mental health problems is minuscule, and falling rather than rising. The percentage of homicides involving mentally disordered offenders has fallen from 43 per cent in 1959–64, to 15 per cent from 1991–5. Admittedly, this is in part because the number of homicides rose significantly overall between those periods, from 691 to 2,524; but the number of homicides involving a mentally ill offender has also dropped in absolute terms in the last fifteen years, from 536 (an average of 107 per year) in the period 1976–80, to 377 (an average of 75 per year) in the period 1991–5.[44] In 1995, sixty people were killed by persons later successfully pleading diminished responsibility, or insanity, or found unfit to plead; that may be compared to 522 homicides overall, or approximately 4,000 road traffic deaths. It is not clear how many of the sixty mentally ill defendants had been in contact with health or social services previously, nor how many, if any, of the deaths would have been prevented by greater legal controls in the community. As Taylor and Gunn comment rather pointedly, 'confining people with a mental illness to hospital to save 40 or so lives would be analogous to abolishing private motoring to prevent the 4000 or so road deaths'.[45]

Viewed in this light, the perceived 'crisis' in community care appears somewhat surprising. The problems appear to be not new, but old. It is therefore appropriate to ask why this is all happening now?

[43] See Wright, n. 31, above, 142 and sources cited therein; Bartlett, n. 5, above, 153–4.
[44] Figures derived from P. Taylor and J. Gunn, 'Homicides by People with Mental Illness: Myth and Reality' (1999) 174 *British Journal of Psychiatry* 9, table1.
[45] Taylor and Gunn, n. 37, above, 10.

Certainly, one reason is editorial opportunism. Homicides related to mental illness may be relatively infrequent, but they sell newspapers when they occur. This results in an editorial bias. In a survey by Philo *et al.* of news coverage of mental illness in April 1993, for example, stories regarding harm to others numbered roughly twice the stories about all other aspects of mental illness combined.[46] The image of failing community care in the early 1990s was given particular public prominence in considerable degree as a result of media coverage of two incidents involving schizophrenics. In one, Ben Silcox entered the lion's enclosure of the London Zoo; in another, Christopher Clunis stabbed Jonathan Zito to death in a London Underground station. These events caught the public eye, and served as a catalyst for the 1995 amendments to the Mental Health Act. Reports of similar events in the press have certainly maintained the public pressure for closer controls on individuals once they have left hospital or are identified as having mental health problems in the community.

At the same time, the history noted above would suggest that an understanding of the development of mental health law requires an understanding of the political context in which the law is created. If Victorian asylums policy is to be understood in a poor law context, and twentieth-century mental deficiency in terms of eugenics, what does the political climate at the end of the twentieth century suggest about the current debate over mental health reform?

The context of reform is, of course, the restructuring of the provision of health care, and the pressures upon and reshaping of the welfare state in general. Amendments made to the National Health Service at the beginning of the 1990s were on their face designed to make the system more efficient. The effect was to introduce a new bureaucrat class to the system, administering an internal market of purchasers and providers. Where previously, doctors had been in control, the system was now to be run by managers. This ethos applied not merely at the level of the service-providing trusts, but also in an increasingly centralized control of the system. Clinical audit was introduced, allowing centralized control of how health care was practised in a much more direct fashion than ever before. Budgets became increasingly stretched; waiting lists grew; and health service staff became demoralized.

Mental health services were not, of course, immune from these influences. Community care is increasingly offered by independent trusts rather than NHS providers. The first move towards increased control of those in the community was supervision registers, introduced by NHS 'guidance' in

---

[46] G. Philo, G. McLauchlin, and L. Henderson, 'Media Content' in G. Philo (ed.), *Media and Mental Distress* (Harlow, 1996), 45, 48. The other categories were comic representations, stories about harm to self, prescriptive stories or advice columns, and criticisms of accepted definitions of mental illness.

1994[47] and enforced by audit. No additional funds were made available to implement this programme; practitioners were simply expected to cope. Discharge under supervision was subsequently introduced by legislation in 1995. Consistently with the retreat from the welfare state evident elsewhere in the last fifteen years, these mechanisms can be seen not merely as designed to identify people at risk, but also to ration (or 'prioritize') care.

The 'efficiency drive' has been having its effect on staff morale. Deahl and Turner claim that the burn-out period for a psychiatric nurse on an adult general psychiatric ward is seven months, and cite a study that 88 per cent of consultant psychiatrists wished to leave the profession.[48] In a context of such pressure, mistakes are inevitably made, with resulting criticisms of staff in the inquiries which are now required by the NHS administration. These errors create a perceived need for greater regulation. Long-term strategy with patients is under threat. Instead, particularly in London, the mental health inpatient system is in the business of dealing with crises.

At least arguably, all this has changed psychiatric practice. Nikolas Rose has argued that a considerable part of the business of psychiatrists is now in risk prediction.[49] Certainly, that is an emphasis of the new centralized administration policies, which require assessment of risk on discharge, and the implementation of structures such as aftercare under supervision or inclusion upon a supervision register in cases of significant risk. Physicians now not merely diagnose, they also assign risk categories to patients: high, medium, or low. Miscategorization to a lower risk runs the risk of criticism, in the event that the patient goes on to injure an individual. Miscategorization to a higher risk group is unlikely to be noticed, or at worst will be perceived as an abundance of caution. The exercise thus risks re-enforcing the traditional and incorrect prejudice that the mentally ill pose special risks with the sheen of scientific respectability.

The attraction of some form of greater control of people with mental health problems in the community can perhaps now be articulated. The perception is that risk can be predicted accurately. 'Failures' of community care are perceived as failures of administration, the doctors, nurses, and social workers failing the client and society. The result is that clients may be forced to be returned as in-patients to an overstretched hospital system.

There are a variety of difficulties with this approach. First, as will be discussed at more length below, risk prediction remains an inaccurate technique. More fundamentally, the perception of 'failures' of community care

[47] National Health Service Management Executive, *Health Service Guidelines*, HSG (94)5.
[48] M. Deahl and T. Turner, 'General Psychiatry in No-man's Land' (1997) 171 *British Journal of Psychiatry* 6.
[49] N. Rose, 'Living Dangerously: Risk-thinking and Risk Management in Mental Health Care' (1998) 8 *Mental Health Care* 263; N. Rose, 'Psychiatry as a Political Science' (1996) 9 *History of the Human Sciences* 1.

as failures of administration places the entire focus on doctors, nurses, and social workers. The patient is removed from the analysis. Evidence-based medicine has recommended a course of treatment; risk analysis has created a scientific account of the patient's future under various scenarios (typically, continuing with medication and failing to continue with medication). A right answer has been derived for the patient's life. What has the patient to add? Patients who do not abide by this truth risk demonization or other forms of marginalization by the popular press and the policy-makers. They are understood as recklessly irresponsible, or pitiable, unable to care for themselves.

It is not obvious why patients should be understood in either of these ways. There is little systematic research done on how patients understand their experiences and their reasons for departing from 'agreed' treatment plans, although the fact that people with mental health problems are as good at concordance with treatment regimes as the remainder of the population suggests that their views may appropriately warrant consideration. A perusal of some of the autobiographical literature of patients and former patients[50] reinforces this point: it simply cannot be assumed that a patient's decision regarding medication is arbitrary, reckless, or irresponsible. The medications may have adverse effects, sometimes severe adverse effects. Equally, patients may have views about the effect on themselves of spending a life on medication. Medical practitioners dealing directly with patients seem often aware of these issues; the pressure at a policy level is nonetheless for the patient's view to be marginalized.

It is difficult to see that further intervention is a recipe for success. It is difficult to see how compliance can be enforced against patients who, perhaps for quite coherent reasons, do not wish to be controlled. The provision of threats or sanctions for non-compliance is at least arguably counter-productive, since it creates a barrier between the patient and the health team: patients are presumably less likely to be forthcoming about problems of medication, if they think they are at risk of legal sanction or further legal control for expressing reservations about their treatment regimen.

Another Approach?

If the objective of this paper is not merely to understand where we are now, but to provoke a broader discussion of the direction of mental health

---

[50] See, e.g., J. Read and J. Reynolds (eds.), *Speaking our Minds: An Anthology* (Basingstoke, 1996); S. Dunn, B. Morrison, and M. Roberts (eds.), *Mind Readings: Writers' Journeys Through Mental States* (London, 1996); L. Hart, *Phone At Nine Just To Say You're Alive* (London, 1995); K. Redfield Jamison, *An Unquiet Mind: A Memoir of Moods and Madness* (London, 1996); J. B. Mays, *In the Jaws of the Black Dogs: A Memoir of Depression* (Toronto, 1995).

policy, it is appropriate to propose a different direction for that policy, a direction which raises some of the fundamental questions about mental health law which should be considered in a major re-evaluation of the Act, and an approach which takes a different view of the patient.

Anti-discrimination has in the last decade or two become central to our understanding and formulation of social policy regarding disability. This is reflected both at the European level in the Treaty of Amsterdam, and domestically, in the Disability Discrimination Act 1995. Abroad, it is reflected in the Americans with Disabilities Act in the United States, and in Canada both by human rights statutes across the country and in the constitutional prohibition of discrimination based on 'mental handicap' contained in the Charter of Rights and Freedoms. Few would now argue against this basic principle, although in the United Kingdom, there is no legal or constitutional bar to passage of legislation which discriminates on the basis of mental disability. The issue here is instead ethical and political.

If we were to develop a Mental Health Act which did not discriminate on the basis of mental disability, what would it look like?

A preliminary point should be made at the outset. Anti-discrimination law does not require that suspect categorizations such as sex or disability can never be used in making decisions. It does not require companies, for example, to hire blind bus drivers. The principle is instead that the use of the criterion must be necessary to achieve a suitably pressing public purpose or objective. If the objective is applied merely to the group of the population identified by the suspect categorization, of course, it will be harder to claim that it is actually a 'pressing' objective as understood by anti-discrimination law and practice. If legislation precluded only black people from driving cars, it would be difficult to defend on the basis that it supported public transit, for example. The public objective cannot be a mask for a discriminatory policy.

Here, the frailty of existing mental health law can be highlighted. We use the law to force people with mental health problems into psychiatric facilities, when we would never do so for those with physical ailments. Even if competent and refusing to give consent, people so confined with mental illness can be treated in their perceived best interests, unlike any physical ailment.[51] And, in jurisdictions with community treatment orders or out-patient confinement, treatment, or other conditions may be enforced outside a hospital setting, in a manner which we would not impose on other groups in society. Unless some reason can be shown why people with mental illnesses are different from those with physical illnesses

---

[51] See Mental Health Act 1983, s. 63 (which allows most treatments without the confined patient's consent, and with no process safeguards, for up to three months), s. 58 (which allows most treatments of confined patients after the three-month period, either with the patient's consent or upon provision of a second opinion that the treatment should be given).

in some socially relevant way, the law in question would appear to be inappropriately discriminatory on the basis of mental illness.

The problem can therefore be rephrased: when, as a matter of social policy, is mental illness really a relevant consideration in the design of a Mental Health Act? The concern here is not in legislation establishing special programmes, or minimum standards of care for those with mental health problems, but instead in the coercive powers of the law noted above: civil confinement and enforced treatment.

Mental illness is not, of course, the same as mental incapacity. There is nothing legally inconsistent in a person with mental health problems still understanding and appreciating the nature and quality of proposed treatment or other decisions, to a degree which makes him or her legally competent to make those decisions.[52] As discussed above, this possibility is already countenanced in the existing Mental Health Act regarding informal patients (whose refusal to consent cannot be overruled) and involuntary patients (whose competent consent removes the need for a second opinion prior to continuation of treatment beyond three months). Similarly, not everyone who lacks capacity has a mental illness.[53] How capacity is to be defined is a complex issue. While in a sense it must go hand in glove with other mental health policy, it is outside the scope of this paper.[54] Existing and, more significantly, proposed law already takes account of those who lack capacity to make specific decisions, and have the advantage of treating people with psychiatric disorders in the same way as all others without capacity.

Distinctions based on incapacity are based on mental disability, but it is submitted that these are an example of acceptable discrimination. Incapacity as a legal concept applies to the specific decision to be made. Thus a patient unable to consent to one treatment is not necessarily unable to consent to a different one, let alone to make decisions about where he or she will live.[55] Decisions on behalf of people lacking capacity do need

[52] See, e.g., Re C (Adult: Refusal of Medical Treatment) [1994] 1 WLR 290.

[53] See, e.g., Re S (Hospital Patient: Court's Jurisdiction) [1995] 3 All ER 290, where the incapacity was the result of a stroke.

[54] Regarding the definition of incapacity, see, e.g., P. Bartlett and R. Sandland, Mental Health Law, Policy and Practice (London, 1999), chs. 10 and 11; M. Gunn, 'The Meaning of Incapacity' (1994) 2 Medical Law Review 8; Law Commission (England), Mental Incapacity, Law Com No 231 (London, 1995); L. Roth, A. Meisel and C. Lidz, 'Tests of Competency to Consent to Treatment' (1977) 134 American Journal of Psychiatry 279; P. Applebaum and T. Grisso, 'The MacArthur Treatment Competence Study', (1995) 19 Law and Human Behavior 105; British Medical Association and the Law Society, Assessment of Mental Capacity: Guidance for Doctors and Lawyers (London, 1996); M. Jones and K. Keywood, 'Assessing the Patient's Competence to Consent to Medical Treatment' (1996) 2 Medical Law International 107.

[55] The exception to this general rule involves financial decisions, when the jurisdiction of the Court of Protection has been invoked. In that event, the individual is precluded from all

to be made. It is the precision which matches incapacity to the specific decision to be made which renders incapacity as a criterion inoffensive to anti-discrimination law.

Certainly, some people (mentally ill or otherwise) will lack the capacity to decide where they will live[56] or will lack capacity to consent to treatment. It would seem that, as a matter of anti-discrimination law, such persons can appropriately be treated, or housed in such facilities as are deemed appropriate. Obviously, there may be serious issues relating to least restrictive alternative and hospital admission, or appropriateness of the treatment proposed, for example, but within the meaning of this paper, those are merely issues about the appropriateness of a decision; they are not about discrimination on the basis of mental disability.

Capacity thus provides an uncontroversial mechanism for dealing with some of the problems of mental health law. If non-discrimination is to be a starting point for analysis, it might be appropriate to ask whether additional regulation of those with capacity is required. Do we need a Mental Health Act at all? It is not something that should be presumed from the existence of people with mental disorders. We do not, by way of analogy, say that there are black people out there; we had better pass a statute to regulate them. An argument based simply on 'protecting the vulnerable' should also be viewed with suspicion, as history provides examples of abuse of this sort of argument. Not long ago, women were thought to be appropriately 'protected' from the stress to their fragile natures which would be caused by, for example, higher education.

Given an adequate legislative framework for incapacity law, a Mental Health Act would bite instead regarding people who have the capacity to make the decision in question. Should it? We respect the right of patients with other medical conditions to refuse hospital admission notwithstanding that it would manifestly be in their best interest, or to refuse treatment or medication against medical advice. They are even allowed to deny the correctness of the medical diagnosis, as with an individual who refuses medication on the manifestly unreasonable belief that they do not have cancer, for example. Is additional law really necessary? Or will it, by definition, be inappropriately discriminatory against people with psychiatric problems?

Lest this be thought too academic a question for serious consideration, it is worth pointing out that the Province of Ontario abolished the legal power to treat competent psychiatric patients without their consent in 1986. That is irrespective of whether the patient is in hospital or in the community, and, if in hospital, whether a voluntary or an involuntary

---

decision-making regarding his or her 'property and affairs': see *Imperial Loan Company* v. *Stone* [1892] 1 QB 599.

[56] See, e.g., *R*. v. *Bournewood Community and Mental Health NHS Trust, ex p. L.* [1998] 3 WLR 107 (HL).

patient. The world did not end. If anything, my suspicion (unprovable, since the absence of data prior to the change makes comparison impossible) is that it has resulted in better communication between patients and doctors, better negotiation of treatment regimes, outcomes acceptable to both, and better rates of continuation of treatment in the long term. If that is correct, the non-discriminatory approach is not merely workable; it provides better health care.

In the treatment area, this might be a convincing argument. It is difficult to come up with any situations where a competent patient's right to consent is overriden regarding physical illness; if we have the courage of our convictions regarding non-discrimination, it is not obvious why the situation should be different regarding mental illness.

The difficulty of applying this approach across all mental health law arises because of the structure of incapacity law, which is directed to the specific decision to be made, not the overall context of the individual's situation. Regarding civil confinement, for example, the argument is not so simple. The physical protection of other members of society is an obvious state interest, and, at least as a theoretical proportion, it seems appropriate to confine an individual who puts other people at physical risk as a result of mental illness. This cannot easily be accommodated using the criterion of capacity. An individual may have capacity to consent to medical treatment and to decide where they will live, but nonetheless as a result of a mental condition be dangerous to others. When people with physical illnesses put others at risk, they can sometimes be confined,[57] suggesting that confinement of the mentally ill in case of danger to others may be justified. The result of reliance on a capacity standard for admission to hospital in this situation would be that society might not be able to intervene, even in the case of clear danger.

There are several difficulties with this approach.

First, the law must not become an instrument of other discriminatory activity. Already, mental health law statistically over-confines defined groups: black men, Irish people, and the poor are obvious examples. There is dispute whether, and about the degree to which, people with mental illness in general and schizophrenia in particular are more likely to behave violently than the general population;[58] but even if such a disparity exists, it is clear that not all—indeed, a relatively small minority—of those with schizophrenia will be violent in the relatively short term. The difficulty is that, within the class of people diagnosed with schizophrenia, it would seem that the best predictors of dangerousness are not diagnostic criteria. Wessely, for example, states:

[57] See, e.g., the Public Health (Control of Diseases) Act 1984.
[58] For a discussion of this literature, see S. Wessely, 'The Epidemiology of Crime, Violence and Schizophrenia' (1997) 170 (supp. 32) *British Journal of Psychiatry* 8.

Schizophrenia *per se*, in other words the experience of mental illness, did contribute to the pattern of offending, as did substance misuse. However, the strongest predictors of criminal behaviour in people with schizophrenia were gender, ethnicity, age of onset and previous offending.[59]

In his study, these predictors were particularly problematic regarding Afro-Caribbean men and class:

The reason for this is that the data show a complex interaction between gender (being male), ethnicity (Afro-Caribbean) and diagnosis. Going back to the original data, the reason is to be found in a small number of young black males with very long histories of both hospital admissions and criminal convictions. The reasons lie beyond the scope of this paper, but differential police response, earlier age of onset, social deprivation and rates of drug misuse may all play a part.[60]

If in fact race and sex are statistically significant as predictors of dangerousness among schizophrenic people, how is this information to be used? The short answer, of course, is that it must not be used: it would be politically and ethically profoundly offensive to place legal restrictions on people based on their race or gender. At the same time, as a matter of practice, how can it not be used? The prevalence of violence in men, and black men in particular, is widely believed. Is it really realistic in practice to expect a human being assessing the dangerousness of an individual to ignore these factors? If not, and if we are serious in our belief that mental health law must not mask discriminatory activity, can we use a dangerousness structure as a basis for mental health law?

Race and sex are perhaps the clearest prohibited categories for the determination of dangerousness in an English context, since discrimination on these bases is generally prohibited by both domestic and European law. As a matter of human rights policy, what criteria ought to be able to be used to determine whether an individual with mental illness is dangerous? Substance abuse, age, age at onset, low social class, being unmarried, criminal record, and age at onset of illness have all been argued to be relevant as predictors. Most are also at least arguably unacceptable in a human rights framework, to determine whether an individual ought to be subjected to legal control.

Secondly, there is an obvious difficulty in assessing responsibility for events which have not yet occurred, and which, perhaps more importantly, may never occur. All the indications from jurisdictions using a dangerousness standard would indicate that dangerousness is consistently over-predicted. Some protection may be afforded by strong statutory language; but it is not clear that the current state of risk prediction can be sufficiently accurate to serve as an appropriate basis for this sort of system, particularly if some of the statistically best predictors such as race and sex are

---

[59] *Ibid.*, 11.   [60] *Ibid.*, 10.

removed from the calculation on policy grounds. All the indications are that dangerousness is significantly over-predicted by psychiatrists. The classic work done by Monahan in the 1980s showed that almost 70 per cent of those predicted to be dangerous in fact did not go on to commit any serious offence.[61] This finding has been controversial, and studies of the accuracy of dangerousness predictions are admittedly methodologically problematic.[62] Nonetheless, even enthusiasts seem to arrive at a false positive rate of roughly 40 per cent.[63] And as the false positive rate drops, the false negative rate—those predicted not to be dangerous who go on to commit violent acts—rises. Thus the studies considered by Monahan tended to have very low false negative rates, in one case as low as 5 per cent; the more recent studies have considerably higher rates. This does not inspire confidence in the accuracy of the process.

Given these figures, it is a fair question whether we should be confining anyone on the basis of risk to others, prior to the commission of an actual offence. The level of certainty would not be acceptable in, say, the criminal system. It is at least arguable that it is also unacceptable in a mental health context.

Finally, a dangerousness standard does not end the discrimination issue. The confinement of those with physical ailments involves the containment of contagion, and mental illnesses are not generally contagious. The justification for confinement of the mentally ill concerns the risk of violence. How should we define those cases where we confine, and those where we await the actual commission of a criminal act? If we take the view that discrimination against those with mental disabilities is inappropriate, it would seem inappropriate to limit the condition expressly to those identified in ICD–10 or DSM–IV, the diagnostic schemes used by psychiatrists in the classification of mental illness. Why should dangerous people with those conditions be dealt with differently from people with other dangerous conditions? The issue would instead appear to be whether the condition is sufficient to constitute removal of responsibility for one's actions, an 'irresistible impulse', to use the old term. If that is the issue, debates of the minutiae of diagnosis, and where the line is between personality disorders and addiction difficulties and mental disease seem in the end to miss the point: the issue is instead whether the individual's will is sufficiently compromised to warrant intervention. Yet that is a philosophical question,

[61] See, e.g., J. Monahan, 'The Prediction of Violent Behaviour: Toward a Second Generation of Theory and Policy' (1984) 141 *American Journal of Psychiatry* 10.

[62] For discussion, see J. Monahan, 'Risk Assessment of Violence Among the Mentally Disordered: Generating Useful Knowledge' (1988) 11 *International Journal of Law and Psychiatry* 249.

[63] For a recent survey of some of the studies, see A. Buchanan, 'The Investigation of Acting on Delusions as a Tool for Risk Assessment in the Mentally Disordered' (1997) 170 (suppl. 32) *British Journal of Psychiatry* 12.

well beyond the specific expertise of medicine. If this approach is adopted, how involved should doctors be in the administration of the act?

Ironically, there are legal difficulties with a *failure* to discriminate on the basis of a medical diagnosis. Article 5 of the European Convention on Human Rights, drafted well before the movement towards non-discrimination on the basis of mental disability, provides a right to liberty and security of the person, with an exception granted for lawful detention of (among other things) 'persons of unsound mind, alcoholics or drug addicts, or vagrants' (Article 5(e)). If we move outside the meaning of the phrase 'person of unsound mind', Article 5 is likely to be offended. While the breadth of the term 'persons of unsound mind' may be open to some interpretation, the European Court of Human Rights in *Winterwep* v. *The Netherlands*[64] adopted a definition reliant almost completely on medicalized criteria. A movement away from a medicalized model of mental illness will be practically problematic. That forces a return to the more fundamental question: is it really justifiable to lock up some dangerous people, and not others? Is this not precisely the sort of approach which a non-discriminatory agenda is to combat?

Conclusion

The debate over mental health law reform may continue for years before legislative action is taken. The risk is that discussion will be dominated by a reflex reaction to perceived problems, rather than a reflective analysis of the broader social and political context. The object of this paper has been to reinforce that the debate is not merely about the subjects of the legislation. It is also about the political context of the reform project, at a time of reformulation of the welfare state. By focusing on different aspects of modern social policy, non-discrimination in the example here, different issues come to the fore for consideration. If we are to achieve appropriate reform, such broader issues should be brought into the discussion.

[64] Series A No. 33, 2 EHRR 387 (ECtHR).

MIND AND BODY:
MEDICINE AND LAW

B. Mahendra

A review of Professor John Searle's recent book noted that 'the way mental occurrences are produced by the brain is the single greatest mystery today facing philosophy, psychology and the neurosciences'.[1]

In this paper I shall concentrate upon the ways clinical medical practice and the courts, in applying legal principles, consider how the mind and body operate and how they interact. Having given a very general account of developments in modern neuroscience, I shall pay attention to the apparent paradox that medical practice, which might reasonably be believed to have ready access to the fruits of neuroscientific research, is reluctant, on the whole, to accept that mental processes originate in the brain, whereas the law, in both its civil and criminal aspects, with no claim to any sophisticated understanding of neurobiological processes, is seemingly able to accept the interaction. I shall conclude by trying to understand and explain these different approaches taken by the two professions.

I need, however, to set the scene with a somewhat oversimplified and very selective survey of philosophical thought as it applies to this matter. The distinction between mind and body can be traced back, at least, to Plato but the modern formulation is generally taken to be that of the French rationalist philosopher, René Descartes. The difference between mind and body he described as follows: '[t]hus extension in length, breadth and depth makes up the nature of physical substance; and thought makes up the nature of thinking substance'.[2] He had a 'clear and distinct' idea of the difference between his own mind—*cogito*—and of physical objects. The essential property of a mind is that it thinks and the essential property of a body is that it is extended. The realms of thought and extension inhabit two completely distinct and discrete universes.

In his original conception Descartes could not allow for any interaction between these two universes. However, he moved on to consider the possibility of interaction in the face of compelling evidence for it. One example from real life which had a powerful impact on him was the phenomenon

---

[1] J. Searle, *Mind, Language and Society: Philosophy in the Real World* (London, 1999). Review by A. C. Grayling in the *Financial Times*, 8 May 1999.

[2] R. H. Popkin, 'Cartesian Theory' in R. H. Popkin and A. Stroll (eds.), *Philosophy Made Simple* (New York, 1956), 74.

of the 'phantom limb' in which an amputee can feel pain and sensation in the area of the severed limb. He was thereby forced to reconsider his formulation of separate and distinct universes harbouring mind and body. His somewhat misconceived and ill-received solution was to place the *locus* of possible interaction in the pineal gland, a lowly organ which, nevertheless, was also believed by Descartes to be the seat of the soul. Even in his time this suggestion of the pineal gland playing a role mediating traffic between mind and body elicited little less than ridicule. Greatly pained, Descartes abandoned any further development of the idea and in a letter written to the Princess Elizabeth of the Palatinates despairingly remarked that the best understanding of any interaction between mind and body was to be achieved by not thinking about it. It might be added that Descartes had some crude notion of physical currents flowing in the nervous system which the mind, in some way, could deflect.

A later thinker to grapple with this Cartesian dualism was the rationalist philosopher, Baruch Spinoza. To him there was but one substance, all-enveloping, infinite, and immanent, in the world. It could be called God or nature, according to taste, but it described the totality of substance with an infinity of attributes. To Spinoza attributes such as thought or consciousness, on the one hand, and extension or occupancy of space, on the other, are like wrinkles on this one, all-inclusive fabric; mere local and temporary formations. These modes, as he called them, may also be likened to the waves of the sea, temporary formations in the eternal ocean. It follows, said Spinoza, that these modes or phases or wrinkles could have two aspects, a mental aspect and a physical aspect, at one and the same time. They are one and the same thing but capable of being viewed from two directions. Likewise, the mind and body are two sides of the same coin or two aspects of one substance.

As Professor T. L. S. Sprigge says:

It would seem rather that for Spinoza the proper study of man involves a unitary treatment of mind and body in which we recognize that we are studying one process with two aspects and use the more obvious aspect of any particular process to illuminate the other, without confusing ourselves with an attempt to find the locus of interaction between them.[3]

Further light is thrown by an attempt to illuminate Cartesian dualism by the British empiricist philosopher, David Hume. The key to understanding these phenomena, according to Hume, is to avoid the meaningless concept of two substances and the vexed search for any necessary connection between them. To Hume it was sufficient that a regular association existed between certain physical events and certain mental events. Thus,

---

[3] T. L. S. Sprigge, 'Spinoza: His Identity Theory' in T. Honderich (ed.), *Philosophy through its Past* (London, 1992), 169.

we may make a connection between the appearance of an apple and its taste, or between the sound of C sharp and the striking of a certain key on the piano. It is unnecessary, said Hume, to seek a relationship between the two events. Indeed, confusion and unintelligibility lie on the road to seeking such connections.

Mind and Body: Perspectives from Medicine

The progress that neuroscience has made since that time, and especially in this century, has placed us in a better position than Descartes, Spinoza, and Hume to try to understand these matters. However, the starting points for our thinking are those phenomena that had been observable long before brain structure and function had been persuaded to yield some of their secrets to skilful and persistent study. Indeed, as we noted, Descartes himself was influenced in his thinking by some of these observations. It has long been known, for instance, that sudden and severe shock of an emotional nature could precipitate a heart attack or stroke or, as the old literature had it, apoplexy. Following such an attack, bodily changes, i.e. morbid pathology, can be seen. Even more commonly, emotional shock is seen to induce a swoon or faint or collapse. Observations made at the time reveal a slowing of the heart and pulse, a pallor of the skin, and a lowering of blood pressure. Moreover, any number of systemic diseases produce psychiatric symptoms such as depression and anxiety. Further, an interesting series of apparently bodily afflictions such as bronchial asthma, peptic ulceration, eczematous dermatitis, and ulcerative colitis, while having discernible physical features, are known also to have strong links to emotional factors. These are called psychosomatic conditions.

In recent months the most dramatic illustration of the interaction between mind and body has been the emergence of the drug Sildenafil (Viagra) which is used in the treatment of male erectile dysfunction. It is widely accepted in clinical practice that the commonest cause of impotence is psychological, with physical illness and injury contributing a much smaller proportion of cases. And, yet, Viagra—a man-made substance made in the laboratory according to chemical specification that exploits known chemical changes in male sexual function—produces significantly successful results with all forms of male impotence, however caused. A more potent case can hardly be made for an interaction between mind and body, and with a conviction that eluded Descartes.

To summarize this section I adopt the words of Lord Browne-Wilkinson in *Page* v. *Smith*:

Medical science has also demonstrated that there are other injuries the body can suffer as a consequence of an accident, such injuries not being demonstrably attributable directly to physical injury to the plaintiff. Injuries of this type may take two forms. First, physical illness or injury not brought about by a chain of demonstrable physical events but by mental or emotional stresses, i.e by a psychiatric route. Examples are a heart attack or miscarriage produced by shock. In this case, the end-product is a physical condition although it has been brought about by a process which is not demonstrably a physical one but lies in the mental or nervous system.[4]

A more detailed study of a psychiatric condition, namely depression, in relation to brain dysfunction has been given elsewhere.[5] Depression is one of the commonest conditions—as well as the commonest symptom—seen in clinical psychiatric practice. In most instances there is no obvious physical basis for the mood change of depression or the associated symptoms of a depressive illness. In a minority of cases, as we have noted already, there may be systemic physical illness that produces depression as an incidental symptom. In fact, in ordinary life, the patient's general practitioner (GP) will rule out these systemic conditions—which include common disorders such as anaemia and thyroid illness as well as the side effects of prescribed drugs—before seeking a specialist psychiatric opinion. And yet we now know, thanks to specialized modern techniques used for the study of the structure and function of the brain, that the seemingly physically intact patient may harbour subtle changes in the brain even with psychiatric conditions such as depression. On the face of it, the traditional distinction between 'organic' illness and 'functional' illness seems no longer tenable.

The more exciting modern studies of brain structure and function are undertaken at a sub-microscopic level. The nerve centre, so to speak, of all this activity is the simple neurone, or nerve cell, a microscopic entity which links up in a network with other nerve cells. Electrical impulses are carried between nerve endings by means of chemicals, and a growing number of these neurotransmitters have been identified, though, doubtless, there are many more to be discovered. One of these in particular, serotonin, has been implicated in the regulation of numerous functions in the brain, and disorders in that chemical's metabolism have been postulated to play a part in conditions as disparate as depression, anxiety, sexual dysfunction, sleep disorders, migraine, pre-menstrual tension, and the state of hangover. Drugs have been manufactured to correct some aspects of serotonin dysfunction in the brain and these are now standard treatment for such common disorders as depression, anxiety, obsessional illness, and bulimia nervosa. Any psychiatrist giving conscious thought to the drug treatment of a condition such as depression with no obvious physical cause for it, hoping the chemical will correct the imbalance in the brain, will be hard put to it to deny there is some form of interaction between mind and body, blurring the 'organic' and the 'functional'. Modern neuroscience lets it be known that the locus for the interaction is the limbic system, not the pineal gland, as favoured by Descartes' speculation.

---

[4] [1995] 2 All ER 736 at 752.
[5] B. Mahendra, *Depression: The Disorder and its Associations* (Lancaster, 1987), 65.

Another approach to the study of the interaction between mind and brain, or at any rate to exploring the neural basis to mental phenomena, is through the analysis of the condition called dementia.[6] This is now a well-recognized condition, thanks to an ageing population. Senile dementia is found in those in the senium, i.e. those over 65 years of age. The commonest cause of senile dementia is believed to be Alzheimer's disease, normally spoken of as a single disease entity but likely in time to be found to be a heterogeneous collection of disorders. A small but significant number of cases is found under the age of 65. At present the diagnosis of Alzheimer's dementia is entirely pathological, i.e. by microscopic study of tissue taken on biopsy or at autopsy. There are obvious microscopic changes in the condition and there is no doubt it is a neuro-degenerative disease, and the symptoms found can broadly be related to the damage to brain structure and resulting dysfunction.

However, the provisional diagnosis of dementia is made by clinical means, undertaken in the consulting room or at the bedside. The clinical assessment finds a constellation of symptoms reflecting a global impairment of intellect, memory, and personality. In a substantial proportion of cases of dementia there is no obvious (i.e. apparent on routine investigation) change in the brain, no destruction of neural tissue as in Alzheimer's disease or other, less common, degenerative causes of dementia. Many of these so-called 'functional' dementias appear to have depression as their cause; other psychiatric disorders are much less often seen. A trial of treatment given in these cases may produce considerable improvement in contrast to the untreatable Alzheimer's dementia. A full cure may indeed be achieved. The traditional diagnostic position is to call these treatable dementias with no obvious organic pathology 'pseudodementias' to contrast them with the 'true' dementias of obvious 'organic' origin.

The traditional approach sits uneasily with the advances in the neurosciences. As was said: '[i]t is precarious terminology, for even the most casual reading of medical history much reveal the changing and improving methods of ascertaining brain pathology. We have seen investigation of the brain move from macroscopic dissection to light microscopy to ultrastructural histology and a histochemical assault on brain disease. What is not revealed today does not necessarily stay unrevealed tomorrow. In any case, several workers might dispute that even today all cases of depression and so-called functional psychiatric disease are truly 'functional' and point to the growing, if admittedly still incomplete, evidence of brain pathology in some of these conditions'.[7]

On grounds of logic one could, therefore, find no place for any conceptualization of 'pseudodementia'. One could also proceed further to try to

---

[6] B. Mahendra, *Dementia: A Survey of the Syndrome* (2nd edn., Lancaster, 1987), 59.

[7] Mahendra, n. 5, above, 60.

unravel the complex relationships between the dementias and depression.[8] There is the possibility of an interrelationship in the Cartesian sense. The dementias due to such degenerative conditions as Alzheimer's disease could produce depression as a symptom in the same way as systemic illnesses do. We could, with equal force, argue for depression as being a cause of dementia, the neurochemical changes of depression giving rise also to the clinical symptoms of dementia. Changing tack, we could, in the manner of Spinoza, say that depression and dementia are the mental phenomena with the causative brain changes as their physical counterparts. With less conviction we could assume the Hume position, observing and listing the mental symptoms and the corresponding physical changes but not striving to seek any interaction or relationship. But the evidence of modern neuroscience, incomplete and tentative though it may be, leaves no doubt that changes at the level of the neurone lead to the symptoms observed in clinical psychiatry. It is submitted that a sustainable hypothesis could be constructed on the basis that pathological processes in the limbic system and related regions of the brain are capable, by means of various permutations and combinations, of producing mental symptoms that are elicited by the ordinary routines of psychiatric examination.

However, it would be misleading to suggest that the medical profession has accepted these arguments to be self-evident propositions. Considerable opposition still exists, especially in the psychiatric speciality, to accepting the view that nervous and mental illness could be explained now, or at a time in the future, as stemming from brain disorders. This position is taken despite the widespread use and understanding of neurological investigatory techniques and psychotropic medication—including among the latter the recently introduced specific anti-depressant agents with actions influencing natural serotonin metabolism—in many forms of psychiatric disorders. The distinction between 'organic' disorders and 'functional' disorders continues to be made and trainee doctors and psychiatrists continue to be instructed in the traditional fashion.

It was not considerations of logic alone that prompted the suggestion that the brain, rather than that vague and nebulous entity, the mind, should be considered the locus of psychiatric illness. It was also believed that, especially where the dementias were concerned, a proper appreciation of the neurobiological basis to the dementias would be a useful therapeutic corrective to the nihilism that pervades the management of the condition. As has been said, for all practical purposes, there is no cure or effective ameliorative treatment of the commonest cause of dementia, namely Alzheimer's disease. However, if the formulation of dementia as a clinical entity is accepted, there is everything to play for since a small but significant

[8] B. Mahendra, 'Depression and Dementia: The Multi-faceted Relationship' (1985), 15 *Psychological Medicine* 227.

proportion of clinical dementias will, upon investigation, turn out to be due to treatable conditions such as depression and be amenable to successful treatment. To seek to find 'functional' causes of 'pseudodementia' while consigning the 'organic' dementias to mere palliation seems not merely illogical but a dispiriting approach to the investigation, study, and management of these illnesses.

The other advantage to accepting the neurobiological basis for psychiatric conditions is that we are enabled to understand certain other conditions, far removed from the dementias, but whose aetiology and pathogenesis are equally uncertain or unknown in the present state of knowledge. I shall here consider two of these which have had an impact on the public consciousness in the past decade or so.

The first of these is myalgic encephalomyelitis (ME) or the chronic fatigue syndrome, or 'yuppie flu' as it was designated in the popular media following its seeming prevalence in a particular social group of individuals. It begins in the most common place of fashions, with symptoms of influenza or a cold. Recovery from these symptoms is rapid and the individual may look forward to resuming social and professional life. Very soon, however, the person is enveloped in a fog of lassitude, malaise, an extreme weariness, which simply will not go away. The sense of fatigue is both profound and persistent, hence the term chronic fatigue syndrome. Rest, which common sense suggests may, in fact, make things worse, the inactivity reinforcing the fatigue. Investigations reveal nothing of significance and, therefore, there is no rational basis for treatment. It is no exaggeration to say that those suffering from the condition feel crippled, their lives disrupted, their social, professional, and domestic existence dislocated. There is no suggestion that a pre-existing vulnerability to nervous illness was present in these patients. There is no evidence of, for want of a better word, hysteria. No one suggests these patients are malingering. To them their suffering is real and undeniably physical but sustained investigation reveals no physical cause. Alternative explanations, built around a psychological framework, are not countenanced. Indeed, considerable anger is generated when it is hinted that a speaker rejects a physical basis, or if he expresses a proper scepticism based on the negative results that have, so far, been yielded.

From the arguments put forward in previous pages, we know it is quite unnecessary to essay rigid demarcations between physical and mental symptoms. While these patients' symptoms may appear to be mental or psychological, there is no reason to believe that the brain is not affected. In fact, there is indirect evidence since similar symptoms are common sequelae of many viral infections, albeit lacking the severity or chronicity of the symptoms in ME. Glandular fever, a mild enough disease in its own right, has long been known to produce persistent malaise and fatigue. A perfectly respectable hypothesis—acceptable, one imagines, to researchers as well as sufferers—is that, perhaps, a viral condition has affected sensitive parts of the brain in ways that are not clear to current methods of neurobiological study. The brain lesion produces symptoms which take a psychological form, in the same way as depression and the dementias due to depression do. Either the interactive or the 'one effect—two phenomena' model already discussed could be productive of a hypothesis that could be put to the test.

A not dissimilar condition is the Gulf War Syndrome. A wide range of symptoms, some physical, some psychological, has been observed in servicemen sent to the Persian Gulf in the conflict in 1991. No convincing explanation is forthcoming for these symptoms though theories, wild as well as plausible, abound. Extraordinary passions are aroused; conspiracies in the armed services are whispered to be behind 'cover ups'. The recent position could be summarized thus:

When the survey of British soldiers who served in the Gulf War of 1991 reported in January 1999, veterans and their representatives ought to have felt vindicated that the incidence of illness suffered during active service in the Gulf is reported to have run at twice the rate for those control servicemen deployed on Bosnian peacekeeping duties or those not deployed at all on active service. In particular, the Gulf veterans seemed to be twice at risk as the other groups to complain of symptoms of psychiatric or psychological nature. In the event, there was a barely concealed sense of disappointment that the study group had not uncovered a specific syndrome relating to factors associated, in particular, with preparations for service in the Gulf and that no specific illness and no specific cause has been discovered. The dismay was due to the likely lay interpretation of the findings—that it was 'all in the mind', a suggestion perceived as verging on the insulting to our brave soldiers'.[9]

If we follow through with the argument put forward in the preceding pages, there will be no need to insult anyone by suggesting that some metaphysical entity is responsible for his or her ills. It is not beyond the bounds of the possible that, as with the chronic fatigue syndrome, the lesion is in some recess of the brain, hidden from us at present but amenable to discovery in the fullness of time. The suggestion that there could be multiple pathogens involved may mean that we are also looking for a diversity of conditions with some shared symptoms.

The antipathy of the medical profession to accepting possible interaction between brain and mind, and that symptoms of a psychological nature could possibly have their origins in brain dysfunction, leads also to confusion when expert evidence is given to the courts, resulting in delay, cost, inconvenience, and possibly even injustice—in fact, all manner of pre-Woolf evils. A case that reached the House of Lords was *Pickford* v. *Imperial Chemical Industries plc*.[10] The plaintiff had obtained employment

---

[9] B. Mahendra, 'Matters of Mind: Gulf War and other Syndromes' (1999), 149 *NLJ* 760.
[10] B. Mahendra, 'Burdens of Judicial Proof' (1998), 148 *NLJ* 1522.

as a secretary. The workload which involved typing increased with time and she had to see her GP for the pain in her hands. He could find no abnormality but signed her off sick. Her work doctor could find no physical explanation for the pain either. Her GP then referred her to a surgeon who confirmed the symptoms were work-related but were 'not susceptible of pathological explanation'. The surgeon said he had no treatment to offer, whereupon she saw several other specialists. Many months of sick leave later she was dismissed. She sued for negligence causing personal injury, contending her condition was 'organic' in origin, had been contracted at work, and was due to excessive typing activity without benefit of periods of rest. The defence was that her condition was a form of conversion hysteria, a 'functional' illness. Much time at trial was evidently taken up with a kind of medieval disputation, asking whether the typist's affliction in the body, in the mind, or both. The actual decision turned on the question of the burden of proof—the trial judge dismissing the action, the Court of Appeal deciding in her favour, and the House of Lords reversing the Court of Appeal and restoring the trial judge's decision—but our interest here is to wonder if it would not have been much more edifying to the trial judge if the medical evidence—described as having been hotly disputed—had been presented in the form of the interactionist model that has been proposed here; that conversion hysteria, a form of neurosis, may have its origins in brain dysfunction leading to chronic physical disability. As I have said, the lack of obvious pathology does not necessitate reaching for a metaphysical explanation for symptoms.

Hysteria, in fact, could serve as a focal point for understanding possible interactions between body and mind. Hysterical mechanisms are still ill-understood despite the interest in them for centuries. The grosser manifestations of hysteria seen in previous centuries have given way to subtler symptoms, such as hysterical pain. The simplistic psychological explanation is that these symptoms are due to unconscious conflicts, which lead to anxiety, which in turn is relieved by the emergence of the symptom. This theory is untestable while neuroscience has yet to throw light on the basic mechanisms of hysteria. What is certain, however, is that some so-called hysterical symptoms may be manifestations of an incubating or latent brain disease which will reveal itself in time. No one denies that multiple sclerosis is due to obvious brain pathology. Yet, in the earliest stages of its presentation, some of the symptoms of the condition, such as transient loss of vision or unexplained paralysis, often suggest 'hysteria' or 'something in the mind' or, worse, 'something put on' or 'malingering'. Some years ago a woman aged 68, previously active and with no hint of any problems, was referred as showing 'hysterical behaviour'. She had started suddenly to crawl on the floor, was unable to stand up, and was incapable of accomplishing the simplest of tasks. A brain scan done later, in fact, revealed a fast growing malignant tumour. She was dead within a week.

Where pain and disability are concerned, there may, therefore, be obvious pathology or subtler mechanisms of hysteria or obvious falsification of symptoms at work. A recent case actually found the trial judge called upon to resolve the issue. *Cooper* v. *P. and O. Stena Line Ltd.*[11] turned on whether an allegation of fraud had to be specifically pleaded under Order 18 of the Rules of the Supreme Court. We are more interested here in the facts and inferences. The plaintiff, a steward on a ship, suffered injuries by slipping and falling in the course of his duties. His injuries did not appear to have an obvious physical basis to his doctors, but treatment was of no avail and he continued to complain of severe and disabling pain which prevented him from working. When he brought an action in personal injury, the defendants alleged the plaintiff ought to have recovered from his injuries, at the latest, within three months, and that since that time he had been fabricating his symptoms and his disability, and distorting physical signs for his own ends. At trial, the procedural technicality aside, the judge found the plaintiff a credible witness and was satisfied his pain was genuine, severe, and disabling. The defence's case in fraud was rejected. The inference from the judge's reasoning must be that the pain complained of was hysterical pain. Perhaps the Woolf reform's requirement for a single joint expert in most civil cases will lead to this resolution of the conflict between 'bodily pain' and 'mental pain' being undertaken by the expert rather than the judge.

Mind and Body: Perspectives from the Civil Law

It was the case of *Page* v. *Smith*[12] that helped to focus our attention on how the law considered those matters we have been discussing. But, as will soon become apparent, the law has been quietly dealing with these issues all this century. In *Page* v. *Smith*, the plaintiff had suffered from ME for some twenty years but the condition was in remission when he was involved in a collision with the defendant's motor vehicle. He was shaken but physically unhurt. The shock led to a relapse of the ME. At first instance, the judge found for the plaintiff, ruling that the recrudescence of the ME could be triggered by the trauma of the accident, and that the aggravation of the condition was a foreseeable consequence of the accident.

The defendant appealed on a point of causation and also that the trial judge had failed to apply the 'reasonable fortitude' test as well as not requiring foreseeability of psychiatric injury to be shown. The Court of Appeal, in a unanimous judgment, held that where psychiatric injury was concerned, it was required to be shown that the defendant could have reasonably foreseen psychiatric injury. It was not sufficient, as the trial

---

[11] *The Times*, 8 Feb. 1999.   [12] [1995] 2 All ER 736.

judge had determined, for the foreseeability required to be of personal injury generally. The appeal was allowed. The plaintiff appealed to the House of Lords.

This, by a three to two majority, allowed the appeal. The majority, applying the principle that a tortfeasor has to take his victim as he found him, agreed with the trial judge that a negligent driver was liable for damages for psychiatric injury suffered by the victim of the accident if personal injury of some kind to that victim was reasonably foreseeable as a result of the accident. The test in all cases, said their Lordships, involving a primary victim was the same, namely whether the defendant could reasonably foresee that his negligent conduct would expose the plaintiff to the risk of personal injury, whether physical or psychiatric. Physical injury need not, in fact, have resulted. The plaintiff was not required to specify that psychiatric injury needed to have been reasonably foreseen by the defendant. It was irrelevant that the defendant could not have foreseen that the plaintiff's prior vulnerability or his 'eggshell personality'. The law had thereby equated psychiatric injury with physical injury. Personal injury did not allow, for the purposes of reasonable foreseeability, any fine distinction to be drawn between bodily and mental injury.

Significant as *Page* v. *Smith* itself was, there was further interest in their Lordships' attempts to trace authority for their reasoning. Lord Lloyd of Berwick supplied a brief historical conspectus of the law's approach. He said:

As long ago as 1901 the courts were already beginning to become aware that there may be no hard and fast line between physical and psychiatric injury, such as had hitherto been supposed.[13]

The case cited was *Dulieu* v. *White and Sons*.[14] In the words of Kennedy J in that case:

For my own part, I should not like to assume it to be scientifically true that a nervous shock which causes serious bodily illness is not actually accompanied by physical injury, although it may be impossible, or at least difficult, to detect the injury at the time in the living subject. I should not be surprised if the surgeon or the physiologist told us that nervous shock is in itself truly an affection of the physical organism.[15]

Four decades from that judgment, in a boldly imaginative speech—this was, after all, 1942, long before substantial advances had been made in the basic neurosciences—Lord Macmillan had noted in *Bourhill* v. *Young*:[16]

The crude view that the law should take cognizance only of physical injury resulting from actual impact has been discarded, and it is now well recognized that an

---

[13] [1995] 2 All ER 736 at 758.   [14] [1901] 2 KB 669.
[15] [1901] 2 KB 669 at 677.   [16] [1942] 2 All ER 396.

action will lie for injury by shock sustained through the medium of the eye or the ear without direct contact. The distinction between mental shock and bodily injury was never a scientific one, for mental shock is presumably in all cases the result of, or at least accompanied by, some physical disturbance in the sufferer's system, and a mental shock may have consequences more serious than those resulting from physical impact.[17]

Another four decades passed, and brought with them the kind of neuro-scientific understanding we have alluded to before until we arrive at the seminal case of *McLoughlin* v. *O'Brian*.[18] This, too, reached the House of Lords where Lord Wilberforce observed:

Whatever is unknown about the mind–body relationship (and the area of ignor-ance seems to expand with that of knowledge), it is now accepted by medical science that recognisable and severe physical damage to the human body and system may be caused by the impact, through the senses, of the external events on the mind. Thus may be produced what is as identifiable an illness as any that may be caused by direct physical impact.[19]

His Lordship was, of course, speaking of nervous shock caused by emotional trauma. In the same case Lord Bridge of Harwich added:

No judge who has spent any length of time trying personal injury claims in recent years would doubt that physical injuries can give rise not only to organic but also to psychiatric disorders. The sufferings of the patient from the latter are no less real and frequently no less painful and disabling than from the former. Likewise, I would suppose that the legal profession well understands that an acute emotional trauma, like a physical trauma, can well cause a psychiatric illness in a wide range of circumstances and in a wide range of individuals whom it would be wrong to regard as having any abnormal psychological make-up. It is in comparatively recent times that these insights have come to be generally accepted by the judiciary. It is only by giving effect to these insights in the developing law of negligence that we can do justice to an important, though no doubt small, class of plaintiffs whose genuine psychiatric illnesses are caused by negligent defendants.[20]

By the time *Page* v. *Smith* reached the House of Lords, it had been, over a period of nearly a century, making an imaginative grasp of mind–body relationships and applying their insights to the particular facts of cases before them. The speeches in *Page* v. *Smith*, in fact, had the air of summaries about them, their Lordships not believing anything ground-breaking was being achieved by them.

Lord Lloyd of Berwick went on to conclude his speech:

In an age when medical knowledge is expanding fast, and psychiatric knowledge with it, it would not be sensible to commit the law to a distinction between physical and psychiatric injury, which may already seem somewhat artificial, and

---

[17] [1942] 2 All ER 396 at 402.   [18] [1982] 2 All ER 298.
[19] (1982) 2 All ER 298 at 301.   [20] [1982] 2 All ER 298 at 312.

may soon be altogether outmoded. Nothing will be gained by treating them as different 'kinds' of personal injury, so as to require the application of different tests in law.[21]

With the greatest respect, one suggests His Lordship was altogether too sanguine in his belief that the medical profession had accepted the progress made in the medical sciences. The actual state of current clinical medical thinking is highlighted in Lord Browne-Wilkinson's speech:

Finally, I would endorse Lord Lloyd's remarks about the dangers of the court seeking to draw hard and fast lines between physical illness and its causes on the one hand and psychiatric illness and its causes on the other. Although medical science has not as yet progressed very far in elucidating the processes whereby psychiatric disorders come about, recent developments suggest a much closer relationship between physical and mental processes than had previously been thought. There is a substantial body of informed medical opinion which attributes some mental illness to physical causes such as chemical or hormonal imbalance.[22]

He then went on to refer to the medical evidence that had been presented in the case, illustrating the point we have been making about the medical profession's antipathy to attempting to bridge the mind–body gap:

In the present case, for example, although all but one of the distinguished doctors who gave evidence were agreed that there was indeed an illness (however mysterious) called ME and the plaintiff suffered from it, they had different views as to its causes. One thought ME was linked to viral infection (physical) and stress (psychological); another to neuroendocrine disturbance (physical) and psychiatric disorder. In cases where distinguished doctors take differing views as to the aetiology of an illness it obviously presents great problems for the court to resolve what was the cause of the recrudescence of such an illness. For the courts to impose different criteria for liability depending upon whether the injury is 'physical' or 'psychiatric' is likely to lead to a growing complication in straightforward personal injury cases. In my judgment, the law will be more effective if it accepts that the result of being involved in a collision may include both physical and psychiatric damage.[23]

Mind and Body: Perspectives from the Criminal Law

Having seen the House of Lords speak definitively on the civil law as it applies to personal injury in terms of mental injury being rooted in brain dysfunction, I turn now to consider recent developments in the criminal law. The starting point here is the reasoning of the Court of Appeal (Criminal Division) in *R. v. Chan-Fook*.[24] The facts were as follows. The victim, suspected of theft, had been locked in a room and vigorously questioned by the assailant. Upon a charge of assault occasioning actual bodily

---

[21] [1995] 2 All ER 736 at 759.
[23] *Ibid.*

[22] [1995] 2 All ER 736 at 754.
[24] [1994] 2 All ER 552.

harm under section 47 of the Offences against the Person Act 1861, the Crown alleged that even if the victim had not suffered any physical injury as a result of the assault, he had suffered mental disturbance which in itself amounted to actual bodily harm. The victim himself reported he had felt abused, humiliated, and frightened. In his direction to the jury, the judge said that a hysterical or nervous condition as a result of an assault was capable of being an assault occasioning actual bodily harm. Conviction and an appeal followed.

The Court of Appeal allowed the appeal on the defective direction to the jury which had not taken account of well-established rules of law, namely that a distinction should be drawn between mere emotions such as fear, distress, and panic and identifiable clinical psychiatric conditions, which the judge had not done, and, further, that medical evidence was needed to establish the presence of that psychiatric condition. Our interest here, therefore, is not in the actual decision but in the Court of Appeal's reasoning on the issue of whether inflicting psychiatric illness amounted to the actual bodily harm that needed to result from the assault to satisfy the statutory provision.

It referred to Lynskey J's observations in *R. v. Miller*.[25] That was a case in which the indictment had originally contained two counts, one of rape and the other assault occasioning actual bodily harm. The rape count was quashed since it was an allegation of marital rape and was before the time of abolition of the marital immunity.

The second count remained since the victim had suffered acute mental and emotional distress. It was contended by the defence that the victim's mental state was not actual bodily harm. Lynskey J cited the contemporary *Archbold* in its 1949 edition that '[a]ctual bodily harm includes any hurt or injury calculated to interfere with the health or comfort of the prosecutor' before going on to say:

> There was a time when shock was not regarded as bodily hurt, but the day has gone by when that could be said. It seems to me now that if a person is caused hurt or injury resulting, not in any physical injury, but in an injury to the state of his mind for the time being, that is within the definition of 'actual bodily harm'.[26]

In *Chan-Fook*, Hobhouse LJ held that the body of the victim includes all parts of his body, including his organs, his nervous system, and his brain. Bodily injury, therefore, may include injury to any of those parts of his body responsible for his mental and other faculties. Citing with approval Lord Wilberforce's observations in *McLoughlin v. O'Brian*, Hobhouse LJ concluded that the phrase 'actual bodily harm' was capable of including psychiatric injury.[27]

---

[25] [1954] 2 All ER 529.   [26] [1954] 2 All ER 529 at 534.
[27] [1994] 2 All ER 552 at 559.

Modern advances in criminal behaviour enabled the House of Lords further to consider the matter when two cases came up to it conjoined in appeal: *R. v. Ireland; R. v. Burstow.*[28] In *R. v. Ireland* the appellant had made repeated silent telephone calls, mostly at night, to three women, as a result of which they went on to suffer psychiatric illness. He was charged with three counts of assault occasioning actual bodily harm under section 47 of the 1861 Act, pleaded guilty, and was given a custodial sentence. His appeal to the Court of Appeal on the ground that psychiatric injury could not amount to actual bodily harm was dismissed.

In *R. v. Burstow*, the appellant had stalked and harassed the victim over an eight-month period. She became ill and suffered a severe depressive illness. He was charged on a count of unlawfully and maliciously inflicting grievous bodily harm contrary to section 20 of the 1861 Act. At trial, following the judge's ruling that a section 20 offence could be committed where no physical violence had been applied directly or indirectly to the body of the victim, the appellant pleaded guilty and was imprisoned. The Court of Appeal dismissed his appeal on the ground that psychiatric injury could amount to bodily harm under section 20. Both appellants appealed further to the House of Lords.

The Court of Appeal, giving leave to appeal, certified the following point as of general importance, namely:

Whether an offence of inflicting grievous bodily harm under section 20 of the (1861 Act) can be committed where no physical violence is applied directly or indirectly to the body of the victim.

In the House of Lords, Lord Steyn, citing Lord Macmillan's observations in *Bourhill* v. *Young* that we have noted already, went on to say:

Moreover, it is essential to bear in mind that neurotic illnesses affect the central nervous system of the body, because emotions such as fear and anxiety are brain functions.[29]

Counsel for both appellants had submitted that bodily harm in Victorian legislation cannot include psychiatric injury, seizing upon some preliminary rhetorical observations of Lord Bingham CJ as to whether the Victorian draftsman of the 1861 Act intended to embrace psychiatric injury within the expressions 'grievous bodily harm' and 'actual bodily harm'. However, as Lord Steyn pointed out, Lord Bingham CJ had actually gone on to welcome the ruling in *R. v. Chan-Fook*.[30] In dealing with the 1861 Act itself, Lord Steyn took as his text that, '[a]n Act of Parliament should be deemed to be always speaking'.[31] Therefore, the 1861 Act had to be interpreted in the light of the best current scientific

---

[28] [1997] 4 All ER 225.   [29] [1997] 4 All ER 225 at 231.
[30] [1997] 4 All ER 225 at 233.   [31] *Ibid.*

appreciation of the link between the body and psychiatric injury. His Lordship was persuaded that bodily harm in sections 18, 20, and 47 had to be interpreted to include recognizable psychiatric illness. There was no practical distinction, at any rate in the context of the 1861 Act, between 'cause' in section 18 and 'inflict' in section 20. Psychiatric injury could be caused as well as inflicted without any intervening physical injury or impact.

To Lord Hope,[32] who agreed with Lord Steyn, the words 'cause' and 'inflict' were interchangeable. Further, it was not a necessary ingredient of the word 'inflict' that whatever causes the harm must be applied directly to the victim. It may be applied indirectly, so long as the result is that the harm is caused by what has been done. In its ordinary meaning, an assailant's actions could inflict psychiatric harm. A unanimous dismissal of both appeals followed.

Comment

It is, therefore, plain that, over a period of a century, in the civil law and, more recently, in the criminal law, the law has accepted that there is no practical distinction to be drawn between bodily injury and mental injury. Given the reluctance of the medical profession to accept that psychiatric illness has a bodily cause, one turns to speculate on the law's embrace of an 'organic' source for all illness and injury.

The following reasons are suggested.

1 The law's thinking normally follows a logical pattern. Obviously, lawyers and judges seldom have first-hand knowledge of the processes of neuroscience and have to resort to logic to make sense of these—where there are gaps in the knowledge, as there assuredly are, an imaginative leap is required to be made. Doctors are more likely to be empiricists, influenced and deterred by the gaps and disinclined to make this imaginative leap. The interaction of mind and body may be better understood, in the present state of knowledge, by the processes of logic than in terms of the available evidence.

2 There are no rigid distinctions of speciality among lawyers and judges dealing with personal injury cases. In fact, at the level of the higher appellate courts, the judges may not even have had a practitioner's experience of personal injury cases. When faced with the kind of problem we have illustrated, they have no alternative but to piece together with the help of logic and authority a picture that aids their grasp of the issues. In medicine, on the other hand, a clear demarcation exists, for instance between the specialties of neurology and

[32] (1997) 4 All ER 225 at 238.

psychiatry and, further, non-medical but therapeutic disciplines such as psychology and psychotherapy are engaged in clinical work. The boundaries are fiercely guarded and any lack of firm and definitive evidence is taken as good enough reason to preserve the traditional dichotomy and jealously protect one's interests. There is also the incentive to pass non-promising clinical material over the boundary.

3 The law is required to find solutions to problems. Even a layman can see that a victim whose illness becomes worse as a result of an unlawful act or one who is subjected to what used to be called mental cruelty must be compensated and/or protected. It is also not unknown for the law to start from the conclusion desired and to strive to find good reasons for reaching that solution. Problem-solving concentrates the mind. The demarcations to be found in clinical medical practice do not allow for this approach to problem-solving. Both neurological and psychiatric practice have a substantial number of problematical cases, whose problems may be insoluble. The smart neurologist passes the less than clear-cut case to the psychiatrist who returns the compliment. Neuropsychiatry is an exceedingly small subspecialty within psychiatry, and not represented at all within neurology.

4 Once a higher court has ruled, its reasoning normally binds all lower courts and itself. A maverick decision is likely to be swiftly overruled as being contrary to authority. The reasoning of the higher courts thereby both is influential and at the same time has practical impact on lower courts. There is no corresponding hierarchical structure, or scope for arbitration, in medicine. Time-honoured methods of thinking can be perpetuated without modification in medicine without recourse to appeal. Oddly, the rigid hierarchy of the courts may be instrumental in advancing new modes of thought, and the reasoning of influential and imaginative appellate judges.

5 For centuries the law has had to deal with mental phenomena, whether in the form of apprehension or fear due to an unlawful act or in such concepts as mental cruelty or nervous shock. Logical solutions may need to be found to adapt the law to changing circumstances. To a lawyer it would be thought anomalous to inform a victim that his fear would constitute an assault, but if the fear was caused to persist and extend into a recognisable clinical psychiatric disorder, the Victorian draftsman's requirements for there to be 'actual bodily harm' or 'grievous bodily harm' would preclude redress. In fact, any other solution would be an open invitation to the informed assailant to proceed to causing or inflicting psychiatric damage and pay the mere price of conviction for assault.

INDEX